JOHN DEWEY AND
AMERICAN DEMOCRACY

John Dewey outside his cabin in Hubbards, Nova Scotia, mid-1940s. Courtesy of the Morris Library, Southern Illinois University at Carbondale.

John Dewey

AND AMERICAN DEMOCRACY

★ ★ ★

Robert B. Westbrook

CORNELL UNIVERSITY PRESS

ITHACA AND LONDON

First published 1991 by Cornell University Press.

Thanks are due to the following for permission to quote from copyrighted works: from the *Collected Works of John Dewey* by permission of Southern Illinois University Press, © Board of Trustees, Southern Illinois University; from the letters of John Dewey by permission of the Center for Dewey Studies, © Center for Dewey Studies, Southern Illinois University at Carbondale. My thanks go as well to Oxford University Press for permission to use portions of Robert Westbrook, "Lewis Mumford, John Dewey, and the 'Pragmatic Acquiescence,'" from Agatha and Thomas Hughes, eds., *Lewis Mumford: Public Intellectual* (New York: Oxford University Press, 1990), in my chapters 5, 11, and 14.

International Standard Book Number 0-8014-2560-3
Library of Congress Catalog Card Number 90-55712

Printed in the United States of America

*Librarians: Library of Congress cataloging information
appears on the last page of the book.*

♾ The paper in this book meets the minimum requirements of the American National Standard for Information Sciences— Permanence of Paper for Printed Library Materials, ANSI Z39.48-1984.

For Shamra

To know where we stand toward Dewey's ideas is to find out, at least in part, where we stand with ourselves.

—CHARLES FRANKEL

Contents

✳

PART THREE   *Toward the Great Community (1918–1929)*

PART FOUR   *Democrat Emeritus (1929–1952)*

Preface

*

I N the spring of 1881, William Torrey Harris, the editor of the *Journal of Speculative Philosophy*, received a manuscript titled "The Metaphysical Assumptions of Materialism" from a young high school teacher in Oil City, Pennsylvania named John Dewey. A diffident note accompanied the manuscript, not only requesting Harris to evaluate the merits of the essay but also asking whether the article showed "ability enough of any kind to warrant my putting much of my time on that sort of subject." The essay displayed considerable dialectical skill, and several months later Harris offered to publish it in the journal and encouraged its author to continue to pursue his interests in philosophy. This was the boost the shy young teacher needed during a difficult year in the classroom, and he resolved to abandon high school teaching and try to make a career of this sort of subject.[1]

Harris proved to be a fine judge. John Dewey would become the most important philosopher in modern American history, honored and attacked by men and women all over the world. His career spanned three generations of American life and thought, and his voice could be heard in the midst of cultural controversies from the 1890s until his death in 1952 at the age of ninety-two. Over the course of this long career, Dewey developed a philosophy that called for the unity of the-

1. JD to William Torrey Harris, 17 May 1881, as quoted in George Dykhuizen, *The Life and Mind of John Dewey* (Carbondale, Ill.: Southern Illinois University Press, 1973), p. 23.

ory and practice and exemplified this unity in his own work as a critical
intellectual and political activist. His was a philosophy of enormous
breadth and a career of remarkable diversity. Taking the whole of
human experience as his field of inquiry, Dewey addressed central
issues in virtually every area of philosophy, and because he held that his
most important role as a philosopher was to "clarify men's ideas as to
the social and moral strife of their own day," he brought his philosophy
to bear directly on the concrete problems he saw plaguing American
society. His social theory was grounded in the moral conviction that
"democracy is freedom," and he devoted his life to the construction of a
persuasive philosophical argument for this conviction and to the pursuit of an activism that would secure its practical realization.[2]

This book examines Dewey's career as an advocate of democracy. I
have sought to make the connections between his social theory and
political activism by placing his thought in the context of the problems
of understanding and action which galvanized his considerable energies. The book is not quite the full intellectual biography that, unfortunately, Dewey has yet to receive. I have focused on Dewey as a social
theorist and, in particular, on his conception of "democracy as a way of
life," offering an interpretation of the meaning of this ideal and explor-
ing its central role in his work. But this perspective is less limited than it
may at first appear. The problems of democratic societies were always
on Dewey's mind, and even when he addressed himself to seemingly
distant issues in metaphysics, logic, or aesthetics, he nearly always managed to work his way toward a consideration of the bearing of such
issues on social and political life. At the same time, Dewey insisted that
an adequate democratic theory required a deep-seated philosophical
anthropology that addressed the fundamental features of human experience. He remarked that "any theory of activity in social and moral
matters, liberal or otherwise, which is not grounded in a comprehensive philosophy seems to me to be only a projection of arbitrary personal preference." For this reason, I have often looked beyond Dewey's
obviously "political" arguments and texts and have extended my discussion to matters apparently far from the concerns of democratic theory,
narrowly conceived. Not to do so would be to fail to do justice to the
centrality democracy had for him, and, like Dewey himself, I have tried
in every instance to wind my way toward the implications for democra-

2. *Reconstruction in Philosophy* (1920), *Middle Works* 12:94; "Christianity and Democracy" (1892), *Early Works* 4:8.

cy of every aspect of his thinking. Thus, I would argue that, while there is much more to be said about Dewey than I have been able to say, my focus on his democratic theory goes to the heart of his philosophy.[3]

This book might be said to be, in important respects, a "Deweyan" book about Dewey, for it is cultural history of the sort he himself favored and, on occasion, wrote. He argued that "the distinctive office, problems and subject matter of philosophy grow out of the stresses and strains in the community life in which a given form of philosophy arises, and, . . . accordingly, its specific problems vary with the changes in human life that are always going on and that at times constitute a crisis and a turning point in human history." Sharing this perspective with Dewey, I have put the development of his democratic theory within the context of the stresses and strains of his own experience and of American culture generally in the last century. I treat Dewey's philosophy as one that developed in the face of the intellectual, social, and political problems he confronted as an engaged intellectual trying both to understand and to transform his world. Rather than abstract Dewey's thought from the occasions that provoked his thinking, I have tried to reconstruct the "problematic situations" that moved him to reflection and action, situations as mundane as his concern about the security of his job at the University of Chicago in the 1890s and as earth-shaking as world war and revolution. I have paid particular attention to those occasions in which Dewey's thinking was formed, transformed, clarified, or found wanting in conversations and debates with others such as George S. Morris, G. Stanley Hall, William James, Sir Henry Maine, Franklin Ford, Jane Addams, Bertrand Russell, David Snedden, Randolph Bourne, Hu Shih, S. O. Levinson, Walter Lippmann, George Santayana, Lewis Mumford, Albert Barnes, Harry Wieman, Alfred Bingham, Leon Trotsky, Sidney Hook, Robert Hutchins, Reinhold Niebuhr, and (not least) his first wife, Alice Dewey. Perhaps surprisingly, my work is unusual in this respect, for, although there is a voluminous secondary literature on Dewey's philosophy, the historical study of his thinking remains relatively unplowed territory, and this is the first book to examine the development of Dewey's democratic theory and activism over the whole of his career.[4]

3. "Nature in Experience" (1940), *Later Works* 14:150.
4. "Introduction: Reconstruction as Seen Twenty-Five Years Later" (1948), *Middle Works* 12:256. On Dewey's considerable abilities as an intellectual historian see Richard Rorty, "Dewey's Metaphysics," in his *Consequences of Pragmatism* (Minneapolis: University of Minnesota Press, 1982), pp. 72–89. One of the ironic features of the literature on

I should perhaps stress that, although the book is biographical and historical in method, it has relatively little to offer the reader in search of a psychological portrait of John Dewey. It thus falls short of the ideal Deweyan examination of Dewey. He often said that human beings are thinkers only in the second instance. In the first instance the self was an "agent-patient, doer, sufferer, and enjoyer." Unfortunately, Dewey left little record of his own private sufferings and enjoyments. I have drawn on what evidence there is of his inner and private life when I found that it helped to explain or illuminate his thinking, but much about the man remains opaque, and given the lacuna in the evidence I doubt that psycho-biographers will ever have much success with Dewey. These limitations have sometimes rendered my explanations of *why* Dewey thought and acted as he did in particular instances more speculative than I would like, especially since some of his more important convictions seem to me to be the product of acts of faith—exercises of a "will to believe" in the face of inconclusive evidence—which call for psychological argument.[5]

I am a great deal less uncertain about my explications of Dewey's ideas, that is, my interpretation of *what* Dewey thought, even though this interpretation departs in important respects from prevailing orthodoxies. This confidence may be misplaced, but it rests on systematic research in the available published and unpublished sources, research that has convinced me that many of those who have written about Dewey's social thought have not read his work with the care it demands. Sharing Morton White's conviction that "if you are going to talk about the causes and consequences of philosophical beliefs, you had jolly well better know a lot about what those beliefs *are*," I have come to sympathize as well with his complaint that, in their eagerness to explore the causes and effects of ideas, American intellectual historians have often failed to undertake a close analysis of the ideas themselves. As a result, we have studies that explore the origins and impact of ideas that never

Dewey is the fact that the best historical study of Dewey's philosophy, Neil Coughlan's *Young John Dewey* (Chicago: University of Chicago Press, 1975), is devoted to his early career as a neo-Hegelian idealist, before he had fully worked out the positions with which he is most closely identified.

5. "Brief Studies in Realism" (1911), *Middle Works* 6:120. Something of the difficulties that await psycho-historians interested in Dewey is suggested by Coughlan's clever but unpersuasive effort to buttress his speculations about the philosopher's inner life by turning from the sparse evidence available to him about Dewey's psyche to the richly documented inner world of George Herbert Mead, which, we are to presume, paralleled Dewey's. See *Young John Dewey*, chap. 7.

existed in the minds of those thinkers to whom they have been attributed.[6]

In the case of Dewey, knowing a lot about what his beliefs were is a difficult task, for precision and clarity often escaped him. Justice Oliver Wendell Holmes's remark that Dewey wrote as "God would have spoken had He been inarticulate but keenly desirous to tell you how it was" is perhaps the most famous of many comments on this opacity. Nonetheless, Dewey's prose is no more (and, in some instances, a good deal less) obscure than that of many modern philosophers, and it suffers only by comparison with the remarkable literary qualities of the work of his fellow pragmatist William James. Much of the difficulty in understanding Dewey's work can be traced, as Edmund Wilson (one of his editors) commented, to his propensity for "generalizing in terms of abstractions." The recovery of the intended meanings of these abstractions requires that one attend carefully to Dewey's own definition of his terms and avoid the temptation to supply inappropriate alternatives. The literature on Dewey's social thought is plagued by a failure to give such key terms as "scientific intelligence," "social control," and "adaptation" the meanings he intended; indeed, by giving such terms meanings Dewey never intended, some interpreters of his work have managed to burden him with positions he explicitly rejected. This is not to say that Dewey's intentions are always clear or that he was always consistent or unambiguous. Nor is it to say that his writing did not, often at critical junctures, escape his intentions and take on new meanings in the minds of his readers. Indeed, Dewey spent a good part of his later life contesting various misreadings of his work, often with limited success. Nonetheless, these things can be sorted out, and I have attempted to do so. Whether the interpretation I have offered of Dewey's democratic theory is more plausible than others is, of course, another question. It is, I believe, a question of some importance, for if I am correct in my interpretation of the meaning of Dewey's thinking, it is high time to reassess his place in the history of modern American culture.[7]

6. Morton White, "Foreword for 1976," *Social Thought in America: The Revolt against Formalism*, 3d ed. (Boston: Beacon Press, 1976), p. xiv.

7. Mark DeWolf Howe, ed., *Holmes-Pollock Letters: The Correspondence of Mr. Justice Holmes and Sir Frederick Pollock, 1874–1932* (Cambridge: Harvard University Press, 1941), 2:287; Edmund Wilson to Arthur Schlesinger, Jr., nd, in Wilson, *Letters on Literature and Politics, 1912–1972*, ed. Elena Wilson (New York: Farrar, Straus and Giroux, 1977), p. 198. Alexis de Tocqueville argued that democrats have a special taste for abstract terms. This, he said, "both widens the scope of thought and clouds it," noting that "an abstract word is like a box with a false bottom; you may put in it what ideas you please and take

The consensus of opinion, including that of those critical of Dewey's social philosophy, is that he was a major influence on the ideology of modern liberalism and that Deweyan pragmatism is the most articulate expression of the philosophical foundation of this ideology, an ideology that has dominated political and social discourse in twentieth-century America. By virtue of the role Dewey purportedly played in the shaping of modern liberalism, many have claimed for him powers second to none among American intellectuals. According to Henry Steele Commager, Dewey became "the guide, the mentor, and the conscience of the American people: it is scarcely an exaggeration to say that for a generation no major issue was clarified until Dewey had spoken." He was, Alfred North Whitehead declared, "the typical effective American thinker" and the "chief intellectual force providing that environment with coherent purpose." A less learned but no less generous estimate of Dewey's importance to liberal Americans came from Lyndon Johnson, who remarked that he had found "a deep and lasting significance in Dr. Johnny's belief that the greatest sin of all is to lose faith in one's fellow man." Such testimony to Dewey's influence has been offered by his detractors as well as his admirers. His most relentless critic among the radical revisionist historians of education, Clarence Karier, has argued that "the pragmatic ethic which Dewey propounded free of rigid principles provided the moral dexterity so necessary for the intellectuals who became the servants of power within the liberal state in twentieth century America." This consensus regarding Dewey's influence was perhaps best summed up in the comment of Morris Cohen, one of Dewey's sharpest critics, that "if there could be such an office as that of national philosopher, no one else could be properly mentioned for it."[8]

Contrary to this prevailing consensus, I argue that Dewey's reputed influence is disproportionate to the actual impact of his most deeply held ideals on American liberalism and on the culture generally. It is more accurate to see Dewey as a minority, not a majority, spokesman within the liberal community, a social philosopher whose democratic vision failed to find a secure place in liberal ideology—in short, a more radical voice than has been generally assumed. Among liberal intellec-

them out again unobserved." *Democracy in America* (New York: Anchor Books, 1969), 2:481–482.

8. Henry Steele Commager, *The American Mind* (New Haven: Yale University Press, 1950), p. 100; Alfred North Whitehead, "John Dewey and His Influence," in Paul Schilpp, ed., *The Philosophy of John Dewey*, 2d ed. (New York: Tudor, 1951), p. 478; Lyndon Johnson to James T. Farrell, 30 November 1966, copy in Dewey Papers; Clarence Karier, "Making the World Safe for Democracy," *Educational Theory* 27 (1977): 26; Morris R. Cohen, *American Thought: A Critical Sketch* (Glencoe, Ill.: Free Press, 1954), p. 290.

tuals of the twentieth century, Dewey was the most important advocate of participatory democracy, that is, of the belief that democracy as an ethical ideal calls upon men and women to build communities in which the necessary opportunities and resources are available for every individual to realize fully his or her particular capacities and powers through participation in political, social, and cultural life. This ideal rested on a "faith in the capacity of human beings for intelligent judgment and action if proper conditions are furnished," a faith, Dewey argued, "so deeply embedded in the methods which are intrinsic to democracy that when a professed democrat denies the faith he convicts himself of treachery to his profession."[9]

It was this ideal and this faith that set Dewey apart from the mainstream of American liberalism. In terms of the criteria of Dewey's testament, much of the history of modern American liberal-democratic theory is a history of treachery, for a rejection of Dewey's democratic faith has become a standard feature of the dominant strain of liberal-democratic ideology. Since early in the century most liberal social theorists in this country have regarded this participatory ideal as hopelessly utopian and potentially threatening to social stability. Unwilling to abandon democracy altogether (although there are some notable exceptions), these liberals have argued, in the name of realism, for revised and more limited conceptions of its ideals. Politically, many have come to favor Joseph Schumpeter's famous definition of democracy as "that institutional arrangement for arriving at political decisions in which individuals acquire the power to decide by means of a competitive struggle for the people's vote," a definition that narrows democracy to little more than an ex post facto check on the power of elites, an act of occasional political consumption affording a choice among a limited range of well-packaged aspirants to office. Socially, democracy has for most liberals come to mean the provision of a minimal level of welfare to every member of a society through a corporate capitalist economy regulated by a centralized state directed by administrative experts, which, even when it works, betrays an identification of the good with the goods. Culturally, liberals have left it to conservatives to worry over the absence of a common culture grounded in a widely shared understanding of the good life and adopted a studied neutrality in ethics and art which favors a segmented market of competing "life styles" in which the good life is reduced, both morally and aesthetically, to a set of more or less arbitrary preferences among bundles of signifying commodities.

9. "Creative Democracy: The Task before Us" (1939), *Later Works* 14:227.

Whereas Dewey called for the shaping of democratic character and the creation of a common democratic culture suffusing schools, factories, political parties, and other institutions, other liberals have moved to strip democracy of its positive, substantive claims in order to render it a purely negative, procedural doctrine. Whereas Dewey urged maximum participation by a responsible public in the direction of human affairs, other liberals have sought to maximize the responsibility of powerful elites while at the same time insulating these elites from most of the pressures of the benighted "masses." They have hoped thereby to render the ordinary citizen the passive beneficiary of decisions made by the leaders of competing interest groups: at best, government *for* but not *by* the people. This is, to be sure, a very realistic notion of democracy, so realistic that it deprives the democratic ideal of most of its critical function by raising the prevailing practice of many nations, including the United States, to normative status.[10]

Dewey did not lose his battle against such realism without a fight, and this book traces not only the development of his democratic theory but also the travails of this theory in the contest with "democratic elitism." In this ideological context Dewey's thought is especially illuminating and instructive, for the tension between liberalism and democracy has been of fundamental importance in the development of modern American society. As Alan Wolfe has said, "The predicament of liberal democracy is that liberalism denies the logic of democracy and democracy denies the logic of liberalism, but neither can exist without the other." I agree with Dewey's radical critics that this tension shaped his social theory and political activism, and I also readily acknowledge that his work, in some of its aspects, provided unintended aid and comfort to those who constructed the dominant liberal-realist position. Where I depart from these critics is in my estimate that, on the whole, Dewey was a deviant among American liberals, a liberal steadily radicalized by his distinctive faith in thoroughgoing democracy. For him, it was always liberalism that had to meet the demands of democracy, not democracy that had to answer to liberalism, and it is·his departures from rather than his contributions to modern liberal orthodoxy I find most significant.[11]

My sympathies for Dewey's democratic ideals are no doubt apparent throughout this work. The battle for the meaning of liberal democracy goes on, and Dewey's democratic theory retains a measure of impor-

10. Joseph Schumpeter, *Capitalism, Socialism, and Democracy*, 3d ed. (New York: Harper and Row, 1962), p. 269.
11. Alan Wolfe, *The Limits of Legitimacy: Political Contradictions of Contemporary Capitalism* (New York: Free Press, 1977), p. 7.

tance for those like myself who are dissatisfied with the limited vision of democratic realism. If, as some political philosophers have argued, democracy is an "essentially contested" concept whose definition is never neutral but always entangled in competing moral and political commitments, then democratic politics is in fundamental respects a never-ending politics of discourse. In such a politics dissenting voices from the past can be silenced by the loss of cultural memory, and it is important, at the very least, to ensure that the more powerful of these voices are not dropped from the conversation or misheard. That Dewey is largely unread today even by those who share his democratic faith is unfortunate, and I am not above hoping that this book might make some modest contribution to a revival of interest in his work.[12]

Sympathy for Dewey's ideals does not entail a withholding of criticism, however, and historians best serve their moral and political commitments when they are willing to be the bearers of bad news as well as good. Among the lessons to be drawn from the study of Dewey's career is an appreciation of the tremendous obstacles that confront the theory and practice of democracy in modern societies. Dewey himself was well aware of these obstacles, and he called for an optimism of will tempered by "a certain intellectual pessimism"—a willingness to "look at the realities of the situation just as they are." He did not himself always sustain this balance of will and insight, but his failure to do so is perhaps as instructive as his argument for its value. It is a tough and demanding stance to maintain, and following Dewey's struggles to hold to it is a sobering experience.[13]

This book bears the marks of the learning, advice, and criticism of a number of unindicted co-conspirators. In researching and writing its first, distant incarnation I benefited enormously from the counsel of Barton Bernstein, who helped as much with the questions he did not ask as with those he did. Later Peter Agree of Cornell University Press took up this role with characteristic grace and sensitivity. Chris Lehmann, Joan Rubin, and Stewart Weaver read the entire manuscript, and I am grateful for their astute criticism and generous encouragement. Thomas Bender, Bruce Kuklick, and William Leach offered helpful comments on portions of my work. A period of animated conversation and debate with Bruce Kuklick proved especially valuable in sharpening my arguments, though I am certain that he remains unpersuaded by much of what I have to say here. Periodic dialogues of

12. On essentially contested concepts in political theory see William E. Connolly, *The Terms of Political Discourse*, 2d ed. (Princeton: Princeton University Press, 1983).
13. *Ethics* (1908), *Middle Works* 5:371.

the sort that only Cornel West can offer boosted my spirits and enhanced my confidence that, despite the current popularity of Parisian fashions, a lot can be said for thinking in an American grain. Marilyn M. Sale provided me with abundant evidence that copyediting is not an entirely lost art.

Financial support for my work was provided by fellowships from the Mrs. Giles Whiting Foundation, the John Dewey Foundation, and the Morse Research Fellowship program at Yale University. A grant from the A. Whitney Griswold Research Fund at Yale helped defray the costs of a research trip to the Midwest, and a timely leave of absence from the University of Rochester enabled me to finish the book before even my own patience ran out. The kind hospitality of Director Jo Ann Boydston of the Center for Dewey Studies and her colleagues Patricia Baysinger, Paul Kolojeski, Barbara Levine, Diane Meierkort, and Kathleen Poulos made my stays in Carbondale enjoyable as well as fruitful. John Dewey is fortunate to have his legacy abide in such hands.

I am most indebted to those friends who have not only read my work but also shared in uncommon fashion their wisdom, good humor, and a commitment to intellectual history informed by moral imagination. Jean-Christophe Agnew, Robert Cummings, Richard Fox, and Christopher Lasch have, each in distinctive ways, afforded me a better sense of what Dewey meant when he said that "democracy is the name of a way of life of free and enriching communion" in which "free social inquiry is indissolubly wedded to the art of full and moving communication."

I am grateful to my parents for the resources, emotional and material, they have committed to my education and work, even though the benefits, as these things are usually reckoned in our culture, were often obscure. Shamra Westbrook provided unflagging support, invaluable criticism, and a concrete exemplification in her teaching of young children of the kind of education on which the fate of a democratic society rests. My children, Rob, Emily, and Charlie, have arrived every nine years or so to remind me of one of the best questions posed in the literature of American democratic thought, that of a disgruntled character in Richard Chase's *Democratic Vista* who asks, "Must the damp diaper suffuse with its urgent reality even the most soaring ideas, the most fervently pure of commitments?" I have found, as did John Dewey, that the answer to this question is yes, and it is a good thing.

ROBERT B. WESTBROOK

Rochester, New York

Abbreviations

✳

Dewey Papers Dewey Papers, Special Collections, Morris Library, Southern
Illinois University, Carbondale, Ill.

Dykhuizen George Dykhuizen. *The Life and Mind of John Dewey.* Carbondale: Southern Illinois University Press, 1973.

Early Works *The Early Works of John Dewey, 1882–1898.* Carbondale:
Southern Illinois University Press, 1967–1972. 5 vols.

Hook Collection Sidney Hook/John Dewey Collection, Special Collections,
Morris Library, Southern Illinois University, Carbondale,
Ill.

Later Works *The Later Works of John Dewey, 1925–1953.* Carbondale:
Southern Illinois University Press, 1981–1991. 17 vols.

Middle Works *The Middle Works of John Dewey, 1899–1924.* Carbondale:
Southern Illinois University Press, 1976-1983. 15 vols.

JOHN DEWEY AND
AMERICAN DEMOCRACY

The Making of a Philosopher

✳

JOHN DEWEY was born in Burlington, Vermont on October 20, 1859, third of the four sons of Archibald and Lucina (Rich) Dewey.[1] Dewey's commitment to democracy has often been attributed to his roots in the egalitarian soil of the homogeneous society of small-town New England. Unfortunately, this simple explanation has little basis in fact. Burlington in Dewey's youth was a rapidly growing city, the second largest lumber depot in the country and the commercial and cultural center of Vermont. It was also a city of considerable social diversity, marked by class, ethnic, and religious divisions between an old-stock bourgeoisie and an Irish and French-Canadian working class that comprised over 40 percent of the population in 1870. Situated between Lake Champlain and the Green Mountains in one of the most beautiful natural settings in America, Burlington was not without the scenery of industrial capitalism as well. The city health officer described the tenements of the poor along the lakeshore in 1866 as "abodes of wretchedness and filth" and "haunts of dissipation and poverty." If anything, it is more accurate to view Burlington as the first of a series of industrializing communities which provided Dewey with an appreciation of the

---

1. John Dewey was born nine months after the first-born son (also named John) died as a consequence of burns suffered when he fell into a pail of scalding water. John's older brother, Davis, became a distinguished economist, while Charles, his younger brother, enjoyed a relatively obscure career as a West Coast businessman. See Dykhuizen, pp. 1–2; Neil Coughlan, *Young John Dewey* (Chicago: University of Chicago Press, 1975), pp. 3, 6.

problems of industrial democracy than it is to argue that it was "out of this early Vermont experience that democracy became part of the marrow of his bones."[2]

Both Dewey's parents were descended from generations of Vermont farmers, but his father had broken with family tradition and moved to Burlington, where he established a grocery business. An easygoing, affable man, he lacked entrepreneurial zeal and was content with modest success in business. His granddaughter later remarked that "his energy was seldom directed toward advancing himself financially and he was said to sell more goods and collect fewer bills than any other merchant in town." He endeared himself to the community not only with his generosity but also with his wit, which often enlivened his advertisements ("Hams and Cigars—Smoked and Unsmoked"). Settling down late in life, he was forty-four years old when he wed the daughter of a well-to-do Vermont squire and nearly fifty when John was born.[3]

The year of Dewey's birth was a momentous one in Western intellectual history, witnessing the publication of Charles Darwin's *Origin of Species* as well as John Stuart Mill's *On Liberty* and Karl Marx's *Critique of Political Economy*. The work of these men would eventually figure prominently in the development of Dewey's social philosophy, but in 1859 it made few ripples on the shores of Lake Champlain. In late October, the attention of the community was riveted not on intellectual controversies but on events in Harper's Ferry, Virginia, where a few days before Dewey's birth John Brown had launched his unsuccessful raid on a federal armory. Dewey's father, a staunch Republican, followed the sectional crisis with great interest and even made it the basis for one of his ads ("To secede or sow seed, that's the question. Those who would sow seed as to succeed and not reseed, will see seeds at Dewey's"). When the Civil War began, Archibald Dewey, despite his age, was among the most eager of Lincoln's volunteers. He sold his grocery business and enlisted in 1861 as a quartermaster in the First Vermont Cavalry, where he was welcomed as a man "of superior intelligence, of strong patriotism, and of a dry humor which made him an entertaining companion."[4]

Dewey's father apparently flourished in the army. Mustered out of his regiment in September 1862, he reenlisted and was promoted to

2. Dykhuizen, pp. 1–2, 328n8; Jerome Nathanson, *John Dewey: The Reconstruction of the Democratic Life* (New York: Frederick Ungar, 1951), p. 2.

3. Jane Dewey, "Biography of John Dewey," in Paul Schilpp, ed., *The Philosophy of John Dewey*, 2d ed. (New York: Tudor, 1951), p. 5.

4. *The Vermont Cynic*, 2 November 1949; G. G. Benedict, *Vermont in the Civil War, 1861–1865* (Burlington, Vt.: Free Press Association, 1888), 2:36.

captain and assistant quartermaster of volunteers. Dewey's mother, however, found separation from her husband unbearable, and in 1864 she moved the family to northern Virginia to be near him. The family did not return to Burlington until 1867, when Archibald went back into business as the proprietor of a cigar and tobacco shop. The devastation and privations of war made a deep impression on the Dewey boys, and according to Sidney Hook, Dewey's youthful impressions of the carnage were an important reference point for his later reflections on the futility of violence in the achievement of human purposes.[5]

In removing herself and three young boys to the battlefields of the Civil War, Lucina Dewey displayed characteristic independence and determination. Although twenty years younger than her husband, she seldom hesitated to assert her will in the affairs of the family. Descended, as Archibald was not, from the social and political elite of Vermont, Lucina had much loftier ambitions for her sons than did her husband. These hopes were fired by the passionate convictions of her evangelical Protestant faith. She had as an adolescent converted to an emotional Congregational pietism that contrasted sharply with the more comforting and rationalistic liberal faith preached in Burlington's First Congregational Church to which her family belonged and with the fun-loving spirit of her husband, whose deepest faith seems to have been in the Republican party. A confirmed "partialist," believing that only a select portion of humanity was destined for salvation, Lucina was constantly inquiring into the state of her sons' souls, asking them—sometimes in the presence of others—whether they were "right with Jesus." Her religious outlook put a premium on feelings of sinfulness and utter dependence on Christ for redemption. When Dewey applied for admission to the church at the age of eleven, he supplied a note attesting, "I think I love Christ and want to obey him," a note written by his mother.

The effect of this relentless maternal solicitude, according to Dewey, was "to induce in us a sense of guilt and at the same time irritation because of the triviality of the occasions on which she questioned us." Under his mother's watchful eye, Dewey grew to be a shy and self-conscious young man, and a certain diffidence was to be a permanent feature of his character. As he matured intellectually, he faced "a trying personal crisis" growing out of "the conflict of traditional religious beliefs with opinions that I could myself honestly entertain." Unfortunately, no record remains of this crisis, only Dewey's carefully guarded recollection of "an inward laceration" produced by an alienating sense

5. Benedict, *Vermont in the Civil War*, 2:580; Sidney Hook, *Education and the Taming of Power* (LaSalle, Ill.: Open Court, 1973), pp. 141–142.

of "isolation of self from the world, of soul from body, of nature from God."[6]

Dewey's mother did not limit her attentions to her own family. Noted especially for her work among the city's poor and her skill as a counselor to young men at the University of Vermont, she was a leader among the women in the church who dedicated themselves to benevolent philanthropy. She sought, as she put it, to "make Burlington a temperate and moral city, a safe clean place for young men, a city of virtuous and happy homes." Her fellow reformers viewed her as an idealist and "a bit of a 'mystic' visionary" who "was always looking forward from things as they *are*, to what they ought to be, and might be." His mother's philanthropy may well have exercised a formative influence on Dewey's social conscience and, at the same time, shaped his lifelong antipathy to "do-gooders," whose altruism, he felt, betrayed a particularly subtle form of egotism.[7]

Although his mother's religious piety placed constraints on Dewey's emotional and intellectual development, her dedication to the education of her sons guaranteed that he would have the resources he needed to work his way out from under her thumb. Building on the connections that came with the Rich family name, she secured a central place for herself among Burlington's "old American" social and cultural elite and made the advantages of cultivated society available to her children. Dewey's father was, despite his limited education, quite well read (he was heard to quote Milton and Shakespeare as he went about his work in his store), but his ambitions extended little beyond the hope that one of his sons would become a mechanic. Lucina, however, was born of a family with many college-educated men, and she was determined that her boys would be the first Deweys to obtain such a degree. She made a wide range of reading available to them to supplement the woeful curriculum of the Burlington public schools, and in the fall of 1875 John and Davis entered the University of Vermont.[8]

6. Dykhuizen, pp. 6–7; Sidney Hook, "Some Memories of John Dewey," in *Pragmatism and the Tragic Sense of Life* (New York: Basic Books, 1974), pp. 102–103; JD, "From Absolutism to Experimentalism" (1930), *Later Works* 5:153. Dewey was perhaps thinking of his mother when he remarked in 1886 that "religious feeling is unhealthy when it is watched and analyzed to see if it exists, if it is right, if it is growing. It is as fatal to be forever observing our own religious moods and experiences, as it is to pull up a seed from the ground to see if it is growing" ("The Place of Religious Emotion," *Early Works* 1:91).

7. *Burlington Free Press*, 28 March 1899; Sarah P. Torrey, "Women's Work in First Church," in *The Hundredth Anniversary of the Founding of First Church* (Burlington, Vt.: First Church, 1905), pp. 62–63. Lucina Dewey's activities as a counselor of collegians were the model for the character of "Mrs. Carver" in a novel by Elvirton Wright, *Freshman and Senior* (Boston: Congregational Sunday School & Publishing Society, 1899).

8. Jane Dewey, "Biography," pp. 5–6.

The university, located in Burlington, was regarded as one of the finest institutions of higher learning in New England. It owed its prominence in large measure to its fifth president, James Marsh, a leading American transcendentalist who had made it a center of intellectual ferment and educational innovation before the Civil War. During the war years, the school had fallen on hard times and become something of an embarrassment to the community, but after it was named the state's land grant institution in 1865, it managed to restore its respectability if not its preeminence. By the time of Dewey's undergraduate years, the university was once again at the heart of Burlington's cultural life, and its faculty, many of them friends of the Dewey family, shared a liberal Christian orthodoxy indistinguishable from that preached from the pulpit of the First Church. L. O. Brastow, minister of the church in Dewey's youth, calmly assured his flock that "liberal evangelicalism assumes that human intelligence may venture to deal with the facts of revelation and of religious experience and bring back valid results," and the faculty of the University of Vermont dedicated itself to the task of demonstrating that this was indeed the case.[9]

For the first two years of college Dewey was a rather halfhearted student, but beginning with his introduction to the natural sciences in his junior year his interest in his studies accelerated. In his second year he took courses in geology (which introduced him to the theory of evolution), biology, and physiology. He later recalled that the physiology course and its textbook, T. H. Huxley's *Elements of Physiology*, provided him with "a sense of interdependence and interrelated unity that gave form to intellectual stirrings that had been previously inchoate, and created a type or model of a view of things to which material in any field ought to conform." The senior-year course of study in moral philosophy—which included instruction in political economy, law, history, psychology, ethics, philosophy of religion, and logic—also captured Dewey's imagination, and he did well enough in his final year to graduate Phi Beta Kappa. He also managed a good deal of extra reading on his own, concentrating in philosophy on the ponderous tomes of Herbert Spencer and in literature on the novels of George Eliot. Sociology was also a special interest, and he was particularly impressed with Frederic Harrison's anglicized version of the social theory of Auguste Comte. His favorite reading, however, was the British periodical press, and he followed the controversies surrounding evolutionary biology in the *Contemporary Review*, the *Nineteenth Century*, and the *Fortnightly Review*.[10]

9. See Julian I. Lindsay, *Tradition Looks Forward: The University of Vermont, a History, 1791–1904* (Burlington: University of Vermont, 1954); Dykhuizen, p. 7.
10. "From Absolutism to Experimentalism," p. 147; Lewis Feuer, "John Dewey's Read-

Instruction in philosophy at Vermont was typical of that offered at most American colleges at the time. The central aim of the curriculum was to fortify the religious and moral convictions of Protestant adolescents. The professor was, as Neil Coughlan has said, "the philosophical arm of the preaching ministry," and his task was "to demonstrate *how* philosophy and human reason tended to support the teachings of Scripture (certainly not to ask *whether* they did)." H. A. P. Torrey, Dewey's mentor, was a graduate of Union Theological Seminary and had served for three years as the pastor of the Congregational church in Vergennes, Vermont, before succeeding his uncle Joseph Torrey in the chair of intellectual and moral philosophy in 1868. He continued to preach after he became a philosopher, and he and his wife were stalwart members of the First Church.[11]

Vermont was unusual, however, in that the college's philosophers had, quite early in the nineteenth century, looked to Kantian and post-Kantian German philosophy for inspiration. By the late nineteenth century, academic philosophy in America had a decided German accent, but before the Civil War (and the Darwinian revolution) most colleges had based instruction in philosophy on Scottish "common-sense" realism. This school of thought rejected the phenomenalism of Lockean epistemology, which had reached an impasse in the corrosive skepticism of David Hume, yet nonetheless set itself firmly in the British empirical tradition. James Marsh had led Vermont on a different path. Marsh, as Dewey said, "was probably the first American scholar to have an intimate first-hand acquaintance with the writings of Immanuel Kant," and in 1829 he brought Kantian philosophy to the attention of his countrymen (including Emerson) with the first American edition of Coleridge's *Aids to Reflection*. In his important introductory essay to this volume Marsh launched an attack on all forms of empiricism, including Scottish realism, arguing that an empirical epistemology could never provide a secure foundation for a spiritual religion. Ignoring the limitations Kant placed on human knowledge of "things-in-themselves" (noumena), Marsh developed a kind of conservative

---

ing at College," *Journal of the History of Ideas* 19 (1958): 415–421. No one, to my knowledge, has ever commented on Dewey's reading of Eliot (including Dewey), but it is worth noting that there are similarities between the social vision in her novels and that of his philosophy. Steven Marcus has observed the remarkable coincidence of Eliot's social theory and that of Charles H. Cooley, the American sociologist who was Dewey's student and whose thinking resembles his in important respects. See "Human Nature, Social Orders and 19th Century Systems of Explanation: Starting In with George Eliot," *Salmagundi* 28 (1978): 20–42.

11. Coughlan, *Young John Dewey*, p. 15; Lewis Feuer, "H. A. P. Torrey and John Dewey: Teacher and Pupil," *American Quarterly* 10 (1958): 35–36.

Transcendentalism which argued that mankind was possessed of a faculty of Reason whose powers exceeded those of the empirical Understanding and which provided the basis for "a quickening communication with the Divine Spirit." At the same time, Marsh was careful to characterize the intuitions of reason in traditional theistic terms and to avoid the radical pantheism of his fellow Transcendentalists in Concord.

Marsh's philosophy was perpetuated at Vermont by his friend and successor in the chair of philosophy, Joseph Torrey, and by Torrey's nephew and successor, Henry, both of whom leaned heavily on *Aids to Reflection* and the *Remains of James Marsh* in their teaching. Immediately after his appointment in 1868, H. A. P. Torrey began a thorough study of Kant's three Critiques, and Dewey was but one of a number of students to express their appreciation for Torrey's undaunted efforts to convey Kant's philosophy to provincial undergraduates. "Thanks to my introduction under your auspices to Kant at the beginning of my studies," Dewey wrote Torrey, "I think I have had a much better introduction into phil. than I could have had any other way. . . . It certainly introduced a revolution into all my thoughts, and at the same time gave me a basis for my other reading and thinking." Dewey later characterized Torrey as "constitutionally timid," and it is true that Torrey's Kantianism was carefully tailored to preserve Christian truth at the expense of speculative rigor. He utilized Kant's epistemology to deflect the threat of Darwinism and put science in its place as knowledge of "mere" phenomena, while at the same time rejecting Kant's conclusion that the noumena of ethics and religion were equally unknowable in favor of an intuitionism that claimed immediate access to these higher things. This straddling, however, was what his role demanded, and it is fair to say that Dewey received as good an undergraduate education in philosophy as was then available in the United States.[12]

It is much more difficult, unfortunately, to determine exactly what Dewey was taught about history, politics, and economics, but surely it was implacably conservative. His instructor in these subjects was President Matthew Buckham, who warned students against "a dangerous tendency toward radicalism. What we call progress is always on the

---

12. Elizabeth Flower and Murray G. Murphey, *A History of Philosophy in America* (New York: Capricorn Books, 1977), pp. 408–409; JD, "James Marsh and American Philosophy" (1929), *Later Works* 5:178–196; Peter Carafiol, *Transcendent Reason: James Marsh and the Forms of Romantic Thought* (Tallahassee: University Presses of Florida, 1982); Feuer, "H. A. P. Torrey and John Dewey," pp. 41–44; *In Memoriam Henry A. P. Torrey, LL.D.* (Burlington: University of Vermont, 1906); JD to H. A. P. Torrey, 17 November 1883, George Dykhuizen Papers and Correspondence, University of Vermont; JD, "From Absolutism to Experimentalism," p. 148.

verge of fanaticism. . . . The very term 'radical' suggests platforms, heated resolutions, angry oratory, fanatics with long hair and fiery eyes, scattering invective and scorn, and investing every cause they advocate with associations of bitterness and hate." One alumnus, reflecting on the prevalence of such sentiments at the university, described Vermont graduates as "the coldest, most indifferent, most immovable body of educated men below the Arctic Circle." Whatever deviant opinions Dewey may have collected in these years, it is likely that he derived them from his own reading and not from his teachers.[13]

After his graduation in 1879, Dewey spent three years teaching high school, first in Oil City, Pennsylvania where a cousin found him a job and then back home in a small town south of Burlington. Oil City was a raw industrial boomtown in the heart of the Allegheny oil fields, and here, amid derricks, refineries, and crowded river wharves, Dewey wrote his first article, "The Metaphysical Assumptions of Materialism," which was accepted for publication by the *Journal of Speculative Philosophy*. It was also in this unlikely setting that he had what he later described to Max Eastman as a mystical experience, an experience of quiet reconciliation with the world, a feeling that "everything that's here is here, and you can just lie back on it." He compared it to the poetic pantheism of Wordsworth and Whitman as an undramatic yet blissful moment of "oneness with the universe." He would never lose touch with this feeling, though his interpretation of its meaning and implications would change dramatically.[14]

After his return to Vermont in 1881, Dewey combined his teaching with a year's tutorial with Torrey in modern philosophy. He had considerable problems with classroom discipline and began to contemplate a switch to an academic career. One of Dewey's students later remarked that she remembered two things about his teaching: "how terribly the boys behaved, and how long and fervent was the prayer with which he opened each school day." Encouraged by the positive response of Harris to his article on materialism and a second essay, "The Pantheism of Spinoza," Dewey applied to Johns Hopkins University for a graduate fellowship in philosophy.[15]

This decision was significant and somewhat risky. The modern American university was only beginning to take shape in the early 1880s, and the well-marked path from secular graduate schools such as

13. Feuer, "H. A. P. Torrey and John Dewey," pp. 48–49. Unfortunately, Dewey's senior commencement oration, "The Limits of Political Economy," has not survived.
14. Dykhuizen, pp. 19–22; Max Eastman, "John Dewey," *Atlantic*, December 1941: 673.
15. Dykhuizen, pp. 25–26.

Johns Hopkins to teaching positions in the nation's colleges had yet to be firmly established. Surveying the condition of philosophy in the United States in 1879, G. Stanley Hall estimated that instruction in the subject in two-thirds of the nation's colleges was "rudimentary and medieval" and that there was but a handful of institutions where "metaphysical thought is entirely freed from reference to theological formula." It was plain, Hall concluded, "that there is very small chance that a well-equipped student of philosophy in any of its departments will secure a position as a teacher of the subject." Although Dewey's initial articles indicated that he had, in Torrey's words, "a marked predilection for metaphysics" and possessed "in a rare degree the mental qualities requisite for its successful pursuit," even someone as talented as he could not be certain of making a career of metaphysical pursuit. Most of the prominent metaphysicians in the United States were, like Harris, philosophers without portfolio, independent gentleman scholars who floated free of affiliations with conventional institutions of higher education, and this was not the sort of life open to the son of a Vermont storekeeper.[16]

Dewey was undeterred by these uncertainties, and he chose to study at the institution that had made a radical break with the traditions of American higher education by committing itself principally to research and advanced study. Built from scratch and bankrolled by the generous bequest of Baltimore businessman Johns Hopkins, the university had opened its doors in 1876 under the aggressive leadership of President Daniel Coit Gilman, and it quickly earned a reputation among such distinguished scholars as Harvard mathematician Benjamin Peirce as "the only American institution where the promotion of science is the supreme object, and the trick of pedagogy is reckoned as of no value." The student at Johns Hopkins, as one of its first graduate fellows, Josiah Royce, remarked, "longed to be a doer of the word, and not a hearer only, a creator of his own infinitesimal fraction of a product, bound in God's name to produce it when the time came." Desperately eager to enlist in this company, Dewey was undaunted when Hopkins offered him admission but not the financial assistance he needed to continue his studies. In the fall of 1882 he borrowed five hundred dollars from an aunt and headed south to join a new breed of academic professionals.[17]

16. G. Stanley Hall, "Philosophy in the United States," *Mind* 4 (1879): 89–91; H. A. P. Torrey to George S. Morris, 11 February 1882, as quoted in Dykhuizen, p. 26. On the institutional dynamics of American philosophy in this period see Bruce Kuklick, *The Rise of American Philosophy* (New Haven: Yale University Press, 1977), pp. 46–62, 129–139.
17. Peirce and Royce quoted in Hugh Hawkins, *Pioneer: A History of the Johns Hopkins University, 1874–1889* (Ithaca: Cornell University Press, 1960), pp. 77, 92.

John Dewey in 1894, photographed at the University of Michigan. Courtesy of the Bentley Historical Library, University of Michigan.

Part One

A Social Gospel
(1882–1904)

Democracy and the one, the ultimate, ethical ideal
of humanity are to my mind synonyms. The idea of
democracy, the ideas of liberty, equality, and
fraternity, represent a society in which the
distinction between the spiritual and the secular has
ceased.

— "The Ethics of Democracy" (1888)

CHAPTER 1

The Hegelian Bacillus

*

Soon after John Dewey arrived at Johns Hopkins to begin his graduate studies in philosophy, President Gilman tried to persuade him to switch to another field. The bulk of the university's resources were committed to the natural sciences, and Gilman regarded philosophy as an insufficiently scientific discipline that remained too closely tied to religious perspectives hostile to the development of scientific knowledge. Hence, the philosophy department was one of the weakest in the university. No full professor had been appointed in the field, and teaching duties were handled by three young lecturers: G. Stanley Hall, George Sylvester Morris, and Charles Sanders Peirce. Dewey, however, was not persuaded by Gilman's arguments, and he quickly gravitated to Morris, the least scientific of Hopkins's trio of philosophers and a neo-Hegelian.[1]

Morris's presence at Hopkins was symptomatic of the growing influence of post-Kantian idealism on American philosophy. A few months before Dewey arrived in Baltimore, William James had filed a brief in the British journal *Mind* against the growing popularity of Hegelianism in the English-speaking world. "We are just now witnessing a singular phenomenon in British and American philosophy," he observed. "Hegelism so defunct on its native soil . . . has found among us so

1. Jane E. Dewey, "Biography of John Dewey," in Paul A. Schilpp, ed., *The Philosophy of John Dewey*, 2d ed. (New York: Tudor, 1951), p. 16; Hugh Hawkins, *Pioneer: A History of the Johns Hopkins University, 1874–1889* (Ithaca: Cornell University Press, 1960), chap. 11.

zealous and able a set of propagandists that today it may really be reckoned one of the most powerful influences of the time in the higher walks of thought." While (after a brief flirtation with materialism) German philosophers rushed "back to Kant," British philosophers led by T. H. Green and F. H. Bradley at Oxford and Edward and John Caird in Scotland had turned to Hegel for support as they worked out a domestic brand of absolute idealism with which to challenge the long-standing dominance of the empirical tradition of Locke, Hume, Bentham, Mill, and Spencer. In the United States, Hegel clubs had sprouted up throughout the country, and in St. Louis an energetic band of Hegelians led by William Torrey Harris had successfully launched the nation's first professional journal of philosophy, the *Journal of Speculative Philosophy*. In addition, absolute idealists including Morris, George H. Palmer, and Josiah Royce had established a foothold in the philosophy departments of leading American universities. These, James felt, were lamentable developments, for "Hegel's philosophy mingles mountain-loads of corruption with its scanty merits." Comparing the spell of absolute idealism to nitrous-oxide intoxication, James hoped he might show "some chance youthful disciple that there *is* another point of view in philosophy."[2]

Dewey may have read James's article, but if so, it had little effect. By the end of his first term at Johns Hopkins he was already committed to "a theory which admits the constitutive power of Thought, as itself ultimate Being, determining objects." For him, Hegel's thought *was* intoxicating; it "supplied a demand for unification that was doubtless an intense emotional craving, and yet was a hunger that only an intellectualized subject-matter could satisfy." He held this commitment to Hegelianism firmly for about ten years; it waned slowly for nearly another decade, and Dewey never completely shook Hegel out of his system. He remarked in 1945, "I jumped through Hegel, I should say, not just out of him. I took some of the hoop . . . with me, and also carried away considerable of the paper the hoop was filled with."[3]

2. William James, "On Some Hegelisms" (1882), *The Will to Believe* (Cambridge: Harvard University Press, 1979), p. 196. At Corpus Christi College, Oxford—a utilitarian island in a sea of idealism—it was said in the 1880s that "all bad German philosophies, when they die, go to Oxford" (Peter Clark, *Liberals and Social Democrats* [Cambridge: Cambridge University Press, 1978], p. 12).

3. "Knowledge and the Relativity of Feeling" (1883), *Early Works* 1:33; "From Absolutism to Experimentalism" (1930), *Later Works* 5:153; JD to Arthur Bentley, 9 July 1945, in *John Dewey and Arthur Bentley: A Philosophical Correspondence, 1932–1951*, ed. Sidney Ratner, Jules Altman, and James E. Wheeler (New Brunswick, N.J.: Rutgers University Press, 1964), p. 439. On the Hegelian residues in Dewey's mature thought see Richard Bernstein, *Praxis and Action* (Philadelphia: University of Pennsylvania Press, 1971), pp. 165–177.

This remark applies as much, if not more, to Dewey's social theory as to other aspects of his philosophy, despite the fact that in his earliest years as a philosopher he devoted relatively little attention to social theory as such. Social and political concerns had little to do with his conversion to absolute idealism, and it was not until the late 1880s that he took much interest in democratic theory or politics. Before this, he centered his attention on more abstruse metaphysical issues and on the threat of experimental psychology to religious faith, believing that the problem of philosophy was one of determining "the meaning of Thought, Nature, and God, and the relations of one to another." But if the problems of democracy had little to do with Dewey's initial attraction to absolute idealism, it is of no small significance that he was an absolute idealist when he began to address these problems, for his early democratic theory was as thoroughly infected as his previous work in metaphysics and psychology with what he later lightly termed the "Hegelian bacillus." Thus it is important to explain why this bacillus found in Dewey such a willing host.[4]

ORGANIC IDEALISM

Many years after he left Vermont, Dewey remarked that the "intuitional philosophy" he learned from Torrey "did not go deep, and in no way did it satisfy what I was dimly reaching for." The evidence that remains from this early period of his career bears him out. The two articles he wrote before graduate school on the metaphysics of materialism and on Spinoza's pantheism are often said to be evidence of an initial intuitionist perspective, but it is difficult to determine from these essays what Dewey's metaphysics were at the time. The critique of the materialists and Spinoza in these articles was strictly logical. In each case Dewey pointed to contradictions in the reasoning of exponents of the offending doctrines, but in neither instance were his own metaphysical convictions readily apparent. Dewey was looking for a philosophy that would free him from the guilt-ridden pietism of his mother, satisfy his hunger for unification, and provide a rational underpinning for the feeling of oneness with the universe which he had experienced in Oil City, but Torrey's intuitionism with its sharp dualisms and question-begging leap of faith could not do so. Without a metaphysics that

---

4. "The Pantheism of Spinoza" (1882), *Early Works* 1:9; JD to William James, 27 March 1903, in Ralph Barton Perry, *The Thought and Character of William James* (Boston: Little, Brown, 1935), 2:522.

could meet his emotional and intellectual needs, philosophy was for Dewey little more than an "intellectual gymnastic."[5]

At Hopkins, Dewey found in George Morris a teacher who had suffered an "inward laceration" similar to his own and discovered in British neo-Hegelianism a cure for the alienation that beset them both. Born in Norwich, Vermont, in 1840, Morris had attended Dartmouth College and Union Theological Seminary, where he studied with Henry Boynton Smith, a leading American theologian. Impressed by Morris's abilities as a scholar, Smith urged him to undertake advanced study in Germany and pursue a career in philosophy rather than the ministry. Morris departed for Europe in 1866 and took up his studies in Germany with Hermann Ulrici of Halle and Friedrich Trendelenburg of Berlin. In the short run, he was ill served by this higher education. His fiancée broke off their engagement because "he had grown so learned and changed so much in his religious opinions that she was afraid of him," and he returned home in 1868 to find that there were no jobs in American colleges for philosophers who had drunk too deeply of the waters of German learning. After a few years spent as tutor to the children of a wealthy New York banker, Morris finally landed a job in 1870 as a professor of modern languages and literature at the University of Michigan, where the chair in philosophy was held by a Methodist minister who had dropped out of school at the age of thirteen.[6]

The early 1870s were also a trying period for Morris intellectually as he wrestled with the challenge of Darwinian science to religious faith and the alienating dualisms meeting this challenge seemed to entail— the same dualisms of self and world, soul and body, God and nature which troubled Dewey. He captured this alienation in a striking metaphor in an 1876 essay, "The Immortality of the Human Soul": "The water-spider provides for its respiration and life beneath the surface of the water by spinning around itself an envelope large enough to contain the air it needs. So we have need, while walking through the thick and often polluted moral atmosphere of this lower world, where seeming life is too frequently inward death, to maintain around ourselves the purer atmosphere of a higher faith." For some, writing off the natural world in this fashion was a satisfactory resolution of the tensions between science and religion, but Morris could not free himself

5. "From Absolutism to Experimentalism," pp. 149, 153; "The Metaphysical Assumptions of Materialism" (1882), *Early Works* 1:3–8; "The Pantheism of Spinoza," pp. 9–18.

6. R. M. Wenley, *The Life and Work of George Sylvester Morris* (London: Macmillan, 1917), passim.

from the force of his teacher Trendelenburg's contention that "thought is suffocated and withers without the air and light of the sensible cognition of the world of real things." As a consequence, the atmosphere inside his envelope of faith grew steadily staler.[7]

By the end of the decade Morris's life had brightened considerably. In 1877 he was invited to lecture in philosophy for a semester at Johns Hopkins, and he subsequently negotiated a regular arrangement whereby he taught philosophy for one semester each year at both Hopkins and Michigan. About the same time Morris discovered in the work of T. H. Green and the other British idealists a philosophy that dissolved the dualisms that had tormented him and a metaphysics that convinced him that nature was not a polluted moral atmosphere but rather the manifestation of divine spirit.

Beginning with Green's long, destructive introduction to a new edition of Hume's *Treatise of Human Nature* published in 1874, the idealists had launched an effort to reconcile religion and Victorian natural science by means of a critique of the agnostic, empiricist epistemology that Herbert Spencer and others contended was the philosophical ally of scientific investigation. Rather than shrink from or deny the accomplishments of natural science or attempt to establish separate spheres of authority for faith and reason as Morris had done, the idealists met science head on and argued that the very successes that natural science could claim in making sense of the world were inexplicable in terms of empiricist epistemology and were explicable only in terms of the metaphysics of objective idealism. As Dewey said, the neo-Hegelians were attempting "to show that there is a spiritual principle at the root of ordinary experience and science, as well as at the basis of ethics and religion; to show, negatively, that whatever weakens the supremacy and primacy of the spiritual principle makes science impossible, and positively, to show that any fair analysis of the conditions of science will show certain ideas, principles, or catagories—call them what you will— that are not physical and sensible, but intellectual and metaphysical."[8]

Empiricists and idealists agreed that science was the knowledge of relations between things, but, the idealists argued, empiricism with its theory of knowledge as the impression of discrete sensations on a passive mind was unable to explain how such relations are known. Insofar as they ordered sensations, these relations could not be the product of

7. G. S. Morris, "The Immortality of the Human Soul," *Bibliotheca Sacra* 33 (1876): 715; Morris, "Friedrich Adolf Trendelenburg," *New Englander* 33 (1874): 332, as quoted in Neil Coughlan, *Young John Dewey* (Chicago: University of Chicago Press, 1975), p. 23.
8. "The Philosophy of Thomas Hill Green" (1889), *Early Works* 3:17.

sensations, for that view would be akin to a geologist's teaching that "the first formation of rocks was the product of all layers built upon it." Thus the empiricists had to admit that ordinary experience as well as scientific knowledge presupposed a constructive function for consciousness which their epistemology did not allow. Far from being the ally of science, empiricism rendered science impossible. "A consistent sensationalism," Green observed, "would be speechless."

This much Kant had shown. The idealists advanced beyond Kant by means of their (controversial) theory of internal relations. This theory held that all the relations of a particular thing were "internal" to it, that is, they were all *essential* characteristics of that thing. Knowledge of any particular thing thus rested on knowledge of a connected whole of which it was a part, and the fact that all the relations of every particular thing were essential implied "the existence of a single, permanent, and all-inclusive system of relations." Moreover, because relations were the product of consciousness, there was further implied the existence of "a permanent single consciousness which forms the bond of relations." This logic showed, at least to the satisfaction of Dewey, Morris, and other idealists, that "in the existence of knowable fact, in the existence of that which we call reality, there is necessarily implied an intelligence which is one, self-distinguishing and not subject to the conditions of space and time." This eternal self-consciousness was the idealists' God. Only this God, the Absolute, could know reality in its totality, but because eternal intelligence was partially and gradually reproducing itself in human experience man could share in this knowledge through science. Science was "simply *orderly* experience. It is the working out of the relations, the laws, implied in experience, but not visible upon its surface. It is a more adequate reproduction of the relations by which the eternal self-consciousness constitutes both nature and our understandings." As such, science posed no threat to religion, for it presupposed "a principle which transcends nature, a principle which is spiritual."9

This "metaphysical analysis of science" released Morris from the doldrums in which he had been mired since his return from Europe, and by the time Dewey arrived at Hopkins, he was in the midst of an enormously productive decade of scholarship which established him as

9. Ibid., pp. 18–24. The difficulty with the idealist theory of internal relations for most philosophers lies in its assertion that all the relations of a thing are essential and hence internal. Most hold that relations can be either essential and internal or accidental and external, a position that derails the idealists' logical express train to the Absolute. See Richard Rorty, "Relations, Internal and External," in *The Encyclopedia of Philosophy* (New York: Macmillan, 1967), 7:125–133, and D. C. Phillips, *Holistic Thought in Social Science* (Stanford: Stanford University Press, 1976), chap. 1.

one of the foremost American philosophers. Dewey succinctly summed up Morris's variant of neo-Hegelianism, which might best be termed "organic idealism," in a letter to Torrey in the fall of 1882:

> Prof. Morris . . . is a pronounced idealist and we have already heard of the "universal self." He says that idealism (substantial idealism as opposed to subjectivistic or agnosticism) is the only positive phil. that has or can exist. His whole position is here, as I understand it. Two starting points can be taken—one regards subject & object as in mechanical relation, relations in and of space & time, & the process of knowledge is simply impact of the object upon the subject with resulting sensation or impression. This is its position as science of knowing. As science of being, since nothing exists for the subject except these impressions or states, nothing can be known of real being, and the result is skepticism, or subj. idealism, or agnosticism. The other, instead of beginning with a presupposition regarding subj. & object & their relation, takes the facts & endeavors to explain them—that is to show what is necessarily involved in knowledge, and results in the conclusion that subject and object are in organic relation, neither having reality apart from the other. Being is within consciousness. And the result on the side of science of Being is substantial idealism—science as opposed to nescience. Knowing is self-knowing, & all consciousness is conditioned upon self-consciousness.[10]

Torrey might well have been disturbed by this letter. Although he acknowledged the intellectual power of Hegelianism, he believed that it was a form of pantheism which threatened the autonomy of the individual moral will. Dewey did not, however, find this objection compelling, for he believed that an organic idealism such as that of Hegel and Morris, unlike the pantheism of Spinoza, did not sacrifice the individual moral will to that of some abstract universal but rather posited a "concrete universal" that not only preserved the reality of individual will but required such individuality for its manifestation. "While pantheism would make the relation of human conscious to the world and to God one of bare identity and absorption, the relation, according to Green [and Morris], is one of spiritual, personal unity, and this implies that there be really spirit, personality on *both* sides of the relation." For Dewey, as for Morris, Hegelianism offered a vision of an interdependent universe that, he later said, "operated as an immense release, a liberation."[11]

10. JD to H. A. P. Torrey, 5 October 1882, George Dykhuizen Papers and Correspondence, University of Vermont.
11. "The Philosophy of Thomas Hill Green," p. 23; "From Absolutism to Experimen-

Despite Torrey's objections to Hegelianism, one should not over-look—as Dewey himself tended to do—the continuity between Ver-mont and Hopkins, Torrey and Morris. Morris's aims as a philosopher were substantially the same as those of Torrey: to provide a philosophi-cal foundation for liberal Protestantism. They differed only in the building blocks they used for this foundation. Morris's philosophy and religious faith, as Dewey said, "were one—vitally and indistinguishably one. . . . In the fundamental principle of Christianity, he found man-ifested the truth which he was convinced of as the fundamental truth in philosophy—the unity of God and man so that the spirit which is in man, rather which is man, is the spirit of God." Absolute idealism, Morris argued, provided a more rational and persuasive argument for Christian belief, and Dewey agreed. As Neil Coughlan has observed, "In Torrey, Dewey had seen a fragmented defense of orthodoxy—part philosophy, part faith, part 'reserved judgment'; in Morris (thanks to Green and the neo-Hegelians) he encountered essentially the same orthodoxy championed by a breathtakingly grandiose system, one that met the empiricists and skeptics on their own grounds and outlogicked them." For Torrey the proof of the existence of God was based on an intuition not subject to rational analysis, while for Morris God was a logical necessity.[12]

Dewey took all of Morris's courses and quickly became the idealist's favorite student. On the other hand, he mustered little enthusiasm for courses in experimental psychology with Hall and mathematical logic with Peirce, and he criticized Johns Hopkins's vaunted history depart-ment for its failure to place historical research in a philosophical con-text, by which he meant Hegel's philosophy of history. Dewey finished his degree in 1884 with his dissertation "Kant's Psychology," which offered the familiar idealist critique of Kant as a halfway revolutionary who failed to see that his own principles pointed beyond the separation of subject and object to an understanding of their "organic relation" as manifestations of Reason. Hegel, of course, saw this, and Kant's phi-losophy found its fulfillment in Hegel's logic, which, Dewey said, was "the completed Method of Philosophy."[13]

Throughout Dewey's years at Hopkins a behind-the-scenes battle was

talism," p. 153. On Torrey's objections to Hegelianism, see the remarks of Edward H. Griffin and John Wright Buckham in *In Memoriam Henry A. P. Torrey, LL.D.* (Burlington: University of Vermont, 1906), pp. 12–13, 24.

12. "The Late Professor Morris" (1889), *Early Works* 3:8–9; Coughlan, *Young John Dewey*, p. 38.

13. Dykhuizen, chap. 3. Dewey's dissertation has been lost, but its substance can be gleaned from "Kant and Philosophic Method," an article drawing on his research which he published in the spring of 1884 (*Early Works* 1:34–47).

determining which of the university's three lecturers would be pro-moted to professor. The obstreperous Peirce was the first to be elimi-nated, and in the end Morris's neo-Hegelianism, sweet disposition, and retiring manner were no match for the scientific psychology, accom-plished academic in-fighting, and back-stabbing of his friend Hall. In January 1884 the part-time lectureships were abolished, and in April Hall was made professor. Morris left Baltimore for a full-time job in philosophy at the University of Michigan, and after a few anxious months of unemployment, Dewey joined his mentor in Ann Arbor as an instructor.[14]

Dewey and Morris worked together in "the most intimate and single-minded cooperation," and together they made Michigan an important center of idealist philosophy. Dewey's work in the mid–1880s was con-tinuous with that he had done in graduate school, and he was clearly the junior partner in this relationship. His essays and books elaborated on and applied the organic idealism he had learned from Morris and the British neo-Hegelians.

Morris's continuing influence is most apparent in Dewey's study *Leib-niz's "New Essays Concerning the Human Understanding"* (1888), which appeared in a series of volumes on "German philosophic classics for English readers and students" initiated by Morris in order to show "in what way German thought contains the natural complement, or the much-needed corrective, of British speculation." Leibniz, Dewey ar-gued, was "the greatest intellectual genius since Aristotle," and his greatness lay in the fact that the ideas of "the unity of the world, the continuity and interdependence of all within it . . . come to their con-scious and delighted birth" in his philosophy. He was the first modern philosopher "to be profoundly influenced by the conception of life and the categories of organic growth." It was "the idea of organism, of life" which provided the "radical" element in Leibniz's thought. Confronted with the stark dualisms of Descartes, Liebniz had offered a new phi-losophy of unity far superior to the pantheism of Spinoza, a philosophy of "unity in and through diversity, not the principle of bare oneness."[15]

The *New Essays* were devoted to a critique of Locke's epistemology,

14. Hawkins, *Pioneer,* pp. 194–201. Gilman did apparently give some thought to keep-ing both Hall and Morris, but Hall was not disposed to share the laurels and effectively blocked any such plan. He wrote Gilman that "my own current & very deep conviction about Prof. Morris is that philosophically he represents just what ought not to be & never can be established & that he never can *touch* our best students" (p. 201). This statement also reflected, by implication, Hall's low opinion of Dewey. See Dorothy Ross, *G. Stanley Hall: The Psychologist as Prophet* (Chicago: University of Chicago Press, 1972), pp. 145–147.

15. *Leibniz's "New Essays Concerning the Human Understanding": A Critical Exposition* (1888), *Early Works* 1:255, 269, 277, 292.

and the bulk of Dewey's book was given over to a sympathetic exposition of Leibniz's attack on Locke's arguments. He reserved any criticism of Leibniz to the final chapter, where he argued that the great polymath had been unable to come up with a philosophic method equal to his insight into the organic nature of reality. Leibniz had come to the substantive conclusions of organic idealism but he employed a method—formal, scholastic logic—that could not sustain them. His philosophy pointed toward the conception of organism, a unity that necessarily involves difference, but the "essentially rigid and lifeless" unity of scholastic logic was one that posited a formal unity that excluded difference. "It is not enough," Dewey concluded, "for intelligence to have great thoughts nor even true thoughts. . . . It must *know* them; it must have a method adequate to their demonstration. And in a broad sense, the work of Kant and of his successors was the discovery of a method which should justify the objective idealism of Leibniz." Had not formal logic "bound him so completely in its toils," Dewey suggested, Leibniz might have anticipated not only Kant but Hegel.[16]

Religion as well as philosophy bound Dewey to Morris in the mid–1880s. He echoed Morris's contention that absolute idealism "in its broad and essential features is identical with the theological teaching of Christianity," and he sought to exemplify this conviction not only in his writing but also in his teaching. One of their colleagues remarked that Morris and Dewey ensured that the philosophy department was "pervaded with a spirit of religious belief, unaffected, pure and independent." Dewey published principally in journals of "progressive orthodoxy" such as the *Andover Review,* and he was active in the affairs of the Student Christian Association and the First Congregational Church in Ann Arbor. He taught Bible classes and lectured students on such topics as "The Search for God," "The Motives of the Christian Life," "Christ and Life," "The Obligation to Knowledge of God," and "The Place of Religious Emotion." Nothing in these early years of his career hinted at the disaffection with institutional religion or the social gospel which were only a few years away; he still firmly believed that "the highest product of the interest of man in man is the Church." Dewey's idealism was, to be sure, far from conventional theism, but his loyalties were clearly with those who, as William James wryly put it, saw neo-Hegelianism as the "quasi-metaphysic backbone" that liberal theology had needed.[17]

16. Ibid., pp. 415, 420, 435.
17. "Ethics and Physical Science" (1887), *Early Works* 1:209; Dykhuizen, p. 47; Willinda Savage, "The Evolution of John Dewey's Philosophy of Experimentalism as Developed at the University of Michigan" (diss., University of Michigan, 1950), pp. 26–27, 121–139;

THE METAPHYSICIAN AS PSYCHOLOGIST

By rationalizing religion and spiritualizing science, absolute idealists hoped to successfully arbitrate the conflict between science and religion without sacrificing the essential interests of either. Edward Caird said: "We must 'level up' and not 'level down'; we must not only deny that matter can explain spirit; but we must say that even matter itself cannot be fully understood except as an element in a spiritual world." In the mid-1880s Dewey made a signal contribution to this project by attempting to merge idealist metaphysics with the experimental findings of the "new psychology" pioneered in Germany and brought to America by William James and G. Stanley Hall, who were seeking to ground psychology in laboratory research in human physiology. He had studied this physiological psychology with Hall in graduate school and was uneasy with the purely logical rapprochement between the science of minds and the Science of Mind offered by Green and other idealists. Even before he left Hopkins he was working to incorporate the new psychology into the metaphysics he had learned from Morris, hoping to provide idealism with a secure footing in the scientific analysis of human experience. It was this effort that earned Dewey his initial renown (and, in some quarters, notoriety) as a philosopher.[18]

Dewey's discussions of the new psychology were aimed at three different audiences, and in each instance he tried to make a different point. First, he addressed himself to the theologians of "progressive orthodoxy," arguing that physiological psychology posed no threat to religious faith. Second, he attempted to convince the new psychologists themselves that their work pointed beyond individual human minds to the ultimate reality of divine Mind. Finally, he hoped to persuade his fellow idealists that psychology should replace logic as the method of philosophy because of its superior ability to explicate the diversity in unity of an organic universe.

Liberal Christians were Dewey's least difficult audience. Led by the "Andover liberals"—George Harris, Theodore Thorton Munger, and Egbert and Newman Smyth—the theologians of progressive orthodoxy had by the 1880s replaced the transcendent, inscrutable God of conservative Congregationalism with an immanent deity that worked

---

"The Obligation to Knowledge of God" (1884), *Early Works* 1:61–63; "The Place of Religious Emotion" (1886), *Early Works* 1:90–92; *Psychology* (1891), *Early Works* 2:295; William James to Charles Renouvier, 27 December 1880, in Elizabeth Hardwick, ed., *The Selected Letters of William James* (Boston: Godine, 1980), p. 113.

18. Caird quoted in Dewey's review of his *Critical Philosophy of Immanuel Kant* (1890), *Early Works* 3:183.

its will through the laws of nature. Most were versed in German transcendentalism and receptive to the idealists' campaign to reconcile natural science and religion by "leveling up." In the mid-1880s Dewey was at home in this company, and his articles "The New Psychology" (1884) and "Soul and Body" (1886) rested comfortably in the pages of the *Andover Review* and *Bibliotheca Sacra*.[19]

Dewey's initial discussion in "The New Psychology" began, predictably, with a slap at British empiricism. Its old faculty psychology of sensationalism, he declared, "gave descriptions of that which has for the most part no existence, and which at the best it but described and did not explain." The chief importance of the new physiological psychology lay in the methodological revolution it had produced by overthrowing the introspection of the sensationalists in favor of laboratory experimentation. Many, however, had mistaken this methodological revolution for a metaphysical coup d'etat that threatened to impose physiological reductionism and materialism, but, Dewey said, "nothing could be further from the truth." Physiology could tell "what and how physiological elements serve as a basis for psychical acts; what the latter *are*, or how they are to be explained, it tells us not at all." Indeed, far from pointing toward a materialistic determinism, the new psychology stressed the importance of the *will* "as a living bond connecting and conditioning *all* mental activity. It emphasizes the teleological element, not in any mechanical or external sense, but regarding life as an organism in which immanent ideas or purposes are realizing themselves through the development of experience." Thus, Dewey concluded, physiology was "intensely ethical" and religious in its tendencies. "As it goes into the depths of man's nature it finds, as stone of its foundation, blood of its life, the instinctive tendencies of devotion, sacrifice, faith, and idealism which are the eternal substructure of all the struggles of the nations upon the altar stairs which slope up to God."[20]

In his essay "Soul and Body" Dewey returned to this discussion of the teleological, antimaterialist implications of the new psychology. Citing

---

19. On progressive orthodoxy see Daniel D. Williams, *The Andover Liberals* (New York: Columbia University Press, 1941), and David E. Swift, "Conservative versus Progressive Orthodoxy in Latter Nineteenth Century Congregationalism," *Church History* 16 (1947): 22–31. Dewey's links with liberal Congregationalism are analyzed in Bruce Kuklick, *Churchmen and Philosophers: From Jonathan Edwards to John Dewey* (New Haven: Yale University Press, 1985), chap. 16. Neil Coughlan has argued for the direct influence of Newman Smyth on Dewey's essay "The New Psychology," but the evidence for this is indirect and, to my mind, unpersuasive (*Young John Dewey*, pp. 41–53). Nonetheless, the conjunction of themes in the work of the two men does, at least, indicate how firmly implanted in liberal Congregational culture Dewey remained in the mid-1880s.
20. "The New Psychology" (1884), *Early Works* 1:48–60.

experiments on frogs by the great German psychologist Wilhelm Wündt and others, he argued that physiological research had shown that nervous activity entailed a process of "purposive adaptation to the stimulus" which was incompatible with materialist explanations. Such explanations rested on physical causality, "the necessities of antecedent and consequent," but the discovery of purposive adaptation in even the simplest forms of nervous action called for teleological explanations in which "the act is not determined by its immediate antecedents, but by the necessary end." This discovery had momentous implications for ethics because "with the appearance of teleological action upon the scene, we have passed from the realm of the material into that of the psychical immanent in the material." By establishing that behavior was purposeful, Dewey argued, physiology had demonstrated that the body was the organ of the soul. The soul directed nervous activity toward "the welfare of the organism" and self-realization, and the body was the indispensable medium through which "the soul expresses and realizes its own nature." In revealing the purposeful immanence of the soul in the body, physiological psychology had uncovered no new truth but had rather confirmed and deepened insight into "the truth divined by Aristotle and declared by St. Paul."[21]

Such conclusions did not promise controversy with liberal Christians. But Dewey's spiritual psychology did provoke his fellow philosophers and psychologists. In 1886 his essays "The Psychological Standpoint" and "Psychology as Philosophic Method" were each given pride of place as the lead article in two successive issues of *Mind*, the leading Anglo-American journal of philosophy, and they elicited a penetrating and highly critical response from English philosopher Shadworth Hodgson—an attack that moved William James to comment "poor Dewey."[22]

The first of these articles was yet another critique of British empiricism. British philosophy, Dewey observed, had prided itself on its adherence to the "psychological standpoint," that is, to the conviction that "the nature of all objects of philosophical inquiry is to be fixed by finding out what experience says about them." This was commendable, and a position Dewey himself was eager to defend. The problem was that empiricists abandoned the psychological standpoint by introducing various unknowable "things-in-themselves" (e.g. sensations) to explain experience, thereby becoming "ontologists of the most pronounced character." To posit such entities was to leave psychology behind be-

21. "Soul and Body" (1886), *Early Works* 1:93–115.
22. William James to Shadworth Hodgson, 15 March 1887, in Perry, *Thought and Character of William James*, 1:641.

cause, for the psychologist, there could be nothing known outside of consciousness to account for it; everything known was within conscious experience. Were empiricists to remain within the bounds of the psychological standpoint, Dewey argued, they would see that it pointed to "the postulate of a universal consciousness," a Mind that manifested itself as an organic unity of subject and object, universal and individual consciousness. Experience, consciousness, showed itself to be at once individual and universal: "the individual consciousness is but the process of realization of the universal consciousness through itself." How experience showed this to be the case Dewey did not "undertake to say," but he was certain that the psychological standpoint would sustain the metaphysics of objective idealism and not that of empiricism.[23]

"Psychology as Philosophic Method" was addressed to Dewey's fellow transcendentalists who held psychology in relatively low esteem as one of the special, partial sciences methodologically subordinate to logic. This stance, Dewey argued, overlooked the real import of psychology as well as the limitations of logic. If, as the idealists believed, man knew the universal intelligence only insofar as it manifested itself in his own consciousness, then psychology, the systematic study of this consciousness, was the only method available to philosophers. To demean psychology as *merely* the study of the manifestation of the Absolute in the individual was to forget that this mere manifestation was the only material mere humans had to think about. For, he said, "if the material of philosophy be the absolute self-consciousness, and this absolute self-consciousness *is* the realization and manifestation of itself, and as material for philosophy exists only in so far as it has realized and manifested itself in man's conscious experience, and if psychology be the science of this realization in man, what else can philosophy in its fullness be but psychology, and psychology but philosophy?"

Here Dewey announced that he was departing in an important respect from idealist orthodoxy. Because only psychology could preserve the character of reality as an "organic unity . . . which lives through its distinctions," it was superior as philosophic method to logic, even, he now held, Hegelian logic. The "leveling up" project, he contended, must rest on the scientific study of human consciousness and not on logic alone. "With a purely logical method, one can end up with the *must be* or the *ought:* the *is* vanishes, because it has been abstracted from. . . . Logic cannot reach, however much it may point to, an actual individual. The gathering up of the universe into the one self-con-

23. "The Psychological Standpoint" (1886), *Early Works* 1:122–143.

scious individuality it may assert as *necessary*, it cannot give it as *reality*."
It was logic, not psychology, that was the special science, and, as such, it
should be subordinated to the careful analysis of actual experience. "If
we start from Reason alone we shall never reach fact," Dewey warned
idealists, but "if we start with fact, we shall find it revealing itself as
Reason."[24]

Dewey's articles made few converts. Neo-Hegelians continued to regard logic as the master method of philosophy, while the empiricist
response to his arguments was made by Hodgson, who remarked that
he was "utterly at a loss to see either how Mr. Dewey justifies on experiential grounds the existence of a universal consciousness, or in what he
imagines the relation between the individual and the impersonal one to
consist." It was a good thing, Hodgson said, that Dewey had not attempted to show how experience manifests the unity of absolute and
individual consciousness because he could not do so without first establishing, as he had made no attempt to do, the existence of the Absolute.
To begin by assuming the identity of universal and individual consciousness "in hopes of showing the *how* afterwards, is fatal to proving
that they are so, because, under cover of assuming their identity only, it
tacitly assumes what it has to prove, the existence of both as realities.
Not even the august companionship of German transcendentalism
could redeem such reasoning from logical perdition." The Absolute
was not a fact of experience but, as Dewey himself had said, a "postulate," and as such it was at best a hypothesis, and "the grounds for
assuming it must be argued." If Dewey wanted to go over to the transcendentalists, Hodgson concluded, he could not do so under the banner of experience and should "frankly own that he does so in deference
to presuppositions which are *a priori* to experience." Dewey responded
weakly that the postulate of universal consciousness to which he had
referred was not his own but that implied in the psychological standpoint of British empiricism. This, of course, was nonsense.[25]

Dewey returned to the fray in 1887 with his textbook *Psychology*, but
even though his book was larded with references in several languages
to the latest experimental work, he failed to meet the empiricists' demand that he show how experience revealed an absolute consciousness
realizing itself in the individual. He continued to hold that knowledge
of God was "implied or involved in every act of knowledge whatever,"
but this argument, on close inspection, rested less on an account of

24. "Psychology as Philosophic Method" (1886), *Early Works* 1:144–167.
25. Shadworth Hodgson, "Illusory Psychology" (1886), *Early Works* 1:xxv–xli; JD, "'Illusory Psychology'" (1887), *Early Works* 1:168–175.

experience than on the idealists' logical doctrine of internal relations, the presupposition that "all facts are related to each other as members of one system." This time Dewey admitted as much. "There is always a chasm between actual knowledge and absolute truth," he said. "There cannot be knowledge that the true reality for the individual self is the universal self, for knowledge has not in the individual compassed the universal." The Absolute was not a fact of experience but it was—if one was a neo-Hegelian—logically implied by it. Dewey's book was less a discussion of developments in scientific psychology than a deductive argument grounded in controversial idealist premises. Even he, it appeared, could not avoid starting with Reason.[26]

This difficulty did not escape reviewers and readers. Hall remarked that Dewey's book "unfolds, with the most charming and unreserved frankness and enthusiasm, the scheme of absolute idealism in a simple yet comprehensive way, well calculated to impress beginners in philosophy." The text was, he admitted, filled with facts, but, he complained, "the facts are never allowed to speak out plainly for themselves or left to silence, but are always 'read into' the system which is far more important than they." Dewey's ability to subordinate fact to system was remarkable: "that the absolute idealism of Hegel could be so cleverly adapted to be 'read into' such a range of facts, new and old, is indeed a surprise as great as when geology and zoology are ingeniously subjected to the rubrics of the six days of creation." Hall predicted that the book would be a hit with adolescents "inclined to immerse themselves in an ideal view of the world" but would be direly disappointing to mature minds hoping to find a reliable account of the methods and results of scientific psychology.[27]

Among the disappointed was William James. He wrote Croom Robertson, the editor of *Mind,* that he had picked up the book with enthusiasm, "hoping for something really fresh," but had abandoned it halfway through. "It's no use trying to mediate between the bare miraculous self and the concrete particulars of individual mental lives," he said, "and all that Dewey effects by so doing is to take all the edge and definiteness away from the particulars when it falls to their turn to be treated." Even H. A. P. Torrey could not resist a similar dig at his

26. *Psychology* (1887), *Early Works* 2:212, 202, 361.
27. G. Stanley Hall, review of Dewey's *Psychology* in *American Journal of Psychology* 1 (1887): 154–159. Hall's nasty review reflected not only his continuing contempt for Dewey's work but also his growing antipathy to idealism. By 1894 he was contending that idealism was the philosophical equivalent to masturbation. See Ross, *G. Stanley Hall,* p. 254.

former pupil. "Psychologically speaking, the world is objectified self; the self is subjectified world," Dewey had written. This, Torrey corrected, was not psychology but metaphysics speaking.[28]

ETHICS AND PHYSICAL SCIENCE

Dewey's failure to find many philosophers willing to share the metaphysical conclusions he derived from his psychological standpoint was a severe setback, and his concession in his *Psychology* that one must abandon experience for logic in order to establish the existence of the Absolute must be counted a retreat. Nonetheless, he held firm to the critique of logic he had advanced in "Psychology as Philosophic Method" and thus found himself torn between a methodological commitment that could not sustain his metaphysics and a metaphysics that could only appeal to an inferior method. Eventually this difficulty would prove fatal to his absolute idealism, but in the late 1880s he continued to cling to the Absolute, and he did so for reasons that were at bottom ethical.

That ethics was at the root of absolute idealism was something William James strongly suspected. Noting that the truth of the logical doctrines of neo-Hegelianism could be known only to the Absolute itself, James contended that absolute idealism was grounded less in rigorous logic than in moral feeling, and he pleaded with the neo-Hegelians to reveal the feelings that fueled their defense of a "through-and-through universe." James freely admitted that his opposition to the absolutists was based on his moral revulsion from this universe, which suffocated him with "its infallible impeccable all-pervasiveness," and he knew that the

28. William James to Croom Robertson (1886) as quoted in Perry, *Thought and Character of William James*, 2:516; H. A. P. Torrey, review of Dewey's *Psychology*, in *Andover Review* 9 (1888): 437–441. Even the undergraduates at Michigan were aware of this criticism. A poem describing the appearance of an apparition called "Psychology" who appears to a man named Dewey was published in a student journal. The apparition declares:

> But first let me say, I'm myself not to blame
> For wearing a mask that should put me to shame.
> But man, daring man, of my folly's the source
> Man,—aspiring to be a Colossus, of course,
> Having one foot in heaven, the other on earth.
> And in lieu of real seeing, his fancy gives birth
> To wild speculations, as solid and fair
> As water on quicksand, or smoke in the air.
> With these fancies he clothed me and called me a science,
> And I—proud of the title, lent him alliance.
> (Quoted in Dykhuizen, pp. 55–56.)

idealists must have "a personal feeling about the through-and-through universe which is entirely different from mine."[29]

Dewey was not disposed to the public revelation of personal feelings, but it is clear from his early work (as well as from his subsequent "deconversion") that he clung to idealism because it seemed to him at the time the only persuasive alternative to philosophies that left the universe utterly bereft of purpose. Like most liberal Protestants, Dewey tailored his God to human needs, and his emotional craving for the through-and-through universe was, above all, a desire for a world in which man could be morally at home. This desire was suggested by the essay "Soul and Body," in which he joyfully welcomed the researches of physiological psychology because they established the teleological character of nervous activity and leaped to the conclusion that this finding implied the presence of spirit and reinforced the teachings of Aristotle and Saint Paul. It was most apparent, however, in his essay "Ethics and Physical Science" (1887), a closely reasoned attack on the efforts of such evolutionary naturalists as Herbert Spencer to construct a positive ethics based on the laws of natural science. Ethical argument, Dewey noted, had become a battle between "an anthropology which sees in man a divine image and superscription, or one which finds him a product of the shaping of earthly clay." In 1887 he was firmly in the first camp, and he argued that the naturalists had failed to establish their claim to have provided man with an ethical ideal.[30]

Spencer and other "physical philosophers" argued that modern science had established man as a natural being subject to the same natural laws as other natural facts. The law of evolution showed man to be the pinnacle of a process at work everywhere in the world. Ethically these facts were said to point to two conclusions. First, because man was not generically different from the rest of nature, ethical science did not require a distinctive set of methods and concepts from those of physical science. Ethics was freed from theology and metaphysics, and the determination of the fundamental law of human conduct was one with the determination of the natural laws of the world. Second, the law of evolution was the fundamental law of both natural science and ethics. Evolution revealed the goal toward which the universe was tending and the means and processes by which it was reaching this goal.

Of particular importance for ethics was the fact, these naturalists

29. William James, "Absolutism and Empiricism" (1884), *Essays in Radical Empiricism* (Cambridge: Harvard University Press, 1976), p. 142.

30. "Ethics and Physical Science," p. 205. Page numbers for further references (EPS) appear in the text.

contended, that evolutionary law showed that human evolution was tending toward the perfection of society. The ethical ideal was thus one with the evolutionary development of human communities. "The law of society, the well-being of the community, is the ideal for all human conduct," according to the naturalists (EPS, 211). "The individual who acts in conformity with it is moral; the individual whose conduct makes against the furthering of the social organism is immoral" (EPS, 211). Human virtues were those characteristics that advanced the evolutionary development of society, and conscience was a manifestation of the identity of individual and social well-being.

Dewey did not disagree with these conclusions, for, as we shall see, they accorded well with his own ethics. What he did dispute was the contention that this ethical ideal could be derived from the natural law of evolution. He denied that "the physical world, as physical, has any end; that nature, as natural, can give birth to an ideal" (EPS, 213). He raised three principal objections to the naturalists' argument. First, Dewey noted that the naturalists' ethical ideal of a cooperative society was incompatible with the process of natural selection which was the natural law of evolution. The ideal of the evolutionists was "contradictory to that out of which it is supposed to be developed. The process is one of conflict; its very condition is opposition, competition, selection, survival. The ideal is harmony, unity of purpose and life, community of well-being,—a good which does not admit of being competed for, but in which all must share" (EPS, 213). Natural selection involved a "struggle for existence" in which various forms of life competed for a limited supply of resources, a struggle in which the fittest survived and the unfit went to the wall. The ethical ideal of cooperative moral community was at odds with the conditions of physical change. The naturalists were faced with the problem "not only of getting the moral out of the non-moral, but out of that which, if it be in the ethical sphere at all, is immoral. The ideal of the physical world is superiority in strength or skill; the ideal in the ethical world is community of good, moral equality" (EPS, 214).

Dewey's second objection was to the naturalists' identification of the terminus toward which evolution was moving as an ethical end. Ethical categories were not to be applied to the evolution of the universe but to the conduct of man, and the naturalists confused two meanings of the term "end." When speaking of the universe, the term meant "its last term, the direction towards which it is actually tending" (EPS, 219). Used ethically, however, "end" means the goal toward which a man directs his attention, "that to which he is, so far as in him lies, to give reality" (EPS, 219). An ethical end, Dewey argued, must be one which a man makes his own and has the power to realize. The evolutionists, Dewey charged, made man a mere means to a cosmic goal, "a link in an endless chain" (EPS, 219). Man was seen as but part of a long series of mechanical changes. It made no sense to talk of the ethical ideal of man as the final outcome of the process of evolution, a process in which man was "absorbed, swallowed up, forever lost" (EPS, 220).

Dewey's final and most fundamental objection to the evolutionary naturalists' attempt to establish a scientific ethics was that in positing an end or ideal for the cosmos they had supplied nature with teleology, something that a purely physical law of nature could not do. "Nature has no end, no aim, no purpose," he declared. "There is change only, not advance towards a goal" (EPS, 213). Scientists, when they were not engaged in constructing ethical systems, freely admitted this fact. Final causes had no place in physical explanations. The idea of an end toward which the universe was tending required a conception of the universe as a whole and a purpose that the universe was fulfilling. Both of these conceptions were foreign to the categories of physical science. "The conception of end," Dewey concluded, "has no place in the lexicon of the physicist. It is consistent only with a teleological interpretation of the world; one which sees it as the embodiment of reason, and the manifestation of intelligent purpose" (EPS, 223–224).

Dewey was not objecting to the notion that there was an ethical ideal to which men ought to direct themselves, nor was he objecting to the evolutionary naturalists' formulation of this ideal. He did object to the contention that this ideal could be derived from an understanding of the natural laws of evolution. "The point is," he said, "that this ethical ideal is a spiritual conception, one which demands for its justification an ideal way of looking at the universe, and that natural processes have no such life in them as will enable them to bring to birth such a principle" (EPS, 221–222). This reasoning demonstrated that "the cause of theology and morals is one, and that whatever banishes God from the heart of things, with the same edict excludes the ideal, the ethical, from the life of man. Whatever exiles theology makes ethics an expatriate" (EPS, 209). Or so Dewey thought in 1887.

CHAPTER 2

Organic Democracy

✱

By the end of the 1880s John Dewey's prolific scholarship had won him wide recognition as "one of the most brilliant, clearly conscious, and enviably confident of all our philosophical writers in America," in Josiah Royce's words. He swiftly moved out of George Morris's shadow. His work in psychology and philosophy distinguished his neo-Hegelianism from that of Morris, who was content with more orthodox idealist deflections of the findings of Victorian science. In 1888 Dewey put physical as well as intellectual distance between himself and his mentor by accepting a position as professor of philosophy at the University of Minnesota. A year later, following Morris's untimely death, he returned to Michigan to head the philosophy department, where he remained until his departure for Chicago in 1894.[1]

During these years the focus of Dewey's work shifted from metaphysics to ethics. Taking seriously his own injunction to idealists to "start with fact," he temporarily stopped speculating freely on what human experience implied about ultimate reality and more closely examined the more mundane aspects of consciousness and action. After his return to Ann Arbor from Minnesota, he turned the teaching of introductory psychology and philosophy over to his assistants, James H. Tufts and, later, George Herbert Mead and Alfred H. Lloyd, and con-

---

1. Josiah Royce, review of *Outlines of a Critical Theory of Ethics* (JD), *International Journal of Ethics* 1 (1891): 503.

centrated his own efforts on courses in ethics and political philosophy. He also found time to take part in the activities of campus organizations such as the Philosophical Society and the Students' Christian Association, before which he lectured on practical issues of religion, ethics, and politics. In these courses and lectures Dewey developed the neo-Hegelian ethics of self-realization which underlay his early democratic theory and formed the ideological foundation for the "Thought News" experiment, his first faltering effort to unify democratic theory and practice.

Students of Dewey's social thought have devoted relatively little attention to these formative years, and as a consequence important historical questions about his career as a democratic theorist remain largely unexplored. If we reject the notion that democratic ideals were at the heart of Dewey's life and work by virtue of his Vermont birthright, then we must look in this period for the origins of these ideals. In addition, because significant aspects of Dewey's social theory remained unchanged from this early period, it is also here that we must begin to explore the reasons he was the sort of democrat he was.

ALICE DEWEY AND T. H. GREEN

Because adoption of the "psychological standpoint" pushed Dewey toward an examination of the concrete particulars of human experience, he might well have made a deeper commitment to psychology as a "special science." That he did not, that instead his thinking took an ethical and political turn in which psychology became the handmaiden of moral argument, owed a great deal to the influence of two individuals: Alice Dewey, his wife, and T. H. Green, the exemplary leader of British idealism.

Alice Chipman Dewey was an extraordinary woman. The daughter of a cabinet maker who had migrated as a boy from Vermont to Michigan, Alice was orphaned at a young age, and she and her sister were raised in Fenton, Michigan, by their maternal grandparents, Frederick and Evalina Riggs. Frederick Riggs, one of Michigan's pioneers, had come to the state as a fur trader for the Hudson Bay Company and was an adopted member of the Chippewa tribe. A champion of Indian rights, Riggs imparted to his granddaughter a disdain for social conventions and a critical social conscience as well as a fiercely independent and self-reliant character. After graduating from high school, Alice studied music at the Fenton Baptist Seminary and taught in the Michigan schools for several years before enrolling at the University of Michigan in 1882. She met Dewey at the boardinghouse where they both lived and was a student of his in the fall of 1884. Although some students characterized Dewey as "cold, impersonal, psychological, sphinxlike, anomalous and petrifying to flunkers," Alice saw the warmth beneath the cool exterior of the young professor. They were married in 1886.[2]

Many observers commented on Alice Dewey's keen intelligence and the breadth and intensity of her social concern. Women who visited the Dewey home, some of them beset by fragile, neurasthenic constitutions, were particularly impressed by her and spoke admiringly, if somewhat ambivalently, of Alice's "masculine" virtues. One visitor, following a conversation in which Alice lectured at length about the importance of Emile Zola, wrote her husband that "she helps me to think of life, real activities, more than the subjectivities of my own communings with self." Alice had much the same effect on Dewey, who credited her with putting "guts and stuffing" into his work. With the exception of a few issues such as educational reform and feminism, her influence is difficult to pinpoint, but it was no coincidence that Dewey's immersion in politics and social reform followed close upon his marriage. According to their daughter Jane, Alice was "undoubtedly largely responsible for the early widening of Dewey's philosophic interests from the commentative and classical to the field of contemporary life. Above all, things which had previously been matters of theory acquired through his contact with her a vital and direct human significance."[3]

In the early years of their marriage Alice's influence was most clearly evident in a shift in Dewey's religious beliefs from the progressive orthodoxy of liberal Congregationalism and a conviction that "the highest product of the interest of man in man is the Church" to a barely Christian social gospel, which held that "it is in democracy, the community of ideas and interests through community of action, that the incarnation of God in man (man, that is to say as organ of universal truth) becomes a living, present thing, having its ordinary and natural

2. Jane Dewey, "Biography of John Dewey," in Paul A. Schilpp, ed., *The Philosophy of John Dewey*, 2d ed. (New York: Tudor, 1951), pp. 20–21; Willinda Savage, "The Evolution of John Dewey's Philosophy of Experimentalism as Developed at the University of Michigan" (diss., University of Michigan, 1950), pp. 12–13; Judy Suratt, "Alice Chipman Dewey," in *Notable American Women*, ed. Edward T James (Cambridge: Harvard University Press, 1971), 1:466–468; Dykhuizen, p. 57.

3. Mabel Castle to Henry Castle, 31 December 1893, as quoted in Neil Coughlan, *Young John Dewey* (Chicago: University of Chicago Press, 1975), p. 92; Max Eastman, "John Dewey," *Atlantic*, December 1941: 678; Jane Dewey, "Biography of John Dewey," p. 21.

sense." Alice, granddaughter of the village freethinker, her daughter noted, "had a deeply religious nature but had never accepted any church dogma," and Dewey "acquired from her the belief that a religious attitude was indigenous in natural experience, and that theology and ecclesiastic institutions had benumbed rather than promoted it." Dewey's own opinion of institutional religion declined steadily after his marriage, and in 1893 he declared that "the function of the church is to universalize itself, and thus pass out of existence." When the Deweys moved to Chicago in 1894 Dewey did not join a church and refused to send his children to Sunday school. This refusal provoked a bitter conflict with his mother, who was living with the family at the time, but Dewey, backed by Alice, stood firm, telling his mother that he had gone to more than enough Sunday school to meet his family's obligations.[4]

In the late 1880s Alice's direct, intimate urging of Dewey to bring his Hegelianism down to earth was joined by the less direct influence of T. H. Green, an influence exercised from beyond the grave. Green had died in 1882, at the outset of Dewey's career as a philosopher, and the young American was thereby deprived of any opportunity to experience at first hand the earnestness the Oxford philosopher transmitted to his followers. But Green remained until the 1890s a thinker of whom Dewey "would not speak without expressing his deep, almost reverential gratitude." Unlike Morris, Dewey took from Green not only a metaphysics that secured religious belief but also the understanding that this metaphysics and faith enjoined a life of public service. Green urged his students to think of absolute idealism as, above all, a philosophy of citizenship, and the influence of his ideas in Great Britain extended well beyond the walls of the academy. At Balliol College in the 1870s, Green had produced a group of unusual Oxford graduates, men who combined deep learning and active social concern. As one of the last major British idealists, R. G. Collingwood, observed, "The school of Green sent out into public life a stream of ex-pupils who carried with them the conviction that philosophy, and in particular the philosophy they had learnt at Oxford, was an important thing, and that their vocation was to put it into practice. . . . Through this effect on the minds of its pupils, the philosophy of Green's school might be found, from about 1880 to about 1910, penetrating and fertilizing every part of the national life."[5]

4. "Christianity and Democracy" (1892), *Early Works* 4:9; Jane Dewey, "Biography of John Dewey," p. 21; "The Relation of Philosophy to Theology" (1893), *Early Works* 4:367; George Dykhuizen, "John Dewey in Chicago: Some Biographical Notes," *Journal of the History of Philosophy* 3 (1965): 218.

5. JD, "Psychology as Philosophic Method" (1886), *Early Works* 1:153; Collingwood as

The philosophy of Green's school could also be found penetrating every part of Dewey's writing and teaching until the early 1890s and fertilizing his initial ventures in social reform. The impression many Americans had that Green's philosophy was remote from life, Dewey argued in 1889, was profoundly mistaken. "Both theoretically and personally, the deepest interests of his times were the deepest interests of Professor Green. The most abstruse and critical of his writings are, after all, only attempts to solve the problems of his times—the problems which meet us in current magazine discussions, in social and political theory, in poetry, in religion, and in the interpretation of the higher results of science. . . . He saw in what is called philosophy only a systematic search for and justification of the conviction by which men should live."[6]

Dewey's commitment to the philosophy of Green's school in the late 1880s and early 1890s was not wholly uncritical, but it is fair to say that his social thought in this period was not especially original. Apart from their considerable importance in the development of his democratic theory, his ethical and political writings in these years stand as minor and largely derivative contributions to idealist social thought. They were, moreover, very bookish exercises that could easily have been written by an Oxford don or an Edinburgh professor; little distinguishes them as the work of an American thinker. The thoroughly British character of Dewey's social philosophy at that time was testimony less to his cosmopolitanism than to his relative isolation, in the provinces of southern Michigan, from the social and ideological ferment of his own society. It was an isolation he was itching to overcome, and Green's conception of the role of the philosopher was one that Dewey himself was beginning to adopt. He too hoped to develop his conscience to the point "in which it became a public and political force as well as a private and 'moral' monitor."[7]

Dewey's social theory in this period drew heavily on two of the fundamental concepts of British idealism: the neo-Hegelian understanding of society as a peculiar kind of moral organism and the related notion of individual freedom within this organic society as the positive freedom to make the best of oneself as a social being and not merely the

---

quoted in John Passmore, *A Hundred Years of Philosophy*, 2d ed. (London: Penguin, 1968), p. 56. Melvin Richter's study of Green, *The Politics of Conscience* (Cambridge: Harvard University Press, 1964), is an outstanding intellectual biography. But for a good, brief summary of the impact of absolute idealism on British culture, see Anthony Quinton, *Absolute Idealism* (London: Oxford University Press, 1971).

6. "The Philosophy of Thomas Hill Green" (1889), *Early Works* 3:15–16.

7. Ibid., p. 30.

negative freedom from external restraint or compulsion. These concepts had been generated in the heat of ideological battle. In the late
nineteenth century, idealists were struggling to protect religious belief
from the incursions of materialism and positivism and also to reconstruct the philosophical foundations of liberalism. When Green enjoined his students to put down their Spencer and look to Kant and
Hegel, he was calling upon them not only to reject empiricism but also
to join the attack on the theory and politics of laissez-faire liberalism.
Dewey was among the many who responded enthusiastically to this call.

THE ETHICS OF DEMOCRACY

Most idealists who fell under Green's spell were professed democrats, believing that progress "has consisted largely just in the widening
of the number of persons among whom there is conceived to be a
common good, and between whom there is a common duty." Dewey
was no exception. His long essay "The Ethics of Democracy" (1888), a
sharp critique of Sir Henry Maine's influential attack on democracy in
Popular Government (1885), contains the fundamentals of his democratic
theory in this period.[8]

Maine, the first of several liberal realists with whom Dewey would
contend in his career, argued that democracy was an unstable and
destructive form of government, which inevitably produced "mon-
strous and morbid forms of monarchy and aristocracy." His critique
was based on a purely instrumental conception of democracy as a set of
political institutions and on criteria of judgment heavily weighted toward social order and stability. A democracy, he insisted, was incapable,
short of demagoguery or corruption, of generating the consensus essential to effective government. It was rule by the masses, a system in
which sovereignty and power were "minced into morsels and each
man's portion is almost infinitesimally small." Democracy was the most
difficult form of government to sustain because it was virtually impossible to generate a common will out of a fragmented multitude of sovereign powers. The only consensus possible in such a situation was one
manufactured by manipulation or corruption, irrational, immoral, and
highly unstable. History, he declared, was a "sound aristocrat," producing only one stable democracy, the United States. Like many of the
realists who followed him, Maine attributed the longevity of the Ameri-

8. Ibid., p. 29.

can republic to an array of constitutional restraints which held popular government in check.[9]

Dewey complained that Maine prejudiced the case against democracy from the outset by defining it as little more than anarchy. "To define democracy simply as the rule of the many, as sovereignty chopped up into mince meat, is to define it as abrogation of society, as society dissolved, annihilated," he said. "When so defined, it may be easily shown to be instable to the last degree." Maine based his definition of democracy on a theory of atomistic individualism that supposed that men in their natural state were nonsocial, individual units that required some external, artificial means, a social contract or the "combined action of the firm of Party and Corruption," to constitute them as a political society manifesting a common will. This, Dewey contended, was an "exploded theory of society" which had since the beginning of the nineteenth century steadily given way to an organic conception of society. The theory that "men are not isolated non-social atoms, but are men only when in intrinsic relations to men, has wholly superseded the theory of men as an aggregate, as a heap of grains of sand needing some factitious mortar to put them into semblance of order" (ED, 231–232). Man had come to be seen as an essentially social being, joined to other men in a social organism by a common will. The state represented men "so far as they have become organically related to one another, or are possessed of unity of purpose and interest" (ED, 232).

Dewey's case against Maine rested heavily on this assumption that society was an organism, an assumption not unique to idealists in the 1880s. The increasing interdependence of individuals and institutions was a social fact in the late nineteenth century, and it was also becoming a root assumption of Anglo-American social theory. As one observer noted, "The educated attention of the present is directed to the relations of individuals rather than to individuals themselves: and these relations are regarded, in a more or less uncertain sense, as essential to if not constitutive of, individuals." So pervasive were organic metaphors in the political discourse of the time that Dewey did not feel compelled to state in any detail the case against the atomistic theory of society which underlay Maine's criticism of democracy; he simply declared it was *passé*. This obsolesence, he admitted, was not conclusive evidence against the theory, but he did not see the necessity of refuting

---

9. "Ethics of Democracy" (1888), *Early Works* 1:228–230; Henry Maine, *Popular Government* (Indianapolis, Ind.: Liberty Classics, 1976), pp. 199–247. Page numbers for further references to "Ethics of Democracy" (ED) appear in the text.

atomism—even Maine himself, he noted, had advanced devastating criticisms of social contract theory (ED, 231–232).[10]

Given a more adequate, organic conception of society and government, Dewey suggested that Maine's concerns about the instrumental efficiency and stability of democracy could be more fairly stated. Simply put, the question was whether democracy as a form of government was a more or less effective means of organizing a common will. Democracy could not be dismissed as anarchy by definition, but it might conceivably be shown to threaten the unity of a social organism. "No one can claim that any society is wholly organized, or possessed of one interest and will to the exclusion of all struggle and opposition and hostility," Dewey remarked. "There are still classes within society, circles within the classes and cliques within the circles. If it can be shown that democracy more than other forms tends to multiply these subdivisions, that it tends to increase this opposition; that it strengthens their efficiency at the expense of the working force of the organism—in short, that its tendencies are towards disintegration, towards mere government by the mass, on the one side, and resolution into infinitesimal fragments, on the other, the case against democracy is amply made out" (ED, 232).

Dewey argued that this case could not be made apart from the outmoded atomistic theory of society. From the perspective of the organic theory, democracy was not only capable of securing the unity of a social organism but was the best means to this end. It entailed participation by every citizen in the affairs of the community. For this reason, Dewey declared, "democracy, so far as it is really democracy, is the most stable, not the most insecure of governments. In every other form of government there are individuals who are not organs of the common will, who are outside of the political society in which they live, and are, in effect, aliens to that which should be their own commonwealth. Not participat-

10. Henry Jones, "The Social Organism," in Andrew Seth and R. B. Haldane, eds., *Essays in Philosophical Criticism* (London: Longmans, Green, 1883), p. 187. Thomas Haskell's penetrating study *The Emergence of Professional Social Science* (Urbana: University of Illinois Press, 1977) demonstrates the central importance of the concept of "interdependence" to late nineteenth-century social theory. See also the important essay by Stefan Collini, "Sociology and Idealism in Britain, 1880–1920," *Archives européenes de sociologie* 19 (1978): 3–50. Of course, the idealists' conception of the society as a "moral organism," a self-conscious unity held together by the ethical consciousness each individual had of his freedom and obligations as part of the community, was but one of several competing notions of the social organism. It contrasted most sharply with that of their chief ideological opponent, Herbert Spencer, which held that society was a distinctive kind of organism constituted by the interactions of discrete, self-conscious individuals but itself lacking a corporate self-consciousness or will. See Spencer, "The Social Organism" in his *Essays*, 2d ser. (New York: Appleton, 1864), pp. 154–184.

ing in the formation or expression of the common will, they do not embody it in themselves. Having no share in society, society has none in them." The source of instability and strife was not the inclusion of all members of a polity as participants in the formation and expression of common purposes but the exclusion of some. "Such," Dewey concluded with satisfying irony, "is the origin of that body of irreconcilables which Maine, with inverted logic, attributes to democracy" (ED, 237–238).

For Dewey, the demonstration that democracy as a form of government was the most effective means of organizing consensus and preserving stability was not enough, for to evaluate it simply in these instrumental terms, as Maine did, was to miss the more fundamental significance of democracy as an end, as an ethical ideal. "To say that democracy is *only* a form of government is like saying home is a more or less geometrical arrangement of bricks and mortar; that the church is a building with pews, pulpit and spire. It is true; they certainly are so much. But it is false; they are so infinitely more." The real importance of democracy lay in its larger ethical meaning. Broadly conceived, democracy was a way of life, "a form of moral and spiritual association," and democratic government was but one of its manifestations (ED, 240).

As an ethical ideal, Dewey identified democracy with "such a development of man's nature as brings him into complete harmony with the universe of spiritual relations," the perfection of both the individual and the social organism through the harmonious development of the powers and capacities of all the individuals in a society (ED, 241). In this respect, he admitted, there was little difference between the democratic ideal and the ideal of Plato and other aristocratic philosophers. Where aristocratic and democratic ethics and politics differed was not in their ends but in their means. According to the aristocrat, most men were incapable of recognizing the harmonious relationship between their real self-interest and the social good and hence were cut off from their own self-realization. It fell to an elite who did recognize the ideal to "see to it that each individual is placed in such a position in the state that he may make perfect harmony with the others, and at the same time perform that for which he is best fitted, and thus realize the goal of life" (ED, 242). For the aristocrat: "The few best, the aristoi; these know and are fitted for rule; but they are to rule not in their own interests but in that of society as a whole, and therefore, in that of every individual in society. They do not bear rule *over* the others; they show them what they can best do, and guide them in doing it" (ED, 242). This was, Dewey remarked, a charming and attractive ideal, as witnessed by "the long line of great men who have reiterated with increasing emphasis that all will go wrong, until the few who know and are strong, are put in power, while others, foregoing the assertion of their individuality, submit to superior wisdom and goodness." Unfortunately for this ideal, things failed to work as promised. "The practical consequence of giving the few wise and good power," Dewey observed, "is that they cease to remain wise and good" (ED 242).

However, Dewey argued, even if philosopher kings of incorruptible virtue could be found, aristocratic politics would still stand condemned, for "the ethical ideal is not satisfied merely when all men sound the note of harmony with the highest social good, so be it that they have not worked it out for themselves":

> Were it granted that the rule of the aristoi would lead to the highest external development of society and the individual, there would still be a fatal objection. Humanity cannot be content with a good which is procured from without, however high and otherwise complete that good. The aristocratic idea implies that the mass of men are to be inserted by wisdom, or, if necessary, thrust by force, into their proper positions in the social organism. It is true, indeed, that when an individual has found that place in society for which he is best fitted and is exercising the function proper to that place, he has obtained his completest development, but it is also true (and this is the truth omitted by aristocracy, emphasized by democracy) that he must find this place and assume this work in the main for himself. (ED, 243)

For the democrat, the realization of the ethical ideal must be entrusted to the self-conscious, freely willed actions of every individual in a society. A good that an individual did not self-consciously recognize and pursue for himself was not a good; men could not be forced to be free. "In one word," Dewey said, "democracy means that *personality* is the first and final reality. It admits that the full significance of personality can be learned by the individual only as it is already presented to him in objective form in society; it admits that the chief stimuli and encouragements to the realization of personality come from society; but it holds, none the less, to the fact that personality cannot be procured for any one, however degraded and feeble, by any one else, however wise and strong" (ED, 244).

POSITIVE FREEDOM

Dewey's argument that the ethical ideal of self-realization was achieved "when an individual has found that place in society for which he is best fitted and is exercising the function proper to that place" echoed the conviction of Green and other idealists that, properly conceived, freedom was the opportunity to make the best of oneself as a social being (ED, 243). Dewey's formulation of this concept in his critique of Maine was so briefly stated, however, that it appeared more conservative than it was. To understand Dewey's concepts of self-realization and positive freedom and the reformist, even radical, implications they held for him, we must turn to the ethical theory he was developing in the classroom in the late 1880s.[11]

The key to Dewey's ethics of self-realization was his notion of "function." He used this term to describe an active relationship between particular individual capacities and the particular environments that advanced the well-being of that individual. It was, then, not a term necessarily describing how a particular person fit or functioned in a given society but a normative concept prescribing how a person *should* fit in that society so as to maximize the development of his capacities. The "moral end," he contended in *Outlines of a Critical Theory of Ethics* (1891), was "the performance by a person of his specific function, this function consisting in an activity which realizes wants and powers with reference to their peculiar surroundings." The critical point is that, for Dewey, the relationship between individual capacities and environments was one of *mutual* adjustment, not a matter of the one-sided accommodation of individual needs and powers to a fixed environment. "True adjustment" did not mean "bare conformity to circumstances, nor bare external reproduction of them." It could often mean asserting oneself against one's surroundings. "The environment must be plastic to the ends of the agent," Dewey said, and often "*transformation* of existing circumstances is moral duty rather than mere reproduction of them." Fitting in to a particular environment might well entail substantially changing it, and this notion of self-realization could— and, in Dewey's case, did—legitimate extensive social reform.[12]

Freedom, Dewey argued, lay simply in the exercise of one's functions, and "every action which is not in the line of performance of functions must necessarily result in self-enslavement." In exercising his

11. That this view *could be* developed in a deeply conservative direction is evident in the thinking of the political sport among British idealists, F. H. Bradley. See his *Ethical Studies*, 2d ed. (Oxford: Oxford University Press, 1927), particularly the chapter "My Station and Its Duties."

12. *Outlines of a Critical Theory of Ethics* (1891), *Early Works* 3:304, 313. Here we see the antecedents of Dewey's concept of "adjustment," which has been so often misunderstood by his critics. An individual's "function" included an ensemble of capacities and interests, a point sometimes obscured by Dewey's use of the term in the singular. Page numbers for further references (*OCTE*) appear in the text.

functions, man realized his individuality, and "only the good man, the man who is truly realizing his individuality, is free, in the positive sense of that word" (*OCTE*, 344).

The most important element in the environment which an individual had to take into account in seeking to exercise his functions was other individuals seeking the same end. A function was thus inherently social, and, by definition, so too was the realization of individuality. The performance of functions entailed "the creation, perpetuation, and further development of an environment, of relations to the wills of others" (*OCTE*, 314). In exercising his function the individual not only developed his particular capacities and interests but did so in a way that contributed to the well-being of the other individuals in his social environment. "Individuality cannot be opposed to association," Dewey told his students. "It is through association that man has acquired his individuality and it is through association that he exercises it. The theory which sets the individual over against society, of necessity contradicts itself."[13] An individual's functions both defined his uniqueness and united him in moral community with the other members of his society. Individuality—"the realization of what we specifically are as distinct from others"—did not mean separation or isolation from others but the "performing of a special *service* without which the social whole is defective" (*OCTE*, 326). Individuals could realize themselves only as members of a community, and only those who did so were truly free.

It is worth repeating that this dialectical relationship between individuality and community, self-realization and social service, did not necessarily require conformity to the practices of one's particular community. Reform could be as much a service to a community as other functions. Dewey did insist, following Hegel's notion of *Sittlichkeit* or concrete ethics, that reform be grounded in the "ought" that was already apparent in the "is" of the prevailing practices of existing communities rather than the abstract and purely formal injunctions of Kantian ethics, but this limitation left plenty for the reformer to do. As he said:

Reflective conscience must be *based* on the moral consciousness expressed in existing institutions, manners, and beliefs. Otherwise it is empty and arbitrary. But the existing moral status is never wholly self-consistent. It realizes ideals in one relation which it does not in an-

13. "Lecture Notes: Political Philosophy, 1892," p. 38, Dewey Papers.

other; it gives rights to "aristocrats" which it denies to low-born; to men, which it refuses to women; it exempts the rich from obligations which it imposes upon the poor. Its institutions embody a common good which turns out to be good only to a privileged few, and thus existing in self-contradiction.

For Dewey, as for Hegel, ethical social change was a matter of "reconstruction," and there was no social service he valued more highly (*OCTE*, 358–359).[14]

Although the idiom of expression would change, an ethics of self-realization and positive freedom would remain an important feature of Dewey's social philosophy for the rest of his life. But one should not overlook the idealist metaphysics that lay beneath Dewey's initial formulation of this moral vision. At the end of the road to self-realization and moral community which Dewey traced in the late 1880s and early 1890s there lay not the self but the Self. In seeking to develop its capacities, he argued in *Psychology*, "the self has always presented to its actual condition the vague ideal of a completely universal self, by which it measures itself and feels its own limitations. The self, in its true nature, is universal and objective. The actual self is particular and unrealized. The self always confronts itself, therefore, with the conception of a universal or completed will towards which it must strive." The universal and objective self against which the actual self measured itself was the Absolute, and, in the final analysis, individual self-realization was but a moment in the larger process of the self-realization of God. Just as idealist logic dictated that the relations of knowledge pointed toward a universal Mind, so too it dictated that the relations of action pointed toward a universal Will. The individual who struggled to exercise his function was a vehicle for the Function of God: "he has renounced his own particular life as an unreality; he has asserted that the sole reality is the Universal Will, and in that reality all his actions take place." These are the sort of sentiments which would later make Dewey shudder, but in these years they were an essential part of his thinking.[15]

The combination of absolute idealism with the positive concept of freedom as freedom to make the best of oneself alarmed many critics, most notably such "negative liberals" as Herbert Spencer, who were the idealists' principal ideological adversaries in the 1880s and early 1890s.

14. On Hegel's concept of *Sittlichkeit* and its political implications see Charles Taylor, *Hegel and Modern Society* (Cambridge: Cambridge University Press, 1979), chaps. 2–3.
15. *Psychology* (1891), *Early Works* 2:290–291, 358, 361.

Liberty, these liberals argued, meant only the absence of coercion or external constraints imposed on an individual by others. Free individuals were free to do as they wished so long as they did not deprive other individuals of this same right. Positive freedom of the sort advocated by idealists, including Dewey, raised the specter of other individuals' or, even worse, the state's coercing an individual into exercising his functions and realizing his "best" or "divine" self. To these defenders of laissez-faire liberalism, the idealists' "functional freedom" seemed to invite authoritarian social engineering. William James voiced this concern nicely in his remark that the neo-Hegelian concept of freedom conjured up for him the image of a "buttoned-up" society ruled by the ministrations of a clergyman certain that he was the Resurrection and the Life. "Certainly, to my personal knowledge, all Hegelians are not prigs," he said, "but I somehow feel as if all prigs ought to end, if developed, by becoming Hegelians."[16]

Anglo-American idealists were sensitive to this criticism, and they attempted to free their concept of liberty from these coercive implications by denying that any human being, even a philosopher, could know the Will of the Absolute with any certainty and hence no man could possess the master plan for the Kingdom of God. Although faith that such a plan existed was a necessary prerequisite of the moral life, it was a plan that mere mortals could view only through a glass darkly. As Anthony Quinton has said, neo-Hegelians were sure only "that all the disharmonies of appearance are *somehow* reconciled in the absolute."[17]

As Dewey's distinction between the means advocated by aristocratic and democratic proponents of positive liberty suggests, idealists also insisted that self-realization was a do-it-yourself project; it was not an

16. William James, "Absolutism and Empiricism" (1884), *Essays in Radical Empiricism* (Cambridge: Harvard University Press, 1976), p. 142. A good discussion of the debate between the advocates of negative and positive liberty in the late nineteenth century is David Nichols, "Positive Liberty, 1880–1914," *American Political Science Review* 56 (1962): 114–128. There were "positive liberals" who were not idealists, for it was possible (as Dewey's later ethics indicates) to disengage positive liberty from the metaphysical underpinning idealists gave it. L. T. Hobhouse is perhaps the best British example, and his "new liberalism" was quite similar to Dewey's postidealist social philosophy. See Stefan Collini's fine study, *Liberalism and Sociology: L. T. Hobhouse and Political Argument in England, 1880–1914* (Cambridge: Cambridge University Press, 1979). As we shall see, one of the most important tasks Dewey undertook when he abandoned idealism—one that occupied Hobhouse as well—was that of constructing a naturalistic argument for positive liberty.

17. Quinton, *Absolute Idealism*, p. 26. This argument did not meet the objections of James, who was concerned primarily about how the purposes of the Absolute determined the self-realization of its human "vehicles." Eventually, Dewey would share this objection to idealism, but, as I indicated in Chapter 1, he saw no alternative in the early 1890s to this sort of "soft determinism" other than the "hard determinism" of materialism.

end that one individual could give to or force on another. The truly moral man was, to be sure, interested in the welfare of others—such an interest was essential to his own self-realization—but a true interest in others lay in a desire to expand their autonomous activity, not in the desire to render them the dependent objects of charitable benevolence. As moral men, Dewey said, "we wish the fullest life possible to ourselves and to others. And the fullest life means largely a complete and free development of capacities in knowledge and production—production of beauty and use." Thus, "our interest in others is not satisfied as long as their intelligence is cramped, their appreciation of truth feeble, their emotions hard and uncomprehensive, their powers of production compressed. To will their good is to will the freeing of all such gifts to the highest degree." To be truly interested in others was to act to create the conditions in which their gifts could be free, conditions in which they might utilize "the self-directed power of exercising, in and by themselves, their own functions." True benevolence in a democratic society, Dewey declared, was indirect, and "the idea of 'giving pleasure' to others, 'making others happy,' if it means anything else than securing conditions so that they may act freely in their own satisfaction, means slavery" (*OCTE,* 318–319).

Although this distinction between directly forcing individuals to be free and indirectly providing them with the conditions of liberty deflected an unduly authoritarian or paternalistic reading of idealist social theory, this theory retained the link between freedom and virtue which troubled negative liberals. Like many idealists, Dewey drew up a list of "cardinal virtues" essential to freedom—"wisdom (practical judgment), temperance (self-control), courage and justice"[18]—and insisted that freedom lay only in virtuous action, that is, "freedom from subjection to caprice and blind appetite, freedom in the full play of activity" (*OCTE,* 383). Insofar as the conditions of liberty were the context for the cultivation of virtue they were not intended to enable individuals to do capriciously whatever they wished but to enable them to exercise their functions and to thwart actions that denied other members of the community the opportunity for effective functioning. Thus, Dewey's critique of direct, coercive benevolence was combined with a call for an indirect benevolence that would empower those who would be free, in this positive sense, to be so.

This sort of indirect benevolence raised important questions, questions that not only divided negative and positive liberals but created

18. *The Study of Ethics* (1894), *Early Works* 4:353.

schisms among positive liberals as well: What were the conditions of liberty, and how were they to be provided? What were the obstacles to liberty, who was responsible for them, and how were they to be removed? What was the role of the state in all this? Green's position on these critical questions was ambiguous, and his followers disagreed about how radical a reform agenda he intended to propose. He asked pregnant questions about the relationship between capitalism and the limitations on the self-realization of working-class men and women and argued that freedom cannot "be enjoyed by one man or one set of men at the cost of a loss of freedom to others." The particular reform measures he advocated, however, were quite moderate, centering on temperance legislation and educational reform. Green's epigone divided into "moral regenerationists" like Bernard Bosanquet and Mrs. Humphrey Ward, who argued that the principal obstacle to liberty was flawed individual character and who proposed to "remoralize" conduct (particularly that of the working class) through voluntary action and such organizations as the Charity Organization Society, and "moral reformists" like D. G. Ritchie, who believed that the obstacles to liberty were structural and systemic and could be overcome only by democratic politics and a measure of socialism.[19]

Dewey's treatment of these issues was, like Green's, both provocative and vague. The substance of democratic politics, he argued in 1894, lay in the effort to secure the conditions for the self-realization of all the individuals in a society. Ethical theory was practically absurd if it did not entail a political commitment to secure the foundations of moral life. "It is self-contradictory," he said, "to say there is not true morality without personal insight and choice, and yet practically endure conditions of social life which shut most men out from the possibility of meeting these requirements." Dewey was loathe in these years to be precise about what constituted the conditions of self-realization or the obstacles to it, but his call for "industrial democracy" suggests he was

19. T. H. Green, "Liberal Legislation and the Freedom of Contract" (1880), in R. L. Nettleship, ed., *Works of Thomas Hill Green*, 3 vols. (London: Longmans, Green, 1885–1888), 3:370–371; Peter Clarke, *Liberals and Social Democrats* (Cambridge: Cambridge University Press, 1978), p. 27. I have borrowed the terms "moral regenerationist" and "moral reformist" from Clarke (pp. 14–15). To moral reformists in the 1880s and early 1890s, "socialism" was a fuzzy term referring to "the principle of association or cooperation in economic and political life" and by no means implying state ownership of the means of production, to which most were opposed. See Collini, *Liberalism and Sociology*, pp. 32–42; and Dorothy Ross, "Socialism and American Liberalism: Academic Social Thought in the 1880s," *Perspectives in American History* 11 (1977–1978): 13.

developing a relatively radical perspective on the problems of his society.[20]

In the conclusion to "The Ethics of Democracy" Dewey declared that "there is no need to beat about the bush in saying that democracy is not in reality what it is in name until it is industrial, as well as civil and political." In this respect, society was most clearly still a "sound aristocrat" and democracy an ideal of the future. Although he did not beat around the bush in saying this, he also did not define carefully what he meant by industrial democracy. He made it clear that he did not mean a simple egalitarian distribution of wealth, nor did he intend the term to imply the sort of socialism in which the term was "interpreted to mean that in some way society, as a whole, to the abolition of all individual initiative and result, is to take charge of all those undertakings which we call economic," that is, state socialism. Industrial democracy rather meant that "all industrial relations are to be regarded as subordinate to human relations, to the law of personality. . . . They are to become the material of an ethical realization; the form and substance of a community of good (though not necessarily of goods) wider than any now known" (ED, 246–247). More than this he did not say, leaving a great deal to the imagination of the reader.

These vague remarks may well have reflected the influence and experience of his Michigan colleague Henry Carter Adams. Adams had studied political economy at Johns Hopkins and was awarded the university's first Ph.D. in 1876, and he returned from a year's study in Germany determined to apply the critical insights of the socialist tradition to the American political economy. In his essay "Democracy" (1881) Adams called for the establishment of a cooperative commonwealth of owner-workers which would "realize socialistic aims by individualistic means." He argued that "the practical plan through which that liberty promised by democracy is to be realized is the abandonment of the wages system and the establishment of industries upon the cooperative basis." These sentiments did not help Adams on the job market. In the early 1880s he held half-time appointments at Michigan and Cornell, and, burdened with suspicions about his political responsibility, he struggled to gain a full-time appointment. In 1886 his public support of the Knights of Labor outraged Cornell trustee Russell Sage, who demanded that Adams be fired. He was able to obtain a permanent appointment at Michigan only after submitting himself to an in-

20. "Ethics and Politics" (1894), *Early Works* 4:373.

terrogation on his political beliefs by the university's president, James B. Angell, in which Adams was forced to admit that his defense of the Knights had been "unwise." Dewey and Adams were quite close, and the fuzziness of Dewey's definition of industrial democracy may well reflect caution in the light of his friend's experience.[21]

In the classroom, Dewey was a bit more precise about what he meant by industrial democracy. He told his students that the class divisions of industrial capitalism were incompatible with the ethics of democracy. The division of labor in industrial capitalism, he argued, fell far short of an ideal division of labor, one that would permit every individual to exercise his functions. The division of labor, Dewey told his class in political philosophy, "is never complete until the laborer gets his full expression": "The kind we now have in factories,—one-sided, mechanical—is a case of class interest; i.e. his activity is made a means to benefit others. It can't be complete till he does that for which he is best fitted,—in which he finds the most complete expression of himself." The exercise of function entailed the conscious control by the individual worker of his own labor for ends he had chosen for himself. In industrial capitalism, "the value of an individual as an organ of activity is appropriated by others," and, as such, capitalism blocked not only the self-realization of the individual but also the perfection of the social organism. "The imperfect realization of the individual means the imperfect realization of the whole and *vice versa*. Class interests not only put a limitation on the individual but also a limitation on the whole."[22]

It is difficult on the basis of these scattered, largely unpublished remarks to categorize Dewey as either a "moral regenerationist" or a "moral reformist." On the one hand, he seemed to conceive of the exercise of class interests as a failure of ethical insight on the part of capitalist employers, requiring little more than their moral regeneration to produce class reconciliation and "the formation of a higher and more complete unity among men" (ED, 248). On the other hand, by arguing that the self-realization of industrial workers was blocked by the capitalist division of labor, he seemed to point toward more fundamental, structural reforms. If this division of labor was the problem, it

21. Henry Carter Adams, "Democracy," *New Englander* 40 (1881): 771–772. Two excellent studies of Adams's life and thought are Ross, "Socialism and American Liberalism," and A. W. Coats, "Henry Carter Adams: A Case Study in the Emergence of the Social Sciences in the United States, 1850–1900," *Journal of American Studies* 2 (1968): 177–197. See also Mary O. Furner, *Advocacy and Objectivity: A Crisis in the Professionalization of American Social Science, 1865–1905* (Lexington: University of Kentucky Press, 1975), pp. 127–142.

22. "Political Philosophy, 1892," pp. 44–45.

was difficult to see how employers and workers could be ethically reconciled unless the social relations of production which made them
distinctive classes in the first place were abolished. This ambiguity
would mark Dewey's thinking about industrial democracy for some
time, but the trajectory of his thought was clearly toward the "moral
reformist" position.

In any case, Dewey's focus on the obstacles to self-realization and
social harmony posed by the dominant class indicates that he was more
critical of his society than were other American neo-Hegelians, most of
whom rushed to the defense of the prerogatives of private property,
and suggests that, in the broader Anglo-American context, he should
be placed on the neo-Hegelian left. Indeed, given the relatively conservative social and political philosophy of William Torrey Harris and
other prominent American absolute idealists, it would not be too much
of an exaggeration to say that in the United States Dewey *was* the neo-
Hegelian left.[23]

"THOUGHT NEWS"

By the early 1890s Dewey was eager to spread his ideas about democracy beyond the classroom. The lecture hall, he complained, had become a "monastic cell" for the modern "Scholastic" in which "he crit-
icizes the criticisms with which some other Scholastic has criticized
other criticisms, and the writing upon writings goes on till the substructure of reality is long obscured." Dewey took as his hero the "Speculator," the thinker who recognized that intelligence must not hoard its
fund of knowledge as the scholastic was inclined to do but "must throw
its fund out again into the stress of life; it must venture its savings
against the pressure of facts." The "merchant of thought" took "action
upon truth" as his first principle. Like William James, who spoke of the
"cash value" of ideas, Dewey called upon market metaphors to make his
point, aware that in a business civilization it was the businessman who
stood as the exemplar of the unity of theory and practice. Life itself was
a business, he said, a transaction between thought and the world: "The
mind must give meaning, ideas to the world that confronts it, and in

23. On the social and political philosophy of the St. Louis Hegelians and other prominent American idealists, see Lawrence Dowler, "The New Idealism and the Quest for
Culture in the Gilded Age" (diss., University of Maryland, 1974), pp. 300–301. For an
accessible sample of Harris's social philosophy see his "Edward Bellamy's Vision," in
William Goetzmann, ed., *The American Hegelians* (New York: Knopf, 1973), pp. 193–201.

return for its investment the world gives back truth and power." Privately, Dewey admitted that the effort to make philosophy an instrument for social action "would sound more or less crazy to a professor of philosophy in good and regular standing," but he intended "henceforth to act on my conviction regardless."[24]

Given this intense desire to escape from a cloistered academic routine, it is no surprise that Dewey proved susceptible to the schemes of Franklin Ford, the first of several eccentrics with whom Dewey would become entangled over the course of his lifetime. Ford, who might best be described as an itinerant journalist, was an editor in the early 1880s of *Bradstreet's*, the New York commercial newspaper. Disgusted by the subservience of his employer and other newspapers to the interests of advertisers, he quit his job and developed a plan for a national "sociological newspaper" that would replace the scattered facts reported by ordinary newspapers with an analysis of the deeper social trends which would give these facts genuine meaning and significance. He had little luck winning the support of other journalists, and in 1888 he turned to the universities, hoping to find "men professedly attached to the principle of intelligence and seeking to follow its dictation." At Michigan he finally met with success. As Ford put it, "I got to John Dewey."[25]

Ford was a minor prophet among late nineteenth-century American utopians, an ideological cousin of Henry George and Edward Bellamy, but unlike them he was interested less in the control of the means of production than in control of the means of communication. His vision rested on a belief that the key to social justice in America was a radical reorganization of the production and distribution of knowledge. The reformer's task was one of freeing the American people, whom Ford referred to as the "Representative Slaves," from the "class interest which found its profit in keeping the common fact covered up." Progress toward a cooperative commonwealth rested on the "socialization

24. "The Scholastic and the Speculator" (1891–1892), *Early Works* 3:150–151, 152, 154; JD to James R. Angell, 11 March 1892, James R. Angell Papers, Yale University.
25. Franklin Ford, "Draft of Action" (1892), pp. 2–3, copy in the library of California State University, Fullerton. The initial studies of the *Thought News* project are Willinda Savage's "Evolution of John Dewey's Philosophy," pp. 140–151, and "John Dewey and 'Thought News' at the University of Michigan," *Michigan Alumnus Quarterly Review* 56 (1950): 204–209. Other interpretations building on Savage's research are Lewis S. Feuer, "John Dewey and the Back to the People Movement in American Thought, *Journal of the History of Ideas* 20 (1959): 548–553, and Coughlan, *Young John Dewey*, pp. 93–112. A view of *Thought News* from the perspective of another important participant, Robert Park, is Fred H. Matthews, *Quest for an American Sociology: Robert E. Park and the Chicago School* (Montreal: McGill-Queen's University Press, 1977), pp. 20–30.

of intelligence." The agency for this reconstruction of society was to be a powerful corporation that Ford called the "Intelligence Trust." This trust—an organization of intellectuals and journalists—would create a giant central clearinghouse of information and analysis, and through its own publications and the material it sold to newspapers throughout the country it would provide the public with the knowledge it needed to free itself from slavery. By making the truth its business, the Intelligence Trust would put publications serving narrow class interests out of business. "In place of discussing 'socialism,'" Ford said, "we put out in the rightful sense of the word, the socialistic newspaper—the organ of the whole."[26]

Dewey was excited by the practical bearing Ford's scheme gave to a central theme in his democratic theory. The freedom of the individual and the full development of the consciousness of the social organism— what Dewey called the "social sensorium"—rested on the ability of individuals to become conscious of their "function" in an interdependent community. "Consciousness is *social* in so far as any individual consciously directs his own activities in view of the social relations involved," Dewey argued. "Freedom is realized insofar as the individual has before him intelligence of the relations involved in his conduct, i.e. so far as society reports to him what it is doing." The social organism was perfected through the development of social consciousness, and one of the critical conditions of self-realization and democracy was the opportunity for every individual in a society to develop such a consciousness. Effective distribution of knowledge was thus essential to the development of the "social sensorium," and democracy rested as much if not more on the egalitarian distribution of knowledge as it did on the egalitarian distribution of wealth.[27]

The prevailing distribution of knowledge, Dewey argued, was far short of democratic, for just as "the dead weight of intrenched class interest" had generated an alienating division of labor which inhibited the exercise of individual functions, so too had it inhibited the development of social consciousness by holding back the socialization of intelligence. Because the agencies for the distribution of intelligence were controlled by class interest, he observed in 1893, "democracy is still untried."[28]

The universities, for their part, had produced too many scholastics and too few speculators, and Dewey vigorously defended the "popular-

26. Ford, "Draft of Action," p. 8.
27. "Political Philosophy, 1892," pp. 60–61.
28. Ibid., pp. 138–139; "Renan's Loss of Faith in Science" (1893), *Early Works* 4:17.

ization" of knowledge while at the same time warning against conceiving of it in paternalistic terms. "The American laborer draws his sustenance from the same great currents of political and commercial life at which the professor or doctor of philosophy must drink," he said in 1891. "Often he feels that while he may not know as much of some abstract principles or as many statistical details as the University man, he is, in truth, nearer to the real sources of knowledge." The important practical question, he told his students, was "whether the tendency of democracy is to produce an adequate social or political science,— meaning by science, not simply an abstract, technical thing but the continual application to the daily social event of the highest principles of interpretation," a social science capable of taking a particular event and putting it in the context of "the main design and general movement." The individual in a democracy required such a science if he was to "really participate, as an organ and member, in the life of the whole organism."[29]

Ford's scheme struck Dewey as a practical plan for creating an essential condition of participatory democracy. He told Henry Carter Adams in 1889 that "no paper can afford now to tell the truth about the actual conduct of the city's business. But have a newspaper whose *business*, i.e. whose livelihood, was to sell intelligence, and it couldn't afford to do anything else, any more than any genuine business can afford to sell spurious goods." Two years later he offered a more effusive estimate of Ford's plan in a long letter to William James:

By some sort of instinct, and by the impossibility of my doing anything in particular, I was led into philosophy and into "idealism"—i.e., the conception of some organism comprehending both man's thought and the external world. Ford, who was a newspaper man (formerly Editor of Bradstreet's in New York) with no previous philosophical training, had been led by his newspaper experience to study as a practical question the social bearings of intelligence and its distribution. That is to say, he was on a paper and wanted to inquire. The paper would not let him: the more he was stopped, the more his desire to inquire was aroused, until finally he was drawn into a study of the whole matter— especially as he found that it was not any one newspaper, but rather the social structure that prevented freedom of inquiry. Well, he identified the question of inquiry with, in philosophical terms, the question of the relation of intelligence to the objective world,—is the former free to

29. "Angle of Reflection" (1891), *Early Works* 3:203; "Political Philosophy, 1892," pp. 138–139.

move in relation to the latter or not? . . . What I have got out of it is, first, the perception of the true or practical bearing of idealism—that philosophy has been the assertion of the unity of intelligence and the external world in idea or subjectively, while if true in idea it must finally secure the conditions of its objective expression. And secondly, I believe that a tremendous movement is impending, when the intellectual forces which have been gathering since the Renascence and Reformation, shall demand complete free movement, and, by getting their physical leverage in the telegraph and printing press, shall, through free inquiry in a centralized way, demand the authority of all other so-called authorities.[30]

Once he had gained Dewey's support, Ford was joined in Ann Arbor by his equally eccentric brother, Corydon Ford, and together with Dewey and Robert Park, then a Detroit newspaperman, they planned a pilot newspaper that would be distributed in southern Michigan. The fruits of this collaboration were revealed in March 1892 in a circular announcing the forthcoming publication of *Thought News:*

In April next will appear the first number of the "Thought News." This will be a newspaper and will aim at performing the function of a newspaper. The world is already supplied, if not burdened, with magazines of philosophy, theology, literature and political science. It is believed there is room, in the flood of opinion, for one journal which shall not go beyond the fact; which shall report thought rather than dress it up in the garments of the past; which instead of dwelling at length upon the merely individual processes that accompany the facts, shall set forth the facts themselves; which shall not discuss philosophic ideas per se but use them as tools in interpreting the movements of thought; which shall treat questions of science, letters, state, school and church as parts of the one moving life of man and hence of common interest, and not relegate them to separate documents of merely technical interest; which shall report new investigations and discoveries in their net outcome instead of in their overloaded gross bulk; which shall note new contributions to thought, whether by book or magazine, from the standpoint of the news in them, and not from that of patron or censor.[31]

30. "Memorandum" in JD to Henry Carter Adams, 29 April 1889, Henry Carter Adams Papers, Michigan Historical Collections, University of Michigan; JD to William James, 3 June 1891, in Ralph Barton Perry, *The Thought and Character of William James* (Boston: Little, Brown, 1935), 2:518–519.

31. Copy of circular in JD to Thomas Davidson, 8 March 1892, Thomas Davidson Papers, Yale University.

Three weeks after this announcement appeared, Ford published another announcement—unbeknownst to Dewey—that characterized the new newspaper in even more grandiose terms:

> On or about April 22 there will issue from the press in this city a new paper, Thought News, conducted by John Dewey of the philosophical department of the university. The date will mark the first appearance in visible merchantable printed types of a new idea in journalism and education. . . . Mr. Dewey calls the paper "A Report of the Social Fact." The social fact is the social organism. Properly, Thought News has but one thing to report and that is a mere announcement—the announcement that the social organism is here.
>
> A report is more than a mere statement. The statement that society is an organism was made long ago and accepted—as a statement. It remains now to point to the fact, the visible, tangible thing, to show the idea in motion. If the social organism is a fact and not a poetic dream it must be studied like a steam engine, in its principle, but also in its practical activity. In order that the social organism may be understood, it is necessary to see the idea in motion—it is necessary to report it, that is, describe it as it moves in life. That is what Thought News will attempt to do. It will report society in order that it may be seen to be an idea in motion. It will report it for thought. . . .
>
> In this the reporter, the fact man, becomes scientific, and the student, the theory man, becomes the reporter. So the chasm between education and real life, between theory and practice, is bridged over once and forever.[32]

This announcement was savagely lampooned in the local press. The *Detroit Tribune* correspondent commented that "just how Mr. Dewey is to report thought no one seems to exactly understand, and Mr. Dewey has not yet explained." It seemed, the reporter said, that "Mr. Dewey proposed to get out an 'extra' every time he has a new thought—in that case the subscribers will be largely dependent on the stability of Mr. Dewey's digestion for their news." Dewey, he joked, "is to be the new Benjamin Franklin," and *Thought News* was to be the "kite" through which "he proposes to bring philosophy down to life and make it, like the lightning, turn the wheels of society." A few days later, the paper's editors complained that existing newspapers were already doing what Dewey's paper proposed to do and wagered "ten to one 'Thought News' will contain

32. Press release quoted in *Detroit Tribune,* 10 April 1892, 3.

news already covered by the newspapers, and twenty to one that its thought will be exclusively that of its editors."[33]

Distressed by this sudden notoriety, Dewey repudiated Ford's expansive view of the aims of *Thought News*. Ford's announcement, he told reporters, "must have been someone's conception of what *Thought News* is to be. It wasn't given out by me." He had not, Dewey said, intended to revolutionize journalism but to inject new life into philosophy, which had become a remote and abstract discipline. He was attempting to give philosophy a practical bearing by putting it in the context of the life of the social organism. "When philosophic ideas are not inculcated by themselves but used as tools to point out the meaning of phases of social life they begin to have some life and value. Instead of trying to change the newspaper business by introducing philosophy into it, the idea is to transform philosophy somewhat by introducing a little newspaper business into it." While it was quite possible that existing newspapers were remiss in failing to treat facts within the context of the movement of the social organism as a whole, "that's not the affair, one way or the other of *Thought News*."[34]

Dewey's hasty retreat from the larger ambitions of their project brought an end to his relationship with Ford. No issue of *Thought News* ever appeared. Near the end of his life, Dewey remembered *Thought News* as "an overenthusiastic project which we had not the means nor the time to carry through." It was an idea ahead of its time and "too advanced for the maturity of those who had the idea in mind." The Ford brothers had a less charitable interpretation of the failure of *Thought News*. Dewey, they charged, had gotten cold feet when faced with the threat that radical journalism would pose to his academic career. "Clogged of the dead institution, he could not move," Corydon Ford scornfully declared; "his salary meant that he was to keep quiet as to the overturning concepts. He must either forego his bribe and become the tramp upon the highway that he might have voice; or he could remain to take the sop of convention and upstew the old ideas with the new as the made dish of apart theory."[35]

There was undoubtedly a good deal of truth in these charges. Professors who engaged in radical journalism did not remain professors

33. *Detroit Tribune*, 10 April 1892, 13 April 1892.
34. Quoted in "He's Planned No Revolution," *Detroit Tribune*, 13 April 1892.
35. JD to Willinda Savage, 30 May 1949, as quoted in Savage, "The Evolution of Dewey's Philosophy," p. 150; Corydon Ford, *The Child of Democracy* (Ann Arbor, Mich.: John V. Sheehan, 1894), p. 175.

for long in the late nineteenth century. It would, however, be a mistake to regard *Thought News* as simply a hard-earned lesson that Dewey prudently put behind him, for the ideals he formulated in planning this project remained an important element in his thinking. Unlike many academics who were busy in the 1890s constructing professional "communities of the competent," Dewey continued to maintain that democracy required all citizens to be offered membership in a single "Great Community" of the competent, and the vision of a "socialized intelligence" survived the Ford debacle. He continued to believe that truth is not truly freed until it "extends and distributes itself to all so that it becomes the Common-wealth." Franklin Ford may have been a scoundrel, as Dewey reportedly claimed, but his character does not diminish his important role in the development of Dewey's social philosophy. If Alice Dewey and T. H. Green were largely responsible for the ethical and political turn Dewey's philosophy took in the late 1880s, it was Ford, more than anyone else, who in the early 1890s directed this turn toward radical democracy.[36]

36. "Christianity and Democracy" (1892), *Early Works* 4:8–9; Dewey's assessment of Ford is reported by Horace Kallen in Corliss Lamont, ed., *Dialogue on John Dewey* (New York: Horizon Press, 1959), p. 30. On the formation of professional "communities of the competent" see Haskell, *Emergence of Professional Social Science*, pp. 65–68, 88–90, 234–240.

CHAPTER 3

Chicago Pragmatism

*

SOMETIME in late 1893 or early 1894 John Dewey's former colleague at Michigan, James H. Tufts, brought his work to the attention of the president of the recently founded University of Chicago, William Rainey Harper, who was assembling an all-star cast of professors with the help of the largesse of the university's chief benefactor, John D. Rockefeller. Describing Dewey as "simple, modest, utterly devoid of any affectation or self-consciousness," Tufts praised his accomplishments as a scholar and teacher and noted his ability "to guide other men into fruitful lines of research." Apparently impressed by this recommendation, Harper offered Dewey the post of head of the philosophy department, and Dewey accepted. Burdened with the costs of raising a growing family, which by this time included three children, Dewey was attracted by Harper's offer of a salary of five thousand dollars as well as by "the chance to build up the department of philosophy, to associate with men whose main interest is in advanced research, the opportunity to devote myself to that kind of work, [and] the living in Chicago." The *University of Chicago Weekly* hailed his appointment, noting that "if we are proud of the reputation of our faculty we are proud of the association of a scholar who enhances and brightens that reputation greatly."[1]

1. James H. Tufts to William Rainey Harper [1894]; JD to Harper, 15 February 1894; *The University of Chicago Weekly,* all as quoted in Dykhuizen, pp. 74–75. On the early years of the University of Chicago see Richard Storr, *Harper's University: The Beginnings* (Chicago: University of Chicago Press, 1966).

When he began work at Chicago, signs that Dewey was weaning himself from neo-Hegelianism were already apparent. Dissatisfied with the remoteness of absolute idealism from the concrete particulars of human experience, he was in search of a philosophy that would provide greater leverage on practical problems. "I presume to think that I am more of a Yankee and less of a 'philosopher' than sometimes may appear," he wrote William James in 1891. By 1905, when he left Chicago for Columbia, Dewey had abandoned idealism and joined James as a leader of the "pragmatists" who proposed to utilize this Yankee sensibility to reconstruct philosophy. This shift from absolute idealism to pragmatic naturalism did not alter Dewey's democratic convictions, but it did transform the philosophical foundations of his democratic theory, placing it on an original and distinctively American footing.[2]

It is difficult to date Dewey's break with neo-Hegelianism because, as he himself observed, this important change in his thinking was a slow "drifting away" from absolute idealism. One consequence of this slow drift is the substantial disagreement among scholars about what exactly Dewey was up to philosophically in the 1890s. Some have argued that he abandoned idealism very early in the decade, as early as 1891. This argument draws on the clear evidence in the early years of the decade that he was disenchanted with the philosophy of T. H. Green and other British idealists, but it ignores the fact that he cast this criticism as a Hegelian critique of what he had come to perceive as a stubborn Kantianism in contemporary idealism. After 1890 Dewey consistently referred to his idealist targets as neo-Kantians and tried to set himself apart from the "purely Anglo-American habit" of "interpreting Hegel as a Neo-Kantian, a Kantian enlarged and purified." He taught a seminar on Hegel's philosophy until 1899, and the careful reader can find residual absolute idealism in his work well into the decade.[3]

Perhaps the dominant interpretation of Dewey's work in the 1890s sees him merging absolute idealism, functional psychology, and instrumental logic into a kind of "experimental idealism." The trouble with

2. JD to William James, 6 May 1891, in Ralph Barton Perry, ed., *The Thought and Character of William James* (Boston: Little, Brown, 1935), 2:516.

3. The boldest statement of the argument for a very early departure from idealism is Michael Buxton, "The Influence of William James on John Dewey's Early Work," *Journal of the History of Ideas* 45 (1984): 451–463. See also Bruce Kuklick, *Churchmen and Philosophers* (New Haven: Yale University Press, 1985), chap. 16. Dewey's defense of Hegel from neo-Kantian misinterpretation can be found in "Self-Realization as the Moral Ideal" (1893), *Early Works* 4:53; "The Metaphysical Method in Ethics" (1896), *Early Works* 5:25; "Beliefs and Existences" (1906), *Middle Works* 3:86. Residual idealism can be seen in *The Study of Ethics: A Syllabus* (1894), *Early Works* 4:293; *Lectures on Psychological and Political Ethics: 1898* (New York: Hafner Press, 1976), p. 197.

this argument is that his published work in the 1890s offers no evidence of an effort to effect this merger. There is some indication that he was attempting this sort of thing in the classroom in the 1890s, but his reluctance to broach this synthesis publicly indicates that it was stillborn.[4]

Given the weaknesses of these prevailing interpretations, it seems to me that a third perspective is in order. By the early 1890s, I would argue, Dewey had not abandoned neo-Hegelianism but he had finally stripped his work of the metaphysical method, the transcendental logic of internal relations, with which idealists established the existence and nature of the Absolute. He held firmly to the "psychological standpoint" applauded in his 1886 essay by that title and to the conviction expressed there that "the nature of all objects of philosophical inquiry is to be fixed by finding out what experience says about them." Attacked by such critics as Shadworth Hodgson and G. Stanley Hall for paying only lip service to this perspective in his psychological writings of the 1880s, Dewey took this criticism to heart and resolved not to stray from the evidence of science and ordinary experience. Moreover, his work with Franklin Ford, despite its practical failures, had firmly convinced Dewey of the superiority of a politically and socially engaged philosophy to the arid scholasticism of hermetic professionalism, and he increasingly came to measure the worth of a philosophical argument not only by the degree to which it was rooted in experience but also by the contribution it made to its enrichment. Idealist metaphysics came up short on both counts. "Metaphysics has had its day," Dewey wrote one of his favorite students in 1893, "and if the truths which Hegel saw cannot be stated as direct, practical truths, they are not true."[5]

But if Dewey repudiated the philosophical method of absolute idealism early in the 1890s, it was not until late in the decade that he openly said farewell to the Absolute. Absolute idealism had satisfied his intel-

4. For a summary of this interpretation see Dykhuizen, pp. 68–71, 82–83. The only time Dewey used the term "experimental idealism" was in his *Study of Ethics* (1894), and proponents of the "experimental idealist" thesis about Dewey's thinking in the 1890s routinely cite this instance. As Dewey uses the term in this case, however, "idealism" does not refer to a metaphysical position but to a conception of the role of ideals in moral behavior—it is contrasted with the "empirical idealism" of hedonism and the "abstract idealism" of Kantian rationalism. Evidence of an attempt to reconcile Hegel and instrumental logic in the classroom can be found in Dewey's own account of his teaching in Jane Dewey, "Biography of John Dewey," in Paul A. Schilpp, ed., *The Philosophy of John Dewey*, 2d ed. (New York: Tudor, 1951), p. 18, and in the lecture notes for his courses "Hegel's Logic" (1894) and "Hegel's Philosophy of Spirit" (1897), H. H. Bawden Collection, Pius XII Library, St. Louis University.

5. "The Psychological Standpoint" (1886), *Early Works* 1:123; JD to James R. Angell, 10 May 1893, James R. Angell Papers, Yale University.

lectual and emotional craving for an organic and purposeful world and provided him with the foundation for a democratic social and political theory that reconciled individuality and community. He was unwilling to relinquish any of this, and he did not give up the Absolute until he convinced himself that he could do so without sacrificing the valuable theoretical and practical benefits it had bestowed. This, it seems to me, accounts for Dewey's continuing touchiness about misreadings of Hegel long after he had given up the quest for the Absolute: he was anxious lest his critique of idealism throw the bathwater out with the baby.

BRACKETING THE ABSOLUTE

The first signs of Dewey's disenchantment with idealist metaphysics appeared in his ethical writings of the early 1890s. The third edition of his *Psychology*, published in 1891, retained the metaphysical linkage of human and divine will, but the *Outlines of a Critical Theory of Ethics*, published that same year, also offered the reader a different, non-metaphysical grounding for the ethics of self-realization. The moral agent, Dewey argued, acted in the faith that the development of his individuality contributed to the well-being of the other members of his society, the faith that "self and others make a true community." All moral conduct was based on this faith, and it was the "postulate" on which moral theory rested as well. Dewey set this postulate off in capital letters to emphasize its importance:

IN THE REALIZATION OF INDIVIDUALITY THERE IS FOUND ALSO THE NEEDED REALIZATION OF SOME COMMUNITY OF PERSONS OF WHICH THE INDIVIDUAL IS A MEMBER; AND, CONVERSELY, THE AGENT WHO DULY SATISFIES THE COMMUNITY IN WHICH HE SHARES, BY THAT SAME CON-DUCT SATISFIES HIMSELF.

The demonstration or refutation of this postulate was a job for metaphysics, he said, but he eschewed the task. Instead, he offered an alternative way of thinking about this ethical postulate which accorded with the way it functioned in the lives of most moral agents and required no metaphysics. The postulate, he said, was akin to the assumption of a uniform and law-bound natural world which governed the work of scientists and, indeed, made science possible. It was, that is, an assumption that moral agents had to make in order to engage in ethical conduct; each had to have faith that "what is really good for me *must* turn out good for all, or else there is no good in the world at all." Like the scientist's assumption that the world was lawlike and that these laws were accessible to human intelligence, this moral postulate was a proposition one had to believe to engage in the action necessary to test it, and the proof was in the pudding of this experimental experience.[6]

Three years later in another, thoroughly revised, ethics textbook, Dewey restated the ethical postulate in somewhat different language: "The conduct required truly to express an agent is, at the same time, the conduct required to maintain the situation in which he is placed; while, conversely, the conduct that truly meets the situation is that which furthers the agent." More important than this more abstract phrasing of the postulate was the fact that Dewey dropped all mention of metaphysics from his account of its verification while retaining the analogy with the scientific postulate. The only proof of such postulates, he now declared, "is in the results reached by making the demand. The postulate is verified by being acted upon. The proof is experimental."[7]

Between these two formulations of the ethical postulate and its verification lay two important essays in which Dewey attacked the "metaphysical ethics" of his one-time hero T. H. Green. Ethical theory, Dewey argued in these articles, had to weave its way between two undesirable conceptions of its task. On the one hand, it should not become a rigid body of rules "erected with the object of having always some precept which will tell us just what to do," for this notion of ethical theory ignored the concreteness and particularity of human action and destroyed "the grace and play of life by making conduct mechanical." Because all conduct was "individualized to the last ell," no casuistry could possibly deal with "the wealth of concrete action," and any attempt to develop one would destroy the spontaneity and breadth of the moral life. On the other hand, ethical reflection had to avoid a metaphysical turn that produced theories too abstract to provide help in determining concrete action. To avoid these pitfalls ethical theory had to play a role in conduct similar to that played by scientific theory in the solution of particular problems of engineering. In such cases theory served as "a general conception which is so true to reality that it lends itself easily and almost inevitably to more specific and concrete statement, the moment circumstances demand such particularization." The special task of ethical theory was to offer "a general statement of

6. *Outlines of a Critical Theory of Ethics* (1891), *Early Works* 3:320–323.
7. *Study of Ethics*, p. 234.

the reality involved in every moral situation. It must be action stated in its more generic terms, terms so generic that every individual action will fall within the outlines it sets forth."[8]

Green's ethical theory, Dewey contended, was a prime example of metaphysical ethics, a theory so remote from contact with experience that it failed to meet the demand that ethical theory prove a useful tool of analysis for concrete action. Green's theory of the "moral motive" (which Dewey had dutifully followed in his *Psychology*) rested on the contention that the moral agent was conscious of a sharp dualism between the ends that would satisfy the unified, Absolute self and those that would satisfy his partial, human self. The ideal self, Green insisted, could never find satisfaction in the particular desires of the partial self, and yet it was the satisfaction of this self standing apart from all human desires that, in his theory, provided the goal of moral conduct. As a consequence, individuals were always striving to attain a moral ideal that could never be realized, for, according to Green, in no possible circumstance could human action satisfy the unified self and thus be truly moral. The upshot of this theory of the moral motive, Dewey said, was that "the moral life is, by constitution, a self-contradiction." Given Green's liberal Christian proclivities, he noted ironically, "no thoroughgoing theory of total depravity ever made righteousness more impossible to the natural man than Green makes it to a human being by the very constitution of his being." More to the point of Dewey's concern with the practical requirements of ethical theory, Green's theory of the moral motive was altogether useless:

> Instead of being a tool which can be brought into fruitful relations to special circumstances so as to help determine what should be done, it remains the bare thought of an ideal of perfection, having nothing in common with the special set of conditions or with the special desire of the moment. Indeed, instead of helping determine the right, the satisfactory, it stands off one side and says, "No matter what you do, you will be dissatisfied. I am complete; you are partial. I am a unity; you are a fragment, and a fragment of such a kind that no amount of you and such as you can ever afford satisfaction." In a word, the ideal not only does not lend itself to specification, but it negates specification in such way that its necessary outcome, were it ever seriously adopted as a controlling theory of morals, would be to paralyze action.[9]

8. "Green's Theory of the Moral Motive" (1892), *Early Works* 3:155–158. See also "Moral Theory and Practice" (1891), *Early Works* 3:93–109.
9. "Green's Theory," pp. 159–163. See also "The Metaphysical Method in Ethics."

Dewey continued to share Green's identification of the moral ideal with the "unified self," but he now refused to treat that self as a metaphysical being standing apart from particular human desires. Properly conceived, "the unity of the self would stand in no opposition to the particularity of the special desire; on the contrary, the unity of the self and the manifold of definite desires would be the synthetic and analytic aspects of one and the same reality, neither having any advantage metaphysical or ethical over the other." The moral self, Dewey argued, did not distinguish itself *from* its special desires but rather defined itself *in* them. The distinction Green drew between the realized, partial self and the ideal, unified self was a hypostatization into separate entities of what were in fact two stages of moral insight, a distinction between a narrow, limited conception of the self's activity and a "more adequate comprehension and treatment" of conduct aiming at "the highest and fullest activity possible." The self, Dewey concluded, should be "conceived as a working, practical self, carrying within the rhythm of its own process both 'realized' and 'ideal' self."[10]

Dewey hinted that, while such a conception of the self was incompatible with Green's dualistic neo-Kantian or "neo-Fichtean" metaphysics, it was not necessarily foreign to neo-Hegelianism. He made no attempt, however, to show how an ethical theory that purged itself of "all conceptions, of all ideals, save those which are developed within and for the sake of practice" might remain Hegelian. For all practical purposes, and these were now what mattered most to Dewey, he was beginning to question the need for metaphysical argument. By 1894 he was confidently proclaiming the possibility and desirability of an ethical theory free of all metaphysics.[11]

THE NATURALIZATION OF ORGANIC EXPERIENCE

Dewey might have made more of an effort to synthesize his ethics of the "working self" with Hegelian metaphysics had he not become increasingly convinced that the functional psychology he had taken on as an ally against the alienating dualisms of empiricism and the moral threat of Spencerian naturalism could slay these dragons without any help from the Absolute. He was rapidly awakening in the early 1890s to

10. "Green's Theory," p. 161; "Self-Realization as the Moral Ideal" (1893), *Early Works* 4:50–53. I shall return in Chapter 6 to the naturalistic ethics of self-realization Dewey forecast here.

11. "Self-Realization as the Moral Ideal," p. 53.

the possibility of a naturalism that could sustain his faith that the world was friendly to human purposes, a naturalism that suffered from none of the practical deficiencies of absolute idealism.

Recounting his intellectual autobiography in 1930, Dewey attributed this reconsideration of the implications of the "new psychology" to the influence of William James's masterful *Principles of Psychology*, published in 1890. James's influence on Dewey has recently been called into question, but if one carefully specifies its character, this influence was as undeniable and important as Dewey claimed it to be. James's book did not, to be sure, offer Dewey much functional psychology that he did not already have, some of it from the articles James had published prior to 1890 (many of which were incorporated into the *Principles*). Dewey had been very sympathetic in the 1880s to the functionalism James was then developing. Following James's contention that the mind was a "fighter for ends," Dewey had argued that consciousness was neither indifferent nor passive but infused with feeling and engaged in purposeful action. The self was "constituted by activities" and was "constantly organizing itself in certain definite, explicit forms" to advance its well-being. In Dewey's account, however, this functional interpretation of consciousness had been subordinated to Green's metaphysics and relentlessly pushed to transcendental conclusions. As he grew dissatisfied with this metaphysics, he retreated from these conclusions and his attempt (as James had put it) to "mediate between the bare miraculous self and the concrete particulars of individual mental lives"; and, in reconsidering the philosophical implications of functional psychology, Dewey found in the *Principles* less an intellectual revelation than "a stimulus to mental freedom" and a "purveyor of methods and materials."[12]

Dewey was selective in what he incorporated into his thought from the *Principles,* for it was a profoundly conflicted, even contradictory, text, torn between epistemological dualism and an antidualistic "radical empiricism" grounded in evolutionary biology. Dewey was sharply critical of remnants of dualism and "subjectivism" in James's thinking, while at the same time he responded enthusiastically to the "objective" biological strain—the rooting of human psychology in organic experience and history—that he found in the *Principles*. Throughout the 1890s Dewey chewed over James's arguments, and they served as the

12. William James, *The Principles of Psychology* (Cambridge: Harvard University Press, 1983), p. 144; JD, *Psychology* (1891), *Early Works* 2:216; William James to Croom Robertson (1886) as quoted in Perry, *Thought and Character of William James*, 2:516; JD to William James, 10 May 1891, in Perry, *Thought and Character of William James*, 2:517.

source of problems and perspectives that enabled him to "naturalize" his organicism and at the same time protect his moral vision from materialism, thereby weaning himself from idealism without giving up the commitments that had made him an idealist. He later remarked that he was unsure that James fully realized the importance of the biological strain in his work, but it was this strain that "worked its way more and more into all my ideas and acted as a ferment to transform old beliefs." By the end of the decade, as Morton White observes, Dewey could "out-James James."[13]

The naturalization of Dewey's organicism followed a pattern evident in his attack on the Kantian dualism in Green's ethics. He began to wonder, that is, whether a whole host of philosophical problems were the consequence of a tendency of philosophers to hypostasize functional divisions within human experience into ontological divisions between supposedly real entities. Faced with these divisions between subject and object, man and nature, reason and fact, absolute idealists had bridged the gap by positing an absolute consciousness within which these divisions were but divisions of organic function. But what if, as biology and psychology now seemed to Dewey to suggest, these ontological divisions were as unreal in human experience as in the putative experience of God? There then would be no need to bring in an Absolute to unify experience by means of logical legerdemain, a procedure that brought with it a whole host of problems, including a retreat from the psychological standpoint he was determined to maintain. If experience was organic in the first place, then the question for philosophers would not be, as it had been for centuries, how things can possibly hang together in experience, but rather why they seem to fall apart and what this apparent falling apart signifies.

Dewey sketched this new perspective in 1896 in "The Reflex Arc

13. Morton White, *The Origin of Dewey's Instrumentalism* (New York: Columbia University Press, 1943), p. 107. For Dewey's statements of James's influence on this thinking see "From Absolutism to Experimentalism" (1930), *Later Works* 5:157–158; Jane Dewey, "Biography of John Dewey," p. 23; "The Development of American Pragmatism" (1925), *Later Works* 2:17. For the skeptical position on this issue see Buxton, "Influence of William James." The competing argument is stated in Andrew J. Reck, "The Influence of William James on John Dewey in Psychology," *Transactions of the Charles S. Peirce Society* 20 (1984): 87–117. On the contradictions Dewey perceived in *The Principles of Psychology*, see "The Ego as Cause" (1894), *Early Works* 4:91–95; "The Vanishing Subject in the Psychology of James" (1940), *Later Works* 14:155–167. One should also not underestimate the importance to Dewey of the simple fact that he found himself working along the same lines as a philosopher whom he respected as much as he did James. This may well have helped sustain his morale as he launched his thinking into unexplored territory. James, on the other hand, seems to have been relatively oblivious to the steady convergence of their work until fairly late in the game.

Concept in Psychology," an article that marked a watershed in the course of his thinking. The reflex arc was the central concept in the new psychology, and as James had done fifteen years earlier in his lecture "Reflex Action and Theism," Dewey made it the focus of an argument with larger philosophical implications. Ten years earlier he had examined research on reflex action to deflect materialism and preserve a place for the soul. Now he returned to the concept to establish grounds for a naturalism that had no use for an "extra-experimental soul."[14]

The concept of the reflex arc and the stimulus-response model of experience it posited, Dewey argued, was plagued by dualisms between sensation and idea, body and soul which were metaphysical survivals deriving little support from "plain science." Sensations, ideas, and motor response were treated as "disconnected existences," and as a result experience was conceived as a "patchwork of disjointed parts, a mechanical conjunction of unallied processes" (RA, 97). An interpretation freed of these metaphysical obstructions, he argued, suggested that experience was a "comprehensive, organic unity" in which stimulus and response should be viewed "not as separate and complete entities in themselves, but as divisions of labor, functioning factors within the single concrete whole" (RA, 97). This concrete whole, the "sensori-motor co-ordination," was the primary reality within which sensation, idea, and movement were functional elements. Stimulus and response existed only within such coordinations and had significance "purely from the part played in maintaining or reconstituting the co-ordination" (RA, 99). Hence experience was not a series of broken arcs but a continuous "circuit," and only those who failed to see the inherent "unity of activity" would feel compelled to call in the "soul" to patch things up (RA, 99–100).

Dewey illustrated his point with an example familiar to readers of James's *Principles* of a child reaching for the flame of a candle and suffering a burn. According to the ordinary interpretation of these events, the sensation of light was the stimulus for the child's grasping response, the burn was the stimulus for the responsive withdrawal of the hand, and the whole affair was a herky-jerky series of discrete acts which began with sensational stimuli existing outside the child's experience. However, Dewey argued, this interpretation misrepresented the process, for it overlooked the fact that these events began not with the light of the candle as a sensation or stimulus standing outside of the child's

14. "The Reflex Arc Concept in Psychology" (1896), *Early Works* 5:99. Page numbers for further references (RA) appear in the text.

activity but with a sensor-motor coordination, the child's act of seeing, within which the sensation of light functioned. Similarly, this act of seeing stimulated the act of reaching, and both seeing and reaching were incorporated in a larger "eye-arm-hand coordination." The burn the child then received was no more an external sensation than the light but rather a further development of the ongoing coordination, one that reacted back upon ("mediated") the "seeing-of-a-light-that-means-pain-when-contact-occurs" (RA, 98). It was by means of this circuit of experience that the child learned not to grasp burning candles. In every instance, "stimulus and response are not distinctions of existence, but teleological distinctions, that is, distinctions of function, or part played, with reference to reaching or maintaining an end" (RA, 104).

Much of experience, Dewey observed, was a smooth-running affair in which there was no consciousness of stimulus and response as such. In the instincts of animals or thoroughly formed human habits, for example, "there is simply a continuously ordered sequence of acts, all adapted in themselves and in the order of their sequence, to reach a certain objective end" (RA, 104). *Conscious* stimuli and responses arose only in situations in which a conflict occurred within a coordination and the agent was uncertain how to complete it. For example, a child who has experienced a variety of consequences, good and bad, when reaching for a bright light would be doubtful about what to do when he again saw such a light. In this situation, "the response is not only uncertain, but the stimulus is equally uncertain" (RA, 106). Both stimulus and response had to be consciously identified or "constituted" for the conflict within the coordination to be resolved. As conscious stimulus, the bright light was not a thing in itself but a function within a problematic coordination; it was that phase of a "disintegrating coordination" which established the problem ("what sort of a bright light have we here?"). Likewise the response in such situations was a function that solved the problem (if the stimuli had been correctly identified) and completed the coordination (RA, 107–108).

This analysis was pregnant with philosophical and practical (particularly pedagogical) implications that Dewey would spend many years developing. Its importance in the context of his shifting philosophical commitments in the 1890s was that not only had he freed himself from soul-talk but had also advanced a critique of dualism without calling upon the assumption of an absolute consciousness and without moving outside of a psychological standpoint. He had, in effect, restated in wholly naturalistic terms the critique of empiricist "ontologism" he had made ten years earlier.

Another notable feature of the "Reflex Arc" essay in this context was the hint it gave of a naturalization of Dewey's functional interpretation of thought. Empiricists and idealists alike tended to equate experience with knowledge, but here Dewey clearly subordinated knowledge to action, clarifying the cryptic statement he had made some years earlier, when trying to come to terms with the philosophical meaning of the reflex arc, that "reality is not to be read in terms of knowledge as such, but in terms of action." This anticipated his pragmatic critique of epistemology and reflected his greatest debt to James, who had in his own essay on reflex action declared that "the current of life which runs in at our eyes or ears is meant to run out at our hands, feet, or lips. The only use of the thoughts it occasions while inside is to determine its direction to whichever of these organs shall, on the whole, under the circumstances actually present, act in the way most propitious to our welfare."[15]

Thought, by these lights, was a natural function that had evolved in order to serve the interests of human survival. It was, moreover, the functional aspect of human experience that distinguished it from that of other natural beings. Man alone was able to mediate his impulses and to engage in intelligent, purposeful action. As Dewey said, "That which was instinct in the animal is conscious impulse in man. That which was 'tendency to vary' in the animal is conscious foresight in man. That which was unconscious adaptation and survival in the animal, taking place by the 'cut and try' method until it worked itself out, is with man conscious deliberation and experimentation." This evolutionary and functional understanding of thought played a significant role in the emergence of Dewey's naturalism, not only because it formed the foundation of his eventual direct attack on absolute idealism but also because it pointed toward the marriage of evolutionary biology and ethics which Dewey had once thought impossible. He now perceived the possibility that one could exile theology *without* making ethics an expatriate.[16]

Dewey had rejected evolutionary naturalism in 1887 because he believed it banished human purposes from the universe. By the turn of the century, armed with a fresh understanding of how man had evolved naturally into a thoughtful, purposeful creature, he left absolute idealism behind for an evolutionary naturalism substantially different from that he had earlier criticized. As James Collins has observed, Dewey continued to believe that "nature has no inherently inscribed values," but

15. "Introduction to Philosophy: Syllabus of Course 5" (1892), *Early Works* 3:229; William James, "Reflex Action and Theism" (1881), *The Will to Believe* (Cambridge: Harvard University Press, 1979), p. 92.
16. "Evolution and Ethics" (1898), *Early Works* 5:53.

now he argued that "nature does give birth to the kind of being which envisions ideals and establishes ends for action." Hence "what makes moral purposes meaningful is not the relating of nature to a universal consciousness, but the relating of it to men in their concrete existence and planning activities." Dewey, that is, discovered that purposeful human action could be explained naturalistically without having to offer a naturalistic argument for a purposeful universe. Nature, apart from man, was not ethical, but, in man, nature had in the course of the evolutionary process produced an ethical being:

> Nature, till it produces a being who strives and who thinks in order that he may strive more effectively, does not know whether it cares more for justice or for cruelty, more for the ravenous wolf-like competition of the struggle for existence, or for the improvements incidentally introduced through that struggle. Literally it has no mind of its own. . . . But when the sentient organism, having experienced natural values, good and bad, begins to select, to prefer, and to make battle for its preference; and in order that it may make the most gallant fight possible picks out and gathers together in perception and thought what is favorable to its aims and what hostile, then and there Nature has at last achieved significant regard for good.

By the early twentieth century, the struggle Dewey had pointed to in 1887 between an anthropology that saw man as a divine superscription and an anthropology that found him the product of the shaping of earthly clay had for him been obviated by a third anthropology that saw man as the emergence of a unique sort of earthly clay.[17]

ATTACKING THE ABSOLUTE

As he indicated to William James, Dewey's psychological writings of the mid-1890s hinted at the replacement of the Absolute with a naturalistic conception of "life activity" as the basis of his philosophy, but he did not make this explicit for some years. He made no attempt publicly to advance the "metaphysical applications" of his newfound understanding of the "active process" of experience until the publication of the collaborative *Studies in Logical Theory*, which appeared in 1903.

17. James Collins, "The Genesis of Dewey's Naturalism," in John Blewett, ed., *John Dewey: His Thought and Influence* (New York: Fordham University Press, 1960), p. 13; "Nature and Its Good" (1909), *Middle Works* 4:29.

There he declared conclusively that he could no longer consent to the proposition that reality "presents itself as a thought-system."[18]

The *Studies in Logical Theory* was the product of nearly ten years of cooperative inquiry by the members of the Chicago philosophy department. Starting virtually from scratch as chairman of the department, Dewey had gathered around him a talented group of younger scholars—James R. Angell, Edward S. Ames, George Herbert Mead, Addison W. Moore, and James H. Tufts—who shared his excitement over the biological strain in James's work and regarded the *Principles* as "the spiritual *progenitor*" of their philosophical enterprise. Together with a number of outstanding graduate students they explored together in their classrooms the "intimate connections of logical theory with functional psychology," and by the end of the decade they had, as James admiringly said, formed "a view of the world, both theoretical and practical, which is so simple, massive, and positive that, in spite of the fact that many parts of it yet need to be worked out, it deserves the title of a new system of philosophy."[19]

It was fitting that Dewey should announce his departure from absolute idealism in an essay in logical theory. Logic was the master science of the idealists, and it was to logic that they retreated when challenged by critics. From the earliest years of his career, he had lamented this logical retreat in idealist argument, though, as we have seen, he found

18. JD to William James, 27 March 1903, in Perry, *Thought and Character of William James*, 2:522; *Studies in Logical Theory* (1903), *Middle Works* 2:333n8.

19. JD to William James, March 1903, in Perry, *Thought and Character of William James*, 2:521; *Studies in Logical Theory*, p. 296; William James, "The Chicago School" (1904), *Essays in Philosophy* (Cambridge: Harvard University Press, 1978), p. 102. For an overview of the work of the Chicago department see Darnell Rucker, *The Chicago Pragmatists* (Minneapolis: University of Minnesota Press, 1969). Mead was the Chicago colleague who exercised the greatest influence on Dewey's thinking in the 1890s. Dewey brought Mead with him from Michigan, where he had been involved with Dewey's earliest efforts to rethink his idealism. Trained in physiological psychology in Germany under such masters as Wilhelm Wündt, Mead played a critical role in what Dewey termed "the biologizing of my approach." Dewey's thinking, in turn, rescued Mead from the turmoil of a spiritual crisis much like that Dewey himself had suffered, and he encouraged the younger man to develop the social psychology implied by their shared philosophical perspective, which Mead did to a degree surpassing Dewey's own efforts along these lines. On the Dewey-Mead relationship see JD, "George Herbert Mead as I Knew Him" (1931), *Later Works* 6:22–28; JD to Joseph Ratner, 9 July 1946, Joseph Ratner Papers, Morris Library, Southern Illinois University; Neil Coughlan, *Young John Dewey* (Chicago: University of Chicago Press, 1975), chaps. 7–8; Hans Joas, *G. H. Mead* (Cambridge: Polity Press, 1985), esp. chap. 2. On Mead's social psychology see, in addition to the Joas book, Gary Cook, "The Development of G. H. Mead's Social Psychology," *Transactions of the Charles S. Peirce Society* 8 (1972): 167–186, and David L. Miller, *George Herbert Mead: Self, Language, and the World* (Chicago: University of Chicago Press, 1973). A good anthology of Mead's work, much of which was unpublished in his lifetime, is Anselm Strauss, ed., *George Herbert Mead on Social Psychology* (Chicago: University of Chicago Press, 1964).

it difficult to extricate himself from its coils. For some time he had asserted the superiority of his "psychological standpoint" to that of transcendental logic, and by the turn of the century he was prepared to demonstrate that superiority by arguing, *on logical grounds*, for a theory of knowledge grounded in functional psychology. Now, however, his psychology had been thoroughly naturalized, and as a consequence not only transcendental logic but transcendentalism itself fell before Dewey's razor. This was no accident, for there is every evidence that it was metaphysical game he was hunting in the first place.[20]

Dewey's contribution to the *Studies in Logical Theory* took the form of a critique of the logical writings of Rudolf Hermann Lotze, a German philosopher who had died in 1881. Lotze is hardly a household name today, and Dewey's approach appears at first glance unduly round-about. Lotze, however, was an extremely important figure for Dewey because he had made a heroic effort to answer the two key questions bedeviling modern epistemology—"how a material formed prior to thought and irrespective of it can yet afford stuff upon which thought may exercise itself" and "how thought working independently and from without upon a foreign material can shape the latter into results which are valid." Lotze did so without questioning the assumption of an ontological distinction between thought and its subject matter which was implied in these questions. Since it was precisely this assumption Dewey wished to challenge, it was important to uncover the difficulties it imposed on logicians, and a critical consideration of Lotze's views was a convenient way to do this.[21]

The full detail of Dewey's critique of Lotze need not concern us. Suffice it to say that Dewey found Lotze's logic continually beset by contradictions that grew out of his preconception that thought had to be differentiated from its unreflective antecedents in "complete, fixed, and absolute or at large" fashion. Doing so either resulted in a conception of the antecedents of thought as wholly undetermined "bare exis-

---

20. See Dewey's remark to James that although his psychological articles in the 1890s bracketed metaphysical questions, he had been at work with his classes "more or less on the metaphysical—or logical side, as I prefer to call it"—of a philosophy that involves "teleological and dynamic conceptions rather than ontological and static ones": JD to William James, 27 March 1903, in Perry, *Thought and Character of Williams James*, 2:522. A good discussion of the priority of metaphysical attack in Dewey's early logical writings is G. M. Brodsky, "Absolute Idealism and John Dewey's Instrumentalism," *Transactions of the Charles S. Peirce Society* 5 (1969): 44–62.

21. *Studies in Logical Theory*, pp. 318–319. Page numbers for further references (*SLT*) appear in the text. A helpful discussion of Lotze's importance in late nineteenth century philosophy is Paul G. Kuntz's introduction to George Santayana, *Lotze's System of Philosophy* (Bloomington: Indiana University Press, 1977), pp. 3–94.

tences" that were inadequate material for thought or in thought's determination of its own antecedents, which, given Lotze's assumption of the independent existence of thought and its subject matter, could only alter this antecedent stuff and "lead the mind farther away from reality" (*SLT,* 327).

Such criticisms were the stock-in-trade of absolute idealists, and Dewey admitted that his critique of Lotze shared features of the idealist attack on epistemological dualism. He agreed with the idealists that thought could not develop out of any sort of bare existences, indeed, that there could be any such thing as "*mere* existence." They agreed, as well, that "reflective thought grows organically out of an experience which is already organized, and that it functions within such an organism." Where they parted company was in their conception of this organized experience. Does belief that thought grows out of organized experience, Dewey asked, necessarily imply that "the organization out of which reflective thought grows is the work of thought of some other type—of Pure Thought, Creative or Constitutive Thought, Intuitive Reason, etc.?" (*SLT,* 333). Once he had himself thought so, but now he demurred.

The problem with the idealist solution to the difficulties of epistemological dualism, Dewey contended, was that it solved these difficulties only at the hypothetical level of the Absolute and left untouched the problems of the relation of finite, reflective thought to its antecedents. Like James, he charged that idealists had worked the world up into "two editions," and the human edition remained a mystery:

> For the more one insists that the antecedent situation is constituted by thought, the more one has to wonder why another type of thought is required; what need arouses it, and how is it possible for it to improve upon the work of previous constitutive thought. This difficulty at once forces idealists from a logic of experience as it is concretely experienced into a metaphysic of a purely hypothetical experience. Constitutive thought precedes *our* conscious thought-operations; hence it must be the working of some absolute universal thought which, unconsciously to our reflection, builds up an organized world. But this recourse only deepens the difficulty. How does it happen that the absolute constitutive and intuitive Thought does such a poor and bungling job that it requires a finite discursive activity to patch up its products? Here more metaphysic is called for: The Absolute Reason is now supposed to work under limiting conditions of finitude, of a sensitive and temporal organism. The antecedents of reflective thought are not, therefore, determinations of thought pure and undefiled, but of what

thought can do when it stoops to assume the yoke of change and of feeling. (*SLT*, 334)

The logical problem with this tale was that it landed human reason right back in the same dilemma with which Lotze wrestled, faced with either bare impressions or with organized experience that was, on idealist as well as empiricist premises, inexplicable. If the antecedents of finite thought could not be bare impressions, as the idealists and Dewey agreed, and if they were not pure determinations of the constitutive thought of the Absolute, as idealist metaphysics conceded, then "we have admitted the possibility of organization in experience, apart from Reason, and the ground for assuming Pure Constitutive Thought is abandoned" (*SLT*, 335).[22]

The source of difficulty for idealists, sensationalists, and those like Lotze who tried vainly to synthesize transcendentalism and empiricism lay in their requirement for "a total contrast of thought as such to something else as such" (*SLT*, 330). This, Dewey argued, was to commit a mistake by now familiar to readers of his work: the erection of functional distinctions within experience into distinct entities. "Epistemological logicians" of all stripes had, like many students of the reflex arc, erected "distinctions that are genetic and historic, and working or instrumental divisions of labor, into rigid and ready-made structural differences of reality" (*SLT*, 348). The result was to state "the terms upon which thought and being transact business in a way so totally alien to concrete experience that it creates a problem which can be discussed only in terms of itself—not in terms of the conduct of life" (*SLT*, 308).

The epistemologists' conception of the relationship of thought and reality was, Dewey noted, totally alien to the conception held by the "plain man" and the scientist who shared an understanding of thought as a "derivative and secondary" function that "comes after something and out of something, and for the sake of something" (*SLT*, 298). The relation of "thought at large" to "reality at large" was of no concern to the man on the street or the scientist in the laboratory, for whom "every reflective problem and operation arises with reference to some *specific* situation, and has to subserve a *specific* purpose dependent upon its own occasion" (*SLT*, 301). As the plain man engaged in reflective activity, he was altogether unaware that he was attempting to bridge two spheres of existence, and the scientist going about his work was igno-

22. See also Dewey's review of Josiah Royce's *The World and the Individual* (1900, 1902), *Middle Works* 1:241–256; 2:120–137.

rant of the ontological gulf he was attempting to cross. "Only the epistemological spectator of traditional controversies," Dewey wryly remarked, "is aware of the fact that the everyday man and the scientific
man in this free and easy intercourse are rashly assuming the right to
glide over a cleft in the very structure of reality" (SLT, 306).

Dewey aligned himself firmly with the everyday man and the scientist
against the epistemologists and argued for a new logic grounded in
functional psychology, a "natural history of thinking as a life-process
having it own generating antecedents and stimuli, its own states and
career, and its own specific objective or limit" (SLT, 309). From this
point of view the antecedents of thought were not bare impressions or
experience organized by thought (or Thought) but rather the sort of
"disintegrating coordinations" within the life process that Dewey had
briefly analyzed in his discussion of the reflex arc concept:

> It is the whole dynamic experience with its qualitative and pervasive
> continuity, and its inner active distraction, its elements at odds with
> each other, in tension against each other, each contending for its prop-
> er placing and relationship, which generates the thought situation. . . .
> There is always as antecedent to thought an experience of subject-
> matter of the physical or social world, or the previously organized
> intellectual world, whose parts are actively at war with each other—so
> much so that they threaten to disrupt the situation, which accordingly
> for its own maintenance requires deliberate redefinition and re-
> relation of its tensional parts. This redefining and re-relating is the
> constructive process termed thinking: the reconstructive situation,
> with its parts in tension and in such movement toward each other as
> tends to a unified arrangement of things, is the thought-situation.
> (SLT, 328–330)

Just as thought arose out of a nonreflective (conflicted) situation, so too
it eventuated, if effective, in a nonreflective (harmonious) situation.
"The test of thought," Dewey held, "is the harmony or unity of experience actually effected, the test of validity of thought is beyond thought,
just as at the other limit thought originates out of a situation which is
not dependent upon thought." Thought was not a thing but a division
of labor within experience, a mediating, "instrumental" function dependent "upon unreflective antecedents for its existence, and upon a
consequent experience for its final test" (SLT, 367).

Dewey's offer to relieve epistemological logicians of their "radically
meaningless" problems in this manner was not particularly well received, but William James was delighted to find in Dewey's interpreta-

tion of the origins and aims of thought evidence of the emergence of a fellow "pragmatist," a term he coined in 1898. He also applauded the Darwinian "radical empiricism" that underlay this interpretation. Dewey had freed himself from belief in an "Absolute behind or around the finite world" in favor of an empiricism in which "'life' or 'experience' is the fundamental conception" and "there is nothing real, whether being or relation between beings, which is not direct matter of experience"— an objective process of interacting variables undergoing constant "reconstruction."[23]

Because of his disappointment with Dewey's early psychology and the latter's lack of "'terseness,' 'crispness,' 'raciness,' and other 'newspaporial' virtues," James had not followed the work of the Chicago philosophers very closely in the 1890s (though he "could discern that Dewey himself was laboring with a big freight, toward the light"). But *Studies in Logical Theory*, he told F. C. S. Schiller, "is splendid stuff, and Dewey is a hero. A real school and real thought. At Harvard we have plenty of thought, but no school. At Yale and Cornell, the other way about." In the course of an exchange of mutually admiring letters, James rejoiced that the Chicago school was "bringing its fruits to birth in a way that will demonstrate its great unity and vitality, and be a revelation to many people, of American scholarship." Dewey modestly replied that he had "funded for my own intellectual capital more of the ideas of other people—students and colleagues—than I can tell," but it was clear to James and others that Dewey was the leader of the Chicago pragmatists and that he had found a voice that was very much his own.[24]

THE NATURALIZATION OF PROGRESS

The "naturalization" of Dewey's psychology, ethics, and logic did not have a dramatic effect on most of the essentials of his democratic theory. Much of "The Ethics of Democracy" could have been written in 1898 as comfortably as in 1888. Of the key components of his early democratic theory, only God failed to survive the recasting of Dewey's philosophy as his faith in the progressive embodiment of the Absolute

23. William James, "The Pragmatic Method" (1898), *Essays in Philosophy*, pp. 123–139; James, "The Chicago School," p. 103.

24. William James to F. C. S. Schiller, 8 April 1903, 15 November 1903; William James to JD, 27 March 1903; JD to William James, 19 December 1903, in Perry, *Thought and Character of William James*, 2:374, 501, 524, 525. For the response of less friendly critics to Dewey's pragmatism and radical empiricism see the sections "Against Epistemology" and "The Meaning of Truth" in Chapter 5.

in social institutions gave way to a faith in the capacities of human will and intelligence for progressive reform, and this divine departure, he insisted, was of little consequence.

As an idealist, Dewey had shared with others in Green's school the belief that not only individual self-realization but also the development of social institutions manifested the "embodiment of divine Reason." History was defined as "the process by which a divine will, determined by reason, has articulated wants, desires, and ideas, by making them organic to its own reproduction." Thoroughgoing democracy, Dewey had argued in 1888, was the end toward which this progressive history was moving, for the idea of democracy represented "a society in which the distinction between the spiritual and the secular has ceased, and as in Greek theory, as in the Christian theory of the Kingdom of God, the church and the state, the divine and the human organization of society are one."[25]

This hitching of democracy to divine providence survived well into Dewey's final years at Michigan, even as his dissatisfaction with Green's ethics and with organized religion grew. His decidedly unconventional social gospel raised a few conservative eyebrows in Ann Arbor and generated considerable excitement among a coterie of undergraduates who credited him with ridding them of the intolerance and superstition of their inherited faith. In the important and influential lay sermon "Christianity and Democracy," delivered to the Students' Christian Association in 1892, Dewey virtually identified Christianity with the growth of scientific inquiry and democracy. Christianity, he argued, was not a religion at all in the sense that religion implied a cult and a body of fixed doctrine, for Christianity proclaimed its universality, its hostility to dogma, and an openness to the progressive revelation of truth as such. "The only truth Jesus knew of as religious was Truth," Dewey declared. "There were no special religious truths which He came to teach; on the contrary, his doctrine was that Truth, however named and however divided by man, is one as God is one; that getting hold of truth and living by it is religion." Prayer, he remarked on another occasion, was identical with "the inquiry of science."

Men were free, Dewey declared, insofar as they appropriated and identified themselves with the Truth that is God, and, in the last analysis, "man's own action, his own life movement, is the only organ he has for receiving and appropriating truth." Because such action was inher-

25. "The Philosophy of Thomas Hill Green" (1889), *Early Works* 3:33, 28; "The Ethics of Democracy" (1888), *Early Works* 1:248–249.

ently social, it was "man's social organization, the state in which he is expressing himself, which always has and always must set the form and sound the key-note to the understanding of Christianity." Democracy was the form of social organization that fully opened the gates to God's revelation, for it was breaking down "the walls of isolation and of class interest" which restricted the flow of truth. "It is in democracy, the community of ideas and interest through community of action," Dewey concluded, "that the incarnation of God in man (man, that is to say, as organ of universal truth) becomes a living, present thing, having its ordinary and natural sense." The Kingdom of God on earth for Dewey was not a kingdom at all but an industrial democracy. "The next religious prophet who will have a permanent and real influence on men's lives," he suggested, "will be the man who succeeds in pointing out the religious meaning of democracy."[26]

At Chicago, Dewey not only refused to join a church but also ceased delivering even unorthodox Christian sermons. As he chased the Absolute from his philosophy he also stripped his social theory of all metaphysical and religious guarantees of progress toward his democratic ideals. He continued to believe that the course of history gave evidence of "a continual movement toward democracy," but having embargoed wholesale teleological arguments, he now rested this belief on what he took to be the power of the superior moral vision of societies experimenting with democracy. Without God at the helm of history, progress was uncertain, and Dewey could no longer place a divine imprimatur on his ideals and view them as the "outworking of God in life."[27]

By the turn of the century, he had come to believe this was just as well. Unlike James, who assaulted the Absolute yet argued for belief in a more modest providential divinity as a spur to a strenuous moral life, Dewey saw no practical benefits to be derived from the postulate of a transcendent God even if the logical deficiencies of this hypothesis could be remedied. "Were it a thousand times dialectically demonstrated that life as a whole is regulated by a transcendent principle to a final inclusive goal," he said, "nonetheless truth and error, health and disease, good and evil, hope and fear in the concrete, would remain just what and where they now are." Indeed, if anything, the idea of a

26. "Christianity and Democracy" (1892), *Early Works* 4:4, 7, 8–9; "The Relation of Philosophy to Theology" (1893), *Early Works* 4:368, 367. On Dewey's impact on his undergraduate followers see Coughlan, *Young John Dewey*, pp. 87–90, and Lillian W. Johnson to Joseph Ratner, March 1947, Ratner Papers.

27. *Lectures on Psychological and Political Ethics: 1898*, p. 327; "Christianity and Democracy," p. 9.

providential God had become a practical liability. "To idealize and rationalize the universe at large is after all a confession of inability to master the courses of things that specifically concern us. As long as mankind suffered from this impotency, it naturally shifted a burden of responsibility that it could not carry over to the more competent shoulders of the transcendent cause." Now, Dewey believed, man was able to carry this burden alone, and "responsible" philosophers should abandon metaphysical speculation for "moral and political diagnosis and prognosis."[28]

Dewey's confidence that democratic community could be achieved without divine assistance did not blind him to the sharp and pervasive social conflicts that beset even progressive societies like his own. Indeed, one of the noteworthy features of his evolutionary naturalism was his insistence that a critique of the cruder laissez-faire applications of Darwinism to human society not ignore the importance of conflict in social life. He believed the elimination of conflict to be "a hopeless and self-contradictory ideal," for social life, like individual life, entailed an ongoing reconstruction of conflict-ridden, "disintegrating coordinations." This view of conflict as an inevitable and potentially functional aspect of social life distinguished Dewey from those reformers, including his friend Jane Addams, who regarded it as unnecessary and thoroughly dysfunctional. Soon after he arrived in Chicago, Dewey reported a conversation with Addams in a letter to his wife in which Addams had remarked that

she had always believed, still believed, that antagonism was not only useless and harmful, but entirely unnecessary; that it lay never in the objective differences, which would always grow into unity if left alone, but from a person's mixing in his own personal reactions—the extra emphasis he gave to the truth, the enjoyment he took in doing a thing because it was unpalatable to others or the feeling that one must show his own colors, not be a moral coward, or any no. of other ways. That historically also only evil had come from antagonisms—she kept asking me what I tho't, and I agreed up to this, but then as to past history I dissented; then she went on that if Jesus drove the money changers out of the temple that accounted for the apparent difference between the later years of his ministry and the earlier, and for much of the falsity of Christianity since; *if* he did it, he lost his faith and reacted; that we

28. "The Influence of Darwinism on Philosophy" (1909), *Middle Works* 4:12, 13. Cf. William James, "The Moral Philosopher and the Moral Life" (1891), *The Will to Believe*, pp. 141–162.

freed the slaves by war and had now to free them all over again individ-ually and pay the costs of the war and reckon with the added bitterness of the Southerner besides, etc., etc. I asked her if she didn't think that besides the personal antagonisms, there was that of ideas and institu-tions, as Christianity and Judaism, and Labor and Capital, the Church and Democracy now and that realization of that antagonism was neces-sary to an appreciation of the truth and to a consciousness of growth, and she said no. The antagonisms of institutions were always unreal; it was simply due to the injection of the personal attitude and reaction; and then instead of adding to the recognition of meaning, it delayed and distorted it.

Addams, Dewey told Alice, "converted me internally, but not really, I fear. At least I can't see what all this conflict and passing of history means if it's perfectly meaningless; my pride of intellect, I suppose it is, revolts at thinking it's all merely negative, and has no functional value."[29]

For Dewey, the persistence of conflict as a fact of social life did not mean that specific conflicts should be left to run their course blindly. If Jane Addams and such "reform Darwinists" as Lester Frank Ward were guilty of ignoring the persistence of the "struggle for existence" in human affairs, such "conservative Darwinists" as Benjamin Kidd were remiss in assuming that this struggle must take the same, irrational form in human communities that it did in the rest of the biological world. In man, after all, an intelligent creature had emerged, and, with the advance of social science, "laissez-faire in society becomes as absurd as would be the refusal to use knowledge of mechanical energy in the direction of steam and electricity." Just as his psychological ethics posited a mediating intelligence capable of discovering "a unity of con-duct which will organize the values respectively presented in the vari-ous competing impulses and desires," Dewey's political ethics was grounded in the hope that conflicts between individuals, groups, and classes could eventually be resolved by the mediation of "socialized intelligence" guided by the findings of social science.[30] Philosophy, as well, had an important role to play in the development of this social capacity, and Dewey made a point of linking his work in logical theory to this task:

29. "Review of Lester Frank Ward, *The Psychic Factors of Civilization,* and Benjamin Kidd, *Social Evolution*" (1894), *Early Works* 4:210; JD to Alice Dewey, 10 October 1894, Dewey Papers. It would not, I think, be too far-fetched to see in the exchange between Dewey and Addams the roots of the later, opposed positions they took on the issue of American intervention in World War I.

30. "Review of Ward and Kidd," p. 208.

The value of research for social progress; the bearing of psychology upon educational procedure; the mutual relations of fine and industrial art; the question of the extent and nature of specialization of science in comparison with the claims of applied science; the adjustment of religious aspirations to scientific statements; the justification of a refined culture for a few in face of economic insufficiency for the mass, the relation of organization to individuality—such are a few of the many social questions whose answer depends upon the possession and use of a general logic of experience as a method of inquiry and interpretation. (*SLT,* 313–314)

In the absence of such a method, social action was subject to the "arbitrary and costly" rule of opinion; "a general logic of experience alone can do for social qualities and aims what the natural sciences after centuries of struggle are doing for activity in the physical realm" (*SLT,* 314).

If Dewey did not blink at the conflicts that beset his society at the turn of the century, he was unduly sanguine about their tractability and the prospects for the "social readjustments" that would meet the needs of "those who can say they are not getting a fair share of social values." His abandonment of absolute idealism may have cost him his faith in automatic progress, but he quickly replaced it with a robust faith in contingent progress which would, over the course of his career, be shaken but never subdued. He admitted that the socialization of intelligence was a distant goal, but he often underestimated the strength of the resistance to this and other democratic reforms by the "vested interests" who were "the particular beneficiaries of the existing social habits." Had he more accurately estimated the strength of this resistance, he might have been more charitable toward those reformers who clung to the comforting certainties of Providence. As it was, his hopes for democracy were sustained by the "vital and sinewy optimism" Josiah Royce had perceived in his ethics as early as 1891. They had to be if they were to survive the defeats that democracy—and Dewey—suffered in Chicago.[31]

31. *Lectures on Psychological and Political Ethics: 1898,* p. 353; Josiah Royce, review of JD, *Outline of a Critical Theory of Ethics,* in *International Journal of Ethics* 1 (1891): 505.

CHAPTER 4

No Mean City

★

THE move from Ann Arbor to Chicago in 1894 had thrust John
Dewey from a relatively pastoral setting into the maelstrom of the
prototypical metropolis of industrializing America. Chicago's population had grown rapidly from a half million in 1880 to over a million in
1890, and by 1900 it would reach nearly 1.7 million. Much of this
increase was due to an enormous influx of immigrants; in 1890 three-
fourths of the city's population was made up of the foreign-born and
their children. The cultural landscape of the city was shaped by class as
well as ethnicity and stretched from lavish lakeside mansions to the
sweatshops and tenements of the West Side. All the pathologies and
possibilities of urban life were on full display in Chicago in the 1890s,
and rapacious entrepreneurs and corrupt politicians struggled with
visionary reformers for control of the city's destiny.[1]

Chicago was everything a philosophical "speculator" like Dewey
could desire, and he responded to the city with awe and enthusiasm.
"Chicago," he wrote his wife, "is the place to make you appreciate at
every turn the absolute opportunity which chaos affords—it is sheer
Matter with no standards at all." Shortly after his arrival Dewey accepted the invitation of a friend to an exploration of some of the less
genteel aspects of urban life. They visited "a salvation meeting out of

1. Ray Ginger's *Altgeld's America* (New York: Funk and Wagnalls, 1958) remains the
best overall portrait of Chicago in the 1890s.

doors, a 'happy gospel' meeting in doors, part of the show at the Park Theatre, the worst one in town, four or five wine rooms, where some of the street women hang around, a ten cent lodging house . . . and three houses of prostitution." In Chicago, he told Alice, "every conceivable thing solicits you; the town seems filled with problems holding out their hands and asking somebody to please solve them—or else dump them in the lake. I had no conception that things could be so much more phenomenal and objective than they are in a country village, and simply stick themselves at you, instead of leaving you to think about them. The first effect is pretty paralyzing, the after effect is stimulating—at least, subjectively so, and maybe that is all chaos is in the world for, and not to be really dealt with. But after all you can't really get rid feeling here that there is a 'method' and if you could only get hold of it things could be so tremendously straightened out." He advised Alice to think of the city as "hell turned loose, and yet not hell any longer, but simply material for a new creation."[2]

Dewey shared this vision of Chicago as "material for a new creation" with the city's other radical democrats, a vision perhaps best expressed in the utopian fable "No Mean City" that reformer Henry Demarest Lloyd concocted in 1894. In this tale, which Lloyd delivered many times as a speech before his death in 1903, the citizens of Chicago undergo a spontaneous moral rebirth a few years after the closing of the Chicago World's Fair of 1893, put aside the differences that had divided them, and decide to rebuild the fair's White City. Working together in "happy harmony," businessmen, workers, professors, ministers, architects, and artists construct a new White City that serves as a laboratory for urban reform. The results of the experiments conducted there are then applied to the larger city, transforming it into a place where "it simply became hopelessly unfashionable, and then absolutely vulgar for any one to threaten or rage against another fellow-being." The unemployment that is a consequence of the social reforms and technological advances developed in the White City is solved by constructing a cooperative community, No Mean City, on the fringes of Chicago. Here the unemployed are put to work in an economy in which "every one had to work and to work at something that was necessary to

2. JD to Alice Dewey, 12 July 1894; JD to Alice Dewey, 23 September 1894; JD to Alice Dewey, 25 August 1894, Dewey Papers. The remarkable letters Dewey wrote to his wife in the summer and fall of 1894 were occasioned by the departure in May of Alice and the three Dewey children for an extended European vacation. Dewey joined them in Europe in January 1895.

the general plan," in which the man who cured a disease was no more necessary or worth no more than the man who dug the ditch that prevented the disease, and in which "as all the work was done by the joint labors of all, it should belong to all." Eventually, No Mean City begins to outcompete Chicago and the surrounding countryside, and people from the parent city seek the shelter of "the wings of their irresistible rival." On the centennial of the great fire of 1871 the people of Chicago vote to put an end to the old city, and it is burned down and transformed into a great park.[3]

Lloyd's utopia expressed the dream of peaceful class reconciliation that was widely shared among the community of Chicago reformers which centered its activities at his home in suburban Winnetka and at Hull House, the settlement founded by Jane Addams and Ellen Gates Starr in 1889. However, despite their aversion to class conflict and their belief in the necessity for a prior transformation of social ethics if reform was to be truly effective, these reformers were realistic enough not to rest content with hope and exhortation but accompanied their pleas for justice and love with practical activism that aimed to push their society along the road to organic democracy. Thus, at the same time he was providing audiences with a vision of No Mean City, Lloyd was organizing a populist political coalition of urban workers, farmers, socialists, and reform intellectuals. And, while Jane Addams was promoting the settlement house as an experimental bridging of class cultures, she and the other women of Hull House were also agitating for factory legislation and improved city services. It was the practical work of these reformers, more than anything else, that convinced Dewey that "Chicago is the greatest place in the world." He had lectured at Hull House for several years before his move to Chicago, and when he moved to the city he was eagerly welcomed into the reform community. Turning his own efforts as an activist to the problems of education, he was soon making a distinctive contribution to the social vision of this community and sharing fully in the modest victories and frustrating defeats of democratic radicalism at the turn of the century.[4]

3. Henry Demarest Lloyd, "No Mean City," in *Mazzini and Other Essays* (New York: G. P. Putnam's Sons, 1910), pp. 201–232. For the context of this speech see John L. Thomas's superb *Alternative America: Henry George, Edward Bellamy, Henry Demarest Lloyd and the Adversary Tradition* (Cambridge: Harvard University Press, 1983), chap. 11.

4. JD to Alice Dewey, 7 October 1894, Dewey Papers; Thomas, *Alternative America*, pp. 267–277; Katherine Kish Sklar, "Hull House in the 1890s: A Community of Women Reformers," *Signs* 10 (1985): 658–677.

THE POLITICS OF PROTECTIVE COLORATION

When Dewey arrived in Chicago to begin his new job in the summer of 1894 it was not the social harmony of Lloyd's utopian scenario which greeted him but the hard realities of class conflict, for he found himself on a train to the city at the height of the Pullman strike. The strike began in the spring of 1894 following a severe wage cut at the Pullman Car Works, a cut unaccompanied by any reduction in the rents, food prices, and service rates George Pullman charged his workers in the model company town he had built for them just south of Chicago in the 1880s. After the company refused to respond to the workers' grievances and fired those who presented them, Pullman's labor force went on strike on May 11. A month later the strikers won the support of Eugene Debs's recently formed American Railway Union, which was fresh from victory in a strike against James J. Hill's Great Northern Railroad, and following Pullman's refusal to submit the dispute to arbitration, the union launched a boycott on June 25 against Pullman sleeping cars, refusing to work on any railroad that did not detach them from its trains. Pullman received support from the powerful General Managers Association of the twenty-four railroads with Chicago terminals, and by July the strike had escalated from a local dispute to an effort by these powerful corporate managers to break the union and assert the superior power of capital.[5]

Dewey followed the progress of the strike closely, and his response to it indicates that the failure of the *Thought News* experiment had not dampened his radical impulses or his commitment to industrial democracy. In his ethical writings he had indicated his belief that strikes could often be progressive, "functional" conflicts, and his sympathies during the Pullman strike were wholeheartedly with the workers. "The trains don't run very regularly any more," he wrote his children, "because the men won't work until some of their friends get paid enough money for their work so that they can live." To Alice he wrote of a moving encounter he had had on his way to Chicago with a union organizer in Durand, Michigan:

I only talked with him 10 or 15 minutes but when I got through my nerves were more thrilled than they had been for years; I felt as if I

5. On Pullman and the strike see Stanley Buder, *Pullman: An Experiment in Industrial Order and Community Planning, 1880–1930* (New York: Oxford University Press, 1974), and Almont Lindsey, *The Pullman Strike* (Chicago: University of Chicago Press, 1942).

had better resign my job teaching and follow him around till I got into life. One lost all sense of the right or wrong of things in admiration of his absolute, almost fanatic, sincerity and earnestness, and in admiration of the magnificent combination that was going on. Simply as an aesthetic matter, I don't believe the world has seen but a few times such a spectacle of magnificent, widespread union of men about a common interest as this strike business. The only point is the Pullman strike; they simply boycott the roads that carry Pullmans and go on a strike if the roads won't stop carrying Pullmans; they say all the labor organizations of all kinds will go into it if Pullman doesn't yield or at least arbitrate. And 19 out of 20 newspapers and well-dressed people have just enough sense of humor to repeat the old chestnut "Of course, every man has a right to leave work himself, but he hasn't any right to keep others from working." The gov't is evidently going to take a hand in and the men will be beaten almost to a certainty—but it's a great thing and the beginning of greater.[6]

Dewey was particularly troubled throughout the strike by the hostility to the strikers expressed by intellectuals and academics, including some of his new colleagues at the University of Chicago. "I think professional people are probably worse than the capitalists themselves," he said. He was especially annoyed by one Chicago minister who "fears lest the strike be settled before some of the men be shot and thus learn a lesson—which is fair for a minister of the gospel of Christ." Such attitudes did little to deter Dewey's growing conviction that organized religion was a drag on social progress and showed "what the Church comes to when Marshall Field and railroad presidents and directors make up the congregation of the righteous." Appalled by attacks on the union in such journals as the *Nation* and *Harper's Weekly*, Dewey remarked that he did not know when he had seen anything that seemed "so hopeless and discouraging." It was, he said, "hard to keep one's balance; the only wonder is that when the 'higher classes'—damn them—take such views there aren't more downright socialists. . . . That a representative journal of the upper classes—damn them again—can take the attitude of that Harper's Weekly and in common with all other journals, think Debs is a simple lunatic or else doing all this to show his criminal control over the criminal 'lower classes'—well, it shows what it is to become a higher class."

6. JD to Children, 5 July 1894; JD to Alice Dewey, 2 July 1894, Dewey Papers. For Dewey's estimate of the positive ethical significance of strikes see "Moral Theory and Practice" (1891), *Early Works* 3:105–106; *Outlines of a Critical Theory of Ethics* (1891), *Early Works* 3:351–352, 360–361.

Touched by an account of the poor that his son Fred had sent him, Dewey contrasted the boy's feelings with the insensitivity of upper-class opinion to the real issues involved in the strike. "Maybe," he mused, "[Fred will] be a social agitator—and maybe he'll get to belong to the higher classes and be strong on law and order and very weak on justice and liberty."[7]

The strike was smashed in early July, when a federal injunction was issued against Debs and the ARU on the grounds that they had interfered with the mails and interstate commerce and President Grover Cleveland dispatched federal troops to Chicago to enforce the injunction. Up to this time the strike had been marked by little violence, but in the week that followed the arrival of the troops riots broke out and substantial railroad property was destroyed. On July 10 Debs and other union officers were arrested on charges of violating the injunction and of conspiracy, and the strike effectively collapsed.

Despite this defeat, Dewey felt the strike had been a success. "The strike is lost and 'labor' is rather depressed," he wrote. "But if I am a prophet, it really won. The business made a tremendous impression; and while there has been a good deal of violent talk—particularly it seems to me by the 'upper classes,' yet the exhibition of what the unions might accomplish, if organized and working together, has not only sobered them, but given the public mind an object lesson that it won't soon forget. I think the few freight cars burned up a pretty cheap price to pay—it was the stimulus necessary to direct attention, and it might easily have taken more to get the social organism thinking." Dewey was prone throughout his life to such hopeful predictions of the unintended consequences of the defeats of democratic reform, and his record as a prophet was undistinguished. Nevertheless, such efforts at prophecy are a telling index to his own political desires.[8]

The Pullman strike was not only a radicalizing experience for Dewey, it also illustrated a key point in his democratic theory, for it opened to view the moral shortcomings of a paternalistic brand of "welfare capitalism" which failed to cultivate workers' capacity for autonomous participation in social life. Dewey did not himself explicitly make the connection between this ethical perspective and the events in Chicago, but his close friend Jane Addams did in her powerful "A Modern

7. JD to Alice Dewey, 5 July 1894; JD to Alice Dewey, 16 July 1894; JD to Alice Dewey, 20 July 1894, Dewey Papers.
8. JD to Alice Dewey, 14 July 1894, Dewey Papers.

Lear," an essay Dewey declared to be "one of the greatest things I ever read both as to its form and its ethical philosophy."[9]

As its title suggests, Addams's essay was based on an extended analogy between the relationships of King Lear and his daughter Cordelia and that of Pullman and his workers. Like Lear, Addams suggested, Pullman exercised a self-serving benevolence in which he defined the needs of those who were the objects of this benevolence in terms of his own desires and interests. Pullman built a model company town, providing his workers with what he took to be all the necessities of life. Like Lear, however, he ignored one of the most important human needs, the need for autonomy. Lear had failed the crucial test with Cordelia, the test of maintaining "the tenderness of the relation between father and child, after that relation had become one between adults." Likewise, Pullman failed to understand the need and the demand of his workers for positive freedom. He gave them houses and parks, and "his conception of goodness for them had been cleanliness, decency of living, and above all, thrift and temperance." He had failed to recognize their "gropings toward justice" and hence took their rejection of his benevolence as the highest form of ingratitude. Pullman, Addams observed, "desired that his employees should possess the individual and family virtues, but did nothing to cherish in them those social virtues which his own age demanded."[10]

These social virtues, Addams said, were incompatible with the social relationships of capitalist production. Pullman's problem was that "he felt himself right from the *commercial* standpoint, and could not see the situation from the *social* standpoint." Industrial capitalism was a vast social operation that nonetheless did little to develop the capacities of the workman for democratic life. The shops were managed "not for the development of the workman thus socialized, but for the interests of the company owning the capital." The labor movement was the expression of the desire of the working class for a fully participatory role in American society. Its "watchwords were brotherhood, sacrifice, the subordination of individual and trade interests to the good of the working class; and their persistent strivings were toward the ultimate freedom

9. JD to Jane Addams, 19 January 1896, as quoted in Christopher Lasch, ed., *The Social Thought of Jane Addams* (Indianapolis, Ind.: Bobbs-Merrill, 1965), p. 176. As Lasch says in his introduction to this essay, "It is difficult to say whether Dewey influenced Jane Addams or Jane Addams influenced Dewey. They influenced each other and generously acknowledged their mutual obligation."

10. "A Modern Lear" (1894), in Lasch, ed., *Social Thought of Jane Addams*, pp. 114–117.

of that class from the conditions under which they now labor." The emancipation of the wage worker was "the social passion of the age," and, Addams declared, "nothing will satisfy the aroused conscience of men short of the complete participation of the working classes in the spiritual, intellectual and material inheritance of the human race."[11]

Addams was among the Chicago reformers most averse to class conflict, and she ended her essay on a conciliatory note, warning workers that "the emancipation of working people will have to be inclusive of the employer from the first or it will encounter many failures, cruelties, and reactions." Although, like Dewey, she believed that capitalists were most in need of instruction in the ethics of democracy, she urged workers as well to recognize the moral interest they shared with their employers. The doctrine of emancipation, she said, "must be strong enough in its fusing power to touch those who think they lose, as well as those who think they gain. Only thus can it become the doctrine of a universal movement."[12]

Despite her plea for class reconciliation, Addams was advised by friends that "A Modern Lear" was too inflammatory for publication as she had written it, and although she did not tone down her remarks, she withheld the essay from publication until 1912. Like many members of the Chicago reform community, Addams depended directly and indirectly on the material support of the city's wealthy and powerful philanthropists, and this dependency kept the lid on a good deal of radical social criticism in the 1890s. While philanthropists and democratic reformers could work together in harmony on many social welfare projects, the support of the latter for labor unions and for an ethic that went beyond charitable benevolence often produced rifts in the alliance. Such a rift is nicely illustrated in a letter Dewey wrote his wife in October 1894, recounting Addams's story of "the first personal flagellation she had ever rec'd":

> She had been to a Mr. Ayers who had given money rather freely, not to Hull House, but to their relief work, and asked him for more money for this winter's relief. He had turned on her, and told her that she had a great thing and now she had thrown it away; that she had been trustee for the interests of the poor, and had betrayed it—that like an idiot she had mixed herself in something which was none of her business and about which she knew nothing, the labor movement and especially Pullman, and had thrown down her own work, etc., etc.[13]

11. Ibid., pp. 110, 115–117, 120.
12. Ibid., pp. 120–123.
13. JD to Alice Dewey, 10 October 1894, Dewey Papers. For a good account of the

At the University of Chicago, the faculty took its cues about what could and could not be said and done about class conflict from the case of economics professor Edward Bemis, a student of corporate corruption, advocate of the municipal ownership of utilities, and a labor supporter during the Pullman strike, who was dismissed from his teaching post in 1895 for what most historians believe were political reasons. This was also Dewey's impression. He reported the Bemis case to Alice and remarked that there was no doubt in his mind that President William Rainey Harper was "afraid of hurting the feelings of the capitalists, and sees the external money side of the Univ. and is relatively purblind to the real advances of life." One of the trustees of the university, Dewey said, had referred to "the victory of our side in the Homestead matter and when asked what side, said 'capitalists' side, of course.'" Dewey noted the irony that at Michigan, a state university, "there was freedom as to social questions, but some restraint on the religious side," whereas at Chicago, an institution with Baptist affiliations, "there is seemingly complete religious freedom, but . . . a good deal of constriction in the social side." Responsible opinion in Chicago in the 1890s was on the side of capital, and Dewey concluded that "Chicago Univ. is a capitalistic institution—that is, it too belongs to the higher classes." He told his wife he was quickly realizing "how 'anarchistic' (to use the current term here) our ideas and especially feelings are" and tried to take some comfort in the fact that Bemis was not, like himself, a department chairman. "There ought to be some compensations for having to lug that title around," he said.[14]

Dewey decided not to risk a test of this proposition and urged a similar prudence on others. He did not abandon social criticism altogether, but he couched it in language carefully designed to avoid giving offense to the powerful. In an essay on academic freedom published at the end of his tenure at Chicago, Dewey advised his colleagues in the social sciences that the injection of moralism and an inflammatory tone into criticism of the established order would get them into hot water.

alliance between democratic reformers and wealthy philanthropists and the tensions created within this alliance by the issue of labor organization, see Steven J. Diner, *A City and Its Universities: Public Policy in Chicago, 1892–1919* (Chapel Hill: University of North Carolina Press, 1980).

14. JD to Alice Dewey, 5 July 1894; JD to Alice Dewey, 16 July 1894; JD to Alice Dewey, 20 July 1894; and JD to Alice Dewey, 25 September 1894, Dewey Papers. On the Bemis case see Harold E. Bergquist, Jr., "The Edward Bemis Controversy at the University of Chicago," *American Association of University Professors Bulletin* 58 (1972): 383–393; Walter P. Metzger, *Academic Freedom in the Age of the University* (New York: Columbia University Press, 1961), pp. 151–162; and Mary O. Furner, *Advocacy and Objectivity* (Lexington: University of Kentucky Press, 1975), pp. 163–204.

He recommended a dispassionate, depersonalized, even Aesopian approach to controversial questions, and his choice of an example of this approach suggests the impact the class conflict that shook Chicago in the 1890s had on his work:

> One might, for example, be scientifically convinced of the transitional character of the existing capitalistic control of industrial affairs and its reflected influences upon political life; one might be convinced that many and grave evils and injustices are incident to it, and yet never raise the question of academic freedom, although developing his views with definiteness and explicitness. He might go at the problem in such an objective, historic, and constructive manner as not to excite the prejudices or inflame the passions even of those who thoroughly disagreed with him. On the other hand, views at the bottom exactly the same can be stated in such a way as to rasp the feelings of everyone exercising the capitalistic function. What will stand or fall upon its own scientific merits, if presented as a case of objective social evolution, is mixed up with all sorts of extraneous and passion-inflaming factors when set forth as the outcome of the conscious and aggressive selfishness of a class.

Dewey's books and articles in this period hardly inflamed passions. He published no political philosophy while he was at Chicago, and although he continued to teach political ethics, his lectures were without the pointed attacks on "entrenched class interest" which had been sprinkled throughout those he delivered at Michigan. His own politics became increasingly circumspect. He confined his "constructive" criticism of those exercising the capitalistic function to lectures and meetings at Hull House and vented his radical spleen only in his private correspondence. Publicly, he refrained from any expression of hostility to the "higher classes," adopting what Randolph Bourne termed "the technique of protective coloration" in a repressive environment in which camouflage seemed essential for survival. Only in his philosophy of education could one hear a hint of the sermon on behalf of radical democracy which Dewey had appeared ready to preach when he arrived in Chicago.[15]

15. "Academic Freedom" (1902), *Middle Works* 2:59; Randolph Bourne, "John Dewey's Philosophy" (1915), in Olaf Hansen, ed., *The Radical Will: Randolph Bourne, Selected Writings* (New York: Urizen Books, 1977), p. 331. See also Jane Addams, "John Dewey and Social Welfare," in *John Dewey: The Man and His Philosophy* (Cambridge: Harvard University Press, 1930), pp. 147–148.

THE CHILD AND THE CURRICULUM

The democratic ideal, Dewey told his class in political ethics, was embodied in the slogan of the French Revolution: liberty, equality, and fraternity. By combining liberty and fraternity one arrived at a positive conception of freedom: "individuality operating in and for the end of the common interest." Equality was a necessary prerequisite for the exercise of such freedom, but this equality did not, Dewey said, require an absolute leveling of social resources but rather that "each individual would of necessity be provided with whatever is necessary for his realization, for his development, whatever is necessary to develop him to enable him to function adequately. . . . He must have certain opportunities provided for him. He must have just the same provision made, the same equipment for enabling him to get all that is in him, that anybody else has." Without such equality, guarantees of individual rights were but empty promises: "An individual does not have the right to life simply because it is laid down in the statutes that he has such a right; it is a matter of conditions, relationships. There is no such thing as a purely abstract capacity or power, it is a question of what anybody can really do. It is a question of where he is, what his position is and what the conditions are in which he is placed." This conception of equality as the provision to each of "whatever is necessary to enable him to put his powers thoroughly at the service of society" made for social differentiation, not homogenization, for the powers and functions of individuals varied widely. Consequently, there would not be an absolute equalization of resources among the members of a just society, but rather no one would be "deprived of whatever was necessary for him to get for himself and to give to society the full benefit of what is in him."[16]

Dewey did not address himself to the assumption that lay beneath this notion of equality that a society could provide every individual in it with the means of self-realization, nor was he specific about what general sorts of resources and opportunities he regarded as essential. Nor did he say how this distribution of resources and opportunities was to be effected or what sort of action might be taken by the state to secure the positive liberty of its citizens, confining his remarks in this regard to criticism of laissez-faire liberals and state socialists who operated with

16. *Lectures on Psychological and Political Ethics: 1898* (New York: Hafner Press, 1976), pp. 441–444.

predetermined, absolute notions of what the state should do in every particular instance. "There is nothing which it is intrinsically desirable for government to do and there is nothing intrinsically which it is not desirable for it to do under certain circumstances," he said. "It is simply a question of what the facts of the case are."[17]

With regard to one condition of liberty Dewey did, however, take a strong and definite public stand in this period. All members of a democratic society, he declared, were entitled to an education that would enable them to make the best of themselves as active participants in the life of their community: "Men will long dispute about material socialism, about socialism considered as a matter of distribution of the material resources of the community; but there is a socialism regarding which there can be no such dispute—socialism of the intelligence and of the spirit. To extend the range and the fullness of sharing in the intellectual and spiritual resources of the community is the very meaning of the community."

For a child to become an effective member of a democratic community, Dewey argued, he must have "training in science, in art, in history; command of the fundamental methods of inquiry and the fundamental tools of intercourse and communication," as well as "a trained and sound body, skillful eye and hand; habits of industry, perseverance, and, above all, habits of serviceableness." In a democratic community children had to learn to be leaders as well as followers, possessed of "power of self-direction and power of directing others, powers of administration, ability to assume positions of responsibility" as citizens and workers. Because the world was a rapidly changing one, a child could not, moreover, be educated for any "fixed station in life," but schools had to provide him with training that would "give him such possession of himself that he may take charge of himself; may not only adapt himself to the changes which are going on, but have power to shape and direct those changes."[18]

This was, Dewey realized, a tall order, but he had set about the task of helping to fill it as soon as he arrived in Chicago. He had taken an active interest in public education at Michigan, where he was a founding member and officer of the Michigan Schoolmasters' Club, which fostered cooperation between high school and college teachers in the state, but he had not been able to teach pedagogy in Ann Arbor. One of the attractions of the position at Chicago was the opportunity it pro-

17. Ibid., pp. 444–445.
18. "The School as a Social Centre" (1902), *Middle Works* 2:93; "Ethical Principles Underlying Education" (1897), *Early Works* 5:59–60.

vided to oversee instruction and research in pedagogy as well as philosophy. Dewey convinced Harper and the university board of trustees that pedagogy should be a separate department, and he was named head of this department as well as that of philosophy.

In the fall of 1894 Dewey wrote a revealing letter to Alice (whose own concerns in these matters remained strong) expressing his growing interest in the problems of education. "I sometimes think I will drop teaching philosophy directly, and teach it via *pedagogy*," he wrote. "When you think of the thousands and thousands of young ones who are practically ruined negatively if not positively in the Chicago schools every year, it is enough to make you go out and howl on the street corners like the Salvation Army." His concern was not only for these anonymous victims of prevailing educational practice but for his own children as well. Fearful of the sorts of schools that he and Alice would have to inflict on them, he sought to ease his wife's anxieties about removing their children from formal schooling for a trip to Europe. "I realize what you say about the evils of their life, and think they need the routine of a school now," he said, "but at least they are still themselves with their own intelligences and their own responses—and that is more than can be said for most children of their age."[19]

Dewey's estimate of the Chicago schools was widely shared not only by reformers but also by many of the city's wealthiest and most influential citizens. Chicago was one of several cities targeted in Joseph Mayer Rice's powerful muckraking articles on urban education published in the *Forum* magazine in 1892 and 1893, and Rice's criticism mobilized the city's elite against the machine politicians who had entangled the schools in a network of patronage and corruption. Chicago was also home to one of the most promising experiments in urban education, the Cook County Normal School of Colonel Francis Parker. Parker, whom Dewey termed "the father of progressive education," had arrived in Chicago in 1883 from Massachusetts, where he had criticized the rigid discipline characteristic of most schools, pioneered innovations in instruction in natural science, and introduced methods of informal classroom instruction. Parker's efforts to transplant these reforms to Chicago elicited a storm of protest from those with an entrenched interest in prevailing practices and initiated a battle that continued until 1899, when wealthy philanthropist Anita McCormick Blaine freed Parker from his annual budget battles with school commissioners by buying him his own school. Throughout his struggles

19. JD to Alice Dewey, 1 November 1894, Dewey Papers.

with school officials Parker was supported by the city's reform community, and Dewey joined this effort, testifying on Parker's behalf before the Chicago Board of Education and sending his own children to the colonel's Cook County school. These efforts in turn enabled Dewey to make valuable contacts with concerned parents, philanthropists, and reformers who helped him sustain his own pedagogical experiments at the university, and by the end of the 1890s Dewey had succeeded Parker as the dominant figure among those seeking to reconstruct education in Chicago.[20]

Dewey's work in education was designed to explore the theoretical implications of his philosophy for pedagogy and also to put this philosophy to an experimental test. As he said, his theory of knowledge emphasized the "necessity of testing thought by action if thought was to pass over into knowledge," and this proviso extended to his theory of knowledge itself. Education, he felt, was an ideal area of experience in which to test a philosophy because "the school is the one form of social life which is abstracted and under control—which is directly experimental, and if philosophy is ever to be an experimental science, the construction of a school is its starting point." Dewey arrived at Chicago with a pretty good idea of the sort of laboratory school he wanted to start. In the same letter in which he decried the deplorable condition of Chicago's public schools he told Alice:

> There is an image of a school growing up in my mind all the time; a school where some actual and literal constructive activity shall be the centre and source of the whole thing, and from which the work should be always growing out in two directions—one the social bearings of that constructive industry, the other the contact with nature which supplies it with its materials. I can see, theoretically, how the carpentry etc. in building a model house shall be the centre of a social training on the one side and a scientific on the other, all held within the grasp of a positive concrete physical habit of eye and hand.

Dewey made a pitch to university officials for a school that would keep "theoretical work in touch with the demands of practice" as the most essential component of a department of pedagogy—"the nerve of the

20. See Joseph Mayer Rice, "The Public Schools of Chicago and St. Paul," *The Forum* 15 (1893): 210–215; Lawrence A. Cremin, *The Transformation of the School: Progressivism in American Education, 1876–1957* (New York: Vintage Books, 1964), pp. 3–8, 129–135; JD, "In Remembrance: Francis W. Parker" (1902), *Middle Works* 2:97; Jack K. Campbell, *Colonel Francis W. Parker: The Children's Crusader* (New York: Teachers College Press, 1967); Merle Curti, *The Social Ideas of American Educators* (Totowa, N.J.: Littlefield Adams, 1959), chap. 11; Robert L. McCaul, "Dewey's Chicago," *School Review* 67 (1959): 258–280.

whole scheme"—and he received the support of Harper, who was himself an important activist in the campaign for educational reform in Chicago. A little over a year later, in January 1896, the Laboratory School of the University of Chicago opened its doors. The school began with sixteen children and two teachers, but by 1903 it was providing instruction to 140 students and was staffed by twenty-three teachers and ten graduate assistants. Most of the students were from professional families, many of them the children of Dewey's colleagues. The enterprise quickly became known as the "Dewey School," for the hypotheses tested in this laboratory were strictly those of Dewey's functional psychology and democratic ethics.[21]

Dewey was convinced that many of the problems of prevailing educational practice grew out of its foundations in the faulty dualistic epistemology he was attacking in his writings on psychology and logic in the 1890s, and he set out to design a pedagogy grounded in his own functionalism and instrumentalism. Having spent a good deal of time observing the growth of his own children, particularly his infant son Morris (who, tragically, had died of diphtheria on the family's trip to Europe in 1895), Dewey was certain that there was no difference in the dynamics of the experience of children and adults. Both were active beings who learned by confronting the problematic situations that arose in the course of the activities engaging their interests. For both, thinking was an instrument for solving the problems of experience, and knowledge was the accumulation of wisdom that such problemsolving generated. Unfortunately, the theoretical insights of functionalism had had little impact on pedagogy, and the identity between the experience of children and that of adults was ignored in the schools. As Dewey said:

> With the adult we unquestioningly assume that an attitude of personal inquiry, based upon the possession of a problem which interests and absorbs, is a necessary precondition of mental growth. With the child we assume that the precondition is rather the willing disposition which makes him ready to submit to any problem and material presented

21. JD to Alice Dewey, 1 November 1894, Dewey Papers; "A Pedagogical Experiment" (1896), *Early Works* 5:244; "Pedagogy as a University Discipline" (1896), *Early Works* 281–289; "The Need for a Laboratory School" (nd), *Early Works* 5:433–435; Katherine Camp Mayhew and Anna Camp Edwards, *The Dewey School* (New York: Atherton Press, 1966), pp. 8, 57, 464; McCaul, "Dewey's Chicago," p. 275. The school was the "Dewey School" in another sense as well: Alice worked there as a teacher and later as principal and four of the Dewey children were among its pupils. This family connection would, as we shall see, become a source of difficulties.

from without. *Alertness* is our ideal in one case; *docility* in the other. With one, we assume that power of attention develops in dealing with problems which make a personal appeal, and through personal responsibility for determining what is relevant. With the other we provide next to no opportunities for the evolution of problems out of immediate experience, and allow next to no free mental play for selecting, assorting and adapting the experiences and ideas that make for their solution. How profound a revolution in the position and service of text-book and teacher, and in methods of instruction depending therefrom, would be effected by a sincere recognition of the psychological identity of child and adult in these respects can with difficulty be realized.[22]

It was precisely this revolution that Dewey aimed to effect. Children did not, he said, arrive at school as passive blank slates on which teachers might write the lessons of civilization. By the time a child entered the classroom, he was "already intensely active, and the question of education is the question of taking hold of his activities, of giving them direction." The child they brought with him four basic "native impulses"—the "impulse to communicate, to construct, to inquire, and to express in finer form"—which were the "natural resources, the uninvested capital, upon the exercise of which depends the active growth of the child." The child also brought interests and activities from the home and neighborhood in which he lived, and it was the task of the teacher to make use of this raw material by guiding the activities of the child toward valuable results.[23]

This argument, advanced in *The School and Society* (1899) and *The Child and the Curriculum* (1902), placed Dewey at odds with both the proponents of a traditional, "curriculum-centered" education and romantic reformers who advocated a "child-centered" pedagogy. The traditionalists, led by William Torrey Harris, now U.S. commissioner of education, favored disciplined, step-by-step instruction in the accumulated wisdom of civilization. It was the subject matter that furnished the end and determined the methods of education. The child was expected simply "to receive, to accept. His part is fulfilled when he is ductile and docile." On the other hand, the advocates of child-centered education such as G. Stanley Hall and prominent members of the National Herbart Society argued that instruction in subject matter should be subor-

22. "Psychology and Social Practice" (1899), *Middle Works* 1:134–135.
23. *The School and Society* (1899), *Middle Works* 1:25, 30. Page numbers for further references (*SS*) appear in the text.

dinated to the natural, uninhibited growth of the child. For them the expression of the child's native impulses were "the startingpoint, the center, the end." These schools of thought waged a fierce battle with one another in the 1890s. Traditionalists defended the hard-won knowledge of centuries of intellectual struggle and viewed child-centered education as a chaotic, anarchistic surrender of adult authority, while romantics celebrated spontaneity and change and charged their opponents with suppressing the individuality of children by means of a boring, routinized, despotic pedagogy.[24]

To Dewey, this debate was evidence that yet another pernicious dualism was afflicting American culture. The dispute could be resolved, he said, if both sides would

> get rid of the prejudicial notion that there is some gap in kind (as distinct from degree) between the child's experience and the various forms of subject-matter that make up the course of study. From the side of the child, it is a question of seeing how his experience already contains within itself elements—facts and truths—of just the same sort as those entering into the formulated study; and, what is of more importance, of how it contains within itself the attitudes, the motives, and the interests which have operated in developing and organizing the subject-matter to the plane which it now occupies. From the side of the studies, it is a question of interpreting them as outgrowths of forces operating in the child's life, and of discovering the steps that intervene between the child's present experience and their richer maturity. (CC, 277–278)

Dewey's critique of the traditionalists for their failure to connect the subject matter of the curriculum to the interests and activities of the child is well known. His attack on the advocates of child-centered education for their failure to connect the interests and activities of the child to the subject matter of the curriculum is, however, often overlooked. Some critics of Dewey's educational theory have confused his position with that of the romantics, but he clearly differentiated his pedagogy from theirs. He said, "Just as, upon the whole, it was the weakness of the 'old education' that it made invidious comparisons between the immaturity of the child and the maturity of the adult, regarding the

24. *The Child and the Curriculum* (1902), *Middle Works* 2:276. Page numbers for further references (*CC*) appear in the text. On the curricular debates in the 1890s see Herbert M. Kliebard, *The Struggle for the American Curriculum, 1893–1958* (Boston: Routledge and Kegan Paul, 1986), chaps. 1–2.

former as something to be got away from as soon as possible and as much as possible; so it is the danger of the 'new education' that it regard the child's present powers and interests as something finally significant in themselves" (*CC*, 280). It would be wrong, he argued, to cultivate the purposes and interests of children "just as they stand." Effective education required that the teacher use these purposes and interests to guide the child toward their culmination in the subject matter of science and history and art. "Interests in reality are but attitudes toward possible experiences; they are not achievements; their worth is in the leverage they afford, not in the accomplishment they represent" (*CC*, 280). The subject matter of the curriculum was the embodied experience of the human race, and, as such, it was that toward which the immature experience of the child pointed. "The facts and truths that enter into the child's present experience, and those contained in the subject-matter of studies, are the initial and final terms of one reality," he concluded. "To oppose one to the other is to oppose the infancy and maturity of the same growing life; it is to set the moving tendency and the final result of the same process over against each other; it is to hold that the nature and the destiny of the child war with each other" (*CC*, 278).[25]

Deweyan pedagogy called upon teachers to perform the extremely difficult task of "reinstating into experience" the subject matter of the curriculum (*CC*, 285). This subject matter, like all human knowledge, was the product of man's efforts to solve the problems that confronted him in experience, but, as a formal body of knowledge, it had been abstracted from the problematic situations that originally occasioned its development. Traditionalists argued that this knowledge should simply be imposed on the child in a sequence of steps determined by the logic of this abstracted body of truth, but presented in this fashion the material was of little interest to children and, moreover, failed to instruct them in the methods of experimental inquiry which had produced this knowledge in the first place. As a consequence, teachers had to resort to an appeal to interests unrelated to the subject matter such as the child's fear of pain and humiliation to produce the appearance of learning. Rather than impose the subject matter on children in this fashion (or

25. In an influential critique of Dewey's philosophy of education Richard Hofstadter claimed Dewey failed to provide teachers with ends toward which to direct the child's impulses, quoting Dewey as urging teachers simply to "let the child's nature fulfill its destiny." This is, however, but half the quotation. Dewey's injunction, in full, was: "Let the child's nature fulfill its own destiny, revealed to [the teacher] in whatever of science and art and industry the world now holds as its own" (*CC*, 291). See Hofstadter, *Anti-Intellectualism in American Life* (New York: Vintage, 1963), p. 375.

simply leave them to their own devices as romantics advised), Dewey called upon teachers to "psychologize" the curriculum by constructing an environment in which the present activities of the child would be confronted with problematic situations in which the knowledge and skills of science, history, and art would be required to resolve these difficulties. "If the subject-matter of the lessons be such as to have an appropriate place within the expanding consciousness of the child, if it grows out of his own past doings, thinkings, and sufferings, and grows into application in further achievements and receptivities," he said, "then no device or trick of method has to be resorted to in order to enlist 'interest'" (*CC*, 288). The curriculum was, in effect, saying to the teacher "such and such are the capacities, the fulfillments, in truth and beauty and behavior, open to these children. Now see to it that day by day the conditions are such that *their own activities* move inevitably in this direction, toward such culmination of themselves" (*CC*, 291).

If teachers were to teach in this fashion, to direct a child's development by indirection, they would, Dewey acknowledged, have to be highly skilled professionals, thoroughly knowledgeable in the subject matter they were teaching, trained in child psychology, and skilled in the techniques of providing the stimulus necessary to make the subject matter part of a child's growing experience. As two of the teachers in the Dewey School remarked, such a teacher had to be capable of seeing the world as both a child and an adult saw it. "Like Alice, she must step with her children behind the looking glass and in this imaginative land she must see all things with their eyes and limited by their experience; but, in time of need, she must be able to recover her trained vision and from the realistic point of view of an adult supply the guide posts of knowledge and the skills of method." Dewey admitted that most teachers did not possess the knowledge and skills necessary to teach in this fashion, but he contended that they could learn to do so, and by the end of the decade he could cite evidence from his own school to prove his point.[26]

At the center of the curriculum of the Dewey School was what Dewey termed the "occupation," that is, "a mode of activity on the part of the child which reproduces, or runs parallel to, some of work carried on in social life" (*SS*, 92). Divided into eleven age groups, the students pursued a variety of projects centered on particular historical or contemporary occupations. The youngest children in the school, who were four and five years old, engaged in activities familiar to them from

26. Mayhew and Edwards, *Dewey School*, p. 312.

their homes and neighborhood: cooking, sewing, and carpentry. The six-year-olds built a farm out of blocks, planted wheat and cotton, and processed and transported their crop to market. The seven-year-olds studied prehistoric life in caves of their own devising while their eight-year-old neighbors focused their attention on the work of the sea-faring Phoenicians and subsequent adventurers like Marco Polo, Magellan, Columbus, and Robinson Crusoe. Local history and geography occupied the attention of the nine-year-olds, while those who were ten studied colonial history, constructing a replica of a room in an early American house. The work of the older groups of children was less strictly focused on particular historical periods (though history remained an important part of their studies) and centered on scientific experiments in anatomy, electro-magnetism, political economy, and photography. The search of the debating club formed by the thirteen-year-old students for a place to meet resulted in the building of a substantial clubhouse, which enlisted children of all ages in a cooperative project that was for many the emblematic moment in the school's history.

Because occupational activities pointed on the one hand toward the scientific study of the materials and processes involved in their practice and on the other toward their role in society and culture, the thematic focus on occupations provided the occasion not only for manual training and historical inquiry but also for work in mathematics, geology, physics, biology, chemistry reading, art, music, and languages. In the Laboratory School, Dewey reported, "the child comes to school to *do;* to cook, to sew, to work with wood and tools in simple constructive acts; within and about these acts cluster the studies—writing, reading, arithmetic, etc." Skills such as reading were developed when children came to recognize their usefulness in solving the problems that confronted them in their occupational activities. "If a child realizes the motive for acquiring skill," Dewey argued, "he is helped in large measure to secure the skill. Books and the ability to read are, therefore, regarded strictly as tools."[27]

Katherine Camp Mayhew and Anna Camp Edwards, who taught in the Laboratory School, later provided a full account of this remarkable educational experiment filled with evidence of the considerable success Dewey and his colleagues achieved in translating his theories into practice, evidence supported by the testimony of less interested observers as

27. "A Pedagogical Experiment," p. 245; JD quoted in Mayhew and Edwards, *Dewey School,* p. 26.

well. It would take us too far afield to examine in any detail how the school established an environment in which the occupational interests of the children were made to serve a wide range of curricular aims, so one example described by Mayhew and Edwards will have to suffice. The six-year-old students in the school, building on the experiences with home activities they had had in kindergarten, concentrated their work on "occupations serving the home." They built a model farm in the sandtable in their classroom, and in the schoolyard they planted a crop of winter wheat. As with most constructive activities in the school, the building of the model farm provided an occasion for learning some mathematics:

> When their sand-table farm had to be divided into several fields for wheat, corn, oats, and also for the house and the barn, the children used a one-foot ruler as a unit of measurement and came to understand what was meant by "fourths and halves"—the divisions made, though not accurate, were near enough to allow them to mark off their farm. As they became more familiar with the ruler and learned the half-foot, and the quarter-foot and inch, finer work was naturally expected of them and obtained. . . . When building the farm-house, four posts were needed for the corners and six or seven slats, all of the same height. In measuring the latter, the children frequently forgot to keep the left-hand edge of the ruler on the left-hand side of the slat, so the measurements had to be repeated two or three times before they were correct. What they did to one side of the house, they also did to the other and naturally worked more rapidly and more accurately as the work was repeated.

In such instances one can see not only how the child's interest in a particular activity of his own (building a model farm) served as the foundation for instruction in a body of subject matter (skills in measurement and the mathematics of fractions) but also how this method introduced children to the methods of experimental problem-solving in which mistakes were an important part of learning. Providing children with firsthand experience with problematic situations largely of their own making was the key to Dewey's pedagogy, for he believed that "until the emphasis changes to the conditions which make it necessary for the child to take an active share in the personal building up of his own problems and to participate in methods of solving them (even at the expense of experimentation and error) mind is not really freed."[28]

28. Mayhew and Edwards, *Dewey School,* pp. 83–84; "Democracy in Education" (1903), *Middle Works* 3:237.

It is difficult to read through descriptions and accounts of the Laboratory School and understand how Dewey came to be seen by critics as a proponent of "aimless" progressive education. He explicitly stated his curricular goals, and they were readily apparent in the classroom practice of the teachers with whom he worked. He valued mankind's accumulated knowledge as much as the most hidebound traditionalist, and he intended that the children in his elementary school be introduced to the riches of science, history, and the arts; here his goals were rather conventional, but they were clearly expressed. He also wanted them to learn to read, to write, to count, to think scientifically, and to express themselves aesthetically. Only his methods were innovative and radical. It may well be true, as Richard Hofstadter said, that much of "progressive education" was methodologically "fertile and ingenious" yet "quite unclear, often anarchic, about what these methods should be used to teach," but this indictment does not, as Hofstadter supposed, apply to Dewey.[29]

THE SCHOOL AND SOCIETY

The shaping of childrens' character, the moral and political agenda of schooling, is sometimes termed the "hidden curriculum," but in Dewey's case this aspect of his educational theory and practice was no less explicit, though a good deal more radical, than his other curricular aims. Important as the Laboratory School was as a testing ground for Dewey's functional psychology, it was even more important as an expression of his ethics and democratic theory. "The social phase of education," as he later said, "was put first." The Dewey School was above all an experiment in education for democracy.[30]

Dewey was not reluctant to assert that "the formation of a certain character" was "the only genuine basis of right living." His deconversion from absolute idealism did not affect his identification of democracy with equal opportunity for all the members of a society to make the best of themselves as social beings, and thus he retained the link between self-realization and social service which was such an important aspect of the neo-Hegelian concept of positive freedom. Individuals, he continued to argue, achieved self-realization by utilizing their peculiar talents to contribute to the well-being of their community, and

29. Hofstadter, *Anti-Intellectualism*, p. 375.
30. *"The Dewey School:* Appendix 2" (1936), *Later Works* 11:205.

hence the critical task of education in a democratic society was to help children develop the character—the habits and virtues—that would enable them to achieve self-realization in this fashion. Schools, Dewey said, must "enable the child to translate his powers over into terms of their social equivalencies; to see what they mean in terms of what they are capable of accomplishing in social life." An "interest in the community welfare, an interest which is intellectual and practical, as well as emotional—an interest, that is to say, in perceiving whatever makes for social order and progress, and for carrying these principles into execution—is the ultimate ethical habit to which all the special school habits must be related if they are to be animated by the breath of moral life."[31]

The failure of American schools to develop in children the character requisite for a democratic society was, Dewey argued, as evident as their failure to integrate the interests of the child with the subject matter of the curriculum. "Upon the ethical side," he said, "the tragic weakness of the present school is that it endeavors to prepare future members of the social order in a medium in which the conditions of the social spirit are eminently wanting" (SS, 10). Most schools employed highly "individualistic" methods that called upon all the students in a classroom to read the same books simultaneously and recite the same lessons. In such schools, Dewey complained, there was little opportunity for "each child to work out something specifically his own, which he may contribute to the common stock, while he, in turn, participates in the production of others." In these conditions the social impulses of the child atrophied, and the teacher was unable to take advantage of the child's "natural desire to give out, to do, and that means to serve." The social spirit was replaced with "positively individualistic motives and standards" such as fear, emulation, rivalry, and judgments of superiority and inferiority, and as a consequence "the weaker gradually lose their sense of capacity and accept a position of continuous and persistent inferiority," while "the stronger grow to glory, not in their strength, but in the fact that they are stronger."[32]

If the school was to foster the social spirit in children and develop democratic character, Dewey argued, it had itself to be organized as a cooperative community. "I believe," he said, "that the best and deepest moral training is precisely that which one gets through having to enter

31. "My Pedagogic Creed" (1897), Early Works 5:93; "Plan of Organization of the University Primary School" (1895), Early Works 5:225; "Ethical Principles Underlying Education," p. 63.
32. "Ethical Principles Underlying Education," pp. 64–65.

into proper relations with others in a unity of work and thought." To educate for democracy, the school had to become "an institution in which the child is, for the time, to live—to be a member of a community life in which he feels that he participates, and to which he contributes." Such a school "must have a *community* of spirit and end realized through *diversity* of powers and acts. Only in this way can the cooperative spirit involved in the division of labor be substituted for the competitive spirit inevitably developed when a number of persons of the same presumed attainments are working to secure exactly the same result."[33]

By all available accounts, Dewey was fairly successful in creating this sort of community in the Laboratory School. Those who worked in the school, he later said, were "animated by a desire to discover in administration, selection of subject-matter, methods of learning, teaching, and discipline, how a school could become a cooperative community while developing in individuals their own capacities and satisfying their own needs." Children shared in the planning of their projects, and the execution of these projects was marked by a cooperative division of labor in which leadership roles were frequently rotated. The following is Mayhew and Edwards's description of the course of a typical school day for the six-year-old children whose farm work I described earlier:

> At the beginning of the period, the children were given time for the exchange of the amenities of the day usual to a group of persons meeting after an absence. The general conversation was soon directed by the teacher to the business of the day. The results of previous work were reviewed in a group process, and plans for further development were discussed. Each child was encouraged to contribute, either out of his past experience or his imagination, ways and means of meeting the problem of needs that might arise under new circumstances. These suggestions were discussed by the group, and with the aid of the teacher, the plans for the work of the day were decided upon and delegated. At the close of the period, there was again a group meeting when the results, if successful, were summarized, and new plans for further work at the next period suggested.

"The process of mental development," Dewey contended, "is essentially a social process, a process of participation," and the children in his school learned not only skills and facts but also how to work as members of a community of cooperative inquiry.[34]

---

33. "My Pedagogic Creed," p. 88; "Plan of Organization of the University Primary School," pp. 224, 225.

34. "*The Dewey School:* Introduction" (1936), *Later Works* 11:192; Mayhew and Edwards,

Democratic community was also fostered (for a time) among the adults who worked there. Dewey was highly critical of the failure of schools to allow teachers to participate in the decisions affecting the conduct of public education. He was particularly disturbed by reformers who wrested control of the schools from corrupt politicians only to invest school superintendents with enormous, autocratic power. The remedy for the evils of the control of schools by politicians, he said, "is not to have one expert dictating educational methods and subject-matter to a body of passive, recipient teachers, but the adoption of intellectual initiative, discussion, and decision throughout the entire school corps." This criticism reflected Dewey's commitment to extending democracy beyond the polity to the workplace. "What does democracy mean," he asked, "save that the individual is to have a share in determining the conditions and the aims of his own work; and that, upon the whole, through the free and mutual harmonizing of different individuals, the work of the world is better done than when planned, arranged, and directed by a few, no matter how wise or of how good intent that few?" In the Laboratory School, he tried to implement this sort of workplace democracy. The work of teachers, he noted, was organized much like that of the children: "cooperative social organization applied to the teaching body of the school as well as to the pupils. . . . Association and exchange among teachers was our substitute for what is called supervision, critic teaching, and technical training." Teachers met weekly to discuss their work and, though no doubt constrained in their criticism by Dewey's commanding presence, they played an active role in shaping the school curriculum.[35]

The role of teachers in the formation of a child's character in the Dewey School was similar to their role in imparting the subject matter of the curriculum: direction by indirection. Dewey had no doubts that the democratic character he hoped children would develop was morally superior to all other possibilities; this was the first principle, the postulate, of his ethics. His critique of oppressive benevolence, however, indicated that the child had to develop this character for himself if education was to be truly moral. Teachers could not directly form a child's character for him, and, even if they could, that molding would not be ethical because "the moral life is lived only as the individual appreciates for himself the ends for which he is working, and does his work in a personal spirit of interest and devotion to these ends." The

---

Dewey School, pp. 80–81; *"Dewey School:* Appendix 2," p. 206. See also Laura L. Runyon, "A Day with the New Education," *Chautauquan* 30 (1900): 589–592.

35. "Democracy in Education," pp. 232, 233; *"The Dewey School:* Statements" (1936), *Later Works* 11:198.

teacher's job was to establish conditions that would enable the child "to interpret his own powers from the standpoint of their possibilities in social use." If such conditions were created, Dewey confidently predicted that the child would come to recognize the link between self-realization and social service just as he came to recognize the utility of reading. In the Dewey School, Mayhew and Edwards reported, "as life flowed on, the child became conscious of his social relationships: that there were others in the group like him who had rights and privileges; that it was far more fun to play games with them even if he must renounce somewhat his own way and consider the way of others in relation to his own. It was more pleasant to work with them, even if he must think of the consequences of what he did in relation to others' plans, and he soon came to see that his consideration of and work with others was to the advantage of all, that by pooling his effort with that of the group, larger and more interesting results were obtained."[36]

Creating the conditions in the classroom for the development of democratic character was no easy task, and Dewey again realized he was placing heavy demands on teachers. "The art of thus giving shape to human powers and adapting them to social service," he said, "is the supreme art; one calling into its service the best of artists; . . . no insight, sympathy, tact, executive power is too great for such service." Perhaps because his philosophy of education called upon teachers to perform such difficult tasks and placed such a heavy burden of responsibility on them, Dewey was given to unusual flights of rhetoric when he spoke of their social role in the 1890s. Occasionally he even called up the language of the social gospel he had otherwise abandoned. Summing up his pedagogic creed in 1897, he declared: "I believe . . . that the teacher is engaged, not simply in the training of individuals, but in the formation of the proper social life. I believe that every teacher should realize the dignity of his calling; that he is a social servant set apart for the maintenance of proper social order and the securing of the right social growth. I believe that in this way the teacher always is the prophet of the true God and the usherer in of the true kingdom of God." As this testament suggests, Dewey's educational theory was far less child-centered and more teacher-centered than is often supposed. His confidence that children would develop a democratic character in the schools he envisioned was rooted less in a faith in the "spontaneous and crude capacities of the child" than in the ability of teachers to create an environment in the classroom in which they possessed the

36. "Ethical Principles Underlying Education," pp. 77, 67; Mayhew and Edwards, *Dewey School*, p. 94.

means to "mediate" these capacities "over into habits of social intelligence and responsiveness." Dewey was calling upon teachers to artfully arrange things in the classroom so that "the right social growth" could be assured, and, given the assembled talent, it is not surprising that the Dewey School achieved the results that it did.[37]

Dewey's conviction that the teacher was the "usherer in of the true kingdom of God" reflected his belief that "education is the fundamental method of social progress and reform." There was a certain logic to this belief. Insofar as schools played an important part in the shaping of the character of a society's children, they could, if they were designed to do so, fundamentally transform that society. The school provided a relatively controlled environment in which the conditions of self-development could effectively shape its course. Indeed, if teachers did their job well, there would hardly be need of any other sort of reform. A democratic, cooperative commonwealth could emerge from the classroom.[38]

The difficulty with this belief was that most schools were designed not to transform societies but to *reproduce* them. As Dewey acknowledged, "The school system has always been a function of the prevailing type of organization of social life." The beliefs about schools and teachers that he outlined in his pedagogic creed were thus less beliefs about what was than about what might be. If schools were to be made agencies of social reform rather than agencies of social reproduction they would themselves have to be radically reconstructed, and this was Dewey's most ambitious aim as an educational reformer: to transform American schools into instruments for the further democratization of American society. The goal of the schools, he said, should not be "to 'adjust' individuals to social institutions, if by adjustment is meant preparation to fit into present social arrangements and conditions. The latter are neither stable enough nor good enough to justify such a procedure." Rather, schools should try "to deepen and broaden the range of social contact and intercourse, of cooperative living, so that the members of the school would be prepared to make their future social relations worthy and fruitful."[39]

Despite these ambitions, Dewey did not really have much of a strategy for making American schools into institutions working on behalf of radical democracy. Although he did not intend nor expect that the methods of the Laboratory School would be "slavishly copied" elsewhere, he did hope that his school would serve as a source of inspira-

37. "My Pedagogic Creed," pp. 94–95.
38. Ibid., p. 93; "The Ethics of Democracy" (1888), *Early Works* 1:242.
39. "Pedagogy as a University Discipline," p. 285; "*Dewey School:* Appendix 2," p. 205.

tion for those seeking to transform public education as well as a training ground and research center for reform-minded teachers and specialists. He tended in this to underestimate the degree to which the success of the Dewey School was attributable to its insulation from the conflicts, divisions, and inequities besetting the larger society, an insulation difficult to replicate. It was, after all, a small school comprised of the children of middle-class professionals and staffed by well-trained, dedicated teachers with access to the intellectual if not the financial resources of one of the nation's great universities. This is not to say that Dewey did not recognize that the schools were heavily contested social terrain, something a citizen of Chicago could hardly fail to see. As a fellow Chicagoan Clarence Darrow observed, the school system in every community "has no independent initiative of its own, but is a reflection of the dominant forces which shape it to their own image." Dewey admitted that educational reform could be "but one phase of a general social modification," but it would be some time before he would give any clear indications of what this general social modification should be.[40]

If Dewey did not have a plan for establishing the schools as powerful adversarial institutions in the heart of American culture, he did have a clear vision of what he thought the schools in a thoroughly democratic society should look like, and he attempted, with some considerable success, to embody that vision in the Laboratory School. This school was clearly not designed for social reproduction. Although Dewey sought to connect the school to larger social life by putting occupations at the heart of his curriculum, he self-consciously purified these occupations of one of their most essential features as they were conducted in American society by removing them from the social relations of capitalist production and putting them in a cooperative context in which they would have been virtually unrecognizable to those who performed them in the larger society. In the school, he said, "the typical occupations followed are freed from all economic stress. The aim is not the economic value of the products, but the development of social power and insight" (SS, 12). Freed from "narrow utilities," occupations in the school were organized so that "method, purpose, understanding shall exist in the consciousness of the one who does the work, that his activity shall have meaning to himself" (SS, 16). The children's work was unalienated labor in which the separation of hand and brain of the nation's factories and offices was nowhere in evidence. Dewey sometimes referred to the Laboratory School as an "embryonic community,"

40. Clarence Darrow quoted in Ginger, *Altgeld's America*, p. 343; *The Educational Situation* (1901), *Middle Works* 1:262.

but it was far from an embryo of the society outside its walls (*SS*, 19). It did not promise the reproduction of industrial America but rather prefigured its radical reconstruction.[41]

Unfortunately there is little evidence of the effect the adversarial education at the Dewey School had on the lives of its students. Mayhew and Edwards did note, however, that their students often underwent a rude awakening to the "real world," finding themselves isolated from and in conflict with the larger society: "In [the Dewey School] intelligent choices had come to mean social choices which were also moral choices. Attitudes had been cooperative in spirit; individual ideals and interests had tended largely toward alignment with those of school society. Now, as then, society brings both shock and conflict to a young person thus trained, even if he be forewarned. His attempts to use intelligent action for social purposes are thwarted and balked by the competitive antisocial spirit and dominant selfishness in society as it is." Deweyan education, the teachers concluded, prepared students for life in a society that did not exist, one in which the welfare of all was regarded as the concern of each—life, that is, in No Mean City.[42]

THE DEATH OF THE DEWEY SCHOOL

The lifetime of Dewey's prefigurative community was brief. It died in 1904, the victim of bureaucratic infighting. In 1901 the Chicago In-

41. Occupations in the Dewey School were free of the capitalist division of labor not only along class lines but also, for the most part, along *gender* lines. Some of the most striking photographs of the school are those picturing little boys cooking and spinning and little girls at work as carpenters. Mayhew and Edwards do report one instance in which the ten-year-old children studying colonial America divided themselves strictly along gender lines for the tasks of building furniture and making fabrics for a seventeenth-century room, but this division was abandoned when the students turned to the construction of a fireplace (*Dewey School*, p. 166). I think, however, that it would be mistaken to see the curriculum of the Dewey School as a self-conscious effort to subvert conventional gender roles in the same fashion as it was intentionally critical of the effect of class divisions on the industrial work process. Dewey was interested in the educative potential of "women's work" for both boys and girls, yet he never challenged the notion that homemaking was women's special sphere. A few years later he commended coeducational colleges for the training they provided in "the distinctive career of women as wives, mothers, and managers of households" ("Is Co-Education Injurious to Girls?" [1911], *Middle Works* 6:163). As Susan Laird has argued, there is a sharp and unacknowledged tension between sentiments such as this and Dewey's educational practice in the Laboratory School in which, among teachers and administrators as well as students, gender had little effect on the distribution of roles ("Women and Gender in John Dewey's Philosophy of Education," *Educational Theory*, 38 [1988]: 111–129). See Chapter 6 for a consideration of what little Dewey had to say about feminist issues.

42. Mayhew and Edwards, *Dewey School*, p. 439. In later versions of "No Mean City" Lloyd included Deweyan education as a feature of life in the cooperative commonwealth. See "No Mean City," pp. 224–225.

stitute, the school for teacher training and educational research which Anita McCormick Blaine had established for Colonel Parker, was incorporated into the university as the School of Education and brought with it the practice school Parker had established. This merger left the university with two elementary schools, which, despite the differences between the two schools, seemed to some administrators, including Harper, to be an expensive duplication of effort, and plans were made to combine Dewey's Laboratory School and the Parker school. This merger was strongly resisted by Dewey and the parents of children in the Laboratory School, and they were able to raise enough money independently to stave it off.[43]

In March of 1902 Parker died, and it was decided to consolidate the Department of Pedagogy (now the Department of Education) and the School of Education under one roof with Dewey as its head. Once again a merger of the two elementary schools was proposed, a proposal Dewey now favored because he felt he had secured the administrative power necessary to guarantee that the school would continue the work of the Laboratory School, and in the fall of 1903 they were merged with Alice Dewey serving as principal of the new school. This merger elicited fierce opposition from the teachers in the School of Education, who feared they would lose their jobs, and from Wilbert Jackman, Parker's right-hand man and dean of the school, who had been waging a running battle for turf with Dewey since 1901. Opponents of the merger were particularly concerned about the appointment of Alice Dewey to the post of principal because she had been an outspoken critic of the Parker school and was not shy about firing teachers she regarded as incompetent. Fearful that a "Mr. and Mrs. Dewey School" was in the offing, many of the faculty in the School of Education threatened to resign if she was appointed principal. Faced with this revolt, Harper worked out a compromise with the faculty which guaranteed the employment of teachers without tenure from the Parker school for at least three years and provided that Alice Dewey's appointment would be for but one year.

Unfortunately, Harper did not make it clear to Dewey or his wife that her job was temporary, and in the spring of 1904 both were shocked when Harper informed Alice Dewey that she would be out of work in the fall. Both husband and wife immediately resigned from the School of Education, and Dewey also resigned from the philosophy depart-

43. My discussion of these events follows the detailed account in Robert McCaul, "Dewey and the University of Chicago," in William W. Brickman and Stanley Lehrer, eds., *John Dewey: Master Educator*, 2d ed. (New York: Atherton Press, 1966), pp. 31–74.

ment. Harper was, in turn, surprised and dismayed by this turn of events and tried, to no avail, to persuade Dewey to reconsider. Almost before the ink was dry on his letter of resignation, Dewey was offered an appointment at Columbia University, and he began work there in February of 1905.

The documents that remain from this train of events make it appear that Dewey resigned from the University of Chicago simply because his wife lost her job, but this apparently was not all there was to the case. Dewey told Harper that he resented the way the president had presented matters so as to make this appear to be the only issue involved. "Your willingness to embarrass and hamper my work as Director by making use of the fact that Mrs. Dewey was Principal is but one incident in the history of years," he said. Unfortunately, Dewey left no account of this "history of years," but it is clear that the apparent civility of the relationship between Harper and Dewey until the spring of 1904 belied some substantial antagonisms, though what they might have been is difficult to say. Like much of Dewey's thinking in his ten years at Chicago, I suspect that these antagonisms, and the deeper reasons Dewey left the university, have been obscured by the politics of protective coloration.[44]

Although Dewey landed on his feet at Columbia, his losses were considerable. He gave up leadership of the collaborative "real school" of philosophy William James had celebrated, and he abandoned the elementary school that was the only practical expression of his philosophy of education. This latter loss seems to me particularly important, for it not only left it to others to interpret, apply, and usually distort Dewey's pedagogical ideas but also deprived him of the one concrete manifestation of his democratic ideals that he could point to and say "*this* is what I have in mind."

44. JD to William Rainey Harper, 10 May 1904, Presidents' Papers, Joseph Regenstein Library, University of Chicago. One sore point between Dewey and Harper was, probably the university's inadequate financial assistance for the Laboratory School. Although most accounts describe Harper's support for the school as enthusiastic, Brian Hendley has recently observed that the money Harper offered to the school on its founding was both limited ($1,000), in kind (tuition for graduate-student assistants), and what administrators term "soft money" (funds shifted on a one-time basis from another use). The school was always financially strapped and survived until the merger only by virtue of the vigorous fund-raising efforts of Dewey, the parents of its students, and other friends and patrons. See Brian Hendley, *Dewey, Russell, Whitehead: Philosophers as Educators* (Carbondale: Southern Illinois University Press, 1986), pp. 18–19.

John Dewey, in a photograph taken during his early years at Columbia.
Courtesy of the Morris Library, Southern Illinois University at Carbondale.

Part Two

Progressive Democracy
(1904–1918)

> Philosophy recovers itself when it ceases to be a
> device for dealing with the problems of
> philosophers and becomes a method, cultivated by
> philosophers, for dealing with the problems of men.
>
> —"The Need for a Recovery
> of Philosophy" (1917)

CHAPTER 5

Reconstructing Philosophy

*

WHEN John Dewey resigned from the University of Chicago in April 1904 he had no job offers, but he was reasonably confident that they would not be long in coming. Despite his difficulties as an administrator in his last years at Chicago, he had mulled over the possibility there of a full-time administrative career, and his papers probe issues of plumbing, heating, and organizational management. The Laboratory School debacle no doubt gave him second thoughts about such ambitions, but had a managerial opportunity come his way Dewey might have taken it. Fortunately for the life of the mind he was diverted by the attractive offer of a position in the philosophy department at Columbia.

The Columbia offer was engineered by James McKeen Cattell, a noted psychologist, and Nicholas Murray Butler, president of the university and himself a former member of the philosophy department. Shortly after Dewey resigned from Chicago, he wrote to Cattell, a friend from graduate school, and inquired about the possibility of a position at Columbia. Recognizing at once the enormous boost that Dewey would give to the reputation of both the Columbia department and the university as a whole, Cattell alerted Butler, who immediately grasped the prestige value of such an appointment. The president expedited an offer through the university bureaucracy and successfully solicited an endowment for a new chair in philosophy from an anonymous donor. After Dewey accepted the offer, his appointment was approved enthusiastically by a committee of trustees who noted that it was a move "of much more than ordinary importance." Dewey, they declared, "is one of the two or three most distinguished students and teachers of philosophy now living" and his presence would make the Columbia department "the most effective and the most distinguished to be found in any university in the world."[1]

Though there were those in Cambridge, Massachusetts (and, indeed, Cambridge, England), who no doubt would have disputed these judgments, they reflected the booster spirit that gripped Columbia in the early twentieth century as it advanced into the front rank of American universities. Until the 1890s Columbia had been, despite its location in New York City, a backwater college, and not until Seth Low assumed its presidency in 1889 was it reorganized along university lines and moved to a new campus in "the great open spaces" uptown. When Low resigned to become mayor of New York in 1901, Butler was appointed president, and under his leadership Columbia initiated a period of rapid growth in which Dewey's appointment was an important moment.

The philosophy department was a special concern for Butler, for during the 1890s he had been its most prominent member. Philosophers at Columbia were among the slowest in the United States to respond to German ideas, and Butler, who had been educated in Germany, was determined to bring the message of neo-Kantian idealism to Morningside Heights. Butler's greatest talents, however, lay less in speculative argument than in organization. As J. H. Randall noted in his history of the department, "His celebrated course in the history of philosophy is remembered not only for its clarity and lucidity, but also for the fact that it began and ended precisely on the hour." The greatest service Butler performed for philosophy at Columbia was not as a philosopher but as the administrator who directed the astute appointments of Dewey and other professors who had by the 1920s established a reputation for the department rivaled among American universities only by Harvard.[2]

When Dewey arrived at Columbia, direction of the philosophy department was already in the capable hands of F. J. E. Woodbridge, and after his years of wrangling with Harper, Dewey was content for the rest of his teaching career to take but a modest leadership role in

1. Dykhuizen, pp. 116–117.
2. J. H. Randall, Jr., "The Department of Philosophy," in Jacques Barzun, ed., *A History of the Faculty of Philosophy of Columbia University* (New York: Columbia University Press, 1957), p. 111.

departmental matters. Other members of the department in 1905 were Felix Adler, William P. Montague, and Wendell T. Bush, and over the course of the next three decades they were joined by a number of their former graduate students ("the younger school of Columbia philosophers"), including Herbert Schneider, J. H. Randall, Jr., Irwin Edman, Horace Freiss, and Ernest Nagel. Dewey also profited over the years by a close association with the members of other Columbia departments, particularly those in the social sciences, including Charles Beard, Ruth Benedict, Franz Boas, James Cattell, Robert MacIver, Wesley Mitchell, and James Harvey Robinson.

Intellectually, the philosophy department at Columbia provided a very different environment for Dewey than that he had had at Chicago. There he had been the leader of a "school" of philosophers committed to cooperative inquiry into the various aspects of a common project defined in large measure by Dewey; here he found himself among men who respected his work but were skeptical of many of his central arguments and presuppositions, an audience not of disciples but of friendly critics. Woodbridge was the most important of these. The son of an Englishman, Woodbridge had grown up in Kalamazoo, Michigan, and was educated at Amherst College, Union Theological Seminary, and the University of Berlin. He had come to Columbia in 1902 after eight years of teaching at the University of Minnesota. Like Dewey, Woodbridge was critical of the epistemological bind into which the tradition of Western philosophy seemed to have delivered philosophers by the turn of the twentieth century, but he had turned back to Aristotle in search of an empirical naturalism capable of rescuing philosophy from the dead end of speculative idealism. Detecting residual idealism in Dewey's metaphysics and theory of knowledge, Woodbridge urged on him the virtues of epistemological realism, descriptive metaphysics, and classical philosophy, and though Dewey was not always persuaded by his colleague, he warmly acknowledged Woodbridge's role as a whetstone against which he sharpened his thinking.[3]

On the face of it, the years between Dewey's move to Columbia and American entry into World War I in 1917 were among the most professional of his career. Although his interest in public affairs and educational reform did not slacken, his activism did. The bulk of his writing in this period was confined to professional journals and dealt with

3. On Woodbridge's philosophy see his "Confessions," in George P. Adams and William P. Montague, eds., *Contemporary American Philosophy* (New York: Macmillan, 1930), 2:415–438, and William F. Jones, *Nature and Natural Science: The Philosophy of Frederick Woodbridge* (Buffalo: Prometheus Books, 1983).

abstruse philosophical issues in which he displayed a skill in technical dialectics with which he is rarely credited. He was, as the effusive praise of the Columbia trustees indicates, at the height of his reputation among his fellow academic philosophers, and in December 1904 he was elected president of the American Philosophical Association (this followed a term as president of the American Psychological Association in 1899).

But the impression one gets from this evidence that Dewey retreated to an ivory tower in these years is misleading, for peeking out of even some of the most technical of his writings is a view of philosophy and of the role of the philosopher critical of the drift of others toward insular professionalism, a view committed to the joining of abstract theory to social and political practice. By the end of World War I, the elements of Dewey's own work that had often moved along separate tracks in the first two decades of his career had clearly begun to come together in a unified vision in which his metaphysics and logical theory were dialectically related to his ethics and democratic faith. As his daughter Jane put it, "For a time Dewey's political philosophy developed as a line of thought independent of his technical philosophical interests. It was inevitable that these currents should gradually fuse in the mind of a man who believed that the influence of the social scene on philosophy should be not merely the unavoidable unconscious one but that of furnishing a testing ground for the correctness of philosophic theory." This fusing of philosophy and politics went against the grain of the development of American philosophy in these years into a highly esoteric discipline isolated from social concerns, and, as a consequence of his insistence that philosophy deal first and foremost with "the problems of men," Dewey's ascendancy as an important voice in the culture as a whole was matched by the steady decline of his reputation among academic philosophers.[4]

AGAINST EPISTEMOLOGY

Most of Dewey's work in his first decade at Columbia consisted of elaborations and refinements of the arguments he had advanced in *Studies in Logical Theory* within the context of a complex, three-sided

4. Jane Dewey, "Biography of John Dewey," in Paul Schilpp, ed., *The Philosophy of John Dewey*, 2d ed. (New York: Tudor, 1951), p. 39. On the professionalization of American philosophy see Bruce Kuklick, *The Rise of American Philosophy: Cambridge, Massachusetts, 1860–1930* (New Haven: Yale University Press, 1977).

debate between proponents of idealism, realism, and pragmatism. This triangular debate reflected the breakup of the domination idealists had exercised in the late nineteenth century over academic philosophy in the United States and elsewhere. By the beginning of World War I this domination had crumbled, and idealism was in full retreat. In the United States, so-called new realists (many of whom were, like Dewey, one-time idealists) and pragmatists led the attack on idealism and fought between themselves for the right of succession to leadership of American philosophy. The controversy filled the pages of the *Journal of Philosophy, Psychology and Scientific Methods* (later simply the *Journal of Philosophy*) founded in 1904 by the Columbia philosophy department, and most of the three dozen or so major articles Dewey published in this ten-year period defending his version of pragmatism appeared in this journal.

The pragmatic and realist camps announced themselves publicly at about the same moment, and each spoke with a decided Harvard accent. The first use of the term "pragmatism" to refer to a philosophical doctrine occurred in an address William James delivered at the University of California in 1898 titled "Philosophical Conceptions and Practical Results," although James there attributed the term to Charles Peirce, who had used it some twenty years earlier in his paper "How to Make Our Ideas Clear" (1878), which had appeared in a series of articles on the logic of science Peirce contributed to *Popular Science Monthly.* James had come to pragmatism and radical empiricism following a long struggle to work himself out from under the absolute idealism of his colleague Josiah Royce, and Royce proved the foil as well for the emergence of American neo-realism, which traced its roots to the critical response in 1902 of two former Harvard graduate students, Ralph Barton Perry and William P. Montague, to the attack on realism in Royce's *World and the Individual* (1900).[5]

James's reference to Peirce, reiterated in *Pragmatism* (1907), sent philosophers scurrying to consult the fugitive publications of his long-forgotten friend, who had been driven from academic life in the 1880s by administrators unappreciative of his unconventional personality, and

5. James's California lecture has been published as "The Pragmatic Method," in James, *Essays in Philosophy* (Cambridge: Harvard University Press, 1978), pp. 123–139; Ralph Barton Perry, "Professor Royce's Refutation of Realism and Pluralism," *Monist* 12 (1902): 446–458; William P. Montague, "Professor Royce's Refutation of Realism," *Philosophical Review* 11 (1902): 43–55. The story of the Harvard department and the emergence of pragmatism and realism therein is well told in Kuklick, *Rise of American Philosophy,* pt. 3. Dewey's own reviews of the two-volume *World and the Individual* are also important documents in the history of pragmatism (*Middle Works* 1:241–256; 2:120–137). See also John Clendenning, *The Life and Thought of Josiah Royce* (Madison: University of Wisconsin Press, 1985), chaps. 6–7.

in the two decades following the Berkeley lecture James, Peirce, Dewey, and others attempted in a steady stream of books and articles to lay out the meaning and implications of pragmatism as they saw it. Efforts by historians of philosophy to treat pragmatism as a movement have faltered in the face of the substantial disagreements that divided the principal pragmatists, disagreements James underplayed, Peirce loudly announced, and Dewey quietly observed. Because it would take us too far afield to unravel the similarities and differences among pragmatists and, in any case, others have examined them in some detail, I make no attempt to deal with the thinking of Peirce and James here except insofar as some of Dewey's disagreements with James illuminate those aspects of his work that are my particular concern.[6]

It is more appropriate to speak of American neo-realism as a collective enterprise since, to a degree and for a time, it was conceived as such. In the spring of 1910, after a decade of debate, six realists—Perry and Edwin B. Holt of Harvard, Dewey's Columbia colleagues Montague and Walter Pitkin, Edward G. Spaulding of Princeton, and Walter T. Marvin of Rutgers—hammered out a set of common positions on methodological and epistemological issues they termed the "New Realism." These were published that year as "The Program and Platform of Six Realists" and followed by a cooperative volume of essays, The New Realism (1912). Although this unity extended only to epistemological questions and eventually succumbed to disagreements centering on the existential status of perceptual illusions, these New Realists (and other realists too) consistently spoke with a common voice when it came to their criticisms of idealism and pragmatism.[7]

6. A useful chronology of the course of American pragmatism is Max H. Frisch, "American Pragmatism before and after 1898," in Robert W. Shahan and Kenneth R. Merrill, eds., American Philosophy: From Edwards to Quine (Norman: University of Oklahoma Press, 1977), pp. 78–110. An excellent critique of efforts to construe pragmatism as a movement and a solid argument for seeing it instead as a family of distinct if related philosophical positions is Garry M. Brodsky, "The Pragmatic Movement," Review of Metaphysics 25 (1971/72): 262–291. Although it is the principal target of Brodsky's strictures, H. S. Thayer, Meaning and Action: A Critical History of Pragmatism, 2d ed. (Indianapolis: Hackett, 1981), remains the best history of this family. See also Murray G. Murphey, "Kant's Children: The Cambridge Pragmatists," Transactions of the Charles S. Peirce Society 4 (1968): 3–33; John E. Smith, Purpose and Thought: The Meaning of Pragmatism (New Haven: Yale University Press, 1978); and Dewey's own perceptive account of the history of American pragmatism: "The Development of American Pragmatism" (1925), Later Works 2:3–21. I will say nothing of the disagreements between Dewey and Peirce since they were confined to issues of logical theory and metaphysics with only the remotest bearing on Dewey's social philosophy, but for an especially illuminating discussion of these issues, see R. W. Sleeper, The Necessity of Pragmatism: John Dewey's Conception of Philosophy (New Haven: Yale University Press, 1986), chap. 3 and passim.

7. See "The Program and First Platform of Six Realists" (1910), Middle Works 6:472–482 (because a number of the exchanges between Dewey and his critics have been republished in his collected works, the reader has convenient access to many of the con-

The neo-realists' critique of idealism centered on what they took to be its central principle: the notion that knowledge was a creative process that conditioned the reality of its objects. This principle was based on what Perry termed the "ego-centric predicament," the fact that all objects as known were objects in the consciousness of a knower and hence it was difficult to know what difference, if any, knowing made in the object known. From this predicament, idealists reasoned that all objects were dependent for their existence on consciousness. But this, realists noted, was to mistake the co-presence of consciousness and real objects for a dependent relationship in which the former determined the existence of the latter and to confuse a tautology (known objects are known objects) for a synthetic truth. Contra idealism, an object might well exist, like a point on each of two intersecting lines, simultaneously within and without the consciousness of a knower. This criticism, realists recognized, did not refute idealism, yet it did undercut what many had regarded as a conclusive argument for it. The realists then went on to argue that from the behavior of objects as known one might reasonably infer that they exist independently of consciousness, are unchanged by knowledge of them, and are presented to and apprehended directly by consciousness.[8]

Although in this period Dewey elaborated on his own quite different critique of idealism in *Studies in Logical Theory*, he devoted most of his energies to extending this critique to neo-realism. Dewey agreed with realism insofar as it meant anti-idealism, "especially in its contention that it is a paralogism to argue that because things must be known before we can discuss knowledge of them, things must themselves always be known (or in relation to mind); and, indeed, with its contention that knowledge always implies existences prior to and independent of their being known." He believed, however, that realism remained trapped along with idealism in the coils of the "alleged discipline of epistemology" and was subject to many of the same criticisms he had advanced against idealism at the turn of the century, criticisms that now became more radical as he extended them to the entire tradition of

troversies in which Dewey was engaged, and whenever this is the case I will cite these republications rather than the originals); Edwin B. Holt et al., *The New Realism* (New York: Macmillan, 1912). Dewey's most persistent realist critic was not one of the "official" realists but Evander McGilvary, chairman of the philosophy department at the University of Wisconsin and president of the American Philosophical Association in 1913. Woodbridge, it is worth noting, refused to join the official New Realists. On the history of this group, see William P. Montague, "The Story of American Realism," *Philosophy* 12 (1937): 140–161, and Kuklick, *Rise of American Philosophy*, chap. 18.

8. Ralph Barton Perry, "The Ego-Centric Predicament," *Journal of Philosophy* 7 (1910): 5–14; Montague, "Story of American Realism," pp. 143–147.

modern philosophy which had since the seventeenth century put epistemological questions at the heart of matters. Realists and idealists
alike, Dewey contended, had inherited a flawed conception of experience from this tradition and derived from it equally flawed conceptions
of knowledge and truth. It was, he believed, time not to offer new solutions to traditional epistemological problems, as the realists proposed,
but to raise corrosive questions about the genuineness of the problems
themselves.[9]

Dewey served notice of this radical project in his presidential address
to the American Philosophical Association in 1905. There he observed
that "modern philosophy is, as every college senior recites, epistemology." The epistemologist was a philosopher committed to "passionless
imperturbability" and "absolute detachment" and determined to replace the mere "beliefs" of the common man—tentative, incomplete,
and compromised by their connection with the everyday world of "weal
and woe" as they were—with knowledge of "Reality, objective, universal, complete." In epistemology "philosophy has dreamed the dream of
a knowledge which is other than the propitious outgrowth of beliefs
that shall develop aforetime their ulterior implications in order to re-
cast them, to rectify their errors, cultivate their waste places, heal their
diseases, fortify their feebleness—the dream of a knowledge that has to
do with objects having no nature save to be known."[10]

The consequences of this swallowing up of modern philosophy by
epistemology, Dewey advised, had been disastrous. Not only had epistemologists not delivered the Reality they promised, but in trying to
grasp it and in contemptuously dismissing ordinary belief, they had cut
philosophy off from science, which was the most reliable method human beings had developed for knowing about their world, a method
continuous with the common man's search for belief. "The whole procedure of thinking as developed in those extensive and intensive inquiries that constitute the sciences," Dewey said, "is but rendering into a
systematic technique, into an art deliberately and delightfully pursued,

9. "The Short-Cut to Realism Examined" (1910), *Middle Works* 6:138; "Brief Studies
in Realism" (1911), *Middle Works* 6:111. For Dewey's critique of absolute idealism in this
period see "Experience and Objective Idealism" (1906), *Middle Works* 3:128–144; "The
Intellectualist Criterion for Truth" (1907), *Middle Works* 4:50–75; "A Reply to Professor
Royce's Critique of Instrumentalism" (1912), *Middle Works* 7:64–78 (a response to Josiah
Royce, "The Problem of Truth in the Light of Recent Discussion" [1911], *Middle Works*
7:413–444); "Voluntarism in the Roycean Philosophy" (1916), *Middle Works* 10:49–52.
The best indication of the shift in the focus of Dewey's critical concern from idealism to
realism is the Introduction to his *Essays in Experimental Logic* (1916), *Middle Works* 10:320–
365.
10. "Beliefs and Existences" (1906), *Middle Works* 3:85–86.

the rougher and cruder means by which practical human beings have in all ages worked out the implications of their beliefs, tested them and endeavored in the interests of economy, efficiency, and freedom, to render them coherent with one another." The future of philosophy, Dewey exhorted his fellow philosophers, lay in an effort to understand and ally with this sort of inquiry. Epistemology was a dead end, and philosophers "should cease trying to construe knowledge as an attempted approximation to a reproduction of reality under conditions that condemn it in advance to failure."[11]

A key mistake of the "epistemological industry," Dewey argued, was its assumption of the "ubiquity of the knowledge relation," its treatment of experience as strictly a "knowledge-affair" in which knowing subjects were set apart from an objective world that they attempted to know. The problems this notion of experience posed for realists were evident, he contended, in the difficulties the closely related assumption that perception was a case of knowledge created for them in their treatment of perceptual illusions. Idealists were fond of using cases of perceptual illusion, such as the apparent convergence of railroad tracks, as conclusive evidence for the transformation of the objects of knowledge by their relationship to a knower. Realists, as I noted, did not dissolve the supposed "egocentric predicament" on which this argument rested, only the conclusions idealists derived from it. As a consequence, they were unable to offer a positive argument for how, if (as they contended) the perceived object (e.g. convergent tracks) was the real object directly presented to consciousness and if perception was a case of knowledge, the physical object (e.g. parallel tracks) and the known object could coincide in such cases. To the idealists, this "duplicity" between reality and perception was evidence of the transformation that consciousness worked on its objects, and though realists could contest the logic of this conclusion, they had no persuasive alternative explanation as long as they held that perception was a case of knowledge. Dewey observed that "when the realist conceives the perceptual occurrence as an intrinsic case of knowledge or presentation to a mind or knower, he lets the nose of the idealist camel into the tent. He has then no great cause for surprise when the camel comes in—and devours the tent."[12]

The realists got themselves into this bind, Dewey advised, because by

11. Ibid., pp. 94, 93.
12. "Brief Studies in Realism," pp. 103–108. As I noted, the problem of perceptual illusions was a source of intramural conflict among realists. See Montague, "Story of American Realism," pp. 151–155.

accepting the alleged ubiquity of the knowledge-relation they could not escape the egocentric predicament. Had they treated perceptions not as cases of knowledge but as "simply natural events having, in themselves (apart from a *use* that may be made of them), no more knowledge status or worth than, say, a shower or a fever," discrepancies between objects and perceptions of those objects would have caused few problems. From this alternative perspective, the numerical duplicity between objects and human perception of them—between parallel railroad tracks and the perception of convergent tracks or between a star and the much later perception of the light it emits (another favorite idealist example)—posed no difficulties: "The astronomical star is *a* real object, but not "the" real object; the visible light is another real object, found, when knowledge supervenes, to be an occurrence standing in a process continuous with the star. Since the seen light is an event within a continuous process, there is no point of view from which its 'reality' contrasts with that of the star." As this example suggests, Dewey was not denying the importance of perceptions *to* knowledge but rather the proposition that, in themselves, they *were* knowledge. "While we do not, in any intelligible or verifiable sense, know *them,* we know all things that we do know *with* or *by* them."[13]

Dewey's analysis of the roots of realist difficulties with perceptual illusions in their assumption of the "ubiquity of the knowledge-relation" pointed to his larger critique of the concept of experience at the heart of traditional epistemology and to a different conception of experience, one congruent with the findings of evolutionary biology and functional psychology and evident in his own logical theory. This alternative conception of experience, which Dewey termed variously "immediate empiricism" or "naive realism," held that experience was not, ubiquitously, a knowledge-affair but rather "an affair of the intercourse of a living being with its physical and social environment" in which that living being was, in the first instance, not a knower but an "agent-patient, doer, sufferer, and enjoyer." Although Dewey acknowledged that things "are what they are experienced as," he did not mean that things are exclusively what they are known as, unless one falsely presumed that "knowing is the sole and only genuine mode of experi-

13. "Brief Studies in Realism," pp. 105, 106, 109. For the realist response by Spaulding, McGilvary, and Durant Drake to this critique and Dewey's rejoinders see *Middle Works* 6:483–500, 143–152, 501–511; 7:445–451, 79–84, 452–453, 79–84, 454–460; 10:431–438, 64–66, 439–449. See also "The Logic of Judgments of Practice" (1915), *Middle Works* 8:49–64.

encing." This latter proposition was "if not the root of all philosophic evil, at least one of its main roots."[11]

Dewey believed that persuasive evidence for his "postulate of immediate empiricism" was provided by evolutionary biology, which had established that experience was a process of interaction between a living being and its environment. In this process the natural energies of the environment sometimes enhanced and sometimes countered the life activities of the organism, and "the human being has upon his hands the problem of responding to what is going on around him so that these changes will take one turn rather than another." Life was a struggle in which the organism used whatever means it had at its disposal to "change the changes going on around it" to further its self-preservation and self-realization. Experience was not a matter of spectatorship but "primarily a process of undergoing: a process of standing something; of suffering and passion, of affection, in the literal sense of these words. The organism has to endure, to undergo, the consequences of its own actions. Experience is no slipping along in a path fixed by inner consciousness. Private consciousness is an incidental outcome of experience of a vital objective sort; it is not its source." Dewey was careful to emphasize that undergoing or "adjustment" was not a passive stance but an active intervention in the environment. "The most patient patient," he observed, "is more than a receptor. He is also an agent—a reactor, one trying experiments, one concerned with undergoing in a way which may influence what is still to happen." The agent-patient of experience "lived forward," for adjustment was an ongoing process requiring an eye to the future. In this view, "success and failure are the primary 'categories' of life; achieving of good and averting of ill are its supreme interests; hope and anxiety (which are not self-enclosed states of feeling, but active attitudes of welcome and wariness) are dominant qualities of experience."[15]

If knowledge was not the whole of human experience, it was cer-

14. "The Postulate of Immediate Empiricism" (1905), *Middle Works* 3:158–160. See also "Reality as Experience" (1906), *Middle Works* 3:101–106.

15. "The Need for a Recovery of Philosophy" (1917), *Middle Works* 10:7–10. I do not wish to belabor this point, but since it has been the source of much confusion and misinterpretation, it bears repeating that throughout his career Dewey clung to a counterintuitive definition of "adjustment" as including "an adaptation of the environment to the individual's needs and ends, rather than vice versa." He reserved the term "accommodation" for "the processes by which the individual assimilates and reproduces the existing environment with a minimum of reaction against it or of effort to change it." For a succinct discussion of these terms see Dewey's definitions of them in his "Contributions to *A Cyclopedia of Education*" (1911), *Middle Works* 6:359–361, 364–366.

tainly a part of it and a critical part. As we have seen, Dewey argued that knowing or inquiry emerged in the course of natural evolution as an important element in human adaptation. The fact "that the brain frees organic behavior from complete servitude to immediate physical conditions, that it makes possible the liberation of energy for remote and ever expanding ends is, indeed, a precious fact, but not one which removes the brain from the category of organic devices of behavior." Knowing was a *mediating* function capable of rendering judgments to guide actions that would transform problematic noncognitive situations into ongoing, unproblematic, noncognitive experience. Reflective inquiry "appears as the dominant trait of a situation when there is something seriously the matter, some trouble, due to active discordance, dissentiency, conflict among the factors of a prior non-intellectual experience." Knowledge was the critical instrument aiding human adjustment, for "the extent of an agent's capacity for inference, its power to use a given fact as a sign of something not yet given, measures the extent of its ability systematically to enlarge its control of the future." Successful adjustment for human beings rested to a considerable degree on effective inquiry.[16]

In *Studies in Logical Theory* Dewey had contrasted this conception of knowledge with that of absolute idealism, pointing to the uselessness of the latter for an understanding of the "human edition" of reality, and called for a reorientation of logical theory toward an investigation of the methods of effective human thinking which had culminated in the procedures of modern science. In subsequent articles including several collected in *Essays in Experimental Logic* (1916), he now argued that the logic derived from realist epistemology was also an inadequate account of how we think.

Like idealists, realists failed to recognize the mediating function of knowledge within a circuit of noncognitive experience. Both epistemological camps overlooked or denied that "things and qualities are present to most men most of the time as things and qualities in situations of prizing and aversion, or seeking and finding, of converse, enjoyment, and suffering, or production and employment, or manipulation and destruction. [Rather they thought] of things as either totally absent from experience or else there as objects of 'consciousness' or knowing." All schools of epistemology were "at one in their devotion to an identification of Reality with something that connects monopolistically with

16. "Does Reality Possess Practical Character?" (1908), *Middle Works* 4:132; "Introduction to *Essays in Experimental Logic*," p. 326; "Need for a Recovery of Philosophy," p. 15.

passionless knowledge, belief purged of all personal reference, origin, and outlook." In contesting this devotion, Dewey readily admitted that his adversarial conception of knowledge entailed the conclusion that "thinking would not exist, and hence knowledge would not be found, in a world which presented no troubles or where there are no 'problems of evil.'" For him, "to be a man is to be thinking desire."[17]

The differences between Dewey's instrumentalism and the realist theory of knowledge turned to a substantial degree on a fundamental disagreement about the place of the "brute existences" of reality in knowledge. For the realists these brute existences were the *objects* of knowledge; thinking was instrumental to a knowledge of these existences. For Dewey, the object of knowledge was not, in any instance, a brute existence but rather "a truth to be stated in propositions," a truth that worked successfully to transform a problematic situation. This is not to say that Dewey denied that brute existences were real or that they "set every problem for reflection and hence serve to test its otherwise merely speculative results." He insisted, however,that "as a matter of fact these brute existences are equivalent neither to the objective content of the situations, technological or artistic or social, in which thinking originates, nor to the things to be known—to the objects of knowledge." In inquiry, Dewey argued, brute existences were changed by intelligence into *signs* in the service of inferences, and the fundamental mistake of realism was to mistake the means of knowledge (brute data) for its objects (the true propositions this data helps us infer and test). Conceiving of knowledge as a simple mirroring of a ready-made reality, realists were gripped by a "kodak fixation." For Dewey the object of knowledge was "a more dignified, a more complete, sufficient, and self-sufficing thing than any datum can be."[18]

Dewey acknowledged that realists found his theory of knowledge unacceptably "idealist" because it asserted that "processes of reflective inquiry play a part in shaping the objects—namely terms and propositions—which constitute the bodies of scientific knowledge." He agreed that "in so far as it is idealistic to hold that objects of knowledge *in their capacity of distinctive objects of knowledge* are determined by intelligence, it is idealistic." Nevertheless, only one who believed in the ubiquity of the knowledge-relation could charge such a theory with holding that existence was *constituted* by thinking. "Thinking is what some of the actual

17. "Introduction to *Essays in Experimental Logic*," pp. 321, 331: "Beliefs and Existences," pp. 86, 100.
18. "Introduction to *Essays in Experimental Logic*," pp. 341, 347; "Does Reality Possess Practical Character?" p. 129.

existences *do. They* are in no sense constituted by thinking; on the contrary, the problems of thought are set by *their* difficulties and its resources are furnished by *their* efficacies; its acts are *their* doings adapted to a distinctive end."[19]

Dewey's arguments largely failed to dent the armor of neo-realism. His realist critics had a difficult time wrapping their minds around a concept of experience which was neither dualistic nor subjective, and some took Dewey's contention that things are "what they are experienced as" to mean that things are *only* what they are experienced as: a clear indication that he had not kicked idealism. Foes of his logic dismissed it as mere psychology, and even friendly adversaries insisted, despite his objections, that a logic that tied knowledge so tightly to the means for producing it was further evidence that he had not entirely shaken out of his system a more thoroughgoing idealism than he admitted. But, the sharp exchanges between Dewey and his opponents on issues of the nature of experience and knowledge were mild compared to the fireworks that exploded over the pragmatic conception of truth.[20]

The Meaning of Truth

At the core of the debate over the pragmatic theory of truth was the contention made variously by James and Dewey that ideas were hypotheses or plans of action, the truth of which rested on their ability to "work" in experience. Truth depended, that is, not on the accuracy with which an idea copied an antecedent reality or on its coherence with other truths but on its capacity to guide thinkers toward a successful or satisfactory resolution of problematic situations. In this sense, the truth of a proposition was not found but "made" through the process by

19. "Introduction to *Essays in Experimental Logic*," pp. 338–339.
20. Dewey's use of the term "experience" was *not* always clear in distinguishing it from "existence," and as a consequence the belief that he was arguing that things are *only* what they are experienced as was not entirely due to the obtuseness of his critics. The preponderance of evidence indicates, however, that he was arguing that, although experience (which in any case is not a "subjective" affair taking place in the mind of man) is the only avenue living beings have for intercourse with things, things do exist in space and time apart from an experiencer (confirming in this regard our experience of them). For a representative sample of the sort of confusion occasioned by Dewey's "immediate empiricism" and his attempts to deal with it, see his exchanges with McGilvary, *Middle Works* 4:295–327, 120–124, 143–155, and the "Introduction to *Essays in Experimental Logic*," pp. 323–324. For a representative response to Dewey's theory of knowledge see Bertrand Russell, "Professor Dewey's *Essays in Experimental Logic*," *Journal of Philosophy* 16 (1919): 5–26. Sleeper offers a useful account of the debate over Dewey's logical theory in this period in *The Necessity of Pragmatism*, chap. 4.

which it was verified. To cite but one of the many homely examples Dewey offered in defense of this theory:

> I hear a noise in the street. It suggests as its meaning a street-car. To test this idea I go to the window and through listening and looking intently—the listening and the looking being modes of behavior—organize into a single situation elements of existence and meaning which were previously disconnected. In this way an idea is made true; that which was a proposal or hypothesis is no longer merely a propounding or a guess. If I had not reacted in a way appropriate to the idea it would have remained a mere idea; at most a candidate for truth that, unless acted upon upon the spot, would always have remained a theory.

James's formulations of these notions, particularly in *Pragmatism*, were much looser than Dewey's, and as a consequence he took the lion's share of criticism. Dewey nonetheless came in for substantial abuse, and he responded vigorously, taking care to distance himself from some of James's more "tender-minded" arguments.[21]

Chief among the latter was James's attribution of truth to "satisfying" ideas, which critics interpreted to mean that any idea that proved emotionally or morally satisfying to an individual could by virtue of that fact be held to be true. As Dewey noted in a polite but nonetheless firmly critical review of *Pragmatism*, there was more than a little truth to these charges. James used the pragmatic maxim that ideas and beliefs should be tested by their consequences in a bewildering variety of ways. At times, when utilizing Peirce's injunction to discover the meaning of an object by observing its conceivable effects, James slid over the differences between "meaning" and "meaningful," between the reference of an idea and its *value*, and attributed meaning to a belief on the basis of its meaningful consequences. As James said, a belief like that in a God that perpetuated existence might have satisfying moral consequences, but, Dewey observed, these consequences did nothing to clarify the meaning or establish the existence of God if they were used as James used them to add value, "meaningfulness," to an already fixed idea of God as an eternal power: "the good or valuable consequences can not clarify the meaning or conception of God; for, by the argument, they

---

21. "The Intellectualist Criterion for Truth," p. 67. See also "The Problem of Truth" (1911), *Middle Works* 6:31–52. A useful guide to the debate over pragmatism is the bibliography in the syllabus for Dewey's course "The Pragmatic Movement of Contemporary Thought," *Middle Works* 4:257–263. See also Addison W. Moore, *Pragmatism and Its Critics* (Chicago: University of Chicago Press, 1910).

proceed from a prior definition of God. They can not prove, or render more probable, the existence of such a being, for, by the argument, these desirable consequences depend upon accepting such an existence; and not even pragmatism can prove an existence from desirable consequences which themselves exist only when and if that other existence is there." As far as Dewey was concerned, pragmatists had no business "finding out the value of a conception whose own inherent significance pragmatism has not first determined" and this criticism most especially included conceptions that posited such consequences as "the eternal perpetuation of existence" which could never be empirically verified.[22]

Even more damaging to the pragmatic cause than James's confusion of meaning and meaningfulness was his related mixing of the true with the good. True ideas, Dewey said, were good in the sense that they solved problems, and the consequences of an idea that established its truth were good in that they did so. This did *not* mean, however, as James sometimes implied (especially, Dewey noted, "when theological notions are under consideration") that *any* good which flowed from acceptance of a belief was evidence of its truth. Dewey noted that, unlike James, he rarely if ever spoke of the "satisfactions" of truth, but, be that as it may, he most certainly "never identified any satisfaction with the truth of an idea, save *that* satisfaction which arises when the idea as working hypothesis or tentative method is applied to prior existences in such a way as to fulfill what it intends." When the issue at stake was truth, the illness and/or death that followed from drinking poisoned water were good and satisfying for testing the idea that the water was poison, but the sense of well-being that followed a belief in a providential God was neither good nor bad, satisfying or unsatisfying in testing that belief. It was, for this purpose, simply irrelevant.[23]

Despite the clear distance Dewey put between himself and James on these matters, his account of truth did not escape the indictment of "subjectivism" and "relativism" on another count. Because he identified truth with ideas and judgments verified in experience, critics who conceived of experience and hence verification as something that went on in individual minds charged him, as one put it, with making truth "a matter wholly of one's individual stream of consciousness. It is not a

22. "What Pragmatism Means by Practical" (1908), *Middle Works* 4:98–107.
23. Ibid., pp. 108–109. For James's own response to his critics, which cleared up some of the ambiguities in his account of truth in *Pragmatism*, see *The Meaning of Truth* (Cambridge: Harvard University Press, 1975).

relation to something outside, it does not transcend the individual experience."[24]

Dewey responded to these charges by pointing to the faulty conception of experience on which they rested, a conception, as we have seen, he was doing his best to subvert. Experience, he repeated in "A Short Catechism Concerning Truth" (1909), was not a purely mental phenomenon, but an interaction between organic beings and their environment and hence "a matter of functions and habits, of active adjustments and readjustments, of coordinations and activities, rather than of states of consciousness." Thinking, cognitive experience, arose in the context of situations in non-cognitive experience presenting "novel and unmastered features" and ideas were "attitudes of response taken toward extra-ideal, extra-mental things." The meaning of ideas was to be found in the modifications—"the differences"—they made in such situations, and their validity was to be measured by their capacity to effect their promised transformations of these situations. Verification was not a subjective matter but, like all human experience, a transaction between an intelligent organism and its environment.[25]

Dewey observed that pragmatists, like the "intellectualists" who charged them with subjectivism, were interested in discerning the relationship between thought and existence, but, unlike the intellectualists, they were able to do so because they were unburdened by their immediate empiricism of a purely mental conception of experience which trapped philosophers in a futile attempt to bring ideas and things together across an ontological chasm separating experience and an unknowable thing-in-itself transcending experience. Unlike the intellectualist, the pragmatist had a correspondence theory of truth that meant something:

He holds that correspondence instead of being an ultimate and unanalyzable mystery, to be defined by iteration, is precisely a matter of cor-respondence in its plain, familiar sense. A condition of dubious and conflicting tendencies calls out thinking as a method of handling it. This condition produces its own appropriate consequences, bearing its own fruits of weal and woe. The thoughts, the estimates, intents, and projects it calls out, just because they are attitudes of response and

24. James Bissett Pratt, "Truth and Ideas," *Journal of Philosophy* 5 (1908): 125. See also Pratt, *What Is Pragmatism?* (New York: Macmillan, 1909).

25. "A Short Catechism Concerning Truth" (1909), *Middle Works* 6:3–5. Page numbers for further references (SC) appear in the text. See also "Valid Knowledge and the 'Subjectivity' of Experience" (1910), *Middle Works* 6:80–85.

of attempted adjustment (*not* mere "states of consciousness"), produce their effects also. The kind of interlocking, of interadjustment that then occurs between these two sorts of consequences constitutes the correspondence that makes truth, just as the failure to respond to each other, to work together, constitutes mistake and error—mishandling and wandering. (SC, 5–6)

On this account, the pragmatist had beaten the advocates of truth as "correspondence" at their own game. "What the pragmatist does is to insist that the human factor must work itself out in *cooperation* with the environmental factor, and that their coadaptation *is* both 'correspondence' and 'satisfaction'" (SC, 10). Properly conceived, the correspondence at work in verification was "between purpose, plan, and its own execution, fulfillment; between a map of a course constructed for the sake of guiding behavior and the result attained in acting upon the indications of the map."[26]

Some intellectualist critics admitted that the pragmatists had elucidated the process of verification, the means by which we knew an idea to be true, but they objected to the pragmatic argument that truths are "made" in this process of verification as one that confused truth and verification. By showing that an idea "worked," inquiry might confirm its truth, but this working was not in itself the truth of the idea. Truth was antecedent to its verification: ideas were not true because they worked, they worked because they were true. For these critics, a favorite case in point of the fallacy of the pragmatists' argument was their treatment of our knowledge of "true" past events, which, contended the intellectualists, could not on the pragmatic theory of truth be said to have in fact occurred unless and until they had been verified. There were, such antagonists as James Pratt asserted, plenty of examples of this fantastic position in the writings of the pragmatists, to wit Dewey's streetcar: "Professor Dewey cites an idea that a certain noise comes from a street-car; this idea being investigated and verified *becomes* true. Had it not been verified it never would have been true—even if as a fact the noise *had* really come from the car." By this same logic, critics said, the fact that Columbus landed in America in 1492 would rest, improbably, on the future working of an idea about his voyage.[27]

Dewey responded to these criticisms by noting that the intellectualists put themselves in a bind by accepting the pragmatic account of verification yet denying any necessary, "organic" connection between truth and

26. "The Control of Ideas by Facts" (1907), *Middle Works* 4:84.
27. Pratt, "Truth and Ideas," p. 125.

verification. If the truth of an idea did not lie in its future consequences but in some antecedent "mysterious static correspondence" between it and existence, how could its truth be established pragmatically by those consequences? If they acknowledged this difficulty, the intellectualists were left without any positive theory of the relationship between truth and verification; they could not trade on the verification procedures identified by the pragmatists for these were not designed to reveal a "ready-made static property" like truth as the intellectualists conceived it (SC, 8). "How does the non-pragmatic view consider that verification takes place?" Dewey asked. "Does it suppose that we first look a long while at the facts and then a long time at the idea until by some magical process the degree and kind of their agreement become visible?"[28]

Dewey acknowledged that there was a sense in which the truth of an idea could be said to antecede its testing. Prior to their verification (as their verification revealed), true ideas had "the property of *ability to work*" (SC, 8). This sort of functional capacity *was* a property of ideas organically connected to verification, but Dewey did not see how any problems were posed for pragmatism by insisting on *this* sort of antecedent truth. He rightly suspected that his intellectualist critics meant to say something more than that an idea worked because it was workable.

The intellectualist criticism of the pragmatists' handling of past events, Dewey observed, revealed the same misunderstanding of the object of thought he attacked in his critique of the realist theory of knowledge. Pratt and other intellectualists confused the occurrence of a bare existence or an event with ideas or judgments about such occurrences. "Truth" was a property only of the latter. "Some conviction, some belief, some judgment with reference to [existences and events] is necessary to introduce the category of truth and falsity," and it was important not to "confuse the content of a judgment with the *reference* of that content" (SC, 6–7). The occurrence of noises from streetcars and of trans-Atlantic voyages by fifteenth-century mariners did not wait upon successful verification of the judgments that "the noise came from the street-car" or "Columbus landed in America in 1492" (that *would be* fantastic) though the truth of our judgments about those occurrences did. Events did not "truly" happen though true judgments about their happening could be made as long as these events left effects against which our judgments could be tested.

Well aware of the problems of the intellectualists with verification, Dewey noted that their theory of truth could not be verified but simply

28. "Control of Ideas by Facts," p. 85.

"has to be accepted as an ultimate, unanalyzable fact" (SC, 8). Pragmatists, on the other hand, were quite willing to submit their theory of truth to the pragmatic test. Thus, when the pragmatist said his theory was true, he meant that it effected the transformations it intended, it solved the problems that occasioned it: "It works, it clears up difficulties, removes obscurities, puts individuals into more experimental, less dogmatic, and less arbitrarily skeptical relations to life; aligns philosophic with scientific method; does away with self-made problems of epistemology; clarifies and reorganizes logical theory, etc" (SC, 9).

Pragmatism, Dewey conceded, was a rather homespun perspective; in its preference for the uncertain truths that were the product of human inquiry, it lacked the grandeur of theories attempting to track down certain Truths and a Reality above and behind such inquiry. It did not therefore answer the supposed human need identified by Bertrand Russell and other critics for absolute truths warranted by something more than the fallible procedures of science. At the time, wedded to what he himself later termed "watered down" Platonism and "mathematical mysticism," Russell most clearly stated this critical case:

> Pragmatism appeals to the temper of mind which finds on the surface of this planet the whole of its imaginative material; which feels confident of progress, and unaware of non-human limitations to human power; which loves battle, with all the attendant risks, because it has no real doubt that it will achieve victory; which desires religion, as it desires railways and electric light, as a comfort and a help in the affairs of this world, not as providing non-human objects to satisfy the hunger for perfection and for something to be worshipped without reserve. But for those who feel that life on this planet would be a life in prison if it were not for the windows into a greater world beyond; for those to whom a belief in man's omnipotence seems arrogant, who desire rather the Stoic freedom that comes of mastery over the passions than the Napoleonic domination that sees the kingdoms of this world at its feet—in a word, to men who do not find Man an adequate object of their worship, the pragmatist's world will seem narrow and petty, robbing life of all that gives it value, and making Man himself smaller by depriving the universe which he contemplates of all its splendour.

Many of Russell's criticisms were directed at those aspects of James's thought to which Dewey also objected, and, on the whole, Russell treated Dewey with more respect than James. Nonetheless, while Dewey's "very genuine scientific temper" appealed to him, he found "there is a profound instinct in me which is repelled by instrumentalism: the instinct of contemplation, and of escape from one's own personality."[29]

For his part, Dewey could not help observing that Russell, G. K. Chesterton, and others who, as a last resort, objected to pragmatism on the grounds that man "needs to be more than a pragmatist" had fallen prey to the very "subjectivism" with which they charged James and Dewey. Perhaps, he mused, the whole debate over the meaning of truth boiled down to the fact that "the pragmatist has spilled the personal milk in the absolutist's cocoanut" (SC, 11).

THE PROBLEMS OF MEN

Dewey was discouraged if not deterred by his failure to convince many philosophers of the fruitfulness of his efforts to break the "intellectual lockjaw called epistemology." Publicly, he observed that "the way the instrumental logician has been turned upon by both idealist and realist is suggestive of the way in which the outsider who intervenes in a family jar is proverbially treated by both husband and wife who manifest their unity by berating the third party." Privately, he wrote, "I have piped my own song, and few have listened, and fewer yet have found a melodic theme. There seems to be little belief in the need of any new musical mode."[30]

Dewey's failure to loosen the stranglehold of epistemology was more than intellectually distressing to him. He believed that philosophy as a cultural practice had reached a fatal turning point, and he had difficulty attracting an audience for his new music in part because his critique of the tradition bore within it not only a proposal for a radical transformation of the substance of philosophy but also of the social role of the philosopher. Philosophy, as he saw it, had two choices. It could become an active participant in "the living struggles and issues of its own age and times" or it could stick to its traditional epistemological conundrums and thereby "maintain an immune monastic impeccability, without relevancy and bearing in the generating ideas of its contempor-

29. Bertrand Russell, "Pragmatism" (1909), in Russell, *Philosophical Essays* (New York: Simon and Schuster, 1966), pp. 110–111; Russell, "Professor Dewey's *Essays in Experimental Logic*," p. 19.

30. "Does Reality Possess Practical Character?" p. 138n; "The Control of Ideas by Facts," p. 78; "Knowledge and Existence" [1908/1909], unpublished ms., Dewey Papers, as quoted in Lewis E. Hahn, Introduction to *Middle Works* 4:ix.

ary present." The consequences of this choice were significant, and Dewey's own inclinations were never in doubt. If philosophy took the first course, he said, "it will be respected, as we respect all virtue that attests its sincerity by sharing in the perplexities and failures, as well as the joys and triumphs, of endeavor." Along the second path lay the genteel satisfaction of being "snugly ensconced in the consciousness of its own respectability."[31]

For the pragmatists, the course was obvious. If their theory of knowledge was correct, if knowing was a mediating function serving human interests and not the means of access to a Reality lying behind the everyday world of weal and woe, then philosophy, as a branch of knowledge, "must take, with good grace, its own medicine." This line of action meant, negatively, that philosophers would have to "surrender all pretension to be peculiarly concerned with ultimate reality, or with reality as a complete (i.e., completed) whole: with *the* real object." Positively, it pointed to the conclusion that "philosophy recovers itself when it ceases to be a device for dealing with the problems of philosophers and becomes a method, cultivated by philosophers, for dealing with the problems of men."[32]

At the heart of Dewey's effort to reconstruct the role of the philosopher was his view of the relationship between philosophy and *science*. He was not alone in thinking that this was an issue of crucial importance, for it was central to the debates surrounding the professionalization of American philosophy in the first third of the twentieth century. Such was the prestige of science among philosophers and in the larger culture in this period that few who participated in these debates had a bad word for it. If philosophers were to establish themselves as a professional community of the competent, it was clear that they had to establish a positive relationship to science. Yet beyond ready agreement that science was a good thing, there was enormous disagreement among philosophers about what exactly science was and what precisely its relationship to philosophy should be. The range of opinion stretched from those who conceived of science as simply rigorously obtained formal knowledge, maintained that philosophy was and always had been scientific in this sense, and advised business as usual, to those who sought to model philosophy on the more restrictive notion of science embodied in the methods and findings of the empirical sciences and called for substantial reform of the way philosophers pursued their calling. The tenor of these reformers' efforts can be seen in Arthur O. Lovejoy's presidential ad-

31. "Does Reality Possess Practical Character?" p. 142.
32. "Need for a Recovery of Philosophy," pp. 38, 46.

dress to the American Philosophical Association in 1916, in which he chided his colleagues for pretending to science but not playing by the rules that prevailed in the truly scientific disciplines. He then outlined a six-point program for "progress in philosophical inquiry" which called for the cultivation of circumspect, inductive inquiry; "a deliberate and systematic attempt at exhaustiveness in the enumeration of the elements of a problem"; cooperative investigation; the adoption of a "common and unambiguous terminology"; the formulation of all problems in hypothetical form; and the compiling of "a modern *Summa Metaphysica*" to incorporate the results of these investigations. These proposals provoked sharp criticism and inconclusive argument, reflecting a diversity of opinion on the relationship between science and philosophy so wide that, as historian Daniel Wilson has remarked, "it is not too much to say that each philosopher had his or her own conception of science and its proper relationship to philosophy."[33]

As a result of these disagreements, strenuous efforts in the first two decades of the century to develop a consensus among American philosophers on the goals, problems, and methods of philosophy failed, and by the end of World War I the discipline had all the institutional trappings of a profession but none of the substantive coherence to which those enamored of the model of the empirical sciences aspired. Academic power filled the vacuum left by the inability of reasoned argument to achieve such coherence, and the advocates of a constricted view of philosophical inquiry, having failed to carry the day in the American Philosophical Association, simply began to flex their considerable muscle in the philosophy departments of the leading American universities. By 1920 momentum clearly lay with those wedded to a relatively narrow conception of "scientific philosophy" which favored the development of a specialized community of esoteric discourse in which the technically rigorous subdisciplines of epistemology and formal logic were privileged.[34]

33. Lovejoy quoted in Daniel J. Wilson, "Science and the Crisis of Confidence in American Philosophy, 1870–1930," *Transactions of the Charles S. Peirce Society* 23 (1987): 250–252, 236. On the prestige of science in this period among American philosophers and other intellectuals see David Hollinger, "Inquiry and Uplift: Late Nineteenth-Century American Academics and the Moral Efficacy of Scientific Practice," in Thomas Haskell, ed., *The Authority of Experts* (Bloomington: Indiana University Press, 1984), pp. 142–156, and Hollinger, "The Problem of Pragmatism in American History," *Journal of American History* 67 (1980): 88–107.

34. Wilson, "Science and the Crisis of Confidence," pp. 252–257. See also Daniel J. Wilson, "Professionalization and Organized Discussion in the American Philosophical Association, 1900–1922," *Journal of the History of Philosophy* 17 (1979): 53–69; and Kuklick, *Rise of American Philosophy,* pp. 451–480.

Dewey, of course, had become unremittingly hostile to epistemology, and although it is inaccurate to portray him (as some have done) as an enemy of formal logic, he certainly did not feel it belonged at the center of philosophical discourse. He had not anticipated that philosophy would march into not-so-splendid isolation under the banner of epistemology and *science,* for he thought science, particularly evolutionary biology, had exploded the fundamental assumptions about experience and knowledge which underlay epistemology. He therefore took little pleasure in the confirmation of his prediction that an unwillingness to close down the epistemology industry would lead American philosophy into cultural irrelevance, for it meant the defeat for his own idiosyncratic vision of the proper alliance between science and philosophy: an alliance of *ethics* and science.

As an idealist, Dewey had eschewed H. A. P. Torrey's defensive Kantian strategy of separate spheres for science and philosophy for T. H. Green's more aggressive attempt to subordinate science to philosophy and prop up its tottering reign as queen of the sciences. Philosophy, he had argued in the mid-1880s, was the science of "all reality as one connected system" and, as such, the basis for every other science, not really a special science at all but "all Science taken in its organic systematic wholeness." One of the most significant consequences of Dewey's deconversion from idealism was a complete reordering in his mind of this relationship between philosophy and the special sciences. By the turn of the century, he was arguing that philosophy as knowledge was wholly parasitic on the special sciences. "Philosophy," he advised, "must go to school to the sciences; must have no data save such as it receives at their hands; and be hospitable to no method of inquiry or reflection not akin to those in daily use among the sciences. As long as it claims for itself special territory of fact, or peculiar modes of access to truth, so long must it occupy a dubious position." Philosophers, in Dewey's view, had to face up to the fact that philosophy could not be a special science, and certainly not Science itself, but instead had a significant role to play as a powerful form of cultural criticism grounded in moral imagination and disciplined by the knowledge provided by the special sciences.[35]

35. "Psychology as Philosophic Method" (1886), *Early Works* 1:158; "'Consciousness' and Experience" (1899), *Middle Works* 1:129; "Some Connections of Science and Philosophy" [1902], unpublished ms. reprinted in *Encounter* 49 (August 1977): 77–82. Insofar as Dewey sought to reorient logic toward the study of the process of "how we think" and science represented that process at its most refined, it could be said that, in this sense, he regarded logic as the science of science, though it would perhaps be more accurate to say that logic was for him the science *about* science, the science that took scientific method itself as its subject matter and as such was parasitic not on the knowledge but on the practices of the special sciences.

Dewey did, to be sure, retain a very important conception of science as such, but it was a strictly *methodological* conception, and a quite loose and expansive one at that. For him, science in its most important sense was not the body of knowledge accumulated by the special sciences but the common method by which this knowledge had been produced. This method he described in very general fashion in order to arrive at a definition of science consistent with the practices of the natural sciences, yet broader than more narrow definitions that insisted that scientific knowledge must take the *forms* characteristic of the results of investigations of physical matters. The scientific attitude of mind, he said, was apparent whenever beliefs were not simply taken for granted but established as the conclusions of critical inquiry and testing. "Our attitude becomes scientific," he said, "in the degree in which we look in both directions with respect to every judgment passed; first checking or testing its validity by reference to possibility of making other and more certain judgments with which this one is bound up; secondly, fixing its meaning (or significance) by reference to its use in making other statements." Although this conception of scientific method did set definite limits on what could count as "science," it was a most liberal formulation. It was so liberal that Dewey often comfortably used science as a synonym for reason, intelligence, and reflective thought, a practice that did not manifest, as some have charged, an unduly narrow notion of the latter terms but rather a willingness to offer relatively relaxed entrance requirements to the house of science.[36]

Scientific thinking, Dewey insisted to popular as well as professional audiences, was but a refinement of the ordinary procedures for fixing belief. For the scientist as for the man on the street, a complete reflective thought proceeded through five distinct steps: (1) a felt difficulty or problem ("thinking begins in what may fairly enough be called a *forked-road* situation"); (2) the location and definition of this difficulty; (3) the suggestion of a possible solution to the problem; (4) reasoned consideration of the bearings of the suggested solution; and (5) further observation and experiment leading to the acceptance (belief) or rejection (disbelief) of the proposed solution. At the heart of this process was the making of inferences, a leap from "what is surely known to something else accepted on its warrant." This leap was subject to a variety of influences that enhanced the chances of a false landing: "past experi-

36. "Logical Conditions of a Scientific Treatment of Morality" (1903), *Middle Works* 3:3–4. Compare, for example, the definition of "reflective thought" offered in *How We Think* (1910): "Active, persistent, and careful consideration of any belief or supposed form of knowledge in the light of the grounds that support it, and the further conclusions to which it tends" (*Middle Works* 6:185).

ence, received dogmas, the stirring of self-interest, the arousing of passion, sheer mental laziness, a social environment steeped in biased traditions or animated by false expectations, and so on." Consequently, the key to better thinking was the negation of these influences through the regulation of the conditions under which inferences were made and tested. Science was, at bottom, just this regulation. Thus science "does not depart from the factors employed in the reflective examination of any topic so far as introducing new operations is concerned, but only by supplying the conditions of increased control and care under which to carry on these operations." Science was but "a purification and intensification of the usual methods" of reflective thought "through making precise and adequate the conditions that enter into their use." To a considerable degree, the development of scientific thinking was no more than a matter of cultivating a set of cognitive virtues, "traits of carefulness, thoroughness, and continuity, . . . ability to 'turn things over,' to look at matters deliberately, to judge whether the amount and kind of evidence requisite for decision is at hand, and, if not, to tell where and how to seek such evidence."[37]

If Dewey's conception of science was latitudinarian it was nonetheless imperial. "Scientific method," he declared, "is not just a method which it has been found profitable to pursue in this or that abstruse subject for purely technical reasons. It represents the only method of thinking that has proved fruitful in any subject—that is what we mean when we call it scientific. It is not a peculiar development of thinking for highly specialized ends; it *is* thinking so far as thought has become conscious of its proper ends and of the equipment indispensable for success in their pursuit." Science, Dewey believed, could and should fix beliefs in all realms of experience, including human conduct. Indeed, his broad conception of scientific method was formulated for the express purpose of elucidating a logic for a scientific treatment of morality which would bring moral judgments within the purview of reflective inquiry, and he took it to be his most important task as a logician to extend the scope of scientific judgment to include ethical reasoning. "If the pragmatic idea of truth has itself any pragmatic worth," he remarked, "it is because it stands for carrying the experimental notion of truth that reigns among the sciences, technically viewed, over into political and moral practices, humanly viewed." This effort to make ethics more scientific is one of the most controversial aspects of Dewey's thought,

37. *How We Think*, pp. 236–237, 201, 232; "Scientific Method," in "Contributions to *A Cyclopedia of Education*" (1913), *Middle Works* 7:339.

but viewed within the context of his own notions of experience, knowledge, and science rather than through the lens of epistemological perspectives he repudiated, it is a somewhat less dubious project than it has appeared to many.[38]

It is critical, first of all, to recall Dewey's anti-epistemological critique of the supposed "ubiquity of the knowledge-relation," his antidualist conception of experience, and his positioning of thinking as a mediating function within this, largely noncognitive, realm of experience. These aspects of his thought were as full of implication for ethics as for the theory of knowledge. Good and evil, Dewey contended, were in the first instance not known but simply experienced as a "primary organic reaction." Hence, the task of moral reasoning was manifestly not to establish the *reality* of the goods of experience; for Dewey, the reality of these goods was unproblematic. Just as the epistemologists' problem of the "existence of the world" vanished in his account of experience, so too did worries about the existence (as opposed to the relative *value*) of particular goods and evils. These worries developed only if one presumed that these goods and evils had to appeal for certification to some transcendent reality beyond experience:

> Goods *are,* a multitude of them—but, unfortunately, evils also *are;* and all grades, pretty much, of both. . . . Until you set up the notion of a transcendental reality at large, you cannot even raise the question of whether goods and evils are or only seem to be. The trouble and the joy, the good and the evil, is *that* they are; the hope is that they may be regulated, guided, increased in one direction and minimized in another. . . . Personally I don't need an absolute to enable me to distinguish between, say, the good of kindness and the evil of slander, or the good of health and the evil of valetudinarianism. In experience, things bear their own specific characters.

As long as things were experienced as unproblematically good or evil, knowledge played no role in moral life. In such experience things were simply "found" to be good and not known or judged to be such: *"finding* a thing good apart from reflective judgment means simply treating

38. "Science as Subject-Matter and as Method" (1910), *Middle Works* 6:78; "The Problem of Truth" (1911), *Middle Works* 6:31. It is tempting to say that scientific method was an absolute for Dewey, and some have done so. I have resisted the temptation because his argument for privileging science over other methods of fixing warranted belief was wholly pragmatic: science worked much better than the available alternatives. In addition, he readily acknowledged that the method of science was not etched in stone and that it, like the conclusions derived from it, had been hammered out over centuries of scientific practice and remained fallible and provisional.

the thing in a certain way, hanging on to it, dwelling upon it, welcoming it, and acting to perpetuate its presence, taking delight in it."[39]

It was only at the point that experiences of good and evil became problematic—when they gave rise to questions of better and worse—that a task was set for thought. Unsettled experience of this sort called for a judgment of practice—a judgment about what to do—in order to enhance goodness and minimize evil, and consequently a doubtful noncognitive experience of prizing gave way to a cognitive experience of appraising—"a process of finding out what we want, what, as we say, we *really* want." Formally, Dewey contended, moral judgments were no different from other kinds of judgments and hence could be made scientifically. They began with a problem—a moral fork in the road—which, like all problems, was subject to definition and to the suggestion of possible courses of action that would resolve it. Deliberation on these suggestions took the form of a "dramatic rehearsal" in the mind of various courses of conduct and an estimate of their consequences. In turn, a judgment of the better thing to do was rendered and subsequently tested in action. Differences between intellectual and moral judgments were thus not differences of method but of subject matter; a value judgment differed from other scientific judgments simply in that "its subject-matter happens to be a good or a bad instead of a horse or planet or curve."[40]

Despite the apparent flippancy of this remark, Dewey recognized that this difference of subject matter was no small difference. In his important yet often damnably opaque essay "Logical Conditions of a Scientific Treatment of Morality" (1903) he observed that, in addition to some important universal features, the logic of scientific judgment varied in significant ways according to the ends it served. Ethical judgments were distinguished by the entrance of the character of the judger into the judgment as a "determinant of *this* content-value of judgment rather than that." The moral judgment was "one which effects an absolutely reciprocal determination of the situation judged, and of the character or disposition which is expressed in the act of judging." In other words, in an ethical judgment assessments of better and worse were determined in significant respects by character, and character was in turn shaped by the ethical judgments made and the consequent actions taken. The sort of person one was or desired to be profoundly affected what one decided one should do, and in deciding what to do

39. "Nature and Its Good: A Conversation" (1909), *Middle Works* 4:19–20; "The Logic of Judgments of Practice," p. 26.
40. "Logic of Judgments of Practice," pp. 35, 26; JD and James H. Tufts, *Ethics* (1908), *Middle Works* 5:292–293.

one was deciding (often implicitly) what sort of person one would be. Scientific reasoning was of inestimable value in determining what one should do to live the life one wished to live and in choosing the proximate ends as well as the means appropriate to such a life, but it could render no definitive judgment about what sort of life one should want to live. This was the work not of scientific intelligence but of moral imagination because, he later remarked, "judgment at some point runs against the brute act of holding something dear as its limit."[41]

It was at this juncture that philosophy distinguished itself from science, and philosophers could make their most important contribution to the solution of the problems of men. Strictly speaking, Dewey argued in "Philosophy and Democracy" (1918), philosophy was not "in any sense whatever a form of knowledge" but rather "a form of desire, of effort at action—a love, namely, of wisdom." Wisdom was not "systematic and proved knowledge of fact and truth, but a conviction about moral values, a sense for the better kind of life to be led." Historically, philosophies "embodied not colorless intellectual readings of reality, but men's most passionate desires and hopes, their basic beliefs about the sort of life to be lived": "They started not from science, not from ascertained knowledge, but from moral convictions, and then resorted to the best knowledge and the best intellectual methods available in their day to give the form of demonstration to what was essentially an attitude of will, or a moral resolution to prize one mode of life more highly than another, and the wish to persuade other men that this was the wise way of living." The fact that philosophy was wisdom and not knowledge explained why one could speak of a national philosophy but not a national chemistry. The cultural variation in philosophies reflected "incompatibilities of temperament and expectation. They are different ways of construing life."[42]

As a vision of "the better kind of life to be led" ethical philosophy was

---

41. "Logical Conditions," pp. 22, 23–24; "Logic of Judgments of Practice," p. 46. It should be said that Dewey did not mean to say that scientific judgments of a nonmoral sort were not dependent in important respects on the character of the judger. As I have suggested, science was to a considerable degree for Dewey a constellation of cognitive virtues. "The system of science," he observed, "is absolutely dependent for logical worth upon a moral interest: the sincere aim to judge truly" ("Logic of Conditions," p. 19). The difference between nonmoral and moral judgments, he argued, was that in the former the character of the judger was a uniform and impartial condition affecting all judgments alike, while in the latter it exercised a preferential effect on particular judgments. In nonmoral judgments "the activity of the agent in the act of judging expresses itself in effort to prevent its activity from having any influence upon the material judged," while in moral judgments the character of the judger "qualitatively colors the meaning of the situation which the judger presents to himself" (21–22).

42. "Philosophy and Democracy" (1918), *Middle Works* 11:43–44. Page numbers for further references (PD) appear in the text.

distinct from the "science of ethics" that Dewey also called for and, as a psychologist, presumed to practice. The latter comprised "psychological ethics" and "sociological ethics" and was a wholly descriptive enterprise "concerned with collecting, describing, explaining and classifying the facts of experience in which judgments of right and wrong are actually embodied or to which they apply." Dewey saw no logical obstacles to the development of such a science, and he believed that "generic propositions" could be developed about human conduct akin to the laws formulated by natural scientists. Such propositions, he argued, would be a valuable resource for moral judgment by affording "insight into the conditions which control the formation and execution of aims." Although reflective moral judgment could proceed apart from this ethical science, Dewey occasionally employed a much narrower notion of science to suggest that until moral reasoning incorporated the kind of causal propositions characteristic of natural science it would not be fully scientific. The modest achievements of social science in generating the sort of laws Dewey hoped for and the conviction of many that human conduct cannot be explained in terms of such laws has rendered this narrower version of scientific moral judgment suspect without, I think, calling into question the broader conception of practical reason Dewey advanced. In any case, he never contended that a descriptive science of ethics could determine particular moral judgments. Ethical *science*, he said, "will never tell us just what to do ethically, nor just how to do it." It was as philosophy rather than science that ethics was concerned with "the ideal, with what ought to be, or with what is absolutely desirable, as distinct from the actual, the existent, the phenomenal."[43]

To view philosophy as wisdom rather than knowledge was not, Dewey was careful to point out, to say that it was an *arbitrary* expression of moral desire. Philosophy "can intellectually recommend its judgments of value only as it can select relevant material from that which is recognized to be established truth, and can persuasively use current knowledge to drive home the reasonableness of its conception of life. It is this dependence upon the method of logical presentation and upon scientific subject matter which confers upon the philosophy the garb, though not the form, of knowledge." This garb was nonetheless essential, and it was what made philosophy hard work and worthwhile. "Scientific form is a vehicle for conveying a non-scientific conviction, but the carriage is necessary, for philosophy is not mere passion but a passion that would

43. "Ethics" (1904), *Middle Works* 3:41; "Psychology and Social Practice" (1900), *Middle Works* 1:150. See also "Logical Conditions," pp. 23–37; *How We Think*, pp. 284–285; and "Psychological Method in Ethics" (1903), *Middle Works* 3:59–61.

exhibit itself as a reasonable persuasion." This combination, Dewey admitted, made philosophy a very tricky business, for the temptation was, on the one hand, to adopt the "conceit of knowledge" and provide moral vision with a set of counterfeit scientific credentials or, on the other hand, to leave moral vision altogether bereft of whatever support science might provide it, in which case "philosophy becomes hortatory, edifying, sentimental, or fantastic and semi-magical" (PD, 46–47).

Dewey conceded it was difficult to avoid these temptations, and he succumbed to each on occasion. Nonetheless, it was, above all, the exercise of this difficult kind of reasonable moral imagination which he sought to put at the heart of the philosopher's vocation. Philosophy was not a science, and it should not aspire to be one. But philosophers had to trade on the fruits and methods of science in articulating their ideals of the good life, for therein lay whatever claims these ideals could stake to rationality. "A philosophy which was conscious of its own business and province would then perceive that it is an intellectualized wish, an aspiration subjected to rational discriminations and tests, a social hope reduced to a working program of action, a prophecy of the future, but one disciplined by serious thought and knowledge" (PD, 43).

PRAGMATISM AND DEMOCRACY

Critics of pragmatism often felt compelled not only to refute it but to explain its emergence on terrain as philosophically unpromising as the United States. In so doing, they moved beyond analysis of what they took to be its logical defects to an effort to explain by means of a loose and condemnatory sociology of knowledge how Dewey and others could possibly believe such a peculiar set of ideas to be true. In a characteristic argument of this sort, one commentator described pragmatism as a "would-be philosophical system" that was a reflex of "such broadly-marked and such well-known American characteristics as the love of the concrete (in preference to the abstract), the love of experiment and experimentation, an intolerance of doctrinairism and of mere book-learning, the general democratic outlook on life and thought, the composite or amalgam-like character of the present culture of the United States, the sociological interest that characterizes its people, and so on."[44]

44. William Caldwell, *Pragmatism and Idealism* (London: Adam and Charles Black, 1913), pp. 172–173. Bertrand Russell was, in this context as well, the most prominent and acerbic critic of pragmatism. See Russell, "Pragmatism," pp. 106–111; Russell, "As a European Radical Sees It," *Freeman* 4 (1922): 608–610.

Dewey had no objections to these efforts to explain pragmatism as Americanism. There was, he said in 1922, "something instructive about our spiritual estate in the fact that pragmatism was born upon American soil." The attempt to explain the origins of philosophical ideas in terms of the cultures in which philosophers were inextricably embedded was, as far as he was concerned, a quite legitimate undertaking. In the debates in which he was engaged in the early twentieth century, Dewey increasingly resorted himself to supplementing strictly logical arguments with a critical intellectual history and sociology of knowledge designed to explain how particular problems (especially those he saw as pseudo-problems) had developed, and the social history of ideas would be a hallmark of his major books of the twenties: *Reconstruction in Philosophy*, *Experience and Nature*, and *The Quest for Certainty*. The polemical uses of this sort of argument were by no means foreign to him either, and he repeatedly charged that absolutist and transcendental philosophies were, in effect if not necessarily in intent, the ideological foundation of "class-codes" that had "done more than brute love of power to establish inequality and injustice among men."[45]

If Dewey did not object to the rooting of pragmatism in American life, he did insist that his critics get it right. He was particularly incensed by Bertrand Russell's efforts to link pragmatism with "obnoxious aspects of American industrialism." This, he said, was on the order of saying that "English neo-realism is a reflection of the aristocratic snobbery of the English; the tendency of French thought to dualism an expression of an alleged Gallic disposition to keep a mistress in addition to a wife; and the idealism of Germany a manifestation of an ability to elevate beer and sausage into a higher synthesis with the spiritual values of Beethoven and Wagner." To say that a philosophy was "American," he observed in 1927, was not to say that it was "merely a formulated acquiescence in the immediately predominating traits" of American life, for cultures embodied conflicting elements. Often the values that a philosophy idealized were those opposed to "the ones most in evidence, the most clamorous, the most insistent," and such oppositional values furnished a set of immanent moral possibilities "upon which criticism rests and from which creative effort springs."[46]

45. "Pragmatic America" (1922), *Middle Works* 13:307; "Intelligence and Morals" (1908), *Middle Works* 4:48–49. The best example of Dewey's own use of the social history of ideas before World War I (if not the best example of his skill in this enterprise) is *German Philosophy and Politics* (1915), which I discuss in Chapter 7.

46. "Pragmatic America," p. 307; "The Pragmatic Acquiescence" (1927), *Later Works* 3:147.

Where Dewey felt his critics were most correct was in their linkage of his thought to democracy, and this was a connection he himself made repeatedly and unapologetically. "American philosophy," he declared in 1904, "must be born out of and must respond to the demands of democracy, as democracy strives to voice and achieve itself on a vaster scale, and in a more thorough and final way than history has previously witnessed." Among other things, democracy required a belief that ordinary men and women might possess the intelligence to effectively direct the affairs of their society. Democracy, he remarked a few years later, was "an absurdity where faith in the individual as individual is impossible; and this faith is impossible when intelligence is regarded as a cosmic power, not an adjustment and application of individual tendencies. . . . To put the intellectual center of gravity in the objective cosmos outside of men's own experiments and tests, and then to invite the application of individual intelligence to the determination of society is to invite chaos." Consequently, "democracy is estimable only through the changed conception of intelligence, that forms modern science." Pragmatism was the logic of this new conception of intelligence, deployed to close down an epistemology industry at odds with both science and democracy in order to erect a philosophy responsive to both. Democracy was the immanent, oppositional value that Dewey's philosophy idealized.[47]

"If democracy be a serious, important choice and predilection," Dewey declared, "it must in time justify itself by generating its own child of wisdom, to be justified in turn by its children, better institutions of life." He believed that the line of thought he had initiated was this child of wisdom and that it was time for Americans to get to work on the better institutions of life toward which it pointed. The only remaining question for American philosophy was "just who will be the philosophers associated with it" (PD, 53). There was no question where Dewey stood. Democracy was the name of his "intellectualized wish."

47. "Philosophy and American National Life" (1904), *Middle Works* 3:74; "Intelligence and Morals," p. 39.

CHAPTER 6

Democracy and Education

*

IN 1894 John Dewey and his family had looked forward to their move to Chicago with eager anticipation; a decade later, they began life in New York in a more somber mood. The rancorous dispute over the Laboratory School left scars that would be long in healing, and, as they had ten years earlier, the Deweys marked new beginnings with a family trip to Europe and returned to America bearing a small coffin.

On the way to England, eight-year-old Gordon Dewey contracted typhoid fever, and after a brief stay in a Liverpool hospital in which he appeared to recover, he suffered a relapse during a trip to Ireland and died shortly thereafter. Gordon and his brother Morris, who had succumbed to diphtheria in Milan in 1895 under eerily similar circumstances, were the most precocious of Dewey's children, and Gordon was fondly remembered by Jane Addams and other family friends for his remarkable maturity and wry sense of humor. Although the pain of Gordon's passing was eased by the adoption a brief time later of an eight-year-old Italian child, Sabino, the Deweys were devastated by the boy's death. God, Dewey mused, seemed to be offering them children on a short-term loan. Afterward, according to her daughter Jane, Alice Dewey "never fully recovered her former energy," and subsequently the Deweys' marriage took a decided turn for the worse as Alice's health deteriorated and her zeal for reform and perfectionism degenerated into resentment and insistent nagging. By the time of her death in

1927, Max Eastman reported, she had become "impossible except for saints to live with."[1]

While he and his family struggled under these conditions to adapt to life in New York (they moved nine times in Dewey's first nine years at Columbia), Dewey devoted himself to his teaching and to his controversial war on the epistemological tradition of modern philosophy and the defense of pragmatism. This left little time for much else, and he was a relative latecomer to the reform efforts of the early decades of the century that we have come to call "progressivism." The Deweys did create a stir in the spring of 1906 when they offered their home as refuge for Russian revolutionary Maxim Gorky, who was refused lodging at New York hotels after he provoked a public outcry not only by seeking support for the revolutionary cause in the United States but also by traveling with a Russian actress who was not his wife. This incident indicated that the Deweys' "anarchism" survived the move to New York ("I would rather starve and see my children starve than see John sacrifice his principles," Alice told the press), but it was not until the eve of the Great War in Europe that Dewey vigorously renewed his own efforts to answer his call to philosophers to address directly the "problems of men."[2]

The Good Democrat

Although Dewey's activism waned somewhat in the early years of the twentieth century, his interest in social reform did not. At Columbia, he continued to teach political philosophy, and in 1908 he and his former

---

1. Dykhuizen, p. 115; Jane Dewey, "Biography of John Dewey," in Paul A. Schilpp, ed., *The Philosophy of John Dewey*, 2d ed. (New York: Tudor, 1951), p. 35; Herbert M. Kliebard, "John Dewey's Other Son," *Teachers College Record* 83 (1982): 453–457; Jane Addams, "Gordon Dewey," in Addams, *The Excellent Becomes the Permanent* (New York: Macmillan, 1932), pp. 59–69; JD, *The Poems of John Dewey*, ed. Jo Ann Boydston (Carbondale: Southern Illinois University Press, 1977), p. 30; Max Eastman, "John Dewey," *Atlantic*, December 1941: 680–681. Eastman's article elicited a bitter denunciation from Dewey's daughters for its portrait of their mother, but as Philip Jackson has suggested in an acute review of *The Poems of John Dewey*, the private poetry Dewey wrote in these years offers substantial evidence that Eastman accurately portrayed life in the Dewey household. See Jackson, "John Dewey's Poetry," *American Journal of Education* 91 (1982): 69–72. Further evidence of Alice Dewey's perfectionism and nagging (and of John Dewey's remarkable abilities as a father) is also available in Sabino Dewey's recollections of this period (Sabino Dewey interview, Sabino Dewey Papers, Morris Library, Southern Illinois University).

2. Dykhuizen, pp. 149, 363n, 150–151.

Chicago colleague James H. Tufts published an innovative *Ethics* text-book combining historical and theoretical analysis with commentary on current social problems that clearly indicated they were attuned to progressive politics. Although it was part of a blockbuster series of Holt and Company textbooks that numbered William James and Henry Carter Adams among its contributors and was used widely in college classrooms, this book attracted little attention from a more general audience, and few historians have examined it carefully. ("No man, I think, with such universally important things to say on almost every social and intellectual activity of the day," Randolph Bourne remarked in 1915, "was ever published in forms more ingeniously contrived to thwart the interest of the prospective public.") It is nonetheless an interesting document in progressive social thought, for here Dewey outlined the moral underpinnings of the positions he took a few years later as he launched his career as a major public intellectual.[3]

As we have seen, the first signs of Dewey's discontent with absolute idealism became evident in his ethical writings of the early 1890s, most notably the *Outlines of a Critical Theory of Ethics* (1891) and *The Study of Ethics: A Syllabus* (1894). But these writings, as the titles suggest, were sketchy, and it was not until the *Ethics* that Dewey returned in any systematic way to the issues of moral philosophy. Here he brought together three strands of argument in ethical theory which he had been developing in fragmentary fashion over the previous twenty years: his metaethical concern with the logic of moral judgment, his contributions as a psychologist to a science of human conduct, and his naturalization of the idealist ethics of self-realization.[4]

3. Randolph Bourne, "John Dewey's Philosophy" (1915), in Olaf Hansen, ed., *The Radical Will: Randolph Bourne, Selected Writings* (New York: Urizen, 1977), p. 331. On the publishing history of the book see "Textual Commentary," *Middle Works* 5:549–554. For a historical account of progressive social thought that does recognize the significance of this text see James T. Kloppenberg, *Uncertain Victory: Social Democracy and Progressivism in European and American Thought, 1870–1920* (New York: Oxford, 1986), pp. 130, 139–144, 350–352, 400–401.

4. My focus here is on the third of these elements of Dewey's ethical theory, though I indicate how Dewey drew on the other two strands of thought (which we have already examined in some detail) to buttress his normative vision of self-realization as the cultivation of democratic character. In the interest of ease of expression I attribute the arguments of the *Ethics* to Dewey alone. Dewey wrote the key middle part titled "Theory of the Moral Life," and the chapters "Social Organization and the Individual" and "Civil Society and the Political State" in the final part ("The World of Action"). Tufts wrote the historical first part, about which I say nothing. The only problem the dual authorship creates here lies with Tufts's authorship of the important concluding sections of the third part on economic life and the family. I simply attribute the views expressed there to Dewey as well on the grounds that Dewey and Tufts said that each had "contributed suggestions and criticisms of the work of the other to sufficient degree to make the book

Dewey advanced his own theory of the moral life through an indirect strategy that first exposed the psychological and logical weaknesses of the principal competing theories: utilitarianism and Kantian formalism. When the shortcomings of each of these theories was repaired, he argued, the differences between them were blurred and the strengths of each could be incorporated into an ethics of self-realization in which both happiness and the dictates of practical reason called for the cultivation of democratic character.

Following his argument about the logic of ethical judgments, Dewey characterized moral action as a particular form of voluntary action or conduct, distinguished from nonmoral conduct by the presence of a choice between competing values. All conscious human life was conduct, but much of it was nonmoral, a "technical rather than a moral affair" in which the questions one faced were those of indifferent preference or means-ends efficiency. As moral, conduct was "activity called forth and directed by ideas of value or worth, where the values concerned are so mutually incompatible as to require consideration and selection before an overt action is entered upon." In a moral situation the problem was one of determining "what *is* really valuable."[5]

In the analysis of the moral situation the differences between utilitarianism and Kantian rationalism appeared at first glance to be fundamental and irreconcilable, for the two schools of thought could not even agree on what constituted the object of moral judgment. For the utilitarians it was the consequences of an action that were to be judged, while the Kantians insisted that the object of moral deliberation was the motives of the actor. Each of these positions found support in the moral discourse of ordinary life, which, on the one hand, held that "a tree is to be judged by its fruits" and noted that "Hell is paved with good intentions" and, on the other, valued the man whose "heart was in the right place" and with Shakespeare believed "there's nothing right or wrong, but thinking makes it so" (*E*, 214–215).

Here as was often the case when Dewey called in the common man for consultation, he was setting the stage for attack on yet another pernicious dualism. Popular appreciation of both sides of this argument led, he said, to the suspicion that philosophers were once again erecting false distinctions and overlooking an inclusive perspective that

---

throughout a joint work," and Tufts's arguments are forecast in earlier sections of the book written by Dewey (*Ethics* [1908], *Middle Works* 5:6).

5. *Ethics*, pp. 191, 194, 192. Page references for further references (*E*) appear in the text.

would resolve their disagreement. In this case, they had split voluntary action, which was "always a disposition, or habit of the agent *passing into an overt act*" producing certain consequences, into two unrelated "inner" (motive) and "outer" (consequences) parts that destroyed its integrity. "A 'mere' motive which does not do anything, which makes nothing different, is not a genuine motive at all, and hence is not a voluntary act. On the other hand, consequences which are not intended, which are not personally wanted and chosen and striven for, are no part of a voluntary act" (*E*, 218–219). Both sides seemed to recognize these difficulties and often hedged their position to shore up its weak flank. Utilitarians emphasized *foreseen* consequences, absolving agents of responsibility for reasonably unforeseen and unintended consequences and focusing judgment on foresight, "a mental act whose exercise depends on character." Kantians linked motives to consequences by regarding motives as forces that worked toward certain results. Each theory thus began with a firm commitment to judge only consequences or motives but, faced with the unity of the two in moral conduct, took account of the concerns of the competing perspective in a fashion that nearly canceled the original opposition. The result was an unacknowledged consensus that the object of moral judgment was "an *outcome, forethought and desired,* and hence attempted" (*E*, 230).[6]

All schools of moral theory agreed that the consequences agents foresaw and desired in a particular moral situation were profoundly shaped by the stable dispositions they brought to it. The sorts of consequences which appealed to a person depended on the sort of person he or she was. Thus, though on the face of it moral situations presented an agent with a decision about what to *do,* they were, at bottom, situations that called for a decision about what one was to *be.* "When ends are genuinely incompatible," Dewey remarked, "no common denominator can be found except by deciding what sort of character is most highly prized and shall be given supremacy" (*E*, 195). Dewey defined "character" as "that body of tendencies and interests in the individual which

6. As this suggests, Dewey required that Kantians give more ground than the utilitarians in defining the object of moral judgment. As we will see, this distribution of relative advantage was also apparent in his discussion of the criteria of moral judgment, though I would not go as far as Charles Stevenson does in his introduction to the *Ethics* in viewing Dewey's position as "a modified but still not unrecognizable form of utilitarianism" (*E*, xxxiii). Nonetheless, utilitarianism did fare consistently better with Dewey than Kantian rationalism, and the neo-utilitarianism of John Stuart Mill came away with the fewest bruises of all. Dewey's antipathy to Kantian formalism was, of course, long-standing, though how deep his aversions ran would not be evident until the polemics of *German Philosophy and Politics* (1915), in which responsibility for German authoritarianism was laid at Kant's doorstep (see Chapter 7).

make him open, ready, warm to certain aims, and callous, cold, blind to others, and which accordingly habitually tend to make him aware of and favorable to certain sorts of consequences, and ignorant of or hostile to other consequences" (E, 234). The selfish man was not a man who consciously gave no weight to the effects of his actions on others but the man who gave no thought to these effects. "The agent intends or wills all those consequences which his prevailing motive or character makes him willing under the circumstances to accept or tolerate" (E, 236). For this reason, an agent's character was the ultimate object of moral judgment. The focus of moral concern was "the disposition of a person as manifested in the tendencies which cause certain consequences, rather than others, to be considered and esteemed—foreseen and desired" (E, 241).

This conclusion, of course, posed the further question of the criteria of moral judgment, the standard by which foreseen and desired consequences (and the character that foresaw and desired them) were to be measured. The utilitarian answer to this question—the identification of the good with "happiness"—was, Dewey felt, intuitively appealing, but as Jeremy Bentham and other utilitarians used it, happiness was plagued by a critical failing as a standard of moral judgment. In utilitarian theory happiness (the pursuit of pleasure and the avoidance of pain) was deployed both to describe the moving spring of all human action and as the standard for moral evaluation, which made it a "highly ambiguous" concept. Dewey observed that "if happiness is the *natural* end of all desire and endeavor, it is absurd to say that the same happiness ought to be the end. . . . If all our acts are moved any way by pleasure and pain, this fact, just because it applies equally to all acts, throws no light upon the rightness or wrongness of any one of them" (E, 245). Moral theory required a standard for distinguishing "the right kind of happiness," and this, Dewey contended, utilitarianism could not provide.

The weakness of utilitarian ethics in this regard was traceable, Dewey argued, to its foundation in hedonistic and atomistic psychology. The hedonistic theory of desire held that the object of desire was pleasure (or the avoidance of pain). The fallacy of this psychological viewpoint, he contended, was to suppose that "the idea of pleasure of exercise arouses desire for it, when in fact the idea of exercise is pleasant only if there be already some desire for it." The object of desire was not pleasure but an object that promised to satisfy desire. Pleasure was "the felt concomitant of imagining a desire realized in its appropriate object" (E, 246–247). Because everyone desired happiness, Dewey said, is not to say that all men desire pleasure but that all men seek to satisfy their desires in appropriate objects. Insofar as the characters of agents differed, their desires differed. Hence, their conceptions of happiness differed:

> If the desire is the desire of an honest man, then the prosperous execution of some honorable intent, the payment of a debt, the adequate termination of a trust, is conceived as happiness, as good. If it be the desire of a profligate, then entering upon the riotous course of living now made possible by inheritance of property is taken as happiness—the one consummation greatly to be wished. If we know what any person really finds desirable, what he stakes his happiness upon, we can read his nature. In happiness, as the anticipation of the satisfaction of desire, there is, therefore, no sure or unambiguous quality; for it may be a token of good or bad character, according to the sort of object which appeals to the person (*E,* 249).

All character types found happiness in the satisfaction of the desires peculiar to that character, and for this reason happiness as a *conceived* good was not an ethical standard. Only happiness as a *rightly conceived* good could serve as such a standard. Since the nature of conceived happiness varied with character, the conceived happiness of the agent of "good character" was the ethical standard.

The hedonistic calculus of Jeremy Bentham, Dewey argued, was not up to providing a measure of true happiness or good character. Bentham held that the standard for judging an action was a calculation of the future pleasures and pains of all those affected by the action. This standard was faulty in two respects. First, it took pleasures to be isolated entities, alike in quality and differing only in quantity, when in fact pleasures were qualitatively distinct and incommensurable (a point made against Bentham even by such sympathetic utilitarians as John Stuart Mill). Second, it misconceived the calculations involved in the moral situation. We do not, Dewey said, measure an act against the *future* quantum of pain or pleasure it will produce but against its effect on our present dispositions or character. "The practical value of our acts is defined to us at any given time by the satisfaction, or displeasure, we take in the ideas of changes we foresee in case the act takes place. The present happiness or distaste, depending on the harmony of the idea in question and the character, defines for us the value of future consequences." This, he observed, still left us with no ethical standard, for "the idea of a certain result warms the heart of each, his heart being what it is. The assassin would not be one if the thought of a murder had not been entertained by him and if the thought had not been liked and welcomed—made at home" (*E*, 254–255). The ethical problem was to distinguish the good heart.

Dewey argued that if one replaced the hedonism, atomism, and sensationalism of utilitarian psychology with the superior scientific understanding of human action afforded by the functional psychology he, James, and others had worked out in the 1890s it would be possible to make this crucial distinction. From the functionalist point of view, pleasure was the result of the realization of some capacity ("function") of the agent in an object. There was no such thing as pleasure itself, only pleasant objects. Pleasure was derived from "the way some object meets, fits into, responds to an activity of the agent": "To say that food is agreeable, means that food satisfies an organic function. Music is pleasant because by it certain capacities or demands of the person with respect to rhythm of hearing are fulfilled; a landscape is beautiful because it carries to fulfillment the visual possibilities of the spectator" (*E*, 257). Functional psychology thus provided a better interpretation of happiness as a conceived good. As such, happiness was not a sum of pleasures but the "agreement whether anticipated or realized, of the objective conditions brought about by our endeavors with our desires and purposes" (*E*, 256).

More important, Dewey asserted, functional psychology pointed to an ethical standard of happiness as rightly conceived, a meaning for real or true happiness. The truly happy agent, he argued, acted so as to develop and express a character that desired ends that *unified* the powers and interests of the whole self. "We can," he said, "distinguish between the false and unsatisfactory happiness found in the expression of a more or less isolated and superficial tendency of the self, and the true or genuine good found in the adequate fulfillment of a fundamental and fully related capacity" (*E*, 246). From the functional perspective, "harmony, reenforcement, expansion are the signs of a true or moral satisfaction." True happiness lay in the pursuit of ends harmonious with all the capacities and desires of the self and which expanded them into a cooperative whole. Unhappiness or false happiness lay in the pursuit of ends that divided the self, failing to take account of some of its capacities or desires. The critical question, Dewey said, was "what is the good which while good in direct enjoyment also brings with it fuller and more continuous life" (*E*, 259).

Dewey argued that the social good—the welfare of all those affected by an action—was the only good that met this demand for an inclusive and expanding end. The human self was inherently social, bound to other selves by instinctive social affections, and these sympathetic affections made the well-being of others the direct object of desire and endeavor. "We cannot think of ourselves save as to some extent *social* beings," he observed. "Hence we cannot separate the idea of ourselves and our own good from our idea of others and of their good" (*E*, 268). Because the self found its good in the good of others, an act that harmed others harmed the agent as well, for it thwarted his social interests and powers, denying him a "full" and "continuous" life. A "selfish" act was not one that set the good of the self against the good of others but an act that set the self against itself by curtailing the social interests and desires. "The fact which constitutes selfishness in the moral sense is not that certain impulses and habits secure the well-being of the self, but that the well-being secured is a narrow and exclusive one" (*E*, 343). The genuinely moral person was thus one "in whom the habit of regarding all capacities and habits of self from the social standpoint is formed and active" (*E*, 271).

Dewey went on to argue that the development of a character that aimed at the social good was not only necessary but sufficient for true happiness. The sympathetic tendencies of the self, he argued, were capable of harmonizing and expanding the capacities and desires of the self into a cooperative whole. The moral ideal—the unified, growing self—could be produced by "a *blending*, a *fusing* of the sympathetic tendencies with all the other impulsive and habitual traits of the self":

> When interest in power is permeated with an affectionate impulse it is protected from being a tendency to dominate and tyrannize; it becomes an interest in *effectiveness of regard for common ends.* When an interest in artistic or scientific objects is similarly fused, it loses the indifferent and coldly impersonal character which marks the specialist as such, and becomes an interest in the adequate aesthetic and intellectual development of the conditions of a common life. Sympathy does not merely *associate* one of these tendencies *with* another; still less does it make one a means to the other's end. It so intimately permeates them as to transform them both into a single new and moral interest. . . .
> The result of this reciprocal absorption is the disappearance of the natural tendencies in their original form *and the generation of moral,* i.e., *socialized interests.* (*E*, 272–273)

This fusion of sympathy with the other capacities and desires of the self was, for Dewey, the task of the moral life. Moral conduct was a process of the self-creation and growth of what might be termed "sympathetic character." Self-realization as an ethical ideal was "the formation, out of the body of original instinctive impulses which compose the natural self, of a voluntary self in which socialized desires and affections are dominant, and in which the last and controlling principle of deliberation is the love of the objects which will make this transformation possible" (*E*, 357). Therein lay true happiness.

Kant had shared Dewey's dissatisfaction with the hedonistic psychology that underlay utilitarianism. His concern, however, was not that it was an inaccurate description of human desire but that it was all too accurate. Consequently he attempted to formulate an ethics designed to counter the heteronomy of desire. Morality required laws that were unqualified, necessary, and universal—categorical imperatives—and hence moral reason had to free itself from experience and substantive desires that were partial, temporary, and relative. Morality should be the product of a reason that operated "*a priori* to all experience of desire, pleasure, and pain"—a purely formal reason. The moral life, for Kant, lay not in happiness but in following the dictates of this purely formal, transcendental faculty of reason.

The trouble with Kantian practical reason was that it was empty; that is, it did not seem capable of indicating in any given case what in general should be done or, more important, what sort of person one should be. It enjoined one simply to follow the law of reason, which was to follow the law of reason. Kant thought that one could derive some more helpful prescriptions from this law, but Dewey argued that he succeeded in this task only by smuggling some important substantive assumptions into his formalism.[7]

For example, Kant's maxim to act as if the motive of one's action were to become a universal law did not, as Kant believed, inhibit such things as lying and selfishness but only less-than-thoroughgoing lying and selfishness. Dewey observed that "there is no *formal* contradiction in acting always on a motive of theft, unchastity, or insolence. All that Kant's method can require, in strict logic, is that the individual always, under similar circumstances, act from the same motive. Be willing to be always dishonest, or impure, or proud in your intent; achieve consistency in the badness of your motives, and you will be good!" (*E*, 287).

---

7. Students of contemporary political philosophy may recognize in Dewey's critique of Kant elements of Michael Sandel's criticism in *Liberalism and the Limits of Justice* (Cambridge: Cambridge University Press, 1982) of the Kantian self at the heart of John Rawls's *Theory of Justice* (1971). Caught in the same dilemma as Kant, Rawls has been accused of smuggling the substantive assumptions of a welfare-state liberal into what appears to be a set of purely formal procedures for determining what is just.

Kant's examples of universalization and the "contradictions" of such things as suicide, sluggishness, and selfishness showed that he was not relying on purely formal reasoning but on an appeal to the agent to consider the ways in which generalizing a particular concrete end would conflict with other concrete ends to which he was committed; the contradictions involved were not formal but substantive, as was their resolution. Thus what Kant was really getting at with his maxim was that "the right as the *rational* good means that which is harmonious with all the capacities and desires of the self, that which expands them into a harmonious whole" (*E,* 285). Similarly, another famous Kantian maxim—always to treat others as an end and not merely as a means—was an ill-disguised version of the substantive proposition that "the good for any man is that in which the welfare of others counts as much as his own" (*E,* 286). When one put these two maxims together one arrived at the injunction to put the "social relations of an act" foremost in moral reasoning and a definition of right action as "that action which, so far as in it lies, combines into a whole of common interests and purposes the otherwise conflicting aims and interests of different persons" (*E,* 286). Stripped of its apparent formalism, Kantian rationalism once again met on common ground with a utilitarianism stripped of its faulty psychology.

When one exposed the substantive, experiential character of Kant's purportedly formal, transcendental reason, Dewey said, one was left with an important lesson about the place of thought, of judgment, in moral situations. What Kant was really insisting on, from Dewey's perspective, was the use of careful deliberation "for such a revision of desire as it casually and unreflectively presents itself as would make the desire a consistent expression of the whole body of the purposes of the self" (*E,* 287). This argument, as Kant's maxim about others as ends indicated, meant that truly moral judgment was informed by social sympathy, for "sympathy supplies the *pou sto* for an effective, broad, and objective survey of desires, projects, resolves, and deeds" (*E,* 303). In reconstructing Kant's theory, Dewey thus provided a normative ideal of scientific practical reason which went beyond the descriptive analysis of moral judgments he offered in his logical writings. Here, that is, he indicated what sort of character *should* enter into ethical reasoning as a "determinant of *this* content-value of judgment rather than that." *Moral* moral reasoning, in brief, was the judgment of an agent possessed of sympathetic character.

In concluding his "theory of the moral life," Dewey briefly assimilated a third tradition of moral argument to his portrait of the good democrat: the Aristotelian tradition of virtue ethics. "The habits of character whose effect is to sustain and spread the rational or common good," he said, "are virtues" (*E*, 359). Virtues were "numberless" because they were intimately connected with all sorts of individual capacities and endowments and varied with changes in social life. Hence, "every natural capacity, every talent or ability, whether of inquiring mind, of gentle affection, or of executive skill, becomes a virtue when it is turned to account in supporting or extending the fabric of social values" (*E*, 360). Nonetheless, all virtuous action displayed wholeheartedness, persistence, and sincerity and required the exercise of a few cardinal virtues: self-control of passions and appetites in the interest of the largest values at stake in any action ("temperance"); a willingness to face often painful obstacles in the pursuit of the common good ("courage"); fairness, impartiality, and honesty in dealings with others ("justice"); and intelligent, deliberate judgment ("conscientiousness") (*E*, 363–379). This latter cardinal virtue was preeminent because "of all the habits which constitute the character of an individual, the habit of *judging* moral situations is the most important, for this is the key to the *direction* and to the *remaking* of all other habits" (*E*, 375). Wisdom ("the nurse of all the virtues") was knowledge as "intimate and well-founded conviction . . . directly connected with the affairs of common associated life"—thoughtfulness infused with sympathetic affections and producing insight into the common good (*E*, 364, 375–376). Whatever their various virtues, all virtuous men and women were temperate, courageous, just, and, above all, wise, for "genuine conscientiousness is guarantee of all virtue" (*E*, 376). Thus, beginning from three very different theoretical starting points, Dewey arrived in each instance at a similar portrait of the good agent.

The elements of continuity between the theory of the moral life advanced in the *Ethics* and Dewey's earlier idealist ethics are clearly evident. Self-realization was no longer conceived as the human approximation of the divine Self, but the more or less *aesthetic* criteria of self-realization characteristic of Hegelian "expressivism" were still very much in evidence. Self-unification, harmony, wholeness, plentitude, richness, and growth remained the key normative terms for Dewey. "The end, the right and only right end, of man," he argued, "lies in the fullest and freest realization of powers in their appropriate objects" (*E*, 273). Powers were full and free in their realization only when they worked together in a complex, diverse, expansive yet unified whole.

Moral man was akin to an artist or craftsman drawing on his powers of judgment and social sympathy to shape his desires into a well-wrought self.[8]

As we saw, Dewey had begun to move in the early 1890s from a grounding of this ethics of self-realization in idealist metaphysics to an appeal to experimental experience for support, and the *Ethics* offered full-scale confirmation of this naturalization of the moral life. This move, as I noted, deprived his ethics of the certainties and guarantees of transcendental authority, but given the problems this authority was having establishing its credentials as well as the abuses to which human beings claiming access to such authority were liable, this did not disturb him. Good reasons—careful argument and the knowledge provided by modern science—were, he believed, sufficient grounds for his moral vision. Functional psychology, in particular, was friendly to his ethics, which was not surprising since he and James had from the beginning forged an alliance between their moral and scientific concerns. Indeed, in the *Ethics* he came perilously close to the "conceit of knowledge" against which he later warned by seemingly suggesting that self-realization as the harmonizing of the desires and capacities of a growing self was an ideal not only consistent with but *authorized by* psycholo-

---

8. On the "expressivist" tradition in romantic and Hegelian thought see Charles Taylor, *Hegel* (Cambridge: Cambridge University Press, 1975), chap. 1. The aesthetic character of Dewey's ideals of self-realization and "consummatory experience" would, as we will see, become fully explicit in the late 1920s and 1930s. In light of the attention that historians led by Jackson Lears and Warren Susman have recently given to the emergence in this period of an ethic of self-realization at the root of the therapeutic self-seeking of modern consumer culture it is perhaps worth distinguishing Dewey's position from it. First of all, Dewey retained a loyalty to the concept of "character"—the stable dispositions of a coherent self—against the blandishments of emerging notions of a more protean "personality." Although his ethic was profoundly social, it was, to use David Riesman's terms, an "inner"- rather than an "other"-directed ethic, an ethic of democratic gyroscopes rather than radar. Moreover, Dewey explicitly criticized notions of self-realization that made the pursuit of a richer self a self-conscious end in itself. "Every moral act in its outcome marks a development or fulfillment of selfhood," he said. "But the very nature of right action forbids that the self should be the end in the sense of being the conscious aim of moral activity. For there is no way of discovering the nature of the self except in terms of objective ends which fulfill its capacities, and there is no *way* of realizing the self except as it is forgotten in devotion to these objective ends" (*E*, 352). Self-realization was thus something one recognized in retrospect and was, as Lears himself would have it, to be found in "commitments outside the self." See T. J. Jackson Lears, *No Place of Grace: Antimodernism and the Transformation of American Culture, 1880–1920* (New York: Pantheon, 1981), and "From Salvation to Self-Realization: Advertising and the Therapeutic Roots of the Consumer Culture, 1880–1930," in Richard Wightman Fox and Lears, eds., *The Culture of Consumption* (New York: Pantheon, 1983), pp. 1–38; and Warren Susman, "'Personality' and the Making of Twentieth Century Culture," in John Higham and Paul Conkin, eds., *New Directions in American Intellectual History* (Baltimore: Johns Hopkins University Press, 1979), pp. 212–226.

gy. In the end, however, it was less the findings of psychology than his ingenious reconstruction of Bentham and Kant that lent the argument of the *Ethics* its power. If Dewey's ethics was now bereft of claims to certitude, it was not relativistic in any crude or simple sense. Some theories—those most fully decked out in the garb of science and logic and capable of appropriating the best insights of their competitors— were clearly superior to others.[9]

The ideal self in Dewey's ethics was one that Green (and young John Dewey) had made available only to God. By the turn of the century, Dewey confidently, too confidently some argued, was offering it to man. Although he admitted elsewhere that "a wholly consistent self is a practical impossibility," his effusive celebration of the powers of social sympathy in the *Ethics* suggested a rather close approximation was not. It might be said that he was advancing a regulative ideal and not a standard to which he anticipated human action would regularly measure up—"unity of personality," he noted, "is a moral ideal rather than a fact." Yet one might fairly expect that he would have made the consequences of this more explicit. William James, in an essay Dewey admired a great deal, had done so. The good man, he said, "must vote always for the richer universe, for the good which seems most organizable, most fit to enter into complex combinations, most apt to be a member of a more inclusive whole." Yet James couched this ideal in terms that lent it a tragic dimension: "that act must be the best act, accordingly, which makes for the *best whole,* in the sense of awakening the least sum of dissatisfactions. In the casuistic scale, therefore, those ideals must be written highest which *prevail at the least cost,* or by whose realization the least possible number of other ideals are destroyed." Dewey's reluctance to admit with James that "some part of the ideal must be butchered" in the quest for wholeness lent a Pollyanish flavor to his ethics, though Dewey no doubt preferred to think of it as the persistence of a sinewy optimism.[10]

9. In an excellent review George M. Stratton took Dewey to task for his use of psychology to pretend to a conceit of knowledge about the standard of ethical judgment. Although published prior to the *Ethics* and addressed to *The Study of Ethics* (1894), the criticisms of Stratton's review apply to the later book as well. See Stratton, "A Psychological Test of Virtue," *International Journal of Ethics* 11 (1901): 200–213.

10. "The Psychology of Social Behavior" (1914), *Middle Works* 7:404; William James, "The Moral Philosopher and the Moral Life" (1891), *The Will to Believe* (Cambridge: Harvard University Press, 1979), pp. 154–155. On Dewey's appreciation of this essay see JD to William James, 3 June 1891, in Ralph Barton Perry, *The Thought and Character of William James* (Boston: Little Brown, 1935), 2:517. Kloppenberg has an excellent discussion of the differences between James and Dewey on this point in *Uncertain Victory,* pp. 132–144. For a persuasive argument that there is nothing inherent in Dewey's ethics that

The persistence of this optimism was also apparent in the social ideal Dewey more briefly advanced in the *Ethics,* an ideal that naturalized his earlier idealist conception of the ethically sound social organism. This ideal, which he termed "moral democracy," was a macrocosm of the ethical standard guiding individual action. The good society was, like the good self, a diverse yet harmonious, growing yet unified whole, a fully participatory democracy in which the powers and capacities of the individuals that comprised it were harmonized by their cooperative activities into a community that permitted the full and free expression of individuality.

The creation and sustenance of such a society was an end dictated by moral reason: "the good is the activities in which all men participate so that the powers of each are called out, put to use, and reenforced" (*E,* 286). The good agent was a good democrat. To act with the social good as the controlling end-in-view was to act with a regard for the consequences of one's action for the happiness of all those affected by this action. The happiness of others was, generally, the same as one's own: "the expression of the active tendencies of the self in their appropriate objects." Thus one should act with regard for "those conditions and objects which permit others freely to exercise their own powers from their own initiative, reflection, and choice" (*E,* 275). This, Dewey admitted, was a very difficult task:

> The chief thing is the discovery and promotion of those activities and active relationships in which the capacities of all concerned are effectively evoked, exercised, and put to the test. It is difficult for a man to attain a point of view from which steadily to apprehend how his own activities affect and modify those of others. It is hard, that is, to learn to accommodate one's ends to those of others; to adjust, to give way here, and fit in there with respect to our aims. But difficult as this is, it is easy compared with the difficulty of acting *in such a way* for ends which are helpful to others as will call out and make effective their activities. (*E,* 275–276)

Reiterating the critique of paternalistic benevolence he had advanced in the 1890s, Dewey suggested that the difficulties of this task were most clearly evident in the failure of many social reformers to meet its demands because they were committed to doing good *for* rather than *with* others. Moral democracy called not only for the pursuit of worth-

---

is inconsistent with a tragic sensibility see the title essay in Sidney Hook, *Pragmatism and the Tragic Sense of Life* (New York: Basic Books, 1974), pp. 3–25.

while ends but for the pursuit of these ends in ways that enlisted the freely cooperative participation of all concerned. Happiness was an *activity;* one person could not confer it on another. "There is," he declared, "no way to escape or evade this law of happiness, that it resides in the exercise of the active capacities of a voluntary agent; and hence no way to escape or evade the law of a common happiness, that it must reside in the congruous exercise of the voluntary activities of all concerned. The inherent irony and tragedy of much that passes for a high kind of socialized activity is precisely that it seeks a common good by methods which forbid its being either common or good" (*E*, 277).

Dewey continued to hold that moral democracy required that the individual be free in a positive as well as a negative sense. Negative freedom, the freedom from restraint, was only an indispensable condition of what he now termed "effective freedom," the opportunity to make the best of oneself by fully realizing one's capacities. Effective freedom also required as the condition of its exercise "positive control of the resources necessary to carry purposes into effect, possession of the means to satisfy desires; and mental equipment with the trained powers of initiative and reflection required for free preference and for circumspect and far-seeing desires" (*E*, 392). In abandoning idealism, he freed himself from the pitfalls of a transcendent and potentially authoritarian conception of "making the best of oneself" which stood apart from the particular powers and particular desires of particular individuals. He did not, however, abandon the conviction that genuine freedom required access to the means of freedom: "The freedom of an agent who is merely released from direct external obstructions is formal and empty. If he is without resources of personal skill, without control of the tools of achievement, he must inevitably lend himself to carrying out the directions and ideas of others. If he has not powers of deliberation and invention, he must pick up his ideas casually and superficially from the suggestions of his environment and appropriate the notions which the interests of some class insinuate into his mind" (*E*, 392).

Effective freedom mandated equality or, to be more precise, what Dewey termed "equality of opportunity." Although, as I noted earlier, he advocated neither an equality of result in which everyone would be like everyone else nor the absolutely equal distribution of social resources, he meant something quite different from the common meaning of the term. For him it meant providing all the members of a society with the means for self-realization. Because people were different, not everyone would have the same resources—greater resources would be committed to those with greater needs—but everyone would have what he needed. Equality of opportunity did not mean for Dewey that everyone would be given an equal chance to run a competitive race with others nor even that such a race would be handicapped so as to equalize the capacities of the runners. For Dewey, the race metaphor was utterly inappropriate to an ethical social life, for it implied that everyone was attempting to cultivate the same capacities (speed afoot) for an exclusive end (winning the race). If anything, a society was more like a track team in which every individual participated in a different event or, better yet (if I may provide my own favored analogy), like a basketball team in which the different skills of the members of a team worked together for a common end. As he defined it, equality of opportunity should enhance rather than inhibit individuality (E, 487–492).[11]

In 1908 modern industrial society was far from providing the conditions for effective freedom for most of its members, a situation, Dewey argued, that called out for democratic reform that would advance equality of opportunity, foster individuality and self-realization and hence secure effective freedom. Here too, though he confessed that such reform "has yet made little progress," Dewey was flush with a confident "optimism of will" (E, 276). Although he lambasted those who continued to believe in automatic, inevitable progress (especially those who tried to reconceive Darwinian theory as an argument for providential "design on the installment plan"), his faith in "the application of intelligence to the construction of proper social devices" was undiminished, and he seldom displayed the "intellectual pessimism" he believed to be "a necessary part of the moral optimism which actively devotes itself to making the right prevail" (E, 371).[12]

11. To continue the basketball metaphor a bit, it seems to me that the virtues and "internal goods" of this practice (to use philosopher Alasdair MacIntyre's term) are quite helpful in illuminating Dewey's ideals of equality and moral democracy. The game calls upon players to develop some common skills and virtues while at the same time specializing in some of each in accordance with individual talents and desires and to coordinate these talents with other members of their team to advance common goals. Because the best teams effect such coordination, some players play better on different teams and a great *team* like the champion 1977 Portland Trailblazers could handily defeat a more talented but ill-harmonized group like the Philadelphia 76ers. Every team has leaders, and these leaders are akin to Dewey's "moral democrats"—players who use their skills to actively draw out and even enhance the skills of their teammates. For this reason Larry Bird and Magic Johnson, exemplary moral democrats, were the best players in the National Basketball Association in the 1980s, and Michael Jordan, "human highlight film" though he was as an individual talent when he entered the league, is rightly said to have become a better player as he has learned to play this leadership role and assumed the mantle of heir apparent to Bird and Johnson. For a persuasive defense of a notion of equality much like Dewey's as the "truly egalitarian attitude" see John Baker, *Arguing for Equality* (London: Verso, 1987).
12. "The Influence of Darwinism on Philosophy" (1909), *Middle Works* 4:9; "Progress" (1916), *Middle Works* 10:239.

SCHOOLS OF TOMORROW

Until World War I, Dewey's own efforts as a reformer to secure the conditions of effective freedom for others moved in familiar channels. He dearly missed Jane Addams and the fellowship of Hull House and maintained a connection to the social settlement movement by taking part in activities at Lillian Wald's Henry Street Settlement in New York. He also played a minor role in the founding of the National Association for the Advancement of Colored People and, with Alice, was more active in promoting equal education for women and woman's suffrage. Asked to comment on the latter issue, he replied that "it is my belief that women's political enfranchisement is necessary not only to complete the democratic movement, but that till so completed many present evils which superficial observers attribute to democracy instead of to the inadequate character of our democracy, will persist." (He is also said to have marched in a suffrage parade unknowingly carrying a banner thrust into his hands which read "Men can vote! Why can't I?")[13]

The primary focus of Dewey's energies, however, remained the nation's schools. His Laboratory School at Chicago was one of several widely publicized precursors to experiments in "progressive education" under way in the early years of the new century, and he followed these experiments closely, lending his support to those with which he felt an affinity. Although his connections to Teachers College were not partic-

---

13. Dykhuizen, pp. 146, 149–150; "A Symposium on Woman's Suffrage" (1911), *Middle Works* 6:153–154. Because Dewey wrote so little on the "woman question" it is difficult to assess the full dimensions of his thinking on this issue, but the available evidence suggests he maintained both that women had a distinct vocation as homemakers and mothers and that the health of a democratic society required that women play an active role as citizens. Moreover, though he believed the home provided women with a special vocation, he did not believe that they were deviants if they failed to practice this vocation or that they should be confined to this "distinctive career." He also vigorously contended that those women who did work outside the home should be granted a full measure of power in the workplace, and he worked tirelessly toward this end on behalf of a largely female teaching profession. In his own home, though he was an attentive father, a conventional division of roles seemed to have prevailed with Alice, in Dykhuizen's words, doing "most of the cooking, baking, cleaning, knitting, and sewing for the family, also seeing to it that the children met their appointments on time and that her husband did not forget to meet his scheduled class" (p. 149). On Dewey's attitudes on feminist issues see "Is Co-Education Injurious to Girls?" (1911), *Middle Works* 6:155–164; "Professional Spirit among Teachers" (1913), *Middle Works* 7:109–112; "Professional Organization of Teachers" (1916), *Middle Works* 10:168–172; *Ethics*, 516–539; JD to Scudder Klyce, 5 July 1915, 8 May 1920, Scudder Klyce Papers, Library of Congress; Jo Ann Boydston, "John Dewey and the New Feminism," *Teachers College Record* 76 (1975): 441–448; Rosalind Rosenberg, *Beyond Separate Spheres: Intellectual Roots of Modern Feminism* (New Haven: Yale University Press, 1982), pp. 22–23, 45–46, 65; and Susan Laird, "Women and Gender in John Dewey's Philosophy of Education," *Educational Theory* 38 (1988): 111–129.

ularly close in his first ten years at Columbia, he took an interest in the schools associated with the college, especially the kindergarten taught by Patty Smith Hill. He continued as well to produce a steady stream of publications on the problems of education, which culminated with *Democracy and Education* (1916)—not only his most important book on education but, as he said, the closest attempt he had made to summarize his "entire philosophical position."[14]

It was no accident, Dewey observed, that the great philosophers had taken a keen interest in the problems of education because there was "an intimate and vital relation between the need for philosophy and the necessity for education." If philosophy was wisdom—a vision of "the better kind of life to be led"—then consciously guided education, broadly conceived, was the praxis of the philosopher. "If philosophy is to be other than an idle and unverifiable speculation, it must be animated by the conviction that its theory of experience is a hypothesis that is realized only as experience is actually shaped in accord with it. And this realization demands that man's dispositions be made such as to desire and strive for that kind of experience." This shaping of disposition might take place through a variety of agencies, but in modern societies the school, with its captive audience of young, unformed minds, was a crucial arena for the shaping of a philosophy into a "living fact."[15]

Dewey's own philosophy of education in this period did not depart significantly from that of the 1890s, though much that was sketchy and allusive then was developed in fuller and more pointed fashion. He continued to try to mediate the conflict between defenders of traditional studies and methods and the romantic advocates of child-centered education, a conflict that now centered on a debate over "interest and effort," with conservatives defending the virtues of imposing mental discipline on students and romantics calling for reforms that would make the school studies more "interesting" to children. He saw this debate as simply a new version of the familiar false dualism between the child and the curriculum. Both groups supposed the need for external incentives—negative in the case of the traditionalists, positive in the case

14. Dykhuizen, p. 137; JD to Horace M. Kallen, 1 July 1916, Horace M. Kallen Papers, American Jewish Archives, Hebrew Union College, Cincinnati. The term "progressive education" was not widely used as a term of self-identification until after the founding of the Progressive Education Association in 1919, which created an official movement for educational reform, a movement toward which Dewey maintained a somewhat distant and often critical stance, as we shall see.

15. "Philosophy of Education," in "Contributions to *A Cyclopedia of Education*" (1912–13), *Middle Works* 7:298, 306–307.

of the romantics—to enlist children's interest in their schoolwork. Providing such incentives, Dewey argued, was not only ineffective but pernicious, for it made for teaching and learning conducted for the sake of these external rewards and punishments alone. Educators had to realize that the subject matter of the curriculum was, like all accumulated thought, at one time the product of "thinking desires" much like those active, if as yet undisciplined, in the child: "human achievements, appealing to tendencies in childhood which are aiming however unconsciously and partially at similar achievements." Consequently the internal link between the interests of the child and the accumulated knowledge of adults must be forged through the creation of a problematic, educative situation in which "the child has a question of his own, and is actively engaged in seeking and selecting relevant material with which to answer it." Establishing this link would "permit the intrinsic wonder and value which attach to all the realities which lie behind the school curriculum to come home to the child, and to take him up and carry him on in their own onward sweep."[16]

In the context of his war on epistemology and his fuller articulation of the ethical ideals of democracy, Dewey sharpened his descriptions of the "mental equipment" and moral character that schools should develop. He suggested that teachers seeking to unify the multiplicity of their tasks should think of their goal as teaching children how to think, by which, of course, he meant how to think *scientifically* in the broad sense I have described. Scientific judgment, he argued, was not an esoteric technique but a refinement of everyday reflection, and "the native and unspoiled attitude of childhood, marked by ardent curiosity, fertile imagination, and love of experimental inquiry, is near, very near, to the attitude of the scientific mind." In *Democracy and Education* he stressed that "without initiation into the scientific spirit one is not in possession of the best tools which humanity has so far devised for effectively directed reflection." Learning to think scientifically was important not only for future scientists but for all members of a democratic society because scientific intelligence was a resource essential to effective freedom. In a democratic society, every man had to be his own scientist.[17]

16. "The Moral Significance of the Common School Studies" (1909), *Middle Works* 4:206; "Teaching That Does Not Educate" (1909), *Middle Works* 4:203; "Education, Direct and Indirect" (1904), *Middle Works* 3:246. See also *Interest and Effort in Education* (1913), *Middle Works* 7:151–197.

17. *How We Think* (1910), *Middle Works* 6:179; *Democracy and Education* (1916), *Middle Works* 9:197. Page numbers for further references (*DE*) appear in the text. One of the latest in a long line of books blaming Dewey for the failures of American education, E. D. Hirsch, Jr.'s *Cultural Literacy* (Boston: Houghton Mifflin, 1987), takes him to task for

Scientific thinking entailed not only the use of a particular method but participation in a community possessed of specific cognitive virtues, and Dewey believed these virtues—free inquiry, toleration of diverse opinion, and free communication—were necessary if not sufficient attributes of a democratic society and polity. Science not only gave man the means for effective thinking, it also exemplified a social group in which intelligence was "socialized." Because scientific thinking was essentially social, the schools should organize themselves as, in part, little scientific communities—"laboratories of knowledge-making." Children should be engaged in ongoing experimentation, communication, and self-criticism, constituting themselves as a youthful commonwealth of cooperative inquiry.[18]

Just as Dewey's writings on the logic of scientific judgment were aimed, above all, at defending a logic of scientific *moral* judgments, so his call for the teaching of scientific thinking in the schools was directed, above all, at cultivating the capacity of children for the exercise of deliberative, practical reason in moral situations. Although he did not slight the importance of learning to make judgments of fact, he devoted the most ink to learning to make judgments of value. Thus, though he was a firm advocate of instruction in the sciences as subject matter, he urged teachers to think of these subjects not as bodies of "ready-made knowledge" but as the fruits of a method that would enhance moral reasoning. "If ever we are to be governed by intelligence, not by things and by words," he said, "science must have something to say about *what* we do, and not merely about *how* we may do it most easily

giving pride of place to instruction in "how to think" at the expense of a consideration of the appropriate content of the curriculum of schools in a democratic society, particularly that body of shared knowledge essential to "cultural literacy." As I hope my account of Dewey's educational thought has indicated, he was not indifferent to the substance of the curriculum and an advocate of "content-neutral" education (nor was he, as Hirsch contends, "a disciple of Rousseau"). Nonetheless, there is something to Hirsch's criticism, for Dewey had very little to say about the particular facts that children should learn. I believe Dewey would have been impressed by the research Hirsch marshals to substantiate a link between such skills as reading comprehension and possession of a "common culture." Hirsch persuasively argues that the teaching of such cultural information is not elitist or incompatible with cultural pluralism (if not separatism), and rightly contends that his call for education in cultural literacy is a democratic proposal. It is, I would say, a reform consistent with Dewey's own vision of American democracy, though I suspect Dewey would be wary of the pedagogy of mechanical information provision which Hirsch's list of "What Literate Americans Know" invites. Despite its distortions of Dewey's thinking, Hirsch's book is, unlike the more celebrated attack on American education with which it is often lumped, Allan Bloom's *Closing of the American Mind* (New York: Simon and Schuster, 1987), a friendly companion to *Democracy and Education*.

18. "Science as Subject-Matter and as Method" (1910), *Middle Works* 6:79.

and economically."[19] Thus the subject to which he devoted the most attention was not the sciences but *history*, because he believed that history was "the most effective conscious tool" for moral instruction. If history was taught not as a mere body of facts about the past but as "indirect sociology" it would "enable the child to appreciate the values of social life, to see in imagination the forces which favor men's effective cooperation with one another, to understand the sorts of character that help and that hold back."[20]

As the remarks suggest, the formation of democratic character remained very much at the heart of Dewey's philosophy of education, though this commitment was occasionally obscured by his discussion of the social aims of education in generic fashion. Statements bereft of further elaboration in which he contended that schools should cultivate in children an interest in "perceiving whatever makes for social order and progress, and in carrying those principles into execution" could (and did) make for a variety of interpretations by his readers of the sort of character to be developed, depending on their competing definitions of "social order" and "progress."[21]

Such ambiguities were, however, altogether absent from *Democracy*

19. "Science as Subject-Matter and as Method," pp. 78–79. Remarks like this are most often misinterpreted to indicate that Dewey believed scientific thinking could determine the ends of the moral life in some conclusive, matter-of-fact way. But Dewey was arguing rather that scientific judgment had something to say not in determining, in this strict fashion, what sort of life one should lead but in estimating the consequences of whatever ends one chose to pursue and the means with which one chose to pursue them in order that the choices one made were reflective rather than impulsive (or, as he later put it, desirable rather than merely desired). As we have seen, he believed the ends one chose were determined by one's character, and insofar as democratic character was infused with sympathy and hence marked by a disposition for the widest possible consideration of the consequences of action it was particularly well suited to the effective exercise of scientific practical reason.

20. "The Moral Significance of the Common School Studies," p. 208; "History for the Educator" (1909), *Middle Works* 4:192. See also *Moral Principles in Education* (1909), *Middle Works* 4:281–283 and *Democracy and Education*, pp. 215–226.

21. *Moral Principles in Education*. p. 274. See also "The Moral Significance of the Common School Studies," p. 213. In one essay published prior to *Democracy and Education* ("Education from a Social Perspective" [1913], *Middle Works* 7:113–127), Dewey did explicitly seek to deflect any misunderstanding of his position, noting that the first task in the advancement of a "social perspective" on education was to "define exactly how we conceive the term 'society'" and identifying his own perspective with a democratic ethos very much at odds with the prevailing social order. As he implied there, the term "social" for him was not merely descriptive but normative; he held that inherent in all social life was an intimation of what it would be at its best, that is, as "truly" social (he made a similar argument in *Democracy and Education* [87–94] and later in *The Public and Its Problems* when he declared that democracy was "the idea of community life itself"). However, Dewey's readers must be forgiven if they overlooked this forceful essay, for it was published in a French journal of education and went untranslated until 1965.

and Education, which opened with a discussion of the way in which all societies utilized the education of children as a means of "social control" by which adults consciously shaped the dispositions of children, but went on to argue that "the conception of education as a social process and function has no definite meaning until we define the kind of society we have in mind" (*DE,* 4–45, 103). Dewey's concern, and he presumed the concern of his fellow Americans, was with "the ideas implied in a democratic society" and the application of these to the problems of education (*DE,* 3). Democratic societies sought to cultivate democratic dispositions in children, to make them good democrats. As in the case of teaching children how to think, the goal not to force "a line of action contrary to natural inclinations" but to configure these inclinations one way rather than another (*DE,* 41). The best way to do this was to initiate school children from the beginning in the form of social life, the "mode of associated living" characteristic of a democracy: a community of full participation and "conjoint communicated experience" in which social sympathy and deliberative moral reason would develop (*DE,* 93). Thus classrooms in a democracy had to be not only communities of inquiry but *democratic* communities of inquiry.[22]

The principal obstacle to democratic education, Dewey argued, was the powerful alliance of class privilege with philosophies of education (beginning with Plato) which sharply divided mind and body, theory

22. Dewey's conception of democratic education as a variant of a generic process of "social control" grounded in the shaping of children's character by adults may seem commonplace, but it is the source of charges by some historians that he was endorsing an insidious and subtle form of "indoctrination" or "manipulation." Christopher Lasch, for example, observes of Dewey and other progressive intellectuals that "the manipulative note was rarely absent from their writings: the insistence that men could best be controlled and directed not by the old crude method of force but by 'education' in its broadest sense." The progressives' faith in education, he says, often served as a rationalization for "a crude will to power on the part of the intellectuals themselves" (Lasch, *The New Radicalism in America* [New York: Vintage, 1965], pp. 146, 169). This argument is flawed in two fundamental respects. First, it reflects a misunderstanding of the meaning of "social control" in the early twentieth century by treating it as a phrase that necessarily implied coercion and manipulation. Second, it fails to distinguish between education that withholds from children (or other adults) full knowledge of what teachers are trying to do to them and education that, as Dewey advocated, is explicit about its ends and openly attempts to enlist the "participating disposition" of children (or other adults) in the pursuit of those ends. I would not, by any means, deny that there were progressive intellectuals who were partisans of manipulation, only that Dewey was among them. There is no doubt that Dewey did what he could to secure schools (and other insitutions) as sites for the testing of his moral vision, but because of his belief that for one to promote the good of others one must do so *with* rather than *for* them, he usually sought democratic means to this democratic end—the notable exception here being his activism in World War I (see Chapter 7, especially the discussion of the Polish-American project), and the grounds for criticism of manipulative power are to be found in his ethics.

and practice, culture and utility. To a considerable degree, prevailing educational practice was the institutionalization of the philosophy of profoundly antidemocratic thinkers. Especially pernicious among educators was the distinction between culture and utility, a dualism "itself imbedded in a social dualism: the distinction between the working class and the leisure class." On the basis of this distinction, two separate and disparate types of education emerged: one—rarely termed "education"—for those who worked with their hands and one for those who worked with their minds or did not work at all. This alliance of privilege and philosophy which equated "the educated class and the ruling class" required that democrats must recognize that "the reconstruction of philosophy, of education, and of social ideas and methods thus go hand in hand" (*DE*, 341): "The price that democratic societies will have to pay for their continuing health is the elimination of an oligarchy— the most exclusive and dangerous of all—that attempts to monopolize the benefits of intelligence and of the best methods for the profit of a few privileged ones, while practical labor, requiring less spiritual effort and less initiative remains the lot of the great majority. These distinctions will ultimately disappear the day that, under the influence of education, science and practical activity are joined together forever." Here Dewey took note of the battles he himself was waging on two fronts and the relationship between them. In the pages of the philosophical journals, he advanced the argument that all knowledge was, in a broad sense, practical; man was "thinking desire." In education, the arena of philosophical praxis, he called for the extension to all children of the tools of social intelligence. The results of these campaigns, if successful, he said, would "not involve a superficial adaptation of the existing system but a radical change in foundation and aim: a revolution."[23]

LEARNING TO EARN

Just how radical Dewey's program for democratic education was became apparent in the arguments he advanced in the debate over vocational education which occupied American educators in the decade before World War I. This debate was touched off in 1906 by the report of the Massachusetts Commission on Industrial and Technical Education which found that thousands of the state's young adolescents did

23. "Education from a Social Perspective," pp. 115–116, 127, 120.

not attend school and were stuck in dead-end industrial jobs without hope of advancement because they lacked the necessary skills. Many of those interviewed indicated that they had left school not because of pressure to contribute to the income of their families but because they were alienated by a school curriculum that had little to offer them. The report concluded that schools were not equipping children with "industrial intelligence" and called for a shift in the orientation of secondary schools from "cultural" to vocational education. This study galvanized critics of the schools, many of whom had cast an admiring glance at Germany, where those deemed unsuited for university study were channeled into vocational and technical education. In its wake an aggressive campaign developed for vocational training programs, headed by a powerful and effective lobbying organization, the National Society for the Promotion of Industrial Education, and supported by a diverse range of interest groups including not only educators but the National Association of Manufacturers, the Chamber of Commerce, the American Federation of Labor, major farm organizations, and settlement workers. This campaign culminated in the passage of the Smith-Hughes Act in 1917, which provided federal support for vocational education. As an important part of a broader effort to address the educational needs of a corporate industrial society, the movement for vocational education helped work a remarkable transformation of the American high school from an elite institution closely tied to the nation's leading colleges and enrolling a mere 6.7 percent of those fourteen to seventeen years of age to an institution of mass education enrolling 32.3 percent of that population and committed to fostering the social efficiency of the children of the nation's working class.[24]

24. *Report of the Massachusetts Commission on Industrial and Technical Education* (1906) quoted in Edward A. Krug, *The Shaping of the American High School, 1880–1920* (Madison: University of Wisconsin Press, 1969), p. 220; Robert L. Church and Michael Sedlak, *Education in the United States: An Interpretive History* (New York: Free Press, 1976), pp. 304–305, 289. The industrial education movement has attracted a great of attention from historians. See Sol Cohen, "The Industrial Education Movement, 1906–1917," *American Quarterly* 20 (1968): 95–110; Berenice M. Fisher, *Industrial Education: American Ideals and Institutions* (Madison: University of Wisconsin Press, 1967); James B. Gilbert, *Work without Salvation: America's Intellectuals and Industrial Alienation, 1880–1910* (Baltimore: Johns Hopkins University Press, 1977), chap. 10; W. Norton Grubb and Marvin Lazerson, eds., *American Education and Vocationalism: Documents in Vocational Education, 1870–1970* (New York: Teachers College Press, 1974); David J. Hogan, *Class and Reform: School and Society in Chicago, 1880–1930* (Philadelphia: University of Pennsylvania Press, 1985), chap. 4; Harvey Kantor, *Learning to Earn: School, Work, and Reform in California, 1880–1930* (Madison: University of Wisconsin Press, 1988); Harvey Kantor and David Tyack, eds., *Work, Youth, and Schooling: Historical Perspectives on Vocationalism in American Education* (Stanford: Stanford University Press, 1982); Daniel T. Rodgers, *The Work Ethic in Indus-*

Although vocational education won wide support, the supporters profoundly disagreed about the direction such industrial training should take. The most prominent issue was whether industrial education should be integrated into the existing public school system or made a separate system under separate control. Business and labor split cleanly on this issue, with businessmen acting as the strongest advocates of a dual system.

Dewey was one of the most vocal opponents of the dual system. He feared, above all, that the kind of vocational education favored by businessmen and their allies was a form of class education which would make the schools a more efficient agency for the reproduction of an undemocratic society. The issue of industrial education, he said, was of great importance for the future of democracy. "Its right development will do more to make public education truly democratic than any other agency now under consideration. Its wrong treatment will as surely accentuate all undemocratic tendencies in our present situation, by fostering and strengthening class divisions in school and out." He noted that "those who believe in the continued existence of what they are pleased to call the 'lower classes' or the 'laboring classes' would naturally rejoice to have schools in which these 'classes' would be segregated. And some employers of labor would doubtless rejoice to have schools, supported by public taxation, supply them with additional food for their mills." Everyone else, however, "should be united against every proposition, in whatever form advanced, to separate training of employees from training for citizenship, training of intelligence and character from training for narrow, industrial efficiency."[25]

trial America, 1850–1920 (Chicago: University of Chicago Press, 1978), pp. 81–87; Selwyn K. Troen, "The Discovery of the Adolescent by American Educational Reformers, 1900–1920: An Economic Perspective," in Lawrence Stone, ed., *Schooling and Society* (Baltimore: Johns Hopkins University Press, 1976), pp. 239–251; David Tyack, *The One Best System* (Cambridge: Harvard University Press, 1974), pp. 182–198; and Arthur G. Wirth, *Education in the Technological Society: The Vocational-Liberal Studies Controversy in the Early Twentieth Century* (Scranton, Pa.: Intertext, 1972).

25. "Some Dangers in the Present Movement for Industrial Education" (1913), *Middle Works* 7:99, 102. See also "Should Michigan Have Vocational Education under 'Unit' or 'Dual' Control?" (1913), *Middle Works* 7:85–92; "A Policy of Industrial Education (1914), *Middle Works* 7:93–97; "Industrial Education and Democracy" (1913), *Middle Works* 7:104–105; "Industrial Education—A Wrong Kind" (1915), *Middle Works* 8:117–122; "Splitting Up the School System" (1915), *Middle Works* 8:123–127; "The Need of an Industrial Education in an Industrial Democracy" (1916), *Middle Works* 10:137–143; "Learning to Earn: The Place of Vocational Education in a Comprehensive Scheme of Public Education" (1917), *Middle Works* 10:144–150; "Vocational Education" (1916), *Middle Works* 10:303–304. See also Randolph Bourne, "In the Mind of the Worker," *Atlantic*, March 1914: 375–382.

Dewey's criticisms brought a wounded response from the Commissioner of Education in Massachusetts, David Snedden, a leading proponent of a dual system of industrial education and a hard-nosed preacher of the gospel of efficiency. Those who had been seeking to promote "the development of sound vocational education," he said, were used to attacks from highbrow academic defenders of Culture but "to find Dr. Dewey apparently giving aid and comfort to the opponents of a broader, richer and more effective program of education, and apparently misapprehending the motives of many of those who advocate the extension of vocational schools designed for that purpose is discouraging."[26]

Dewey responded that Snedden had misunderstood his criticisms and overlooked the "profoundly political and social" differences that separated them: "The kind of vocational education in which I am interested is not one which will adapt workers to the existing industrial regime; I am not sufficiently in love with the regime for that. It seems to me that the business of all who would not be educational timeservers is to resist every move in this direction, and to strive for a kind of vocational education which will first alter the existing industrial system, and ultimately transform it."[27]

As these comments suggest, beneath Dewey's opposition to the proposal for dual control lay a deeper antagonism to the dominant perspective on vocational education and a radical vision of industrial democracy. "I object," he told Snedden, "to regarding as vocational education any training which does not have as its supreme regard the development of such intelligent initiative, ingenuity, and executive capacity as shall make workers, as far as they may be, the masters of their own industrial fate." Most American workers, Dewey observed, had no direct interest in their work and were merely the tools of their employers, appendages of the machines they tended. He told a gathering of teachers that "for some years I preserved a little piece of cast iron taken from a typical American factory, one of our large agricultural machinery works. I preserved it as a

26. David Snedden, "Vocational Education," *New Republic*, 15 May 1915: 40. Walter Drost, *David Snedden and Education for Social Efficiency* (Madison: University of Wisconsin Press, 1967), is an excellent biography. See also Herbert M. Kliebard, *The Struggle for the American Curriculum, 1893–1958* (Boston: Routledge and Kegan Paul, 1986), chap. 4.

27. "Education vs. Trade-Training: Reply to David Snedden" (1915), *Middle Works* 8:412. A good discussion of the Dewey-Snedden debate is Arthur G. Wirth, "Philosophical Issues in the Vocational-Liberal Studies Controversy (1900–1917): John Dewey vs. the Social Efficiency Philosophers," *Studies in Philosophy and Education* 8 (1974): 169–182. Dewey and other advocates of a single system won a Pyrrhic victory in this controversy. Vocational education was incorporated into the existing public school system, but the result, as many have noted, was the development of class education *within* this system.

sort of Exhibit A of our social and educational status. The iron came out of the casting with a little roughness upon it which had to be smoothed before it could become part of the belt for which it was designed. A boy of fifteen or sixteen spent his working day in grinding off this slight roughness—grinding at a rate of one a minute for every minute of his day." The "stupefying monotony," routine, and total lack of intellectual and imaginative content of such work was, Dewey contended, endemic to a class society.[28] Such workers "do what they do, not freely and intelligently, but for the sake of the wage earned." Their activity was "not free because not freely participated in." Industrial education designed to train children for such work was "illiberal and immoral" (DE, 269).

Dewey had, of course, been a long-standing proponent of the integration of manual training into the curriculum; "occupations" were at the center of life in the Dewey School. But manual training was not, for him, trade training but rather a key component of a pedagogy that "psychologized" the curriculum by tying together a body of knowledge and the interests of the child—a task often best served by such activities as carpentry, cooking, and weaving which conjoined hand and mind. The sort of vocational education advocated by Snedden and other "administrative progressives" would continue to divide the education of hand and mind and perpetuate the class divisions it reflected. This was "to treat the schools as an agency for transferring the older division of labor and leisure, culture and service, mind and body, directed and directive class, into a society nominally democratic" (DE, 328). Administrative progressives were in a sense the unknowing and third-rate descendants of Plato, who had argued that individuals fell into three fixed social classes (laborers and merchants, citizen subjects, and philosopher kings) by virtue of the particular faculties and dispositions that predominated in their nature (appetites, courage, reason) and had devised a distinct education for each (DE, 127, 96).[29]

The sort of "vocational" education Dewey had in mind would prepare children for rewarding work in which they would be more than factors of production and, in so doing, "help on such a reorganization of industry as will change it from a feudalistic to a democratic social order." He contended that "an education which acknowledges the full intellectual and social meaning of a vocation would include instruction

28. "Education vs. Trade-Training," p. 411; "Culture and Industry in Education" (1906), Middle Works 3:288.
29. I borrow the term "administrative progressives" from David Tyack. See The One Best System, pp. 126–133, 177–198, and Tyack and Elisabeth Hansot, Managers of Virtue: Public School Leadership in America, 1820–1980 (New York: Basic Books, 1982), pt. 2.

in the historic background of present conditions; training in science to give intelligence and initiative in dealing with material and agencies of production; and study of economics, civics, and politics, to bring the future worker in touch with the problems of the day and the various methods proposed for its improvement. Above all, it would train power of readaptation to changing conditions so that future workers would not become blindly subject to a fate imposed upon them" (*DE*, 328). Such an education would prepare children not only for their work in life but for the other functions and vocations required of them in a democratic society, including citizenship. It would obliterate distinctions between culture and utility by providing all children with an education that integrated the two. Nothing drew Dewey's contempt more than the claims of businessmen and technocratic reformers in the vocational movement that their plans were more democratic than existing educational practice because they made no effort to force "culture" down the throats of the working class and provided children of that class with "no-frills" schooling suited to their station in life. "Nothing in the history of education is more touching," he commented, "than to hear some successful leaders denounce as undemocratic the attempts to give all the children at public expense the fuller education which their own children enjoy as a matter of course."[30]

Dewey's writings on vocational education did signal an important shift in emphasis in his thinking about industrial democracy. In the 1890s, despite the critique of wage labor implicit in the "vocations" of the Laboratory School, he had suggested that all that was required to enable industrial workers to have morally satisfying work was to "socialize" the perspective of employers and employees and thereby give each a full sense of how the work they did fit into the larger productive and social relations of their society. "The world in which most of us live," he wrote in *School and Society* (1899), "is a world in which everyone has a calling and occupation, something to do. Some are managers and others are subordinates. But the great thing for one as for the other is that each shall have had the education which enables him to see within his daily work all there is in it of large and human significance."[31] In *Democracy and Education* he still maintained that it was important for workers to have this sense of significance, but now he argued further that they must also have *control* of their work if this work was to contribute to their self-realization, an argument posing a more fundamen-

---

30. "Learning to Earn," pp. 150, 146.
31. *School and Society* (1899), *Middle Works* 1:16.

tal challenge to the social relations of capitalist production, especially as these had been "rationalized" by scientific management since the 1890s by a process that, as radical labor leader Bill Haywood put it, took the brains out from under the workman's cap."The great majority of workers," Dewey observed, "have no insight into the social aims of their pursuits and no direct personal interest in them. The results actually achieved are not the ends of *their* actions, but only of their employers." The work could not be free until they had "direct participation in control" (*DE*, 268–269). That Dewey believed that the kind of participation essential to workers' freedom was not possible in a capitalist society was suggested by his remark that the intellectual and emotional limitation on the work of both employers and workers was "inevitable" when the "animating motive is desire for private profit or personal power" (*DE*, 327–328).

What remained absent in the treatment of industrial work in *Democracy and Education* and thereby limited its radicalism was anything resembling a *political* strategy for the redistribution of power Dewey proposed. He remained wedded to moral exhortation as the sole means to ends that required democratic politics. He advanced impeccable arguments about the ways in which industrial capitalism directed the intelligence not only of workers but also of capitalists and managers into "non-humane, non-liberal channels," yet relied all too heavily on the force of such arguments to overcome the appeal of the tangible, if morally shortsighted benefits employers derived from exploitation (*DE*, 327). Thus, though he now argued that industrial democracy necessitated structural changes in the distribution of power in the workplace, he had yet to envision a politics commensurate with this radical vision.

The differences between Dewey and the "administrative progressives" were not always as clear as they were in the debate with Snedden. Because he employed—with different definitions—many of the same terms, like "social efficiency," superficial observers (and some subsequent historians), could see him as their ally rather than their deadly enemy. More important, some of the pedagogical reforms he advocated were, when removed from the context of his larger democratic philosophy, adaptable to quite different purposes, including those of the administrative progressives. Consequently, some of the "schools of tomorrow" he saw springing up in the antebellum decade were, despite their adoption of some Deweyan reforms, very much "schools of today."

The best case in point was the school system of Gary, Indiana, which Dewey and his daughter Evelyn applauded in *Schools of Tomorrow* (1915) and which Dewey's disciples including Alice Barrows and Randolph Bourne celebrated as, in Barrows's words, evidence that "Dewey's philosophy could be put into practice on a large scale in the public schools." Built from scratch in the new industrial city founded by U.S. Steel in 1906, the Gary system was the creation of Superintendent of Schools William A. Wirt, an imaginative and energetic administrative progressive who took full advantage of this rare opportunity to design an urban school system and instituted the "Gary Plan," the most widely discussed of progressive educational innovations.[32]

At the heart of the Gary Plan was the "platoon system," in which students in each school were divided into two platoons. For part of the day students in one platoon filled classrooms where they studied traditional academic subjects, while students in the other platoon worked in the school shops, exercised in the gymnasium or swimming pool or on the playing fields, studied in the library or laboratories, participated in fine arts activities, went on field trips, or took part in communal gatherings in the school auditorium. Later in the school day the two platoons switched roles. This division accommodated twice as many students in school buildings as would ordinarily be the case and permitted full-time use of all the facilities of the school plant (programs extended into the evening, when well-attended adult education classes were held). The flexibility of this scheduling also enabled the schools to adapt to the needs of individual children by creating a schedule that allowed for remedial work, additional work in areas of special interest, Saturday classes, and part-time or full-time, full-year attendance.

Although these features of the Gary schools were appreciatively noted by Dewey and the Deweyans, it was Wirt's effort to make each of his schools "a self-sustaining child community" which most captured their imagination. They liked the way children were allowed to proceed through the curriculum at their own pace and the "helper system" in which older children aided younger students with their work. Above all, Dewey and Bourne were excited by the combination of intellectual and practical instruction in Gary. In the schools' manual training facilities children learned a variety of skills, including printing, electrical

32. Barrows quoted in Ronald D. Cohen and Raymond A. Mohl, *The Paradox of Progressive Education: The Gary Plan and Urban Schooling* (Port Washington, N.Y.: Kennikat Press, 1979), p. 25. This is the fullest historical study of the Gary Plan, but see also Raymond Callahan, *Education and the Cult of Efficiency* (Chicago: University of Chicago Press, 1962), chap. 6; Lawrence Cremin, *The Transformation of the School: Progressivism in American Education, 1876–1957* (New York: Vintage, 1964), pp. 153–160; and Christopher Lasch, "Educational Structures and Cultural Fragmentation," in Lasch, *World of Nations* (New York: Knopf, 1973), pp. 256–261.

repair, carpentry, and metalworking, and they put these skills to use in the school itself. They built desks, tables, bookcases, and cabinets, handled all of the schools' printing needs, made repairs on buildings, took care of school grounds, helped prepare school lunches, and applied the skills they learned in commercial courses in the administrative routines of the schools. The aim of vocational education of this sort, Dewey said, "is not to hurry the preparation of the individual pupil for his individual trade" but "to give practical value to the theoretical knowledge that every pupil should have, and to give him an understanding of the conditions and institutions of his environment." And it did so, he believed, in the context of a fully participatory, little democratic commonwealth.[33]

Administrative progressives, given to discussions of schooling in terms of "raw material and finished products," were much taken with the organizational efficiencies of the platoon system but were often critical of the inefficiency of the Deweyan features of the schools, commenting, for example, on the poor spelling and arithmetic errors of student administrators. More important, though, is the different perspective Wirt had on what Dewey and others took to be a school system at odds with the dominant thrust of industrial education. Wirt valued his little commonwealth of student/workers less as a participatory democracy than as a way of indoctrinating children in the work ethic and as a means of cutting the costs of maintenance of the expansive facilities the platoon system required. Moreover, he required children to learn a wide variety of manual skills not as a way of "giving practical value to theoretical knowledge" at odds with trade training but because he thought the development of aptitude in a variety of skills was a more effective kind of trade training. It is not then surprising that there is little evidence that U.S. Steel exercised much direct influence on Wirt's program; the corporation had no need to do so since his values were fully in accord with its own. Wirt's conception of social efficiency was very much that which Dewey attacked as "defined in terms of rendering external service to others" and distant from Dewey's own notion of social efficiency as "the cultivation of power to join freely and fully in

33. JD and Evelyn Dewey, *Schools of Tomorrow* (1915), *Middle Works* 8:320–328, 365–378, 402–403. See also Randolph Bourne, *The Gary Schools* (Cambridge: M.I.T. Press, 1970, originally published in 1916). In the case of *Schools of Tomorrow* its dual authorship may be of significance since Dewey himself did not visit any of the schools described in the book except one in New York, leaving the task of research and description to Evelyn. Firsthand observation might have led to a more critical perspective on Wirt's handiwork, though one cannot imagine that he could have chosen two observers who saw more as with his own eyes than his daughter and Bourne did.

shared or common activities" (*DE*, 130). As two recent historians of the Gary Plan observe, Wirt "wanted an educated populace, but educated to take orders cheerfully and positively; above all he desired order, voluntary or otherwise." Thus the Gary schools showed that some of the innovative pedagogical methods that emerged from Dewey's laboratory could be put to social uses quite other than those he intended.[34]

More often than not, however, the differences between Dewey and the administrative progressives were not obscured. Reviewing *Democracy and Education* in 1918, one hard-boiled sociologist remarked critically that "while it is true that citizens of a democracy need to be taught to think, it is even more important, especially in the present crisis, that they be trained to revere and to obey." He took comfort in the fact that Dewey's book would be "greatly handicapt" because it was too hard for the average educator to read.[35]

A New Republic

As the foregoing discussion suggests, the task of placing Dewey's thought in this period in the larger context of "progressivism" is rendered difficult by the utter lack of consensus among historians of the reform initiatives of the early twentieth century about what exactly progressivism was. Some have argued it was a movement of "old middle class" reformers suffering from "status-anxiety" who sought to use state power to curb the threat both of the growing power of big business and of an immigrant working class which had them caught in an uncomfortable squeeze. Others have contended that it was a movement of confident, technocratic, "new middle class" professionals eager to seize power in state and society in the name of expertise and efficiency. Still others have argued that progressive reform was a conservative movement led by big business, rationalized by "corporate liberal" intellectuals, and designed to create a "political capitalism" friendly to the giant corporation. Not all of these historians can be right, and thus an assessment of Dewey's "progressivism" requires a bit of the sort of historiographical discussion I have otherwise tried to confine to my notes.[36]

34. Cohen and Mohl, *Paradox of Progressive Education*, p. 17. For a typical example of the response of administrative progressives to the Gary Plan see the 1918 report by Abraham Flexner and Frank P. Bachman republished in the reprint edition of Bourne's *Gary Schools*, pp. 217–313.

35. Ross Finney as quoted in Krug, *Shaping of the American High School*, p. 422.

36. The classic versions of these arguments are (1) Richard Hofstadter, *The Age of Reform* (New York: Vintage, 1955), chaps. 4–7; (2) Samuel Hays, *The Response to Industrial-*

Of late, there seems to be general agreement among historians that the obituary Peter Filene offered in 1970 for progressivism as a *movement*—a self-conscious collective group with a clear membership and consistent and shared goals—was appropriate, but no clear alternative has emerged. Although this is not the place to argue fully the case for any such alternative, I would like to offer a sketch of the terrain of American reform in the period between 1890 and World War I in order to give some sense of where I think Dewey belongs among his contemporaries.[37]

First of all, I think one should look at reform in this period as the product of not one but three efforts to reshape the contours of American society: the reconstruction of American capitalism by the leaders of the nation's large corporations and their allies; a wide variety of middle-class reform initiatives for which we might reserve the term "progressivism"; and the attempt of American labor organizations ranging from American Federation of Labor trade unions to the syndicalists of the Industrial Workers of the World to preserve the traditional prerogatives of labor and, in some cases, to establish new forms of workers' control. Each of these reform efforts was marked by internal divisions and by complicated relationships of opposition and cooperation with the other two. They did share in what Martin Sklar has termed the "anti-competitive consensus," a belief in the need to curb the effects of an unregulated competitive market; the only real "conservatives" in this era were the defenders of proprietary, competitive capitalism, and even they made considerable concessions to the critique of the market.[38]

---

ism (Chicago: University of Chicago Press, 1957), and Robert Wiebe, *The Search for Order, 1877–1920* (New York: Hill and Wang, 1967); and (3) Gabriel Kolko, *The Triumph of Conservatism* (New York: Free Press, 1963), and James Weinstein, *The Corporate Ideal in the Liberal State* (Boston: Beacon Press, 1968). There are also useful, if conflicting, essays on the historiography of progressivism. See Robert Wiebe, "The Progressive Years, 1900–1917," in William H. Cartwright and Richard L. Watson, Jr., eds, *The Reinterpretation of American History and Culture* (Washington, D.C.: National Council for Social Studies, 1973), pp. 425–442; David M. Kennedy, "Overview: The Progressive Era," *Historian* 37 (1975): 453–468; John D. Buenker, John C. Burnham, and Robert M. Crunden, *Progressivism* (Cambridge, Mass.: Schenkman, 1977); Daniel T. Rodgers, "In Search of Progressivism," *Reviews in American History* 10 (1982): 113–132; and Richard L. McCormick, "Progressivism: A Contemporary Reassessment," in McCormick, *The Party Period and Public Policy* (New York: Oxford University Press, 1986), pp. 263–288.

37. Peter Filene, "An Obituary for the 'Progressive Movement,'" *American Quarterly* 22 (1970): 20–34.

38. Martin J. Sklar, *The Corporate Reconstruction of American Capitalism, 1890–1916: The Market, the Law and Politics* (Cambridge: Cambridge University Press, 1988), p. 17. Although Sklar focuses exclusively on the first of these reform efforts, this sketch owes a great deal to his argument—a sophisticated rethinking of the "corporate liberal" view of progressivism. I have also found Michael McGerr's unpublished paper sketching out

Within the loose constraints of this anticompetitive consensus, ideological differences within each reform camp were substantial, and nowhere more substantial than among the middle-class progressives, as is evident in the unsuccessful efforts of historians to characterize progressivism as an ideology grounded simply in either old middle-class Protestant moralism or the new middle-class scientific gospel of efficiency. Some progressives spoke one of these "languages of social vision and discontent" and some the other—and many spoke both simultaneously. Moreover, each of these languages and its combinations was loose enough to allow for the articulation of decidedly different social ideals. This looseness of progressive language has contributed to the shortcomings of efforts to categorize Dewey.[39]

Robert Crunden, for example, has seen Dewey as exemplifying the "displaced Protestantism" he finds at the heart of progressivism. Dewey was one of "a group of people who had internalized Protestant moral norms, but who often could not find psychological satisfaction within the ministry, or even within religious institutions generally" and consequently "displaced" this moral concern in social reform. Much can be said for this argument. As we have seen, there is a great deal of continuity in Dewey's ethical thought despite his break with institutional religion. It is not, I think, too extreme to say with Crunden that for Dewey the school replaced the church in the 1890s as "the key institution in the saving of souls for democracy."[40]

---

some of the arguments of a forthcoming book on the period quite helpful, though his characterization of middle-class progressivism as an "intentionally conservative program" leaves no place for the likes of Dewey ("Confinement, Liberation, and Social Class: Synthesizing Early Twentieth-Century American History," paper delivered at the Annual Meeting of the American Historical Association, December 1986). On labor activism in the period see David Montgomery, *The Fall of the House of Labor* (Cambridge: Cambridge University Press, 1987).

39. The phrase "languages of social vision and discontent" is Daniel Rodgers's ("In Search of Progressivism," p. 123). On the progressives as Protestant moralists see Robert M. Crunden, *Ministers of Reform: The Progressives' Achievement in American Civilization, 1889–1920* (New York: Basic Books, 1982). On them as proponents of science and bureaucratic thought see Wiebe, *Search for Reform*, chap. 6; Samuel Haber, *Efficiency and Uplift: Scientific Management in the Progressive Era, 1890–1920* (Chicago: University of Chicago Press, 1964); and R. Jeffrey Lustig, *Corporate Liberalism: The Origins of Modern American Political Theory, 1890–1920* (Berkeley: University of California, 1982). A recent survey that sharply divides progressives into these two groups, yet often admits the artificiality of the division, is David Danbom, *"The World of Hope": Progressives and the Struggle for an Ethical Public Life* (Philadelphia: Temple University Press, 1987). Danbom's book is marked by a refreshing absence of contempt for the moral concern of his favored progressives.

40. Robert M. Crunden, "Essay," in Buenker, Burnham, and Crunden, *Progressivism*, pp. 75–76, 96.

On the other hand, as I have indicated, Dewey's break with conventional Protestant notions of progress and the absolute ethical authority of God had important consequences for his thought. Most important, perhaps, this break sharpened his critique of the sort of paternalistic benevolence that clothed itself in this authority and was prominent among many Protestant progressive reformers, displaced or not, whose biographical trajectory from religion to reform was similar to his own. This criticism, which he had voiced even as a Protestant, was powerfully restated in the *Ethics:*

> The vice of the social leader, of the reformer, of the philanthropist and the specialist in every worthy cause of science, or art, or politics, is to seek ends which promote the social welfare in ways which fail to engage the active interest and cooperation of others. The conception of conferring the good upon others, or at least attaining it for them, which is our inheritance from the aristocratic civilization of the past, is so deeply embodied in religious, political, and charitable institutions and in moral teachings, that it dies hard. Many a man, feeling himself justified by the social character of his ultimate aim (it may be economic, or educational, or political), is genuinely confused or exasperated by the increasing antagonism and resentment which he evokes, because he has not enlisted in his pursuit of the "common" end the freely cooperative activities of others. This cooperation must be the root principle of the morals of democracy. (*E,*276)

As Dewey perceived, the language of middle-class benevolence often betrayed a view of the masses as inert material on which reformers might work their will, and he called instead for a reconstructed conception of helping others which enlisted their full and willing participation in the provision of social welfare.

Efforts to tie Dewey tightly to the gospel of efficiency are even more questionable. On this view, his advocacy of "scientific intelligence" is seen to have provided, either knowingly or unknowingly, a philosophical underpinning for the ambitions of new-middle-class experts. Pragmatism pointed toward an antipolitics in which, according to R. Jeffrey Lustig, "scientists would constitute a neutral bar before whom people of differing outlooks could bring their conflicts, and by whose verdicts they would willingly be bound." Dewey's philosophy, in brief, was a "bureaucratic epistemology" that "dovetailed" with the thinking of the father of scientific management, Frederick W. Taylor. In even more extreme fashion, Clarence Karier has declared that Dewey offered a "philosophic justification for the dominant economic organization of the period" and "never seriously challenged the power sources within American society." Committed to "expert knowledge over populist opinion," Dewey advocated the "use of unchecked state power to control the future through shaping the thought, action, and character of its citizens." Pragmatism "provided the moral dexterity so necessary for the intellectuals who became servants of power within the liberal state," offering a philosophy that translated questions of moral value into "problems of strategy" and defined principles as "the expedient within a given set of social circumstances."[41]

Most interpretations of this sort attempt to derive sustenance from the remark of a disillusioned Randolph Bourne in 1917 that World War I had

revealed a younger intelligentsia, trained up in the pragmatic dispensation, immensely ready for the executive ordering of events, pitifully unprepared for the intellectual interpretation or the idealistic focusing

41. Lustig, *Corporate Liberalism*, pp. 153, 173, 155; Clarence Karier, "Liberal Ideology and the Quest for Orderly Change," in Karier, Paul Violas, and Joel Spring, *Roots of Crisis: American Education in the Twentieth Century* (New York: Rand McNally, 1973), pp. 85, 86, 87, 93, and "Making the World Safe for Democracy: An Historical Critique of John Dewey's Pragmatic Liberal Philosophy in the Warfare State," *Educational Theory* 27 (1977): 25–26. Many of Lustig's criticisms of Dewey's thought are apt and similar to my own. Yet his efforts to establish that Dewey was not really a democrat and that pragmatism was a philosophy of administrative reason are based on what I find to be extremely tendentious readings. Ironically, it seems to me that Dewey's political vision is, in important respects, quite similar to the democratic alternative to corporate liberalism Lustig offers at the end of his book. Karier's readings are not merely tendentious but often just plain wrong. He seems to have an almost visceral dislike for Dewey, reflected in arguments that build on a crude kind of social determinism to suggest that because Dewey was a member of the bourgeois class (he owned stock!) his reform proposals were necessarily bourgeois. Karier is a leader of what might be called the "Illinois school" of revisionist educational historians, which is distinguished by its attacks on Dewey, Jane Addams, and other democratic progressives. (See e.g. Paul Violas's contribution to *Roots of Crisis;* Walter Feinberg, *Reason and Rhetoric: The Intellectual Foundations of Twentieth Century Liberal Educational Policy* [New York: John Wiley, 1975]; and Walter Feinberg and Henry Rosemont, Jr., eds., *Work, Technology, and Education: Dissenting Essays in the Intellectual Foundation of American Education* [Urbana: University of Illinois Press, 1975].) My criticisms here apply only to this particular wing of revisionist history of American education. Much revisionist scholarship is quite persuasive, and some revisionists have taken a view of Dewey quite similar to mine. See, for example, Samuel Bowles and Herbert Gintis, *Schooling in Capitalist America* (New York: Basic Books, 1976), pp. 20–26 (Karier takes them to task for this in a review of this book, "The Odd Couple: Radical Economics and Liberal History," *Educational Studies* 7 [1976]: 185–193). David J. Hogan, a one-time student of Karier's and the other Illinois revisionists, has advanced a penetrating critique of their perspective and offered a far more sophisticated radical interpretation of progressive educational reform (Hogan, *Class and Reform*, p. 230). For a taste of the sort of nasty polemics this revisionist historiography has generated with liberal and neoconservative historians see Diane Ravitch, *The Revisionists Revised: A Critique of the Radical Attack on the Schools* (New York: Basic Books, 1978), and Michael Katz, *Reconstructing American Education* (Cambridge: Harvard University Press, 1987), chap. 5.

of ends. . . . The formulation of values and ideals, the production of articulate and suggestive thinking, had not, in their education, kept pace, to any extent whatever, with their technical aptitude. . . . It is true, Dewey calls for a more attentive formulation of war-purposes and ideas, but he calls largely to deaf ears. His disciples have learned all too literally the instrumental attitude toward life, and being immensely intelligent and energetic, they are making themselves efficient instruments of the war-technique, accepting with little question the ends as announced from above.

Often overlooking Bourne's exemption of Dewey himself from many of his strictures, some historians have blamed him for the sins of his disciples and linked the corruption of reason Bourne identified to his conception of "scientific intelligence" and this in turn to a rationale for the power of amoral technocrats. But Dewey's notion of scientific thinking cannot be construed as a commitment to purely technical rationality. Indeed, he valued scientific thinking most because of the support he believed it provided for the consideration of competing ends, of clashing values. At the same time, he did not construe science as "substantive reason" that could simply determine value choices as if this were a matter of identifying some brute (or transcendental) existence. Dewey did not believe such substantive reason existed; this was the burden of his attack on the epistemology industry. "The good can never be demonstrated to the senses," he said. "It involves a radical venture of the will in the interest of what is unseen and prudentially incalculable" (*E*, 371). In the moral life, to use Aristotle's terms, science was neither *sophia* nor *techne* but *phronesis,* practical reason.[42]

Dewey's call for scientific intelligence was not a call for the rule of intelligent scientists but for the egalitarian distribution of the capacity for scientific thinking and its incorporation into democratic decision making in the polity, workplace, and elsewhere. He continued to be wary of centralized state power and though he firmly believed that ex-

42. Randolph Bourne, "Twilight of Idols" (1917), *Radical Will*, pp. 342–343. A similar reading of Dewey's philosophy, free of Bourne's qualifications, which seems to have had some influence on the interpretation I criticize here is that of Max Horkheimer in *Eclipse of Reason* (New York: Seabury Press, 1974, originally published in 1947). Like the rest of the first generation of the Frankfurt School, Horkheimer did not know what he was talking about when it came to pragmatism. This is not true of the leading figure in the next generation of the school, Jürgen Habermas (see e.g. "The Scientization of Politics and Public Opinion," in Habermas, *Toward a Rational Society* [Boston: Beacon Press, 1970], pp. 62–80). One would have thought Dewey's controversial and proto-postpositivist treatment of *natural science* as a "practical" community would have drawn more attention from historians, but it has not because most have wrongly assumed that his philosophy of science as well as his ethics was a species of positivism.

perts performed indispensable functions in complex societies, he explicitly consigned them to an advisory role and advocated the subordination of expert administration to fully participatory, deliberative, democratic publics. Although he said relatively little about political democracy in this period, Dewey did nonetheless argue in the *Ethics* that the political "function" common to all citizens in a democracy was of particular importance because it stood for "direct and active participation in the regulation of the terms upon which associated life shall be sustained, and the pursuit of the good carried on. Political freedom and responsibility express an individual's power and obligation to make effective all his other capacities by fixing the social conditions of their exercise" (*E*, 424). This argument suggested at once a commitment to an active state that would oversee the provision of the conditions of effective freedom and to a state in which every citizen had the opportunity to take part in that oversight, "an organ by which people associated in pursuit of common ends can most effectively cooperate for the realization of their own aims" (*E*, 425). The principal task of progressive politics, as Dewey saw it, was not that of enhancing the power of experts but of "safeguarding the democratic ideal against the influences which are always at work to undermine it, and with building up for it a more complete and extensive embodiment" (*E*, 424).[43]

This analysis suggests that historians should be attentive to the way particular progressives defined a widely shared set of terms. Although Dewey spoke of the need for "social control," he, like many progressives, meant by the term only a generic "capacity of a society to regulate itself according to desired principles and values" and he distinguished democratic social control from other forms of control. Although he used the term "social efficiency" occasionally, his meaning, as we have seen, was something quite different from that of the administrative progressives. Although he, like nearly everyone else at the time, celebrated science, there were many different celebrations going on of which his was but one. Although he assumed a functionally differentiated division of labor, he carefully distinguished functions from classes and argued for the compatibility of functional differentiation and shared democratic authority. Although he called for equality of opportunity, this was not for him a matter of a well-run race for riches, and he stressed the unique ways in which each individual in an egalitarian

43. Those who charge Dewey with commitment to the antidemocratic power of experts are never able to cite a direct statement from him to this effect, always overlook an abundance of direct evidence to the contrary, and consistently rely on an indirect approach grounded in a misreading of his conception of scientific thinking.

society would make use of the opportunities afforded him or her. Most important, at a time when the meaning of "democracy" was beginning to be constricted by many to describe government for the people by benevolent elites or, at best, a negative popular check on the extensive powers of such elites, Dewey called for a radical extension of the power of the common man and woman in the polity and the workplace.[44]

I would then place Dewey in the radical wing of progressivism. Among middle-class intellectuals of the era he was, I believe, one of the most, if not the most, thoroughly democratic. He opposed the administrative progressives and *ipso facto* the masters of the corporate reconstruction of American capitalism with whom they often aligned. His own alliances were formed in the other direction, with labor, especially with those elements of the labor movement committed to workers' control. He flirted with socialism, but because many socialists were no more democratic than corporate liberals (and, indeed, might be said to constitute an anticapitalist wing of administrative progressivism), he was wary of identifying himself with them.[45]

44. The quotation about social control is from Chicago sociologist George Vincent in 1896, quoted in Morris Janowitz, *The Last Half-Century: Societal Change and Politics in America* (Chicago: University of Chicago Press, 1978), p. 28. See also JD, "Education and Social Direction" (1918), *Middle Works* 11:54–57. As Janowitz says, "social control" in this period signified opposition to laissez-faire market controls; thus its use was a badge of membership in the "anti-competitive consensus," which, as I have suggested, tells us little about where any particular reformer stood. On the use and abuse of the concept of social control by historians see William A. Muraskin, "The Social Control Theory in American History: A Critique," *Journal of Social History* 9 (1976): 559–569. A useful discussion of some of the differences between the pragmatists' conception of science and that of their contemporaries is David Hollinger, "The Problem of Pragmatism in American History," *Journal of American History* 67 (1980): 88–107. Martin Schiesl offers a solid discussion of the constriction of "democracy" in one setting in the period in *The Politics of Efficiency: Municipal Administration and Reform in America, 1800–1920* (Berkeley: University of California Press, 1977), chap. 10.

45. I am sure Dewey was not, like Roger Williams, a church of one, but I am not entirely sure who I would place with him on the radical wing of progressivism, though his friends Jane Addams, Randolph Bourne, and George Herbert Mead seem to me to belong there. (On the largely unfamiliar story of Mead's politics see Dmitri N. Shalin, "G. H. Mead, Socialism, and the Progressive Agenda," *American Journal of Sociology* 93 [1988]: 913–951 and Andrew Feffer, "Sociability and Social Conflict in George Herbert Mead's Interactionism, 1900–1919," *Journal of the History of Ideas* 51 [1990]: 233–254.) Elsewhere I have linked Dewey's vision of "moral democracy" with that of the great progressive photographer Lewis Hine ("Lewis Hine and the Ethics of Progressive Camerawork," *Tikkun*, May 1987: 24–29). Herbert Croly is an especially interesting figure because within the space of a few years he argued at length for a more constricted (*The Promise of American Life*) and a more expansive (*Progressive Democracy*) view of democracy, and the latter volume seems to me one of the most important documents of what I am calling radical progressivism. For a view of progressive social thought close to my own see David Price, "Community and Control: Critical Democratic Theory in the Progressive Period," *American Political Science Review* 68 (1974): 1663–1678.

This argument accords with the view of some of Dewey's contemporaries including Bourne, the young hunchback who overcame his painful handicap to become a brilliant cultural critic, and Max Eastman, the fair-haired Adonis of American radicalism, both of whom studied with Dewey at Columbia. But perhaps most interesting in this respect was the appropriation of Dewey's thought by renegade socialist William English Walling. Walling anticipated Dewey himself in tying his version of pragmatism to a socialism that, as Dewey would later put it, was not state socialism. In the second volume of his important trilogy on socialist thought and politics, *The Larger Aspects of Socialism* (1913), Walling argued that "pragmatism is Socialism, if taken in what seems to me to be its most able and consistent interpretation, that of Professor John Dewey." The object of this book, as well as of its companion volumes, was to attack the socialism of many American, British, and European socialists as state socialism, a collectivist, technocratic authoritarianism that threatened democracy and "true socialism." True socialism, Walling contended, was decentralized, egalitarian, classless, and radically democratic. State socialism and its less radical counterpart, state capitalism, were simply new forms of class rule. "It is evident," he argued, "that collectivism, government ownership of monopolies, the appropriation of the land rent by the state, and the placing of labor on maximum efficiency, are not socialism. . . . The 'State Socialism' of the immediate future promises to leave the present class culture intact. It remains for the Socialist movement to supply the principles and the forces required to create a new type of man and society."[46]

Walling proposed to socialists a heretical definition of "class" which, unlike that of conventional Marxism, divided society not into capitalists

46. William English Walling, *The Larger Aspects of Socialism* (New York: Macmillan, 1913), iii–iv, xix–xxi. The other volumes in the trilogy were *Socialism as It Is* (1912) and *Progressivism—and After* (1914). On Bourne and Dewey see Bourne, "John Dewey's Philosophy" (1915), in *The Radical Will*, pp. 331–335; Bruce Clayton, *Forgotten Prophet: The Life of Randolph Bourne* (Baton Rouge: Louisiana State University Press, 1984); and Casey Blake, *Beloved Community: The Cultural Criticism of Randolph Bourne, Van Wyck Brooks, Waldo Frank, and Lewis Mumford* (Chapel Hill: University of North Carolina Press, 1990). On Eastman and Dewey see William O'Neill, *The Last Romantic: A Life of Max Eastman* (New York: Oxford University Press, 1976), and John Diggins, *Up from Communism: Conservative Odysseys in American Intellectual History* (New York: Harper and Row, 1975), chap. 1. On Walling see James Gilbert, *Designing the Industrial State: The Intellectual Pursuit of Collectivism in America, 1880–1940* (Chicago: Quadrangle, 1972), chap. 8. Walling and Dewey were both members of the famous "X" club, a group of New York intellectuals organized in 1903 by W. J. Ghent which met weekly to discuss socialism and other contemporary issues. Other members included Charles Beard, Morris Hillquit, Algernon Lee, Lincoln Steffens, J. G. Phelps Stokes, and Walter Weyl (James Weinstein, *The Decline of Socialism in America, 1912–1925* [New York: Monthly Review Press, 1967], pp. 80–81).

and workers but into the privileged and the non-privileged. This definition of class was based on wealth and power rather than on the relationship to the means of production, and it set as its goal the end of class rule by the privileged in whatever form—capitalist or pseudosocialist—it might take and its replacement by a self-governing industrial democracy, a new and "higher" form of individualism. State socialism sacrificed the individual and his need for creative political action to a specious belief in the inevitability of centralization and bureaucratic control. This was not "real" socialism, which for Walling, as James Gilbert has said, was "'true democracy,' in which there were no social classes and divisions and all men enjoyed equal opportunity. Socialism did not mean that the industrial state, with its insatiable demands for efficiency and centralization, be allowed to swallow the political state whole." State socialism was no less antidemocratic than state capitalism; it merely offered a new set of masters.[47]

What Walling valued most in Dewey's work was his attack on philosophical absolutism and his concept of science as an experimental, hypothetical form of inquiry on which to model democratic life. He had freed science from nineteenth-century conceptions of inevitable law and from the deterministic evolutionary thinking that still befuddled the minds of state socialists. Dewey's science offered a democratic method to replace science as law and scientists as lawgivers. "If Dewey expects science to guide us," Walling noted, "this does not mean that he expects the scientists to guide us. Only in so far as the true spirit has been grasped by the community at large, can science actually guide our social life; and only as life and science are truly social is true science possible. . . . The application of science to social and ethical questions means nothing less than the abolition of class rule in society." Walling also saw the importance of Dewey's educational theory to libertarian socialists like himself, for the "new education," he said, was best seen as schooling for participation in a democratic community. "The child is to be trained," he observed, "not only to have interest in the community welfare but to reshape and remodel the community. The child is not taught to regard even society or the human race as authorities which stand above him, but as things over which he will have a voice and some control." Walling's treatment of Dewey's philosophy was not only per-

47. Walling, *Larger Aspects of Socialism*, x–xi; Gilbert, *Designing the Industrial State*, pp. 200–201. As this discussion of Walling's work suggests, a focus on the conceptions of democracy held by intellectuals and reformers in this period introduces divisions that cut across those conventionally made between progressives and socialists on the basis of their attitudes toward capitalism.

ceptive but also prescient in that it offered a remarkable anticipation of the reasoning that would lead Dewey himself to an unorthodox democratic socialism some years later.[48]

By the eve of World War I, Dewey was more fully aware that the democratic reconstruction of American society he envisioned could not take place simply by a revolution in the classroom, that, indeed, the revolution in the classroom could not take place until the society's adults had been won over to radical democracy. He could not, like William Wirt and U.S. Steel, start from scratch. It remained true that "we may produce in schools a projection in type of the society we would like to realize," but this achievement presumed a "we" committed to thoroughgoing democracy, and here the democratic ideal "has to contend not only with the inertia of existing educational traditions, but also with the opposition of those entrenched in command of the industrial machinery, and who realize that such an educational system if made general would threaten their ability to use others for their own ends." This opposition may, as he said, be taken as testimony to the "dependence of social reorganization on educational reconstruction," but it was not necessarily, as he hopefully predicted, "the presage of a more equitable and enlightened social order" (*DE*, 326, 328–329).

Dewey's awareness of the limits of school reform pointed to a larger public role for himself and other democratic intellectuals, more inclusive in its concerns than American schools but still largely educative in character. The democratic voice had to reach "all the agencies and influences that shape disposition," for "every place in which men habitually meet—shop, club, factory, saloon, church, political caucus—is perforce a school house, even though not so labelled." These schoolhouses were, however, even tougher places for a democrat to teach in than the conventional classroom because the task here was less to make minds than to change them, and in an environment not conducive to democratic debate. One had to convince one's fellow citizens, many of them lacking in "sympathetic character," to construct the institutions of moral democracy and to do so without resorting to undemocratic means, especially to a politics in which intellectuals became "a class which is especially expert in the manipulation of their fellows and skilled in the 'acceleration' of public opinion" (*E*, 426). Convincing them, of course, presumed the capacity of one's fellow citizens for reasoned moral deliberation, something Dewey was never willing to doubt, and an unshakable faith that the "radical venture of the will"

48. Walling, *Larger Aspects of Socialism*, pp. 37–38, 266–267.

democracy required would bear fruit, something he was never willing to relinquish.[49]

In 1914 Dewey found the platform that for two decades would serve him as his principal medium for the larger task of public education. In that year a new weekly magazine, the *New Republic*, was launched, bankrolled by Willard and Dorothy Whitney Straight and edited by the impressive troika of Herbert Croly, Walter Lippmann, and Walter Weyl. Dewey quickly became one of the journal's regular contributors, and from its pages Bourne, a junior editor, sang the praises of Deweyan education. By virtue of Croly's paean to executive power in *The Promise of American Life* (1909) and Lippmann's unmatched contributions to liberal elitism, the *New Republic* might not be imagined to be the most congenial home for a radical democrat like Dewey, but in its early years the editors carefully balanced their appeal for expert public administration with an insistence that experts act as the servants of "guiding democratic control," and Croly's second book, *Progressive Democracy* (1914), was substantially more democratic than its predecessor. Although Dewey's position on the ideological spectrum at the *New Republic* matched the one he held in the larger arena of reform, its editorial stance was close enough to his own thinking not to cause discomfort.[50]

Describing the role in American politics they saw for their magazine, the editors of the *New Republic* laid out the task of public intellectuals in terms very similar to those Dewey used to characterize the intervention of the philosopher in the problems of men. That task—"social education" or "opinion formation"—was distinguished from the work of both those Dewey termed manipulative "accelerators" of public sentiment and the Olympian detachment of the scholar. The former were "not speaking in order so much to convince us as to make us act or vote or feel with them. Their words are chains of phrases strung together

49. "Philosophy of Education," pp. 303–304.
50. "Training for Public Service," *New Republic*, 8 July 1916: 241; Herbert Croly, *Progressive Democracy* (New York, Macmillan, 1914), esp. chap. 19. On the founding of the *New Republic* and its editorial direction in these years see Charles Forcey, *Crossroads of Liberalism: Croly, Weyl, Lippmann and the Progressive Era, 1900–1925* (New York: Oxford, 1961), chaps. 5–6; Paul F. Bourke, "The Status of Politics 1909–1919: The *New Republic*, Randolph Bourne and Van Wyck Brooks," *Journal of American Studies* 8 (1974): 171–202; James A. Neuchterlein, "The Dream of Scientific Liberalism: The *New Republic* and American Progressive Thought, 1914–1920," *Review of Politics* 42 (1980): 167–190; John Patrick Diggins, "The New Republic and Its Times," *New Republic* 10 December 1984: 23–26; David Levy, *Herbert Croly of "The New Republic"* (Princeton: Princeton University Press, 1985), chap. 7; and David Seideman, *The New Republic: A Voice of Modern Liberalism* (New York: Praeger, 1986), pp. 19–45.

almost undesignedly with a view to pulling us to the cause or party or idea they are supporting." The latter, often possessed of the knowledge that would provide opinion with "grounds just short of proof," were fearful of falling prey to the sins of the manipulators and hence refused to take a stand while they awaited conclusive proof of moral and political propositions. Thus "those who have the 'grounds just short of proof' will not form opinions" and "those who will loosely express their opinions have not the grounds." Genuine opinion, the editors contended, was "neither cold, logical judgment nor irrational feeling" but "provisional conviction" unafraid to "show you the foundations of the categories and terms in which it is expressed." It was "an interpretation with a definite slant and bias" buttressed by good reasons. Formation in themselves and others of "conviction, gripped after the widest possible survey of the field," was the aim of intellectuals. "Quixotic as the enterprise may seem," the editors concluded, "it is the formation of opinion and not dusty scholarship and solemn cant that will enlist the good-will and best endeavors of those who aim to think worthily."[51]

Under the banner of the *New Republic* Dewey began to express his opinions about national politics. He had been distressed by the election of Woodrow Wilson in 1912 (like his colleagues at the *New Republic*) and had himself voted for Eugene V. Debs, the Socialist candidate. But over the next four years he found himself (like his colleagues at the *New Republic*) "warming up to [Wilson] more and more every day." In the wake of the passage of the reform legislation of Wilson's first term, Dewey foresaw the possibility that under the president's leadership the Democratic party might become "a party which in effect is as nationalistic as the Republican, but which allies its nationalism with the interests of the masses and not of the privileged pecuniary classes."[52] He thus threw his support to Wilson in the presidential campaign of 1916. How much Dewey had warmed up to the president would not, however, be clear until the onset of Mr. Wilson's War.

51. "What Is Opinion?" *New Republic*, 18 September 1915: 171–172.
52. "The Hughes Campaign" (1916), *Middle Works* 10:253–254. On Dewey's voting record see his "American Youth, Beware Wallace Bearing Gifts" (1948), *Later Works* 15:242.

CHAPTER 7

The Politics of War

*

By the second decade of the twentieth century, John Dewey had firmly established his credentials as a major philosopher and a leading theorist of educational reform. He had, on the other hand, published very little formal political philosophy or popular political commentary, though his work was rich with political implications. Recognizing these implications, Randolph Bourne urged Dewey in 1915 to broaden his audience and address himself to current affairs. "A prophet dressed in the clothes of a professor of logic," Bourne remarked, "he seems almost to feel shame that he has seen the implications of democracy more clearly than anybody else in the great would-be democratic society about him, and so been forced into the unwelcome task of teaching it. . . . I feel a savage indignation that Professor Dewey should not be out in the arena of the concrete, himself interpreting current life."[1]

Within two years of Bourne's remarks, Dewey *had* placed himself squarely in the center of the arena of the concrete as he struggled to bring his democratic theory to bear on the politics of World War I. This struggle led him from support of American intervention in the war and Woodrow Wilson's "new diplomacy" to a critical postwar appraisal of American foreign policy and a leading role in the Outlawry of War movement in the 1920s. Dewey's attempt to relate his social philosophy

1. Randolph Bourne, "John Dewey's Philosophy" (1915), in Olaf Hansen, ed., *The Radical Will: Randolph Bourne, Selected Writings* (New York: Urizen, 1977), pp. 332, 334.

to foreign policy resulted in a radically democratic variant of the "open-door" theory that had served as an important component of the ideology of American foreign policy since the late nineteenth century. He initially used this theory to justify his support for American participation in the war, but by the twenties it served him as a critical counter to both traditional balance-of-power conceptions of world order and to the liberal-capitalist version of open-door ideology which guided the thinking of Wilson and other American policymakers. His embrace of the war on behalf of radical democracy also generated a bitter confrontation with Bourne which, as an almost obligatory historical reference point, has shaped modern debate about the political responsibility of intellectuals.[2]

2. The consistent ideological elements in Dewey's thinking about issues of war and peace are slighted in the substantial literature on his activism in these years, a literature that focuses on the merits of the shifting political commitments he made in the service of this world view. Some critics, particularly those in the "realist" school of foreign policy analysis, have attacked Dewey's positions on the war and his role in the postwar outlawry-of-war movement as representative of the naive moralism that, in their view, has forever blighted American relations with the rest of the world. Some sympathetic pacifist students of his work have lamented his support of the war and commended his later antiwar stance. Dewey's less sympathetic critics on the left have echoed Bourne's attack on him, but have often overlooked the in-house, Deweyan nature of much of Bourne's critique and the extent to which Dewey's postwar writings and activism constituted, in effect, a concession to Bourne's arguments. Focusing on Dewey's most short-sighted efforts to find the means of action appropriate to the creation of a democratic world, they have ignored the radicalism that animated these efforts. For the realist perspective see John C. Farrell, "John Dewey and World War I: Armageddon Tests a Liberal's Faith," *Perspectives in American History* 9 (1975): 299–342. In his *Politics of John Dewey* (Buffalo: Prometheus Books, 1983), chaps. 3–7, Garry Bullert attempts unsuccessfully to provide Dewey with a set of realist credentials. The friendly pacifist perspective is that of the fullest study of Dewey's involvement in foreign affairs, Charles F. Howlett, *Troubled Philosopher: John Dewey and the Struggle for World Peace* (Port Washington, N.Y.: Kennikat Press, 1977). For the more critical radical argument see Sidney Kaplan, "Social Engineers as Saviors: Effects of World War I on Some American Liberals," *Journal of the History of Ideas* 17 (1956): 247–269; Clarence Karier, "Making the World Safe for Democracy: An Historical Critique of John Dewey's Pragmatic Liberal Philosophy in the Welfare State," *Educational Theory* 27 (1977): 12–47; and Christopher Lasch, *The New Radicalism in America* (New York: Knopf, 1965), pp. 181–224. A more sympathetic analysis of Dewey's politics from a radical perspective is Alan Cywar, "John Dewey in World War I," *American Quarterly* 21 (1969): 578–595, and "John Dewey: Toward Domestic Reconstruction, 1915–1920," *Journal of the History of Ideas* 30 (1969): 385–400. Although my interpretation is somewhat different from Cywar's, I am in full accord with his remark that "the character and content of [Dewey's] response to World War I, frequently viewed as the moment of truth for progressivism, reveal a tenacity and radicalism in the American mind of that era for which a careful examination of most of the relevant literature would leave the student unprepared" (400). There are several studies of the open-door theory and its influence on American foreign policy, but the source of this argument, William Appleman Williams, *The Tragedy of American Diplomacy,* 2d ed. (New York: Delta, 1972), remains indispensable.

OPEN DOORS AND FLEXIBLE MINDS

The intergenerational intellectual alliance Dewey had formed with a number of young radicals in the prewar years was ruptured by his support for American intervention in the war. Bourne was a leader of these young intellectuals, and in 1917 he turned his savage indignation on his former teacher. The Bourne-Dewey confrontation, one of the classic set pieces in American intellectual history, was very much a family affair. As Bourne saw it, the manner in which Dewey supported the war was treason to the principles and method of Deweyan democracy. Bourne did not, as is often said, so much reject Dewey's philosophy as turn it, with a vengeance, back upon his mentor. In the first years of the war, prior to American intervention, Dewey had set up standards for the critical analysis of international relations, and it was these very standards that Bourne would charge him with abandoning in 1917.

Democracy, Dewey argued in 1916, could not be conceived simply as a national or American affair. A nation could no longer be an isolated island unto itself; involvement in the affairs of other nations was not a matter of choice but an unavoidable fact of life in the modern world. The atomistic nation, like the atomistic individual, was a myth. Interdependence was inescapable. "Facts have changed," he remarked. "In actuality we are part of the same world as that in which Europe exists and into which Asia is coming. Industry and commerce have interwoven our destinies. To maintain our older state of mind is to cultivate a dangerous illusion."[3]

Isolation was not only an illusion but an illusion that foreclosed what Dewey saw as an important American mission. Although the United States stood apart from the war, the effort of Americans to build a democratic community marked by cultural, ethnic, and racial pluralism within their own borders was immediately relevant to the international situation, for it presented problems and possibilities analogous to those facing the world at large. Americans were thus in a unique position to aid in the reconstruction of international politics, but the situation called for "radical thinking" on their part. "We have to recognize that furtherance of the depth and width of human intercourse is the measure of civilization; and we have to apply this fact without as well as within our national life." This furtherance demanded more than intervening to secure peace among nations, which was essentially a negative

3. "The Schools and Social Preparedness" (1916), *Middle Works* 10:193.

enterprise. It entailed as well a commitment to the positive ideal of "promoting the efficacy of human intercourse irrespective of class, racial, geographical and national limits" and opening the door to "the fruitful processes of cooperation in the great experiment of living to-gether." It was uncertain whether Americans had the courage and the wisdom to "make the accident of our internal composition into an idea, an idea upon which we may conduct our foreign as well as our domestic policy," but Dewey was convinced that "an intelligent and courageous philosophy of practice" pointed toward "a future in which freedom and fullness of human companionship is the aim, and intelligent coopera-tive experimentation the method."[4]

Only in these very general terms did Dewey articulate his vision of a pluralistic, international democracy in the early years of the war, and prior to 1917 he offered few specific plans for the creation of this open-door world or even any clear indication of what role he believed the United States should play in the European conflict. Apart from expressing his vigorous opposition to proposals for universal com-pulsory military training for American schoolboys, he did not take an active part in the "preparedness" debates of 1915–1916. He concen-trated instead on providing general methodological guidelines and caveats for formulating policy which he urged Americans to consider when thinking about the United States' role in the war.[5]

Dewey was chiefly concerned that Americans would fall prey to a home-grown variety of the ideological absolutism he believed had gripped Germany. In *German Philosophy and Politics* (1915), his most thoroughly polemical venture into the social history of ideas, he of-fered a surprising analysis of the relationship between the German philosophical tradition and that nation's foreign policy, an analysis claiming to have uncovered an ideological dissociation of ideals and action in Germany which demonstrated that "philosophical absolutism may be practically as dangerous as matter of fact political absolutism" (*GPP*, 182).

Surprising in Dewey's dissection of the ideology behind German mili-tarism was his tracing its roots not to Nietzsche, as many had done, but to that notorious warmonger Immanuel Kant, the author of *Perpetual Peace*. Dewey acknowledged that Kant's own politics had been liberal

4. *German Philosophy and Politics* (1915), *Middle Works* 8:203–204. Page numbers for further references (*GPP*) appear in the text.
5. For Dewey's opposition to universal military training see "Universal Service as Education" (1916), *Middle Works* 10:183–190; and "Universal Military Training" (1917), *Middle Works* 20:377–393.

and cosmopolitan, but he argued that the key to the German mind nonetheless lay in Kant's philosophy and, in particular, in his division of the world into two distinct realms: the outer realm of phenomena and necessary causation and the inner realm of noumenal ideals and freedom. The inner realm was superior to the outer, and it was governed by a purely formal concept of duty which stood apart from the phenomena of human desire and the consequences of human action. Rehashing in a more polemical context his earlier criticisms of this substantively empty, wholly inner notion of moral duty, Dewey argued that it was at the root of German authoritarianism. Because Kant's ethics "tells men that to do their duty is their supreme law of action, but is silent as to what men's duties specifically are," it was not a useful moral guide, and the temptation (which even Kant could not entirely resist) was to fill it up with empirical, concrete duties. More often than not, the state led the way in filling this void. "When the practical political situation called for universal military service in order to support and expand the existing state," Dewey remarked, "the gospel of a Duty devoid of a content naturally lent itself to the consecration and idealization of such specific duties as the existing national order might prescribe. The sense of duty must get its subject-matter somewhere, and unless subjectivism was to revert to anarchic or romantic individualism (which is hardly in the spirit of obedience to authoritative law) its appropriate subject-matter lies in the commands of a superior. Concretely what the State commands is the congenial outer filling of a purely inner sense of duty" (*GPP,* 164). Hence the curious phenomenon of cavalry generals like Friedrich von Bernhardi who buttressed militarist appeals with quotations from the *Critique of Pure Reason.*[6]

On this account, Kant was not himself guilty of linking moral duty and unquestioning obedience to the state, but he had opened the door to this rendering of obligation by effectively cutting German culture off from an appreciation of the virtues of a pragmatic, consequentialist ethics: "Morals which are based upon consideration of good and evil consequences not only allow, but imperiously demand the exercise of a discriminating intelligence. A gospel of duty separated from empirical purposes and results tends to gag intelligence. It substitutes for the work of reason displayed in a wide and distributed survey of consequences in order to see where duty lies an inner consciousness, empty of content, which clothes with the form of rationality the demands of

6. For Dewey's critique of the effort to link German militarism to Nietzsche see "On Understanding the Mind of Germany" (1916), *Middle Works* 10:216–233.

existing social authorities" (*GPP*, 164). It was the post-Kantian idealists, most notably Fichte and Hegel, who put the imprimatur of philosophy on this perversion of the categorical imperative. Unhappy with Kant's separation of the noumenal and the phenomenal, they joined the two realms and subjected the empirical world to the will of Absolute spirit embodied in the commands of its agent, the State. As a result, Dewey wrote, since the early nineteenth century Germans had been "instructed by a long line of philosophers that it is the business of ideal right to gather might to itself in order that it may cease to be merely ideal. The State represents exactly this incarnation of ideal law and right in effective might" (*GPP*, 182). Since the State was "God on earth," patriotism was a religious obligation, and a willingness to engage in the sacrifice of war was "the final seal of devotion to the extension of the kingdom of the Absolute on earth" (*GPP*, 187, 182).

Dewey offered little evidence beyond a few quotations from the notorious Bernhardi for the link he attempted to establish between Kantian ethics and German policy making, and his effort to hold Kant responsible for the conjoining of philosophical absolutism and German nationalism was less compelling intellectual history than further evidence of Dewey's unabated hostility to the sage of Königsberg. More persuasive was his contention that the persistent influence of philosophical idealism on German culture had played an indispensable ideological role in German politics by allowing the nation's elites to pursue *Realpolitik* under the banner of "an unconditional obligation to fulfill an historic mission as organ of the Absolute," hence freeing them from the need to justify their actions in terms of consequences. "The prevalence of an idealistic philosophy full of talk of Duty, Will, and Ultimate Ideas and Ideals, and of the indwelling of the Absolute in German history for the redeeming of humanity," Dewey observed, "has disguised from the mass of the German people, upon whose support the policy of the leaders ultimately depends for success, the real nature of the enterprise in which they are engaged."[7]

Although *German Philosophy and Politics* left no doubt as to where Dewey's sympathies lay in the European war, he claimed that it was not intended to be a piece of Allied propaganda or a call to arms but a cautionary tale for his fellow citizens as they faced the tough decisions that lay ahead. The threat of absolutism, Dewey was careful to point

7. "Reply to William Ernest Hocking's 'Political Philosophy in Germany'" (1915), *Middle Works* 8:420, 419. For a useful summary of Dewey's ongoing war with Kant see A. H. Somjee, *The Political Theory of John Dewey* (New York: Teachers College Press, 1968), pp. 41–72.

out, was not confined to Germany, though this was the most arresting case. His book, Dewey told a reviewer, aimed "to make Americans conscious of the discrepancy which exists between the tenor of our activity and our current theory and phraseology about that activity." He lamented the appeals of such American leaders as Woodrow Wilson and William Jennings Bryan to "'immutable principles,' waiting ready-made to be fastened upon the situation" as much as he did the Kantian mystifications of Bernhardi. American absolutism, he believed, was in some respects even worse than that of the Germans because of its "deplorable thinness and unreality." War required the abandonment of absolutism and of the obfuscations of high-blown rhetoric for the application of critical analysis to the ends as well as the means of action. "Instead of confining intelligence to the technical means of realizing ends which are predetermined by the State," Dewey commented, "intelligence must, with us, devote itself as well to the construction of the ends to be acted upon" (*GPP*, 202). There was no room for ideological absolutism in this process, which had to be critical and reflexive. As Dewey saw it, "What is at issue is the difference between an activity which is aware of its own character, which knows what it is about, which faces the consequences of its activities and accepts responsibility for them, and an activity which disguises its nature to the collective consciousness by appeal to eternal principles and the eulogistic predicates of pure idealism."[8]

In his plea for a "consequentialist" approach to the war, Dewey devoted particular attention to the issue of the use of force in the pursuit of ideals. The use of force, he argued, was purely a question of means-ends efficiency. All action required the use of force, which he defined as nothing more than the energy required to bring purposeful action to fruition. Violence was the wasteful use of force, the use of means inappropriate or counterproductive for the desired end. Dewey criticized pacifists for a blindly absolute prohibition of the use of force, a prohibition that rendered them quiescent and impotent. "No ends are accomplished without the use of force. It is consequently no presumption against a measure, political, international, jural, economic, that it involves a use of force. Squeamishness about force is the mark not of idealistic but of moonstruck morals." Dewey was even more critical of militarists who tied the use of force to vague concepts like honor, liberty, civilization, divine purpose, and destiny, "forgetting that war, like anything else, has specific concrete results on earth." This being the

8. "Reply to Hocking," pp. 418, 420.

case, "unless war can be shown to be the most economical method of securing the results which are desirable with a minimum of the undesirable results, it marks waste and loss; it must be adjudged a violence, not a use of force."[9]

Dewey gave few indications before 1917 of his own feelings as to the specific conditions in which World War I would come under the category of the efficient use of force rather than violence, but it seemed obvious that, if faced with the necessity of deciding the issue, Dewey's answer would be grounded in a critical, concrete analysis of means and ends, purposes and consequences. The war would be severely tested as a means to a democratic world. As it turned out, however, it was Randolph Bourne, not John Dewey, who provided this kind of critical analysis.

THE TWILIGHT OF IDOLS

Dewey's support for American intervention in World War I was rooted less in pragmatic reason than in blind hope. This is not to say that he entirely abandoned his critical intelligence during the war, as did many of his fellow academics, but rather that this intelligence was constantly fighting a losing battle with his uncritical optimism. The signs of this struggle were scattered throughout his war essays, and they were clearly marked for him by Bourne in the summer and fall of 1917.

In the early spring of 1917, as Woodrow Wilson mulled over his response to the German resumption of unrestricted submarine warfare, Dewey observed that the nation had reached a "plastic juncture," a critical moment when democratic hopes required concrete formulation into specific purposes and the question of the nature of the war as force or violence demanded a careful answer. The country hesitated on the brink of entry into the war, he said, not because of apathy or cowardice but because of the need for intelligent, deliberate evaluation of the situation. "It is easy to be stampeded; it is easy to be told what one's mind is, and humbly to accept on trust a mind thus made up. It is not easy to make up the mind, for the mind is made up only as the world takes on form. We have hesitated in making up our mind just

9. "Force and Coercion" (1916), *Middle Works* 10:248–249; "Force, Violence, and Law" (1916), *Middle Works* 10:214–215.

because we would make it up not arbitrarily but in the light of the confronting situation, and that situation is dark, not light."[10]

It was at this plastic juncture that Dewey's own scientific judgment faltered. Moved by Wilson's rhetoric, he defended American intervention in the war on the grounds that it might provide a unique opportunity to reorganize the world into a democratic social order, guaranteeing a future of peace. This could be, he thought, the war to end all wars, a prospect he had intimated earlier might be the one motive that would induce Americans to take up arms. They would not devote themselves to a war for European civilization; they would fight with unreserved energy only "for another democracy and another civilization." When Wilson declared that this would be a "people's war," a war to make the world safe for democracy, Dewey jumped on the bandwagon. "Ever since President Wilson asked for a breaking of relations with Germany and afterwards for war against that country, more and more as he has stated why we are in this war," Dewey said, "I have been a thorough and complete sympathizer with the part played by this country in this war and I have wished to see the resources of this country used for its successful prosecution. As has been said over and over again, this is not merely a war of armies, this is a war of peoples."[11]

As this statement suggests, Dewey based his decision to support the American war effort less on the scientific empiricism he continued to advocate than on the "footless desires" he continued to attack. In so doing, he fell victim to fuzziness of purpose, ideological idealization of an American mission, and uncritical adoption of inefficient, counterproductive technique. He was not alone in this; he was joined by a host of progressive and socialist intellectuals and reformers, many of them former members of pacifist organizations. But what made Dewey's support of the war particularly noteworthy and especially devastating to those who, like Bourne, had marched in step with him until April 1917 was his falling prey to the very mistakes his philosophy was designed to prevent.[12]

10. "In a Time of National Hesitation" (1917), *Middle Works* 10:258.
11. Ibid.; "Democracy and Loyalty in the Schools" (1917), *Middle Works* 10:158; "Universal Service as Education" (1916), *Middle Works* 10:190.
12. On the effect of the war on American progressive intellectuals and reformers see Allen F. Davis, "Welfare, Reform, and World War I," *American Quarterly* 19 (1967): 516–533; Charles Forcey, *The Crossroads of Liberalism* (New York: Oxford University Press, 1961), chaps. 7–8; Charles Hirschfeld, "Nationalist Progressivism and World War I," *Mid-America* 45 (1963): 139–156; Kaplan, "Social Engineers as Saviors"; Christopher Lasch, *The New Radicalism in America* (New York: Vintage, 1965), chap. 6; and Stuart

For most of the war, Dewey defined his ideal, open-door world in such general terms that his concept of democracy was virtually useless as a practical ethical tool. As Bourne complained, "I search Professor Dewey's articles in vain for clues as to the specific working-out of our democratic desires, either nationally or internationally." Instead, he used "democracy" as one of those vague concepts tied blindly to the use of force, "an unanalyzed term, useful as a call to battle, but not an intellectual tool, turning up fresh sod for the changing future. . . . Dewey says our ends must be intelligently international rather than chauvinistic. But this gets us little along our way." Some of Dewey's statements early in the war gave clear evidence that his open-door for international democracy was quite different from that of Woodrow Wilson. "Industrial democracy is on the way," he told a *New York World* reporter in July 1917. "The rule of the Workmen and the Soldiers will not be confined to Russia; it will spread through Europe; and this means that the domination of all upper classes, even of what we have been knowing as 'respectable society,' is at an end." This provocative statement cried out for concrete elaboration of means and ends, but none was forthcoming from Dewey until well into 1918. A clearer formulation of his ends might have alerted him to the inappropriateness of the war, even Wilson's war, to their fulfillment. As it was, Bourne ruefully observed, Dewey and other prowar intellectuals had "assumed the leadership for war of those very classes whom the American democracy has been immemorially fighting. Only in a world where irony was dead could an intellectual class enter war at the head of such illiberal cohorts in the avowed cause of world-liberalism and world-democracy."[13]

Rochester, *American Liberal Disillusionment in the Wake of World War I* (University Park: Pennsylvania State University Press, 1977), chaps. 1–5. On the response of American socialists and pacifists see James Weinstein, *The Decline of American Socialism, 1912–1925* (New York: Monthly Review Press, 1967), chap. 3, and Nick Salvatore, *Eugene Debs: Citizen and Socialist* (Urbana: University of Illinois Press, 1982), chap. 9; Charles Chatfield, "World War I and the Liberal Pacifist in the United States," *American Historical Review* 75 (1970): 1920–1937; and C. Roland Marchand, *The American Peace Movement and Social Reform, 1898–1918* (Princeton: Princeton University Press, 1973). The best place to begin a consideration of the impact of the war on American political culture is the superb chapter "The War for the American Mind" in David Kennedy's *Over Here: The First World War and American Society* (New York: Oxford University Press, 1980), pp. 45–92—an account somewhat less critical of Dewey than my own.

13. Randolph Bourne, "Twilight of Idols" (1917), *Radical Will*, p. 340; Dewey quoted in "Professor Dewey of Columbia on War's Social Results," *New York World*, 29 July 1917; Bourne, "War and the Intellectuals" (1917), *Radical Will*, p. 308. In view of the argument I am making here about the Deweyan character of Bourne's polemics, it is worth noting that in "War and the Intellectuals," published before Dewey had made his position on the

In the midst of the crisis of war, Dewey also proved susceptible to an idealization of the moral qualities of his country, the very sort of ideological blindness against which he had warned in the period of neutrality. Dewey had argued before the war that the task of building a pluralistic democracy in the United States must go hand in hand with the internationalization of this ideal. During the war, the ideal appeared in his rhetoric as a settled American reality that was to be spread to the rest of the world. For example, speaking of the problem of the rights of nationalities, he remarked: "We have solved the problem by a complete separation of nationality from citizenship. Not only have we separated the church from the state, but we have separated language, cultural traditions, all that is called race, from the state—that is, from problems of political organization and power. To us language, literature, creed, group ways, national culture, are social rather than political, human rather than national interests. Let this idea fly abroad; it bears healing in its wings." Thus the need to put the struggle for pluralism at home in an international context became the need to spread to the rest of the world a triumphant American solution to the problems of racial and ethnic conflict. "The task of making our own country detailedly fit for peace," Bourne commented bitterly, had been abandoned amid a "gradual working up of the conviction that we were ordained as a nation to lead all erring brothers towards the light of liberty and democracy."[14]

Dewey also assumed as real the rational public that was a regulative ideal of his social theory—an intelligent, democratic community immune to manipulation in the name of "nationalistic patriotism." "To create a war motivation by resort to 'patriotic' appeal when large numbers of people are convinced that nationalistic patriotism was chiefly responsible for the outbreak of war is to operate against the tide of events and almost to invite failure," he counseled policy makers. "Burnt-out ashes cannot be made to glow, no matter how fervid the appeal." Americans had approached the war in a "businesslike way," and "conventional heroics and self-hypnotism were replaced by a serious earnestness." This approach lacked the "glamour and impetuous rush of traditional war psychology," but it had "infinitely more potential for intelligence." These sentiments left Dewey somewhat bewildered by the bonfire of

war clear and directed primarily at other "new republicaners," Bourne pointed to *German Philosophy and Politics* as one of the few examples of "original and illuminating interpretation" advanced by American intellectuals in the neutrality period (p. 310).

14. "America in the World" (1918), *Middle Works* 11:71; Bourne, "The War and the Intellectuals," p. 313.

patriotic repression that soon engulfed the country, including his own university.[15]

Dewey's failure to clarify his ends and his tendency to confuse real and ideal America contributed to his insensitivity to the difficulties and dangers of using war as a means to social change. In two articles attacking absolute pacifism in July 1917, he argued that for the "intelligent pacifist" like himself if "the moving force of events is always too much for conscience the remedy is not to deplore the wickedness of those who manipulate events. . . . The remedy is to connect conscience with the forces that are moving in another direction." Noting that "in a world organized for war there are as yet no political mechanisms which enable a nation with warm sympathies to make them effective, save through military participation," he saw pacifists in "the dilemma of trying to accomplish what only definite political agencies could effect, while admitting these agencies had not been created." In this situation, Dewey contended, the immediate future of pacifism lay "in seeing to it that the war itself is turned to account as a means for bringing these agencies into being. . . . Failure to recognize the immense impetus to reorganization afforded by this war; failure to recognize the closeness and extent of true international combinations which it necessitates, is a stupidity equaled only by the militarist's conception of war as a noble blessing in disguise." This argument lacked a convincing demonstration that there were forces in the war moving in the right direction. Dewey rested his faith in their existence on the belief that Wilson's open-door ideals were consistent with his own, as well as on a shortsighted confidence in the efficacy of American power and the rationality of the American public. The available evidence, however, pointed to a different conclusion, and such evidence mounted as the war continued.[16]

Bourne brought this evidence to Dewey's attention in a series of slashing polemics that hoist the philosopher with his own petard. "The 'liberals' who claim a realistic and pragmatic attitude in politics have disappointed us in setting up and then clinging wistfully to the belief that our war could get itself justified for an idealistic flavor, or at least for a world-renovating social purpose," Bourne remarked. "If these realists had had time in the hurry and scuffle of events to turn their philosophy on themselves, they might have seen how thinly disguised a rationalization this was of their emotional undertow." Bourne turned

15. "What America Will Fight For" (1917), *Middle Works* 10:273–274.
16. "Conscience and Compulsion" (1917), *Middle Works* 10:264; "The Future of Pacifism" (1917), *Middle Works* 10:266, 267–268.

pragmatic realism back upon Dewey and effectively challenged him for the right to the title of "intelligent pacifist."[17]

Bourne relentlessly amassed evidence and argument to dispute the contention of Dewey and others that the war could be controlled in the service of democratic ends. He rested his analysis on pragmatic, not absolutist, grounds. He brought the war before the bar of means-ends rationality and found it wanting. In a brilliant article titled "The Collapse of American Strategy" published in August 1917, Bourne employed Deweyan ethical analysis in exemplary fashion to shatter Dewey's case for American participation in the war. If the end for which the United States entered the war was the creation of an international order that would prevent the recurrence of world war, it was worth asking, Bourne reasoned, how entering the war was to serve and, since April, had served as a means to this end. The country entered the war in the face of the resumption of German submarine attacks, prowar progressives argued, not to secure an Allied victory but to prevent a German victory and secure a negotiated "peace without victory" which could serve as the basis of the international organization necessary to prevent future conflicts. At the time, Bourne said, "realistic pacifists" like himself had argued for the use of naval force to keep the shipping lanes free, a policy of "armed neutrality" aimed directly at the submarine problem. If it was successful in rendering submarine warfare ineffectual, such a policy might have convinced the Germans that they could not win while at the same time it might preserve the possibility of a negotiated settlement mediated by the United States. By entering the war, the United States lost any leverage it may have had for securing "peace without victory" and, indeed, lifted the hopes of the Allies for "la victoire intégrale," a "knockout blow" against the Germans. If American participation in the war was supposed to liberalize the war aims of the Allies, it had thus far been a miserable failure. Instead, American war aims themselves had been transformed. The nation had been effectively enlisted on behalf of the reactionary goal of an Allied "peace with victory," and "American liberals who urged the nation to war are therefore suffering the humiliation of seeing their liberal strategy for peace transformed into a strategy for a prolonged war."[18]

The collapse of American strategy was compelling evidence, Bourne argued, that war was as nearly inexorable as a social phenomenon could be. "War-technique" set its own end, victory, and its own means,

17. Bourne, "A War Diary" (1917), *Radical Will*, pp. 321–322.
18. Bourne, "The Collapse of American Strategy" (1917), in Carl Resek, ed., *War and the Intellectuals* (New York: Harper and Row, 1964), pp. 22–35.

whatever was necessary to that end, and it rode roughshod over any attempt to control it for other ends or to tame the bloodshed and repression it brought to the single-minded pursuit of its goal. Tied to any but its own purposes, war approached the status of an absolutely inefficient means, the paradigm, in Deweyan terms, of violence. True to his pragmatism, Bourne declared that he would not yield his fear of such inefficient means. He would resist the war-technique even when it came "bearing gifts," and any philosopher "who senses so little the sinister forces of war, who is so much more concerned over the excesses of the pacifists than over the excesses of military policy, who can feel only amusement at the idea that any one should try to conscript thought, who assumes that the war-technique can be used without trailing along with it the mob-fanaticisms, the injustices and hatreds, that are organically bound up with it, is speaking to another element of the younger intelligentsia than that to which I belong."[19]

Bourne's arguments could not easily be dismissed as the work of an unworldly, evangelical conscience, for they were grounded not in mere "amiable sentiment" but in hardheaded, empirical criticism. Bourne was asking Dewey to acknowledge that in the war he had run up against the sort of social force his philosophy admitted in the abstract but seldom acknowledged in the concrete, a social force that could not be controlled or "reconstructed" through active "adaptation" or "adjustment" but only passively "accommodated" or resisted in toto. In wartime, Bourne said, "one's pragmatic conscience moves in a vacuum. There is no leverage to clutch. To a philosopher of the creative intelligence, the fact that war blots out the choice of ends and even of means should be the final argument against its use as a technique for any purpose whatever. . . . War is just that absolute situation which is its own end and its own means, and which speedily outstrips the power of intelligent and creative control."[20]

In view of the withering ironies of Bourne's critique, it is worth

---

19. Bourne, "A War Diary," pp. 324–325; Bourne, "Twilight of Idols," p. 336.
20. Bourne, "Conscience and Intelligence in War," *Dial* 63 (13 September 1917): 194. Again, on Dewey's distinctions between "accommodation," "adjustment" and "adaptation" see his entries on these subjects in *A Cyclopedia of Education* (1911), *Middle Works* 6:359–361, 364–366. Bourne's argument here pointed to his famous contention in "Twilight of Idols" that pragmatism had degenerated in the war into a form of purely technical reason detached from moral vision, a charge I examined briefly in Chapters 5 and 6 and return to in Chapters 10 and 11. I would only note here that Bourne's conviction of the degeneration of pragmatic intelligence in 1917 was belied to a degree by its importance in his own critique, which was grounded more in pragmatic truth than in "poetic vision." A good example of a thoroughly antipragmatic criticism of Dewey's writings on war which, by contrast, shows how close Bourne and Dewey remained in their thinking is John Patrick Diggins, "John Dewey in Peace and War," *American Scholar* 50 (1981): 213–

noting that Dewey's war essays were not without their own flashes of skepticism about the way events were proceeding. He did not completely abandon a critical perspective, although at times he came close. He never argued that the war had in fact become a war for democracy, but he insisted on its continuing potential to be such. "War to put a stop to war is no new thing," he acknowledged. "History shows a multitude of wars which have been professedly waged in order that a future war should not arrive. History also shows that as a pacifist, Mars has not been a success. But a war to establish an international order and by that means to outlaw war is something hitherto unknown. In just the degree in which the American conception of the war gains force and *this* war becomes a war for a new type of social organization, it will be a war of compelling moral import." Dewey conceded that a critical opportunity to shape the war to these ends had been wasted when the United States had entered the war without securing any quid pro quo on war aims from the Entente (though he blamed the absence of intelligent pacifist leadership for this), and he expressed some worries that, for Americans as well as for the Allies, the war was becoming a punitive crusade against Germany, which he admitted would have disastrous consequences. Still he insisted, without specifying where the opportunity now lay, that the war provided an "opportunity which justifies the risk."[21]

Dewey did quickly retract his optimistic assessment of American immunity to wartime hysteria and manipulation. He could hardly do otherwise, as widespread repression of dissent and free speech became prevalent in the United States. School districts banned the teaching of German; teachers were required to take loyalty oaths; textbooks were censored; and the federal Bureau of Education distributed war study courses that were thinly veiled Allied propaganda. Immigrants were compelled to pledge their loyalty to "100 percent Americanism," and those unfortunate enough to be of German descent were ostracized, beaten, and occasionally lynched. Patriots formed such government-sanctioned groups as the American Protective League which spied on

---

230. For a view of the Bourne-Dewey confrontation from Bourne's perspective see Bruce Clayton, *Forgotten Prophet: The Life of Randolph Bourne* (Baton Rouge: Louisiana State University Press, 1984), chap. 11. Clayton's title seems to me a misnomer. Bourne has never been forgotten but repeatedly remembered, especially in the midst of subsequent wars (by other pragmatic critics of degenerate pragmatism such as Dwight Macdonald and Noam Chomsky) as the exemplar of a conception of the responsibility of intellectuals profoundly adversarial to that of the American mandarinate. For some recent examples see Henry Fairlie, "A Radical and a Patriot," *New Republic*, 28 February 1983: 25–32, and George Scialabba, "Bourne in Flames," *Village Voice Literary Supplement*, February 1985: 6–7.

21. "Morals and the Conduct of States" (1918), *Middle Works* 11:125–126; "The Future of Pacifism," pp. 268–270; "Fiat Justitia, Fiat Coleum" (1917), *Middle Works* 10:281–284.

their neighbors and launched vigilante raids against dissenters, draft resisters, and other "slackers." Under the authority of the Espionage Act of 1917 and the Sedition Act of 1918, Postmaster General Albert Burleson banned socialist literature from the mails and Attorney General Thomas Gregory did his best to see that speech critical of the war effort as well as antiwar activism was silenced. Dissent and radicalism were equated with treason, and the principal victims of these witch-hunting campaigns such were radical organizations as the Industrial Workers of the World and the Socialist party. Prowar progressive publicists gathered together in George Creel's Committee on Public Information, where they used the latest public relations and advertising techniques to enlist the less savory public emotions on behalf of the war. In the face of these events, Dewey admitted in November 1917 that his earlier efforts to deflect concern about domestic repression now appeared "strangely remote and pallid," for "the increase of intolerance of discussion to the point of religious bigotry has been so rapid that years might have passed. In the face of such intense and violent reactions as now prevail, commendation of sanity is no more audible than is any other still small voice of reason amid howling gales of passion."[22]

Perhaps nothing did more to shake Dewey's conviction that irrational appeals to patriotism would have little effect in the United States than the warm reception such appeals received in American universities, including Columbia. The war quickly changed Columbia's reputation as a bastion of academic freedom. Alert to public suspicion of the wayward opinions of the university's faculty, President Nicholas Murray Butler and the university trustees adopted a policy warning that faculty members who expressed views or engaged in activities detrimental to the war effort would be fired. Sharply narrowing the boundaries of free speech and academic freedom, Butler declared that Columbia had no room for those "who are not with whole heart and mind and strength committed to fight with us to make the world safe for democracy." He advised his faculty that "what had been tolerated before becomes intolerable now. What had been wrongheadedness was now sedition. What had been folly was now treason."[23]

Two professors, James McKeen Cattell and Henry Wadsworth Longfellow Dana, fell victim to these strictures and were dismissed. Cattell, Dewey's old friend who had been instrumental in his coming to Col-

22. "In Explanation of Our Lapse" (1917), *Middle Works* 10:292. Kennedy provides an excellent summary account of this repression in *Over Here*, pp. 53–88.

23. Butler quoted in Carol Gruber, "Academic Freedom at Columbia University, 1917–1918: The Case of James McKeen Cattell," *American Association of University Professors Bulletin* 58 (1972): 302.

umbia, was fired for sending a letter to members of Congress urging support of a bill prohibiting the sending of draftees to fight in Europe without their consent. Dana was dismissed for his participation in a peace organization. The Columbia faculty was given little say in these actions, and the faculty committee established to hear such charges of disloyalty was bypassed. Dewey was a member of this committee, and in the wake of the firings he resigned from it and condemned the actions of the trustees. It was, he said, "idle to appeal to reason" in the face of Butler's views. "For the time being the conservative upholders of the Constitution are on the side of moral mob rule and psychological lynch law. In such an atmosphere a sober effort to locate the real abode of folly and wrongheadedness would itself appear treasonable."[24]

Faced with the facts of domestic repression, Dewey reached for very wistful explanations and dismissed out of hand any suggestion of an "organic" connection between war and intolerance. Intolerance, he suggested, was simply a sign of American inexperience with the ways of war, comparable with the "riotous gambolings of youth." Domestic repression and the trampling of democratic ideals and procedures were "merely a part of our haste to get into the war effectively, a part of the rush of mobilization, which, thank heaven, had to be improvised because of our historic and established unmilitarism." This explanation carried little conviction, and Dewey admitted, "It may be my hope is the source of my belief." More compelling was his warning to liberals who would wink at the repression of civil liberties in the interest of the war effort that such action could well prepare the way for "a later victory of domestic Toryism."[25]

None of Dewey's reservations led him to give Bourne's criticism the serious attention it demanded. While he acknowledged that there were pacifists like Jane Addams who were not subject to his strictures against hapless conscience, he made no reference at all to Bourne's arguments nor did he attempt to meet the fundamental objections they posed to his position on the war. Rather than return Bourne's fire Dewey did what he could to silence him by securing his dismissal from the editorial

24. "In Explanation of Our Lapse," p. 292. Dewey did not match the protest of Charles Beard, who resigned from the university. See also JD, "The Case of the Professor and the Public Interest" (1917), *Middle Works* 10:164–167; Bourne, "Who Owns the Universities," *Radical Will*, pp. 216–218; "Professor Beard's Letter of Resignation from Columbia University," *School and Society* 6 (1917): 446. For full accounts of the suppression of dissent at Columbia see Carol Gruber, *Mars and Minerva* (Baton Rouge: Louisiana State University Press, 1975), pp. 187–212; Gruber, "Academic Freedom at Columbia," 297–305; and William Summerscales, *Affirmation and Dissent: Columbia's Response to the Crisis of World War I* (New York: Teachers College Press, 1970).
25. "In Explanation of Our Lapse," p. 295.

board of the *Dial,* which by 1918 was the only important forum Bourne had left for the expression of his views.[26]

THE POLISH QUESTION

Debate among historians—particularly historians of education—about Dewey's political ideology has concentrated to an inordinate degree on what has come to be known as the "Polish question": Dewey's involvement in a wartime investigation of the politics of Poles in the United States. While this single episode in a long career has taken on exaggerated importance, it is also undeniable that this unlikely adventure clearly revealed some of the key principles of Dewey's democratic theory and some of the central difficulties he encountered in tying his vision of a democratic world to the American war effort.[27]

To put this incident in perspective it is necessary to say something more than I have about the vision of cultural pluralism that was central to Dewey's open-door ideology. As I noted, he viewed the American effort to build an ethnic and racial democracy to be a model for international politics. But he was a sharp critic of "Americanization" programs that sought to strip immigrants of their ethnic culture. Noting that "the theory of the melting pot always gave me rather a pang," he, along with Bourne, was one of the few American intellectuals to support Horace M. Kallen's effort during the war to formulate a theory of cultural pluralism with which to contest melting-pot enthusiasts and proponents of conformity to strictly Anglo-American cultural values. American nationalism, he argued, had to be international and interracial: "No matter how loudly any one proclaims his Americanism, if he

26. For Dewey's brief comments on Addams's "intelligent pacifism," see "Future of Pacifism," pp. 266–267. For a discussion of the *Dial* incident see Chapter 8 and the literature cited there. The only occasion on which Dewey and Bourne openly confronted each other during the war was in a debate over the merits of the posture therapy and attendant philosophy of F. Matthias Alexander in which their opposing positions on the war were aired obliquely and sub rosa. See Bourne, "Making over the Body: Review of *Man's Supreme Inheritance* by F. Matthias Alexander" (1918), *Middle Works* 11:359–360, and JD, "Reply to a Reviewer" (1918), *Middle Works* 11:353–355.

27. The literature and debate on this issue includes Karier, "Making the World Safe for Democracy," pp. 31–47; Walter Feinberg, "Progressive Educators and Social Planning," *Teachers College Record* 73 (1972): 485–505; and a symposium in the *History of Education Quarterly* 15 (1975): Paul F. Bourke, "Philosophy and Social Criticism: John Dewey, 1910–1920," pp. 9–12; Charles L. Zerby, "John Dewey and the Polish Question: A Response to the Revisionist Historians," pp. 17–30; J. Christopher Eisele, "John Dewey and the Immigrants," pp. 67–85; Feinberg, "On Reading Dewey," pp. 395–415; and Karier, "John Dewey and the New Liberalism: Some Reflections and Responses," pp. 417–443.

assumes that any one racial strain, any one component culture, no matter how early settled it was in our territory, or how effective it has
proved in its own land, is to furnish a pattern to which all other strains
and cultures are to conform, he is a traitor to an American nationalism.
Our unity cannot be a homogeneous thing like that of the separate
states of Europe from which our population is drawn; it must be a unity
created by drawing out and composing into a harmonious whole the
best, the most characteristic which each contributing race and people
has to offer." The implications of this for international democracy were
clear. "If there is to be lasting peace," Dewey declared, "there must be a
recognition of the cultural rights and privileges of each nationality, its
right to its own language, its own literature, is own ideals, its own moral
and spiritual outlook on the world, its complete religious freedom, and
such political autonomy as may be consistent with the maintenance of
general social unity."[28]

Although Dewey's commitment to cultural pluralism cannot be
doubted, this commitment was not without its reservations. He favored
pluralism consistent with "general social unity," but worried about pluralism that threatened "harmony." This concern was apparent in his
response to Kallen's important essay "Democracy versus the Melting
Pot" (1915), in which Kallen used the striking metaphor of an orchestra
to define his ideal for American civilization. Kallen said:

> As in an orchestra, every type of instrument has its specific timbre and
> tonality, founded in its substance and form; as every type has its appro-
> priate theme and melody in the whole symphony, so in society each
> ethnic group is the natural instrument, its spirit and culture are its
> theme and melody, and the harmony and dissonances and discords of
> them all make the symphony of civilization, with this difference: a
> musical symphony is written before it is played; in the symphony of
> civilization the playing is the writing, so that there is nothing so fixed
> and inevitable about its progressions as in music, so that within the
> limits set by nature they may vary at will, and the range and variety
> may become wider and richer and more beautiful.

In a letter to Kallen, Dewey remarked: "I quite agree with your orchestra idea, but upon [the] condition we really get a symphony and not
a lot of different instruments playing simultaneously. I never did care
for the melting pot metaphor, but genuine assimilation *to one another—*

---

28. "The Principle of Nationality" (1917), *Middle Works* 10:288–289; "Nationalizing
Education" (1916), *Middle Works* 204. See also Bourne, "Trans-National America" (1916),
and "The Jew and Trans-National America" (1916), in *War and the Intellectuals*, pp. 107–
133.

not to Anglosaxondom—seems to be essential to an America. That each cultural section should maintain its distinctive literary and artistic traditions seems to me most desirable, but in order that it might have more to contribute to others. I am not sure that you mean more than this, but there seems to be an implication of segregation geographical and otherwise. That we should recognize the segregation that undoubtedly exists is requisite, but in order that it may not be fastened upon us."[29]

As this comment suggests, Dewey was considerably more concerned than Kallen about the threats of "discord" and "segregation" cultural pluralism posed. For him there was no point in cultivating ethnicity if the various groups involved did not communicate with one another and enrich the common life. He wanted no atonal music in the repertoire of his cultural orchestra and, here as elsewhere when he was confronted by potentially divisive conflict, he confidently presumed that pleasing harmonies could be scored. Moreover, though he shared Kallen's pragmatic preference that the orchestra not be confined to prearranged music, Dewey was insistent that there were core ideals in American nationalism which stood apart from the particular values of the country's composite cultures, had priority over them, and ought to shape the lives of all the groups in the society. These ideals were those of democracy: "friendly and helpful intercourse between all and the equipment of every individual to serve the community by his own best powers in his own best way." Hence, as the Polish investigation revealed, he was willing to put the orchestra in the hands of a conductor—the democratic state and the public schools at home and a democratic international organization in the world at large—which would, if necessary, constrain group autonomy in order to foster, even impose, the conditions of democracy.[30]

The Polish investigation grew out of a seminar in social and political philosophy Dewey taught at Columbia in 1917–18. Participating in the class as a special student (though he is said to have slept through most of the sessions) was Albert Barnes, a Philadelphia millionaire who had been impressed with *Democracy and Education* and was eager to know Dewey and his philosophy firsthand. Barnes was especially interested, as a man of affairs, in the practical applications of Dewey's philosophy.

29. Horace M. Kallen, "Democracy versus the Melting-Pot," *Nation,* 25 February 1915: 220; JD to Horace M. Kallen, 31 March 1915, Horace M. Kallen Papers, American Jewish Archives, Hebrew Union College, Cincinnati.
30. "Nationalizing Education," p. 210. One of the best indications on the priority Dewey gave communications between groups was his vision of a nationalized education in

Intrigued by class discussions of the relationship of social science to social action, he proposed to Dewey that he finance research on the Polish community of Philadelphia.[31]

The inquiry got under way in May 1918, but it proceeded rather aimlessly for a couple of months, plagued by tensions between the irascible Barnes and the other members of the inquiry. In July, Paul Blanshard, a graduate student who wanted to turn the project toward social settlement work, was dropped from the group, and more organized inquiry was begun. Although participants were assigned various aspects of Polish-American social life for study—religion, family life, education, and intellectual and cultural activities—the focus of the study quickly became political when investigation showed that the Polish community was split into factions struggling to mobilize Polish-American support for one or another of the groups battling for control of the independent Poland that Woodrow Wilson had included among his war aims.[32]

This was, Dewey reported, a very uneven struggle in which the advantage lay, as he saw it, with the forces of corruption and conservatism which had been largely successful in manipulating the Polish-American public into support of reactionary elements at home and abroad. The main object of the inquiry became "to ascertain the forces and conditions which operate against the development of a free and democratic life among the members of this group, to discover the influences which kept them under external oppression and control." As it became apparent that conditions on the local level were intimately related to international events, the scope and ambitions of the inquiry expanded. Divisions and conflicts within the Polish-American community reflected divisions and conflicts within Poland itself, and Dewey and Barnes sought to put their inquiry in the service of the war for democracy. As Barnes, who was a bit less squeamish than Dewey about the overt politicization of the project, put it, "The idea would be to work out a practical plan based upon first hand knowledge to eliminate forces alien to democratic internationalism and to promote American ideals in accor-

which every illiterate foreign immigrant "had not only the opportunity but the obligation to learn the English language"—English being regarded here not as an element of Anglo-Saxon culture but as the medium of discourse between various ethnic groups ("Universal Service as Education," p. 186).

31. JD, *Conditions among the Poles in the United States: Confidential Report* (1918). This once rare document has now been conveniently reprinted in *Middle Works* 11:259–330. For more on the Dewey-Barnes relationship see Chapter 11.

32. William Schack, *Art and Argyrol* (New York: Thomas Yoseloff, 1960), p. 104; JD to Alice Dewey, 13 July 1918; JD to Family, 21 July 1918; JD to Alice Dewey, 1 August 1918, Dewey Papers.

dance with the principles announced by President Wilson in his various communications."[33]

For Poles, World War I revived the long-buried dream of a united, independent Poland. Two major groups emerged as rivals for control of the new Poland. The first of these was the Polish National Committee, established in 1914. This faction, dominated by conservatives, was centered in Russian Poland. It had close ties with the tsar, and after the Russian Revolution it moved its headquarters to Paris and was thereafter known as the Paris Committee. Its leader was Roman Dmowski, a reactionary, antisemitic Polish imperialist. He and his supporters favored the restoration of the monarchy in Poland and wide territorial claims for the new Polish state. Because of its tsarist sympathies, this group supported the Allies in the war, and in return the Allies gave the Paris Committee semiofficial status.[34]

The other major faction in Poland was headquartered in Austrian Poland and was led by liberals and social democrats. This faction, the Committee of National Defense (KON), hoped to establish a democratic socialist state for the new Poland. Their platform called for: "An independent Polish democratic republic based on the following principles: Direct, general and secret suffrage; legislation by the people, including the initiative and referendum; equality of all citizens, regardless of sex, race, nationality and religion; progressive income tax; an eight-hour working day, minimum wages, equal pay for men and women, prohibition of child labor; gradual socialization of land, of the means of transportation and production and of communication." Regarding the tsar as the principal enemy, this group had given its support to Austria at the beginning of the war. After the Russian Revolution, this policy changed, and in 1918 the leader of the liberals, General Joseph Pilsudski, was in a German prison. This faction was not represented on the Paris Committee and clearly had less influence on Western policy makers.[35]

The Paris Committee's most important representative in the United States was the famous pianist Ignace Paderewski. In this country, Paderewski exerted tremendous influence on Poles and non-Poles alike. Through his friendship with Colonel Edward M. House he had access to the highest circles in the Wilson administration, and he used his

33. JD to Alice Dewey, 13 July 1918; JD to Alice Dewey, 3 August 1918, Dewey Papers; Barnes quoted in *Conditions among the Poles,* 260.

34. Louis L. Gerson, *Woodrow Wilson and the Rebirth of Poland, 1914–1920* (New Haven: Yale University Press, 1953), is the standard source on American policy toward Poland in this period.

35. KON platform quoted in *Conditions among the Poles,* p. 265; Jan Kobiet, "America and the Polish Question," *New Republic,* 10 August 1918: 44–46.

power with great skill. The American government had given the Paris Committee the official authority to raise relief funds in the United States and to direct the distribution of this money in Poland. At the time Dewey completed the report of his group on the Polish-American community, the Hitchcock bill was before Congress, proposing to grant the Paris Committee American recognition as the official government-in-exile of Poland and give the committee the authority to decide which nonnaturalized Poles in the United States would or would not be designated as enemy aliens. According to Dewey, the power of the Paris Committee in the United States was further bolstered by its alliance with the political machines of large cities and with "that portion of the Polish clergy which is opposed to and admittedly afraid of Americanization." Dewey also charged that the conservatives were in control of the major sources of information on Polish affairs, including the Polish Press Bureau in Washington.[36]

To generate popular support for the Hitchcock bill, the American supporters of the Paris Committee called for a Polish Congress in Detroit in late August 1918. This convention was described by its organizers as "the greatest possible political and national occurrence for all Poles in America without exception, a visible, external embodiment of the will of the whole immigration." Dewey disputed this claim in the *New Republic,* noting that the convention had been called by a self-constituting group of men from such conservative organizations as the Polish National Alliance and the Roman Catholic Polish Alliance. Both the process for selecting delegates to the convention and the rules of the convention itself were designed to exclude the effective participation of liberals and radicals. The selection of delegates, Dewey said, was analogous to a situation in which "the bosses of a political machine like Tammany should graciously decide that all of its own minor and local clubs should be allowed to select delegates to a thoroughly representative convention, the leading officers being thrown in as delegates ex officio." The rules of the convention made it apparent that "no chances are to be taken even with a packed convention."[37]

Dewey's sympathies were clearly with the KON and its American supporters. He saw the Paris Committee as the embodiment of the very forces the United States had gone to war to combat. "In view of a war waged on behalf of democracy and the freedom of oppressed nationalities, the query naturally persists as to why a group which is mo-

---

36. *Conditions among the Poles,* p. 262; "Second Preliminary Confidential Memorandum" (1918), *Middle Works* 11:255–258.

37. Paris Committee quoted in *Conditions among the Poles,* p. 302; "Autocracy under Cover" (1918), *Middle Works* 11:243.

narchical, representative of conservative economic interests and largely anti-Semitic should occupy such an important semi-official political status?" Dewey believed that the main reason why the Wilson administration lent its support to the Paris Committee was that the committee was its only source of information on the Polish situation. If the facts were known, the administration would, he presumed, support the KON, which was obviously the Wilsonian party in Poland. At the very least, he believed, the government would see the need for more democratic methods of gathering information on Polish affairs and mobilizing the support of the Polish-American community for the war.[38]

Dewey was up against stiff opposition. The Paris Committee and its clerical and political allies were in firm control of Polish-American politics. Dewey admitted that not only American policy makers but most American Poles supported Paderewski and the committee. The KON was badly outnumbered, although, Dewey commented, "it contains by the common consent of its adversaries the 'ablest and brainiest' among Poles in this country, and has the greatest influence among all of the more intelligent and skilled workingmen."[39]

The practical problem, as Dewey defined it, was one of overcoming the power of the Paris faction to manipulate public and official opinion in the United States. This involved publicizing the findings of the Philadelphia study and convincing the government that these findings called for curbs on the controlling influence of the Paris Committee. As he wrote his wife:

> Aside from general articles, what needs to be done practically is to get this convention postponed, get the Hitchcock bill changed to complete recognition of some organization which shall be really representative, and in connection with both of these things have the US government employ its moral authority to make the Poles get together, and get them under the control of representative Americans, instead of under the manipulation via Paderewski and the priests of a little clique in Paris. Of course, I don't anticipate much success in the practical parts of this program, but the whole experience is a revelation of what can be done.

Dewey and other members of the study group published articles in liberal magazines detailing the ideology and tactics of the Paris Committee, and Dewey, at the request of the U.S. Military Intelligence Bureau, which got wind of the Philadelphia project, submitted two

38. *Conditions among the Poles,* p. 282.
39. Ibid., p. 296.

brief reports and a longer one to the government, outlining the results of the inquiry and offering some policy recommendations. Dewey and Barnes also attempted to persuade Colonel House to use his influence to revise the Hitchcock bill.[40]

In his policy recommendations to the government, Dewey called for an investigation of the Polish Press Bureau and its connections with the Committee for Public Information. In order to provide a more accurate picture of the issues at stake among American Poles, he recommended a careful evaluation of all claims, charges, and interpretations of these issues, including his own. Dewey also called upon the administration to attempt to postpone the Detroit convention "until there is adequate assurance that it is genuinely representative in its make-up and truly parliamentary in its procedure, and is committed to a policy which has the antecedent sanction of the State and War Department." If such a postponement proved impossible, he recommended that the group controlling the convention be "guided" by the government to reorganize the control of the collection, distribution, and accounting of relief funds. Dewey also advised the administration to press for the establishment of "an American commission which shall have as its object the unification of all Polish groups and parties in behalf of the declared policies of President Wilson, and which shall—through authorized representatives—get in touch with similar groups abroad, including those in Poland itself." The willingness of a group to agree to such a commission, Dewey said, "would be an acid test of whether the interests of the United States primarily, and of Poland secondarily, are uppermost, or whether these interests are subordinate to something personal and factional."[41]

These latter recommendations are particularly interesting, for Dewey was not simply calling for policies to guarantee a freer circulation of information on Polish affairs but was recommending that the American government take an active, indeed a controlling, role in Polish-American politics. He was, that is, seeking a policy that would counter the manipulative politics of the conservatives with a policy of manipulation by liberal Wilsonians. He justified such tactics on the grounds that

40. JD to Alice Dewey, 3 August and 9 August 1918, Dewey Papers; "Autocracy under Cover," pp. 241–247; Irwin Edman, "The Fourth Part of Poland," *Nation,* 28 September 1918: 342–343; Albert Barnes, "Democracy, Watch Your Step!" *Dial,* 28 December 1918: 595–597; *Conditions among the Poles;* "Preliminary Confidential Memorandum" (1918), *Middle Works* 11:248–254; "Second Preliminary Confidential Memorandum"; Colonel Edward M. House Diary, 5 August 1918, Edward M. House Papers, Sterling Library, Yale University.

41. "Second Preliminary Memorandum," pp. 257–258; *Conditions among the Poles,* pp. 298–299; "Preliminary Confidential Memorandum," pp. 252–253.

all concerned agreed that the interests of Poland were inextricably tied to Wilson's "completely disinterested" foreign policy. Given this fact, he argued, leadership by the American government in Polish-American affairs was "natural." Seeking to circumvent the politics of the Polish community itself—a politics dominated by conservatives—Dewey was attempting to persuade Wilson to use his authority to impose a set of procedures and policies on this community which would guarantee the KON a voice in Polish-American policy and secure the commitment of American Poles to Wilsonianism.[42]

Frustrated by the power of the Paris Committee, Dewey, in the name of democratic self-determination, called for the state to intervene undemocratically in the undemocratic politics of the Polish-American community. The fact that democracy in this community had been corrupted by the reactionaries justified, to his mind, such an intervention. Resistance to it, he advised the government, should not be seen as resistance to outside interference in the affairs of the Poles but as an indication that those who resisted did not have the best interests of the United States and Poland at heart.

The "Polish question" dramatically points up what is perhaps the most distinctive feature of Dewey's politics during World War I. At no other time did he regard an existing American state as committed to the same vision of democracy as he was. During the war, Dewey linked his democratic project to Wilsonianism, and, periodically, he became lightheaded with the thought that his own world view was that guiding the ship of state. Like his colleagues at the *New Republic,* who were more overt in their quest for association with men of power, Dewey thought he had found his man in Wilson, and the temptation to practically align himself with the American state proved irresistible. Given this identification of Deweyan democracy with Wilsonian democracy, the ideal with the real, it is not surprising that he could not resist the temptation to call upon the government to intervene in the politics of the Polish-American community. Had his recommendations been limited to calls for procedural reform of Polish politics and freedom of the Polish press this episode might not have been particularly ironic. As I noted, his cultural pluralism left room for a democratic state that might contravene group autonomy in order to establish the conditions of democracy. But in this case, Dewey was identifying democracy with the adoption by Poles of substantive policies that had "the antecedent sanction of the State and War Department." He, no less than the Polish reactionaries he was battling, was anxious to secure a rigged convention. Just as

42. "Preliminary Confidential Memorandum," p. 252.

he supported a war to end war, Dewey here called for manipulation to end manipulation.[43]

Dewey's determined effort to intervene in the politics of the Polish-American community was fueled not only by the excitement of what Bourne scornfully called "the elemental blare of doing something aggressive" for the war effort but also by the passion of a brief love affair with Anzia Yezierska, a budding novelist of Polish-Jewish descent some twenty-five years younger than he. The two met when Yezierska registered in the fall of 1917 for the same course that Barnes attended. The following summer she joined the Polish investigation as a translator and engaged as well in research on the conditions of women and the family in the Philadelphia community. Physically, the relationship appears not to have advanced beyond light petting, but emotionally it deeply affected both Dewey and Yezierska. For our purposes, the most interesting thing about this romance is the way both parties construed it as the sort of "harmonizing" of cultures about which Dewey wrote abstractly in his essays on American nationalism. By the time she encountered Dewey, Yezierska had begun to publish the stories of ghetto life which would subsequently earn her a place in American literary history, and Dewey was clearly drawn to her power to evoke this world. In a poem he wrote for her he spoke of

> Generations of stifled worlds reaching out
> Through you,
> Aching for utt'rance, dying on lips
> That have died of hunger,
> Hunger not to have, but to be.
> Generations as yet unuttered, dumb, smothered,
> Inchoate, unutterable by me and mine,
> In you I see them coming to be,
> Luminous, slow revolving, ordered in rhythm.
> You shall not utter them; you shall be them,
> And from out the pain
> A great song shall fill the world.

For her part, Yezierska considered ethnicity to be a crucial aspect of the love she and Dewey shared. In a thinly veiled fictionalization of their romance in a later story, she wrote: "Now and then threads of gold have spun through the darkness—links of understanding woven by fearless souls—Gentiles and Jews—men and women who were not afraid to

43. Ibid., p. 253. On the quest of the *New Republic*'s editors for influence see Charles Forcey, *The Crossroads of Liberalism* (New York: Oxford, 1961), pp. 221–272, and Lasch, *New Radicalism*, pp. 181–224.

trust their love. . . . It's because he and I are of a different race that we can understand one another so profoundly, touch the innermost reaches of the soul, beyond the reach of those who think they know us." Yezierska regarded Dewey as a godlike figure blessed with an intuitive understanding of and compassion for the immigrant, and to have been seen as such in the eyes of a lover no doubt animated Dewey's efforts to rescue the Poles from Paderewski.[44]

The efforts of Dewey and Barnes to influence American Polish policy failed. The two men slowly awakened to the fact that Wilson's rhetoric about international democracy often belied the policies of his administration. "If the US government prefers to let a lot of small shysters and self-seekers run its foreign policies for it, probably they might as well do it," Dewey wrote his wife. "We gave them a run for their money for a few weeks however and it was good sport while it lasted." In January 1917 Wilson had declared before the Senate "for a free, united, and autonomous Poland," Barnes observed, but the most interesting feature of the Polish situation to Americans should be "the contrast between the Polish policy of President Wilson as he stated it to the Senate and the manner in which it was antagonized within the knowledge of the highest administration political circles." The Detroit Convention was not postponed; the government refused to intervene in Polish-American politics; the Wilson administration continued its support of the Paris Committee; and Dewey and Barnes were investigated by the Justice Department for "pro-German" sympathies.[45]

---

44. Jo Ann Boydston, ed., *The Poems of John Dewey* (Carbondale: Southern Illinois University Press, 1977), pp. 4–5; Anzia Yezierska, "Wild Winter Love," *Century* 113 (February 1927): 490. The Dewey-Yezierska romance came to an end in the fall of 1918 for reasons that remain obscure, though it seems to have been Dewey, constrained by the "iron band" binding him to Alice and his family ("those who made, and own"), who broke it off. The story of the relationship is told in Jo Ann Boydston's Introduction to the *Poems*, and to Boydston goes the credit for the clever detective work that uncovered what details there are of the affair. Boydston's researches are incorporated in a recent biography of Yezierska by her daughter, Louise Levitas Henriksen, *Anzia Yezierska: A Writer's Life* (New Brunswick, N.J.: Rutgers University Press, 1988), and Mary V. Dearborn, *Love in the Promised Land: The Story of Anzia Yezierska and John Dewey* (New York: Free Press, 1988). Dewey never intended his poems—the basis of our understanding of his side of the romance—to see the light of day, and they survived only by virtue of some questionable archival acquisition practices by Columbia librarian Milton Thomas, who rescued some of them from Dewey's wastebasket and kept them, unbeknownst to Dewey, and philosopher Herbert Schneider, who found others in Dewey's desk when he inherited his office and turned them over to Thomas without informing Dewey. For a sensitive and insightful reading of the poems see Philip W. Jackson, "John Dewey's Poetry," *American Journal of Education* 91 (1982): 65–78.

45. JD to Alice Dewey, 6 September 1918, Dewey Papers; Barnes, "Democracy, Watch Your Step!" pp. 595, 597.

In late August, Dewey wrote his children that his work on the Polish question was nearly completed and "my activities in saving the nation—or nations—will have come to an end, the rest of my work will be merely the kind of intellectual study which is more in my line. I shall be glad and sorry; if this sort of thing could be strung out more instead of being so highly concentrated and intensified I should be mainly sorry." Had his recommendations to the Wilson administration to intervene in the affairs of the Polish community been more favorably received, he might well have been sorrier than he suspected.[46]

Unintended Consequences

Despite his growing uneasiness with the way the war was progressing, Dewey remained hopeful until the end of the conflict that it would advance the development of radical democracy at home as well as abroad. Neither Bourne's powerful polemics nor his own nagging doubts in the wake of the failure of his modest efforts to curb repression and shape Polish-American affairs substantially inhibited his search for silver linings.

The destructive ends to which wartime mobilization were directed should not, Dewey maintained, be permitted to totally obscure the positive aspects of the experience which might point the way toward more humane social action. For one thing, the war had demonstrated that social control of a complex, interdependent society was not beyond human capacities. At the outset of the war, many had believed that human affairs had grown to a scale "too big to be got in hand." The war had, however, "put the immensity of things in a new light," revealing an inchoate power for control that lay in the hands of private interests and might readily be centralized in the hands of the national government. "The economists and businessmen called to the industrial front," he declared, "accomplished more in a few months to demonstrate the practicable possibilities of governmental regulation of private business than professional Socialists had effected in a generation." Domestic mobilization for violence, as Dewey saw it, had proved that it was "possible for human beings to take hold of human affairs and manage them, to see an end which has to be gained, a purpose which must be fulfilled, and deliberately and intelligently to go to work to organize the means, the resources and the methods of accomplishing these results." The

46. JD to Children, 20 August 1918, Dewey Papers.

question was no longer whether social control was possible but what kind of social control was desirable and for what ends.[47]

Dewey admitted that "to say that the world will be better organized is not—unfortunately—the same thing as to say that it will be organized so as to be a better world," but even here he was sanguine. During the war, science and the scientific community had been put in the service of social ends; men had become conscious of the "interdependence of all peoples"; and "in every warring country there had been the same demand that in the time of great national stress production for profit be subordinated to production for use." This latter development was of particular significance, for it pointed to some deep-seated weaknesses of capitalism, most notably its failure to guarantee its members steady and useful employment, its inability to provide an adequate standard of living for much of the industrial population, and its inefficient utilization of natural and human resources. The war suggested to Dewey that Americans might be capable of aggressively addressing these weaknesses instead of trusting to the drift of "so-called evolution." These weaknesses were not the product of "nature" but of capitalism, and, casting his remarks in a Veblenian vein, Dewey argued that "the war, by throwing into relief the public aspect of every social enterprise, has discovered the amount of sabotage which habitually goes on in manipulating property rights to take a private profit out of social needs."[48]

The weaknesses of American society and their roots in the structure of the political economy, Dewey argued, called for at least three legitimate demands for postwar reconstruction. The first demand was for the right of every individual to work: "not the mere legal right, but a right which is enforceable so that the individual will always have the opportunity to engage in some form of useful activity." Second, Dewey demanded that every individual be provided with a decent standard of living: "not merely of economic livelihood, but of physical, moral, intellectual, and aesthetic livelihood." Finally, Dewey demanded "greater industrial autonomy," by which he meant the "greater ability on the part of the workers in any particular trade or occupation to control that industry, instead of working under these conditions of external control where they have no interest, no insight into what they are doing, and no social outlook upon the consequences and meaning of what they are doing."[49]

47. "The New Paternalism" (1918), *Middle Works* 11:117; "Internal Social Reorganization after the War" (1918), *Middle Works* 11:82.

48. "What Are We Fighting For?" (1918), *Middle Works* 11:98–102; "Internal Social Reorganization," pp. 74–83.

49. "Internal Social Reorganization," pp. 83–84.

This last demand not only reflected Dewey's position in the prewar industrial education debate but also his growing concern that postwar reconstruction in the West would take the form of state capitalism or state socialism, both of which encouraged a centralization of power which posed a threat to participatory democracy. "Socialization, as well as the kindred term socialism, covers many and diverse alternatives," he said. "Many of the measures thus far undertaken may be termed in the direction of state capitalism, looking to the absorption of the means of production and distribution by the government, and to the replacement of the present corporate employing and directive forces by a bureaucracy of officials. So far as the consequences of war assume this form, it supplies another illustration of the main thesis of Herbert Spencer that a centralized government has been built up by war necessities, and that such a state is necessarily militaristic in its structure."[50] Dewey hoped that this sort of centralization could at least be forestalled in favor of a transitional form of political capitalism which would serve as a way station on route to a decentralized, democratic socialism centered on workers' control of production. This transitional stage would "not involve absolute state ownership and absolute state control, but rather a kind of conjoined supervision and regulation, with supervisors and arbiters, as it were, to look after the public interests, the interests of the consumer, the interests of the population as a whole, others to represent those who have their capital immediately invested, and others to represent those who have their lives (in the form of work) immediately invested." During this intermediate period production for profit would be dismantled, and both white- and blue- collar labor would be educated in the ways and means to guide production in the public interest. Centralized authority would have to be exercised only to effect an initial "transfer of power from the more or less rapacious groups now in control."[51]

Beyond the transition for Dewey lay a quasi-guild socialist ideal, a political economy consisting of "a federation of self-governing industries with the government acting as adjuster and arbiter rather than as direct owner and manager, unless perhaps in the case of industries occupying such a privileged position as fuel production and the railways. Taxation will be a chief governmental power through which to produce and maintain socialization of the services of the land and of industries organized for self-direction rather than for subjection to

---

50. "What Are We Fighting For?" p. 104. In this article Dewey called "state capitalism" what most would term "state socialism," a terminological confusion he later cleared up. See "The New Paternalism," p. 117.
51. "Internal Social Reorganization," p. 85; "What Are We Fighting For?" p. 105.

alien investors." Dewey was, in fact, quite taken with British guild socialism, and insofar as there is a familiar socialist model with which to
identify his thinking about the political economy after World War I, this
would be it.[52]

The most notable feature of his early efforts to formulate a democratic socialist vision is that he focused on capitalism less as a badly
managed economic system than as a system of *power*. This view led him
to a critique that retained its strength even in periods of prosperity. He
had a good deal to say, to be sure, about the limitations of capitalism as
a means of producing and distributing goods, but these limitations
could be corrected as well, perhaps even better, by state capitalism or
state socialism as by his own decentralized socialism. Dewey's central
concern, reflected in his preoccupation with workers' control and the
parceling-out of decision-making authority, was with power and, in
particular, with the power needed by all men to develop their individual capacities. State socialism as well as state capitalism took this power
from the individual, especially the individual laborer. Dewey attacked
those liberals who sought a solution to the injustices of American society simply through a redistribution of wealth, important as this was.
He pointed out that most capitalists would be offended if it were suggested that they worked wholly for the material benefits of their labor.
Would Herbert Hoover, he asked after the war, "be contented under
the charge that the animating spring of his own activities had been the
material products of his work?" Wage earners were no different in this
respect: "Not idealism but human psychology proclaims the fact that
man does not live by wages alone. What men need is an outlet for what
is human in them. Not for any long period can they be bribed to be
quite lacking such an outlet. At present, the period is almost zero. For
the workers realize that an increase in wages is now a testimony to their
power; and an awakened sense of power is just what demands opportunity for exercise. And this means a responsible share in the management of activities."

Although Dewey underestimated the power of bribery and overestimated the interest of American organized labor in self-management,
his own antagonism to "economism" was clear. "Only as modern society
has at command individuals who are trained by experience in the control of industrial activities and relationships can we achieve industrial

52. "What Are We Fighting For?" p. 105. Guild socialism was well publicized and
widely discussed in the United States in 1918 and 1919, and guild socialists including G.
D. H. Cole regularly contributed articles to the *New Republic, Nation, Dial,* and other
American magazines.

democracy, the autonomous management of each line of productive work by those directly engaged in it," he declared in 1918. "Without such democratization of industry, socialization of industry will be doomed to arrest at the stage of state capitalism, which may give the average laborer a greater share in the material rewards of industry than he now enjoys, but which will leave him in the same condition of intellectual and moral passivity and perversion as that in which he now lives."[53]

These proposals for domestic reconstruction Dewey offered in 1918 went a good way toward addressing Bourne's complaint about the vagueness of his democratic ideals, but he remained captivated by an extraordinarily naive faith that the war could be placed in service of his radical vision. Perhaps most striking is the indirect and perhaps unconscious testimony he offered throughout the war to Bourne's thesis about the inhospitability of war to conscious human purposes, for he based his most radical hopes on an appeal to the *unintended* consequences of the conflict:

> Just now we are fighting for democracy. Democracy is a fact in the minds of most Americans. They think, at least, that they know what it means. It seems certain that the Allies will be victorious and I believe they will find democracy. But that democracy will be as different from the democracy of their concepts as the New World was different from the Orient which Columbus sought. We are fighting to do away with the rule of kings and kaisers. When we have finished the job we may find that we have done away with the rule of money and trade. We are fighting for freedom to transact business; but this war may easily be the beginning of the end of business. In fifty years, it is altogether probable, the whole system which we know as "business" today will have vanished from the earth.[54]

For an instrumentalist to appeal in this fashion to the history made behind men's backs was, at the very least, tacit testimony to Bourne's argument that the war would negate the designs of peaceful men. It was also to come perilously close to the "militarist's conception of war as a noble blessing in disguise" which Dewey had labeled "a stupidity."

53. "Freedom of Thought and Work" (1920), *Middle Works* 12:8–9; "Creative Industry" (1918), *Middle Works* 11:335.
54. Dewey quoted in "Professor Dewey of Columbia."

Portrait of John Dewey by Edwin Burrage Child, painted in 1929. Courtesy of Columbia University in the City of New York.

Part Three

Toward the Great Community (1918–1929)

Regarded as an idea, democracy is not an
alternative to other principles of associated life.
It is the idea of community life itself.
— *The Public and Its Problems* (1927)

CHAPTER 8

The Politics of Peace

★

In December 1918, Randolph Bourne died, a victim of an influenza epidemic that killed thousands. "If any man has a ghost," wrote John Dos Passos, "Bourne has a ghost, a tiny twisted unscared ghost in a black cloak hopping along the grimy old brick and brownstone streets still left in downtown New York, crying out in a shrill soundless giggle: *War is the health of the state*." After Bourne's untimely death, John Dewey never admitted to being haunted by this ghost, but in the immediate postwar years his thinking about war and international politics underwent a substantial revision that amounted essentially to a reconsideration of positions he had taken during the war along lines suggested by Bourne's criticisms of them.[1]

Dewey never publicly or privately conceded the power of Bourne's antiwar arguments; there remains evidence only of the deep personal bitterness their confrontation engendered. Yet, whatever the emotional consequences may have been for Dewey of covertly conceding to Bourne, it was not particularly wrenching intellectually. For him to admit the cogency of Bourne's war essays largely meant to reexamine his wartime sentiments in light of his own philosophical ideals. One could regard the war as a failed experiment without seeing it as a failure of experimentalism, and, for Dewey, confrontation with the

1. John Dos Passos, *1919* (New York: New American Library, 1969), p. 121.

unintended consequences of "war-technique" energized a renewed quest for ways to make the world safe for democracy.[2]

THE DISCREDITING OF IDEALISM

As early as the fall of 1917 Dewey expressed concern that the war in which he had enlisted was becoming a war quite other than that promised by Woodrow Wilson. But he was unwilling to admit that the opportunity to turn the war to democratic ends had been lost, and when the president announced his Fourteen Point peace plan in January 1918, Dewey quickly lent his voice to the campaign for Wilson's "new diplomacy." In forging the peace, he said, Americans had to ensure that the Allies "accept and are influenced by the American idea rather than ourselves by the European idea." In this case a particularly important feature of the "American idea" was embodied in Wilson's proposal for a League of Nations: the commitment to a federalism in which "the unity does not destroy the many, but maintains each constituent factor in full vigor"—*e pluribus unum*. "It is not an accident," he noted, "that the conceptions of a world federation, a concert of nations, a supreme tribunal, a league of nations to enforce peace, are peculiarly American contributions."[3]

Depending on whether American or European ideas shaped the peace process, Dewey foresaw two likely consequences of the international interdependence revealed and enhanced by the Great War:

> We shall have either a world federation in the sense of a genuine concert of nations, or a few large imperialistic organizations, standing in chronic hostility to one another. . . . The choice between these two alternatives is the great question which the statesmen after the war will

2. I have found no evidence of whatever direct consideration Dewey may have given to Bourne's war essays. Shortly after Bourne's death *Alice* Dewey did offer her daughter a condescending assessment of Bourne's work. "We had not heard of the death of Randolph Bourne," she wrote, "and are saddened by it. It brings acutely to my mind the same pathetic fact that his talented life illustrated. I mean the fact that he might have been happy where he was and where he made others happy if only his early misfortunes might have been related to his life in different fashion. One can see he would have very little chance in a battle with pneumonia. I hope his writings will be gathered up by his friends for they give proof of real talent. The trouble came when he attempted to deal with the facts of actual life which represented a struggle that he shrunk from and hated. Literature in its academic and esthetic sense should have been his field. It is always hard to see the young ones die; even if you think his would have been an experience of increasing bitterness" (Alice Dewey to Evelyn Dewey, 2 January 1919, Dewey Papers).

3. "America in the World" (1918), *Middle Works* 11:70–71.

have to face. If it is dodged, and the attempt is made to restore an antebellum condition of a large number of independent detached and "sovereign" states allied only for purposes of economic and potential military warfare, the situation will be forced, probably, into the alternative of an imperially organized Balance of Power whose unstable equilibrium will result in the next war for decisive dominion.

The statesmen and politicians of the world were divided into those who thought primarily in negative terms of national security and defense and those who thought positively in terms of "association for the realization of common interests." Throughout 1918 Dewey regarded Wilson as the principal spokesman for the latter and delivered unwavering support for the president's efforts to end the war on American terms.[4]

In the spring of 1918 Dewey was offered an important platform for the delivery of this support when Martyn Johnson, owner and editor of the *Dial*, asked him to serve with Thorstein Veblen and Helen Marot as an associate editor of that magazine, with a special responsibility for addressing the issues of postwar "reconstruction" at home and abroad. This offer was made as part of one of the sleaziest episodes of double-dealing in American magazine history.[5]

Published in Chicago since 1880, the *Dial* had by the beginning of the war become a moribund publication engaged in a rear-guard defense of the genteel tradition in literature. But in 1916 Johnson, a young midwestern journalist, bought the magazine, and he was determined to move it to New York as soon as possible and transform it into a voice of literary modernism and progressive politics. One of Johnson's most decisive moves in the latter regard was to appoint Randolph Bourne a contributing editor in March 1917, and by 1918 the *Dial* was virtually the only magazine willing to publish Bourne's work. To escape from Chicago, Johnson needed a financial angel, and he worked his way into the good graces of Scofield Thayer, scion of a wealthy Worcester, Massachusetts, family, who was looking to invest in a magazine and was a great admirer of Bourne's essays in the *Dial*. At the same time, unbeknownst to Thayer and Bourne—both of whom thought a larger role for Bourne in the magazine's editorial direction was in the offing as a result of Thayer's support—Johnson initiated negotiations to put Dew-

4. "What Are We Fighting For?" (1918), *Middle Works* 11:101; "The Approach to a League of Nations" (1918), *Middle Works* 11:128.

5. My account of Dewey's relationship with the *Dial* follows that in Nicholas Joost, *The Dial: Years of Transition, 1912–1920* (Barre, Mass.: Barre Publishers, 1967), chaps. 4–6, and Joost, "Culture vs. Power: Randolph Bourne, John Dewey, and *The Dial*," *Midwest Quarterly* 9 (1968): 245–259.

ey, Veblen, and Marot, three decidedly prowar intellectuals, at the top of his masthead.

Like Dewey, Veblen had lent a helping hand to the American war effort in both word and deed, and the thinking of these two major figures in American intellectual life converged in significant ways during the war. Veblen's *Imperial Germany and the Industrial Revolution* (1915) characterized German culture in terms remarkably similar to those of Dewey's *German Philosophy and Politics* (published the same year) as an "unstable cultural compound" comprised of transcendental idealism and technical efficiency, and his *Nature of Peace and the Terms of Its Perpetuation* (1917) anticipated and perhaps influenced Dewey's own subsequent proposals for a more equitable international order. During the war Veblen offered advice to Walter Lippmann and the other members of Wilson's famous "Inquiry" that formulated American plans for peace, and he worked on several studies for other government agencies, including a plan for a submarine defense system. Marot, the least known of the prospective editorial triumvirate, was a socialist, the former executive secretary of the New York Women's Trade Union League, and a member of the editorial board of the *Masses* until that journal was suppressed by the government in 1917 for its antiwar stance. Despite this latter connection, Johnson assured Dewey that Marot was in accord with "vigorous editorial backing of the President in his entire war policy."[6]

In the early summer of 1918 Johnson secured Thayer's financial support (Thayer was also made an associate editor), and in July the *Dial* moved to New York and began to reorganize its editorial staff. At about this time Dewey, who was not, in any case, completely sold on taking part in the "new *Dial*," noticed that Bourne was to remain a contributing editor and wrote Johnson that he would have nothing to do with a publication with which Bourne was associated. Because Thayer's check was in hand, because he was aware of and uneasy with the unpopularity of Bourne's criticism of the war, and because Dewey was a bigger and safer name than Bourne, Johnson quickly responded to Dewey's objec-

6. Martyn Johnson to JD, 10 April 1918, Joseph Ratner Papers, Morris Library, Southern Illinois University. On Veblen's work during the war see Joseph Dorfman, *Thorstein Veblen and His America* (New York: Viking, 1934), chaps. 18–22; and John P. Diggins, *The Bard of Savagery: Thorstein Veblen and Modern Social Theory* (New York: Seabury, 1978), chap. 10. Many of Veblen's important wartime essays and his government reports are collected in *Essays in Our Changing Order*, ed. Leon Ardzrooni (New York: Viking, 1934), pp. 245–470. On Helen Marot see Sol Cohen, "Helen Marot," in *Notable American Women*, ed. Edward T. James (Cambridge: Harvard University Press, 1971), 2:499–501; and Joost, *The Dial*, pp. 199–203. Marot was the author of a book on industrial education, *Creative Impulse in Industry* (1918), which Dewey admired. See JD, "Creative Industry" (1918), *Middle Works* 11:333–335.

tions and fired Bourne. Both Bourne and Thayer reacted to this turn of events with bitter anger, but the best Thayer could do was to persuade Johnson to keep Bourne on as a reviewer confined to nonpolitical, literary subjects. This was fine with Dewey, who ended up with not only a new forum for his views but also a muzzle on his most astute critic.[7]

Dewey backed Wilson's new diplomacy not only through his articles in the *Dial* and other publications but also by endorsing the work of the League of Free Nations Association (LFNA), the most important organization of progressives supporting the president. In November 1918 the LFNA, which had begun work in the spring, published its "Statement of Principles" in the leading progressive magazines. Signed by Dewey and other notables including Charles Beard, Herbert Croly, Felix Frankfurter, Learned Hand, Norman Hapgood, Sidney Hillman, Paul Kellogg, and James Harvey Robinson, this statement declared that Wilson's proposed League of Nations was the cornerstone of a "sounder future international order." The principal purpose of such a league would be to provide security and equality of economic opportunity for all the nations of the world. Heretofore the security of nations had been seen to rest on the competitive pursuit of preponderant power between nations, but the war had made it clear that such a system of competitive nationalism inevitably gave rise to "covert or overt competitions for power and territory dangerous to peace and destructive to justice." Competitive nationalism had to give way to "cooperative nationalism" in which "the price of secure nationality is some degree of internationalism." The second pillar of a lasting peace, equality of economic opportunity, was essential not only to the "maximum economic development" of every nation but to international security as well. Equality of opportunity, the LFNA contended, required "a gradually increasing freedom of mutual exchange with its resulting economic interdependence," and this in turn mandated equal access for all nations to raw materials and markets, to international transportation systems, and to the resources and customers in "non-self-governing territories." The effective pursuit of these goals, the LFNA argued, required the sacrifice of a considerable measure of national sovereignty

---

7. JD to Alice Dewey, 13 July 1918; JD to Family, 7 September 1918, Dewey Papers. After Bourne's death in December 1918, Thayer resigned from the *Dial*. In late 1919 he and his friend James Sibley Watson, Jr., purchased the magazine from Johnson, and under their leadership it became a leading voice of modernism in art and literature in the twenties. See William Wasserstrom, *The Time of the Dial* (Syracuse, N.Y.: Syracuse University Press, 1963).

and the establishment of "a universal association of nations based upon the principle that the security of each shall rest upon the strength of the whole." Fearful of the power of "deep-seated forces of reaction," the group urged "all liberal-minded men to stand behind the principles which the President has enunciated."[8]

Though the LFNA statement was denounced by conservatives as a Marxist critique of imperialism, it might well have been written by Woodrow Wilson himself and was an especially clear statement of liberal, open-door ideology. Though Dewey signed the statement, he told a friend that his "personal connection with the document was nil," and by the fall of 1918 his own thinking about the postwar order was becoming considerably more radical than that of the LFNA. At the same time the group's statement appeared, Dewey was publishing a series of articles on the prospective league in the *Dial* which offered a quite different vision of what the open-door and international equality of economic opportunity should mean.[9]

In these articles Dewey called for a transfer of authority in international affairs from aristocratic leaders possessed by the "ethics of dignity" to "men whose habitudes of thought have been formed by dealing with the facts of modern industry and the give and take, for common interests, of modern commerce." But despite this hymn to men trained by the market, he revealed that, for him, an open-door world was not the liberal-capitalist political economy envisioned by Wilson and the LFNA. To Wilson opening the door in the international economy meant providing all nations with *formal* equality of opportunity, and hence the key reforms were such things as the abolition of preferential trade agreements, freedom of the seas, and access to ports for landlocked countries. But to Dewey, who here drew on his larger ethical critique of purely formal, negative freedom, opening the door meant providing all nations with a more substantive "effective freedom" akin to that required for the self-realization of individuals:

> It has been demonstrated that more is needed to secure freedom and equality of conditions between individuals than to declare them legally all free and equal, while leaving them to unrestricted competition with

8. "League of Free Nations Association: Statement of Principles," *Dial*, 30 November 1918: 493, 495. An excellent discussion of the LFNA is Wolfgang J. Helbich, "American Liberals in the League of Nations Controversy," *Public Opinion Quarterly* 31 (1967): 568–596.

9. JD to S. O. Levinson, 30 December 1918, S. O. Levinson Papers, Joseph Regenstein Library, University of Chicago.

one another. Immense inequality of power is compatible with formal equality. The same thing will surely develop with respect to any merely legal equality among nations. Certain nations have a tremendous superiority in population, natural resources, technical progress in industry, command of credit, and shipping. Nothing better calculated to develop actual inequality of trade relationship among nations could well be found than a system which set up a nominal mathematical equality and then threw matters practically into the hands of the present big nations.[10]

Genuine equality among nations required not "free" trade but trade carefully regulated to take account of prevailing inequalities of power. Hence Dewey called for the creation of an international economy managed by democratically controlled international bodies committed to production for use and the elimination of imperialism. This, he admitted, would require that the wealthy nations of the world surrender power in order to develop the wealth and capacity for self-government of the poor nations. This surrender was ultimately in the interests of the strong nations, he argued, because it would eliminate the costs of wars between competing imperial powers and promote the growth of prosperous trading partners. Trade and business contracts would be exchanges between equals for mutual advantage, not unequal bargains struck between rich and poor nations. Control of the international economy on these terms, Dewey concluded, required "powerful international commissions dealing with such matters as equality of labor standards, the regulation of shipping, and, for some time to come, of food, raw materials and immigrants, and above all of the exportation of capital and distribution of the available credit of the world. Equality of trade conditions means *equalization* of conditions." Thus, though Dewey continued to support Wilson throughout 1918, by the end of the year he was clearly attempting to persuade the president to initiate efforts to make the world safe for a democracy far different, and far more radical, than anything Wilson had in mind.[11]

By the time the "Reconstruction" editors of the *Dial* began their work in earnest in the fall of 1918 it was already apparent that the new diplomacy of Wilson and the LFNA, let alone the more radical vision of Dewey and Veblen, was in trouble. By December the *Dial* trio acknowledged that "the high hopes which the world has entertained for a peace

10. "The League of Nations and the New Diplomacy" (1918), *Middle Works* 11:133; "The League of Nations and Economic Freedom" (1918), *Middle Works* 11:139.
11. "The League of Nations and Economic Freedom," p. 142.

settlement that will make future wars impossible do not seem likely to be realized." Dewey himself, who had the year before attributed wartime repression and hysteria to American inexperience with the ways of war, now intimated darkly that the nation's ruling class had self-consciously cultivated irrationality in order to deflect the war from Wilsonian purposes and to protect their interests. For progressives "to win the war was to bring about the state of things which should make any similar war impossible in the future," but the reactionaries had effectively persuaded many that "a military defeat of Germany had only to be complete enough to be of itself a winning of the war irrespective of any further consequences." As Bourne had warned, progressives had made some strange bedfellows when they threw their support to the war. Now, Dewey admitted, their dreams were threatened by a powerful flanking movement by American enemies of democracy who were forging an alliance with "those elements in the [Allied] governments which have shown themselves as most nearly imperialistic and unreconstructed." In December he reiterated this argument, privately predicting that "probably the more imperialistic factors will dictate the peace settlement, ably assisted by Knox, Lodge, Roosevelt, et al. in this country, tho there will be some of the clothing of an alleged democratic settlement along Wilsonian lines."[12]

By the late winter and spring of 1919 the news from Paris made it clear that the fears of progressives had been realized. "America has won the war; America has lost the peace, the object for which she fought," the *Dial* editors wrote in May. Wilson had achieved a thoroughly pyrrhic victory at Versailles, securing the League of Nations at the expense of the principles that were to be its foundation. "Peace without victory," self-determination, freedom of the seas, disarmament, racial equality, anti-colonialism, equality of economic opportunity among nations—all were sacrificed. Wilson, the editors contended, was either a hypocrite or a fool who had fallen among thieves. They charitably opted for the latter explanation and extended the blame to all who had blindly followed him into the trap. "The proper mood for the reception of President Wilson

12. "Reconstruction Editorial," *Dial*, 14 December 1918: 561; "The Cult of Irrationality" (1918), *Middle Works* 11:109–110; JD to S. O. Levinson, 30 December 1918, Levinson Papers. In this letter Dewey again showed his weakness in the face of defeat for compensatory prophecy about unintended consequences. "The Bourbons are always Bourbons, even when victorious," he said, "and the greater the reactionary victory now, the greater the democratic reaction later—tho I wish the latter policy could be established without the confusion and conflict this wasteful method entails. I didn't set out to play the role of a prophet, but the situation is so clear that it is hard to realize the stupidity that makes the present reactionaries unable to see it."

on his return," they concluded, "is that of the old Puritan day of fasting, humiliation, and prayer." The *Dial* was second to none in its resistance to ratification of the peace treaty, which, its editors argued, "should be rejected as a matter of national honor, of national safety, and of national service to the world."[13]

A few days after the peace conference opened, Dewey departed for a vacation in Asia. He was thereafter a *Dial* editor in name only, and in the spring of 1919 the magazine was very much Veblen's organ. But Dewey fully shared his coeditor's sentiments about the peace treaty and the League. The Far East was, after all, not the best vantage point to see any virtue in the machinations at Versailles, for the grant of German territorial concessions in China to Japan was one of the most blatant accommodations to imperialism and secret treaties made by Wilson and the other peacemakers.[14]

By early 1919 Dewey was advancing a grudging bit of self-criticism for his enthusiastic support of Wilson's fool's errand. "It will be interesting," he wrote his children, "to see what will happen if the American people should wake up to wonder what we went into the war for after all"—a remark that reflected Dewey's growing second thoughts about his own commitment to the war. Those like himself who were converted to war, he publicly admitted, were "obliged to undertake an unusually searching inquiry into the actual results in their relation to their earlier professions and beliefs. Were not those right who held that it was self-contradictory to try to further the permanent ideals of peace by recourse to war? Was not he who thought they might thus be promoted one of the gullible throng who swallowed the cant of idealism as a sugar coating for the bitter core of violence and greed?" Dewey acknowledged the power of this criticism, though he was unwilling to accept the separation of idealism and force it implied. It was not the combination of idealism and force that the Versailles Treaty condemned, he said, but the failure of Americans to "use force adequately

13. "Reconstruction Editorial," *Dial*, 17 May 1919, 31 May 1919: 511–513, 565. On the *Dial*'s position on the spectrum of liberal opinion on the peace settlement see Helbich, "American Liberals in the League of Nations Controversy," pp. 580–596; and Stuart I. Rochester, *American Liberal Disillusionment in the Wake of World War I* (University Park: Pennsylvania State University Press, 1977), chaps. 6–7.

14. See "The Student Revolt in China" (1919), *Middle Works* 11:186–191; "The International Duel in China" (1919), *Middle Works* 11:192–198; and "Militarism in China" (1919), *Middle Works* 11:199–204. Because of Dewey's visit to Asia, he and Veblen worked together only for a few months, and it does not appear to have been a very collaborative relationship. The successful purge of Bourne forestalled the even more intriguing possibility of a Bourne-Veblen partnership. Dewey resigned from the editorial board of the *Dial* in September 1919.

and intelligently" on behalf of their ideals. The United States had given up its leverage when it entered the war on its allies' terms. Wilson, Dewey argued, should have made American entry into the war contingent on the adoption of democratic war aims by its allies, and the nation's economic power should have been used to achieve these aims. By failing to use their power when it would have been most effective, Americans had put themselves in the position of having fought a war that did little to advance the cause of international democracy, a war that was instead a setback for democrats. Thus Dewey, in effect, admitted the logic of Bourne's pragmatic critique of his "sentimentalism." He had yet to recognize the power of Bourne's deeper insights into the inexorability of "war-technique." But that too would come.[15]

Traveling Theory

Dewey spent the better part of the important years between 1919 and 1921 in the Far East, amid revolutionary social change and far from his own nation's "return to normalcy." In the fall of 1918 he was on leave from Columbia teaching at the University of California in Berkeley, and he and Alice decided that they "may never again get as near Japan as we are now and that as the years are passing, it is now or never with us." In late January 1919 they sailed for a short Japanese vacation that was unexpectedly to become an Asian sabbatical of more than two years, most of it spent in China. Thus, while in the United States Herbert Croly wrote despairingly of the "eclipse of progressivism" on the eve of the election of Warren G. Harding, Dewey found himself speaking to Chinese audiences eager to hear the progressive message. Chinese liberals attempting to reconstruct their society in the wake of the Revolution of 1911, which had overthrown the Manchu dynasty only to replace it with a chaotic "republic" ruled by corrupt warlords and foreign imperialists, accorded Dewey a warm, enthusiastic welcome and hailed him as the philosopher of democracy. This reception recharged his political energies, which had been drained by the controversies of the war years, and the activities of the May Fourth Movement of young Chinese students and intellectuals sustained his hopes for the progress of international democracy. China would henceforth be "the country nearest his heart after his own," his daughter Jane

15. JD to Children, 20 January 1919, Dewey Papers; "The Discrediting of Idealism" (1919), *Middle Works* 11:180–185.

reported, and "the change from the United States to an environment of the oldest culture in the world struggling to adjust itself to new conditions was so great as to act as a rebirth of intellectual enthusiasms."[16]

Dewey's Far Eastern sojourn began, however, with a more dispiriting visit to Japan. When two prominent Japanese businessmen with American connections, Ono Eijiro and Baron Shibusawa Eiichi, learned that Dewey and his wife were planning a trip to Asia, they arranged for him to deliver a series of lectures at Tokyo Imperial University. The Deweys arrived in Japan in early February 1919. Dewey delivered his lectures at the university in late February and March (later published as *Reconstruction in Philosophy*), and the couple departed for China in late April. Their impressions of Japan were recorded in several articles Dewey wrote for the *Dial* and privately in letters to the Dewey children.[17]

Dewey's work was little known in Japan and pragmatism was a philosophy with few Japanese exponents. The only American philosopher granted much respect in Japan was Josiah Royce, whose absolute idealism was thought to blend nicely with the traditional values of Japanese culture. The kind words Royce had written about the feudal-militarist code of Bushido added to his reputation among Japanese philosophers. As Lewis Feuer has pointed out, "The philosophical distance between Royce and Dewey corresponded in Japan to the political distance between militarist absolutism and liberal democracy. Dewey's philosophy was not falling on friendly soil."[18]

Dewey was clearly aware he was in hostile territory. Although he reported optimistically on the few signs of democratic activity in Japan, he was deeply troubled by a society that was the antithesis of nearly everything he believed to be just. Japanese society was marked by deep class divisions, held together by the mythology of the emperor cult and the repression of a military state. The free expression of opinion and the scientific analysis of social problems which were at the heart of Deweyan democracy were impossible under these conditions. More-

16. JD to S. O. Levinson, 9 December 1918, Levinson Papers; Herbert Croly, "The Eclipse of Progressivism," *New Republic*, 27 October 1920: 210–216; Jane Dewey, "Biography of John Dewey," in Paul Schilpp, ed., *The Philosophy of John Dewey*, 2d ed. (New York: Tudor, 1951), p. 42.
17. "Liberalism in Japan" (1919), *Middle Works* 11:156–173; "On Two Sides of the Eastern Sea" (1919), *Middle Works* 11:174–179; "Public Opinion in Japan" (1921), *Middle Works* 13:255–261; and *Letters from China and Japan*, ed. Evelyn Dewey (New York: E. P. Dutton, 1920). A full account of the Deweys' visit to Japan is Lewis Feuer, "John Dewey's Sojourn in Japan," *Teachers College Record* 71 (1969): 123–145.
18. Feuer, "Dewey's Sojourn," p. 126.

over, Japanese liberals were not disposed to risk their necks for the cause of democracy.

Dewey alternated between an impatience with the liberals' lack of "moral courage" and a sensitive awareness of the dangers that the exercise of such courage entailed. "It takes more force, more moral courage to be an outspoken critic of the politics and social condition of one's nation, to be a dissenter, in Japan than in any other country in the world," he said. Publicly, Dewey expressed the belief that Japanese militarism and imperialism could be curtailed, and he called upon American policy makers to put an end to the racist immigration policies that were an embarrassment to international liberalism and an important source of hostile Japanese nationalism. Privately, he was a good deal less sanguine about the potential for democratization in Japan. "Dewey, the political philosopher and political reformer," as Feuer has observed, "finally found himself baffled by Japanese society. The advocate of the method of intelligence, the believer in the ethics of democracy, the teacher with faith in the common man, found Japanese society immovable, mythridden, class congealed, and recalcitrant to liberal influences." When the Japanese emperor announced his intention to confer on Dewey the Order of the Rising Sun, the philosopher politely refused the honor.[19]

China was an entirely different story. "It is three days' easy journey from Japan to China," Dewey reported. "It is doubtful whether anywhere in the world another journey of the same length brings with it such a complete change of political temper and belief." Dewey's arrival in China in early May 1919 coincided with the eruption of what came to be known as the May Fourth Movement, a nationwide student movement of protest against Japanese imperialism and the corruption of domestic politics. The immediate occasion for the protest was the announcement of the treaty provisions at the Versailles Peace Conference granting territorial concessions in China to Japan. It was revealed that a weak and corrupt Peking government had secretly promised these concessions to the Japanese in exchange for a series of loans. In the protest that followed these revelations, student nationalists demanded a purge of the government and an end to Japanese domination of China. They

19. *Letters from China and Japan*, pp. 166–169; "Public Opinion in Japan," p. 257; Feuer, "Dewey's Sojourn," p. 140; Dykhuizen, p. 194. The Japanese translation of Dewey's *Democracy and Education* was published as *Introduction to the Philosophy of Education* because the word "democracy" was outlawed. The translator, Riichiro Hoashi, was later sentenced to prison for publishing articles on democracy, and his book on ethics was banned because it made no mention of the Imperial Household.

formed an alliance with Chinese merchants and shopkeepers, and throughout Dewey's stay in China the country was rocked by mass demonstrations, strikes, and boycotts of Japanese goods. The student movement made a great impression on Dewey, and he told his children "to think of kids in our country from fourteen on, taking the lead in starting a big cleanup reform politics movement and shaming merchants and professional men into joining them. This is sure some country."[20]

The groundwork for Dewey's visit to China had been carefully laid by several of his former students, led by Hu Shih, a prominent liberal philosopher. Hearing of Dewey's visit to Japan, Hu Shih arranged an invitation to him to teach for a year at the National University in Peking as well as to lecture in other parts of the country, an invitation Dewey eagerly accepted. When he was later offered the opportunity to teach in Peking yet another year, he agreed enthusiastically to extend his Chinese sojourn. "Nothing western looks quite the same any more," he wrote a Columbia colleague in 1920, "and this is as near to a renewal of youth as can be hoped for in this world."[21]

Hu Shih and many of Dewey's other students in China were active in the New Culture Movement, which was seeking to democratize Chinese culture and foster a vernacular literary renaissance. By 1919 hundreds of new periodicals had sprung up all over China, reflecting the activism of the intellectuals in both the May Fourth and the New Culture movements. These periodicals carried transcripts of Dewey's lectures and many articles explicating his thought. The lectures were also published in book form in China and went through numerous editions. Dewey was met by large and attentive audiences wherever he went, and his courses were exempted from the boycott of classes at Chinese universities instituted by May Fourth student activists. One Shanghai journal

20. "On Two Sides of the Eastern Sea," p. 174; *Letters from China and Japan*, p. 247. Dewey also did what he could to assure the U.S. State Department that the student radicals were not Bolshevists. See JD to Colonel Alexander Drysdale, 1 December 1920 ("Bolshevism in China: Service Report"), *Middle Works* 12:253–255. On the May Fourth Movement see Chow Tse-tung, *The May Fourth Movement* (Cambridge: Harvard University Press, 1960); Lin Yü-Sheng, *The Crisis of Chinese Consciousness: Radical Antitraditionalism in the May Fourth Era* (Madison: University of Wisconsin Press, 1979); and Vera Schwarcz, *The Chinese Enlightenment: Intellectuals and the Legacy of the May Fourth Movement of 1919* (Berkeley: University of California Press, 1986). Since I have repeatedly made light of Dewey's record as a prophet, it is worth recording his accurate prediction that in China "the fourth of May, nineteen hundred and nineteen, will be marked as the dawn of a new day" ("The Student Revolt in China" [1919], *Middle Works* 11:191).

21. JD to John Jacob Coss, 13 January 1920, Special Collections, Butler Library, Columbia University, New York.

reported that "Professor Dewey, by means of his lectures which are interpreted as they are given, has reached thousands of Chinese. These lectures are translated into Chinese and are published in the leading magazines and newspapers of the country. These printed lectures are carefully studied by many. It may be guessed that by means of the spoken and the written, or printed word Professor Dewey has said his say to several hundred thousand Chinese." In New York, the *Chinese Students' Monthly* reported that "Mr. Dewey's career in China is one of singular success. From the time of his arrival to the present, continual ovation follows his footprints. Bankers and editors frequent his residences; teachers and students flock to his classrooms. Clubs compete to entertain him; to hear him speak; newspapers vie with each other in translating his latest utterances. His speeches and lectures are eagerly read, his biography has been elaborately written. The serious-minded comment on his philosophy; the light-hearted remember his name." As historian Barry Keenan has observed, "Dewey became a fad." For many Chinese intellectuals he was quite a serious fad, for they "closely associated his thought with the very definition of modernity."[22]

For our purposes, the lectures Dewey delivered in China on social and political philosophy are particularly important. As Hu Shih said, they were Dewey's first public attempt to "formulate a coherent statement of a social and political philosophy based in pragmatism" and an effort to sketch out some of the implications of such a philosophy for the reform of Chinese society. In addition, the lectures gave further evidence of Dewey's interest in pluralism, guild socialism, and other recent developments in Anglo-American radicalism which addressed the worries about state capitalism and state socialism he had expressed during the war.[23]

22. JD to John Jacob Coss, 22 April 1920, Special Collections, Butler Library, Columbia; Chinese journals quoted in Barry Keenan, *The Dewey Experiment in China: Educational Reform and Political Power in the Early Republic* (Cambridge: Harvard University Press, 1977), pp. 30, 34. This is the best account of Dewey's visit to China and his influence there. On Dewey's students and the "New Culture" movement see Jerome B. Grieder, *Hu Shih and the Chinese Renaissance: Liberalism in the Chinese Revolution, 1917–1937* (Cambridge: Harvard University Press, 1970), esp. pp. 75–128, and *Intellectuals and the State in Modern China* (New York: Free Press, 1981), chap. 6; and Lin, *Crisis of Chinese Consciousness*, chap. 5.

23. *John Dewey: Lectures in China, 1919–1920*, ed. Robert W. Clopton and Tsuin-chen Ou (Honolulu: University Press of Hawaii, 1973), pp. 43–44. Page numbers for further references to these lectures (*LC*) appear in the text. Another series of Dewey's Chinese lectures has been published as *Types of Thinking* (New York: Philosophical Library, 1984). Transcripts of other unpublished lectures are available in the Gregg M. Sinclair Library, University of Hawaii. Alice Dewey also lectured extensively in China, stirring up audiences with her call for equality for Chinese women (Dykhuizen, p. 200).

A pragmatic social theory, Dewey told the Chinese, was neither radical nor conservative in the means it proposed for social change, for it abandoned the quest for either wholesale change or wholesale social preservation. The theory looked for "particular kinds of solutions by particular methods for particular problems which arise on particular occasions" (*LC*, 53). For the instrumentalist, progress toward desired ends, even revolutionary ends, was an incremental process of experimental problem solving. "Progress is not automatic, nor is it progress *en bloc*," he declared, "it is cumulative, a step forward here, a bit of improvement there. It takes place day by day, and results from the ways in which individual persons deal with particular situations; it is a step-by-step progress which comes by human effort to repair here, to modify there, to make a minor replacement yonder. Progress is retail business, not wholesale. It is made piecemeal, not all at once" (*LC*, 62). "Reconstruction," not revolution, was the byword of Deweyan politics.

The theory of social conflict and the state which Dewey proposed in his Chinese lectures reflected his sympathy for pluralism and the pluralist critique of state sovereignty which had been an important current in British political philosophy since World War I and was popularized in the United States by Harold Laski. Dewey argued that most social philosophers had obscured the basis of social conflict by resorting to "generalized antimonies" such as the individual versus society, the people versus the government, or freedom versus authority to explain conflict when its origins lay rather in the antagonistic relationships of groups. A group was a "collection of people who are united by common interests." Society was made up of a multiplicity of groups, and social conflict was at bottom "conflict between classes, occupational groups, or groups constituted along ideational, or perhaps even ethnic lines" (*LC*, 65).

Conflict arose in a society, Dewey said, because of the inequities in the relationships between the groups that comprised it. "Social conflict occurs not because the interests of the individual are incompatible with those of his society, but because the interests of some groups are gained at the disadvantage of, or even by the suppression of, the interests of other groups" (*LC*, 73) This conflict between groups was the source of social instability and injustice, and it set the task of instrumental social theory:

We need to observe, first of all, the causes of social conflict, to find out what groups have become too dominating and have come to exercise disproportionate power, as well as to identify the groups that have been oppressed, denied privilege and opportunity. Only by making such an accurate diagnosis can we hope to prevent social infection and build a healthier society. We must devise means for bringing the interests of all the groups of a society into adjustment, providing all of them with the opportunity to develop, so that each can help the others instead of being in conflict with them. We must teach ourselves one inescapable fact: any real advantage to one group is shared by all groups; and when one group suffers disadvantage, all are hurt. Social groups are so intimately interrelated that what happens to one of them ultimately affects the well-being of all of them. (*LC*, 71)

From this point of view, social reform was not an attack by dis-gruntled individuals on "society," but an effort to better meet the needs of society by harmonizing the interests of the groups that comprised it. Dewey recommended that reformers "dispassionately determine which needs of their society are not being reasonably met; which elements in the society are not being afforded opportunity to develop themselves so as to contribute to the enrichment of the total society; and what sorts of abilities are being wasted or inadequately utilized." If reformers adopt-ed this strategy, Dewey suggested, the need for revolution would be obviated because the dominant groups in a society would then find it "immeasurably more profitable" to adopt a rational approach to prob-lem solving. All the groups in a society would develop an "openness to conviction" and come to see themselves as "helpful participants in an ongoing process of social reconstruction" (*LC*, 80).

The theory of the state which Dewey articulated for his Chinese audiences also reflected a pluralist perspective. The state, he argued, was simply a mechanism for mediating the conflicts between the groups in a society. Groups existed prior to the state, and the state was but an instrument for adjudicating the disputes arising among them. The state, he observed elsewhere, was not an absolute power absorbing all the interests in a society, and to conceive of it as such was to threaten social freedom: "To become state-minded instead of socially-minded is to become a fanatic, a monomaniac, and thus to lose all sense of what a state is. For a state which shall give play to diversity of human powers is a state in which the multitude of human groups and associations do *not* dissolve. It is a mechanism, up to the present a rather clumsy one, for arranging terms of interplay among the indefinite diversity of groups in which men associate and through active participation in which they become socially-minded." The fundamental problem in politics, Dewey said, was "to build a state which consistently works for the welfare of all its people" (*LC*, 132). Social reform was thus in large measure a matter of building such a state and using it to harmonize the relationships of various groups.[24]

This strategy of social reform obviously required criteria by which to judge social relationships. The "act of judging," Dewey declared, was the central problem of instrumental social action. "We cannot judge what is good or what is bad, what is better or what is worse, unless we have criteria on which to base our judgments" (*LC*, 84). The highest ideal of social development—the ideal that should provide the criteria for the act of judging—was, he asserted, the ideal of "associated living," and all societies should strive toward this end. Habits, customs, and social institutions were to be judged according to the degree to which they contributed to "the development and qualitative enhancement of associated living" (*LC*, 90). Associated living was living that fostered the growth of the individuality of all the members of a society, and a social practice was "to be judged good when it contributes positively to free intercourse, to unhampered exchange of ideas, to mutual respect and friendship and love—in short, to those modes of behaving which make life richer and more worth living for everybody concerned; and conversely, any custom or institution which impedes progress toward these goals is to be judged bad" (*LC*, 90).

The chief obstacle to the development of associated living, Dewey argued, were systems of class and caste which isolated different segments of society from one another and established exploitative relationships between social groups. At the opposite pole of the ideal of associated living stood the master-slave relationship, which Dewey defined broadly as "a system of relationship which effectively places one person in subjugation to another—children subject to their parents, wives to their husbands, subjects to their rulers, laborers to their employers." Recalling the criticisms he had long ago made of the realism of Sir Henry Maine, Dewey argued that the master-slave relationship

24. "Social Absolutism" (1921), *Middle Works* 13:313. Dewey used a characteristic pluralist metaphor in his Japanese lectures to describe this process. The "supremacy" of the state, he said, "approximates that of the conductor of an orchestra, who makes no music himself but who harmonizes the activities of those who in producing it are doing the thing intrinsically worthwhile" (*Reconstruction in Philosophy* [1920], *Middle Works* 13:196). As I indicated in my discussion of Dewey's cultural pluralism in Chapter 7, this formulation deceptively underplays the considerable state power that "harmonizing" might entail. In his discussions of the state, Dewey was inclined to return with one hand what he had apparently taken away with the other, and in a few years he would abandon this notion of the state as mere conductor. See the discussion of *The Public and Its Problems* in Chapter 9.

produced unstable societies and alienated individuals. "When people exist under arrangements which call for some to rule and others to be ruled, some to command and others to obey," he said, "integration of the society cannot proceed, nor can the society hope to remain stable, because this disparity of status and function breeds conflict and induces disorder. At the same time, this pattern of dominance-subservience makes the development of personality extremely difficult, if not impossible—and strangely enough, this is as true of members of the dominant group as it is of those in the subservient group" (LC, 92).

Authoritarian societies were those that rested on the various forms of the master-slave relationship, societies held together by force rather than consensus. For this reason, Dewey argued, they were, despite the appearance of order and efficiency they often conveyed, poorly integrated and unstable societies. The institutions of authoritarian societies also perverted the personalities of both masters and slaves. For the latter, social relationships of dominance and subordination produced individuals who lacked opportunities for developing their individual potentialities. Caste and class societies generated slaves who were often "mean and despicable," but Dewey was contemptuous of those who used the evil effects of authoritarian institutions to defend these institutions by arguing that "because the inferiors are dependent, crafty, servile, ignorant and obsequious, they are thereby incapable of participation in associated living." Such theorists were, he said, unable or unwilling to see that "servility, ignorance, craftiness and obsequiousness are not innate qualities, but are the fruits of a system which forces men into subservience. Evil institutions bear bitter fruit, and this bitter fruit is then used to justify the institutions which produced it" (LC, 96–97).

The effect of authoritarian social relationships on the character of the masters was, Dewey argued, no less debilitating. The moral dispositions of the ruling classes were subject to rapid decay, and power over other men produced cruelty, arrogance, and extravagance. Above all, the privileges of "superiors" made them insensitive to the needs and feelings of others, depriving them of the social sympathy essential to self-realization. Their intellectual horizons were narrowed as well because of the limitation of their social contacts to fellow rulers, and, as a result of their moral and intellectual underdevelopment, ruling classes were historically subject to decadence, dissipation, and corruption (LC, 97–98).

Associated living was then but another name for "moral democracy," a society in which the good of each was the good of all and the good of all the good of each. "Free and open communication, unself-seeking and reciprocal relationships, and the sort of interaction that contributes to mutual advantage, are the essential factors in associated living" (*LC*, 92). Democracy was the embodiment of the possibilities inherent in social life as such because democratic societies, insofar as they were truly democratic, were held together by consensus rather than force and were dedicated to securing the opportunities for self-development for all the members of the society. A true democracy would be "a society in which there would be opportunities for individual development, opportunities for free communication of feeling, knowing, and thinking. The foundation of such a society would be free participation by each member of the society in setting its goals and purposes, full and willing contribution by each person toward the fulfillment of these goals" (*LC*, 98).

Dewey observed that even the United States, with its rich democratic tradition, fell well short of the ideal of associated living, particularly in the social relationships of capital and labor. He offered a sympathetic discussion of socialism to the Chinese, and although his distaste for state socialism and Marxism was clear, he was very positive in his analysis of guild socialism, which he saw as a plan for a society composed of an association of democratic associations, free of overweening government authority. He warned the Chinese not to mortgage their future by permitting an entrepreneurial minority to gain control of the country's material resources, and he suggested that the Chinese guild system might serve as an important institutional basis for popular control of economic development. "Socialism, no matter what its shade," he concluded, "is centered on the one concept of the welfare of the total society, and this, rather than individual profit, should be the criterion according to which economic organization and economic enterprises are judged" (*LC*, 124).

Despite the warm reception Dewey received in China and the wide circulation his ideas were given by Chinese liberals, the impact of his social theory on China was limited. It was a theory decidedly inappropriate to Chinese conditions, and its weaknesses were quickly apparent to many Chinese radicals. As Dewey acknowledged, if social reform was to be as rational, relatively conflict-free, and nonrevolutionary as he suggested it could be, the criteria of the acts of judging at the heart of such reform had to be shared by all the groups in a society, especially those at odds with one another. A widespread consensus on the values of associated living was one of the "laboratory conditions" for experimental reform. As he said (to repeat), "We must teach ourselves one inescapable fact: any real advantage of one group is shared by all groups; and when one group suffers disadvantage, all are hurt. Social groups are so intimately interrelated that what happens to one of them ultimately affects the well being of all of them." The kind of reform Dewey advocated required the assent of the conflicting groups to this "inescapable fact."

This was not a fact at all, however, but an ethical postulate of which many remained unpersuaded, an axiom the masters in particular could not be presumed to accept. Although Dewey's argument that domination hurt the master as much as the slave was cogent, the benefits of domination—however short-term, limited, and, in the end, self-destructive they might be from Dewey's ethical point of view—were undeniable. Dewey's reform strategy thus required a transformation of cultural values difficult to contemplate in the United States, let alone in China. In the United States one could at least build on the democratic traditions of the country. A commitment to democracy was a deep-seated part of the nation's political traditions (its *Sittlichkeit*), and the most effective American radicals played on the gap between democratic aspiration and the realities of politics and social life. In China, this possibility was not available to reformers. As historian Maurice Meisner has said, "Applied to China, Dewey's program was neither conservative nor radical but largely irrelevant. After the Revolution of 1911 China was confronted with a crisis of social, cultural, and political disintegration of massive proportions. The extreme poverty and widespread illiteracy of the masses of the Chinese people and the lack of even the rudiments of responsible political authority negated the possibility of the general social consensus that Dewey's program presupposed."[25]

Dewey's Chinese followers realized that this consensus did not exist in China, and for this reason they argued that a cultural revolution must precede political action. Chinese Deweyans were cool to the political radicalism of the May Fourth Movement, and Hu Shih went so far as to call for a twenty-year moratorium on political discussion while

25. Maurice Meisner, *Li Ta-Chao and the Origins of Chinese Marxism* (Cambridge: Harvard University Press, 1967), pp. 107–108. Dewey himself was skeptical about his influence in China. He wrote a colleague that, though the Chinese were teaching him a great deal, he was uncertain that his message was getting through to them. "China remains a massive bland and impenetrable wall, when it comes to judgment. My guess is that what is accomplished is mostly by way of 'giving face' to the younger liberal element. It's a sort of outside reinforcement in spite of its vagueness. Other times I think Chinese civilization is so thick and self centred that no foreign influence presented via a foreigner even scratches the surface" (JD to John Jacob Coss, 13 January 1920, Special Collections, Butler Library, Columbia).

cultural reconstruction was under way. This strategy, however, as Keenan has observed, was extremely shortsighted in that "it assumed that educational and cultural improvements could both avoid repression and begin the process leading gradually to desirable political consequences." In this sense, the program of Hu Shih and other Chinese Deweyans suffered from the same strategic weaknesses as Dewey's own hopes to make the school the unsteepled church of democracy. Both assumed that cultural reconstruction could be separated from politics and thereby circumvent the democratic reformer's problem of powerlessness, ignoring the fact that any effort to establish a democratic culture was itself a political act and would entail a struggle for power. One could not assume that the masters would teach themselves the virtues of participatory democracy, nor could one expect the masters to permit the free development of cultural institutions and values subversive of their rule. Culture was not an unprotected flank that democrats could easily seize. "Politics is rotten," wrote the chastened Deweyan editor of the *New Education*, Chiang Monlin, in 1922, "but how can we *not* talk politics?"[26]

Dewey was not the man to talk politics with the Chinese in the early twenties. Securing the society he urged them to create required both politics and education or, to be more exact, a strategy that would simultaneously make and empower democratic citizens—a political movement that would prefigure the democratic society it sought in its own institutions and "movement culture," and would struggle for the power to extend those institutions and that culture. But while he repeatedly called in the abstract for the steeling of idealism with force, Dewey had yet to conceive of an exercise of force, a politics, which would be at once effective and democratic. When confronted with particular political problems during the war and its immediate aftermath, he had fluctuated wildly between sentimental moral exhortation and hard-boiled defense of the counterproductive violence of war without carefully considering the combinations of idealism and force which might lie between these extremes. To the Chinese, Dewey proposed radically democratic ends without proposing means commensurate with those ends, and—though it is unlikely, given the situation in China, that creative political thinking by a visiting American philosopher would have made much difference—he did little to help resolve the strategic dilemmas of his disciples. Although the Deweyans dominated Chinese

---

26. Keenan, *Dewey Experiment*, p. 154; Chiang Monlin quoted in Grieder, *Intellectuals and the State*, p. 277.

educational theory from 1919 until 1927, they were subsequently swept aside with ease by revolutionaries who thought first of power and whose movement culture was far from democratic.[27]

IMPERIALISM IS EASY

At the same time Dewey attempted to bring an American philosophy to China, he was also interpreting events in China for an audience at home. In dozens of articles, which he referred to with undue modesty as "pot boilers," he offered American readers a sympathetic view of the May Fourth Movement and of Chinese nationalism generally, as well as sharp denunciations of Japanese imperialism. Although it would take us too far afield to examine these articles in great detail, they are significant here as the most important concrete instance in which Dewey argued for his notion of an egalitarian, open-door international order and differentiated his ideals from those guiding American foreign policy.[28]

As I noted, Dewey's vision of just relations between nations was homologous with the vision of just relations between individuals which he advanced in his ethical writings: an egalitarian world, one might say, in which all nations participated so that the "powers of each are called out, put to use, and reenforced." The burden of responsibility for creating such a world lay with wealthy and powerful nations such as the United States. These nations were required to shoulder the difficult task of the Deweyan reformer, not only to abandon imperialism but to avoid paternalism, to act "for ends which are helpful to others as will call out and make effective their activities." Such a foreign policy, Dewey contended, was in the long-term interest of the powerful as well as the less powerful nations, for, to extend the homology, it fostered an international community that permitted the full and free expression of the individuality of all.[29]

27. The term "movement culture" is that of Lawrence Goodwyn, whose arguments about the requirements of a democratic politics have deeply influenced my own thinking. See *The Populist Moment* (New York: Oxford University Press, 1978), Introduction. For a brief but thoughtful consideration of the dilemmas of Chinese liberals see Jerome B. Grieder, "The Question of 'Politics' in the May Fourth Era," in *Reflections on the May Fourth Movement: A Symposium*, ed. Benjamin I. Schwartz (Cambridge: Harvard University Press, 1972), pp. 95–101.

28. JD to John Jacob Coss, 7 November 1920, Special Collections, Butler Library, Columbia. For a different view of Dewey's Chinese reportage see Jerry Israel, *Progressivism and the Open Door: America and China* (Pittsburgh: University of Pittsburgh Press, 1971), pp. 181–185.

29. *Ethics* (1908), *Middle Works* 5:275–277.

American policy in China, Dewey argued, should aim to thwart European and Japanese imperialism and foster democratic nationalism. The Chinese, he told his readers in the summer of 1919, felt trapped between competing imperial powers and, forced to chose between masters, might well cast their lot with their fellow Asians. "Let there be a resumption of the old diplomacy of the western nations with respect to China," he warned, "and it is conceivable that bitter as would be the dose, China would accept the domination of Japan as the lesser of two evils." Chinese democrats were looking to the United States for a way out of this dilemma. America symbolized "the free democracy that progressive China would be and is not," and the idealization of the United States (and, he might have added, the lionizing of Dewey) were a projection of "China's democratic hopes for herself."[30]

This situation presented the United States with a unique opportunity to intervene, and Dewey lamented American unwillingness to seize it. "We readily emit large and good schemes," he noted, "but we are ineffectual when it comes to the test of action." He initially proposed that Americans try to make an end run around the Japanese in China by "undertaking big things on a large scale." Such projects as the unification of the currency and railroad system and the reconstruction of the inland waterway system were huge tasks for which "the United States is the only country that combines the requisite capital, engineering ability, and executive talent." Of course, if such projects were not to become the opening wedge of American imperial hegemony in China, American leaders would have to treat their Chinese counterparts as equals and "the plans must be on such a scale that it is evident while ample security and reasonable profit are given foreign investors the outcome will be to make China the mistress of her own economic destinies." Although concerned that Westerners who brought aid to China also brought "a voracious appetite," Dewey's dispatches from Asia assumed that Americans could be persuaded to curb their appetites in the interests of Chinese self-determination.[31]

Dewey's proposal that the United States unilaterally join the Chinese in rebuilding the nation's economic infrastructure presumptuously assumed both American and Chinese willingness to undertake such grandiose joint projects and Japanese willingness to allow them to go forward without protest. Perhaps for this reason (as well as a rapidly growing respect for the capacities of the Chinese), he quickly dropped

30. "The International Duel in China," pp. 195–197.
31. "The American Opportunity in China" (1919), *Middle Works* 11:231, 233–234; "Transforming the Mind of China," *Middle Works* 11:214.

this idea in favor of support of more modest cooperative schemes designed to deter Japanese expansion and nurture Chinese independence without substantial unilateral American intervention in Chinese affairs. By 1921 he was arguing that the best United States policy was to help the Chinese work out their own destiny. "The hope of the world's peace as well as of China's freedom," Dewey declared, "lies in adhering to a policy of Hands Off. Give China a chance. Give her time. The danger lies in being in a hurry, in impatience, possibly in the desire of America to show that we are a power in international affairs and that we too have a positive foreign policy. And a benevolent policy of supporting China from without, instead of promoting her aspirations from within, may in the end do China about as much harm as a policy conceived in malevolence."[32]

In 1919 the Wilson administration asked Wall Street bankers led by Thomas Lamont of J. P. Morgan and Company to establish a banking consortium that would enable the United States to cooperate with Great Britain, France, and Japan in controlling the financing of Chinese economic development. Dewey supported the consortium, and although he knew that it was denounced by many American liberals as "financial imperialism, committing the United States to embark upon a career of foreign financial exploitation," he defended it on the grounds that it would serve to curtail the use of loans by the imperial powers to wring concessions and spheres of influence from corrupt Chinese officials. "As long as China is dependent upon foreign loans," he said, "it is much better for her to be dependent upon a combination of powers that have agreed to forgo special privileges, and who will have to use their funds to build up China as a whole, than upon single separate powers that loan money only in response for special concessions and a command of strategic points." From the point of view of the United States government, the consortium was less an economic than a political instrument, a means of preserving Chinese territorial integrity. Even if the group never made a loan, Dewey concluded, it might serve a most useful political function. "If a blockade or embargo can be established for even five years upon predatory foreign loans to China, the consortium meantime doing nothing, a precedent may be established which will make such loans difficult, if not impossible, in the future. The effect may be to throw China back upon her own resources. The best thing that could happen to China would be for her to be put on a starvation diet for a while and have to face her own problems with her

32. "Federalism in China" (1921), *Middle Works* 13:155.

own capacities." Far from a stalking horse for American imperialism, the consortium, as Dewey saw it, was designed to deter imperialism and might advance Chinese autonomy.[33]

In his defense of the consortium, Dewey suggested a coincidence of perspective between himself and U.S. policy makers. He said he was "credulous enough" to believe that the American government meant what it said when it indicated that it was committed above all to "the maintenance of the Open Door and the preservation of the territorial integrity of China." Although Dewey's reading of American intentions slighted related commercial motives, it was, on the whole, accurate. But what he apparently failed to recognize was how far apart his own understanding of the relationship between the Open Door and democratic nationalism in China stood from that of the men in charge of U.S. foreign policy. This would, however, become clear to him in the wake of the Washington Conference.[34]

The Washington Conference of 1921–22 was regarded by many at the time and many since as one of the triumphant moments in American diplomacy. Through bold initiatives and skillful negotiating, Secretary of State Charles Evans Hughes secured three treaties that restructured the relationship between the Western powers and Japan in the Pacific and China. The Four-Power Treaty between the United States, Great Britain, France, and Japan replaced the Anglo-Japanese alliance with a nonaggression pact between the signatories which committed them to consultations in the event of disagreements among themselves or a threat from others to their interests in the Pacific. In the Five-Power Treaty, Italy joined these four nations in an agreement to limit naval arms. Finally, the Nine-Power Treaty laid out principles designed to stabilize competition between the powers in China. In effect, it inter-

---

33. "Chinese National Sentiment" (1919), *Middle Works* 11:226; "The Consortium in China" (1921), *Middle Works* 13:87, 90, 92. On the establishment and operations of the consortium see Warren I. Cohen, *The Chinese Connection: Roger S. Greene, Thomas W. Lamont, George E. Sokolosky and American-East Asian Relations* (New York: Columbia University Press, 1978), chap. 2; Roberta Dayer, *Bankers and Diplomats in China, 1917–1925* (London: Frank Cass, 1981); and Lloyd C. Gardner, *Safe for Democracy: The Anglo-American Response to Revolution, 1913–1923* (New York: Oxford University Press, 1984), pp. 224–228, 295–303, 315–318. As it turned out, the consortium made few Chinese loans, but this inaction had neither of the desired effects Dewey anticipated. Although Dewey was largely correct in his estimate of the overriding political concerns of the American government in setting up the consortium, Lamont, to the consternation of his friends in Washington, saw the arrangement as, in the first instance, a business operation. Consequently, he not only promoted few Chinese loans but did what he could to secure safer and more profitable loans to the *Japanese* government, which, if anything, advanced the imperial interests of Japan.

34. "The Consortium in China," p. 90.

nationalized the Open Door by committing the signatories, Japan among them, to eschew further meddling in the internal affairs of China, to establish equality of economic opportunity for all competitors in the China market, and, as the treaty put it, to "respect the sovereignty, the independence, and the territorial and administrative integrity of China."[35]

Dewey returned to the United States in July 1921, but he continued to follow Chinese affairs closely. In the fall he agreed to contribute a series of articles on the Washington Conference to the *Baltimore Sun*, and in these commentaries he sharply criticized the manner in which the assembled powers were handling the China question. "If the American people are going to bring an enlightened public opinion to bear on the Conference," he said, "we need more sob sisters and fewer joy brothers to report the Conference." In his articles, Dewey complained about the treatment of China by the diplomats and tried to explain to Americans why, despite the apparently favorable provisions of the Nine-Power Treaty, Chinese nationalists were so distressed by the course of events at the Conference.[36]

The negotiators in Washington, Dewey protested, were treating China "too much as a patient and too little as an active living force" and thereby failing to understand that "the interest of China is that she have an opportunity to develop and to develop in her own way." The commitment of the great powers to the Open Door was a limited one: concessions were made to Japanese interests in Manchuria, and, in general, the Nine-Power Treaty promised only no *future* infringements of Chinese sovereignty. Prior encroachments—foreign control of tariffs, extraterritoriality, and the presence of foreign troops—were, at best, left to later discussions. The treaty might "improve China's condition for the future," Dewey said. "But the forces which are operating because of the things that have been done in the past will not stop operating because a conference of powers in Washington decides that such and such things will be done differently in the future. . . . To consecrate the status quo in China and then to resolve that things will

35. On the Washington Conference see Thomas H. Buckley, *The United States and the Washington Conference, 1921–1922* (Knoxville: University of Tennessee Press, 1970); Frank Costigliola, *Awkward Dominion: American Political, Economic, and Cultural Relations with Europe, 1919–1933* (Ithaca: Cornell University Press, 1984), pp. 80–87; Roger Dingman, *Power in the Pacific: The Origins of Naval Arms Limitation, 1914–1922* (Chicago: University of Chicago Press, 1976); Gardner, *Safe for Democracy*, chap. 13; and Akira Iriye, *After Imperialism: The Search of a New Order in the Far East, 1921–1931* (Cambridge: Harvard University Press, 1965), pp. 13–22.

36. "The Conference and a Happy Ending" (1921), *Middle Works* 13:204.

be done differently in the future is another of these miracles of diplomacy."[37]

More fundamental for Dewey was an apparent misunderstanding by American policy makers of what the Open Door meant or, at least, what it meant to him. As articulated at the Conference, Dewey said, "the open door policy is not primarily a policy about China herself but rather about the policies of foreign powers toward one another with respect to China. It demands equality of economic opportunity for different nations. Were it enforced, it would prevent the granting of monopolies to any one nation: there is nothing in it to render impossible a conjoint exploitation of China by foreign powers, an organized monopoly in which each nation has its due share with respect to others." Dewey acutely perceived the lack of concern of the imperial powers with the interests of China. Although American policy makers were arguably more sensitive to the demands of Chinese nationalists than leaders of other nations, Hughes's principal goal was to stabilize big-power competition on a new footing. The basic objective of the conference, as historian Akira Iriye has said, "was to redefine relations among Japan, the United States, Britain, and other powers. China entered the picture only insofar as these powers agreed to limit their expansion and renounce particularistic agreements."[38]

For Dewey the Open Door signified (idiosyncratically) more than the preservation of Chinese territorial integrity and the replacement of the formal imperialism of spheres of influence with the informal imperialism of exploitative market relationships between unequal nation-states. To him it meant opening opportunities for Chinese self-determination and, he hoped, democracy. He feared the "conquest of China by economic penetration that will reduce her population to a proletariat working for foreign capitalists backed by superior military resources." He also expressed his appreciation for the "sound instinct" of the Chinese in resisting the rapid industrialization of their nation. "The

37. "The Issues at Washington" (1921), *Middle Works* 13:175, 182; "Conference and a Happy Ending," p. 208. For the Chinese perspective on the Conference see Wunsz King, *China at the Washington Conference, 1921–1922* (New York: St. John's University Press, 1963). Dewey continued throughout the twenties to press for the restoration of full sovereignty to the Chinese government. See "Is China a Nation or a Market?" (1925) and "We Should Deal with China as Nation to Nation" (1926), *Later Works* 2:181–188. He also sharply criticized the racist American immigration policies that excluded Asians and heightened tensions between Japan and the United States. See "Racial Prejudice and Friction" (1922), *Middle Works* 13:242–254, and "Highly Colored White Lies" (1925), *Later Works* 2:176–180.

38. "A Parting of the Ways for America" (1921), *Middle Works* 13:161; Iriye, *After Imperialism*, pp. 21–22.

imagination cannot conceive a worse crime than fastening western industrialism upon China before she has developed within herself the means of coping with the forces which it would release." China's "sole way out" lay in "transformation from within," and the best thing the United States could do was "to see to it that she gets the time she needs in order to effect this transformation whether or not we like the particular form it assumes at any particular time."[39]

Repeating, on a regional scale, arguments he had made in November 1918 in his call for a democratic League of Nations, Dewey proposed the establishment of a "permanent international commission for Far Eastern affairs," designed to ensure that the people and resources of China would not be exploited. "Let us try out international regulation on one another," he said, "before we try it out on China." For starters, such a commission would cancel all existing foreign monopolies and prohibit further monopolistic contracts; put an end to the unproductive, "administrative" loans with which corrupt Chinese officials lined their pockets; pool and refund Chinese debts; provide maximum publicity about and open bidding for public-works projects; and restore Chinese control over tariffs. As these measures suggest, Dewey believed "a solution should be sought which involves the minimum of international supervision and control of China, while it involves the maximum of practicable international supervision and control of individual nation's activities toward China."[40]

Still wedded to a faith in American exceptionalism, Dewey was reluctant, even in the wake of the Washington Conference, to acknowledge fully the complicity, indeed the leadership, of the United States in the construction of a new imperial order in the Pacific. He admitted there were "grounds for apprehension" that the United States was on the verge of establishing an imperial course "as bad as that of any of the rest of them," and he was particularly troubled by the alliances that had been forged between the State Department and big banking interests. But, on the whole, he attributed the shortcomings of American policy at the conference less to a desire to join in the exploitation of China than to a shortsighted preoccupation with American interests in Europe which allowed China to be "lost in the shuffle." Dewey was especially resistant to the pessimism of radicals whose fears of an emerging

39. "As the Chinese Think" (1922), *Middle Works* 13:226; "Parting of the Ways for America," pp. 170–171.
40. "The Issues at Washington," pp. 185–189.

American imperialism were grounded in "a fatalistic formula as to how a 'capitalistic nation' must conduct itself."[41]

A trip to Mexico later in the mid-twenties profoundly altered Dewey's convictions. Here American politicians and businessmen were engaged less in keeping the door open for prospective investments, as they were in China, than in protecting very tangible material interests, and Dewey lamented the manner in which American state capitalism used the sanctity of contract to establish its hegemony in Latin America and disrupt promising revolutions. He noted that he had once thought of imperialism as the product of a consciously imperialistic policy, but "a visit to Mexico, a country in which American imperialism is in the making, knocked that notion out of my head":

> Given, on the one hand, a nation that has capital and technical skill, engineering and financial, to export, plus manufacturers in need of raw material, especially iron and oil, and, on the other hand, an industrially backward country with large natural resources and a government which is either inefficient or unstable, or both, and it does not require intention or desire to involve the first nation in imperialistic policies. Even widespread popular desire to the contrary is no serious obstacle. The natural movement of business enterprise, combined with Anglo-American legalistic notions of contracts and their sanctity, and the international custom which obtains as to the duty of a nation to protect the property of its nationals, suffices to bring about imperialistic undertakings.

Conditions had combined, Dewey now contended, to make imperialism easy for the United States. Protest was unavailing; only "a permanent change of our habits" would suffice. But at the moment he doubted that many of his compatriots would join him in calling for a rewriting of the Monroe Doctrine to state that "American citizens who invest in backward foreign countries do so at their own risk."[42]

Views such as this made it clear that the brief romance Dewey had begun with the American state during World War I was over. He was no longer willing to give American elites the benefit of the doubt as he had in China. *American* imperialism was now for him conceivable, indeed apparent. There would be no more dispatches to the State Department, for this sort of thinking left him far distant from those in the

41. "Parting of the Ways for America," pp. 160, 165.
42. "Imperialism Is Easy" (1927), *Later Works* 3:158, 162.

centers of established power. This, as Bourne had contended, was where a man of his democratic convictions had belonged all along.

OUTLAWING WAR

No one more eagerly welcomed Dewey back to the United States in 1921 than Salmon O. Levinson. A wealthy Chicago corporate lawyer and friend of the Deweys since the 1890s, Levinson had in the aftermath of World War I almost singlehandedly organized an American movement to outlaw war. Dewey had helped Levinson publish his initial proposal for outlawry in the *New Republic* in 1918, and now Levinson was eager to enlist his friend as a major spokesman for the cause. If Dewey had let him, Levinson would have consumed all of his energies in the twenties, and even as it was, the outlawry crusade was the principal focus of Dewey's activism in that decade. In this context, he began at last to conceive of a politics appropriate to his democratic ideals.[43]

In the initial statement of the outlawry idea in his March 1918 *New Republic* article, Levinson pointed out that while most people regarded war as a crime it was in fact recognized under international law as the final method for settling conflicts between nations and hence was legal. There was an abundant body of law that tried to constrain wars once they began but no law against initiating warfare. Drawing an analogy that was to become a staple of outlawry argument, Levinson compared the effort to regulate war to earlier efforts to regulate dueling, the last vestige in domestic law of a nonjudicial method for the coercive settling of disputes. Just as efforts to regulate dueling had been abandoned in favor of outlawing the practice, so too should efforts to legally circumscribe the practice of war be abandoned in favor of declaring war illegal. "In one case as the other," Levinson said, "we want not laws *of* war, but laws *against* war, just as we have laws *against* murder, not laws *of* murder." Any attempt at the reorganization of the world through a League of Nations required the "specific outlawing of war by the code of nations." Outlawing war would not guarantee that wars would not

43. The most detailed account of the Outlawry movement is John E. Stoner, *S. O. Levinson and the Pact of Paris* (Chicago: University of Chicago Press, 1943), but for a succinct summary see Dewey's own "Outlawry of War" (1933), *Later Works* 8:13–18. Other useful studies of the movement include Robert H. Ferrell, *Peace in Their Time: The Origins of the Kellogg-Briand Pact* (New Haven: Yale University Press, 1953), esp. pp. 31–37; Charles F. Howlett, *Troubled Philosopher: John Dewey and the Struggle for World Peace* (Port Washington, N.Y.: Kennikat Press, 1977), chaps. 6–7; and Charles C. Morrison, *The Outlawry of War* (Chicago: Willett, Clark and Colby, 1927).

occur, but it would mean that war "would be branded as a crime and the force of the world would be organized to deal with the criminal."[44]

Levinson, like Dewey, had been an enthusiastic supporter of Wilson's foreign policy in early 1918, and the proposal to outlaw war was offered as an essential component of an "American" peace. Levinson looked forward to a peace settlement that would be grounded in outlawry and felt he had every reason to expect such a treaty from Wilson. But in the wake of the Treaty of Versailles, Levinson became an implacable opponent of the League, and outlawry became not a supplement to Wilsonian diplomacy but an alternative to it. Throughout the immediate postwar years, Levinson peddled his idea to Senate "irreconcilables" such as Philander C. Knox and William E. Borah, who used the plan as a weapon in their fight against the League.

Dewey was no less an opponent of the League than Levinson, though in neither case can their position be attributed to isolationism. Writing from China, Dewey argued that Americans were faced with a troubling dilemma. Isolation from the affairs of the world was no longer possible, but participation in international politics "still conducted upon a basis and by methods that were instituted before democracy was heard of as a political fact" threatened the measure of democracy that had been achieved in the United States. Americans were thus confronted with the difficult task of losing their innocence without losing their integrity. Dewey recommended that the nation exercise extreme caution and "avoid all general commitments, and confine ourself to the irreducible minimum, and that most specifically stated" until "the labor parties of European democracies or some other liberal organization supervise and direct the foreign policies of those nations with jealous regard for democratic principles, and until we have ourselves attained not merely greater knowledge of foreign and international politics but have developed the sure means of popular control."[45]

44. S. O. Levinson, "The Legal Status of War" (1918), *Middle Works* 11:388–392. This article originally appeared in the *New Republic* on 9 March 1918. On Dewey's efforts to run interference for Levinson with Herbert Croly, see the extensive correspondence between Dewey and Levinson in February 1918, Levinson Papers. Dewey followed Levinson's article two weeks later with a companion piece arguing that outlawing war was essential to the creation of an international organization that would "align the moral code of state behavior with the best which obtains as to personal conduct" ("Morals and the Conduct of States" [1918], *Middle Works* 11: 122–126). Most experts disputed Levinson's contention that international law held war to be legal. Rather, they held, war was akin to a natural disaster like an earthquake, a *nonlegal* contingency to be provided against. Had Levinson acknowledged this, his argument would have lost some of its polemical force but (logically) the significance of making war illegal would have been undiminished. See Stoner, *Levinson*, p. 186.

45. "Our National Dilemma" (1920), *Middle Works* 12:5–7.

After his return from China, Dewey emerged as one of the most vocal opponents of renewed efforts to promote American participation in the League of Nations. On the face of it, he said, League proponents had a plausible argument that took the form of a syllogism: isolation meant the continuance of war and international cooperation its cessation, international cooperation meant joining the League, therefore the United States should join the League. League advocates were also able to appeal to Americans' sense of their special mission to other nations: "saving the world is the part we most like to enact in the drama of history." Finally, the League was, after all, an American idea, and it was shameful to repudiate it. A friend, he said, had called this "the Great Refusal of history, fit to go on record by the side of that of the rich young man of the New Testament."

No intelligent person, Dewey countered, favored isolation for its own sake or opposed cooperation, but League advocates were insufficiently attentive to the questions of "with whom and for what?" implied by cooperation with the League. The League of Nations was really a league of *governments*, reactionary governments "whose policies played a part in bringing on the war and that have no wish to change their policies." Dewey was deeply fearful that the United States (and he himself) would be suckered into the same mistake he felt had been made in World War I. As things stood in the early twenties, he concluded, "any specific move toward international cooperation on our part will be but a repetition of what happened when we plunged into the war without having first come to an understanding with our associates, only to find in the end our hands tied in the execution of our own policies by conflicting European policies in general, and secret agreements in particular." There was no reason to "repeat the experiment without even the excuse of wartime excitement, without the warning of an experience of which we were then innocent."[46]

Dewey's critics, among them Arthur Lovejoy, charged him with demanding perfection from the League and damning it for failing to meet an impossibly high standard. "Mr. Dewey has taken the visions of the more naïf supporters of the League; he has exaggerated even these; and finding that the reality does not and cannot correspond to the exigent ideal thus generated, he bids us have nothing to do with the contrivance." The question, Lovejoy said, was not whether the League was a perfect international organization but whether it was a step toward the control of war-generating tensions in Europe.[47]

46. "Shall We Join the League?" (1923), *Middle Works* 15:78–81.
47. Arthur O. Lovejoy, "Shall We Join the League of Nations?" (1923), *Middle Works* 15:378–382.

Accepting Lovejoy's formulation of the question, Dewey responded that he regarded the League as offering no significant prospect for sustained peace. It was, if anything, a step in the wrong direction. "The steps have all been taken under the war system. It is not a step that we need, it is a right-about-face." The League was merely a reorganization of the insidious balance of power politics that had led to the Great War, and "only stupendous thoughtlessness will assume that if we whip up these same means into increased energy or manipulate them in some mechanical way, they will suddenly begin to operate for totally different ends." European statesmen wanted American participation "for the same reason that they wanted us during the war—to add power to *their* policies." Moreover, pursuing international cooperation did not necessarily mean joining the League. Levinson's outlawry plan afforded the United States a far more attractive alternative. American idealism, Dewey declared, "is waiting for the discovery of a channel through which it can operate, a channel that does not conduct to the political system of Europe which is at bottom bound up at every point with the war system—a system of deceit and intrigue, predation and violence. Such a proposition has at last been put before the American people. Its short name is the Outlawry of War."[48]

By 1921 Levinson's outlawry idea had taken form as a simple three-part program, what historian John Stoner has termed the "three commandments of outlawry":

1. That war be outlawed and declared a crime, under the law of nations, and that its use as a means of settlement of disputes be abolished.

2. That a conference of civilized nations be held for the creation and codification of international law on the basis of equity and right.

3. That a court be established with jurisdiction over all purely international disputes as defined by the international code.

In December 1921 Levinson established the American Committee for the Outlawry of War to promote this program and published his widely circulated pamphlet, *Outlawry of War*, which featured a foreword by Dewey. In addition to Levinson and Dewey, the leading figures in the movement were Raymond Robins, the wartime head of the American

48. "Reply to Lovejoy's 'Shall We Join the League of Nations?'" (1923), *Middle Works* 15:83–86; "Shall the United States Join the World Court?" (1923), *Middle Works* 15:98, 88; "Political Combination or Legal Cooperation?" (1923), *Middle Works* 15:107. The exchange with Lovejoy appeared originally in the *New Republic*. Levinson felt Dewey scored a clear victory in this debate, suggesting that he should henceforth be called "Killjoy" (Levinson to JD, 28 March 1923, Levinson Papers).

Red Cross in Russia and outlawry's most effective and charismatic orator; Charles Clayton Morrison, editor of the *Christian Century*, the nation's most influential liberal Protestant magazine; John Haynes Holmes, pacifist minister of New York's Community Church; and Justice Florence E. Allen of the Ohio Supreme Court. By the early twenties, Levinson was resting his political hopes in the United States on William Borah, and, after months of coaxing, the Idaho senator and "Hamlet" of the movement introduced a resolution in the Senate on February 23, 1923, embodying the principles of outlawry. Until 1927 the efforts of the movement focused on passage of this resolution ("the Magna Carta of the outlawry movement") and on deflecting challenges from pro-League forces and from advocates of American participation in a World Court that fell short of the requirements of the outlawry plan and, to outlawry forces, appeared to be a back door into the League.[49]

From the outset, the outlawry movement was subjected to sharp criticism from its opponents. The most common of these criticisms—that the movement was attempting to abolish war simply by passing a law against it—was easily met. "Criminal law has not prevented crimes," Dewey observed. "I should hesitate to claim that the outlawry of war will absolutely ensure us against the crime of war." Although Dewey had few doubts that, if the outlawry program were adopted, the likelihood of war would diminish, the immediate aim of outlawry was not to abolish war but to deprive it of legal sanction. The proposition was "not the moral proposition to abolish wars. It is the much more fundamental proposition to abolish the war system as an authorized and legally sanctioned institution. The first idea is either utopian at present or merely sentiment. This other proposition, to abolish the war system as an authorized, established institution sanctioned by law, contemplated by law, is practical." Providing a judicial substitute for war as the meth-

---

49. Stoner, *Levinson*, p. 187. Dewey's understanding of the outlawry commandments differed in important respects from those listed here, which Stoner draws from a speech by Justice Florence Allen (see JD, "Outlawry of War," pp. 16–17), and I shall turn to the most significant of these differences momentarily. I use this formulation here because I believe it closely approximates the most widespread understanding of the outlawry program (by historians as well as contemporaries). I shall not relate the long story of Borah's relationship to the outlawry movement: I am convinced by those who have argued that he did not believe in the movement but rather attempted to use the movement for obstructionist or partisan purposes. See Robert J. Maddox, *William E. Borah and American Foreign Policy* (Baton Rouge: Louisiana State University Press, 1969), chaps. 6–7, and John C. Vinson, *William E. Borah and the Outlawry of War* (Athens: University of Georgia Press, 1957). As Maddox says, that Levinson "considered Borah 'our' man for as long as he did bears greater testimony to Levinson's patience than to his wisdom" (p. 139).

od for settling international disputes would not guarantee an end to war, anymore than domestic courts had put an end to violent crime. But it would have the effect of delegitimating the international equivalent of murder as the court of last resort.[50]

Two other related elements of the outlawry program—its position on sanctions and self-defense—proved much more difficult to explain and persuasively defend. In his initial formulation of outlawry, Levinson had argued (and Dewey had agreed) that "if war is made criminal international force is required for prevention and punishment. The power to enforce any law must always be adequate." The outlawing of war had to be accompanied by "the ability by force to execute the decrees of the international tribunal." By 1921 Levinson and Dewey had changed their minds about sanctions. To invoke sanctions, they now decided, was to use war to enforce a statute outlawing war, which was both illogical and counterproductive. They went to great lengths to counter the efforts of their critics to compare international sanctions with domestic police power, claiming that the use of police power against a recalcitrant individual was "radically different" from the use of coercive force against a recalcitrant nation. Dewey said: "The latter is war, no matter what name you give it. . . . You cannot coerce an entire nation save by war and in the same measure to provide for war is to guarantee the perpetuation of the war system." To those who advocated an international army to keep peace, he declared: "Abolish war, and at the same time keep war up our sleeves! The contradiction is more than merely logical. It means the perpetuation of that attitude of mind that perpetuates war. If the moral conviction of the world will not restrain a nation from resort to war after its case has been publicly heard and adjudged and after it has given its own consent to the outlawry of war and to abiding by the decisions of the Court, the world will not get rid of war under any system." This argument puzzled many, who could not understand why the outlawry movement was anxious to drop the domestic analogy at this crucial point. Moreover, it seemed to leave outlawry a toothless and sentimental program.[51]

Outlawry advocates were at great pains to make it clear that their opposition to sanctions was not an interdiction of the right of a nation

---

50. "Political Combination or Legal Cooperation," p. 109; "Shall the United States Join the World Court?" p. 90.

51. Levinson, "Legal Status of War," pp. 391, 392; JD, "Morals and the Conduct of States," pp. 125–126; "Shall the United States Join the World Court?" p. 94; "If War Were Outlawed" (1923), *Middle Works* 15:113–114. See also Levinson, "Can Peace Be 'Enforced'?" *Christian Century*, 8 January 1925: 46–47.

to defend itself when attacked by another nation. Self-defense was not a sanction. "The right of self-defense," Levinson argued, "is not an institution; it is not a method of settling disputes; it is not a brand of war. It is a right inherent in nations as in individuals, and is indispensable to both liberty and life. It is impossible to abolish or outlaw the right of self-defense." Yet, if outlawry advocates did not rule out national self-defense, they did adamantly oppose any effort to distinguish between "aggressive" and "defensive" war. To admit the legitimacy of the latter, they argued, was to leave the war system untouched, for by their own lights all nations had always fought only defensive wars and could, with a little imagination, construe any war other than the strict exercise of self-defense as such. The considerable energy they were forced to devote to these distinctions was frustrating for Levinson, Dewey, and others, for they believed that the fact that one of the first and principal concerns their program raised centered on its provisions for a legitimate response to war was compelling evidence of the hold the war system had over the moral imagination of their audience.[52]

Dewey was the most skilled polemicist in the outlawry movement, and Levinson repeatedly called upon him to take on the toughest critics. Perhaps the most important service he performed lay in his deflection of the barbs of one of outlawry's most influential opponents, Walter Lippmann. By the twenties, Lippmann, only in his early thirties, was already one of the nation's preeminent journalists. After wartime service as secretary to the Inquiry, Wilson's planning committee for the Paris peace negotiations, and later as a captain in army intelligence on General John J. Pershing's staff, he had assumed charge of the editorial page of the *New York World*, specializing in articles and commentary on foreign affairs. In March 1923 he authored a *World* editorial that seemed favorable to the outlawry movement and told Dewey that he had been persuaded to do so by one of Dewey's articles. But in August of that year he published a withering critique of the movement in the *Atlantic Monthly* that was cause for great consternation among outlawry partisans.[53]

Skillfully deploying wit and innuendo and leaning heavily on legitimate doubts about Borah's motives, Lippmann characterized the histo-

---

52. Levinson, "The Sanctions of Peace," *Christian Century*, 25 December 1929: 1604. See also JD, "'As an Example to Other Nations'" (1928), *Later Works* 3:163–167; "Outlawing Peace by Discussing War" (1928), *Later Works* 3:173–176.

53. JD to Levinson, 25 April 1923, Levinson Papers; Stoner, *Levinson*, p. 115. On this stage of Lippmann's career, see Ronald Steel, *Walter Lippmann and the American Century* (Boston: Little, Brown, 1980), chaps. 11–12, 16.

ry of outlawry as "a perfect record of irreconcilability." Outlawry was "first employed in order to strengthen a league, before there was a League. It was used to defeat the League after there was a League, and to advocate an international court before there was a Court. Now that the Court has been created, it is being used to defeat the Court, and to advocate another court which does not exist." Lippmann chided outlawry proponents for hedging their opposition to war by allowing for wars of self-defense and national liberation. "The only war outlawed under this plan," he said, "is a war openly announced to be a war of aggression. There are no such wars." He also suggested that the movement was far too cavalier about the conference that would codify international law. Such a conference, he said, would amount to a world legislature, required "to lay down laws affecting the very existence of governments and the destiny of nations." Finally, Lippmann criticized outlawry for contending that the only alternatives for the settlement of disputes were war and judicial procedures. This left diplomacy out of account, and the reform of diplomacy, he argued, was far more essential to peace than courts and codes. He closed with a slap at the outlawry camp for its rigid refusal to practice the cooperation it celebrated rhetorically. "To say to the world, as Mr. Borah's associates have in effect done from the start, that mankind must meet our terms or none, and coöperate on our principles or none, is to perpetuate precisely that temper of mind which the outlawry of war will most need to outlaw."[54]

Dewey responded to Lippmann's attack by charging him with gross misrepresentation and misunderstanding. Lippmann construed the outlawry notion of self-defense far too broadly, confusing it with the very idea of the "defensive war" they opposed. "Self-defense," as the outlawry movement saw it, was "the right to defend one's self *when actually attacked*." Wars of liberation, moreover, were civil wars and consequently beyond the purview of international law. Furthermore, the outlawry movement did not intend to deprecate diplomacy; it argued that war and law were the only alternatives for the *coercive* settlement of disputes. Outlawing war would contribute to the very reform of diplomacy Lippmann advocated. "The friends of outlawry of war," Dewey said, "believe that the most effective way to reform diplomacy is to make recourse to war a crime and provide a court for the settlement of disputes when diplomats come to an impasse." Lippmann's point about the codification of international law dealt with a genuine difficulty, but, Dewey contended, it overlooked the degree to which existing international law

54. Walter Lippmann, "The Outlawry of War" (1923), *Middle Works* 15:404–417.

would suffice in most war-breeding disputes, and settlement of such disputes would require little new legislation. Citing a number of historical instances in which disputes led to war, he observed that "the existing state of international law, whatever its imperfections, would have sufficed to secure a judicial hearing and decision, were it not for the fundamental imperfection in that code against which the outlawry project is directed; namely, its legalizing of resort to force which enables any nation that thinks it can get away with it to constitute itself the final judge in its own cause."[55]

Dewey failed to convince Lippmann, but the outlawry forces believed he had won a decisive victory. Levinson proposed to circulate 40,000 copies of Dewey's articles. John Haynes Holmes, who had found Lippmann's article very disturbing, wrote Levinson that he was "in a state almost of hysterics" after reading Dewey's reply. "All in all," he said, "Dewey's article is one of the most brilliant pieces of controversial writing that I have ever seen and one more evidence that Dewey's mind is well neigh unmatched in our world today. Think what it means to have such an intellect on your side!"[56]

Under Levinson's steady, diplomatic guidance, the outlawry movement was marked by little internal discord. Although this harmony was no doubt a boon to organizational efficiency, it tended to obscure the differences between Dewey's conception of outlawry and that of others in the movement. Nonetheless, Dewey tended to emphasize aspects of the program that others downplayed or ignored. And he embedded outlawry in a larger democratic vision and political strategy far more radical (and more utopian) than anything Levinson envisioned. An article Dewey wrote later on the movement for *The Encyclopedia of Social Sciences* (1933) suggests as much. Here he added a fourth commandment to the outlawry program I cited earlier, and his version of the first three commandments was different in significant respects:

First, modification of international law to take war out of the category of legitimate means of solving disputes, this change to be effected or attended by national plebiscites to insure the education and registration of public opinion; second, revision and codification of international law to insure harmony of all its parts with the new action; third, the

55. "What Outlawry of War Is Not" (1923), *Middle Works* 15:115–121; "War and a Code of Law" (1923), *Middle Works* 15:122–127. Because the editor of the *Atlantic* would not entertain further debate on this matter, these articles appeared in the *New Republic*.

56. John Haynes Holmes to Levinson, 1 October 1923; Levinson to JD, 4 October 1923, Levinson Papers.

formation of an international court of justice which should have affirmative jurisdiction with respect to disputes likely to lead to war; fourth, provision that, in accord with the tenor of article 1, section 8 of the Constitution of the United States, each nation should make offenses against the law of nations crimes under domestic law, so that war breeders be tried and punished in their own country.

The most important difference in Dewey's version of outlawry lay in its concern with the means by which war would be outlawed. For Dewey, it was absolutely essential that this be the act of democratic publics. Insofar as such publics did not exist, they had to be created if outlawry was to work. Although Levinson also argued vigorously in the mid-twenties that the outlawing of war should be the result of national plebiscites, this aspect of the outlawry program proved far less essential for him than for Dewey, as the decidedly different responses of the two men to the Kellogg-Briand Pact would indicate. Levinson was a fixer, most comfortable behind the scenes arranging deals between powerful men. Public opinion was for him a tool to be manipulated to bring pressure to bear on elites. He seemed amused that Dewey supported Robert La Follette rather than Calvin Coolidge in the presidential race in 1924, and he never recognized the radically democratic tinge Dewey gave to outlawry. For Dewey, outlawing war was both an end of and a means to the democraticization of politics, not only in the United States but throughout the world.[57]

The operative assumption of Dewey's commitment to outlawry was the conviction that the peoples of the world were overwhelmingly against war. He believed that much of the power of the outlawry idea lay in its ability to close "by far the greatest gap that exists in any realm of life

57. "Outlawry of War," pp. 14–15; Levinson, "Can Peace Be 'Enforced'?" p. 47. Two other differences in Dewey's version of the first three outlawry commandments are worth mentioning. First, as a sympathetic observer in the twenties of revolutionary nationalism in the world outside the West, Dewey did not confine participation in the codification of international law to so-called civilized nations. Second, in their debates with World Court advocates, Dewey and others came to insist on the importance of vesting the international tribunal with "affirmative" (not just optional) jurisdiction over international disputes, that is with the authority to hear any case a party to a dispute asked it to hear, an authority that could not simply be ignored by the other party or parties to the dispute as it could if jurisdiction were merely optional (see JD, "Shall the United States Join the World Court?" pp. 92–93). Dewey seems, in the interests of friendship and movement harmony, to have suppressed and underplayed his differences with Levinson. In 1939 he did "consent" to the publication of a commentary on outlawry by Joseph Ratner which more or less accused Levinson of an "opportunism" verging on "perfidy" for his endorsement of the Pact of Paris ("Editor's Note," in Ratner, ed., *Intelligence in the Modern World: John Dewey's Philosophy* [New York: Modern Library, 1939], p. 560).

between moral sentiment and authorized practise." Abhorrence of war had created a "community of moral feeling" and "the outlawing of war provides a common centre for the expression of this community of moral emotion and desire. International law against war would produce the same condensing, precipitating, crystallizing effect for morals with respect to international relations that law has supplied everywhere else in its historic development." [58]

As Dewey conceived it, the means for securing the outlawry plan—the creation of active, well-informed, vigilant, democratic publics in the nations of the world—was subsequently to serve as the means for making it effective. Dewey's vision of outlawry, as Joseph Ratner showed in an astute essay, drew on the argument for a mutually reinforcing relationship between means and ends which was an essential part of his moral philosophy. "The *means necessary* for securing the worldwide adoption of the Plan and the creation of its legal instrumentalities are also *the means sufficient* for enacting or making effective those instrumentalities. The *means* to be used to create the Court (in which the plan heads up) are to be the very support of its decisions—*the ends*; and *the ends* (the decisions) in turn would (because supported) further strengthen, deepen, and further organize the already (partially) organized moral sentiment of the world—*the means*." Thus though the scale of the plan was breathtaking and utopian, Dewey's writings on outlawry did for the first time envision a politics consistent with his ethics, a politics that dialectically related democratic means and ends and might well be applied to more modest projects than the democratization of the world.[59]

Dewey's fourth commandment of outlawry shows also how essential democratic publics were for him in the enforcement as well as the establishment of outlawry, for it vested the sanctions against war which he denied to the community of nation-states in the hands of a plurality of democratic, national polities. His plan was not toothless. It appeared so because critics were looking in the wrong place for the incisors. He foresaw the day when "the warlike people will be the non-patriotic and the criminals. The pacifist then becomes the active patriot-loyal citizen, instead of an objector, a nuisance and a menace, or a passive obstructionist."[60]

As these remarks suggest, Dewey regarded outlawry as a popular

58. "Ethics and International Relations" (1923), *Middle Works* 15:62–63.
59. Ratner, "Editor's Note," p. 529.
60. "If War Were Outlawed," p. 111.

revolt against political elites. Optimistically putting his own stamp on things, he declared that it was "a movement for peace that starts from the peoples themselves, which expresses their will, and demands that the legislators and politicians and the diplomats give effect to the popular will for peace." There was no basis for hope for the responsible organization of international politics, he had told the Chinese, "unless there are democratic foreign policies within the nation-states that will make up the international organization" (*LC*, 161). And though he was given to bouts of American exceptionalism, Dewey acknowledged that a democratic foreign policy had to begin at home: "We have no right to demand 'open diplomacy' of other nations until we ourselves have shown that we have at least a kindergarten notion of what it implies. . . . Our conduct of our foreign policy is in working fact, if not in form, as irresponsible as that of any autocracy or monarchy. In fact, if not in form, it is still being determined for us behind our backs, and without our knowledge or consent, by a small clique of persons." If one took the conduct of foreign policy as the measure, he concluded, "the United States has still to go to school to learn democracy."[61]

Dewey admitted that "unless the moral sentiment of the world has reached the point of condemning war there is nothing that can be done about it." But unlike Lippmann, who maintained that the common man was as entangled in the traditions and institutions of war as his leaders, he believed that the convictions of most people were on his side and that no radical "moral disarmament" was required if war was to be outlawed. Without the exercise of coercion and manipulation by elites, he contended, publics would not go to war against the dictates of conscience. Hence truly democratic polities would not go to war if it were outlawed, and they would punish those who attempted to have them do so. It made an enormous difference, he contended, "whether you begin with the people and end with the politicians, or begin with the politicians and end by putting something over on the people."[62]

In 1927 the campaign to outlaw war took a turn that most in the outlawry movement found heartening, but which Dewey saw as a potential disaster. In April of that year the French foreign minister, Aristide Briand, proposed that the United States and France enter into a bilateral pact to "condemn recourse to war and renounce it respectively as

61. "Shall the United States Join the World Court?" p. 100; "Reconstruction Editorial," *Dial*, 28 December 1918: 619.

62. "If War Were Outlawed," pp. 110–111; "Shall the United States Join the World Court?" p. 100. Cf. Lippmann, "Outlawry of War," p. 408.

an instrument of their national policy towards each other." In December, U.S. secretary of state Frank Kellogg suggested instead a multilateral pact in which all the principal powers of the world renounced war. Although this was not at all what the French had in mind, further negotiations eventually produced the Kellogg-Briand Pact, signed on 27 August 1928 by France, the United States, Great Britain, Japan, and a number of secondary powers. The agreement condemned war as a means of solving international disputes, and the signatories joined in renouncing war as an instrument of national policy and agreed to settle conflicts among themselves by peaceful means.[63]

Although Levinson worked diligently on behalf of the pact and believed it was an important advance toward outlawry, Dewey's response to it was lukewarm at best. His friend Joseph Ratner later reported that he had said on the day the pact was signed that "he was convinced the Pact would hinder not help the realization of the outlawry objective." He worried over the notes exchanged in the negotiations which hedged the apparently straightforward language of the treaty with reservations and exceptions designed to ensure that the pact posed no threat to colonial empires and prior security arrangements in Europe. He was also deeply troubled that the French had muddied the treaty with ambiguous notions of self-defense all too close to that bête noire of outlawry, "defensive war." But above all he objected to the treaty because it was the work of the very political elites he most distrusted rather than the educated publics he favored. The pact, he said, "should have been the conclusion of an irresistible public demand; to a considerable extent it was the termination of the manuevers of diplomats. There has, therefore, always been the danger that official adoption of the outlawry idea would turn out to be an embalming of the idea rather than an embodiment of it."[64]

At best, the pact was only the first step toward outlawry, and perhaps because of his disappointment with it, Dewey disappeared from the outlawry movement for nearly four years. But after the Japanese seizure of Manchuria in late 1931, he reluctantly agreed in the face of this crisis involving his beloved China to try to pump new life into the cause. In the spring of 1932 he accepted the invitation of James G. McDonald, chair of the Foreign Policy Association, to respond to a lengthy article

63. On the pact negotiations see Stoner, *Levinson*, chaps. 13–18, and Ferrell, *Peace in Their Time*, chaps. 5–17.

64. Ratner, "Editor's Note," p. 547n; "Peace—by Pact or Covenant?" (1932), *Later Works* 6:190–191. See also "'As an Example to Other Nations,'" pp. 163–167; "Outlawing Peace by Discussing War," pp. 173–176.

by the group's research director, Raymond Buell, defending the use of collective sanctions to enforce international law and arguing that had sanctions been invoked, as provided for by Article 16 of the League of Nations charter, Japanese aggression might well have been forestalled. In his reply, Dewey argued that sanctions against Japan were impracticable, both because divisions among the other great powers made united coercive measures impossible and because sanctions would probably have increased Japanese intransigence and enhanced the power of the militarists in that country. Moreover, he contended, even if sanctions were practical, they would do little to advance the cause of peace, leaving "the war system as the ultimate means of settling international controversies." In a forceful counterargument to the domestic "police" analogy favored by outlawry opponents, he contended that, given the scale of collective sanctions, the better analogy was civil war, and he could not imagine anyone's believing that civil war was intrinsically desirable or that it should be provided for in advance. As he saw it, war could not be disguised by calling it a "police action," for "if the animal looks like a frog, jumps like a frog, and croaks like a frog, it *is* a frog."[65]

Dewey's response to Buell was one of his most effective summary arguments for the outlawry program. He remained convinced, he concluded, that "if the peoples of nations *want* to have done with war, the outlawry idea is the best method for giving expression to that desire which has yet been discovered." The fighting in Manchuria had raised an issue much larger than the particulars of that local conflict. The question it posed was "whether the measures which the world has taken since the end of the Great War to develop means for settling international disputes without resort to war have any force, or whether they can be blown aside like feathers when the air of animosity and national ambition is fanned into a breeze." Knowing as we do of the hurricane that followed, we find it perhaps all too easy to wonder that Dewey still believed this was an open question and to stand amazed at his persistent faith that time had not run out on the outlawry of war.[66]

As he had throughout the twenties, Dewey made clear in 1932 the

65. James G. McDonald to JD, 5 April 1932; Raymond J. Buell, "Are Sanctions Necessary to International Organization? Yes" (1932), *Later Works* 6:450–484; JD, "Are Sanctions Necessary to International Organization? No" (1932), *Later Works* 6:196–223. See also JD to Levinson, 1 March 1932, 8 March 1932, Levinson Papers. The Buell-Dewey debate was originally published by the Foreign Policy Association as a pamphlet titled *Are Sanctions Necessary to International Organization?* (1932).

66. "Are Sanctions Necessary? No," p. 221; "Group Here Votes Boycott on Japan," *New York Times*, 13 December 1931, 30.

fearful analogy that lay on the underside of his hope: "The assumption that threats of coercive force would have really restrained [Japan's] militarism sound to me much like the pleas we gave way to during the World War, that militaristic opposition to and conquest of German militarism would sound the death knell of all militarism. Instead we have a world more completely armed than in 1914. I submit that by this time we ought to have got beyond the notion that resort to coercive force is going to weaken the tendency to resort to coercive force; it only shifts its focus." As a pacifist, Mars had once again proved a failure in World War I, and a war to end war was now for Dewey inconceivable.[67]

In arguing for the removal of the sanction of law from war, Dewey was now banning war from the realm of efficient means to anything other than morally indefensible ends. In terms of his earlier distinction between force and violence, war was now inevitably violence. This, of course, had been Bourne's contention, and Dewey was now using the term "war system" in much the same acidly ironic way that Bourne had used the term "war technique." Alas, Bourne was not around to see it.

67. "Are Sanctions Necessary? No," pp. 207–208.

CHAPTER 9

The Phantom Public

✳

In 1918 many radicals and liberals shared John Dewey's hopes for the reconstruction of American society after World War I. They believed that the war had greatly weakened the established order and opened the way for the development of one form or another of industrial democracy. George Soule, an editor of the *New Republic*, later recalled that at war's end

> the world seemed more in flux, more ready for fundamental changes, than it ever has since. Many of us had before that time felt not only the injustice but the meaninglessness of a haphazard civilization in which the survival of institutions and the effectiveness of personalities depended more and more on the ability to connect with profit and commercial success. During the War we had sensed the possibilities of planning and communal effort, hastily and crudely organized though they were under such agencies as the War Industries Board and the Food Administration. The shock of the War itself produced a conviction that the world was plunging to disaster. We had read avidly Wells, Shaw, Sidney Webb, G. D. H. Cole and others who proposed new types of society under socialism, guild socialism, syndicalism, or some other logical system. There had been the Communist revolution in Russia, the Socialist revolution in Germany, and the tremendous growth of the British Labor party, with its ambitious Nottingham program. The labor movement in the United States was strong, aggressive and fermenting with ideas.

As a consequence, Soule remembered, many progressive intellectuals "were seized in this current of ideas and were ready to take part in a reorganization of society."[1]

Dewey was seized by some of these ideas and a leader among those eager to take part in social reorganization. He was particularly impressed by the awakening to the progressive potential of social science which the war seemed to him to bring. "We have gained a presentiment that what the public wants there is the intelligence and skill to make good," he said. One of the most salutary effects of this "awakened and altered sense of human affairs" was the exposure of the ideological character of the "natural laws" of conservative social science. This unmasking opened the door, he thought, for an empirical, experimental social science that would treat notions of any inherent laws of social structure, function, and growth with the contempt such "mythologies" deserved. The new social sciences would thereby be free to serve the cause of reform, coupling the interests of the hand worker with those of the brain worker. The war, he concluded, had "cleared the way for a science of ideas in action which will trust not to negative forces, to bankruptcy, to bring about what is desired, but to positive energy, to intellectual competency, to competency of inquiry, discussion, reflection and invention organized to take effect in action in directing affairs."[2]

Occasionally, Dewey tempered his optimism during the war with a realistic estimate of the obstacles radicals faced in postwar America. The demobilization of soldiers and war workers raised the specter of unemployment and a reduction of wages. The war had also consolidated capital and done little to further the organization of labor, which was "hampered by a fixed habit of thinking and acting in terms of immediate wages and hours of labor instead of in terms of control of economic conditions." The American Constitution remained a powerful bulwark of the status quo, and the opportunities for effective political action were restricted by other established institutions. "To see the property-less man in the saddle under such conditions," Dewey remarked, "requires a peculiarly exuberant imagination."[3]

As the politics of peace took shape, Dewey's doubts about the possibilities of postwar domestic reconstruction deepened, and he began to call into question his own "glowing prophecies of an inevitable social

1. George Soule, "Hard-Boiled Radicalism," *New Republic*, 21 January 1931: 262.
2. "A New Social Science" (1918), *Middle Works* 11:88–92.
3. Ibid., p. 88.

reconstruction to follow the war." He and others, he said, had counted too much on "the community of emotional consciousness generated by war." This was "the sandiest of foundations" on which to build reform, and by the end of 1918 he could perceive that its erosion was well advanced. "Men will resume the opposition of interests where they laid them down," he predicted. "We may indeed count ourselves lucky if these are not intensified by the truce, by the stirrings of hate and suspicion bred by war, and by the extraordinary and abnormal read-justments that have to be undertaken." Forecasting the issue that would be at the heart of debates among democratic theorists in the twenties, Dewey voiced a particular concern over the manipulation of public opinion during the war, a feature of wartime management he felt sure would survive the conflict. The war had witnessed an alliance of "be-nevolent paternalists" among powerful elites in business, government, and the news industry whose motto was: "Let us make democracy safe for the world by a careful editing and expurgation of the facts upon which it bases the opinions which in the end decide social action."[4]

Dewey, the pessimist, proved a better prophet than he wished. Wil-sonian progressivism had exhausted itself before the war, and the con-servative Republican ascendancy forecast in the elections of November 1918 was sealed with the election of Warren Harding to the presidency in 1920. Reaction swept over the country, and, as Soule said, many intellectuals became "tired radicals," who "surrendered by going out for conventional success, perhaps tucking away some reservations in a dark closet of the mind."[5]

As he turned sixty, Dewey was entitled to more weariness than most intellectuals, but he did not abandon his radical convictions in the twen-ties. As we have seen, his participation in the Outlawry of War move-ment was of a piece with these convictions, and trips to Turkey, Mexico, and the Soviet Union in mid-decade resulted in each case in favorable reports to the American public on the prospects of revolutionary na-tionalism. At home, he remained a vigorous advocate of social action that would create the conditions for thoroughgoing democracy and began to develop the socialist conclusions to which his vision of democ-racy pointed, though he remained reluctant to identify himself as a socialist. He did join the League for Industrial Democracy, newly formed in 1921 from the ashes of the Intercollegiate Socialist Society,

4. "The Post-War Mind" (1918), *Middle Works* 11:114–115; "The New Paternalism" (1918), *Middle Works* 11:120–121.
5. Soule, "Hard-Boiled Radicalism," p. 262.

the most important prewar organization of American socialist intellectuals. Like others in the LID, Dewey supported the Progressive party of Robert La Follette in the presidential campaign of 1924, arguing that the Republicans and Democrats were doing little more than "handing out bunkum." In 1928, though his heart was with Norman Thomas and the Socialist party, he backed Al Smith, feeling that the American people were not "ripe" to confront the issues of economic reconstruction the Socialists were posing and that the best one could hope for at the moment was the injection of some "humane sympathy" into American politics. Smith's considerable administrative abilities, he said, were "as much controlled by a human sense of his fellow beings as [Herbert Hoover's] are by a hard 'efficiency' which works out to strengthen the position of just those economic interests that most need weakening instead of strengthening." By the end of the twenties he was supporting local Socialist candidates in New York City and working for the establishment of a third party that would advocate democratic socialism without the burden of the "socialist" name.[6]

Throughout the twenties Dewey denounced the political repression and coercive Americanization that persisted long after the Red Scare of the immediate postwar years had passed, and his voice was a particularly strong one in efforts to weather the climate of fear in the nation's schools, colleges, and universities. He played a leading role, along with Charles Beard, Herbert Croly, Alvin Johnson, Wesley Mitchell, James Harvey Robinson, and Thorstein Veblen, in the founding in 1919 of the New School for Social Research, designed to provide a center of learning free from the constraints on academic freedom apparent during the war. Concern about wartime suppression of civil liberties also led Dewey to join Jane Addams, Roger Baldwin, Clarence Darrow, Felix Frankfurter, Norman Thomas, and others in helping to establish the American Civil Liberties Union in 1920.[7]

6. Dykhuizen, pp. 224–225, 232, 235–239; "Dewey Aids La Follette" (1924), *Middle Works* 15:317; "Why I Am for Smith" (1928), *Later Works* 3:184–185; "Dewey Supports Vladeck" (1930), *Middle Works* 5:443. On the League for Industrial Democracy see *The League for Industrial Democracy: A Documentary History*, ed. Bernard K. Johnpoll and Mark R. Yerburgh (Westport, Conn.: Greenwood Press, 1980). For a brief account of its history and ideology see my review of this book in *International Labor and Working Class History* 20 (1981): 73–78. On Dewey's role in third-party politics in the thirties see Chapter 12, and on his trip to the Soviet Union see Chapter 13.

7. "The School as a Means of Developing a Social Consciousness and Social Ideals in Children" (1923), *Middle Works* 15:150–157; "Social Purposes in Education" (1923), *Middle Works* 15:158–169; "The Liberal College and Its Enemies" (1924), *Middle Works* 15:205–211; "Why I Am a Member of the Teacher's Union" (1928), *Later Works* 3:269–275. On the founding of the New School see Herbert Croly, "A School of Social Re-

As he often did when confronted with the power of conservatives, Dewey argued in the early twenties that reactionaries might well be inadvertently helping the cause of democracy in their campaign to stamp out Bolshevism. Beneath the postwar reaction Dewey sensed there lay the fear of conservatives of growing support for industrial democracy. "Freedom of speech and of the franchise is now significant," he said, "because it is part of the struggle for freedom of mind in industry, freedom to participate in its planning and conduct." He predicted that reactionary attacks on free speech would in the end be counterproductive because conservative power rested on ignorance of the facts these attacks brought to light, in this case the intimate relationship between freedom of thought and workplace democracy. "The stupidity of the reactionary," he said, "is that at critical junctures he strives to entrench himself by doing things which force attention to facts that he has every interest in keeping concealed."[8]

By the end of the twenties and the denouement of the decade's civil liberties *cause célèbre*—the execution of Nicola Sacco and Bartolomeo Vanzetti for two murders committed during the robbery of a South Braintree, Massachusetts, shoe factory in 1920—Dewey was no longer clinging to this wistful hope. Following the execution in 1927, he carefully analyzed the "psychology of the dominant cultivated class of the country" evident in the report of the committee of leading citizens appointed by Governor Alvan Fuller to assess the trial proceedings, which put the imprimatur of respectable opinion on a guilty verdict that seemed to many to owe less to the strength of the evidence than to an aversion to the politics of the immigrant anarchist defendants. Reading the report, Dewey said he found himself "profoundly humiliated" by the attitudes apparent there. "The sense of humiliation is akin to that of guilt, as if for a share in permitting such a state of mind as is exhibited in the record to develop in a country that professes respect for justice and devotion to equality and fraternity." If Dewey was by no means a tired radical at decade's end, he was a decidedly defensive one.[9]

---

search," *New Republic*, 8 June 1918: 167–171, and Peter M. Rutkoff and William B. Scott, *New School: A History of the New School for Social Research* (New York: Free Press, 1986), chaps. 1–3. On the origins of the ACLU see Donald O. Johnson, *The Challenge to American Freedom: World War I and the Rise of the American Civil Liberties Union* (Lexington: University of Kentucky Press, 1963).

8. "Freedom of Thought and Work" (1920), *Middle Works* 12:11; "How Reaction Helps" (1920), *Middle Works* 12:18.

9. "Psychology and Justice" (1927), *Later Works* 3:186, 195.

GOVERNMENT FOR THE PEOPLE

For Dewey the conservative attack on civil liberties was, in the long run, less distressing than the reconstruction of democratic theory by fellow liberals which picked up a full head of steam in the twenties. He returned from China to find his expansive conception of democracy under attack by "democratic realists," who were assuming command of American democratic thought and thereby beginning to force him to the margins of liberal social theory. Ironically, the arguments of democratic realism were often cast in a Deweyan idiom, and its ascendancy went hand-in-hand with the rapid development of the new social sciences he had hoped would play a leading role in radical social change.

During the early twentieth century, social scientists located in the newly emergent universities and national professional societies had established a fresh agenda for the scientific study of American social and political life, calling, like Dewey, for an empirical and experimental science of human society to replace the abstract, a priori approach that characterized nineteenth-century studies in the human sciences. In the twenties, a new generation of scholars, led by Charles Merriam, professor of political science at the University of Chicago and one of the greatest academic entrepreneurs in American history, further nationalized their disciplines by means of the formation of such interdisciplinary organizations as the Social Science Research Council and the skillful use of corporate philanthropy. By the end of the decade, the expansive research infrastructure of modern American social inquiry—the network of academic associations, government and industrial research bureaus, and private foundations which has since become a taken-for-granted part of the intellectual landscape—was well established.[10]

By the twenties, the steady drift of American democratic theory into

10. My discussion here of American social science and democratic theory in the twenties follows closely that in three fine studies: Edward A. Purcell, Jr., *The Crisis of Democratic Theory: Scientific Naturalism and the Problem of Value* (Lexington: University of Kentucky Press, 1973); David M. Ricci, *The Tragedy of Political Science: Politics, Scholarship, and Democracy* (New Haven: Yale University Press, 1984); and Raymond Seidelman, *Disenchanted Realists: Political Science and the American Crisis, 1884–1984* (Albany: SUNY Press, 1985). On Merriam and his influence see Barry D. Karl's excellent biography, *Charles Merriam and the Study of Politics* (Chicago: University of Chicago Press, 1974), and Karl, "The Power of Intellect and the Politics of Ideas," *Daedalus* 97 (1968): 1002–1035. Although less germane to my concerns because its focus is sociology rather than political science, Robert C. Bannister, *Sociology and Scientism: The American Quest for Objectivity, 1880–1940* (Chapel Hill: University of North Carolina Press, 1987), is also an important study of the formative years of modern American social science.

the hands of academic social scientists was also well advanced. Although voices could already be heard arguing for "value-free" social science, this did not, as yet, mean a full-fledged retreat into a specious objectivity. Many social scientists, particularly those whose research had some bearing on the fate of American democracy, shared Dewey's conviction that social science without social philosophy was blind. Science, he said, "can describe and record natural phenomena, but it cannot guide them or change them according to human ideals. But social philosophy cannot stop with mere recording and description; it must direct with thoughtful understanding the conclusions and recommendations which grow out of the records and descriptions of science. . . . The relationship between the social sciences and social philosophy is thus one of interpenetration." Although leading social scientists now argued that they might best serve the interests of democracy by distancing themselves from direct involvement in reform politics, they still considered their disciplines to be "applied" sciences. For Merriam and other prominent students of American democracy, the science of politics remained a science for politics.[11]

But the politics that political scientists sought to serve after World War I was not the same democratic politics that Dewey had in mind when he argued that political science must "provide the material by means of which man can improve his lot and move towards the goal of peace and happiness." The marriage of democratic values and objective science on which American political science had been founded (which had never been an altogether happy one) came unraveled in the twenties. Rather than afford one another mutual support, as Dewey had supposed they would, democratic ideals and the findings of empirical research were placed increasingly at odds. As David Ricci has said, political scientists began to produce studies that served "to undermine the very object which the discipline was professionally committed to support, namely, the democratic polity."[12]

The democratic realists of the twenties focused their criticism of

11. *John Dewey: Lectures in China, 1919–1920*, ed. Robert W. Clopton and Tsuin-chen Ou (Honolulu: University Press of Hawaii, 1973), pp. 57, 59; Seidelman, *Disenchanted Realists*, chap. 4. The manifesto of the "new political science" of the twenties was Charles Merriam, *New Aspects of Politics* (Chicago: University of Chicago Press, 1925).

12. *Lectures in China*, p. 59; Ricci, *Tragedy of Political Science*, p. 78. As several analysts of Merriam's work have argued, it is important to distinguish his democratic theory and his defense of objective science—both of which were closer to Dewey's than that of most social scientists in the twenties and thirties—from that of his more hard-boiled students such as Harold Lasswell. See Siedelman, *Disenchanted Realists*, pp. 109–133, and Karl, *Merriam*, chap. 6.

democracy on two of its essential beliefs: the belief in the capacity of all men for rational political action and the belief in the practicality and desirability of maximizing the participation of all citizens in public life. Finding ordinary men and women irrational and participatory democracy impossible and unwise under modern conditions, they argued that it was best to strictly limit government by the people and to redefine democracy as, by and large, government for the people by enlightened and responsible elites.

One of the great enthusiasms of American political science in the twenties was the application of psychological theory to the study of politics. This was one of Merriam's pet projects, and he encouraged the work in this field of his students Harold Gosnell and Harold Lasswell, and the latter became the most prominent American practitioner of a psychological approach to political behavior. By the late twenties a wide consensus had emerged among political scientists that the alliance of psychology and political analysis was an indispensable feature of their discipline. This alliance provided the theoretical foundation for much of the democratic realist critique of participatory democracy.

The application of psychological theory and research to politics in the twenties did not bode well for radical democracy. Americans were still reeling from the results of intelligence tests administered by the army to 1,700,000 soldiers during World War I, which purported to demonstrate that 60 to 70 percent of the soldiers tested were mentally deficient. A fierce debate raged over the reliability of the tests and their implications. Prominent psychologists, led by Lewis M. Terman, Edwin G. Boring, and William S. McDougall, defended the tests as compelling evidence of the limited intelligence of most Americans. McDougall drew on the tests to support a racialist theory of the politics of cultural degeneration, arguing that democracy permitted equality between unequal races and was a dangerous form of government. In insisting on its preservation, the United States was "speeding gaily, with invincible optimism, down the road to destruction." The resurgence of nativism during and after the war provided fertile soil for such racialist attacks on social equality and democracy. Racial biology, some argued, dictated that multiracial societies like the United States abandon democratic ideals and vest control in those of superior, Anglo-Saxon racial stock. Although such racism defined the outer limits of the attack on democracy, it does suggest the hostile environment in which an unreconstructed democrat like Dewey was forced to operate in the twenties.[13]

---

13. William McDougall, *Is America Safe for Democracy?* (1921), as quoted in Purcell, *Crisis of Democratic Theory*, p. 98. On intelligence tests see also Daniel Kevles, "Testing the

The dominant psychological theories of the twenties also gave little comfort to democrats, for they raised serious questions about the capacity of most human beings for the sort of rational deliberation and judgment theorists such as Dewey found essential to democratic politics. By 1930 Freudian and behaviorist psychologies were exerting a dominant influence on American social science. Freudians emphasized the unconscious, irrational, and instinctual elements of human behavior, while behaviorists reduced human behavior to the mechanical, automatic, and subrational operations of stimulus and response. Neither school had any good news for democrats, though many academics were excited about the prospects they afforded for social science. Summing up the influence of such theories in 1930, Beardsley Ruml observed that "the shift in emphasis from rational to irrational motivation is a contribution of the first order to our understanding, and it is affecting profoundly the social sciences."[14]

Those social scientists who assessed the implications of contemporary psychological theory and research for democracy came to predictable conclusions. Sociologist Harry Elmer Barnes declared that psychology "has given scientific confirmation to the old Aristotelian dogma that some men are born to rule and others to serve, and makes it clear that we can have no efficient and progressive social system unless we recognize the real value of leadership and make it possible for the actual intellectual aristocracy to control society." Elton Mayo suggested that most social behavior was determined by irrational factors, which he termed the "night mind," and argued that democratic politics served only to enhance the influence of the night mind on social life. Building on a study of wartime propaganda, Lasswell observed that the intense interest policy makers and social scientists displayed in propaganda "testifies to the collapse of the traditional species of democratic romanticism and to the rise of the dictatorial habit of mind":

> Familiarity with the ruling public has bred contempt. Modern reflections upon democracy boil down to the proposition, more or less contritely expressed, that the democrats were deceiving themselves. The public has not reigned with benignity and restraint. The good life is not in the mighty rushing wind of public sentiment. It is no organic

Army's Intelligence: Psychologists and the Military in World War I," *Journal of American History* 55 (1968): 565–581, and Clarence J. Karier, "Testing for Order and Control in the Corporate Liberal State," in Karier, Paul Violas, and Joel Spring, eds., *Roots of Crisis: American Education in the Twentieth Century* (Chicago: Rand McNally, 1973), pp. 108–137.

14. Beardsley Ruml, "Recent Trends in Social Science," in Leonard D. White, ed., *The New Social Science* (Chicago: University of Chicago Press, 1930), p. 101.

secretion of the horde, but the tedious achievement of the few. The lover of the good life no longer consults Sir Oracle; he pulls the strings of Punch and Judy. Thus argues the despondent democrat. Let us, therefore, reason together, brethren, he sighs, and find the good and when we have found it, let us find out how to make up the public mind to accept it. Inform, cajole, bamboozle and seduce in the name of the public good. Preserve the majority convention, but dictate to the majority.

Lasswell employed psychoanalytic theory directly in case studies of political activists and concluded that public, political action was a projection of private, unconscious, and irrational psychological drives. "Political movements," he said, "derive their vitality from the displacement of private affects upon public objects, and political crises are complicated by the concurrent reactivation of specific primitive motives." Most men were blind to their own best interests, and democratic politics only increased the opportunities for psychopathological projection and fruitless efforts to satisfy irrational private hatreds and desires on the public stage.[15]

Empirical studies of voting behavior further enhanced this portrait of democratic man as irrational man. Social scientists noted the sharp decline in participation of eligible voters in American elections and observed that those who did vote rarely acted as rational decision makers. A study of the 1924 presidential election by Norman C. Meier concluded that "the successful campaign was the one which dealt least with rational motives and most with simple appeals directed toward the arousal of specific, instinctive, emotional, and habit pattern-responses." The results of his research, Meier believed, "lay open to question anew the fundamental assumption of democracy that there be accorded every member of the electorate adequate and relatively unbiased information for his guidance in considering men and issues." These conclusions were echoed by Carroll D. Wooddy, whose study of the Chicago primary of 1926 demonstrated that "voting was indiscriminate and unintelligent, and the primary practically meaningless as an expression of public opinion."[16]

15. Harry Elmer Barnes, "Some Contributions of Sociology to Modern Political Theory," in Charles E. Merriam and Harry E. Barnes, eds., *A History of Political Theories: Recent Times* (New York: Macmillan, 1924), p. 373; Elton Mayo, "The Irrational Factor in Human Behavior: The 'Night Mind' in Industry," *Annals of the American Academy of Political and Social Science* 110 (November 1923): 117–130; Harold Lasswell, *Propaganda Technique World War I* (original ed. 1927, Cambridge: MIT Press, 1971), pp. 4–5. I am indebted here to the fuller discussion of the application of psychology to the study of politics in Purcell, *Crisis of Democratic Theory*, pp. 97–109.

16. Norman C. Meier, "Motives in Voting: A Study in Public Opinion," *American Jour-*

Few of the social scientists who denounced the irrationality and impracticality of democratic government believed that democracy should be totally abandoned. Rather, they argued that the role of the public in decision making should be severely restricted and power placed in the hands of those few men who *were* rational and intelligent (often described as men much like the social scientists themselves). Lasswell, the most thoroughgoing, influential, and extremist of those who described the psychopathology of politics, recommended a "politics of prevention" in which therapeutic social scientists would advise elites who in turn would "reorient minds" in order to control political conflict. Harold Gosnell more modestly suggested that political scientists determine the qualities of good citizenship and then work with psychologists to devise an examination "which would be more useful than a literacy test in weeding out undesirable voters." Summarizing such sentiments in his presidential address to the American Political Science Association in 1934, Walter Shepard declared that it was clear that

> the dogma of universal suffrage must give way to a system of educational and other tests which will exclude the ignorant, the uninformed, and the anti-social elements which hitherto have so frequently controlled elections. We must frankly recognize that government demands the best thought, the highest character, the most unselfish service that is available. We must admit, as did Aristotle, that an aristocratic as well as a democratic element is necessary in government—not an aristocracy of wealth, or class, or privileged position, but an aristocracy of intellect and character.

Shepard ended his speech with a ringing call to his fellow academics to assume the responsibility for leading the nation, imploring "men of brains" to "seize the torch!"[17]

By the end of the twenties, as Ricci has said, the discipline of political science "had reached a point where its scientific findings could not be discounted as separate curiosities but constituted, instead, a coherent body of testimony to the notion that something in democracy either

---

nal of Sociology 31 (1925): 210–212; Carroll D. Wooddy, *The Chicago Primary of 1926* (Chicago: University of Chicago Press, 1926), p. 275; Purcell, *Crisis of Democratic Theory*, pp. 107–108. See also Charles E. Merriam and Harold Gosnell, *Non-Voting* (Chicago: University of Chicago Press, 1924). For an overview of voting studies in the twenties and their political context see Michael E. McGerr, *The Decline of Popular Politics: The American North, 1865–1928* (New York: Oxford University Press, 1986), chap. 7.

17. Harold Lasswell, *Psychopathology and Politics* (Chicago: University of Chicago Press, 1930), chap. 10; Harold Gosnell, "Some Practical Applications of Psychology in Government," *American Journal of Sociology* 28 (1923): 742; Walter Shepard, "Democracy in Transition," *American Political Science Review* 29 (1935): 18–19, 20.

needed radical repair or—always a possibility when old faiths are challenged—a new and reassuring explanation." Most social scientists opted for the latter. The problem, they argued, was less with American democracy than with participatory democratic theory. Rather than radical repair, they contended, American democracy required a redefinition of its essentials, a redefinition that considerably closed the gap between the ideal and reality. Democracy should be conceived less as a republic of active citizens than as a system of responsible elites, a system well within reach in the United States.[18]

From Dewey's perspective, the conclusions of these "democratic elitists" were bleak. They saw themselves as repudiating the hopelessly utopian dreams of radical democrats in the interest of a more realistic, "modernized" model of democracy, but as far as he was concerned, their model drained democracy of its essentials. By the end of the twenties a chorus of voices among democratic theorists and social scientists was singing the praises of the wedding of democracy and "organized intelligence" as Dewey had since the 1890s, but he found himself in the difficult position of arguing that, though the words were the same, the song they were singing was quite different from his own.

HABITUAL INTELLIGENCE

Dewey had begun to work out a full statement of the psychological foundations of his own democratic politics in the spring of 1918 in a

---

18. Ricci, *Tragedy of Political Science*, p. 88. Ricci sees Dewey as a contributor to this "new and tough-minded version of liberalism"—indeed he says that the "matrix of discourse" in which it took shape was "Deweyism" (pp. 101–111). Yet he acknowledges that, unlike the political scientists whose work he surveys, Dewey argued for an expansion rather than a constriction of participatory democracy. The burden of his argument thus rests on the contention that Dewey provided the philosophical grounding for political scientists' turn from an ethical argument for the value of democracy to what he takes to be a nonethical argument on its behalf. This turn enabled them to say that democracy may not be all it is cracked up to be but it sure works better than the alternatives. "Deweyism," he says, "suggested considering the world of politics, rather than principles, and concentrating on very practical considerations concerning the capacity of liberal or authoritarian regimes, rather than theorists, to deal with that world. In the process, it might be possible to portray democracy as an imperfect but necessary mechanism, in words so plain that recourse to the tricky ground of ethical analysis and explication could be avoided entirely." As it happens, even if this were an accurate rendering of Dewey's thinking, which it is not, it does not avoid the "tricky ground of ethical analysis," for it poses the (ethical) questions of "capacity for *what*?" and "necessary for *what*?" Ricci's analysis suggests (correctly I believe) that the predominant answer to these questions for political scientists was "stability," which clearly was not Dewey's answer. Edward Purcell, Jr., also believes Dewey made an important contribution to the ethical dilemmas of

series of lectures he delivered at Stanford University. Although not directly conceived as such, these lectures, rewritten, expanded, and published in 1922 as *Human Nature and Conduct*, amounted to a forceful challenge to the psychological underpinnings of democratic realism.

Human Nature and Conduct was written against the background of the preeminence of instinct theory among American social psychologists in the antebellum years, and, in particular, the influence of William McDougall's *Introduction to Social Psychology* (1908). Dewey's book, itself subtitled *An Introduction to Social Psychology*, was dedicated to the proposition that it was not instinct but habit that was the key to social psychology.[19]

"Habit" was yet another of those commonplace terms Dewey insisted on defining against the grain of ordinary usage. For him, it meant not simply routinized behavior (though that could be a component of a habit) but something much broader. Habit was "human activity which is influenced by prior activity and in that sense acquired; which contains within itself a certain ordering or systematization of minor elements of action; which is projective, dynamic in quality, ready for overt manifestation; and which is operative in some subdued subordinate form even when not obviously dominating activity." Repetition was not the essence of habit. This lay rather in "an acquired predisposition to *ways* or modes of response, not to particular acts except as, under special conditions, these express a way of behaving. Habit means special sensitiveness or accessibility to certain classes of stimuli, standing predilections and aversions, rather than bare recurrence of specific acts. It means will."[20]

Habits were, in effect, social functions. Like physiological functions such as breathing and digesting they were an interaction between human organisms and their environment. The principal difference between habits and physiological functions was that they were always social. "It is not an ethical 'ought' that conduct *should* be social," Dewey

---

American democratic theory, but he does not contend that Dewey sought to avoid tricky moral questions but rather that, though he tried, he did not answer them very well (*Crisis of Democratic Theory*, pp. 42–43). I do not pretend to venture any conclusive response to this criticism (which, in any case, takes the form of a mere assertion), though I do offer what can only be called a sympathetic account of Dewey's mature effort to supply democracy with an ethical foundation in Chapters 10 and 11.

19. On McDougall and his influence see Reba Soffer, *Ethics and Society in England: The Revolution in the Social Sciences, 1870–1914* (Berkeley: University of California Press, 1978), chaps. 10–11.

20. *Human Nature and Conduct: An Introduction to Social Psychology* (1922), *Middle Works* 14:31–32. Page numbers for further references (*HNC*) appear in the text.

said. It *is* social, whether bad or good." The human self was constituted by habits; it was a more or less integrated collection of habitual dispositions. Individual character was an "interpenetration of habits" (*HNC*, 16, 21, 29).

The customs of any society were its prevailing habits, and Dewey argued strenuously that individual minds were the product of custom and not vice versa. "Customs persist," he said, "because individuals form their personal habits under conditions set by prior customs. An individual usually acquires the morality as he inherits the speech of his social group." Given this fact, "the problem of social psychology is not how either individual or collective mind forms social groups and customs, but how different customs, established interacting arrangements, form and nurture different minds" (*HNC*, 43, 46). A proper social psychology must then begin with the settled habits, the social environment, not with individual minds. The latter were a dependent variable, and a habit-based psychology denied the existence of a separate and individual consciousness. Rather, it fixed its attention on "the objective conditions in which habits are formed and operate" (*HNC*, 61).

Dewey did not deny the existence of instincts or, as he preferred to call them, impulses, just their priority. He admitted instincts were, strictly speaking, primary—habits being a secondary structuring of impulses. Yet he insisted on the prior importance of habits, for, he contended, the "natural activities" or impulses of human beings were, of themselves, completely unorganized and hence meaningless. "The *meaning* of native activities is not native; it is acquired. It depends upon interaction with a matured social medium" (*HNC*, 65). Men and women were wholly creatures of habit, that is, of culture:

> In the case of a tiger or eagle, anger may be identified with a serviceable life-activity, with attack and defense. With a human being it is as meaningless as a gust of wind on a mudpuddle apart from a direction given it by the presence of other persons, apart from the responses they make to it. It is a physical spasm, a blind dispersive burst of wasteful energy. It gets quality, significance, when it becomes a smoldering sullenness, an annoying interruption, a peevish irritation, a murderous revenge, a blazing indignation. And although these phenomena which have a meaning spring from original native reactions to stimuli, yet they depend also upon the responsive behavior of others. They and all similar human displays of anger are not pure impulses; they are habits formed under the influence of association with others who have habits already and who show their habits in the treatment

which converts a blind physical discharge into a significant anger. (*HNC*, 65–66)

Impulses, on this account, were completely plastic—"any impulse may become organized into almost any disposition according to the way it interacts with surroundings" (*HNC*, 69).[21]

Despite their inherent meaninglessness, impulses were very important to Dewey's social psychology. They provided him with an explanation of individuality and social change and rescued his psychology from "oversocialization." They were "the pivots upon which the re-organization of activities turn, they are agencies of deviation, for giving new directions to old habits and changing their quality" (*HNC*, 67). Impulses, he argued, could never be wholly contained by habits, especially under conditions of rapid change when habits became ill adapted to their environment. Uncontained impulses were the levers of reform. "There always exists a goodly store of non-functioning impulses which may be drawn upon," he said. The task of the reformer was to take advantage of the clash between impulse and habit in order to reconstruct habits. Contrary to the belief of conservatives, it was not instinct ("old human nature") that stood in the way of change, but encrusted habit. "Impulse is a source, an indispensable source, of liberation; but only as it is employed in giving habits pertinence and freshness does it liberate power." In Dewey's theory the chicken (habit) came before the egg (impulse), but "this particular egg may be so treated as to modify the future type of hen" (*HNC*, 73, 75, 68).

Dewey acknowledged that there remained a difficulty in this explanation of social change. If the direction of impulses depended on acquired habits, and yet acquired habits could be changed only by *re*-directing impulses, it was not clear how impulses could be employed to break the cake of custom if they required adversarial habits to redirect them. Dewey suggested two ways out of this vicious circle. First, not surprisingly, he noted that reformers often focused their efforts on children, whose habits were relatively unformed. "The cold fact of the situation," he said, "is that the chief means of continuous, graded, economical improvement and social rectification lies in utilizing the opportunities of educating the young to modify the prevailing types of thought and desire" (*HNC*, 89). At its best, education would provide

21. Dewey preferred the term "impulse" to "instinct" because the latter was "too laden with the older notion that an instinct is always definitely organized and adapted—which for the most part is just what it is not in human beings" (*HNC*, 75n).

children with habits of flexible response, and they would enter adulthood with a disposition for a creative response to a changing environment and emergent impulses.

True though this was, it failed to account for the habits of adult reformers themselves. Just as the eggs of impulse required the hens of adversarial habits if they were to play a role in the reconstruction of culture, so children required adults who could educate them in the habits of social transformation. Here Dewey located the source of a disposition for reform in the conflict among prevailing habits which marked any complex culture. "Different institutions foster antagonistic impulses and form contrary dispositions," he said. Contemporary civilization presented just such a scene of "internal frictions and liberations." For example, "political and legal institutions are now inconsistent with the habits that dominate friendly intercourse, science and art." The task of reformers was to appeal to the habits characteristic of the latter (which, presumably, were their own) in order to provide the "intelligent direction" necessary to "turn the elements of disintegration into a constructive synthesis" (*HNC*, 90).

Human Nature and Conduct was, as I say, directed principally against theories that treated human behavior simply as the expression of instincts, among which Dewey included psychoanalysis. Although Dewey saluted psychoanalysts for their emphasis on the "profound importance of unconscious forces," he argued that they were hamstrung by an insufficiently social psychology that posited a psychic realm apart from the determinations of habit and by a reductionist theory of instincts which privileged sexual impulses as the key to human behavior (*HNC*, 61). There were, he insisted, simply no "definite, independent, original instincts which manifest themselves in specific acts in a one-to-one correspondence." Even in the expression of the most apparently straightforward impulses—hunger and sex—"the actual content and feel of hunger and sex are indefinitely varied according to their social contexts" (*HNC*, 104, 106). The psychoanalytic treatment of sex exhibited the consequences of both "artificial simplification and the transformation of social results into psychic causes." In this case, "writers, usually male, hold forth on the psychology of women, as if they were dealing with a Platonic universal entity, although they habitually treat men as individuals, varying with structure and environment. They treat phenomena which are peculiarly symptoms of the civilization of the West at the present time as if they were the necessary effects of fixed native impulses of human nature" (*HNC*, 106–107).

Having exposed the weaknesses of psychoanalysis to his own satisfaction, Dewey then moved boldly to incorporate some of its insights into his own social psychology via a typically American embrace of the concept of "sublimation":

> In the career of any impulse activity there are speaking generally three possibilities. It may find a surging, explosive discharge—blind, unintelligent. It may be sublimated—that is, become a factor coordinated intelligently with others in a continuous course of action. Thus, a gust of anger may, because of its dynamic incorporation into disposition, be converted into an abiding conviction of social justice to be remedied, and furnish the dynamic to carry the conviction into execution. Or an excitation of sexual attraction may reappear in art or in tranquil domestic attachments and services. Such an outcome represents the normal or desirable functioning of impulse; in which, to use our previous language, the impulse operates as a pivot, or reorganization of habit. Or again a released impulsive activity may be neither immediately expressed in isolated spasmodic action, nor indirectly employed in an enduring interest. It may be "suppressed." (*HNC*, 108)

The suppression of impulse, Dewey contended, was "the cause of all kinds of intellectual and moral pathology" (*HNC*, 109). But unlike Freudian "repression," Deweyan "suppression" was not the normal course of things. Rather, sublimation, which Freud regarded as an extraordinary and relatively rare process, was taken as the normal, or at least a readily available, course for psychic events. Moreover, rather than an unconscious process, sublimation was for Dewey a conscious, rational operation. "Breach in the crust of the cake of custom releases impulses," he said, "but it is the work of intelligence to find the ways of using them" (*HNC*, 118).[22]

Philip Rieff has offered an excellent discussion of the differences separating Dewey and Freud which bears repeating here, especially since Rieff regards Dewey's analysis in *Human Nature and Conduct* as "the most penetrating critique of Freud's instinct theory." For Dewey, as we have seen, an instinct was "only a neutral potentiality . . . without effect until it becomes an element in social habits." Freud, on the other hand, posited a more dialectical relationship between instinct and culture. Instincts have "their own built in vicissitudes" that always threaten to defeat culture. For Freud, Rieff says, "residues of instinctual contradiction persist, crude and threatening, beneath the surface of so-

22. On the American appropriation of sublimation see Nathan G. Hale, Jr., *Freud and the Americans: The Beginnings of Psychoanalysis in the United States, 1876–1917* (New York: Oxford University Press, 1971), chap. 13.

cially acceptable behavior; there is always the hazard of a renewal of conflict." For Dewey, "the individual is not, as in Freud's conception, under a constant threat from the instincts lying in wait below the surface of consciousness, ready at any moment to claim their original autonomy"—they have no such original autonomy. For Freud there was the possibility of a compromise in the conflict of instinct and culture but not of a resolution; faith in such a resolution was a first principle of Dewey's social psychology. Dewey, as Rieff concludes,

> locates in society the critical principle that Freud assigns to human nature, and this divergence accounts for a difference of ethical vision. Dewey sees the impulses as capable of rescuing a society in which habits in institutional structures (i.e., collective habit) have become petrified and therefore impediments to progress, where Freud sees the instincts as themselves the force which limits progress by threatening a renewal of conflict; by their very existence, the instincts serve notice of the inadequacies of all social arrangements. Thus Dewey and Freud meet back-to-back. It becomes clear why the meliorist Dewey accused Freud of reducing "social results" to "psychic causes." But with equal justification Dewey may be accused of reducing psychic results to social causes; for his analysis traces all failures of personality back to their faulty social context thereby shoring up the liberal hope for progressively more intelligent fusions of impulse and situation.[23]

Just so.

Dewey's critique of behaviorism, the other psychological theory underlying democratic realism, was more oblique. Behaviorists were themselves sharp critics of prevailing instinct theories. Like them, Dewey was a sworn enemy of all theories positing a "ready-made consciousness" standing apart from human behavior. Yet, unlike them, Dewey did not try to reduce human behavior to a simple chain of stimulus and response but gave conscious thought—intelligence—a central place in his social psychology. One did not have to subscribe to a superstitious psychology to appreciate the power of rational deliberation in human action, he argued. Intelligence was itself a collection of habits: "concrete habits do all the perceiving, recognizing, imagining, recalling, judging, conceiving, and reasoning that is done" (HNC, 124). Indeed, thoughtfulness was the most important of the habits human beings had developed for it permitted a flexible, adaptative response to novel sit-

---

23. Philip Rieff, *Freud: The Mind of the Moralist*, 3d ed. (Chicago: University of Chicago Press, 1979), pp. 30–33.

uations. The reflective disposition was a custom "capable of exercising the most revolutionary influence on other customs" (*HNC*, 58).[24]

Dewey did not deny that many habits tended to check thought and eventually to produce routinized thoughtless action in which "stimulus and response are mechanically linked together in an unbroken chain." He claimed only that such thoughtless behavior was not the necessary lot of the masses, as democratic realists who drew on behaviorism claimed. Two kinds of habit were in conflict in modern American society: "routine, unintelligent habit, and intelligent habit or art" (*HNC*, 55). Democracy, which he said "should be a means of stimulating original thought, and of evoking action deliberately adjusted in advance to cope with new forces," had served, he admitted, mainly to "multiply occasions for imitation" (*HNC*, 48). But a democracy that was anything less than rule by citizens possessed of the habits of intelligence was a perversion, and consequently, Dewey argued, democratic reformers should bend their efforts to cultivating the capacity for deliberation which was well within reach of most citizens, "fostering those impulses and habits which experience has shown to make us sensitive, generous, imaginative, impartial in perceiving the tendency of our inchoate dawning activities" (*HNC*, 144). Men and women were not white rats, and they need not behave as if they were. Under the right conditions, intelligence might become habitual.

THE CHALLENGE OF WALTER LIPPMANN

If Dewey's social psychology offered an alternative to the psychologies of the democratic realists, which attributed the failure of a society such as the United States to approximate his ideals for a democratic polity to the irredeemable irrationality of its people, it remained for

24. The most important behaviorist critique of instinct theory in the twenties was Luther L. Bernard, *Instinct: A Study in Social Psychology* (New York: Holt, 1924). For an explicit critique of behaviorism from the point of view of pragmatic, functional psychology see George Herbert Mead, *Mind, Self, and Society* (Chicago: University of Chicago Press, 1934), pp. 90–109, and Mead, *Movements of Thought in the Nineteenth Century* (Chicago: University of Chicago Press, 1936), pp. 386–404. One might well say that Mead rather than Dewey himself provided the fullest social psychology for Deweyan democratic theory, and I regret it would take me too far afield to make this case here. It is suggested in much of the literature on Mead cited in Chapter 3, note 19; Dmitri N. Shalin, "G. H. Mead, Socialism, and the Progressive Agenda," *American Journal of Sociology* 93 (1988): 913–951; and Andrew Feffer, "Sociability and Social Conflict in George Herbert Mead's Interactionism, 1900–1919," *Journal of the History of Ideas* 51 (1990): 233–254.

him to explain how the culture's habits, institutions, and "established interacting arrangements" had caused this failure. For help in formulating such an explanation he turned to the democratic realist with whom he had the greatest affinity, Walter Lippmann, trading on Lippmann's descriptions and explanations of the plight of democracy while rejecting his solutions to it.

Lippmann, the wunderkind of prewar progressivism, now one of the nation's most influential journalists, was the most widely read of the democratic realists of the twenties. Having served in the propaganda apparatus of the American army in World War I and devoted himself in the immediate postwar years to a study of the ways in which a distorted view of international affairs found its way into the hands of American newspaper readers, Lippmann found prevailing democratic theory woefully inadequate both as a description of and a prescription for modern politics. In two important books, *Public Opinion* (1922) and *The Phantom Public* (1925), he drew together the work of European and American critics of democracy and added many sharp insights of his own to produce what many considered a damning indictment of participatory democracy. Unlike many realists, Lippmann did not rely on Freudian or behaviorist conceptions of human nature but on psychological and philosophical premises similar to those of Dewey and William James, and Dewey credited Lippmann with "a more significant statement of the genuine 'problem of knowledge' than professional epistemological philosophers have managed to give." For this reason, among others, he regarded *Public Opinion* as "perhaps the most effective indictment of democracy as currently conceived ever penned." As was the case in the debates over the outlawry of war, Lippmann was for Dewey, as we shall see, a critic who could not go unappreciated or unanswered.[25]

Lippmann began his analysis in *Public Opinion* with a simple epistemological point: men did not know their environment directly but through the "fictions" or representations they made to themselves of that environment. These fictions, Lippmann said, comprise a "pseudo-

---

25. "Public Opinion" (1922), *Middle Works* 13:337. On the context for Lippmann's work see D. Steven Blum, *Walter Lippmann: Cosmopolitanism in the Century of Total War* (Ithaca: Cornell University Press, 1984), chap. 3; Heinz Eulau, "From Public Opinion to Public Philosophy: Walter Lippmann's Classic Reexamined," *American Journal of Economics and Sociology* 15 (1955/56): 439–451, and Ronald Steel, *Walter Lippmann and the American Century* (Boston: Little, Brown, 1980), chaps. 12, 14, 17. Lippmann's initial study of public opinion, *Liberty and the News* (New York: Harcourt, Brace, 1920), was far more Deweyan in its conclusions than the later, more famous books, and I shall not consider it here.

environment" standing between man and the world. Despite the invidious sound of these terms, Lippmann made it clear that fictions and pseudo-environments were unavoidable features of human experience. "To traverse the world men must have maps of the world. Their persistent difficulty is to secure maps on which their own need, or someone else's need, has not sketched in the coast of Bohemia." The way in which men represented the world to themselves determined their action, and as a consequence the principal concern of the student of public opinion was to know how men conceived the political environment and how this environment could be more accurately conceived.[26]

Lippmann observed that men were often misled by their conceptions of the political environment, and thus the central concern of analysts and reformers should be "why the picture inside so often misleads men in their dealings with the world outside." There were, he suggested, two sorts of causes for misconception. The first lay in the limited access to the relevant factual environment which most men possessed. The environment of most modern political perceptions was expansive and only indirectly accessible to citizens. They had to rely on others for information, and their sources of contact with the world were often inadequate. Their vision of the "real world" was limited by "artificial censorships, the limitations of social contact, the comparatively meager time available in each day for paying attention to public affairs, the distortion arising because events have to be compressed into very short messages, the difficulty of making a small vocabulary express a complicated world, and finally the fear of facing those facts which would seem to threaten the established routine of men's lives" (PO, 18).

The second cause for the misconceptions of public opinion lay in the way in which the facts to which men did have access were distorted by the mind itself. As Lippmann said, "In the great blooming, buzzing confusion of the outer world we pick out what our culture has already defined for us, and we tend to perceive that which we have picked out in the form stereotyped for us by our culture" (PO, 55). Again, despite the invidious term, Lippmann did not believe that stereotypes were necessarily good or bad, for they were unavoidable and necessary features of human experience:

What matters is the character of the stereotypes, and the gullibility with which we employ them. And these in the end depend upon those

26. Walter Lippmann, *Public Opinion* (New York: Free Press, 1965), p. 11. Page numbers for further references (PO) appear in the text.

inclusive patterns which constitute our philosophy of life. If in that philosophy we assume that the world is codified according to a code which we possess, we are likely to make our reports of what is going on describe a world run by our code. But if our philosophy tells us that each man is only a small part of the world, that his intelligence catches at best only phases and aspects in a coarse net of ideas, then, when we use our stereotypes, we tend to know that they are only stereotypes, to hold them lightly, to modify them gladly. (*PO*, 60)

This latter philosophy of life reflected a scientific code that held stereotypes to be tentative hypotheses subject to test and verification. A scientific habit of mind could thus counteract the baleful effects of stereotypes, if not their existence. Unfortunately, few men possessed such habits, and as a result in most public opinions "real space, real time, real numbers, real connections, real weights are lost. The perspective and the background and the dimensions of action are clipped and frozen in the stereotype" (*PO*, 100).

The circumstances under which most people formed their public opinions were well known to political leaders, Lippmann noted, even if these circumstances were ignored by democratic theorists. This knowledge formed the basis for the "manufacturing of consent" which legitimated, stabilized, and mobilized ostensibly democratic societies. Leaders relied on vague, conventional symbols to tie the varied interests of a polity together. They realized that such symbols in themselves signified nothing in particular but could be associated with almost anything, and for this reason the symbol could become "the common bond of common feelings, even though those feelings were originally attached to disparate ideas." Building a consensus was not a matter of obtaining rational agreement on policies but of finding effective symbols that would disguise disagreement and deflect conflict. "He who captures the symbols by which the public feeling is for the moment contained," Lippmann observed, "controls by that much the approaches of public policy." The symbol was the instrument of solidarity and exploitation. "It enables people to work for a common end, but just because the few who are strategically placed must choose the concrete objective, the symbol is also an instrument by which a few can fatten on many, deflect criticism, and seduce men into facing agony for objects they do not understand." Consent was manufactured from above; it did not well up from below. "In the crystallizing of a common will, there is always an Alexander Hamilton at work" (*PO*, 132–133, 151, 140).

Since the eighteenth century, Lippmann argued, the great failing of radical democratic theory had been its belief that every citizen, by virtue of his "natural endowment," possessed the knowledge of the world necessary for governing. This belief immediately ran up against the fact that the knowledge of the world any citizen could possess as a self-sufficient individual was very limited, and the political environment he was asked to understand and control in a modern nation was very large and, for the most part, invisible. Democrats were faced with an insoluble dilemma. "Their science told them that politics was an instinct, and that the instinct worked in a limited environment. Their hopes bade them insist that all men in a very large government could govern. In this deadly conflict between their ideals and their science the only way out was to assume without much discussion that the voice of the people was the voice of God" (PO, 165).

In theory, Lippmann said, democrats had never come to terms with the problem of the limited knowledge of the citizen. In practice, they relied heavily on the newspaper to put the citizen in touch with the invisible world. "Practically everywhere," he noted, "it is assumed that the press should do spontaneously for us what primitive democracy imagined each of us could do spontaneously for himself, that every day and twice a day it will present us with a true picture of all the outer world in which we are interested." The newspaper was not, however, up to this task, and the belief that it was fostered a further democratic delusion. On the one hand, the limitations of the newspaper were economic. People expected the newspaper to provide them with the truth but they were unwilling to pay for it. As a result, newspapers depended on advertising to survive, so that they depended ultimately on the support of the public who purchased the goods advertised in the newspaper. "Roughly speaking," Lippmann said, "the economic support for general news gathering is the price paid for advertised goods by the fairly prosperous sections of cities with more than one hundred thousand inhabitants" (PO, 203, 206).

Even more debilitating than the economics of newspaper publishing was the nature of news itself. The news and truth were two very different things, Lippmann observed. Before a series of events became news it had to make itself visible as an overt act, generally in a crudely overt act. "The course of events must assume a certain definable shape" before it became news. The important facts of social life did not, of course, always or even usually take the form of news, and reporters were ill prepared to give them the shape of truth. "The function of news is to signalize an event, the function of truth is to bring to light the hidden facts, to set them into relation with each other, and make a picture of reality on which men can act." Newspapers could report truth but they could not discover it, and the failure of newspapers to bear the burden imposed on them by democratic theory grew out of "the failure of self-governing people to transcend their casual experience and their prejudice, by inventing, creating, and organizing a machinery of knowledge" (*PO*, 226, 230).

The lesson of Lippmann's analysis of public opinion was clear. "In the absence of institutions and education by which the environment is so successfully reported that the realities of public life stand out sharply against self-centered opinion, the common interests very largely elude public opinion entirely, and can be managed only by a specialized class whose personal interests reach beyond the locality. This class is irresponsible, for it acts upon information that is not common property, in situations that the public at large does not conceive, and it can be held to account only on the accomplished fact" (*PO*, 195).

Thomas Jefferson and other pioneers of democratic theory could not solve the dilemma of an uninformed citizenry, Lippmann said, but they should not be expected to have been able to do so. The means for making the vast invisible environment accessible to the public was simply not conceivable to them. "It would have been visionary to suppose that a time would come when distant and complicated events could conceivably be reported, analyzed, and presented in such a form that a really valuable choice could be made by an amateur." Times had, however, changed. There was no longer any doubt, Lippmann asserted, that "the continuous reporting of an unseen environment is feasible. It is often done badly, but the fact that it is done at all shows that it can be done, and the fact that we begin to know how badly it is often done, shows that it can be done better" (*PO*, 166).

The key to the development of the "machinery of knowledge" capable of making the world accessible for public decision making, Lippmann argued, lay in the development of the social sciences into policy sciences. There was a need to interpose "some form of expertness between the private citizen and the vast environment in which he is entangled" (*PO*, 238). The social scientist should take his place in front of decisions instead of behind them:

To-day the sequence is that the man of affairs finds his facts and decides on the basis of them; then, some time later, the social scientist deduces excellent reasons why he did or did not decide wisely. This ex post facto relationship is academic in the bad sense of that fine word. The real sequence would be one where the disinterested expert first finds and formulates the facts for the man of action, and later makes what wisdom he can out of the comparison between the decision, which he understands and the facts, which he organized. (*PO*, 236)

Lippmann admitted that there were very real difficulties in assuring that such policy sciences would be truly disinterested, but he argued that by strictly separating investigation from policy making they could be overcome. He also admitted that there were many issues of technique and organization to be worked out. Nonetheless, he declared, it was clear from work already done that "unseen environments can be reported effectively, that they can be reported to divergent groups of people in a way which is neutral to their prejudice, and capable of overcoming their subjectivism" (*PO*, 248).

In suggesting this method for making public opinion more rational, Lippmann was advancing an argument similar in most respects to Dewey's effort to link participatory democracy to a morally and politically engaged social science. Lippmann's analysis, however, took a definite elitist turn that sharply distinguished his thinking from that of Dewey. It was clear that the "men of action" in his ideal society would be few in number. Expert opinion was not to be directed to the ordinary citizen but to governing elites. The purpose of the organization of intelligence was "not to burden every citizen with expert opinion on all questions, but to push that burden away from him towards the responsible administrator." The making of decisions should be left to insiders, and the general public should confine its interest to procedural concerns. "The broad principles on which the action of public opinion can be continuous are essentially principles of procedure" (*PO*, 250–251).

Lippmann's democratic elitism was even more apparent three years later in *The Phantom Public*. Popular participation in public affairs, he argued in this book, should be held to an absolute minimum. Democracies were haunted by a dilemma: "they are frustrated unless in the laying down of rules there is a large measure of assent; yet they seem unable to find solutions of their greatest problems except through centralized governing by means of extensive rules which necessarily ignore the principle of assent. The problems that vex democracy seem to be unmanageable by democratic methods." He repeated his contention that the public should intervene only on issues of procedure, but he now narrowed the scope of even this limited role by insisting that the public should not concern itself with the nature or substance of rules, only with the guarantee that *some* rule exists. The public "will contribute its part to the solution of social problems if it recognizes that some system of rights and duties is necessary, but that no particular system is peculiarly sacred." Other than this, the most that the ordinary citizens of a democracy could do was throw their support to one or another of the powerful interests contending for control. "To support the Ins when things are going well; to support the Outs when they seem to be going badly," Lippmann declared, "this, in spite of all that has been said about tweedledum and tweedledee, is the essence of popular government."[27]

Behind Lippmann's elitism lay an ethical position that was common to many democratic realists. Self-determination, he argued, was only one of the many interests of a human being, and not a particularly strong one. Mankind was interested "in all kinds of other things, in order, in rights, in prosperity, in sights and sounds and in not being bored." Men do not desire "self-government for its own sake. They desire it for the sake of results." Democratic theorists had erred in asserting the primacy of self-government. The criterion that should be used to assess a government was not the extent to which citizens were self-governing but "whether it is producing a certain minimum of health, of decent housing, of material necessities, of education, of freedom, of pleasures, of beauty." For the democratic realist, substantial self-government was a minor good, readily expendable in a complex industrial society (*PO*, 196–197).

DISCOVERING THE STATE

Much of Dewey's political writing in the twenties attempted to come to terms with the challenge democratic realists such as Lippmann posed for his own ideals of participatory democracy. This was particularly evident in *The Public and Its Problems* (1927), his only work of formal political philosophy, which was in part a reply to the realist indictment of democracy. In general, Dewey applauded the realists for exposing the shortcomings of democratic government and the bewilderment of the ordinary citizen, but he denied that this criticism delivered a death blow to participatory democracy. It was less the elitists' description of the state of American democracy that he contested than their prescriptions for reforming it, which seemed to him to threaten its fundamentals.[28]

27. Walter Lippmann, *The Phantom Public* (New York: Macmillan, 1925), pp. 189, 106, 126.

28. For Dewey's explicit acknowledgment of his debt to Lippmann see *The Public and Its Problems* (1927), *Later Works* 2:308n. Page numbers for further references (*PP*) appear in the text.

For the democratic political philosopher and political scientist, Dewey argued, the tasks were to determine the theoretical conditions essential for a public life consonant with democratic ideals, to point out the obstacles to the establishment of these conditions, and to suggest "political technologies" that might remove these obstacles and sustain the conditions for democracy. But before I turn to Dewey's own efforts to complete these tasks, it is necessary to explicate briefly the unique generic concepts of the "public" and the "state" which he developed in *The Public and Its Problems* as a preliminary to these efforts. Here he again made clear his debt to contemporary pluralist thinking, though, in the end, he deviated significantly from pluralist precepts.[29]

As a work of formal political theory, *The Public and Its Problems* aimed to explain the origins and functions of the state. This was, of course, a long-standing preoccupation of political philosophers, and, Dewey warned, "the moment we utter the words 'The State' a score of intellectual ghosts rise to obscure our vision," threatening to draw the analyst into a web of abstractions and away from concrete human activities. Better, he said, to begin with the latter and see what explanations of the state might be derived therefrom. This meant eschewing any quest for "state-forming forces" or political "instincts," which tended to result in tautologies akin to that which attributed the sleep-inducing effects of opium to its "dormitive power," in favor of beginning with characteristic forms of human action and their consequences (*PP*, 241–242).

Following this approach, Dewey observed that, like all natural objects, human beings existed in association with other natural objects, including other human beings. Human action had consequences on other natural objects and usually on other human beings, for "conjoint, combined associated action is a universal trait of the behavior of things." Human action differed from the behavior of other things in that it was intelligent, that is, an effort was made, in light of perceived consequences, to control action so as to secure some consequences and avoid others. In actions affecting other human beings, consequences were of two sorts: those affecting only the individuals directly engaged

29. Dewey's active engagement with pluralist theory is also apparent in the political philosophy course he taught in the twenties. See Sidney Hook, "Notes on Dewey's *Political Theory*" (1926), Hook Collection. On the character of pluralist theory in the United States in the twenties see G. David Garson, "On the Origins of Interest-Group Theory: A Critique of a Process," *American Political Science Review* 68 (1974): 1505–1519. Pluralism was European in origin and its major interpreter for Dewey and other American intellectuals was Harold Laski. See his *Studies in the Problem of Sovereignty* (New Haven: Yale University Press, 1917) and *The Foundations of Sovereignty* (New York: Harcourt Brace, 1921). By the mid-twenties Laski himself was drifting away from pluralism toward what would become a decidedly "statist" political philosophy.

in a transaction and those indirectly affecting other individuals not immediately concerned in the transaction. Transactions thought to be confined in their consequences mainly to those directly engaged in them were "private" transactions. Transactions perceived to have extensive, enduring, and significant indirect consequences for those not directly engaged in them took on a "public" character (*PP*, 243–244).

Acknowledging that the line between public and private transactions was indistinct and subject to dispute, Dewey argued that it was nonetheless "drawn on the basis of the extent and scope of the consequences of acts which are so important as to need control, whether by inhibition or promotion." He therefore defined the "public" as "all those who are affected by the indirect consequences of transactions to such an extent that it is deemed necessary to have those consequences systematically cared for." In organizing themselves to deal with the indirect consequences of associated action, publics formed a "state" and established officials (who might include their own members acting as citizens) to serve their interests. These officials comprised the "government." The government was not the state, which included the public as well as its representatives, but apart from its organization as a state the public was formless. "By means of officials and their special powers [the public] becomes a state. A public articulated and operating through representative officers is the state; there is no state without a government, but also there is none without the public." The worth of a state was measured by "the degree of organization of the public which is attained, and the degree in which its officers are so constituted as to perform their function of caring for public interests" (*PP*, 245–253, 277, 256).

The problems a public faced in attempting to organize itself into a state were difficult and complex. State organization demanded the power to perceive the consequences of associated behavior and to trace these consequences to their source. It called for the selection of the officials to represent the public interest and a definition of their functions. It also required careful measures to ensure that the government served the public rather than particular private interests. Given these problems, it was not surprising that historically there had been so many and so many types of states, for "there have been countless forms of joint activity with correspondingly diverse consequences. Power to detect consequences has varied especially with the instrumentalities of knowledge at hand. Rulers have been selected on all kinds of different grounds. Their functions have varied and so have their will and zeal to represent common interests." The only general statement one could make about the state was a formal one: "the state is the organization of the public effected through officials for the protection of the interests shared by its members." The important questions this definition left open—"what the public may be, what the officials are, how adequately they perform their function"—were historical questions about particular societies and states, not philosophical questions about the nature of the state (*PP*, 255–256).

The practical difficulties of state formation were exacerbated by the changing modes of associated behavior which often generated new, extensive, and enduring indirect consequences and hence new publics. These changes took place beyond the ken of existing political organization, and as a result a new public often remained inchoate and unorganized because the existing state was inadequate to its needs. Indeed, the existing state was often actively hostile to the needs of new publics. If inherited political agencies were well institutionalized, Dewey noted, they obstructed the organization of a new public:

> They prevent that development of new forms of the state which might grow up rapidly were social life more fluid, less precipitated into set political and legal molds. To form itself, the public has to break existing political forms. This is hard to do because these forms are themselves the regular means of instituting change. The public which generated political forms is passing away, but the power and lust of possession remains in the hands of the officers and agencies which the dying public instituted. This is why the change of the form of states is so often effected only by revolution. The creation of adequately flexible and responsive political and legal machinery has so far been beyond the wit of man.

The process of state formation was thus an ongoing, experimental process. "By its very nature," Dewey said, "a state is ever something to be scrutinized, investigated, searched for. Almost as soon as its form is stabilized, it needs to be re-made" (*PP*, 255).

In this theory, Dewey remained committed to the pluralist conception of the state as a "distinctive and secondary form of association, having a specifiable work to do and specified organs of operation." The state did not engross all other associations monopolistically into itself, nor were all social values political values. Other social groups existed prior to the state, and the state was, in effect, an artifact of their transactions. But Dewey now rejected the pluralist notion that the state was or should be a neutral mechanism—an umpire or conductor—standing apart from associated life and designed only to adjudicate conflicts between the social groups in a society, and he replaced it with a conception of the state as the organization of one key group, the public (*PP*, 279, 281).

Even more significantly, Dewey departed from pluralist norms in arguing that no predetermined limitations could be set on state action and in granting the state superior powers to other social organizations. The state, he argued, was obliged to intervene in the activities of any primary group when the public interest was at stake. Dewey acknowledged that such state action could be extensive, for public officials "may act so as to fix conditions under which *any* form of association operates." Dewey further violated pluralist orthodoxy in arguing that the state might even intervene in the internal affairs of a group if the public interest was seen to dictate such action. "At times," he said, "the consequences of the conjoint behavior of some persons may be such that a large public interest is generated which can be fulfilled only by laying down conditions which involve a large measure of reconstruction within that group" (*PP*, 280–281).

Even though Dewey's state remained a "conductor" of sorts, most pluralists would have regarded the regulatory powers he assigned to it as fearful, given the tendency of states to abuse their power. Dewey was well aware of this tendency, and he stressed that the most serious problem of government was that of devising means whereby the abuse of state power by government officials could be controlled. On the whole, he favored a minimum of government intervention in the affairs of private groups and a voluntary coordination of intergroup relations. But he was unwilling to set any inherent limitations on the activity of the state, for such limitations could, under certain conditions, be harmful to the public interest. The consequences of the action of private associations varied, and so might state action vary from laissez-faire to extensive intervention. "There is no antecedent universal proposition which can be laid down because of which the functions of a state should be limited or should be expanded," he said. "Their scope is something to be critically and experimentally determined" (*PP*, 281).

Dewey readily agreed that "only through constant watchfulness and criticism of public officials by citizens can a state be maintained in integrity and usefulness," but he believed pluralists neglected the valuable role the state might play in the life of private associations. "When a state is a good state, when the officers of the public genuinely serve the public interests," he said, the "reflex effect" of the state upon other social groups was very important and, potentially, very beneficial (*PP*,

278, 279). This was not to say that state action was necessarily benign, but it did indicate that Dewey was unwilling to grant private groups inviolable rights that would limit the power of the state to protect the public interest.

Dewey's imaginative theory of the generic process of the formation of publics and states suffered from several ambiguities he never explicitly addressed. First, his usage of the definite and indefinite articles tended to obscure his contention that in any given society *the* Public was, at most, a collective noun designating plural publics that concerned themselves with the indirect consequences of particular forms of associated activity. His book might better have been titled "Publics and Their Problems" or "A Public and Its Problems." Consequently, *the* State was also a plural phenomenon, a collection of publics organized into representative institutions (though presumably one institution or collection of officials might serve several publics). For this reason Dewey's statement that a new state was created every time a public organized itself was less bizarre than it sounded. For it did not mean that the governing institutions of the state of previous publics were replaced wholesale but rather that they were supplemented or themselves took on new functions.

Even more ambiguous was Dewey's use of the term "the public interest." By this he meant the interest of *a* public, not the interest of the society as a whole, as the term is often taken to mean. Moreover, the "interest" he referred to was, for the most part, the formal interest a particular public took in the indirect consequences of the associated activity that affected it. But he also used the term to refer to a substantive interest in these consequences, especially when he was discussing state intervention in the activities of social groups, though he had next to nothing to say about the formation of this interest. This substantive "public interest" was presumably much more difficult to determine than the simpler fact that there was at any given time a public with an interest in particular consequences.

This second, substantive use of the "public interest" suggests that for Dewey the work of a public amounted to more than recognizing itself and organizing a government to represent its interest in the regulation of certain indirect consequences. Presumably, the members of a public would want to determine *how* these consequences would be regulated by the government, particularly since they often would not be of one mind, at least initially, on the answer to this question of where "the public interest" lay. If a state was to be representative of a public it would seem necessary that it represent this substantive public interest (or interests) as well. Otherwise it would be impossible for the public to determine whether or not the state was regulating indirect consequences in its interest or had been captured by private interests. A public had to know more than that it was interested; it had to judge what its interests were. Thus, Dewey's theory pointed to the need for a public to organize itself not only to serve its interests but to define them.

This was not the only instance in Dewey's formal theory in which the public seemed underorganized to meet the demands he placed on it. In considering the particular problems of modern democratic publics, he himself observed that a public might have to organize itself merely to recognize that it was a public (which is not as difficult as it sounds if one recognizes that a public is not a thing but a group of individuals, some of whom might be aware of the need for such organization). In addition, it would seem that a public would have to organize in order to incorporate itself into a state, especially if, as Dewey acknowledged was often the case, existing political agencies resisted the efforts of a new public to build a new state that met its needs. Political agencies outside the existing government such as new political parties or revolutionary conspiracies might serve to organize a public for this purpose, but whatever form such organization might take it is hard to see how any new public could do without it.

GOVERNMENT BY THE PEOPLE

A public, Dewey argued, acted only through its officers, including, conceivably, citizen voters. Since all such officials were also members of private associations, the public was faced with the difficult task of organizing itself in such a way as to hold its officials accountable to its interests. Its officials were torn between private and public interests, and, he noted, "rarely can a person sink himself in his political function." The best one could hope for were officials in whom the desire to serve the public welfare dominated their other desires. "Representative government" was the means by which publics had been organized in order to secure this dominance. Political democracy was the best means yet devised by publics to ensure that the "insight, loyalty, and energy" of its officials was "enlisted on the side of the public and political role" (*PP*, 283, 286).

For Dewey, there was nothing sacred about the institutional machinery of those states that called themselves political democracies, and democrats were free, indeed they were obliged, to criticize these institutions for their inadequacies. Historically, this machinery had not been produced by men seeking to realize democracy as an ethical and social ideal (which was much broader in its implications than mere political democracy). It had been, for the most part, the creation of a nineteenth-century bourgeoisie "deeply tinged by fear of government," whose interest in the ethics of democracy was minimal (*PP*, 289). The only legacy of the history of political democracy Dewey believed to be clearly essential to the democratic ideal was the doctrine that "government exists to serve its community, and that this purpose cannot be achieved unless the community itself shares in selecting its governors and determining their policies" (*PP*, 327).

Ironically, existing forms of democratic government became obsolete almost from the moment they were created, victims of forces unleashed by the economic activities of the very class that created them. Following Lippmann and Lippmann's mentor, Graham Wallas, Dewey argued that the industrial revolution had created a "Great Society" in modern nations marked by vast and impersonal webs of interdependent relationships. The creation of the Great Society had ushered in what Woodrow Wilson termed a "new era of human relationships" by enormously multiplying the quantity and complexity of the indirect consequences of associated behavior. This new society had called into existence a new public, but this new public had, unfortunately, been unable to understand these consequences, and as a result it was in no position to begin to organize itself to control them. As Dewey put it:

> Indirect, extensive, enduring and serious consequences of conjoint and interacting behavior call a public into existence having a common interest in controlling these consequences. But the machine age has so enormously expanded, multiplied, intensified and complicated the scope of the indirect consequences, has formed such immense and consolidated unions in action, on an impersonal rather than a community basis, that the resultant public cannot identify and distinguish itself. And this discovery is obviously an antecedent condition of any effective organization on its part. (*PP*, 314)[30]

The institutions of political democracy in the United States, designed to meet the needs of the publics of a decentralized, agrarian, simple-market society, were completely inadequate for the organization of this

---

30. Compare Graham Wallas, *The Great Society* (New York: Macmillan, 1914), pp. 3–19.

new public. "The same forces which have brought about the forms of democratic government, general suffrage, executives and legislators chosen by majority vote, have also brought about conditions which halt the social and human ideals that demand the utilization of government as the genuine instrumentality of an inclusive and fraternally associated public. The 'new age of human relationships' has no political agencies worthy of it." Americans had inherited "local town-meeting practices and ideas. But we live and act and have our being in a continental nation-state" (*PP*, 303, 306).

Before the public created by industrial capitalism could organize itself into a new state, it had first to find itself and define its interests. For the moment, Dewey contended, "the problem of a democratically organized public is primarily and essentially an intellectual problem, in a degree to which the political affairs of prior ages offer no parallel." An "inchoate public" such as that in modern America could organize itself as a state "only when indirect consequences are perceived, and when it is possible to project agencies which order their occurrence." But, as things stood in the 1920s, "many consequences are felt rather than perceived; they are suffered, but they cannot be said to be known, for they are not, by those who perceive them, referred to their origins." The public was "amorphous and unarticulated," and until the intellectual problems of the public were solved, issues of organization and control had to be postponed. "If a public exists," he concluded, "it is surely as uncertain about its own whereabouts as philosophers since Hume have been about the residence and make-up of the self" (*PP*, 314, 317, 308).

The eclipse of the public, Dewey argued, provided the occasion for the emergence of democratic realism among political theorists. They argued that the phantom public was not a problem because an active public was neither necessary nor desirable for modern democratic government. Government had become a matter of questions best left to experts, and the prime obstruction to effective government was "the superstitious belief that there is a public concerned to determine the formation and execution of general social policies" (*PP*, 312).

The chief weakness of the realist argument, Dewey observed, was that its indictment of the public was filed against the inchoate, unorganized public produced by industrial capitalism and the outmoded political machinery that ill served its needs. These targets accounted for the realists' "depreciation of the machinery of democratic political action in contrast with a rising appreciation of the need for expert administrators." But participatory democrats like himself, he said, must insist that democracy not be identified with the flounderings of a bewildered public or the failures of this machinery: "The old saying that the cure for the ills of democracy is more democracy is not apt if it means that the evils may be remedied by introducing more machinery of the same kind as that which already exists, or by refining and perfecting that machinery. But the phrase may also indicate the need of returning to the idea itself, of clarifying and deepening our sense of its meaning to criticize and re-make its political manifestations." The "candid believer" in democracy could not say that he was completely untouched by criticisms of its existing political mechanisms, but he might well "object to the common supposition of the foes of existing democratic government that the accusations against it touch the social and moral aspirations and ideas which underlie the political forms" (*PP*, 319, 325). Dewey recognized that this criticism of realism made it incumbent on him to indicate how the public could escape its confusion and organize itself for effective political action. But this was not something he did in very compelling fashion, when he tried to do it at all.

Dewey averted many issues of this sort by choosing not to address the problems of the political organization of the public, confining himself to its "intellectual problem." If the public was not to remain in eclipse, Dewey said, the Great Society had to be converted into what he termed the Great Community. Or, to use a bit of Marxist jargon, the "public-in-itself" had to become a "public-for-itself." The first task of democratic reformers was to discover "the means by which a scattered, mobile and manifold public may so recognize itself as to define and express its interests," and this was in the first instance a problem of inquiry and communication. The Great Society was marked by extensive webs of interdependence; the Great Community would be marked by a shared understanding of the consequences of this interdependence. The conversion of the Great Society into the Great Community required "the perfecting of the means and ways of communication of meanings so that genuinely shared interest in the consequences of interdependent activities may inform desire and effort and thereby direct action" (*PP*, 327, 332).[31]

Dewey agreed with Lippmann that democratic theory had been bur-

---

31. Of course, many of the indirect consequences of the creation of the Great Society transcended national boundaries, creating international publics. As the outlawry program suggested, the "state" and "government" that such publics might create might differ in significant respects from those characteristic of nations, and analogies drawn from the latter could be misleading. See Dewey's Introduction to the second edition of *The Public and Its Problems* (1946), *Later Works* 2:375–381.

dened by the illusion of an "omnicompetent" citizen who could, by his own devices, gain the understanding of the vast environment of the Great Society necessary for governing it. The problem for the democratic theorist, he said, was to disentangle "faith in the dignity of human nature, the need that every human being rise to his full stature, from the dogma that individuals can of themselves get the knowledge required to render democratic government effective and competent."[32]

Dewey further agreed with Lippmann that modern society required the organization of intelligence and the development of the social sciences into policy sciences. "The prime condition of a democratically organized public," he declared, "is a kind of knowledge and insight which does not yet exist." If the public was to find itself it would have to rely on "effective and organized inquiry." Genuinely public policy could not be formulated unless it was informed by scientific knowledge, and such knowledge "does not exist except where there is systematic, thorough, and well-equipped search and record" (*PP*, 339, 346).

But at the crucial point where Lippmann's argument had taken its elitist turn, Dewey dissented. The enlightenment of the public, he said, took precedence over the enlightenment of government administrators. "Democracy," he observed, "demands a more thoroughgoing education than the education of officials, administrators and directors of industry."[33] For this reason, social science should be tied not to elite but to popular media. "A genuine social science would manifest its reality in the daily press, while learned books and articles supply and polish tools of inquiry" (*PP*, 348).

Dewey complained that Lippmann had dismissed the social possibilities of the newspaper all too readily, assuming "that what the press is it must continue to be." It was possible, he contended, to treat news events "in the light of a continuing study and record of underlying conditions."[34] Lippmann was unfair to the reporter because he slighted the difficulties these professionals encountered in a capitalist society, and Dewey offered a distinctly Veblenian comment to support this complaint:

> Just as in the conduct of industry and exchange generally the technological factor is obscured, deflected and defeated by "business," so specifically in the management of publicity. The gathering and sale of

32. "Public Opinion," p. 338.
33. Ibid., p. 344.
34. Ibid., p. 343.

subject-matter having a public import is part of the existing pecuniary system. Just as industry conducted by engineers on a factual technological basis would be a very different thing from what it actually is, so the assembling and reporting of news would be a very different thing if the genuine interests of reporters were permitted to work freely.

Dewey admitted that "a newspaper which was only a daily edition of a quarterly journal of sociology or political science would undoubtedly possess a limited circulation and a narrow influence." But, he predicted, the material in the newspapers he imagined would "have such an enormous and widespread human bearing that its bare existence would be an irresistible invitation to a presentation of it which would have a direct popular appeal." Consequently, the "freeing of the artist in literary presentation" was as much a condition of the creation of an effective public as the freeing of social inquiry (*PP*, 348–349).

This union of social science, effective news gathering, and skillful literary presentation of the fruits of social inquiry was, Dewey admitted, not easy to achieve. It was up against not only the overt power of powerful interests "who have ability to manipulate social relations for their own advantage" but also such deeper obstructions as the adverse emotional and intellectual "habituations" of a poorly educated public and the failure of increasingly cloistered social scientists to recognize that "a fact of community life which is not spread abroad as to be a common possession is a contradiction in terms" (*PP*, 341, 345). But, he concluded, if the Great Community was to become a reality, "the highest and most difficult kind of inquiry and a subtle, delicate, vivid and responsive art of communication must take possession of the physical machinery of transmission and communication and breathe life into it." Democracy, he declared, "will have its consummation when free social inquiry is indissolubly wedded to the art of full and moving communication" (*PP*, 350). *Thought News* redivivus.

As this vision suggests, Dewey was at once a proponent of an expanded role for social science in American politics and a sharp critic of those who called for the rule of an intellectual aristocracy. If he was a cynic, he said, he might well say that the call for the men of brains to seize the torch was "a revery entertained by the intellectual class in compensation for an impotence consequent upon the divorce of theory and practice, upon the remoteness of specialized science from the affairs of life: the gulf being bridged not by the intellectuals but by inventors and engineers hired by captains of industry" (*PP*, 363).

Apart from this cynical response, Dewey saw major flaws in the arguments of democratic elitists. In the first place, if the masses were as "intellectually irredeemable" as these critics implied, they would in any case have too many desires and too much power to permit rule by experts. "The very ignorance, bias, frivolity, jealousy, instability, which are alleged to incapacitate them from share in political affairs, unfit them still more for passive submission to rule by intellectuals." Rule by an economic class could be concealed, but rule by experts would have to be an open affair. "It could be made to work," Dewey suggested, "only if the intellectuals became the willing tools of big economic interests. Otherwise they would have to ally themselves with the masses, and that implies, once more, a share in government by the latter" (*PP*, 363–364).

An equally serious objection to the rule of experts, Dewey argued, was that, without the participation of the public in the formulation of policy, such policy could not reflect the common needs and interests of the society because these needs and interests were known only to the public. "It is impossible for high-brows to secure a monopoly of such knowledge as must be used for the regulation of common affairs. In the degree in which they become a specialized class, they are shut off from knowledge of the needs which they are supposed to serve." The role of the expert was not as a policy maker but as a technician who would discover and make known to the public and its representatives the facts on which policy making depended. Only the public could define its interests. For experts to define those interests for the public was not democratic elitism but elitism pure and simple (*PP*, 364–365).

Dewey also argued that just as experts could not make policy that was truly public, so too policy makers need not be experts. Democratic realists tended to "ignore forces which have to be composed and resolved before technical and specialized action can come into play." It was not necessary for the many to have the knowledge and skill to conduct inquiries essential to intelligent public decisions. Such knowledge could be left to the few. But the many must have the capacity to "judge the bearing of the knowledge supplied by others upon common concerns." This was a capacity Dewey believed most men and women possessed, and he charged that elitists had greatly exaggerated the amount of intelligence and ability it took to render these kinds of judgments. In any case, it was impossible to tell, on the basis of prevailing conditions, whether or not the public possessed the necessary intelligence, for even the most brilliant of citizens faltered in the absence of adequate information on which to base judgments. "Until secrecy, prejudice, bias, misrepresentation, and propaganda as well as sheer ignorance are replaced by inquiry and publicity," Dewey noted, "we have no way of telling how apt for judgment of social policies the existing intelligence of the masses may be" (*PP*, 366).

Elitists also failed to recognize that "*effective* intelligence is not an original, innate endowment." The important consideration was not "native intelligence" but "*embodied* intelligence," the knowledge embedded in the social and technical conditions of action. "A more intelligent state of social affairs, one more informed with knowledge, more directed by intelligence, would not improve original endowments one whit, but it would raise the level upon which the intelligence of all operates. The height of this level is much more important for judgment of public concerns than are differences in intelligence quotients." IQ tests were relevant to democratic politics only insofar as they directed the attention of the democrat to the pretensions to class rule of those who claimed "superior" intelligence. "The notion that intelligence is a personal endowment or personal attainment," Dewey said, "is the great conceit of the intellectual class, as that of the commercial class is that wealth is something which they personally have wrought and possess" (*PP*, 366–367).[35]

Although Dewey criticized this aspect of democratic realism, he was not satisfied with the quality of the popular mind. He found Lippmann's analysis of "stereotypes" penetrating and agreed that they were more responsible for public misinformation than was consciously distorted news. Propagandists, he noted, often believed their own propaganda. Consequently, though he gave it slight mention in *The Public and Its Problems*, a radical reform of education remained an essential if not a sufficient condition for a revitalized public. Schools, he observed in 1922, had fostered a "systematic, almost deliberate, avoidance of the spirit of criticism in dealing with history, politics, and economics." This avoidance was perversely taken to be essential to the training of good citizens. Yet Dewey imagined a day when "teachers become sufficiently courageous and emancipated to insist that education means the creation of a discriminating mind." They would "cultivate the habit of suspended judgment, of skepticism, of desire for evidence, of appeal to observation rather than sentiment, discussion rather than bias, inquiry rather than conventional idealizations." Then, he said, schools would become "the dangerous outposts of a humane civilization" and "begin to be supremely interesting places."[36]

In the concluding pages of *The Public and Its Problems*, Dewey alluded

35. See also "Mediocrity and Individuality" (1922), *Middle Works* 13:289–294, and "Individuality, Equality, and Superiority" (1922), *Middle Works* 13:295–300.

36. "Education as Politics" (1922), *Middle Works* 13:331–334.

all too briefly to one further condition for the development of a self-conscious, modern, democratic public. The creation of the Great Community, he contended, had in the end to go hand-in-hand with the revitalization of the local community because "in its deepest and richest sense a community must always remain a matter of face-to-face intercourse" (*PP*, 367). Publics must literally stay in *place*, for attachments "are bred in tranquil stability; they are nourished in constant relationships. Acceleration of mobility disturbs them at their root. And without abiding attachments associations are too shifting and shaken to permit a public readily to locate and identify itself" (*PP*, 322–323). The capstone of the creation of the Great Community would be the restoration of the public life of the local associations which had been invaded and partially destroyed by the forces of industrialization creating the Great Society. "Democracy must begin at home, and its home is the neighborly community" (*PP*, 368).

Only in local, face-to-face associations could members of a public participate in dialogues with their fellows, and such dialogues were critical to the formation and organization of the public. "The connections of the ear with vital and out-going thought and emotion are immensely closer and more varied than those of the eye," Dewey remarked. "Vision is a spectator; hearing is a participator. Publication is partial and the public which results is partially informed and formed until the meanings it purveys pass from mouth to mouth. There is no limit to the liberal expansion and confirmation of limited personal intellectual endowment which may proceed from the flow of social intelligence when that circulates by word of mouth from one to another in the communications of the local community" (*PP*, 371).

Nothing about the forces that had created the Great Society, Dewey asserted, prevented a clear understanding of their consequences from being developed on the local level. The "vast, innumerable and intricate currents of trans-local associations" could be "banked and conducted" so that they would "pour the generous and abundant meanings of which they are potential bearers into the smaller intimate unions of human beings living in immediate contact with one another." Unless these forces were so banked and conducted, the democratic public would remain in eclipse. Only in the participatory context of local communities could the public's education be consummated, an education that would "render nugatory the indictment of democracy drawn on the basis of the ignorance, bias and levity of the masses" (*PP*, 367, 371).[37]

37. See also "Americanism and Localism" (1920), *Middle Works* 12:12–16.

"Perhaps to most, probably to many," Dewey admitted as he closed his analysis, "the conclusions which have been stated as to the conditions upon which depends the emergence of the Public from its eclipse will seem close to denial of the possibility of realizing the idea of a democratic public" (*PP*, 351). This would not have been a surprising judgment for his readers to reach, for he gave them little choice. The conditions he laid out for the emergence of the public from its eclipse were strenuous, and establishing these conditions was a matter of overcoming formidable obstacles. The sort of organized social inquiry he envisioned faced the resistance of powerful, entrenched interests, and he offered no strategy for defeating them. It also went against the grain of the concerted effort of American social science to distance itself from the very role he proposed for it. For Dewey, the ideal social scientist remained someone like Henry George, the self-taught economist and social reformer whose *Progress and Poverty* (1879) brought together unorthodox economics, republican moralism, and religious conviction into a searing jeremiad against the unearned wealth and power of the rentier class. Even in his own day, George had met with nothing but harsh criticism in the halls of American universities, and Dewey's estimate of George as the greatest American social philosopher was shared by few social scientists in the twenties. Most academics were eager to dissociate their disciplines from the taint of the mix of scholarship and journalism (and politics) which George had practiced so well and which served Dewey as a model of the social scientist as public intellectual.[38]

Dewey's assertion that the local community might be reconstructed in the midst of the Great Society also seemed wistful in the absence of specific suggestions for doing so. It was unclear how a public that was the product of a social transformation showing no respect for place could remain strongly attached to local settings. Dewey said it was "easy to point to many signs which indicate that unconscious agencies as well as deliberate planning are making for such an enrichment of the experience of local communities as will conduce to render them genuine centres of the attention, interest and devotion for their constituent

38. "An Appreciation of Henry George" (1928), *Later Works* 3:359–360; "Foreword to *The Philosophy of Henry George*" (1933), *Later Works* 9:299–302. The latter is prefatory to a study of George's career by George Geiger (*The Philosophy of Henry George* [New York: Macmillan, 1933]), a revision of a doctoral dissertation which Dewey had supervised. The contempt of social scientists for public intellectuals was not directed only to radicals such as George. Although Lippmann probably did more than anyone else to gain a hearing for democratic realism in the twenties, some academics who shared his perspective dismissed him as a mere litterateur. See the review of *The Phantom Public* by Arnold Hall in the *American Political Science Review* 20 (1926): 199–200.

members," but easy though it may have been, he pointed to no such signs (*PP*, 369). In their absence, what stood out was his powerful descriptions of how the Great Society had invaded face-to-face communities and stripped them of control over their own destiny.[39]

Everything about Dewey's analysis pointed to the need for a politics of knowledge that would end the bewilderment of the public, but this politics remained, at best, an implicit, wholly undeveloped element of his argument. In laying out the "infinitely difficult" conditions for the emergence of the Great Community and offering little guidance for overcoming them, he inadvertently and ironically made almost as good a case as Lippmann had that the phantom public would not materialize. Although he had helped clarify the sad state of American democracy, Dewey proved no exorcist.

Equally debilitating for Dewey's critique of realism were his neglect of the politics necessary for contemporary publics to solve their intellectual problem and to build a new state and his refusal to speculate on the forms this state might take. Dewey said nothing about the former (indeed, as I indicated, he left no place for it in his theory), and little about the latter. He justified this omission on the grounds that the search for the conditions under which the Great Society could become the Great Community had priority and that until these conditions came about it was "somewhat futile to consider what political machinery will suit them" (*PP*, 327). But his own activism in the Outlawry of War movement suggested that the separation of the intellectual problems of

39. For a keen analysis of the unacknowledged difficulties of Dewey's effort to designate the "neighborly community" as "the site upon which the knowledge of modern science is to fuse with the virtues that can only be cultivated within intimate surroundings" see Timothy Kaufman-Osborn, "John Dewey and the Liberal Science of Community," *Journal of Politics* 46 (1984): 1142–1165. One difficulty Dewey did comment upon was the resistance that local communities might well offer to enlightenment afforded by organized scientific inquiry. In a fairly evenhanded commentary on the fundamentalist controversy of the twenties, he noted the close connection in the United States between local democracy and evangelical religion. William Jennings Bryan represented the people who formed the "backbone" of American social reform, people who intimately associated evangelicalism with "impulses to neighborliness and decency." There was, therefore, an "element of soundness" in the fundamentalist fear of science. "The forces which are embodied in the present crusade would not be so dangerous were they not bound up with so much that is necessary and good. We have been so taught to respect the beliefs of our neighbors that few will respect the beliefs of a neighbor when they depart from forms which have become associated with aspiration for a decent neighboring life. This is the illiberalism which is deep-rooted in our liberalism." A defense of science which rested content with Menckenesque sneers at "boobs" like Bryan was, Dewey said, doomed to cultural defeat. Liberal defenders of science like himself had to make the case that science did not threaten but rather sustained the aspiration for a decent, neighborly life ("The American Intellectual Frontier" [1922], *Middle Works* 13:301–305).

publics from their political problems, however useful for purposes of analysis, was practically debilitating. What democracy required, he had astutely argued in that context, was a strategy that at once educated and empowered publics. Moreover, the fact that a public could not begin to construct its government until it found itself did not mean that the theorist of public life could not intimate what forms this government might take.

Especially important to the democratic theorist, one would think, was the role that one particular set of officials—those Dewey termed "citizen-voters"—would play in the government of a democratic public. Clearly, unlike Lippmann, Dewey found the prevailing modest function of these officials as a periodic electorate to be inadequate (*PP*, 320). And though equally clearly he believed that modern democratic government would continue to rely heavily on accountable officials other than citizen voters, the logic of Dewey's political theory and ethics pointed to a government that would include, indeed maximize, agencies of direct democracy, that is, agencies through which the public would choose to govern itself. Government was one of the associated activities of society, and hence in a democratic society the democratic ideal—which afforded to every individual "a responsible share according to capacity in forming and directing the activities of the groups to which one belongs and in participating according to need in the values which the groups sustain"—would presumably serve as the regulative ideal for it as well as for other groups (*PP*, 327–328). For Dewey, unlike the realists, self-government in the broadest sense was not a relatively insignificant good; it was essential to self-realization. Hence we might expect him to have had more to say about self-government in its narrower, strictly political sense. Presumably, the advantages that the local, face-to-face community provided to a public trying to discover itself would apply as well to a public seeking to organize itself to define, protect, and advance its interests. Decentralizing power would also, of course, raise difficulties of the sort Dewey fudged in merely asserting the easy interdependence of local communities with the Great Community, difficulties inherent in any effort to preserve a measure of direct democracy in a large nation state. Yet, despite the implications of his own argument, he appeared to have given little thought to the problems and possibilities of participatory government. For a philosopher who put democratic ideals at the center of his thinking, Dewey had surprisingly little to say about democratic citizenship.

Perhaps most troubling about the questions Dewey avoided in *The Public and Its Problems* is his own concession of their undeniable importance. As he said, it was essential to answer the question "By what means shall [the public's] inchoate and amorphous estate be organized into effective political action relevant to present social needs and opportunities?" (*PP*, 313). Moreover, he was himself constantly railing against those who were guilty of wishful thinking because of an inattentiveness to means. A wish, he said, "becomes an aim or end only when it is worked out in terms of concrete conditions available for its realization, that is in terms of 'means'" (*HNC*, 161). Much of what passed for moral ends, he complained, "do not get beyond the stage of fancy of something agreeable and desirable based upon an emotional wish. . . . Unless ideals are to be dreams and idealism a synonym for romanticism and phantasy-building, there must be a most realistic study of actual conditions and of the mode or law of natural events in order to give the imagined or ideal object definite form and solid substance—to give it, in short, practicality and constitute it a working end" (*HNC*, 162). Dewey's failure to constitute participatory democracy as a compelling "working end," as well as the demanding conditions he set for its realization, made *The Public and Its Problems* a less than effective counter to democratic realism. Too many questions were left unanswered.

Dewey never returned in any systematic fashion to these unanswered questions. One has to dig out his subsequent thinking about the public and its problems from the enormous flow of journalism which issued from his battered typewriter in the extraordinary years of political activism he began as he entered the eighth decade of his life. But this reluctance to think abstractly about politics is, I suppose, as it should be for a philosopher who insisted that ideas arose in the context of particular, concrete, and problematic situations.

CHAPTER 10

Philosophy and Democracy

✳

A familiar impatience crept into John Dewey's discussion of the institutions of political democracy in *The Public and Its Problems*, as if somehow consideration of such matters was really beside the point or at least not properly at the heart of a democratic philosophy. Echoes resounded in the text not only of *Thought News* but also of his maiden contest with realism in the person of Sir Henry Maine some forty years earlier. Contemporary debate about the shortcomings of democratic theory and practice had, he felt, failed—as Maine had—to distinguish between democracy as a way of life and political democracy as a system of government. The two were closely related, of course, but the idea of democracy in the former sense was "a wider and fuller idea than can be exemplified in the state even at its best. To be realized it must affect all modes of human association, the family, the school, industry, religion. And even as far as political arrangements are concerned, governmental institutions are but a mechanism for securing to an ideal channels of effective operation." If Dewey talked too little of "political machinery," it was perhaps because he believed others tended to talk of nothing else. Like Maine before him, Walter Lippmann confused one of the houses of democracy with its home.[1]

This perspective reflected not only Dewey's interest in the democratization of social institutions other than the state—the school and

---

1. *The Public and Its Problems* (1927), *Later Works* 2:325.

the factory in particular—but also his fear that the triumph of realism would threaten not merely the political forms of democracy but its ethical substance. For in its "generic social sense" democracy was an inherently participatory ideal; the realist proposal for democracy without a maximum of self-government was a contradiction in terms. Whatever his weaknesses as a political theorist and strategist, Dewey was never guilty of shortchanging democracy as a moral ideal. And though this is not usually the way in which it is read, much of his more technical philosophical work during the twenties, including *Experience and Nature* (1925) and *The Quest for Certainty* (1929), comprised his most concerted effort to date to strengthen the case for this ideal by providing metaphysical warrants on its behalf.[2]

Dewey had advanced what amounted to a prospectus for this project in an important (and neglected) lecture entitled "Philosophy and Democracy" delivered at the University of California in the fall of 1918. Here he made the distinction between the wisdom of philosophy and the knowledge of science to which I have alluded, and argued for a mutually sustaining relationship between them. Scientific knowledge was partial and incomplete, he said, until it was placed "in the context of a future which cannot be known but only speculated about and resolved upon." Insofar as it was a democratic future one wished to speculate about and resolve upon, several questions arose for a philosopher like himself:

> Is democracy a comparatively superficial human expedient, a device of petty manipulation, or does nature itself, as that is uncovered and understood by our best contemporaneous knowledge, sustain and support our democratic hopes and aspirations? Or, if we choose to begin arbitrarily at the other end, if to construct democratic institutions is our aim, how then shall we construe and interpret the natural environment and natural history of humanity in order to get an intellectual warrant for our endeavors, a reasonable persuasion that our undertaking is not contradicted by what science authorizes us to say about the structure of the world? How shall we read what we call reality (that is to

2. Ibid., p. 327. *Experience and Nature* and *The Quest for Certainty* are often the only books of Dewey's read by philosophers nowadays (if those), and few read them, as I do here, as an effort to provide a philosophical anthropology for democracy (which is not to say that this is all they are). A major exception, and a book from which I have profited enormously, is James Gouinlock, *John Dewey's Philosophy of Value* (New York: Humanities Press, 1972). On the other hand, virtually no one interested principally in Dewey's social philosophy and political activism pays much attention to these texts. See, for example, my own inadequate "John Dewey and American Democracy" (diss., Stanford University, 1980).

say the world of existence accessible to verifiable inquiry) so that we may essay our deepest political and social problems with a conviction that they are to a reasonable extent sanctioned and sustained by the nature of things? Is the world as an object of knowledge at odds with our purposes and efforts? Is it merely neutral and indifferent? Does it lend itself equally to all our social ideals, which means that it gives itself to none, but stays aloof, ridiculing as it were the ardor and earnestness with which we take our trivial and transitory hopes and plans? Or is its nature such that it is at least willing to cooperate, that it not only does not say us nay, but gives us an encouraging nod?

Dewey went on to argue that in the radical empiricism of William James one could find a powerful vision of a universe friendly to democracy, but by the end of the 1920s one could find its equal in Dewey's own "empirical naturalism."[3]

EXPERIENCE AND NATURE

In *Experience and Nature*, his most important book of the twenties, Dewey returned to metaphysics on a grand scale. At first glance, this was surprising. Since the early 1890s, he had, after all, bad-mouthed metaphysics as often as epistemology. Yet his experimental logic and his criticisms of idealism and realism rested on controversial, if often implicit, metaphysical propositions, and under the influence of his Columbia colleague F. J. E. Woodbridge he had begun to appreciate the uses of a descriptive, neo-Aristotelian metaphysics. In a signal prewar article "The Subject-Matter of Metaphysical Inquiry" (1915), he indicated that his dissatisfaction was less with metaphysics as such than with the sort of metaphysics that underlay the epistemological preoccupations of most professional philosophers, metaphysics that took as its task the search for some "temporally original," ultimate, causal Being. Causal analysis, he argued, should be left to science, which had no use for a First Cause. Still, there remained a place for a metaphysics that would, like that of Aristotle, describe "certain irreducible traits found in any and every subject of scientific inquiry," yet, unlike that of Aristotle, free these traits from "confusion with ultimate origins and ultimate

---

3. "Philosophy and Democracy" (1919), *Middle Works* 11:48. In the twenties Dewey reiterated and refined the distinction between philosophy as wisdom and science as knowledge. See "Philosophy and Civilization" (1927), *Later Works* 3:3–10; "Philosophy" (1928), *Later Works* 3:115–132; and "Philosophy" (1929), *Later Works* 5:161–177.

ends—that is, from questions of creation and eschatology." Science should tell us how we came to have the world we do, but metaphysics could help us understand what sort of world it was that we had.[4]

Experience and Nature was a full, rich, and, at times, exasperated argument for the "immediate empiricism" Dewey had sketched before the war and for the idiosyncratic conception of "experience" that had given his opponents fits. Here Dewey again inveighed forcefully against any and all efforts to separate nature and experience and contended for a recognition of their continuity. Experience was not a veil or screen shutting man off from nature, as many philosophers believed, but a path into the world: "Experience is *of* as well as *in* nature. It is not experience which is experienced, but nature—stones, plants, animals, diseases, health, temperature, electricity, and so on. Things interacting in certain ways *are* experience; they are what is experienced. Linked in certain other ways with another natural object—the human organism—they are *how* things are experienced as well. Experience thus reaches down into nature; it has depth. It also has breadth and to an indefinitely elastic extent. It stretches." Experience was an aspect of nature by means of which nature disclosed itself to man—a disclosure that in turn enriched experience.[5]

This understanding of experience and nature was that of the common man. But it was also the understanding of experimental science, which provided "naive realism" with a powerful ally, and here, as always, Dewey was eager to cement an alliance of science and common sense. In the natural sciences, the union of experience and nature was taken for granted. Scientific investigators assumed that "experience, controlled in specifiable ways, is the avenue that leads to the facts and laws of nature." The empirical method that guided their experiments began and ended in "directly experienced subject-matter." A long train of theoretical reasoning might intervene between the direct experience of nature which initiated a scientific inquiry and that which tested and

4. "The Subject-Matter of Metaphysical Inquiry" (1915), *Middle Works* 8:4–5, 13. In this essay Dewey suggested that metaphysics would confine itself to generic traits found in scientific inquiry. *Experience and Nature* broadened the project to include generic traits evidenced by aesthetic, moral, and religious experience as well, a broadening of fundamental importance for Dewey's mature metaphysics. On Woodbridge's influence see Dykhuizen, pp. 173–174, 209, and R. W. Sleeper, *The Necessity of Pragmatism: John Dewey's Conception of Philosophy* (New Haven: Yale University Press, 1986), chap. 4.

5. *Experience and Nature* (1929), *Later Works* 1:12–13. This is the second edition of the book, which includes a preface not found in the first edition (1925) and a completely revised first chapter. For my purposes, the differences between the two editions are of little moment. Page numbers for further references (*EN*) appear in the text.

verified its hypotheses, but "the vine of pendant theory is attached at both ends to the pillars of observed subject-matter" (*EN*, 11).

This view of knowledge suggested that one need not limit the empirical investigation of what experience might tell us about nature to those of its aspects that were of greatest interest to natural scientists but could extend such inquiry to the whole of experience. Thus "if experience actually presents esthetic and moral traits, then these traits may also be supposed to reach down into nature, and to testify to something that belongs to nature as truly as does the mechanical structure attributed to it in physical science." These traits, no less than those that occupied the scientist, were real. "They are *found*, experienced, and are not to be shoved out of being by some trick of logic. When found their ideal qualities are as relevant to the philosophic theory of nature as are the traits found by physical inquiry." It was this broader use of an empirical method which Dewey recommended to philosophers. "The theory of empirical method in philosophy," he said, "does for experienced subject-matter on a liberal scale what it does for special sciences on a technical scale" (*EN*, 13–14).

Empirical investigation of the implications of experience should begin, Dewey argued, with a distinction between "gross, macroscopic, crude subject-matters in primary experience and the refined, derived objects of reflection." Primary experience set the problems and furnished the initial data for reflection, which constructed secondary objects that explained primary objects by locating them in a set of unapparent relationships and thereby enriched and expanded their meaning. In the wake of reflection, primary objects might in immediate contact be just what they were before—hard, painful, delightful, etc. But when one returned to these experienced things by a path laid out by the secondary objects of reflection "these qualities cease to be isolated details; they get the meaning contained in a whole system of related objects; they are rendered continuous with the rest of nature and take on the import of the things they are now seen to be continuous with" (*EN*, 15–16).

Thus the path of reflection in both science and philosophy should be *from* the things of primary experience and then back *to* them, not only for purposes of verification but also because the whole point of reflection was to enlarge and enrich the meaning of such things. Herein lay the measure of the value of a philosophy:

Does it end in conclusions which, when they are referred back to ordinary life-experiences and their predicaments, render them more significant, more luminous to us, and make our dealings with them more fruitful? Or does it terminate in rendering the things of ordinary experience more opaque than they were before, and in depriving them of having in "reality" even the significance they had previously seemed to have? Does it yield the enrichment and increase of power of ordinary things which the results of physical science afford when applied in every-day affairs? Or does it become a mystery that these ordinary things should be what they are; and are philosophic concepts left to dwell in separation in some technical realm of their own?

By these standards, most philosophies failed to measure up. Rather, they terminated in "conclusions that make it necessary to disparage and condemn primary experience" and, consequently, led "cultivated common sense to look askance at philosophy" (EN, 18).

At the root of the failure of most philosophers to do justice to experience were confusions occasioned by what William James termed the "double-barreled" nature of the word "experience"—a term that denoted both the subject-matter experienced and the processes of experiencing. This usage, Dewey contended, betokened that in primary experience act and material were contained in an "unanalyzed totality." Empirical method would take this "integrated unity" as its starting point and ask how and why this whole was so often reflectively distinguished into experiencing subject and experienced object (EN, 19). It would find, he suggested (anticipating his own conclusions), that such a distinction was essential for the effective regulation of primary experience and was made for this purpose. "Until some acts and their consequences are discriminatingly referred to the human organism and other energies and effects are referred to other bodies, there is no leverage, no purchase, with which to regulate the course of experience." In this sense, the reflective constitution of "subjects" as centers of experience was a necessary condition for "subjecting the energies of nature to use as instrumentalities for ends" (EN, 22).

Most philosophers had not followed this path of analysis. Rather they had taken as their starting point the reflective division of primary experience into subject and object and mistakenly treated this reflective product as if it was primary. They consequently asked not how and why subject and object came to be distinguished but rather how one might possibly bridge the ontological gap they had themselves obtusely constructed between these separate sorts of existence. In such "nonempirical" philosophy:

Object and subject, mind and matter (or whatever words and ideas are used) are separate and independent. Therefore it has upon its hands the problem of how it is possible to know at all; how an outer world can affect an inner mind; how the acts of mind can reach out and lay hold of objects defined in antithesis to them. Naturally it is at a loss for an answer, since its premises make the fact of knowledge both unnatural and unempirical. One thinker turns metaphysical materialist and denies reality to the mental; another turns psychological idealist, and holds that matter and force are merely disguised psychical events. Solutions are given up as a hopeless task, or else different schools pile one intellectual complication on another only to arrive by a long and tortuous course at that which näive experience already has in its own possession. (*EN*, 19–20)

As a result of this artificial separation of the subject-matter of experience from the process of experiencing, nature was drained of qualities and conceived as an "indifferent dead mechanism" and experiencing was conceived to comprise the whole of experience. "When objects are isolated from the experience through which they are reached and in which they function, experience itself becomes reduced to the mere process of experiencing, and experience is therefore treated as if it were also complete in itself. We get the absurdity of an experiencing which experiences only itself, states and processes of consciousness, instead of the things of nature." Since the seventeenth century, such "subjectivism" had created havoc among philosophers and was largely responsible for the belief that "'nature' and 'experience' are names for things which have nothing to do with each other" (*EN*, 21).[6]

In addition to subjectivists, the chief villains among philosophers who contravened the facts of primary experience were Dewey's old enemies, the intellectualists of one sort or another. He again blasted idealists and realists alike for their supposition of the "ubiquity of the knowledge relation"—their identification of experience with knowing and their failure to recognize that "what is really 'in' experience extends much further than that which at any time is *known*." In primary experience "things are objects to be treated, used, acted upon and with, enjoyed and endured, even more than things to be known. They are things *had* before they are things cognized" (*EN*, 27–28). Indeed, having was prior to knowing, and knowing was essentially the servant of

6. As these statements suggest, Dewey regarded many philosophies that were conventionally termed "empiricist" as nonempirical in method.

having. "*Being* and *having* things in ways other than knowing them, in ways never identical with knowing them, exist, and are preconditions of reflection and knowledge." It was a "context of non-cognitive but experienced subject-matter which gives what is *known* its import" (*EN*, 377, 29).

The pseudo-problems of subjectivism and intellectualism were intimately connected with one another. The functional separation of subject and object essential to knowing was taken by both subjectivists and intellectualists to be primary and ubiquitous. Moreover, if only knowledge-objects were held to be real objects (as intellectualists contended), then all "affectional and volitional objects" were excluded from the "real" world and forced to find refuge in the private world of the experiencing subject (as subjectivists argued). One was forced into "the denial to nature of the characters which make things lovable and contemptible, beautiful and ugly, adorable and awful" (*EN*, 28). And at the same time, the experiencing subject that feels and acts as well as knows was rendered unnatural: "the self becomes not merely a pilgrim but an unnaturalized and unnaturalizable alien in the world" (*EN*, 30). Short of the introduction of some extranatural or supernatural agency or principle, the only way to avoid walling off an experiencing subject from an experienced natural world in this fashion was to "acknowledge that all modes of experiencing are ways in which some genuine traits of nature come to manifest realization" (*EN*, 30–31).

Subjectivism and intellectualism were but two instances of a more general malady afflicting nonempirical philosophy, an abuse of the "principle of selective emphasis." In any inquiry, some aspect of experience was selected out as relevant for some particular purpose or problem. Ordinarily, the circumstances of selection were readily acknowledged with no thought of denying the reality of what was left out by the selection. Nonempirical philosophers, however, tended to exhibit "a cataleptic rigidity in attachment to that phase of the total objects of experience which has become especially dear to a philosopher. *It* is real at all hazards and only it; other things are real only in some secondary and Pickwickian sense" (*EN*, 31). Usually a moral impulse lay behind this attachment: philosophers transformed those experienced traits of nature they found to be good into "fixed traits of real Being" (*EN*, 33). As a result, such traits as certainty, simplicity, and permanence had usually been privileged over uncertainty, complexity, and change, and the latter traits banished from the realm of the really Real.

To counter such selective emphasis, Dewey proposed in his own metaphysics to make use of an empirical or denotative method that would begin "with no presuppositions save that what is experienced, since it is a manifestation of nature, may, and indeed, must be used as testimony of the characteristics of natural events" (*EN*, 27). He would offer not a causal or teleological account of Being, but a "descriptive metaphysics" that would indicate in the most general terms what the world must be like such that we have the experience (of all kinds) that we do. Beginning with ordinary experience, Dewey proposed to infer the "generic traits" of nature. These inferences—the reflective products of metaphysical inquiry—would then be referred back to ordinary experience for verification. Those that passed the test, he predicted, would both enrich and explain ordinary experience. Nonempirical philosophies, he believed, had "cast a cloud over the things of ordinary experience" and obscured their possibilities. Empirical naturalism, he hoped, would clear away this cloud and create "a respect for concrete human experience and its potentialities" (*EN*, 40–41). Dewey's metaphysics, as James Gouinlock has said, "made nature whole again in a way which philosophers had not known since Aristotle. Beauty and value, triumph and defeat, knowing and doubting—the entire spectrum of qualitative and cognitive experience—were once again characteristic of nature, and were discriminated in such a way that the philosopher could indicate the methods by which such things could be subject to human reckoning."[7]

GENERIC TRAITS

Dewey began his description of the generic traits of nature with the critical claim that precariousness and contingency were as real as stability and predictability. Nature was in every instance a combination of these traits, and neither could be overlooked. Experience made it clear, he said, that "we live in a world which is an impressive and irresistible mixture of sufficiencies, tight completenesses, order, recurrences which make possible prediction and control, and singularities, ambiguities, uncertain possibilities, processes going on to consequences as yet indeterminate" (*EN*, 47). Uncertainty was a fact of life, and it could not be dialectically drummed out of existence simply because it made life difficult and dangerous.

Anthropological investigation, especially the widely noted preeminence in primitive cultures of innumerable sayings, proverbs, and aphorisms concerned with *luck*, provided particularly telling evidence for

7. Gouinlock, *Dewey's Philosophy of Value*, pp. 13–14.

Dewey that "man finds himself living in an aleatory world." The fears of primitive man—the source of superstition, magic, and religion—were not subjective feelings projected on the world but a very realistic response to a fearful environment, an uncertain, unpredictable, uncontrollable, and hazardous world of disease, famine, crop failure, death, defeat in battle, and other dangers. Feelings of fear were a function of a larger situation enclosing both man and his environment which was, as a whole, fearful. "Man fears because he exists in a fearful, an awful world. The *world* is precarious and perilous" (*EN*, 42–44).

Reflective thought was the most promising of mankind's responses to the contingencies of existence; indeed, thinking itself, which arose in doubtful, uncertain situations, was perhaps the best evidence of the precariousness of nature. Uncertainty was thus the source of both philosophy and science. Unfortunately, many philosophers had lost sight of the origins of their quest for wisdom in nature's intricate mix of the stable and the precarious and had responded to uncertainty by dividing existence into two realms of being and then enshrining and protecting its stable aspects in a higher realm of the really Real while banishing its precarious dimensions to a merely illusory or phenomenal realm. "Variant philosophies," Dewey suggested, "may be looked at as different ways of supplying recipes for denying to the universe the character of contingency which it possesses so integrally that its denial leaves the reflecting mind without a clew" (*EN*, 46).[8]

On the other hand, science, which was the fruit of the intellectual labor required to regulate this mix rather than deny its existence, had given modern man greater powers for the prediction and control of uncertainty. But it had not erased contingency. Hence, the self-confidence of modern "scientism" was as talismanic as—if more "sophisticated" than—the fearful superstitions of our ancestors. "Our magical safeguard against the uncertain character of the world," Dewey observed, "is to deny the existence of chance, to mumble universal and necessary law, the ubiquity of cause and effect, the uniformity of nature, universal progress, and the inherent rationality of the universe. . . . But when all is said and done, the fundamentally hazardous character of the world is not seriously modified, much less eliminated. Such an incident as the last war and preparations for a future war

8. Dewey extended this indictment to such exponents of a metaphysics of change as Heraclitus, Hegel, and Bergson because these philosophers, while taking note of a trait of nature "whisked out of sight" by many, made change itself into something universal, regular, and sure rather than, as experience showed it to be, something contingent, uncertain, and "a potential doom of disaster and death" (*EN*, 49–50).

remind us that it is easy to overlook the extent to which, after all, our attainments are only devices for blurring the disagreeable recognition of a fact, instead of means of altering the fact itself" (*EN*, 45).

The conjunction of the stable and precarious in existence pointed to another generic trait of nature to which Dewey gave particular emphasis: change or temporality. His was a metaphysics of "events" rather than "substances"; indeed, he denied that there were any immutable substances in nature. Everything was subject to change because every existent was lodged in surroundings that were "only in part compatible and reinforcing." Even the greatest mountains had appeared and would disappear like the most fleeting cloud—it would just take longer. "A thing may endure *secula seculorum* and yet not be everlasting; it will crumble before the gnawing tooth of time, as it exceeds a certain measure." All existence was eventful. A "thing" was not an immutable substance but an "affair"—a "diversified and more or less loose interconnection of events." Nature itself was "an affair *of* affairs" (*EN*, 63, 83–85).[9]

This view suggested that even the stable features of nature were only relatively so. Stable things were those that changed relatively slowly, regularly, or rhythmically. Such events lent "structure" to the world. Structure was therefore not a thing but a character of events, a persistent ordering of changes. The same was true of "matter" (and "mind" for that matter), which was not a substance but that feature of natural events that gave them "a characteristic rhythmic order." Matter was "no cause or source of events or processes; no absolute monarch; no principle of explanation; no substance lying behind or underlying changes—save in that sense of substance in which a man well fortified with this world's goods, and hence able to maintain himself through vicissitudes of surroundings, is a man of substance" (*EN*, 65). Dewey contended the time had come to stop thinking of matter and mind as "static structures instead of functional characters." He predicted that "if there were an interdict placed for a generation upon the use of mind, matter, consciousness as nouns, and we were obliged to employ adjectives and adverbs, conscious and consciously, mental and mentally, material and physically, we should find many of our problems much simplified." Given this view, the concerns of life (and philosophy)

9. Dewey drew support for his contention that things were events not only from evolutionary biology (a long-standing ally) but also from post-Newtonian physics. As he noted, "The fixed and unchanged being of the Democritean atom is now reported by inquirers to possess some of the traits of his non-being and to embody a temporary equilibrium in the economy of nature's compromises and adjustments" (*EN*, 63).

should be with "the rate and mode of the conjunction of the precarious and the assured, the incomplete and the finished, the repetitious and the varying, the safe and sane and the hazardous. If we trust to the evidence of experienced things, these traits, and the modes and tempos of their interaction with each other, are fundamental features of natural existence" (*EN*, 64–67).

Aesthetic experience provided Dewey with clues to another generic trait of nature that was significant in his mature philosophy: quality. Aesthetic experience, broadly conceived, involved the immediate appreciation of things—things directly possessed, enjoyed, and suffered in and of themselves. Although largely ignored by philosophers fixated on cognitive experience, the "direct appropriations and satisfactions" of experience preoccupied most men and women, who were intensely interested in life's consummations. To empirical philosophers willing to concede the occasional wisdom of "näive common sense," these immediate enjoyments and sufferings of experience provided compelling evidence that nature had "terminating qualities" (*EN*, 69, 87).

Aesthetic experience—the appreciation of these qualities—was fundamentally different from cognitive experience. Qualities, Dewey argued, were not known but immediately felt or had. As such, they were not only not known but not knowable, for to know was to deal in relationships—mediations—not immediacies:

> Immediacy of existence is ineffable. But there is nothing mystical about such ineffability; it expresses the fact that of direct existence it is futile to say anything to one's self and impossible to say anything to another. Discourse can but intimate connections which if followed out may lead one to *have* an existence. Things in their immediacy are unknown and unknowable, not because they are remote or behind some impenetrable veil of sensation of ideas, but because knowledge has no concern with them. For knowledge is a memorandum of conditions of their appearance, concerned, that is, with sequences, coexistences, relations. Immediate things may be *pointed to* by words, but not described or defined. (*EN*, 74–75)

The immediate experience of qualities was at the heart of noncognitive experience, which was a prior and necessary condition of knowledge. Of course, to say that such experience was ineffable was not to say that we could not know *that* we experience qualities immediately. But to know that one had had an experience and having that experience were two very different matters. Immediate experience and knowledge claims *about* immediate experience were not to be confused.

Immediate experience indicated that there was more to nature than the spare, nonqualitative relationships posited by modern scientific knowledge. "In every event there is something obdurate, self-sufficient, wholly immediate, neither a relation nor an element in a relational whole, but terminal and exclusive." Nothing, to be sure, existed in isolation, but a set of relationships between things presupposed the existence of those things apart from these relationships. "Without immediate qualities those relations with which science deals would have no footing in existence and thought would have nothing beyond itself to chew upon or dig into. Without a basis in qualitative events, the characteristic subject-matter of knowledge would be algebraic ghosts, relations that do not relate. . . . Only if elements are more than just elements in a whole, only if they have something qualitatively their own, can a relational system be prevented from complete collapse." In aesthetic experience—"in all immediately enjoyed and suffered things, in things directly possessed"—things in effect "speak for themselves" and proclaim "I may *have* relatives but *I* am not related" (*EN*, 74–76).[10]

Unless one ignored aesthetic experience, one could not deny the existence of objects of direct grasp, possession, use, and enjoyment or gainsay the qualities found in the immediate experience of these objects. These, Dewey contended, included not only so-called primary and secondary qualities (like number and color) but also "tertiary" qualities (like fearfulness). "Empirically, things are poignant, tragic, beautiful, humorous, settled, disturbed, comfortable, annoying, barren, harsh, consoling, splendid, fearful; are such immediately and in their own right and behalf. If we take advantage of the word esthetic in a wider sense than that of application to the beautiful and ugly, esthetic quality, immediate, final, or self-enclosed, indubitably characterizes natural situations as they empirically occur. These traits stand in themselves on precisely the same level as colors, sounds, qualities of contact, taste and smell. Any criterion that finds the latter to be ultimate and 'hard' data will, impartially applied, come to the same conclusions about the former" (*EN*, 82).

For Dewey, it is important to emphasize, the qualities immediately found in experience were not "in" the organism or "in" the extra-organic environment but rather in "interactions in which both extra-

10. Here Dewey was criticizing the idealist theory of internal relations which, as we have seen, was an important part of his thinking at the beginning of his career. As he later said, his metaphysics sought "a *via media* between extreme atomistic pluralism and block universe monisms" ("Experience, Knowledge, and Value: A Rejoinder" [1939], *Later Works* 14:29).

organic things and organisms partake." Qualities were thus the qualities of affairs or "situations." As such, they were as much qualities of the things experienced as of the experiencer. Qualities were felt, but they were not merely feelings; they were objective features of natural events. "*Things* are beautiful and ugly, lovely and hateful, dull and illuminated, attractive and repulsive. Stir and thrill in us is as much theirs as is length, breadth, and thickness" (*EN*, 199, 91). The qualities of experience required an experiencer but they did not belong exclusively to that experiencer. They belonged to the experience, to a natural transaction.[11]

Qualities were final, and the qualitative distinctiveness of events suggested that nature, though constantly changing, was not endless but was marked by a wealth of "ends" or conclusions. "If experienced things are valid evidence," Dewey said, "then nature in having qualities within itself has what in the literal sense must be called ends, terminals, arrests, enclosures" (*EN*, 82). Qualities were the endings (and beginnings) of affairs. The experience of quality indicated that every natural affair was bounded: it had a beginning, a direction, and a conclusion. Situations were thus "histories" possessed of sequential order that lent them direction. "Anything denoted is found to have temporal quality and reference; it has movement from and towards *within* it" (*EN*, 385). Nature was the scene of incessant beginnings, ongoings, and endings, "a history which is a succession of histories, and in which any event is at once both beginning of one course and the close of another" (*EN*, 85).

In saying that nature had ends and histories, Dewey was not (as many had) asserting that nature had purposes (ends-in-view) or that the ends of nature's histories were necessarily happy or "progressive" ones. "We may conceive the end, the close, as due to fulfillment, perfect attainment, to satiety, or to exhaustion, to dissolution, to something having run down or given out. Being an end may be indifferently an ecstatic culmination, a matter-of-fact consummation, or a deplorable tragedy. Which of these things a closing or terminal object is, has nothing to do with the property of being an end" (*EN*, 83). It was only human beings that had ends-in-view, and it was only human reflection, deliberate

11. At the time he wrote *Experience and Nature*, Dewey used the term "interaction" to characterize natural affairs. Late in life, he reserved this term for the faulty, Newtonian notion of events as action among permanent, fixed entities or substances. He then used the term "transaction" to characterize his own, more "organic" view, which held that it was the action or event that was primary and that the elements in transactions were not independent existents but functions of transactions. See JD and Arthur Bentley, *Knowing and the Known* (Boston: Beacon Press, 1949), pp. 103–118.

choice, and directed effort that converted the terminations of natural histories into "conclusions and fulfillments" entitled to the "honorific status of completions and realizations" (*EN*, 86).

Everything of worth and significance in life was to be found in the immediate qualities of experience—the goods of life were, in the first instance, simply had. Unfortunately, immediate qualities, because they marked the terminations of complicated sequences of events in an ever-changing world, were precarious and fleeting—"immediate objects are the last word of evanescence" (*EN*, 94). Yet these qualities were the ends of sequentially ordered events in which, as in all of nature, the stable and predictable were inextricably mixed with the precarious and uncertain. By virtue of their unique capacity to know the ends of experience as conclusions of histories (and not merely have them as such), human beings could intervene in events and attempt to shape their course in order to secure (or avoid) situations having particular qualities. At best, such control was partial, for an element of contingency was always present. There was always "something unpredictable, spontaneous, unformulable and ineffable" in every terminal object; consummatory objects were "infinitely numerous, variable and individualized affairs." Nonetheless, by making use of the stable elements in events as manipulable means, man could, in some measure, render immediate qualities less precarious and arrive at an "approximation to what is unique and unrepeatable" (*EN*, 96–97).

This sort of regulation of experience required insight into the ordering of experience. Qualities were had, not known, but the conditions under which qualities were had could be known. Indeed, this was what knowledge was all about. All we could do with qualities themselves directly was to enjoy and suffer them, but indirectly we could reflect on "the order which conditions, prevents and secures their occurrence." Knowledge dealt with "the instrumentalities, the efficacious conditions, of the occurrence of the unique, unstable and passing" (*EN*, 96).

If man was not to take his pleasures in haphazard, uncontrollable fashion, he had to work at knowing the efficacious conditions of good and evil and at making use of this knowledge. Knowing thus originated in "the enforced penalty of labor" (*EN*, 100). It was rooted in the useful, instrumental arts, and it was through such arts—"arts of control based on study of nature"—that "objects which are fulfilling and good" were "multiplied and rendered secure." Artisans were the world's first knowers. The sciences, in turn, were children of the useful arts, and "the distinctively intellectual attitude which marks scientific inquiry was

generated in efforts at controlling persons and things so that consequences, issues, outcomes would be more stable and assured" (*EN*,
104–105).[12]

The capacity of human organisms to know about and artfully intervene in natural histories was an extraordinary feature of the situations
in which they were involved, but Dewey insisted that this remarkable
feature of human experience did not mark any breach in the continuity
of nature. He contended that one could account for it without positing
any ontological breaks in nature, and he did so with a version of the
theory of "emergent" evolution.[13]

Just as every natural event had its unique qualities, so too the interaction of various natural events resulted in further events with their own
unique, unpredictable qualities. One could discern in nature at least
three plateaus of existence whereupon an increasingly complex interaction of natural events had produced affairs with dramatically new
characteristics. From the level of events of a purely physicochemical
sort emerged events marked by life, vitality—a psychophysical character. And from interactions at the psychophysical level there emerged
events possessed of mental features. Matter, life, and mind were not
then separate kinds of Being. Rather, the distinction between them was
one of "levels of increasing complexity and intimacy of interaction
among natural events" (*EN*, 200). Life was not something mysterious
added to matter. The difference between the inanimate and the animate lay in "the *way* in which physico-chemical energies are intercon-
nected and operate, whence different *consequences* mark inanimate and
animate activity respectively. . . . Psycho-physical does not denote an
abrogation of the physicochemical; nor a peculiar mixture of something physical and something psychical (as a centaur is half man and
half horse); it denotes the possession of certain qualities and efficacies
not displayed by the inanimate" (*EN*, 195–196). Although nature's
plateaus were continuous with one another, each level was charac-

12. Though knowing was in its origins a tool and an instrumental art, Dewey readily
acknowledged that cognitive experience was not without immediate qualities to be had in
direct and unmediated fashion for their own sake. Tools could be beautiful as well as
useful, and "intellectual meanings may themselves be appropriated, enjoyed and appreciated." But "contemplation" of such meanings was not itself knowing; it was an aesthetic
not a cognitive experience (*EN*, 105).

13. Theories of emergent evolution did not necessarily serve to establish a continuity
between experience and nature. They could be used as a device to explain (emergent)
discontinuity. As J. E. Tiles notes in his fine discussion of Dewey's notion of emergence,
"one can offer up a theory under this banner which amounts to little more than dualism
back from the laundry" (*Dewey* [London: Routledge, 1988], p. 49).

terized by unique emergent qualities, and hence it was a mistake to attempt to reduce one level to another. Physicochemical events were no more real than vital or mental events. Dewey's naturalism was not a reductive materialism but rather a metaphysics that stressed the continuity of existence without denying the qualitative distinctiveness of its various forms.[14]

Both inanimate and animate things interacted with their environments to establish a state of dynamic equilibrium. But an organism differed from an inanimate thing in attempting to do so in a manner that sustained itself as a "characteristic organized activity." Pure iron was indifferent to becoming iron oxide, whereas a plant tended to interact with its environment in such a way as to retain the characteristics of a plant. In an organism—a complex, integrated ("organized") history—a "selective bias in interactions with environing things is exercised so as to maintain *itself*." Organisms thus displayed a selective and discriminatory set of responses in their interactions with the rest of nature. Organisms had sensitivity, interests, and values (even those that were not aware of them), and more complex organisms had feelings, that is a "premonitory" sensitivity to that which was useful or harmful in its surroundings. And the more complex the organism (and its organs of discrimination and motor response) the more varied its feelings (*EN*, 195–198).

Complex animals had a wide range of feelings, but they did not know that they had them. Their experience was without *meaning*. With the emergence of organisms whose lives were meaningful—human beings—a new qualitative level of natural existence was reached: mental life. At this level, feelings were not just had but differentiated, named, and rendered significant. For a creature such as man, "feelings are no longer just felt. They have and they make *sense*; record and prophesy" (*EN*, 198).

The bridge between organic life and meaningful organic life was language; indeed, "mind" might best be defined, Dewey said, as "an added property assumed by a feeling creature, when it reaches that organized interaction with other living creatures which is language, communication." It was language that "changed dumb creatures—as we so significantly call them—into thinking and knowing animals and created the realm of meanings." Language was thus the antecedent—

14. On the distinctions between Deweyan naturalism and materialism see JD, Sidney Hook, and Ernest Nagel, "Are Naturalists Materialists?" *Journal of Philosophy* 42 (1945): 515–530.

not a consequence—of thought. Language did not express ideas, rather ideas were a soliloquy that was "the product and reflex of converse with others" (*EN*, 133–135). Thinking was talking to ourselves, which presupposed a prior talking with our fellows. It was not because they had minds that some creatures had language, but because they had language that they had minds.

On this account, language was a natural function of human association, "the peculiar form which interaction sometimes assumes in the case of human beings." All existents were associated, bound up in relationships with other existents, but human association had some most unusual consequences: "the significant consideration is that assemblage of organic human beings transforms sequence and coexistence into participation" (*EN*, 138). That is, in a situation shared with others human beings could—unlike other organisms—view the situation from the standpoint of all concerned. In associated human action "something is literally made common in at least two different centres of behavior" (*EN*, 141). Only transactions between human beings were "participative" or, to use a term Dewey might have found handy, "intersubjective."

Language originated, Dewey contended, in the use made by human beings of gestures and cries (in themselves meaningless modes of organic behavior) in intersubjective contexts of "mutual assistance and direction." The "establishment of cooperation in an activity in which there are partners, and in which the activity of each is modified and regulated by partnership" was at the root of language. To understand was to act together, to fail to understand was to thwart shared action, to misunderstand was to act at cross-purposes. Language emerged as the "tool of tools" for an organism capable of assuming the standpoint of another in order to act with that other. Events and things took on their initial meanings in the course of these cooperative transactions; words and other signs became names—things with significance—when they established "a genuine community of action." Meaning, in brief, was symptomatic of a "community of partaking" (*EN*, 139–141, 145–146).

Things acquired meaning in social life "by having their potential consequences identified with them as their properties." Events that had acquired meaning in the course of communication became *objects*, events-with-meaning. "Without language, the qualities of organic action that are feelings are pains, pleasures, odors, colors, noises, tones, only potentially and proleptically. With language they are discriminated and identified. They are then 'objectified'; they are immediate traits of things" (*EN*, 198). Meaning was therefore an added trait that things took on in human experience; they became literally *marked* by their meanings.

The capacity to invest nature with meaning was, by Dewey's lights, the jewel in the crown of man's estate. "Of all affairs," he said, "communication is the most wonderful. That things should be able to pass from the plane of external pushing and pulling to that of revealing themselves to man, and thereby to themselves; and that the fruit of communication should be participation, sharing, is a wonder by the side of which transubstantiation pales" (*EN*, 132). Meaningful things could lead a "double life," for once things had meaning inference and reasoning were possible. "In addition to their original existence, they are subject to ideal experimentation: their meanings may be infinitely combined and re-arranged in imagination, and the outcome of this inner experimentation—which is thought—may issue forth in interaction with crude or raw events. Meanings having been deflected from the rapid and roaring stream of events into a calm and traversable canal, rejoin the main stream, and color, temper and compose its course." Once funded with meaning, the qualitative immediacies of experience ceased to be "inarticulate consummations" because "when something can be said of qualities they are purveyors of instruction" (*EN*, 132–133).

Meaningful existence was potentially artful existence, for an awareness of the potential consequences of things opened the door to the control of those consequences. In acquiring meaning, things became "infinitely more amenable to management, more permanent and more accommodating, than events in their first estate" (*EN*, 132). When a consummatory experience became articulate, it revealed the relationships that comprised its history and thereby rendered itself subject to intentional approximation. A meaningful world opened the possibility of consummations of choice. Art, broadly conceived, was the production of consummations of choice, the intelligent direction of the processes and materials of nature into "achieved and enjoyed meanings" (*EN*, 269).

In art, relationships of cause and effect, antecedent and consequent, were converted into bonds of means-ends, a conversion of "physical and brute relationships into connections of meanings characteristic of the possibilities of nature" (*EN*, 277). Means and ends, that is, were causes and effects of a special sort, those produced by the arts of an organism able to invest the world with meaning. "Means are always at least causal conditions; but causal conditions are means only when they possess an added qualification; that, namely, of being freely used, because of perceived connection with chosen consequences. . . . Similarly consequences, ends, are at least effects; but effects are not ends unless thought has perceived and freely chosen the conditions and processes that are their conditions" (*EN*, 275).

Because its experience was meaningful, the human organism could grasp the tendencies of things. The artist grasped "tendencies as possibilities" and directed these tendencies as means toward chosen goals or ends-in-view. The relationship of means and ends in this process was not an extrinsic, mechanical relationship of simply "antecedent to" and "consequent of" but an intrinsic, organic relationship of "instrument for" and "fulfillment in." In building a house, for example:

> The end-in-view is not just a remote and final goal to be hit upon after a sufficiently great number of coerced motions have been duly performed. The end-in-view is a plan which is *contemporaneously* operative in selecting and arranging materials. The latter, brick, stone, wood and mortar, are means only as the end-in-view is actually incarnate in them, in forming them. Literally, they *are* the end in its present stage of realization. The end-in-view is present at each stage of the process; it is present as the *meaning* of the materials used and acts done; without its informing presence, the latter are in no sense "means"; they are merely extrinsic causal conditions. (*EN*, 280)

In the work of art, ends and means were constitutive of each other, and distinctions between them were analytic, not material or even chronological.

Fine art, Dewey argued, was not to be distinguished from useful art, for art at its best was at once consummatory and instrumental. Indeed, "great art" was marked by the capacity of its objects to afford "continuously renewed delight," to be "indefinitely instrumental to *new* satisfying events." Its capacity to provide satisfaction under changing conditions and on repeated approach was the source of its staying power. "A consummatory object that is not also instrumental turns in time to the dust and ashes of boredom. The 'eternal' quality of great art is its renewed instrumentality for further consummatory experiences." Those who said that fine art was "good in itself" often meant that it had "an indefinitely expansive and radiating instrumental efficacy." In this sense, fine art comprised more than what were conventionally termed the "fine arts" such as painting, literature, and music. "Any activity that is productive of objects whose perception is an immediate good, and whose operation is a continual source of enjoyable perception of other events exhibits fineness of art. There are acts of all kinds that directly

refresh and enlarge the spirit and that are instrumental to the production of new objects and dispositions which are in turn productive of
further refinements and replenishments" (*EN*, 274). Things of use
were not without beauty, and things of beauty were not without their
uses—though each might typically be primarily perceived as useful or
beautiful. "The only *basic* distinction is that between bad art and good
art, and this distinction, between things that meet the requirements of
art and those that do not, applies equally to things of use and of beauty.
Capacity to offer to perception meaning in which fruition and efficacy
interpenetrate is met by different products in various degrees of fullness; it may be missed altogether by pans and poems alike. The difference between the ugliness of a mechanically conceived and executed
utensil and of a meretricious and pretentious painting is one only of
content or material; in form, both are articles, and bad articles" (*EN*,
283).

Dewey was eager not only to contest distinctions between fine and
useful art but to broaden the definition of art to include all "action that
deals with materials and energies outside the body, assembling, refining, combining, manipulating them until their new state yields a satisfaction not afforded by their crude condition" (*EN*, 267). In particular,
he was anxious to establish the claim that "thinking is preeminently an
art" and thereby to call into question rigid distinctions between art and
science. The propositions produced by thinking were as much works of
art as were symphonies. "Conclusion and premise," he said, "are
reached by a procedure comparable to the use of boards and nails in
making a box; or of paint and canvas in making a picture. If defective
materials are employed or if they are put together carelessly and awk-
wardly, the result is defective. In some cases the result is called unwor-
thy, in others, ugly; in others, inept; in others, wasteful, inefficient, and
in still others untrue, false. But in each case, the condemnatory adjective refers to the resulting work judged in the light of its method of
production." Indeed, because thinking—"the art of constructing true
perceptions"—was so essential to the practice of other arts, it occupied
a privileged position among them, which should not set knowledge
apart from other works of art but more securely establish its rightful
place in the museum of life (*EN*, 283–284).

Apart from the exercise of its capacity for insight into the tendencies
of nature and its ability to direct them toward ends-in-view, the human
organism lived at the psychophysical level of existence. Apart from art,
that is, human life was brutish, a life of meaningless feelings, appetites,
satisfactions, and sufferings. Unfortunately, much of life was lived at

this level, bereft of art. "Our liberal and rich ideas, our adequate appreciations, due to productive art are hemmed in by an unconquered domain in which we are everywhere exposed to the incidence of unknown forces and hurried fatally to unforseen consequences" (*EN*, 278–279). Sometimes these forces produced consequences in which we delighted, but, Dewey advised, before we took these goods as altogether good we should face up to their capricious nature compared to the goods of art. "The goods of art are not the less good in their goodness than the gifts of nature; while in addition they are such as to bring with themselves open-eyed confidence. They are fruits of means consciously employed; fulfillments whose further consequences are secured by conscious control of the causal conditions which enter into them. Art is the sole alternative to luck" (*EN*, 279).

Art rendered human beings the most fortunate of organisms by providing them with an unparalleled control over their fate. But this control was not, and could not be, absolute. A proper appreciation of the powers and limitations of art—particularly the art of knowledge—should, Dewey suggested, forestall both hubris and despair and engender both humility and faith. "A mind that has opened itself to experience and that has ripened through its discipline knows its own littleness and impotencies; it knows that its wishes and acknowledgments are not final measures of the universe whether in knowledge or in conduct, and hence are, in the end, transient." But such a mind knows as well that its sense of power and achievement "are also the doing of the universe, and they in some way, however slight, carry the universe forward" (*EN*, 313–314). Man was not the measure of all things, but neither he nor his aspirations were unnatural:

> Fidelity to the nature to which we belong, as parts however weak, demands that we cherish our desires and ideals till we have converted them into intelligence, revised them in terms of the ways and means which nature makes possible. When we have used our thought to its utmost and have thrown into the moving unbalanced balance of things our puny strength, we know that though the universe slay us still we may trust, for our lot is one with whatever is good in existence. We know that such thought and effort is one condition of the coming into existence of the better. As far as we are concerned it is the only condition, for it alone is in our power. To ask more than this is childish; but to ask less is a recreance no less egotistic, involving no less a cutting of ourselves from the universe than does the expectation that it meet and satisfy our every wish. To ask in good faith as much as this from ourselves is to stir into motion every capacity of imagination, and to exact from action every skill and bravery. (*EN*, 314)

Neither optimism and self-aggrandizing arrogance nor pessimism and self-denigrating abasement but rather meliorism and hope were the appropriate responses to "the peculiar intermixture of support and frustration of man by nature which constitutes experience" (*EN*, 314).

If man would live as man and not as a brute, Dewey said, he must struggle to live by his intelligence in a world that "induces and partially sustains meanings and goods, and at critical junctures withdraws assistance and flouts its own creatures." Nature, as any philosopher who refused to privilege a "special impulse or staked-off section of experience" had to admit, was an unavoidable mix of limits and possibilities, constraints and prospects. It denied to man the roles of either "ruthless overlord" or "oppressed subject" (*EN*, 314–315). Intelligence—"the use of science in criticizing and re-creating the casual goods of nature into intentional and conclusive goods of art"—offered amelioration but not domination. "Thoughtful valuation" offered hope against suffering and contingency but, as William James had often said, no guarantee against shipwreck: "faith in wholesale and final triumph is fantastic." Critical intelligence claimed no absolute virtues. It professed to be only a relatively better method than the alternatives for constructing "freer and more secure goods," and, as such, Dewey concluded, it was "the reasonable object of our deepest faith and loyalty, the stay and support of all reasonable hopes" (*EN*, 325–326).

Experience and Nature was widely greeted as one of the most important philosophical works of the new century. In what would become the most cited estimate of the book, Oliver Wendell Holmes, Jr. (himself quoted extensively in the closing pages of the text) remarked that, though "incredibly ill written," it had "a feeling of intimacy with the inside of the cosmos that I found unequaled. So methought God would have spoken had He been inarticulate but keenly desirous to tell you how it was." An even more enthusiastic reviewer declared that Dewey's metaphysics broke upon the intellectual landscape "like a new sun—shedding life-giving light and warmth over the very human world—on rich and poor, alike, on the just and on the unjust." But not all hearts were warmed by the book, and professional philosophers in particular remained cool to Dewey's radical dissolution of their prized problems.[15]

Some of this opposition was the fault of Dewey's prose: as Holmes complained, his language was loose, his definitions slippery, and his arguments often elusive. Yet many of Dewey's critics understood his

15. Oliver Wendell Holmes, Jr., to Frederick Pollock, 15 May 1931, in *Holmes-Pollock Letters: The Correspondence of Mr. Justice Holmes and Sir Frederick Pollock, 1874–1932*, ed. Mark DeWolf Howe (Cambridge: Harvard University Press, 1941), 2:287; Joseph K. Hart, *Survey*, 15 November 1925: 239, as quoted in Dykhuizen, p. 214.

metaphysics well enough, and their objections were substantive. He promised a systematic and full description of the generic traits of nature, they noted, but offered instead a selective discussion largely neglectful of and seemingly uncurious about what the world might be like apart from situations involving the human organism. Dewey offered no evidence that his list of traits was exhaustive, and less than a third of the way into the book he was focusing almost exclusively on a discussion of what experience might tell us about those natural transactions involving human beings rather than on what it might tell us about more inclusive features of existence. Dewey conceded there was more to nature than experience but had little to say about this "more," and even sympathetic critics expressed disappointment that his metaphysics was so decidedly anthropocentric. "We hoped that the experience which men have and have had would be surveyed, analyzed, and interpreted so as to throw light upon—not the experiences which are 'had'—but upon the nature of that world or worlds which comprise the environment of human life and experience," George P. Adams said. But instead Dewey offered "an inquiry into the nature of human goods and meanings and the possibility of their intelligent liberation and control."[16]

The most pointed, and influential, criticism along these lines was George Santayana's. Dewey's metaphysics, Santayana charged, was marked and distorted by a "dominance of the foreground," that is, by an exclusive concern with human experience and with nature as experienced, and the result was a "half-hearted and short-winded" naturalism. Santayana, who considered himself a wholehearted, long-winded naturalist, contended that "in nature there is no foreground or background, no here, no now, no moral cathedra, no centre so really central as to reduce all other things to mere margins and mere perspectives. A foreground is by definition relative to some chosen point of view, to the station assumed in the midst of nature by some creature tethered by fortune to a particular time and place. If such a foreground becomes dominant in a philosophy naturalism is abandoned." Dewey, in short, was himself guilty of the fallacy of "selective emphasis," not in privileging some aspect of experience over others but in privileging experience itself.[17]

Dewey responded that if his humanistic naturalism appeared half-hearted to Santayana, Santayana's own decentered naturalism seemed

16. George P. Adams, *International Journal of Ethics* 36 (1926): 201, as quoted in Dykhuizen, p. 215.

17. George Santayana, "Dewey's Naturalistic Metaphysics" (1925), *Later Works* 3:373–375.

"broken-backed" to him because it excluded most of human experience from nature. Santayana's assertion that nature had no foregrounds and backgrounds was sheer dogmatism. He offered no evidence for it, and, on the face of it, it contradicted the evidence of nature as experienced. Only by the dictatorial banishment of experience from nature could this view be sustained, thereby setting up the very sort of ontological break between man and nature that naturalism was presumably designed to preclude. Santayana's removal of foregrounds and backgrounds from nature struck Dewey as an "adjuration of all that is human," a "denaturing" of the distinctively human simply because it was so. "It is in virtue of what I call naturalism," he said, "that such a gulf as Mr. Santayana puts between nature and man—social or conventional man, if you will—appears incredible, unnatural and, if I am rightly informed as to the history of culture, reminiscent of supernatural beliefs. To me human affairs, associative and personal, are projections, continuations, complications, of the nature which exists in the physical and pre-human world. There is no gulf, no two spheres of existence, no 'bifurcation.' For this reason, there are in nature both foregrounds and backgrounds, heres and theres, centres and perspectives, foci and margins. If there were not, the story and scene of man would involve a complete break with nature, the insertion of unaccountable and unnatural conditions and factors." The foreground of human experience is not a screen, it is a "foreground *of* nature." It does not block our passage to the background; it conducts us there:

The main features of human life (culture, experience, history—or whatever name may be preferred) are indicative of outstanding features of nature itself—of centres and perspectives, contingencies and fulfillments, crises and intervals, histories, uniformities, and particularizations. This is the extent and method of my "metaphysics": the large and constant features of human sufferings, enjoyments, trials, failures and successes together with the institutions of art, science, technology, politics, and religion which mark them, communicate genuine features of the world within which man lives.

It was precisely because experience was the foreground of nature that we are able to "come to reasonable terms with its constituents and relations" and not "merely fall back on an 'animal faith' that there is some adorable substance behind."[18]

18. "Half-Hearted Naturalism" (1927), *Later Works* 3:73–76. See also "Philosophy as a Fine Art. Review of George Santayana's *The Realm of Essence*" (1928), *Later Works* 3:287–293. Some years later Dewey engaged in notable exchanges with Morris R. Cohen and

Although this reply was effective, criticisms such as those Santayana advanced clearly troubled Dewey (and subsequent interpreters of his metaphysics). For a second edition of *Experience and Nature* published in 1929, he completely rewrote the first chapter of the book to try to take account of them. There was, of course, more to nature than the foreground of experience, he acknowledged there. But experience provided our only route into nonexperiential existence, as the practice of many natural scientists indicated. "A geologist living in 1928 tells us about events that happened not only before he was born but millions of years before any human being came into existence on this earth. He does so by starting from things that are now the material of experience." It would be foolish to deny that "experience as an existence is something that occurs only under highly specialized conditions, such as are found in a highly organized creature which in turn requires a specialized environment. There is no evidence that experience occurs everywhere and everywhen." But at the same time, a decent respect for the discoveries of science required that one recognize that "when experience does occur, no matter at what limited portion of time and space, it enters into possession of some portion of nature and in such a manner as to render other of its precincts accessible" (*EN*, 12).

This methodological claim was important and compelling. Yet it did not change the fact that Dewey himself engaged in very little of this foreground to background movement in the chapters that followed his methodological prolegomenon. Rather, he devoted most of his attention to demonstrating how all sorts of difficulties about experience which had bedeviled philosophers for centuries might be cleared up if one assumed that experience was in and of nature. If experience was so, then to analyze experience was, to be sure, to analyze nature, but it was not to analyze it generically. Thus, to cite perhaps the most important example of this ambiguity, Dewey claimed that every natural event possessed unique qualities, yet centered his analysis on those types of quality which could be characteristic only of experiential transactions. Sometimes he justified this focus by arguing that it was best to observe nature functioning at its most complicated and complex level, that is, in human society. Yet, insofar as the emergence of new plateaus of exis-

---

Sholom J. Kahn which moved along similar lines. See Cohen, "Some Difficulties in Dewey's Anthropocentric Naturalism" (1940), *Later Works* 14:379–410, and JD, "Nature in Experience" (1940), *Later Works* 14:141–150; Kahn, "Experience and Existence in Dewey's Naturalistic Metaphysics," JD, "Experience and Existence: A Comment," and Kahn, "The Status of the Potential: A Reply to Professor Dewey," *Philosophy and Phenomenological Research* 9 (1948): 316–321, 709–716.

tence entailed qualitative changes in natural events, a long-winded naturalism had to advance and test some inferences about the qualities events would have at less complex levels of existence if the claim that all existents had distinctive qualities (apart from those that appeared in experiential situations) was to be sustained. One could not presume these qualities were the same as those experienced at the "mental" level—indeed, one could safely assume they were not. Yet Dewey said next to nothing about what *these* qualities might be, and what he did say failed to convince many of his critics that "quality" was a generic trait inclusive of experiential and nonexperiential transactions.[19]

Dewey himself believed that other philosophers had so much difficulty appreciating his metaphysics because they were unable to wean themselves from subjectivist, dualistic notions of experience, and late in life he said that, had he known better, he would have titled his book *Culture and Nature* and avoided the term "experience" as much as possible. Theoretically, "experience" was precisely the term he needed because of its double-barreled meaning, but historically this term, which had begun life as part of an effort to liberate philosophy from "desiccated abstractions," had itself become a desiccated abstraction designating a private, mental, psychic way of experiencing. "My insistence that 'experience' also designates *what* is experienced was a mere ideological thundering in the Index for it ignored the ironical twist which made this use of 'experience' strange and incomprehensible." The term "culture," on the other hand, seemed to Dewey to have retained the double-barreled meaning he was after:

> The name "culture" in its anthropological (not its Matthew Arnold) sense designates the vast range of things experienced in an indefinite variety of ways. It possesses as a name just that body of substantial references which "experience" as a name has lost. It names artifacts which rank as "material" and operations upon and with material things. The facts named by "culture" also include the whole body of beliefs, attitudes, dispositions which are scientific and "moral" and which as a matter of cultural fact decide the specific uses to which the "material" constituents of culture are put and which accordingly deserve, philosophically speaking, the name "ideal" (even the name "spiritual," if intelligibly used).

19. For an influential critical discussion of Dewey's analysis of quality see Richard Bernstein, "John Dewey's Metaphysics of Experience," *Journal of Philosophy* 58 (1961): 5–14. As Bernstein notes, Dewey sometimes argued that qualities were not intrinsic possessions of things but potentialities of natural transactions, but here again he seemed interested almost exclusively in those potentialities released in transactions involving human beings. See "The Inclusive Philosophic Idea" (1928), *Later Works* 3:41–54.

"Culture" not only posited a reciprocity of the ideal and material, it brought together the too often compartmentalized realms of experience—religion, politics, art, economics, etc.—into a "human and humanistic unity." Finally, it argued for the very sort of *social* psychology outlined in *Human Nature and Conduct*. As the great anthropologist Bronislaw Malinowski had put it, "Culture is *at the same time* psychological and collective." Dewey's fascination with and respect for anthropology already evident in the twenties in the pages of *Experience and Nature* (and in his appreciative response to such studies as Robert and Helen Lynd's *Middletown*) had by the late forties reached the point that he believed that adoption of the concept of culture was "of utmost importance if philosophy is to be comprehensive without becoming stagnant."[20]

The persistent misunderstandings of Dewey's metaphysics by idealists and realists and the ongoing efforts to place him in one or the other of these conventional pigeonholes suggests that Dewey's sense of the debilitating effects of his idiosyncratic notion of "experience" was a keen one. A switch from "experience" to "culture" might have had the clarifying effect Dewey hoped for, though "culture" has proved as slippery a term as "experience." At least, one can lament that what appears on the basis of the fragments that remain to have been the beginning of some extremely fertile thinking on Dewey's part about "culture" and its potential as an analytic tool never saw the light of day.

Yet such a terminological switch would not, on the face of it, have addressed the contention that his metaphysics (if not his metaphysical method) was anthropocentric—even such self-styled Deweyans as Sidney Hook admitted as much. Cultural anthropology, after all, was par excellence the study of objects, events-with-meaning. Intersubjective though it might be, "culture" was as much "foreground" as "experience." Whatever Dewey's ambitions and intentions, *Experience and Nature* was, for the most part, a rich and original philosophical anthropology that fell short of a "wholehearted" investigation of the generic traits of nature. But for his democratic theory, it was enough that Dewey's metaphysics was "merely" a rich and original philosophical anthropology. Indeed, as I will suggest, Dewey's concerns about democracy in the twenties may well have had something to do with its being that above all else.[21]

---

20. "Experience and Nature: A Reintroduction" (1951), *Later Works* 1:361–364. See also "Anthropology and Ethics" (1927), *Later Works* 3:11–24; *Individualism Old and New* (1930), *Later Works* 5:45–49.

21. See Sidney Hook, "Introduction" (1981), *Later Works* 1:vii–xxiii. R. W. Sleeper offers a vigorous riposte to Hook, Bernstein, and others who claimed Dewey offered only

THE QUEST FOR CERTAINTY

In addition to offering a full and explicit alternative to the "bad metaphysics" that plagued Western philosophy, Dewey also worked up an extended historical explanation in the twenties of the origins and persistence of such spurious thinking. In the antebellum years, he had challenged idealism and realism dialectically, and his opponents had often responded with a reductionist intellectual history that tried to dismiss his work as a peculiarly American delusion. After the war, Dewey himself sought to exploit more fully the polemical possibilities of intellectual history. Having shown how empirical naturalism could dissolve the conundrums that bedeviled philosophers, he sought as well to show how it was that philosophers had put themselves in these binds in the first place by revealing the circumstances in which they arose and the rationalizations they performed—thereby extending the sort of history of ideas he had ventured in a more limited way in *German Philosophy and Politics*.

As a historian of philosophy, Dewey displayed considerable talent for what Richard Rorty has coyly termed "first-rate" criticism of philosophy, that is, criticism that takes philosophers at their best (unlike second-rate criticism that pokes holes in their thinking at its worst) only to show that, for the critic and his readers, these philosophers are not of much use. As Rorty says, the most effective form of such "robustly external" criticism is a "dramatic narrative" like that to be found in *Reconstruction in Philosophy* and *The Quest for Certainty*; that is to say, a narrative that "displays the historical situation in which the philosopher being criticized worked, the contemporary historical situation in which the critic himself is working, the connecting links between these two situations, and the inefficacy of the philosopher's means to achieve the goals which the critic (and, by the time they have finished reading the narrative, his readers) are trying to achieve. . . . Such narratives typically tell us that the tradition has exhausted its alternatives, and that it is time to start afresh—to achieve new ends with new means." Dewey was well aware that such dramatic narratives were self-serving. "Common frankness," he said, required him to admit that his own destructive account of the Western philosophical tradition was "given with malice prepense."[22]

---

a "metaphysics of experience" rather than a successful "metaphysics of existence" in *The Necessity of Pragmatism*, but, as my remarks suggest, I am unconvinced.

22. Richard Rorty, "Posties," *London Review of Books*, 3 September 1987: 11; *Reconstruction in Philosophy* (1920), *Middle Works* 12:93.

Dewey began his intellectual history as he began his metaphysics, with an account of the crucial role that the precariousness and uncertainty of nature played in human experience. Indeed, in a nutshell, one could say his narrative was the story of an inevitably unsuccessful pursuit by philosophers of a therapeutic quest for absolutely certain knowledge of truth, goodness, and beauty in an unavoidably contingent world. And the moral of this story was to abandon this quest and substitute "a search for security by practical means in place of quest of absolute certainty by cognitive means."[23]

Pushing the beginning of his story back beyond the mystifications of modern epistemology he had attacked before the war, Dewey now argued that philosophy got off on the wrong foot from the outset. His interest in classical philosophy renewed by the Aristotelian turn in his own metaphysics, he dwelt at greatest length in his pugnacious intellectual history on the remarkable achievements and unfortunate defects of Greek civilization, calling for a recovery of the classical appreciation of qualitative experience while at the same time arguing that responsibility for many of the shortcomings of Western philosophy could be laid at the feet of Plato and Aristotle, who, each in his own fashion, had hypostatized the aesthetic realm of "secure and self-possessed meaning" into a transcendent reality and confused the immediate enjoyment of form with knowledge of eternal objects.[24]

At the dawn of human culture, Dewey's narrative began, primitive men and women faced the perils of a universe largely beyond their control. They searched for any means that would protect them from the hostile forces surrounding them and provide a measure of well-being. To some degree they found relief in the practical arts they developed, but the knowledge that accompanied such arts was itself, at best, probable and hence precarious, and the limited range of experience

23. *The Quest for Certainty* (1929), *Later Works* 4:20. Page numbers for further references (*QC*) appear in the text.
24. As was the case with Dewey's appreciation of descriptive metaphysics, his enthusiasm for classical philosophy owed much to Woodbridge's influence. In addition to the sweeping narrative in such books as *Reconstruction in Philosophy* and *The Quest for Certainty*, Dewey also undertook more specialized studies in intellectual history in the interwar years, contributing several essays to the philosophy department's *Studies in the History of Ideas*. See, for example, "The 'Socratic Dialogues' of Plato" (1925), *Later Works* 2:124–140. On Dewey's treatment of the Greeks see Walter Veazle, "John Dewey and the Revival of Greek Philosophy," *University of Colorado Studies in Philosophy* 2 (1961):1–10; John Anton, "John Dewey and the Ancient Philosophies," *Phenomenological Research* 25 (1965): 477–499; Frederick Anderson, "Dewey's Experiment with Greek Philosophy," *International Philosophical Quarterly* 7 (1967):86–100; Joseph Betz, "Dewey and Socrates," *Transactions of the Charles S. Pierce Society* 16 (1980): 329–356.

subject to such knowledge paled before the extraordinary and unaccountable events beyond the reach of human powers. As a result, a "fundamental dualism of human attention and regard" emerged, two distinct and unequal realms of experience and belief. "The inferior was that in which man could foresee and in which he had instruments and arts by which he might expect a reasonable degree of control. The superior was that of occurrences so uncontrollable that they testified to the presence and operation of powers beyond the scope of everyday and mundane things" (QC, 11). The practical arts were confined to the former realm, while religious rites and ceremonies circumscribed the more prestigious and sublime matters.

Philosophy, which began with the Greeks, inherited this latter, religious realm and gave it a rational formulation and justification. Plato and Aristotle destroyed the imaginative forms of Greek popular religion but not its substance: "The belief that the divine encompasses the world was detached from its mythical context and made the basis of philosophy." Mythic gods were replaced by a supreme Reality of logical forms with necessary and immutable characteristics, and "pure contemplation of these forms was man's highest and most divine bliss, a communion with unchangeable truth" (QC, 13).

Greek philosophy thus had the salutary effect of eliminating myths and superstitions and setting up the ideals of science and a life of reason (for some), but it did so without challenging the dualism of attention and regard established by primitive religion. The Greeks retained the notion of "a higher realm of fixed reality of which alone true science is possible and of an inferior world of changing things with which experience and practical matters are concerned." Change in nature was discerned qualitatively as movement toward inherent ends, a fulfillment in perfect objects. Greek science thus posited no sharp break between imperfect nature and transcendent form: the former was not unreal but less real, infected by "non-Being." Philosophy or theoretical knowledge—the highest and purest kind of knowledge—was exclusively concerned with the superior realm, with "the disclosure of the Real in itself, of Being in and of itself." Practical matters—those infected with non-Being—were left to lower forms of wisdom, judgment, and technical expertise. Such lower forms of knowledge were inferior because they were not knowledge of the fully and purely Real. Only by contemplative philosophical insight could man find the certainty he sought beyond the contingencies of ordinary experience. Thus Greek philosophy "translated into a rational form the doctrine of escape from the vicissitudes of existence by means of measures which do not demand an active coping with conditions. For deliverance by means of rites and cults, it substituted deliverance through reason. This deliverance was an intellectual, a theoretical affair, constituted by a knowledge to be attained apart from practical activity" (QC, 13–14). Plato and Aristotle were the first great philosophical escape artists, turning their backs on the precariousness of human experience to dwell in a more perfect and certain world of rational forms. They gave the deprecation of practice an ontological justification and established the predisposition of subsequent philosophers toward "the universal, invariant, and eternal" (QC, 16).

Dewey's narrative skipped lightly over the centuries separating Aristotle and Descartes. Thinkers in the intervening period, he contended, had made no significant intellectual contributions to the quest for certainty. Rather, they had leaned heavily on the root assumptions of classical philosophy to provide refuge for favored objects of value (which were, to be sure, often quite different from those of the Greeks). Medieval thinkers, in particular, Dewey quickly dispatched as derivative, though he did pay the church a backhanded compliment for its decisive influence in the popularization of the wayward thinking of the Greeks. Christian theologians, he noted, effectively adapted to their own purposes the Greek glorification of "a life of knowing apart from and above a life of doing." In medieval thought "the perfect and ultimate reality was God; to know him was eternal bliss. The world in which man lived and acted was a world of trials and troubles to test and prepare him for a higher destiny. Through thousands of ways, including histories and rites, with symbols that engaged the emotions and imagination, the essentials of the doctrine of classic philosophy filtered its way into the popular mind" (QC, 233–234).

In Dewey's treatment of the history of Western thought the most important watershed was the scientific revolution of the seventeenth century, which demolished the qualitative, aestheticized natural science of the Greeks and replaced it with a far more instrumentally effective science grounded in abstract mathematical and mechanical relationships. But, by Dewey's lights, this was a halfway revolution, for it failed to depose the classical metaphysical equation of the known with the real and, as a consequence, engendered many of the pseudo-problems of modern philosophy. The quest for certainty might have—and should have—ended in the seventeenth century were it not for the continued power of the assumption that "what is known, what is true for cognition, is what is real in being" (QC, 17).

The great achievement of modern science, Dewey argued, was to have stripped nature of its qualities in order that the relationships between things might be better understood. Effective thinking, such scientists as Galileo and Newton recognized, required a turning away from the immediate qualities of things to a consideration of things as signs. This bracketing of immediacy set knowledge on the path of abstraction, which eventually resulted in the highly abstract objects of knowledge of modern science, objects denuded of all that was immediate, qualitative, final, and self-sufficient. In the wake of the scientific revolution, nature had been effectively conceived as a "mathematical-mechanical object." This conception marked an enormous advance in the capacity of human beings to regulate experience: genuine science had been impossible as long as the object of knowledge was taken in its immediacy (as the Greeks did), for this immediacy defeated "its use as indicating and implying." In their immediacy, things could not signify; to signify, things had to be drained of immediacy. Bracketing qualities for the purposes of knowledge did not logically mean denying their existence as the ends of natural transactions. Properly conceived, the abstractions of science posed no threat to noncognitive experience. Indeed, they should serve to render immediately appreciated ends more secure and extensive because science revealed "the state or order upon which the occurrence of immediate and final qualities depends. It adds to the casual having of ends an ability to regulate the date, place and manner of their emergence" (*EN*, 106, 110).

But unfortunately the scientific revolution came burdened with a bad metaphysics that confused scientific abstraction as a mediating, instrumental move in the service of experienced qualities with a radical redescription of reality which banished qualities from nature:

> The notion of knowledge as immediate possession of Being was retained when knowing as an actual affair radically altered. Even when science had come to include a method of experimental search and finding, it was still defined as insight into, grasp of, real being as such, in comparison with which other modes of experience are imperfect, confused and perverted. Hence a serious problem. If the proper object of science is a mathematico-mechanical world (as the achievements of science have proved to be the case) and if the object of science defines the true and perfect reality (as the perpetuation of the classic tradition asserted), then how can the objects of love, appreciation—whether sensory or ideal—and devotion be included within true reality? (*EN*, 109–110)

If the real was the known and only the known, as even scientists continued to believe, then nature as known was now a machine with no place for everything that made life worth living.

The scientific revolution thus broke the continuity between Being and non-Being, the transcendent and the empirical, found in classical philosophy. Nature was now not qualitatively imperfect, but not qualitative at all. Having ceded the knowledge of nature to Newtonian science, philosophers rushed to assure their readers that their values remained well protected in a transcendent realm. "Qualities, excellencies, and ends that were extruded from nature by the new science found their exclusive abode and warrant in the realm of the spiritual, which was above nature and yet which was its source and foundation" (QC, 43). In this context, philosophy became "a species of apologetic justification for belief in an ultimate reality in which the values which should regulate life and control conduct are securely enstated" (QC, 23). Yet now philosophers faced the difficult task of demonstrating how this ultimate reality could be known now that science wanted nothing to do with it, for their metaphysical premises dictated that unless values could be known they could not be real. "According to the religious and philosophic tradition of Europe," Dewey observed, "the valid status of all the highest values, the good, true, and beautiful, was bound up with their being properties of ultimate and supreme Being, namely God. All went well as long as what passed for natural science gave no offence to this conception. Trouble began when science ceased to disclose in the objects of knowledge the possession of any such properties. Then some roundabout method had to be devised for substantiating them" (QC, 34).

Much of the subsequent history of philosophy could be well told, Dewey argued, as the unsuccessful pursuit of various such roundabout methods to substantiate values without giving up the conception of knowledge as the grasp of ultimate Being, a conception that doomed this effort to failure. The scientific revolution had apparently divided matter and spirit, nature and ultimate ends and goods, science and moral reflection, and "the tension created by the opposition and yet necessary connection of nature and spirit gave rise to all the characteristic problems of modern philosophy. It could neither be frankly naturalistic, nor yet fully spiritualistic to the disregard of the conclusions of physical science. Since man was on the one hand a part of nature and on the other hand a member of the realm of spirit, all problems came to a focus in his double nature" (QC, 43).

A variety of solutions to this dualism had come and gone since the seventeenth century. Spinoza had offered a breathtaking synthesis that brought the true and the good together under the reign of rational natural law, but some found that this reign granted too many concessions to science and others found it neglectful of the experimentalism at the heart of the new science. Kant, building on older distinctions between the province of faith and reason, had argued for a "two-fold nature of truth," divided between the cognitive certitudes of science and the moral assurances of a higher reason—a clever job of intellectual carpentry in which, unfortunately, "morals become an affair of formulas, often sublime in themselves, but without possibility of effective translation, intellectual or practical, into the affairs of the workaday world."[25] Others, dissatisfied with Kant's convenient rationalization of the dualism between scientific knowledge and moral conviction and the empty formalism of his ethics, had laid claim to a higher science that would reintegrate the realms of fact and value. Absolute idealists such as Hegel had tried to spiritualize nature, while evolutionary naturalists such as Spencer had tried to materialize spirit. Each of these diverse and incompatible resolutions of the cultural predicament attendant on the cognitive triumphs of modern science had been plagued with difficulties and none had carried the day. As a result, philosophy, and Western culture at large, had been afflicted by a seemingly interminable and irresolvable "conflict of authorities" (QC, 40–53).

By the early twentieth century, some influential voices among philosophers were arguing that they should stick to the apprehension of the only certain and universal knowledge available, that of formal logical and mathematical propositions. The great mistake of philosophy, from this point of view, had been "to admit values in any shape within the sacred enclosure of perfect science." This perspective, Dewey said, had the virtue of owning up to the inherently contingent character of values (and, indeed, of existence) and hence was the "logical development of that strain in historic philosophy which identifies its subject-matter with whatever is capable of taking on the form of cognitive certainty" (QC, 53–54). But it also foreshadowed a severing of philosophers from the problems of their culture, and even more important, it signified the presence within that culture of "intellectual confusion, practically chaos, in respect to the criteria and principles which are employed in framing judgments and reaching conclusions upon things of most vital importance" (QC, 57). Dividing up knowledge between scientists who studied a nature without qualities and philosophers who studied forms without existence and relegating desire to the no-know land of subjectivity, this flight from ethical judgment in the quest for certainty cut the tie between knowledge and values and left the direc-

25. "Kant after Two Hundred Years" (1924), *Middle Works* 15:11.

tion of the moral life to "custom, external pressure and the free play of impulse" (QC, 55). Seeking to solve their conflicts by running away from them, philosophers threatened to leave their culture bereft of intellectual authority where it was most needed. "Old beliefs have dissolved as far as definite operative hold upon the regulation of criticism and the formation of plans and policies, working ideals and ends, is concerned. And there is nothing else to take their place" (QC, 57).

This situation had brought some secular intellectuals to the brink of existential despair, perhaps most evident in Joseph Wood Krutch's book *The Modern Temper* (1929), a widely discussed meditation on the crisis of belief engendered by modern science published the same year as Dewey's *Quest for Certainty*. Few captured better than Krutch the apparently stark consequences of the triumphs of scientific knowledge and the failures of religion and philosophy to provide human values with the certainty demanded by the metaphysical paradigm established by the Greeks:

> We went to science in search of light, not merely upon the nature of matter, but upon the nature of man as well, and though that which we have received may be light of a sort, it is not adapted to our eyes and is not anything by which we can see. Since thought began we have groped in the dark among shadowy shapes, doubtfully aware of landmarks looming uncertainly here and there—of moral principles, human values, aims, and ideals. We hoped for an illumination in which they would at last stand clearly and unmistakably forth, but instead they appear even less certain and less substantial than before—mere fancies and illusions generated by nerve actions that seem terribly remote from anything we can care about or based upon relativities that accident can shift. We had been assured that many troublesome shadows would flee away, that superstitious fears, irrational repugnances, and all manner of bad dreams would disappear. And so in truth many have. But we never supposed that most of the things we cherished would prove equally unsubstantial, that all the aims we thought we vaguely perceived, all the values we pursued, and all the principles we clung to were but similar shadows, and that either the light of science is somehow deceptive or the universe, emotionally and spiritually, a vast emptiness.

Science, Krutch concluded, had rendered humanism and nature utterly incompatible. Unable to deny its most urgent desires and no longer vulnerable to the tricks of faith which had suggested that its values might have a place in the world, humanity was, at best, consigned to a "tragic existence in a universe alien to the deepest needs of its nature."[26]

This sort of despair, Dewey admitted, was understandable given the premises on which it rested. But these premises were faulty, and Krutch's dark vision confirmed Dewey's warning that the combination of good science and bad metaphysics would render the human self "an unnaturalized and unnaturalizable alien in the world." Science did seem to strip reality of the qualities that lent value to human experience, but this claim (or fear) could be sustained only if one conflated experience and knowing:

> If and as far as the qualitative world was taken to be an object of knowledge, and not of experience in some other form than knowing, and as far as knowing was held to be the standard or sole valid mode of experiencing, the substitution of Newtonian for Greek science (the latter being but a rationalized arrangement of the qualitatively enjoyed world of direct experience) signified that the properties that render the world one of delight, admiration, and esteem have been done away with. There is, however, another interpretation possible. A philosophy which holds that we experience things as they really are apart from knowing, and that knowledge is a mode of experiencing things which facilitates control of objects for purposes of non-cognitive experiences, will come to another conclusion. (QC, 79)

On this latter interpretation, what happened in the scientific revolution was that scientists, for the purposes of explanation, prediction, and control, bracketed the qualities of natural objects in order to better understand the relationships between them. Science did not know things but relations, and "the relations a thing sustains are hardly a competitor to the thing itself." In this view, "the physical object, as scientifically defined, is not a duplicated real object, but is a statement, as numerically definite as is possible, of the relations between sets of changes the qualitative object sustains with changes in other things— ideally of all things with which interaction might under any circumstances take place" (QC, 105). Science treated qualities as effects. It sought to understand how these effects were produced, not to deny their reality. Scientific objects were instruments of knowledge, and it was a grievous mistake to take these tools as substitutes for "objects as

26. Joseph Wood Krutch, *The Modern Temper: A Study and a Confession* (New York: Harcourt Brace Jovanovich, 1957, originally published in 1929), pp. 47–48, xi.

directly perceived and enjoyed." As if responding directly to Krutch, Dewey remarked that "the man who is disappointed and tragic because he cannot wear a loom is in reality no more ridiculous than are the persons who feel troubled because the objects of scientific conception of natural things have not the same uses and values as the things of direct experience" (QC, 109).

Thus it was not science but the metaphysical quest for certainty in which science had become entangled which led Krutch and others to believe that "the findings of science are a disclosure of the inherent properties of the ultimate real, of existence at large" and was to blame for the anxieties of the modern temper. "It is because of injection of an irrelevant philosophy into interpretation of the conclusions of science that the latter are thought to eliminate qualities and values from nature." Not the least of the disastrous effects of this injection was the failure to recognize that, properly conceived, science was "a search for those relations upon which the *occurrence* of real qualities and values depends, by means of which we can regulate their occurrence" (QC, 83).

Not surprisingly, Dewey eagerly welcomed the second scientific revolution fostered by the post-Newtonian physical theory of Albert Einstein and others, for he believed it lent powerful support to his instrumental conception of knowledge. Newtonian science had itself contributed to the bad metaphysics of the quest for certainty by sticking to a spectatorial notion of knowledge despite the obviously active, experimental character of its own practice and by insisting that its laws were fixed properties of unchangeable substances. Post-Newtonian physics had acknowledged the unavoidably practical character of scientific knowledge and repudiated Newton's metaphysics of fixed substances and laws. Werner Heisenberg's principle of indeterminacy, which established that the act of scientific observation made a difference in what was observed, dealt a death blow to the notion of knowledge as passive spectatorship. And physicists now conceived of laws not as properties of natural substances (which they, with Dewey, now viewed as "events" rather than substances) but as tools for the understanding of correlated changes in nature—"formulae for the prediction of the probability of an observable occurrence" (QC, 156–166).

Dewey hoped the new physics foreshadowed a broader cultural reconstruction in which the claims of reason would be supplanted by the judgments of intelligence. Reason—the artifact of the quest for certainty—"designates both an inherent immutable order of nature, superempirical in character, and the organ of mind by which this universal order is grasped. In both respects, reason is with respect to changing things the ultimate fixed standard the law physical phenomena obey, the norm human action should obey." Intelligence—the way of knowing in a world without certainty—was, by contrast, "associated with *judgment*; that is, with selection and arrangement of means to effect consequences and with choice of what we take as our ends. A man is intelligent not in virtue of having reason which grasps first and indemonstrable truths about fixed principles, in order to reason deductively from them to the particulars which they govern, but in virtue of his capacity to estimate the possibilities of a situation and to act in accordance with his estimate. In the large sense of the term, intelligence is as practical as reason is theoretical." Replacing reason with intelligence meant exchanging "a loss of theoretical certitude for a gain in practical judgment," supplanting a spectatorial, transcendent knowledge that had never been able to deliver the goods with a knowledge that had "a foothold and function within nature" and had a proven track record in directing nature's changes (*QC*, 170).

Among the proponents of reason he targeted for criticism, Dewey was more charitable to Plato and Aristotle than to their modern successors because the former had better excuse for privileging reason over intelligence. The Greeks had few means for regulating nature, and "as long as man was unable by means of the arts of practice to direct the course of events, it was natural for him to seek an emotional substitute; in the absence of actual certainty in the midst of a precarious and hazardous world, men cultivated all sorts of things that would give them the *feeling* of certainty," including philosophy (*QC*, 26). It was perfectly understandable for mankind to wish to safeguard that for which it cared the most, to save its values from the vicissitudes of experience. And, given the absence of alternatives, it was perhaps inevitable that philosophers would rush in to provide the illusion of protection by dialectically transporting these values to a transcendent realm. But, he argued, to cling to this illusion of protection when real protection (if not certain guarantees) of values was available elsewhere—in intelligent action—was the height of folly. Not only did the quest for certainty not help matters, it made things worse because it diverted energy from the efforts necessary to make values relatively secure. The philosophy most needed in the wake of modern science was not one that sought out new versions of reason but one that argued for a more expansive exercise of intelligence—"the securer, freer, and more widely shared embodiment of values in experience by means of that active control of objects which knowledge alone makes possible"

(*QC*, 30). What was needed, in brief, was pragmatism, a conception of "*both* knowledge and practice as means of making goods—excellencies of all kinds—secure in experienced existence" (*QC*, 30n). Thus, as the dramatic narratives of philosophers usually do, Dewey's intellectual history ended with himself.

Dewey was well aware of the radical challenge he was posing to his fellow philosophers. If they abandoned their commitment to the ubiquity of the knowledge relation and adopted his conviction that "the world as we experience it is a real world," they would, he rather immodestly suggested, launch a "Copernican Revolution" in thought (*QC*, 235). And the consequences of such a revolution would affect not only philosophers, for the quest for certainty was, from the outset, intimately connected to the social and political institutions of Western societies. It was sustained not only by the necessary anxieties attendant on life in a contingent world but also by class interest. That is, these anxieties had often been exploited by some to advance their interests at the expense of those of others. On the whole, philosophy had played a profoundly conservative cultural role, serving "to justify on rational grounds the spirit, though not the form, of accepted beliefs and traditional customs." The superiority Greek philosophers attributed to purely speculative, theoretical knowledge reflected the contempt of the leisured class for artisans and the contingent, useful knowledge that marked the work of the world. The supposed preeminence of the certain knowledge available to this ruling class served ideologically to legitimate their power over those whose knowledge was at best probable. Substantively, the science the Greeks grounded in philosophical insight posited a "universe with a fixed place for everything and where everything knows its place, its station and class, and keeps it."[27] Subse-

---

27. *Reconstruction in Philosophy*, 90, 113. According to Sidney Hook, it was this sort of social interpretation of the causes and consequences of transcendental metaphysics that had initially attracted him, as a young radical, to Dewey's philosophy. Reading *Reconstruction in Philosophy* in college, he saw it as a "brilliant application of the principles of historical materialism, as I understood them then as an avowed young Marxist, to philosophical thought, especially Greek thought. Most Marxist writers, including Marx and Engels themselves, made pronouncements about the influence of the mode of economic production on the development of cultural and philosophical systems of thought, but Dewey, without regarding himself as a Marxist or invoking its approach, tried to show in detail how social stratification and class struggles got expressed in the metaphysical dualism of the time and in the dominant conceptions of matter and form, body and soul, theory and practice, truth, reason, and experience" (*Out of Step: An Unquiet Life in the Twentieth Century* [New York: Harper and Row, 1987], p. 81). See also Hook, *John Dewey: An Intellectual Portrait* (New York: John Day, 1939), pp. 29–38.

quent transcendental philosophies generally sustained this conservative function and "apologetic spirit." Philosophies that attempted to protect values by spiriting them away to a certain realm beyond ordinary experience were usually seeking to safeguard prevailing social arrangements (though occasionally such a move might be made by a philosopher interested in undermining these arrangements). "A moderate amount of acquaintance with these philosophies discloses that they have been interested in justifying values drawn from current religious faiths and moral codes, not just eternal values as such:—that they have often used the concept of universal and intrinsic values to cover those which, if not parochial, were at least exponents of temporal social conditions" (QC, 54).

Unfortunately, those philosophers, like the utilitarians critical of this sort of arbitrary dogmatism or "*ipse dixitism*," as Jeremy Bentham called it, reinstated values in experience only to wall them off in a subjective realm no less inaccessible to intelligent judgment than values others had removed from nature. If transcendentalists had advanced unsubstantiated claims to certain knowledge of values, many empiricists had (as scientifically minded thinkers in the approved mode) declared themselves agnostics when it came to values and simply equated goods with subjective feelings, the desirable with the desired. As a result, modern men and women were forced to choose between "a theory that, in order to save the objectivity of judgments of values, isolates them from experience and nature, and a theory that, in order to save their concrete and human significance, reduces them to mere statements about our own feelings" (QC, 210). The first of these theories usually vested cultural authority over values in an intellectual class of one sort or another, while the second left such matters to the market, that is, to a class of a different sort. And by 1929 the market was well on its way toward colonizing the vacuum left by the waning authority of transcendentalism.

Dewey's hoped-for "Copernican revolution" offered a quite different resolution to the modern crisis of intellectual authority in the realm of values. Given the understanding central to his naturalism that science was not alien to objects of value but was instead essential to their security, he proposed that philosophers shift their focus as moral theorists from the ends or goods that should be sanctioned to the means or method by which such values should be authorized. This, he argued, meant a concerted effort to develop and institute methods for judging values "congruous with those used in scientific inquiry and adopting their conclusions; methods to be used in directing criticism and in forming the ends and purposes that are acted upon" (*QC*, 57). If one acknowledged that the search for certain, fixed, ultimate, transcendent goods was misconceived, then the crucial general question for moral theory was not what it was desirable to do in every case requiring a judgment of value—which, given the unique qualities and circumstances of each case, it was impossible to know in advance—but rather how, in every case, to decide what it was desirable to do. This would "place *method and means* upon the level of importance that has, in the past, been imputed exclusively to ends" (*QC*, 222). "Morals," he said, "is not a catalogue of acts nor a set of rules to be applied like drugstore prescriptions or cook-book recipes. The need in morals is for specific methods of inquiry and of contrivance to form plans to be used as working hypotheses in dealing with them. And the pragmatic import of the logic of individualized situations, each having its own irreplaceable good and principle, is to transfer the attention of theory from preoccupation with general conceptions to the problem of developing effective methods of inquiry."[28] If such methods of inquiry were not established, Dewey concluded, the consequences were easily foreseen. "If intelligent method is lacking, prejudice, the pressure of immediate circumstance, self-interest and class-interest, traditional customs, institutions of accidental historic origin, are *not* lacking, and they tend to take the place of intelligence" (*QC*, 211–212).

For Dewey, substituting intelligence for transcendent reason or uninterrogated desire in the moral life of a culture required vesting authority not in the insights of philosophers (or scientists) but in the deliberations of ordinary men and women skilled in the art of practical judgment—the lowly artisans with their humble, contingent, probable knowledge would claim the temple denied them by Plato and nearly every philosopher since. Philosophers might help their fellow citizens understand the logic of practical judgment, but the day-to-day exercise of that logic was the responsibility of the public. In such a culture, as one latter-day pragmatist has said, "social experimentation is the basic norm, yet it is operative only when those who must suffer the consequences have effective control over the institutions that yield the consequences, i.e., access to decision-making process. . . . The claim is that once one gives up on the search for foundations and the quest for certainty, human inquiry into truth and knowledge shifts to the social and communal circumstances under which persons can communicate

28. *Reconstruction in Philosophy*, p. 177.

and cooperate in the process of acquiring knowledge."[29] Or, as Dewey himself more elegantly put it,

> the ulterior problem of thought is to make thought prevail in experience, not just the results of thought by imposing them upon others, but the active process of thinking. The ultimate contradiction in the classic and genteel tradition is that while it made thought universal and necessary and the culminating good of nature, it was content to leave its distribution among men a thing of accident, dependent upon birth, economic, and civil status. Consistent as well as humane thought will be aware of the hateful irony of a philosophy which is indifferent to the conditions that determine the occurrence of reason while it asserts the ultimacy and universality of reason (*EN*, 99).

The proponents of intelligence had to be democrats if they were to avoid the hypocrisy of the partisans of universal reason.

A METAPHYSICS OF DEMOCRATIC COMMUNITY

Dewey's metaphysics was, as he said, a metaphysics of the common man. With this, at least, many of his critics agreed, though they hardly took this to be a virtue. The "master-burden" of Dewey's philosophy, the aristocratic Santayana sniffed, "is a profound sympathy with the enterprise of life in all lay directions, in its technical and moral complexity, and especially in its American form, where individual initiative, although still demanded and prized, is quickly subjected to overwhelming democratic control. This, if I am not mistaken, is the heart of Dewey's pragmatism, that it is the pragmatism of the people, dumb and instinctive in them, and struggling in him to a labored but radical expression."[30]

Dewey's metaphysics was also a metaphysics *for* the common man, that is, a metaphysics that attempted to provide an "intellectual warrant" for democracy. To be sure, *Experience and Nature* and *The Quest for Certainty* were in no direct sense about democracy. Yet they were, in

29. Cornel West, *The American Evasion of Philosophy: A Genealogy of Pragmatism* (Madison: University of Wisconsin Press, 1989), p. 213. See also the imaginative use and extension of Dewey's critique of the antidemocratic intentions and implications of classical philosophy and the skeptical treatment of modern "back to the polis" philosophers such as Leo Strauss, Hannah Arendt, and Hans-Georg Gadamer in Timothy V. Kaufman-Osborn, "Politics and the Invention of Reason," *Polity* 22 (1989): 679–709.

30. JD, "Half-Hearted Naturalism," p. 76; Santayana, "Dewey's Naturalistic Metaphysics," p. 370.

part, an effort to establish that the world we have is one in which a faith in democracy was reasonable. As Gouinlock has noted, Dewey's moral philosophy—including his democratic theory—"possesses its distinctive character precisely because it is an integral part of a far more inclusive philosophy," and Dewey himself insisted on this connection. It was, he said, what made his democratic theory more than "a projection of arbitrary personal preference."[31]

If democracy was to be a "reasonable persuasion," Dewey argued in "Philosophy and Democracy," a particular reading of the meaning of liberty, equality, and fraternity had to be "sanctioned and sustained by the nature of things" and those metaphysical systems that thwarted this reading had to be subverted. His metaphysics performed just this sanctioning and subverting, and, I believe, that was precisely its point.[32]

The quest for certainty had produced a notion of liberty which held that to be free was to act in accord with the fixed laws of Being: "men are free when they are rational and they are rational when they recognize and consciously conform to the necessities which the universe exemplified" (PD, 49). This notion held that "reality exists under the form of eternity." It was an "an all at once and forever affair, no matter whether the all at once be of mathematical-physical laws and structures, or a comprehensive and exhaustive divine consciousness." Characteristic of both metaphysical scientism and the idealist flight from its barren reality, this conception of freedom was "not one which is spontaneously congenial to the idea of liberty in a society which has set its heart on democracy" (PD, 50). Democracy required, rather, a world like that described in *Experience and Nature*: "a universe in which there is real uncertainty and contingency, a world which is not all in, and never will be, a world which in some respect is incomplete and in the making, and which in these respects may be made this way or that according as men judge, prize, love and labor." In such a world, men and women would not be subject to the transcendental pronouncements of philosophers or other lawgivers, nor would they despair in the face of a world denuded of value by scientistic metaphysicians. Rather, as hopeful meliorists they would act together to secure the goods of experience, "humbly grateful that a world in which the most extensive and accurate thought and reason can only take advantage of events is also a world which gives room to move about in, and which offers the delights of consumma-

31. Gouinlock, *Dewey's Philosophy of Value*, p. iii; JD, "Nature in Experience," p. 150.
32. "Philosophy and Democracy," pp. 48–49. Page numbers for further references (PD) appear in the text.

tions that are new revelations, as well as those defeats that are admonishments to conceit" (PD, 50–51).

Liberal empiricists in revolt against the conception of freedom as conformity to necessary law had attempted to protect free choice and action by grounding liberty in a metaphysics that "thought of individuals as endowed with an equipment of fixed and ready-made capacities, the operation of which if unobstructed by external restrictions would be freedom." But, Dewey argued, such a philosophy overlooked the part played by human society in the generation of wants, desires, and rights and in the development of capacities for action and, as a result, posed a less obvious but no less serious threat to democracy than its metaphysical adversaries. For—because human capacities were, to a significant degree, socially determined—the removal of obstructions to action in pursuit of "natural rights" disproportionately benefited in practice those who, by virtue of the "past accidents of history," happened to possess superior resources and "left all others at the mercy of the new social conditions brought about by the free powers of those advantageously situated." An "adjectival/adverbial" metaphysics, which held that freedom was not a substantive property of presocial human atoms but a functional characteristic of social transactions, was, Dewey contended, far more congenial to democratic reform. "Since actual, that is, effective rights and demands are products of interactions, and are not found in the orginal and isolated constitution of human nature, whether moral or psychological, mere elimination of obstructions is not enough." For democrats eager to broaden and deepen liberty, "the only possible conclusion, both intellectually and practically, is that the attainment of freedom conceived as power to act in accord with choice depends upon positive and constructive changes in social arrangements."[33]

As we have seen, Dewey regarded the quest for certainty as hostile not only to freedom but to equality (sometimes by intention and always in effect). Philosophers had repeatedly marshaled distinctions between superior and inferior realities into legitimations of social hierarchy. Largely committed to "a metaphysics of feudalism," philosophy has often "become unconsciously an apologetic for the established order, because it has tried to show the rationality of this or that existent hierarchical grading of values and schemes of life." On those rarer occasions when philosophy took a socially radical form, it usually did not contest this hierarchical grading but simply sought a rival principle of

33. "Philosophies of Freedom" (1928), *Later Works* 3:99–101.

highest authority. Even democrats had mistakenly tried to beat the enemy at its own game by mythologizing the voice of the people into the voice of God, but this strategy had failed because "the people are too close at hand, too obviously empirical, to be lent to deification" (PD, 51–52).

A better metaphysical argument for democratic equality, Dewey contended, lay in exploiting the implications of the qualitative uniqueness of existents which his naturalism had described. For the democrat, equality was qualitative not quantitative. It meant that "every existence deserving the name of existence has something unique and irreplaceable about it": "In social and moral matters, equality does not mean mathematical equivalence. It means rather the inapplicability of considerations of greater and less, superior and inferior. It means that no matter how great the quantitative differences of ability, strength, position, wealth, such differences are negligible in comparison with something else—the fact of individuality, the manifestation of something irreplaceable" (PD, 52–53). Democracy, in brief, needed "a metaphysical mathematics of the incommensurable in which each speaks for itself and demands consideration on its own behalf" (PD, 53). For, properly conceived, democracy was not a society of identical, interchangeable, atomized quantitative units as such scientistic philosophies as Bentham's utilitarianism suggested, but a community of unique individuals striving to express their qualitative individuality. Democracy did not seek to level out individuality but rather sought such leveling—of legal, political, and economic resources—as would prevent "the untoward workings of native differences of power" and thereby release the unique capacities of all concerned.[34]

Metaphysically, democracy also required (and Dewey provided) support for fraternity—a world in which qualitatively unique existences were also necessarily related to like existences and in which individuality was expressed only in the context of such transactions, a world in which "what is specific and unique can be exhibited and become forceful or actual only in relationship with other like beings." Democracy was concerned, above all, with "associated individuals in which each by intercourse with others somehow makes the life of each more distinctive" (PD, 53).

In light of his desire to establish metaphysical warrants for democratic fraternity, the centrality of language, meaning, and communication in Dewey's metaphysics and the sudden warming of his prose as he took

34. "Individuality, Equality and Superiority" (1922), *Middle Works* 13:299.

up these topics in *Experience and Nature* becomes explicable. "Shared experience," he declared, "is the greatest of human goods" (*EN*, 145). If language was what made the human organism distinctive, then men and women could realize their humanity only insofar as they were able to participate in the experiences that language made possible. "To learn to be human is to develop through the give-and-take of communication an effective sense of being an individually distinctive member of a community; one who understands and appreciates its beliefs, desires and methods, and who contributes to a further conversion of organic powers into human resources and values."[35]

Discourse was among the finest of arts, at once instrumental and consummatory, and democracy universalized this art, making its means and ends available to all:

> Communication is uniquely instrumental and uniquely final. It is instrumental as liberating us from the otherwise overwhelming pressure of events and enabling us to live in a world of things that have meaning. It is final as a sharing in the objects and arts precious to a community, a sharing whereby meanings are enhanced, deepened and solidified in the sense of communion. Because of its characteristic agency and finality, communication and its congenial objects are objects ultimately worthy of awe, admiration, and loyal appreciation. They are worthy as means, because they are the only means that make life rich and varied in meanings. They are worthy as ends, because in such ends man is lifted from his immediate isolation and shares in a communion of meanings. . . . When the instrumental and final functions of communication live together in experience, there exists an intelligence which is the method and reward of the common life, and a society worthy to command affection, admiration, and loyalty. (*EN*, 159–160)

In Dewey's metaphysics, democracy was the full realization of the possibilities of human society as such. It was not "an alternative to other principles of associated life. It is the idea of community life itself. It is an ideal in the only intelligible sense of an ideal: namely, the tendency and movement of some thing which exists carried to its final limit, viewed as completed, perfected." Since such perfection was impossible in a precarious, uncertain world, democracy was a regulative ideal, not a fact, yet it was an ideal rooted in the most essential features of human experience. "Whenever there is conjoint activity whose consequences

35. *The Public and Its Problems*, p. 332.

are appreciated as good by all singular persons who take part in it, and where the realization of the good is such as to effect an energetic desire and effort to sustain it in being just because it is a good shared by all, there is in so far a community. The clear consciousness of a communal life, in all its implications, constitutes the idea of democracy."[36]

If we read *Experience and Nature* and *The Quest for Certainty* as an effort to fulfill the program laid out in "Philosophy and Democracy," then we have at least a partial explanation for why Dewey's metaphysics was so anthropocentric. For if he was most interested in a metaphysics of democratic community, there was no need to dwell on Santayana's "background" except insofar as it had some bearing on the fate of democracy, and he dwelt most on those traits of the background— contingency and quality—he had previously identified as most pertinent to a metaphysical support of democracy. Dewey, I must admit, covered his tracks. He gave no explicit indication that he was construing and interpreting nature in order to sustain a reasonable argument that democracy was not contradicted by the structure of the world. To have done so would perhaps have come too close to the sort of special pleading of which he accused other metaphysicians, and, indeed, some have detected in *Experience and Nature* a whiff of this sort of bad faith. But it must be said in Dewey's defense that he never tried as a metaphysician to secure his most cherished values as "fixed traits of real Being." His attempt to establish that democracy was a reasonable regulative ideal in a hazardous world in which such ideals often came to grief was a far cry from the efforts of others to forge for their ideals a false passport to certainty.[37]

---

36. Ibid., p. 328.
37. On Dewey's "slightly bad faith" see Richard Rorty, *The Consequences of Pragmatism* (Minneapolis: University of Minnesota Press, 1982), p. 74. Rorty believes that Dewey's mistake lay in believing that he *could* avoid such special pleading, which is (Rorty argues) unavoidable. Elsewhere, Rorty contends that Dewey, in his more clear-headed moments, believed this as well. "Those who share Dewey's pragmatism," he says, "will say that although [democracy] may need philosophical articulation, it does not need philosophical backup. On this view, the philosopher of liberal democracy may wish to develop a theory of the human self that comports with the institutions he or she admires. But such a philosopher is not thereby justifying these institutions by reference to more fundamental premises, but the reverse: He or she is putting politics first and tailoring a philosophy to suit." Now, while I would agree with Rorty that Dewey tailored his philosophy to suit his politics, I would note that (1) Dewey rarely admitted as much, usually preferring as a strategy of argument what he took to be the more powerful rhetorical approach of tailoring his politics to suit his philosophy; (2) Dewey regarded both sorts of tailoring as legitimate—what mattered was the quality of the tailor's work; and (3) Dewey, from whatever end he approached things, did think he was providing democracy with "philosophical backup," if not the metaphysical foundations that others had tried to establish for their politics. Dewey, unlike Rorty, believed that democrats had something of con-

BOURNE AGAIN

If, as Dewey said, the spirit of William James animated his construction of a democratic metaphysics, he was perhaps egged on, though he did not say so, by another familiar spectre. In "Twilight of Idols," his last and most famous wartime foray against Dewey, Randolph Bourne had ventured beyond a pragmatic critique of Dewey's support of the war to a complaint about the more general contours of Dewey's philosophy—a complaint that, as I noted, has profoundly influenced subsequent interpreters. Dewey's "philosophy of intelligent control," Bourne contended, was desperately lacking in "poetic vision." During the war, it had become the watchword of young administrative experts with "no clear philosophy of life except that of intelligent service, the admirable adaptation of means to ends." But what was required in the midst of a crisis like the war was less of this technical rationality and more clear articulation of "democratic desires." Although he was clear about where his own desires lay, Dewey had to be held partially responsible, Bourne concluded, for a generation that had no idea of what sort of society it wanted, though it was admirably equipped with the administrative talents to attain it. To one-time Deweyans like himself, this was deeply disillusioning:

> To those of us who have taken Dewey's philosophy almost as our American religion, it never occurred that values could be subordinated to technique. We were instrumentalists, but we had our private utopias so clearly before our minds that the means fell always into its place as contributory. And Dewey, of course, always meant his philosophy, when taken as a philosophy of life, to start with values. But there was always that unhappy ambiguity in his doctrine as to just how values were created, and it became easier and easier to assume that just any growth was justified and almost any activity valuable as long as it achieved ends.

---

siderable significance at stake in metaphysics; they had not only to articulate the metaphysics that comported with their politics but arrive at conclusions that enabled them to "essay our deepest political and social problems with a conviction that they are to a reasonable extent sanctioned and sustained by the nature of things." The key words here are "to a reasonable extent," which distinguish the relationship Dewey sought to establish between metaphysics and politics from both the metaphysical foundationalism of those he was attacking in *Experience and Nature* and the "post-philosophical" antifoundationalism of Rorty. Rorty's contention that "no such discipline as 'philosophical anthropology' is required as a preface to politics" may be true, but it is not, as a matter of intellectual history, "the Deweyan view." Cf. Rorty, "The Priority of Democracy to Philosophy," in Merrill D. Peterson and Robert C. Vaughan, eds., *The Virginia Statute for Religious Freedom* (New York: Cambridge University Press, 1988), pp. 260, 262.

Bourne charged that Dewey's epigoni and, during the war, Dewey himself, had failed the country as "value-creators." It was thus time to write off "optimism-haunted philosophies" in favor of a "skeptical, malicious, desperate, ironical mood." Appealing to the shade of William James as well as Nietzsche, Bourne called upon his fellow "malcontents" to launch intellectual "war and laughter" in behalf of new values: "it is the creative desire more than the creative intelligence that we shall need if we are ever to fly."[38]

"Twilight of Idols" stretched Bourne's Deweyan critique of Dewey to the breaking point, though, as the invocation of James suggests, he was not necessarily turning his back on pragmatism and radical empiricism. Had Dewey chosen to respond to Bourne's charges, he might well have pointed to work he had written before the war about "how values were created" and perhaps even laid claim to a measure of poetic vision. As we have seen, Dewey had explicitly distinguished his conception of scientific intelligence from merely technical rationality, and his logic was designed, above all, to serve as a logic for moral judgments. Yet Bourne was correct to point up the ambiguity of Dewey's prewar reflections on the "quality of life"—much of what he had to say on the subject before the war was obscure. And, despite his appreciative evocations of noncognitive experience and his conception of human beings as "thinking desire," Dewey had had a great deal more to say about thinking than about desire. I suspect most of the young "instrumentalists" whom Bourne indicted had not read a word of Dewey's work and, if they thought of him as "their" philosopher, it was because someone like Lippmann had told them they might do so. But this situation was partly Dewey's responsibility. As Bourne had complained in 1915, Dewey could hardly be said to have made his thinking very accessible before the war. If technocrats mistakenly thought themselves Deweyans, they could not be censured for failing to attend carefully to Dewey's articles in the *Journal of Philosophy*.[39]

After the mid-twenties, it would be far more difficult to make

38. Randolph Bourne, "Twilight of Idols" (1917), in Olaf Hansen, ed., *The Radical Will: Randolph Bourne, Selected Writings* (New York: Urizen, 1977), pp. 341–347.
39. "Nature and Its Good: A Conversation" (1909), *Middle Works* 4:15–30, reprinted in *The Influence of Darwin on Philosophy* (1910), was probably the most accessible of Dewey's prewar discussions of the origin of values. Indeed, even in the context of the whole of his work, it remains a very good place to begin. As it happens, ironically, the years immediately preceding World War I appear to have been Dewey's most active as an amateur poet (see *The Poems of John Dewey*, ed. Jo Ann Boydston [Carbondale: Southern Illinois University Press, 1977]). But had Bourne been able to read them, I doubt he would have seen them as compelling evidence that Dewey possessed much poetic vision.

Bourne's case that Dewey's philosophy was marred by "an exaggerated emphasis on the mechanics of life at the expense of the quality of living" (although, as we will see, some tried). By then, Dewey had offered an accessible (if not a popular) account of human experience which clearly demonstrated that, no less than Bourne, he felt the allure of "intelligence suffused by feeling, and feeling given fibre and outline by intelligence."[40]

Indeed, by the end of the decade, as was the case in his thinking about international politics, Dewey could be found advancing sentiments much like those Bourne had expressed in attacking him during the war. Although he insisted that philosophers not advance propositions inconsistent with the knowledge of science, he emphasized that this did not mean that they should confine themselves only to scientifically verifiable ideas. Philosophy should respect truth, but its central concern was with meaning, and meaning was "wider in scope as well as more precious in value than is truth." There was a great difference, he said, "between an imagination that acknowledges its responsibility to meet the logical demands of ascertained facts, and a complete abdication of all imagination in behalf of a prosy literalism." Philosophy was, at bottom, creative intelligence in service of creative desire, and, like Bourne, Dewey chastised American intellectuals in general and philosophers in particular for a lack of "imagination in generating leading ideas." Thus he entered "a plea for the casting off of that intellectual timidity which hampers the wings of imagination, a plea for speculative audacity, for more faith in ideas, sloughing off a cowardly reliance upon those partial ideas to which we are wont to give the name of facts."[41]

Although Dewey's wariness of "intellectual aristocracies" extended to the sort of Nietszchean transvaluation of values by a coterie of malcontents which Bourne proposed, he shared Bourne's contempt for those who uncritically took the values of their culture for granted. If his was not, like Bourne's, a call to alienation, it was a call for unsparing social appraisal. Having relieved philosophy of its grander pretensions, Dewey continued his effort to redefine its mission as cultural criticism.

Criticism was discriminating judgment, and judgment was best termed criticism "wherever the subject-matter of discrimination con-

---

40. Bourne, "Twilight of Idols," pp. 345–46. Again, there is no direct evidence that Bourne's critique affected Dewey's thinking, though as I indicate in Chapter 11 Dewey finally did take up some of Bourne's criticisms after they appeared secondhand in 1927 in Lewis Mumford's *Golden Day*.
41. "Philosophy and Civilization," pp. 4, 9–10.

cerns goods or values." Values—the goods of belief, conduct, and appreciation—were, in the first instance, immediate qualities of experienced things. Primary experience was inherently value-laden. Such immediate value, like all immediacy, was ineffable: "values are values, things immediately having certain qualities. Of them as values, there is accordingly nothing to be said; they are what they are. . . . Value as such, even things having value, cannot in their immediate existence be reflected upon; they either are or are not; are or are not enjoyed" (*EN*, 297–298). But the having of values inevitably gave way to thinking about them: "Possession and enjoyment of goods passes insensibly and inevitably into appraisal. First and immature experience is content simply to enjoy. But a brief course in experience enforces reflection; it requires but brief time to teach that some things sweet in the having are bitter in aftertaste and in what they lead to. Primitive innocence does not last. Enjoyment ceases to be a datum and becomes a problem. As a problem, it implies intelligent inquiry into the conditions and consequences of a value-object; that is, criticism" (*EN*, 298). Critical appraisal produced goods different from those of initial immediate value, goods funded with the meaning supplied by inquiry into their antecedents and consequences.

The function of criticism was to subject immediate values to this sort of inquiry and replace them with reflective values. It was not a matter of distinguishing the immediate goods and bads of experience, for which criticism was unnecessary, but of distinguishing apparent and real goods. In matters of belief, conduct, and appreciation—that is, in cognitive, moral, and aesthetic judgments—there was, in each instance, a conflict between an immediate and an ulterior value-object, between given goods and those justified on reflection. Criticism turned from the apparent good of things to consider their *eventual* goodness; it aimed to institute and perpetuate "more enduring and extensive values" (*EN*, 301–302). Criticism provided goods with credentials; reflective goods were better than unreflective goods (though both were immediately good) because they bore the value-added stamp of criticism.

Philosophy, Dewey contended, could be nothing other than criticism pursued at a high level of self-consciousness and generality. Conceived as such, philosophy

> starts from actual situations of belief, conduct and appreciative perception which are characterized by immediate qualities of good and bad, and from the modes of critical judgment current at any given time in all the regions of value; these are its data, its subject-matter. These values, criticisms, and critical methods, it subjects to further criticism as

comprehensive and consistent as possible. The function is to regulate the further appreciation of goods and bads; to give greater freedom and security in those acts of direct selection, appropriation, identification and of rejection, elimination, destruction which enstate and which exclude objects of belief, conduct and contemplation. (*EN*, 302)

But if the business of philosophy was "criticism of beliefs, institutions, customs, policies with respect to their bearing upon good," this did not mean "their bearing upon *the* good, as something attained and formulated in philosophy." Goods inhered in "the naturally generated functions of experience"; they were not locked up in some transcendental closet to which only philosophers had the key. "For as philosophy has no private store of knowledge or of methods for attaining truth, so it has no private access to good. As it accepts knowledge of facts and principles from those competent in inquiry and discovery, so it accepts the goods that are diffused in human experience. It has no Mosaic or Pauline authority of revelation entrusted to it. But it has the authority of intelligence, of criticism of these common and natural goods" (*EN*, 305).

In an important sense then, Dewey was countering Bourne's call to philosophers and intellectuals to be "value creators" if this was taken to mean sages who claimed access to values apart from those available or possible in experience. The latter, as Dewey saw it, were the only values possible (which did not mean they were always readily apparent or fully realized). It was the task of the philosopher to "clarify, liberate and extend" them. For this reason, cultural criticism required not only "a heightened consciousness of deficiencies and corruptions in the scheme and distribution of values that obtains at any period" but also "a heightened appreciation of the positive goods which human experience has achieved and offers." Such positive goods were "the basic subject-matter of philosophy as criticism; and only because such positive goods already exist is their emancipation and secured extension the defining aim of intelligence" (*EN*, 308). Philosophers did not travel "a special road to something alien to ordinary beliefs, knowledge, action, enjoyment, and suffering." But they could afford "a criticism, a critical viewing, of just these familiar things."[42]

In the best of all possible worlds, there would be no need for philosophers. The "organon of criticism" belonged to nature and life, not to philosophy. One could conceive of "a happier nature and experience

---

42. "Construction and Criticism" (1930), *Later Works* 5:141. See also "The Determination of Ultimate Values or Aims through Antecedent or A Priori Speculation or through Pragmatic or Empirical Inquiry" (1938), *Later Works* 13:255–280.

than flourishes among us wherein the office of critical reflection would be carried on so continuously and in such detail that no particular apparatus would be needed." Yet until that day arrived, there would remain a need for thinkers who could cut across the barriers thrown up by an overspecialization of interests and occupations, barriers that isolated and petrified the goods of experience. In such a situation, philosophy could become "a messenger, a liaison officer, making reciprocally intelligible voices speaking provincial tongues, and thereby enlarging as well as rectifying the meanings with which they are charged" (*EN*, 306). If philosophers must abandon the search for Truth-at-large, they might remain critics-at-large.

Philosophy was thus different from other forms of cultural criticism—indeed from criticism as such—only by virtue of its generality. "It differs from other criticism only in trying to carry it further and to pursue it methodically. . . . As soon as anyone strives to introduce definiteness, clarity, and order on any broad scale, he enters the road that leads to philosophy. He begins to criticize and to develop criteria of criticism, that is, logic, ethics, esthetics, metaphysics." This meant, as Dewey's own practice indicated, not the abandonment but the reconstruction of logic, ethics, aesthetics, and metaphysics by reconceptualizing these branches of philosophy as "a generalized theory of criticism" (*EN*, 9). Unlike some contemporary "Deweyans" such as Richard Rorty, who applaud Dewey's notion of philosophy as cultural criticism yet disparage him for holding onto even an unorthodox metaphysics, Dewey himself believed that "ground-maps" at the level of generality he offered in *Experience and Nature* were essential to the more "intricate triangulations" of criticism. For "the more sure one is that the world which encompasses human life is of such and such a character (no matter what his definition), the more one is committed to try to direct the conduct of life, that of others as well as of himself, upon the basis of the character assigned to the world" (*EN*, 309). Although Dewey, like Rorty, held the search for certain foundations for social hope to be futile and counterproductive, he could not rest easy, as Rorty does, with "*unjustifiable* hope, and an *ungroundable* but vital sense of human solidarity." If he did not seek certainty for his social hope, he did feel compelled to establish its possibility. Hope, he believed, required at least the "encouraging nod" from experience and nature which he believed only metaphysics could provide.[43]

---

43. "Construction and Criticism," p. 141; Rorty, *Consequences of Pragmatism*, p. 208 (my emphasis). For some further comparisons of Rorty and Dewey see the Epilogue.

Dewey realized that, in stripping philosophy of any claim to access to a truth beyond that assayed by science or to a good greater than the goods of ordinary experience and in confining the philosopher's task to the exercise of critical imagination and intelligence, he was leaving philosophers with a far more modest cultural role than that to which they had traditionally aspired. It was, nonetheless, a role requiring great courage, for, in the service of their culture, philosophers might well call into question its apparent goods and thereby risk, at least figuratively, the fate of Socrates. Humble roles boldly performed were nothing to be ashamed of. For, as Dewey saw it, "a combination of such modesty and courage affords the only way I know of in which the philosopher can look his fellow man in the face with frankness and with humanity."[44]

As the United States skidded into the Great Depression, Dewey argued that the nation was in desperate need of critic-philosophers of modesty and courage. The culture that had fostered economic collapse lacked a discriminating self-consciousness about the values it had enstated, and therein lay its greatest weakness. "The standardized factory and the automobile racing from nowhere in particular to nowhere else in particular with no special purpose except to get there and back as fast as possible are the Siamese twins of our civilization," he observed. "We do not know what we really want and we make no great effort to find out. We allow our purposes and desires to be foisted upon us from without. We are bored by doing what we want to do, because the want has no deep roots in our own judgment of values."[45] It was in awakening such a judgment of values that American philosophers might serve their culture at a critical juncture in its history and find their true calling. It was there that Dewey had found his.

44. "Philosophy and Civilization," p. 10.
45. "Construction and Criticism," p. 133.

John Dewey at eighty. Courtesy of the Morris Library, Southern Illinois University at Carbondale.

Part Four

Democrat Emeritus
(1929–1952)

Forty years spent wandering in a wilderness like
that of the present is not a sad fate—unless one
attempts to make himself believe that the wilderness
is after all itself the promised land.

—"From Absolutism to Experimentalism" (1930)

CHAPTER 11

Consummatory Experience

＊

THE late twenties was a period of pivotal endings and beginnings in John Dewey's long and eventful life. Most notable among these was Alice Dewey's death on 14 July 1927. Alice had begun having trouble with her heart on the couple's visit to Mexico in the summer of 1926. Her health deteriorated rapidly over the following year, and a series of strokes eventually led to her death. Although she apparently never fully recovered her energy and spirit after young Gordon Dewey's death in 1904 and the Dewey marriage was subsequently rockier than it appeared to most, Alice had continued to stimulate her husband's thought and activism while at the same time attending to the affairs of day-to-day family life which often eluded the easily distracted professor. Soon after her death, Dewey remarked that the "deepest source of happiness in life comes to one, I suppose, from one's own family relations; and there, though I have experienced great sorrows, I can truly say that in my life companion, in my children, and in my grandchildren, I have been blessed by the circumstances and fortunes of life."[1]

Another transition, though less sorrowful than that to life without Alice, was nearly as significant. Shortly before the beginning of the academic year 1929–1930, Dewey announced that he would retire from the Columbia faculty effective at the end of the spring term.

1. Dykhuizen, pp. 232–233.

Although university officials talked him into staying on as Professor Emeritus of Philosophy in Residence for another nine years, his duties were confined to occasional consultations with graduate students. This schedule allowed him to devote most of his time and effort to the heavy burden of political activism he assumed with the onset of the Great Depression as well as to major books on aesthetics and logic and several lesser volumes he still had in him at an age when most other men might have considered truly retiring.

Dewey's retirement from Columbia brought to an end a teaching career of some forty-five years. By conventional standards, he was a miserable teacher, but as several accounts of their classroom experience by some of his more astute students have suggested, his teaching could provide unequaled rewards to those willing patiently to bracket the conventions. The best of these accounts, that of Irwin Edman, not only nicely captures the character of Dewey's teaching but also shows that as a teacher Dewey exemplified some of the virtues he believed essential to democratic character and culture.

Having read much of Dewey's work and found there "a philosophy that was not only a vision but a challenge," Edman eagerly anticipated his first class with Dewey in 1915. But Dewey was not what he had expected, and instead of intellectual excitement, Dewey's first lecture left him with "a shock of dullness and confusion":

> He had none of the usual tricks or gifts of the effective lecturer. He sat at his desk, fumbling with a few crumpled yellow sheets and looking abstractedly out of the window. He spoke very slowly in a Vermont drawl. He looked both very kindly and very abstracted. He hardly seemed aware of the presence of a class. He took little pains to under-line a phrase, or emphasize a point, or, so at first it seemed to me, to make any. . . . He seemed to be saying whatever came into his head next, and at one o'clock on an autumn afternoon to at least one under-graduate what came next did not always have a very clear connexion with what had just gone before. The end of the hour finally came and he simply stopped; it seemed to me he might have stopped anywhere.

But Edman stuck it out, and soon he discovered "it was my mind that had wandered, not John Dewey's." Looking over his notes, he found that "what had seemed so casual, so rambling, so unexciting, was of an extraordinary coherence, texture, and brilliance. I had been listening not to the semi-theatrical repetition of a discourse many times made—a fairly accurate description of many academic lectures—I had been lis-tening to a man actually *thinking* in the presence of a class": "To attend a lecture of John Dewey was to participate in the actual business of thought. Those pauses were delays in creative thinking, when the next step was really being considered, and for the glib dramatics of the teacher-actor was substituted the enterprise, careful and candid, of the genuine thinker. Those hours came to seem the most arresting educational experiences, almost, I have ever had."

Edman believed Dewey to be at his best in small seminars as did most of his students. Here, true to his philosophy, he proceeded as if the group was a democratic, cooperative community of inquiry. He never dominated the proceedings, often saying very little. But, Edman recalled, "one remembered what he said" and particularly admired "his capacity for sympathetically seeing what a student was driving at, even when he did not quite succeed in saying it." For many of those who were his students and colleagues, as J. H. Randall wrote, "Dewey became a part of their very lives and selves. . . . It was not alone what he did and thought, it was what he was, that drew men to him—simple, sturdy, unpretentious, quizzical, shrewd, devoted, fearless, genuine." Other members of Columbia's great department received admiration, respect, and affection from their students, but "for Dewey it was unashamed love."[2]

In part as a result of these feelings, Dewey was honored every ten years of the last thirty years of his life with several *festschriften*. But these memorial tributes were not without sharp criticism of their honored subject, and as R. W. Sleeper has said, not all of the many excellent essays in these volumes "can have added to the conviviality of the occasion for which they were written." Dewey's thought remained controversial, and in his final years he was constantly fencing with opponents, new and old. In this, as always, he usually gave as good as he got, and, in the process, both refined and broadened his philosophy.[3]

2. Irwin Edman, *Philosopher's Holiday* (New York: Viking, 1938), pp. 138–143; J. H. Randall, Jr., "The Department of Philosophy," in Jacques Barzun, ed., *A History of the Faculty of Philosophy of Columbia University* (New York: Columbia University Press, 1957), p. 129. See also Sidney Hook, *Out of Step: An Unquiet Life in the Twentieth Century* (New York: Harper and Row, 1987), pp. 80–94; Harold A. Larrabee, "John Dewey as Teacher," in William W. Brickman and Stanley Lehrer, eds., *John Dewey: Master Educator* (New York: Society for the Advancement of Education, 1959), pp. 50–57; and Herbert Schneider, "Recollections of John Dewey," in Robert B. Williams, *John Dewey Recollections* (Washington, D.C.: University Press of America, 1982), pp. 139–141, 148–149.

3. R. W. Sleeper, *The Necessity of Pragmatism: John Dewey's Conception of Philosophy* (New Haven: Yale University Press, 1986), p. 10–11. Dewey *festschriften* include *Essays in Honor of John Dewey on the Occasion of His Seventieth Birthday* (New York: Holt, 1929); *John Dewey: The Man and His Philosophy* (Cambridge: Harvard University Press, 1930); Sidney Ratner, ed., *The Philosopher of the Common Man* (New York: G. P. Putnam's Sons, 1940); Kenneth D. Benne and William O. Stanley, eds., *Essays for John Dewey's Ninetieth Birthday* (Urbana:

THE "PRAGMATIC ACQUIESCENCE"

If Dewey thought *Experience and Nature* would diminish the sway of Randolph Bourne's "Twilight of Idols," he was sorely disappointed. After the war, prominent young intellectuals, many of whom viewed Bourne as a martyred hero, continued to pound away at Dewey. In 1926 one of these writers, Lewis Mumford, reiterated and extended Bourne's criticisms in a chapter in his book *The Golden Day* titled "The Pragmatic Acquiescence"—an assault, as the title suggests, on the supposed compliant conformity of the philosophies of James and Dewey to the prevailing values of a degraded civilization and a critique that has exercised nearly as much influence on interpreters of Dewey's thought as Bourne's essay.[4]

Mumford's foray against pragmatism was embedded in the sad tale he told in *The Golden Day* of the declension of American culture since the mid-nineteenth century. The Civil War, he argued there, had "cut a white gash through the history of the country." On the far side of the conflict lay the culture of the "Golden Day" of Emerson, Thoreau, Melville, Hawthorne, and Whitman: "the period of an Elizabethan daring on the sea, of a well balanced adjustment of farm and factory in the East, of a thriving regional culture, operating through the lecture-lyceum and the provincial college; an age in which the American mind had flourished and had begun to find itself." The war had sealed the doom of this culture and had ushered in the reign of industrial exploitation and mammon.[5]

University of Illinois Press, 1950); Sidney Hook, ed., *John Dewey: Philosopher of Science and Freedom* (New York: Dial Press, 1950); Harry Laidler, ed., *John Dewey at Ninety* (New York: League for Industrial Democracy, 1950); and *In Honor of John Dewey on His Ninetieth Birthday* (Madison: University of Wisconsin Press, 1951). Paul Schilpp, ed., *The Philosophy of John Dewey* (Evanston, Ill.: Northwestern University Press, 1939), one of the best (and most critical) collections of essays on Dewey, was not technically a *festschrift* even though it was published in Dewey's eightieth year. In addition to these volumes, magazines and journals with which Dewey was associated including the *New Republic*, the *Teachers College Record*, and the *Journal of Philosophy* published special Dewey issues on the philosopher's decennial anniversaries. These were almost uniformly celebratory.

4. For a fuller revisionist account of the Mumford-Dewey relationship in the twenties and thirties than I offer here see my "Lewis Mumford, John Dewey, and the 'Pragmatic Acquiescence,'" in Thomas and Agatha Hughes, eds., *Lewis Mumford: Public Intellectual* (New York: Oxford University Press, 1990). Other critical treatments of Dewey's philosophy by Bourne's heirs include Van Wyck Brooks, "Letters and Leadership" (1918), in Brooks, *Three Essays on America* (New York, E. P. Dutton, 1970), pp. 169–173; Waldo Frank, "The Man Who Made Us What We Are," *New Yorker*, 22 May 1926: 15–16, and *The Re-Discovery of America* (New York: Scribner, 1929), pp. 168–177; Harold Stearns, *Liberalism in America* (New York: Boni and Liveright, 1919), chap. 8.

5. Lewis Mumford, *The Golden Day*, 3d ed. (New York: Dover, 1968), p. 79. Page numbers for further references (*GD*) appear in the text.

In the Gilded Age, Mumford said, industrialism ruled the American mind as well as the political economy. The "guts of idealism" went out of late nineteenth-century writers and intellectuals, and they lacked a belief in the "process of re-molding, re-forming, re-creating, and so humanizing the rough chaos of existence" (GD, 83). Having lost this faith, these intellectuals were paralyzed, and they bowed to the inevitable, idealized the real, and drifted with the prevailing currents of their culture. William James was among the most important of these intellectuals because he named this acquiescence: "he called it pragmatism: and the name stands not merely for his own philosophy, but for something in which that philosophy was deeply if unconsciously entangled, the spirit of a whole age" (GD, 92).

James, in Mumford's account, translated the "animus of the pioneer" into philosophical argument by portraying an unfinished universe of boundless possibility and by celebrating the combative instincts and a life of struggle at the expense of a consideration of the ends for which these instincts were marshaled and the struggle waged. In sanctioning "this digging and dogging at the universe," James was doing little more than "warming over again in philosophy the hash of everyday experience in the Gilded Age" (GD, 96, 95). He was less a creative philosopher than a "reporter," for he offered no *Weltanschauung* that challenged the premises of his culture; in his philosophy one got "an excellent view of America" (GD, 95, 93). His new ideas were far less significant and influential than those he took for granted: "protestantism, individualism, and scientific distrust of 'values'" (GD, 95). Mumford acknowledged that James's philosophy had been caricatured by many into "a belief in the supremacy of cash-values and practical results" and admitted that "there is an enormous distance between William James and the modern professors who become employees in advertising agencies, or bond salesmen, or publicity experts, without any sense of degradation" (GD, 97, 98). Nevertheless, James's thought was "permeated by the smell of the Gilded Age," and Mumford felt that he had to bear a substantial measure of responsibility for the reinforcement his work provided for those whose eye was on the main chance. James, Mumford concluded, "built much worse than he knew" (GD, 97, 98).

Though Mumford doubted the value of the substance of James's work, he did admit that it had a "homely elegance" of style, unlike the prose of fellow pragmatist John Dewey, whose writing afforded the reader an experience "as depressing as a subway ride" (GD, 130–131). Apart from matters of style, however, Mumford found more to praise in Dewey's "instrumentalist" version of pragmatism than he did in

James's philosophy. He applauded, in particular, Dewey's commitment to the cooperative and experimental procedures of science and his efforts to replace a spectatorial "leisure-class notion of thinking" with a conception of creative thought which conjoined ideas and action, ends and means. Critical of speculation with no practical issue and of practice bereft of reflection, Dewey had cleared the ground for an ideal of human activity "in which facts and values, actualities and desires, achieve an active and organic unity" (GD, 133).

But despite these promising initiatives, Dewey himself had failed to articulate such an ideal, and therein lay the key to *his* acquiescence to the crude utilitarianism of his culture. Dewey's philosophy, Mumford said, effectively conveyed an appreciation of but half of this desired organic unity—and not the more essential half. He had succumbed to a fixation with facts at the expense of values, actualities at the expense of desires, means at the expense of ends, technique at the expense of moral imagination, invention at the expense of art, practicality at the expense of vision. Bourne had, of course, said much of this a decade before, and Mumford acknowledged his debt to Bourne by reproducing the essentials of his critique. But while Bourne had criticized Dewey for caving in to war, Mumford considerably expanded the scope of Dewey's purported acquiescence, rendering him an accomplice to the dominance in American culture of the "utilitarian type of personality" (GD, 134). Without "the values that arise out of vision," Mumford observed, "instrumentalism becomes the mere apotheosis of actualities: it is all dressed up with no place to go" (GD, 137). In taking values for granted and engaging in a "one-sided idealization of practical contrivances," Dewey had lent a hand to "tendencies which are already strong and well-established in American life" and underplayed "things which must still be introduced into our scheme of things if it is to become thoroughly humane and significant" (GD, 137, 136). Dewey's pragmatism continued to bear the marks of its birth amidst "the shapelessness, the faith in the current go of things, and the general utilitarian idealism of Chicago." His complacent philosophy, bred in the "maw of the Middle West," gave the game away to those like Sinclair Lewis's George Babbitt who practiced "so assiduously the mechanical ritual of American life" and treated bathroom fixtures and automobile accessories as ends in themselves "as if a life spent in the pursuit of these contrivances was a noble and liberal one" (GD, 131, 121, 135–136).[6]

6. For Mumford's estimate of Bourne's significance see "The Image of Randolph Bourne," *New Republic*, 24 September 1930: 151–152.

Mumford reserved some of his sharpest barbs for Dewey's aesthetics. Dewey, he said, had little to say about art, and when he did consider it, he failed to see anything other than its instrumental value and consequently missed its essence. He did not seem to realize that inventions and fine art were different: "the invention is good for what it leads to, whereas a scene in nature, a picture, a poem, a dance, a beautiful conception of the universe, are good for what they are" (GD, 47). Finding utilitarianism "thoroughly agreeable," Dewey had kind words for Bacon, Locke, and Bentham, but nothing to say of Shakespeare, Milton, Shelley, Keats, Wordsworth, and Blake: "a Goodyear and a Morse seem to him as high in the scale of human development as a Whitman and a Tolstoi." This was not to say that Dewey was wrong to point out the uses of art, but "the essential criterion of art is that it is good without these specific instrumental results, good as a *mode of life*, good as a beatitude" (GD, 47).[7]

If American culture were to see a new golden day, Mumford concluded, the "idola of utilitarianism" to which James and Dewey had acquiesced had to be supplanted by a new idolum, one that recognized, as Emerson and Whitman had, that "in proportion as intelligence was dealing more effectually with the instrumentalities of life, it became more necessary for the imagination to project more complete and satisfying ends" (GD, 140–141). Pragmatism had "given depth to the adventure of industrialism," but it "offered no clue as to what made a proper human life outside the mill of practical activity" (GD, 100). Man need not accommodate himself pragmatically to external circumstance, for he had the capacity to act creatively, as an artist, to shape the aims and necessities of his world. "Practical intelligence and a prudent adjustment to externalities are useful only in a secondary position: they are but props to straighten the plant when it begins to grow: at the bottom of it all must be a soil and a seed, an inner burgeoning, an eagerness of life" (GD, 143). Rescue from the sterility, boredom, and despair of "the sinister world" of modern American culture could come only by means of "the double process of encountering more complete modes of life, and of reformulating a more vital tissue of ideas and symbols to supplant those which have led us into the stereotyped interests and actions which we endeavor in vain to identify with a full human existence" (GD, 144).

Dewey's response to his portrait in *The Golden Day* was not as effective

---

7. For a further instance of Mumford's criticism of Deweyan aesthetics see "Metaphysics and Art," *New Republic* (18 December 1929): 117–118.

as it might have been. He accused Mumford of perpetuating an accretion of myths around pragmatism and instrumentalism but devoted most of his attention to Mumford's shaping of James's thought into "a pattern which inverts his whole spirit" rather than to a consideration of the criticisms Mumford had made of his own thinking. Near the end of his reply he briefly acknowledged that it was "a not unreasonable hypothesis" to suppose that a preoccupation with natural science and the technology that issued from it and transformed the American landscape had played a part in the development of his thinking. But, he commented acerbically, he would have thought that it would be clear to "a mind not too precommitted" that in calling his philosophy of knowledge "instrumentalism" and in conceiving of science and technology as instruments he did not intend to substitute instruments for ends. Instruments implied ends to which they were to be put:

> It would require a mind unusually devoid both of sense of logic and a sense of humor—if there be any difference between them—to try to universalize instrumentalism, to set up a doctrine of tools which are not tools for anything except for more tools. The counterpart of "instrumentalism" is precisely that the values by which Mr. Mumford sets such store are the ends for the attainment of which natural science and all technologies and industries and industriousness are intrinsically, not externally and transcendentally, or by way of exhortation, contributory. The essential and immanent criticism of existing industrialism and of the dead weight of science is that instruments are made into ends, that they are deflected from their intrinsic quality and thereby corrupted.

Dewey was not, he said, preoccupied with science and technology for their own sake but because he was as committed as Mumford to "ideal values which dignify and give meaning to human life" and was concerned that science and technology be used as instruments to render valued experience less "precarious in possession, arbitrary, accidental, and monopolized in distribution."[8]

This response, as Mumford noted in his subsequent reply, missed the force of the criticism he had directed at Dewey's work. Mumford had not contended that Dewey's effort to explore the bearing of science and technology on the pursuit of ideal ends was, in itself, troubling. The difficulty lay in the insufficiency of this inquiry to a "complete philo-

---

8. Dewey, "Pragmatic Acquiescence" (1927), *Later Works* 3:147, 150–151. This reply originally appeared in the *New Republic*.

sophic orientation." Dewey had devoted inadequate attention to the ends to which these means should be turned and seemed to believe that ideals would simply come into existence of their own accord and that the critical task was one of devising means to their achievement. This, Mumford said, got things backward: "We are faced by the fact that knowledge of the necessary technique is common enough to be taken for granted, and that the ability to conceive new forms and channels for life to run in, the ability to think creatively with the artist who says 'I will' rather than with the scientist who says 'It must' is what is lacking. The desiccation and sterilization of the imaginative life has been quite as important an historic fact as the growth of a sense of causality, an insight into what Mr. Dewey calls 'means-consequences.'" Mumford and the other young critics who had criticized pragmatism were not so much rejecting Dewey's philosophy as calling for a more expansive philosophical vision: "We seek for a broader field and a less provincial interpretation of Life and Nature than he has given us."[9]

Dewey had much more to say about the ends of life and hence a considerably broader interpretation of "Life and Nature" to offer than Mumford apparently realized or Dewey let on in his criticisms of *The Golden Day*, but the only place in their exchange where this was at all apparent was in their disagreement about Dewey's interpretation of art, which was the only instance in which Mumford produced textual evidence for his reading of Dewey's philosophy. The ninth chapter of *Experience and Nature*, the basis for Mumford's contention that Dewey appreciated only the "utility" of art, was not the most lucid of texts, but Mumford's reading of its discussion of art and aesthetic experience as a claim that art was merely instrumental was simply blind. As Dewey said, his argument was clearly that "art which is really fine exhibits experience when it attains completion or a 'final,' consummatory character, and, while it is urged that such art is also contributory, that to which it is held to be auxiliary is 'renewal of spirit,' not, it would seem, a base end, and certainly not a utilitarian one." The finest art, he had argued, was both consummatory and instrumental, and that to which it was instrumental were further consummations. Dewey's notion of consummatory, aesthetic experience as one of the "immediate enjoyed intrinsic meaning" of an object was little different from Mumford's own conception of aesthetic objects as "good for what they are."[10]

9. Mumford, "The Pragmatic Acquiescence: A Reply," *New Republic*, 19 January 1927: 250–251.

10. Dewey, "Pragmatic Acquiescence," p. 146; *Experience and Nature* (1925), *Later Works* 1:271, 274.

Mumford's criticisms of Dewey's discussion of art suggested that he was determined not to find there what he believed to be lacking. He severed Dewey's theory of knowledge and truth—his instrumental-ism—from the broader naturalism of which it was a part and hence missed the central place in his philosophy of noncognitive experience in general and aesthetic experience in particular. In 1920 Dewey had anticipated Mumford's conclusion to *The Golden Day*, arguing that "surely there is no more significant question before the world than this question of the possibility and method of reconciliation of the attitudes of practical science and contemplative esthetic appreciation. Without the former man will be the sport and victim of natural forces which he cannot use or control. Without the latter, mankind might become a race of economic monsters, restlessly driving hard bargains with nature and with one another, bored with leisure or capable of putting it to use only in ostentatious display and extravagant dissipation." But such remarks fell on deaf ears, for Mumford was certain that Dewey's philosophy had "no place for art." Dewey's "exertions in trying to open up a wedge for it," he remarked privately, "are painful to behold."[11]

Although he hinted in *The Golden Day* and in the subsequent ex-change with Dewey that in addition to the utilitarian Dewey he was aware of "another Dewey, still thinking experimentally and freshly, who is reaching out to wider sources of experience," Mumford gave no account of this Dewey (*GD*, 139). Had he done so, he would have seriously compromised the architecture of *The Golden Day*. This seems the best explanation of Mumford's almost willful misreading of Dewey. His book was built around the contention that the happy wedding of fact and value, science and art, tradition and creativity which marked the American Renaissance had come undone in the work of the nation's subsequent writers, and Mumford needed Dewey to stand in as the representative philosopher of half of the sundered unities of the Gold-en Day (as he needed George Santayana to represent the other half). Hence, he invented a one-eyed Dewey that would fill the bill while at the same time advancing a plea for cultural reconstruction very similar to that Dewey himself had advocated.[12]

Yet, for all its limitations and misreadings, Mumford's criticisms of Dewey did, at least, point to those regions of his thinking that required some elaboration if the "other" John Dewey "reaching out to wider

11. *Reconstruction in Philosophy* (1920), *Middle Works* 12:152; Mumford to Victor Bran-ford, 3 March 1926, Lewis Mumford Papers, Van Pelt Library, University of Pennsyl-vania. I am grateful to Casey Blake for bringing this letter to my attention and to Sophia Mumford for permission to quote from it.

12. Mumford, "Pragmatic Acquiescence: A Reply," p. 251.

sources of experience" was to be more apparent to his readers. Above all, it seemed, he had to say more about life's consummations if he was ever to escape the charge that his was a philosophy that left its readers all dressed up with no place to go.

THE ARTFUL LIFE

Ironically, at the very moment Mumford was claiming that Dewey's philosophy had no place for art Dewey was beginning to move art—both broadly and narrowly conceived—to the center of his thinking. The chapter on art in *Experience and Nature* which Mumford misread so badly was the first fruit of this fresh turn in Dewey's work, and Mumford's failure to grasp what he was trying to say there may have helped to push him to expand and clarify his thinking about aesthetic experience. While searching for a subject for the talks that would inaugurate the William James Lectures at Harvard in 1931 and form the basis for *Art as Experience* (1934), he remarked to Sidney Hook, "I still feel the desire to get into a field I haven't treated systematically and art & esthetics has come to me. One reason is the criticism for neglecting them and the consummatory generally."[13]

Another reason was the close relationship Dewey had developed with Albert Barnes, the wealthy sponsor of the ill-fated Polish investigation of 1918, who was also one of the world's greatest art collectors. Barnes, a doctor, chemist, and pharmaceutical entrepreneur, had made his considerable fortune in his early thirties through his role in the development and marketing of Argyrol, a silver compound that became a standard antiseptic used by physicians throughout the world. In 1910, bored with running his business, Barnes began to collect art, aided by a high-school friend, the painter William Glackens. Barnes had himself done some painting in his youth, and though at first he relied heavily on Glackens's judgment, he quickly developed a sharp eye of his own. When Barnes crossed paths with Dewey during the war, he had already become a familiar figure in the salons and galleries of Paris, where he had boldly and bluntly bought up some of the best modern art on the market.[14]

13. JD to Sidney Hook, 10 March 1930, Hook Collection.
14. For Barnes biography, see William Schack, *Art and Argyrol* (New York: Thomas Yoseloff, 1960); John Lukacs, "Albert Coombs Barnes; or, The Methodist as Aesthete," in Lukacs, *Philadelphia: Patricians and Philistines, 1900–1950* (New York: Farrar, Straus, Giroux, 1981), chap. 8; and Howard Greenfield, *The Devil and Dr. Barnes* (New York: Viking, 1987).

By the early twenties Barnes had amassed a remarkable collection. At a time when respectable opinion in the United States still regarded modern art as scandalous, Barnes courageously purchased dozens of Impressionist and Post-Impressionist paintings, focusing his collecting on the work of Renoir, Cézanne, and Matisse but also whipping out his checkbook to pick up such lesser-known modernists as Soutine and Modigliani. He housed his collection in the galleries of the Barnes Foundation he established on his estate in Merion, Pennsylvania, just outside Philadelphia. Here he launched the experiment in aesthetic education that formed the main work of the foundation, an experiment strictly grounded in the highly formalist philosophy of art he developed alongside his collection. From the outset, Barnes made it clear that his was not a collection to be viewed by casual visitors, and he carefully restricted access to his paintings and to the foundation's classes to those willing to subject themselves to his prescribed curriculum. For decades, he waged an abusive campaign against those who regarded the art he loved as degenerate, as well as those who had no less enthusiasm than he did for the works he had collected yet were unwilling to pay the price he asked if he was to share his collection with them.[15]

As these remarks suggest, Barnes was a difficult man. His personality, as Arthur Danto has recently noted, "was defined by a degree of irascibility so outside the common measure that his crusade for esthetic education was accompanied by an obbligato of fits and tantrums comically disproportionate to their many occasions. . . . He is remembered today for the spectacular collection of early modern art that bears his name, for the enthusiasm with which he kept people from viewing it, and for the terrible temper he expended on behalf of these two projects. He was a gifted but an extremely tiresome man." Because so few people could stand Barnes, Dewey's friendship with him was a source of perplexity to the philosopher's other friends and remains difficult to explain. Hook, who despised Barnes, commented that for him this "indulgent friendship" was something of a relief because it showed that Dewey's character was not without at least one serious flaw that rendered him human.[16]

15. The fullest guides to Barnes's theories about art are his *Art in Painting*, 2d ed. (New York: Harcourt Brace, 1928), and the monographs on Cézanne, Matisse, and Renoir he wrote with his chief assistant, Violette de Mazia. But for a brief summary of his thinking see his "Method in Aesthetics," in Ratner, *Philosopher of the Common Man*, pp. 87–105.

16. Arthur Danto, "Every Straw Was the Last," *New York Times Book Review*, 22 November 1987: 13; Sidney Hook, *Pragmatism and the Tragic Sense of Life* (New York: Basic Books, 1974), p. 108.

Barnes claimed to be a democrat, and to a degree he was. Admission to his galleries followed a rough standard of reverse snobbery: he usually passed favorably on requests for admission from ordinary people and unfavorably on those from the wealthy and privileged. He was an active proponent of racial equality, a supporter of the New Negro movement in the twenties, and an astute and appreciative student of African and Afro-American art and culture. After years of failed negotiations with the University of Pennsylvania, he left custody of his invaluable collection after his death to Lincoln University, a leading black college. Yet though he often declared that his system of aesthetic education was based on Dewey's democratic philosophy, it would be difficult to conceive of a less Deweyan method of instruction than the authoritarian indoctrination Barnes's offered his students at Merion, a pedagogy in which those who asked critical questions were booted out of class. As Hook said, "Barnes made a profession of complete devotion to the principles of Dewey's philosophy, especially his philosophy of democracy. But there never was a man more undemocratic in his personal way of life, which for Dewey was the essence of democracy."[17]

Nonetheless, "Jack" and "Al"—as they referred to one another—got along quite famously for more than thirty years. In part, theirs was a relationship of mutual exploitation. Barnes basked in the prestige Dewey's name lent to the educational program of his foundation, and he was forever calling upon Dewey to testify on his behalf in his running battles with the Philadelphia art establishment in the press and in the courts. Dewey, in turn, benefited from the extraordinary access Barnes provided him to his paintings and from the substantial retainer he was paid as a consultant to the Barnes Foundation. Yet these conveniences alone fail to explain the genuine affection that developed between the two men, an affection that led each to withhold sharp criticism from the other when they disagreed. Dewey quickly realized the futility of arguing with Barnes and learned to live with this, while Barnes forgave Dewey the sort of unintended minor slights that sent him into a towering rage where other, soon-to-be-former friends were concerned. The most important bond between the two men was that they learned a great deal from each other, and this, more than anything else, held them together. Barnes dedicated his first theoretical tome, *The Art in Painting* (1925), to Dewey, and Dewey, in turn, dedicated *Art as Experience* "in gratitude" to Barnes and made reference to Barnes's work throughout the book.

---

17. Hook, *Pragmatism and the Tragic Sense of Life*, p. 108. See also Corliss Lamont, ed., *Dialogue on John Dewey* (New York: Horizon Press, 1959), pp. 44–49.

Though Dewey's aesthetics differed from Barnes's stringent formalism in important respects, no one did more than Barnes to help him understand the character of the artful experience that he believed made life most worth living.

At the heart of Dewey's aesthetics was an effort to break down the barriers erected by many philosophers between art and the rest of experience and to trace the continuities between the work of art and the doings and undergoings of everyday life. He had argued in *Experience and Nature* that art was best conceived broadly as the purposeful production of consummatory experience of all sorts and thus must be seen as something more than the creation of what were conventionally viewed as aesthetic objects—paintings, poems, plays, and so forth. By the same token, he argued, aesthetic quality was not confined to these objects alone and was to be had across a broad spectrum of experience (including that of thinking). These arguments were extended and refined in *Art as Experience*, which sought to shift the focus of the philosophy of art from the "art product" as an object standing apart from the experience of artists and their audiences to the (literal) "work" of art— "what the product does with and in experience." Separating works of art from the experiential conditions of their origin and the consequences of their appreciation had obscured their general significance, Dewey contended. Too often "art is remitted to a separate realm, where it is cut off from that association with the materials and aims of every other form of human effort, undergoing, and achievement." To recover the import of art, aesthetic theory had to "restore continuity between the refined and intensified forms of experience that are works of art and the everyday events, doings, and sufferings that are universally recognized to constitute experience."[18]

This perspective required a "detour" from the normal course of thinking about art, which presumed that one began with art products of the best sort. If great works of art were continuous with the rest of life, if they served to "idealize qualities found in common experience," then philosophers had to begin with those qualities and not with their idealization:

> In order to *understand* the esthetic in its ultimate and approved forms, one must begin with it in the raw; in the events and scenes that hold the attentive eye and ear of man, arousing his interest and affording him

18. *Art as Experience* (1934), *Later Works* 10:9. Page numbers for further references (*AE*) appear in the text.

enjoyment as he looks and listens: the sights that hold the crowd—the fire engine rushing by; the machines excavating enormous holes in the earth; the human-fly climbing the steeple-side; the man perched high in air on girders throwing and catching red-hot bolts. The sources of art in human experience will be learned by him who sees how the tense grace of the ball-player infects the onlooking crowd; who notes the delight of the housewife in tending her plants, and the intent interest of her goodman in tending the patch of green in front of the house; the zest of the spectator in poking the wood burning on the hearth and in watching the darting flames and crumbling coals. (AE, 10–11)

Approaching art from this angle of vision promised a reciprocal illumination of art and ordinary experience. It would further the understanding of fine art while at the same time "indicate the factors and forces that favor the normal development of common human activities into matters of artistic value" (AE, 17).

Thus Dewey's philosophy of art began with a detour into the experience not of artists but of ordinary men and women. Indeed, in the initial chapters of Art as Experience he offered the clearest and most compelling account of his view of what the "experience" and "growth" of a live creature amounted to. Although much of this is familiar, it bears brief repetition.

Life, he said, was an ongoing transaction between an organism and its environment. This transaction was marked by recurrent phases of equilibrium and disequilibrium: "the organism falls out of step with the march of surrounding things and then recovers unison with it—either through effort or by some happy chance." If the transaction between an organism and its environment became too disharmonious, the organism died. If the rhythm of alienation and restored equilibrium did not enhance the activity of the organism, it merely subsisted. Growth occurred when the organism was enriched by recovery from temporary disequilibrium. "Life grows when a temporary falling out is a transition to a more extensive balance of the energies of the organism with those of the conditions under which it lives" (AE, 19–20). Growth was then not merely quantitative but qualitative, the development of "a higher powered and more significant life," and when growth occurred "the moment of passage from disturbance into harmony is that of intensest life" (AE, 22).

In human beings the transaction between organism and environment was conscious and purposeful. Emotions signaled actual or impending breaks in harmonious experience, and this discord provided the occasion for reflective thought. Desire for the restoration of equilibrium converted emotion into an interest in ends-in-view which would realize harmony. Achieving these ends brought (or did not bring) renewed equilibrium and growth. Lacking the instinctual mechanisms for restoring equilibrium possessed by other organisms and relying instead on the more flexible resources of thought, language, and culture, human beings were capable both of sinking below the level of beasts and of rising to an unprecedented level of growth because of their ability to saturate the world with meaning. "As an organism increases in complexity, the rhythms of struggle and consummation in its relation to its environment are varied and prolonged, and they come to include within themselves an endless variety of sub-rhythms. The designs of living are widened and enriched. Fulfillment is more massive and more subtly shaded" (*AE*, 29).

Experience did not always bring fulfillment. Much of it was inchoate, winding down to a conclusion that was a cessation but not a consummation. Only when events ran a course to a culmination, only when they were marked by wholeness and self-sufficiency, did one speak idiomatically of having *an* experience. Often "things are experienced but not in such a way that they are composed into *an* experience" (*AE*, 42). In *an* experience of this honorific sort "every successive part flows freely, without seam and without unfilled blanks, into what ensues. At the same time there is no sacrifice of the self-identity of the parts. . . . In an experience, flow is from something to something. As one part leads into another and as one part carries on what went on before, each gains distinctness in itself. The enduring whole is diversified by successive phases that are emphases of its varied colors" (*AE*, 43). Any experience insofar as it was characterized by "internal integration and fulfillment reached through ordered and organized movement" had an aesthetic quality that "pervades the entire experience in spite of the variation of the constituent parts," and "no experience of whatever sort is a unity unless it has esthetic quality" (*AE*, 44, 45, 47).

As these comments suggest, aesthetic experience as a distinctive sort of experience was not to be distinguished from intellectual and practical experience by virtue of its possession of aesthetic quality, for every unified, consummatory experience had this quality. Without it, it would not be a single, coherent experience; it would not be *an* experience. "The most elaborate philosophic or scientific inquiry and the most ambitious industrial or political enterprise has, when its different ingredients constitute an integral experience, esthetic quality. For then its varied parts are linked to one another, and do not merely succeed one another. And the parts through their experienced linkage move toward a consummation and close, not merely to cessation in time" (*AE*, 61). In this respect, the proper contrast was not between the esthetic and the intellectual or the practical but between the esthetic and the anesthetic: "the humdrum; slackness of loose ends; submission to convention in practice and intellectual procedure" (*AE*, 47).

What rendered some experiences distinctively aesthetic was not their aesthetic quality but the interest and purpose that initiated and controlled them. An aesthetic experience was one in which the aim was the production or appreciation of aesthetic quality. In consummatory intellectual and practical experience aesthetic quality was an unintended by-product of the pursuit of other ends. Thinking at its best was beautiful, but it was not its purpose to be beautiful. The artist, on the other hand, aimed to produce an object that would be appreciated for its aesthetic quality. "In distinctively esthetic experience, characteristics that are subdued in other experiences are dominant; those that are subordinate are controlling—namely, the characteristics in virtue of which the experience is an integrated complete experience on its own account" (*AE*, 62). In aesthetic experience "the factors that determine anything which can be called *an* experience are lifted high above the threshold of perception and are made manifest for their own sake" (*AE*, 63).

Herein, Dewey argued, lay the general significance of works of art for philosophy. They opened a window on "experience in its integrity" (*AE*, 278). In art one confronted experience as a complex yet unified whole steeped in values, which for Dewey was experience at its best, and the analysis of distinctively aesthetic experience—the creation and appreciation of works of art—that he offered was controlled throughout by his more inclusive notion of organic, consummatory experience. He aimed, that is, to make the case that art manifested "what actual existence actually becomes when its possibilities are fully expressed." It was to aesthetic experience, he argued, that "the philosopher must go to understand what experience is" because aesthetic experience was "experience freed from the forces that impede and confuse its development as experience; freed, that is, from factors that subordinate an experience as it is directly had to something beyond itself" (*AE*, 285, 278). As Edman noted, "The whole of Dewey's philosophy of art is not so much what is commonly called 'esthetics' as it is a work on experience *in excelsis*, a comment upon, and an analysis of experience as it is when it is what it always is in possibility: rich, rounded, ordered and directly and immediately enjoyable."[19]

19. Irwin Edman, "Dewey and Art," in Hook, ed., *John Dewey*, p. 50. James Gouinlock has astutely observed that "*Art as Experience* might more accurately have been titled

I will sketch Dewey's argument for aesthetic experience as the model of consummatory experience here without the wealth of detail he offered as evidence for it, which I fear renders it unduly abstract (even for Dewey). But it is worth at least noting that this analysis was not bereft of concrete readings of particular works of art, especially of paintings and poems. Although Dewey leaned heavily on Barnes, particularly in his comments on the visual arts, *Art as Experience* was also an impressive yet unpretentious display of his own prodigious reading in aesthetics and his deep and abiding appreciation of a wide range of works of art. Moreover, though his taste in literature was decidedly old-fashioned, Dewey (thanks again to Barnes) exhibited considerable enthusiasm and understanding of Post-Impressionist painting. If nothing else, *Art as Experience* offered conclusive evidence that Dewey was not the utilitarian philistine Mumford took him to be. This was a book in which the informing voices were not those of Locke, Bacon, and Bentham but those of Shakespeare, Shelley, Matisse, and, above all, Keats.

"The real work of art," Dewey argued, "is the building up of an integral experience out of the interaction of organic and environmental conditions and energies" (*AE*, 70). Art was "nature transformed by entering into new relationships where it evokes a new emotional response," an expression of "esthetic emotion," which was "native emotion transformed through the objective material to which it has committed its development and consummation" (*AE*, 85). Art provided experiences that served to clarify and concentrate "meanings contained in scattered and weakened ways in the material of other experiences" (*AE*, 90). Science, of course, might be said to do the same thing, but there was a fundamental difference in the ways science and art illuminated experience. Scientific statements provided a symbolic roadmap to experience, directions leading to an experience. Aesthetic expression, on the other hand, did not give directions to an experience, it *constituted* one. "Through art, meanings of objects that are otherwise dumb, inchoate, restricted, and resisted are clarified and concentrated, and not by thought working laboriously upon them, nor by escape into a world of mere sense, but by creation of a new experience" (*AE*, 138).

Aesthetic expression was a conjunction of past and present, of old

---

Consummatory Experience in Nature, for the book is precisely that: a study of consummatory experience, of which the fine arts provide only the most conspicuous example" (*John Dewey's Philosophy of Value* [New York: Humanities Press, 1972], p. 250n).

experience and new vision. "Aspects and states of [the artist's] prior experience of varied subject matters have been wrought into his being; they are the organs with which he perceives. Creative vision modifies these materials. They take their place in an unprecedented object of a new experience" (AE, 95). In art "that which is given here and now is extended by meanings and values drawn from what is absent in fact and present only imaginatively" (AE, 276). Imagination afforded the artist a vision of possibilities in experience heretofore unseen, and these possibilities were then embodied in objects that communicated them to others. "Art throws off the covers that hide the expressiveness of experienced things; it quickens us from the slackness of routine and enables us to forget ourselves by finding ourselves in the delight of experiencing the world about us in its varied qualities and forms. It intercepts every shade of expressiveness found in objects and orders them in a new experience of life" (AE, 110). If science ventured from the unknown to the known, the path of art was the reverse. "Art departs from what has been understood and ends in wonder" (AE, 274).

Dewey made a particular point of emphasizing that appreciating a work of art was as much an active, often prolonged, process as creating one. "The work of art tells something to those who enjoy it about the nature of their own experience of the world; it presents the world in a new experience that they undergo" (AE, 89). But for the consummatory experience of art to be had by its audience, this audience had to bring together prior experience and imaginative insight in a fashion similar to that of the artist. "We lay hold of the full import of a work of art," he said, "only as we go through in our own vital processes the processes the artist went through in producing the work" (AE, 328). Appreciating art, in other words, was hard work, if not as hard as making it. One simply could not, for example, appreciate great paintings by rushing through a museum gathering up the momentary sensations they excited. Dewey himself, as his daughter-in-law noted following their trip to the museums of Leningrad in 1928, would stand for a long time in intense concentration before a painting attempting to appreciate fully the experience it afforded. The appreciation of art required cultivated taste. But because of the continuity between works of art and everyday experience, aesthetic appreciation was not an esoteric capacity confined to a favored few; it could be learned. Critics had the privilege of fostering the communication between artist and audience, but more often than not, Dewey complained, they arrested it. A few, however, had shown that even the most difficult works of art were not beyond the appreciative capacities of ordinary men and women, and his friend Barnes favored such students not only to thumb his nose at the Philadelphia gentry but to make this very point.[20]

If the work of art was a successful one, the experience it afforded was *an* experience, that is, experience distinguished by the organic form of consummatory experience generally. "There is," Dewey said, "an old formula for beauty in nature and art: Unity in variety" (*AE*, 166). And this was the formula to which he adhered in defining aesthetic objects and estimating their quality. "Mutual adaptation of parts to one another in constituting a whole is the relation which, formally speaking, characterizes a work of art," he argued, and occasionally he went so far as to describe the work of art literally as an organism (*AE*, 140, 196–197). The measure of greatness in art was the degree to which it constituted a complex—that is, an internally differentiated yet unified—organism: "the variety and scope of factors which, in being rhythmic each to each, still cumulatively conserve and promote one another in building up the actual experience" (*AE*, 176). The finest art was marked by "the capacity of the whole to hold together within itself the greatest variety and scope of opposed elements" (*AE*, 184).

These Hegelian-sounding sentiments, combined with some of the more effusive, even mystical, passages in *Art as Experience* in which Dewey suggested that works of art, because of the quality of wholeness they imparted, elicited a sense of "belonging to the larger, all-inclusive, whole which is the universe in which we live," led such critics as Stephen Pepper and Benedetto Croce to the conclusion that he had either returned to the idealist fold or, as some had suspected, had never really abandoned idealism. Dewey responded acidly to this supposition. In the text itself he warned against drawing the wrong conclusion from the fact that he often spoke of "a quality of an intense esthetic experience that is so immediate as to be ineffable and mystical." Only "an intellectualized reading of this immediate quality of experience," he cautioned, "translates it into the terms of a dream-metaphysics" (*AE*, 297). In response to Pepper he observed that just because he used words like "whole, complete, coherence, integration, etc." did not necessarily mean he was an idealist. Idealists had no monopoly on these terms, and they employed them to quite different purposes than he did. He was convinced that "the school of objective idealism has borrowed these traits from esthetic experiences, where they do have application, and has then illegitimately extended them till they became categories of the universe at large, endowed with cosmic import." He

20. Greenfield, *Devil and Dr. Barnes*, p. 64.

himself had applied such terms only to experiences with esthetic quality, using them in "a sense which is *special* just because it belongs to experiences as esthetic and *not* to experiences of other kinds, and certainly not to the world at large as objects of distinctively *cognitive* experience."[21]

But if Dewey did not intend to render the world at large as a unity in *Art as Experience*, it could at least be said that this text was the best place to find him carrying the remnants of the Hegelian hoop through which he had jumped on his way to empirical naturalism. If he no longer believed God was at work shaping nature into an organic whole, he did affirm that this was the work of the artist on a more modest scale. Art provided human beings a glimpse of what the world would be like if they had godlike powers and were not subject to the contingency and uncertainty that were generic traits of nature. He observed:

Through selection and organization those features that make any experience worth having as an experience are prepared by art for commensurate perception. There must be, in spite of all indifference and hostility of nature to human interests, some congruity of nature with man or life could not exist. In art the forces that are congenial, that sustain not this or that special aim but the process of enjoyed experience itself, are set free. That release gives them ideal quality. For what ideal can man honestly entertain save the idea of an environment in which all things conspire to the perfecting and sustaining of the values occasionally and partially experienced? (*AE*, 190)

For our purposes, the most significant arguments in *Art as Experience* were those considering the cultural role of art and the artist. Because the objects of art were expressive, Dewey said, they necessarily communicated. This function need not require that the artist intend to communicate, and indeed the less artists were committed to expressing a particular message the more expressive their work was likely to be.

21. JD, "Experience, Knowledge and Value: A Rejoinder," in Paul Schilpp, *The Philosophy of John Dewey*, 2d ed. (New York: Tudor, 1951), pp. 549–554. These pages are a response to Stephen Pepper, "Some Questions on Dewey's Esthetics," in the same volume (pp. 369–389). See also Pepper, "The Concept of Fusion in Dewey's Aesthetic Theory," *Journal of Aesthetics and Art Criticism* 12 (1953): 169–176; Benedetto Croce, "On the Aesthetics of Dewey," and JD, "A Comment on the Foregoing Criticisms" (1948) *Later Works* 15:438–444, 97–100; and Croce, "Dewey's Aesthetics and Theory of Knowledge," *Journal of Aesthetics and Art Criticism* 11 (1952): 1–6. For a good discussion of this debate and a more detailed consideration of Dewey's aesthetics than I can offer here see Thomas M. Alexander, *John Dewey's Theory of Art, Experience, and Nature: The Horizons of Feeling* (Albany: SUNY Press, 1987).

Moreover, this function did not require artists to tailor their work to the appreciative capacities of a current audience, for because they were communicating a new experience, at first few would probably appreciate their work. Great artists were "animated by a deep conviction that since they can only say what they have to say, the trouble is not with their work but those who, having eyes, see not, and having ears, hear not. Communicability has nothing to do with popularity." Yet over time it was true, as Tolstoy said, that "no man is eloquent save when some one is moved as he listens," and artists should work to create an audience that could appreciate their work. For in the end, Dewey believed, "works of art are the only media of complete and unhindered communication between man and man that can occur in a world full of gulfs and walls that limit community of experience" (*AE*, 110).

Because art was "the means of keeping alive the sense of purposes that outrun evidence and of meanings that transcend indurated habit," artists had an extremely important place in the moral life of their culture, one at least as important as that of philosophers. As Dewey indicated in *Experience and Nature*, philosophers were trespassing on the territory of the artist when they attempted to bring home the goods of experience to perception, and he elaborated on this important ethical function of art in *Art as Experience*, concluding his aesthetics with the assertion that "imagination is the chief instrument of the good" (*AE*, 350). Philosophers and artists alike might function as moral critics, he said, but, whereas philosophers best did so directly and self-consciously, when artists ventured direct, self-conscious moral criticism the result was usually bad art. Art best served as a criticism of life "not directly, but by disclosure, through imaginative vision addressed to imaginative experience (not to set judgment) of possibilities that contrast with actual conditions. A sense of possibilities that are unrealized and that might be realized are when they are put in contrast with actual conditions, the most penetrating 'criticism' of the latter that can be made. . . . Only imaginative vision elicits the possibilities that are interwoven within the texture of the actual" (*AE*, 349, 348). Shelley, Dewey concluded, was correct to proclaim poets the unacknowledged legislators of the world, for "the first intimations of wide and large redirections of desire and purpose are of necessity imaginative. Art is a mode of prediction not found in charts and statistics, and it insinuates possibilities of human relations not to be found in rule and precept, admonition and administration" (*AE*, 352).[22]

22. See also *Experience and Nature* (1929), *Later Works* 1:322.

Cultures, Dewey asserted, were best estimated by the depth and breadth of the aesthetic experience they afforded. "Neither the savage nor the civilized man is what he is by native constitution but by the culture in which he participates. The final measure of the quality of that culture is the arts which flourish" (*AE*, 347). By this criteria, he observed with dismay, modern industrial civilization was sadly wanting, not because it lacked great artists and great works of art but because art was so isolated from the rest of life. Modern society was afflicted with a "museum conception" of art which built a wall around works of art and rendered their significance "almost opaque" (*AE*, 9). The communication by artists of imagined possibilities of experience to most other members of their culture had broken down badly; the lives of most individuals were without significant aesthetic experience; and the critical moral function of art had been substantially weakened. Art had become an insignificant diversion from the business of life, which was business.

If Dewey's analysis of the continuity between art and the rest of experience was correct, there was nothing inherent in art which fostered its contemporary isolation, a conclusion buttressed by evidence from earlier civilizations in which art and ordinary life were far more closely integrated. This evidence, as he said, raised some crucial questions. "*If* artistic and esthetic quality is implicit in every normal experience, how shall we explain how and why it so generally fails to become explicit? Why is it that to multitudes art seems to be an importation into experience from a foreign country and the esthetic to be a synonym for something artificial?" (*AE*, 18).

The answer to these questions, Dewey contended, was to be found primarily in the effects of capitalism on the relationship between art and common life. It was no accident, he said, that the consolidation of "museum culture" coincided closely with the emergence of fully developed market societies. Individual capitalists and capitalist societies collected fine works of art as signifiers both of their wealth and of their capacity to commit themselves to something more refined than the accumulation of capital which absorbed them in everyday experience. In capitalist cultures works of art "reflect and establish superior cultural status, while their segregation from the common life reflects the fact that they are not part of a native and spontaneous culture. They are a kind of counterpart of a holier-than-thou attitude, exhibited not toward persons as such but toward the interests and occupations that absorb most of the community's time and energy" (*AE*, 14–15). Floating free of such interests and occupations, works of art lost the connection with the *"genius loci* of which they were once the natural expression," a process vastly enhanced by the production of art for sale on what had become a world market. "Objects that were in the past valid and significant because of their place in the life of a community now function in isolation from the conditions of their origin. By that fact they are also set apart from common experience, and serve as insignia of taste and certificates of special culture" (*AE*, 15). Finding their work isolated in this fashion, artists took refuge in an ideology of "self-expression" which made a virtue of their alienation and enhanced the esoteric status of art. Finally, philosophers who believed this separation to be the normal state of affairs arrived to locate art "in a region inhabited by no other creature," after which followed "much applause for the wonders of appreciation and the glories of the transcendent beauty of art indulged in without much regard to capacity for esthetic perception in the concrete" (*AE*, 15–16).[23]

But industrial capitalism fostered an even greater "chasm between ordinary and esthetic experience" by draining everyday social life of aesthetic quality. In modern society, "the hostility to association of fine art with normal processes of living is a pathetic, even a tragic, commentary on life as it is ordinarily lived. Only because that life is usually so stunted, aborted, slack or heavy laden, is the idea entertained that there is some inherent antagonism between the process of normal living and creation and enjoyment of works of esthetic art" (*AE*, 34).

The debilitating effects of capitalism in this regard were particularly evident in the workplace, arguably the most important site in which to assess the diffusion of consummatory experience in a society. Modern work, Dewey said, was not work but labor, that is, an activity in which means and ends were related externally and not intrinsically. "The toil of a laborer is too often only an antecedent to the wage he receives, as consumption of gasoline is merely a means to transportation. The means cease to act when the 'end' is reached; one would be glad, as a rule, to get the result without having to employ the means. They are but a scaffolding" (*AE*, 201). This inorganic relationship of means and ends was not only not aesthetic but the very definition of the nonaesthetic,

23. Dewey's critique of museum culture and his call for a reintegration of art and everyday life had a significant influence on one of his former students, Holger Cahill, who served as director of Federal Art Project of the Works Progress Administration in the thirties. See Cahill, "American Resources in the Arts," in Francis V. O'Connor, ed., *Art for the Millions: Essays from the 1930s by Artists and Administrators of the WPA Federal Art Project* (Greenwich, Conn.: New York Graphic Society, 1973), pp. 33–44, and Jane De Hart Mathews, "Arts and the People: The New Deal Quest for a Cultural Democracy," *Journal of American History* 62 (1975): 322–323.

and this nonconsummatory labor was the lot of most industrial workers. Work in which means and ends were intimately linked had, like art,
become a sideshow.[24]

Blame for this, Dewey maintained, lay not with the "machine," as
many contended, but with a political economy in which "prestige goes
to those who use their minds without participation of the body and who
act vicariously through control of the bodies and labor of others" (*AE*,
27). The problem was less one of the technological forces of production
than of the social relations of production, less one of wealth than of the
power that wealth granted some to control the work of others. As such
it could not be solved by higher wages or more leisure. "No permanent
solution is possible save in a radical social alteration, which effects the
degree and kind of participation the worker has in the production and
social disposition of the wares he produces" (*AE*, 345):

> Oligarchical control from the outside of the processes and the products
> of work is the chief force in preventing the worker from having that
> intimate interest in what he does and makes that is an essential prereq-
> uisite of esthetic satisfaction. There is nothing in the nature of machine
> production *per se* that is an insuperable obstacle in the way of workers'
> consciousness of the meaning of what they do and enjoyment of the
> satisfactions of companionship and of useful work well done. The
> psychological conditions resulting from private control of the labor of
> other men for the sake of private gain, rather than any fixed psycho-
> logical or economic law, are the forces that suppress and limit esthetic
> quality in the experience that accompanies processes of production.
> (*AE*, 346)

Industrial civilization had thus severely limited the participation of its
working class in aesthetic as well as material goods. Rectifying the adverse effects of an inegalitarian distribution of social power was thus
impossible "by any revolution that stops short of affecting the imagination and emotions of man" (*AE*, 346).

As these comments suggest, *Art as Experience* was not incidental to the
radical politics that absorbed Dewey in the 1930s. Indeed, it was one of
the most powerful statements of that politics, for it clearly indicated

---

24. This argument, which, as we have seen, can be found in Dewey's earliest writings,
was one he developed throughout the twenties. In the major books of that decade he
turned to an account of modern industrial labor whenever he required an example of the
dissociation of means and ends characteristic of human activity that fell short of the
artful. See, for example, *Human Nature and Conduct* (1922), *Middle Works* 14:82–87, 100–
103, 208, 211, and *Experience and Nature*, pp. 272, 275–279.

that his was not a radicalism directed solely to the material well-being of the American people but directed as well to the provision of consummatory experience that could be found only outside the circulation of commodities. The "esthetic politics" he called for in this book required not only that "the products of art should be accessible to all" but also that "the values that lead to production and intelligent enjoyment of art have to be incorporated into the system of social relationships." Art itself, he concluded, "is not secure under modern conditions until the mass of men and women who do the useful work of the world have the opportunity to be free in conducting the processes of production and are richly endowed in capacity for enjoying the fruits of collective work" (*AE*, 347).

CONSTRUCTING GOOD

Nothing frustrated the literary intellectuals who criticized Dewey's philosophy more than his refusal, as Waldo Frank put it, to "hierarchise" his values. Philosophers and intellectuals, these critics argued, should do more than Dewey had done to specify and rank those "ideal values which dignify and give meaning to human life." Those prescriptions Dewey did seem willing to offer, they complained, were merely methodological. He had strong views about how one should form values, but little to say about which values one should form. He talked a great deal about evaluation, they protested, but said little about the ideals that should guide such evaluation.[25]

There was something to this criticism, though not as much as its proponents believed. Dewey *was* wary of wholesale (if not particular) ethical prescriptions and vigorously resisted any hierarchical ranking of values. But he offered good reasons for this wariness, if not reasons that carried much weight with critics worried more than he was about relativism and less than he was about absolutism. He did believe that the preeminent task of the moral life was that of developing and institutionalizing intelligent methods of judgment. But his methodological prescriptions carried more ethical power than his critics were willing to admit. Dewey could never satisfy those who believed that there were

25. Frank, *Re-Discovery of America*, p. 172. At times, others defended Dewey from such charges more effectively than he defended himself. See Philip M. Glick, "The Philosophy of John Dewey," *New Republic*, 1 August 1928: 281–282; James Farrell and Joseph Ratner, "Letters to the Editor," *Saturday Review*, 12 July 1930: 1194; and Sidney Hook, "John Dewey and His Critics," *New Republic*, 3 June 1931: 73–74.

absolute, certain, "hierarchised" values that could and should guide the moral life—such a stance, in his view, betrayed a woeful misunderstanding of human experience. But it cannot be said that his ethics left his readers without a clue as to where he thought the good life lay. And, in the face of the claim by some influential philosophers in the 1930s that terms like "good" and "right" were meaningless expressions of emotion and hence beyond rational dispute, he continued to venture arguments for tightly binding values to intelligence.

The contention that moral language was meaningless or nonpropositional—a position termed variously "emotivism" or "noncognitivism"—was closely associated in the interwar years with logical positivism, an important school of emigré philosophers from Germany and Austria seeking a foothold in the United States and Great Britain in the thirties. Many philosophers in this school hoped to establish common ground with American pragmatism and the leading American pragmatist. The positivists were especially eager to enlist Dewey's participation in their Unity of Science project, which centered on publication of an extremely ambitious *International Encyclopedia of Unified Science* in which they proposed to explore the foundations of the various special sciences in order to advance their integration. Dewey's student Ernest Nagel has recounted an amusing story about the efforts of editor Otto Neurath to solicit a contribution to the *Encyclopedia* from Dewey which suggests the ardor with which the positivists courted him:

I accompanied Neurath and Sidney Hook when they called on Dewey at his home; and Neurath was having obvious difficulty in obtaining Dewey's participation in the *Encyclopedia* venture. Dewey had one objection—there may have been others, but this is the only one I recall—to Neurath's invitation. The objection was that since the Logical Positivists subscribed to the belief in atomic facts or atomic propositions, and since Dewey did not think there are such things, he could not readily contribute to the *Encyclopedia*. Now at that time Neurath spoke only broken English, and his attempts at explaining his version of Logical Positivism were not very successful. Those of us who knew Neurath will remember his elephantine sort of physique. When he realized that his efforts at explanation were getting him nowhere, he got up, raised his right hand as if he were taking an oath in a court of law (thereby almost filling Dewey's living room), and solemnly declared, "I *swear* we don't believe in atomic propositions." This pronouncement won the day for Neurath. Dewey agreed to write the monograph, and ended by saying, "Well, we ought to celebrate," and brought out the liquor and mixed a drink.

As it turned out, Dewey's objections to the views of the logical positivists were manifold, and the celebration was premature (though Dewey sustained his affection for Neurath). He did eventually contribute the *Theory of Valuation* (1939) and one other article on science and ethics to the *Encyclopedia*, but he made a point in these contributions and elsewhere of sharply distinguishing his value theory from that of his Central European suitors and their Anglo-American allies. In so doing, he elaborated on and clarified his logical theory of practical and moral judgments, which, as I noted, was one of the muddiest and most controversial aspects of his initial formulation of instrumentalism.[26]

In the mid-thirties the most prominent statement of the emotivist position was that advanced by British philosopher A. J. Ayer in his *Language, Truth and Logic* (1936), and Dewey subjected Ayer's arguments to critical scrutiny in his *Theory of Valuation*. Statements of ethical value, Ayer argued, were not, in any sense, statements of empirical fact, but rather simple expressions of emotion and hence could not be judged scientifically to be true or false. Moral predicates like "good" and "bad" or "right" and "wrong" were "pseudo-concepts" that added no factual content to propositions but only evinced moral approval or disapproval. Such terms did not make assertions about objects but merely expressed feelings about them. "In fact," Ayer said, "we may define the meaning of the various ethical words in terms of the different feelings they are ordinarily taken to express, and also the different responses they are calculated to provoke." Ayer was not even willing to grant that ethical language was propositional language in that it asserted the mere existence of certain feelings. When one said that a certain object was "good," that is, one was not, according to Ayer, asserting the proposition that one had certain feelings about that object

26. Nagel in Corliss Lamont, ed., *Dialogue on John Dewey* (New York: Horizon Press, 1959), pp. 11–13. For some further discussion of Dewey's differences with the logical positivists see Chapter 14. See also the critical comments about this school in JD to Corrinne Chisholm Frost, 22 July 1939, in "Reflections of John Dewey: Excerpts from Unpublished Correspondence," *Daedalus* 88 (1959): 552, and JD to James Farrell, 2 March 1941, Dewey Papers. Dewey's initial contribution to the *International Encyclopedia of Unified Science* was "Unity of Science as a Social Problem" (1938), *Later Works* 13:271–280. On the history of the *Encyclopedia* see "International Encyclopedia of Unified Science," *Science* 86 (29 October 1937): 400–401, and Charles Morris, "On the History of the International Encyclopedia of Unified Science," *Synthese* 12 (1960): 517–521. In Neurath's most grandiose vision the *Encyclopedia* was to contain twenty-six volumes comprised of 260 monographs. In the end, only the first two volumes (nineteen monographs), titled *The Foundations of the Unity of Science*, were published. Dewey's *Theory of Valuation* was not the only contribution to the series to distance itself decidedly from logical positivism; the most important of these monographs was Thomas Kuhn's *Structure of Scientific Revolutions* (1962).

but rather merely "evincing" one's feelings. "Ethical statements are expressions and excitants of feeling which do not necessarily involve any assertions." Because sentences that expressed moral judgments were but expressions of feeling, one could not determine whether they were true or false. "They are unverifiable for the same reason as a cry of pain or a word of command is unverifiable—because they do not express genuine propositions." Because of this unverifiability, questions of value were not subject to reasoned argument, and ethical philosophy (as distinct from psychology or sociology) could merely observe that "ethical concepts are pseudo-concepts and therefore unanalysable."[27]

To Dewey, this emotivist argument was not only weak but culturally disastrous. He himself had spilled a great deal of ink challenging both absolutist claims to a higher Reason that could judge the truth and falsity of ethical judgments and utilitarian formulations of a hedonistic calculus which offered a false promise of moral certainty to ordinary intelligence. But he had done so in order to clear a path for a genuinely fruitful logic of evaluation, not to set up an impassable barricade between science and values. Logical positivism, he observed in 1946, had converted "the practical neglect by modern philosophies of political and moral subjects into systematic theoretical denial of the possibility of intelligent concern with them. It holds that the practical affairs of men which are of highest and deepest significance are matters of value and valuations, and that *therefore* they are by their very nature incapable of intellectual adjudication; of either justification or condemnation on rational grounds." At the very least, one had to hope that arguments like Ayer's were mistaken, for, Dewey asked, "what is the probable destiny of man on earth if regulation of the concrete conditions under which men live continues to increase at its present rate, while the consequences produced by them are necessarily left at the mercy of likes and dislikes that are, in turn, at the mercy of irrational habits, institutions, and a class and sectarian distribution of power between the stronger and the weaker?" Should the emotivist perspective become widespread, all disagreements on matters of value would be presumed beyond reasoned dispute and subject entirely to the vagaries of power. Moral argument would give way to "bashing in of heads." But the more likely effect of this view would be to drive people in reaction into the arms of the supernaturalists. "In a time as troubled as the present," he re-

27. A. J. Ayer, *Language, Truth and Logic,* 2d ed. (New York: Dover, 1946), pp. 102–112.

marked, "a philosophy which denies the existence of any natural and human means of determining judgments as to what is good and evil will work to the benefit of those who hold that they have in their possession super-human and super-natural means for infallible ascertainment of ultimate ends, especially as they also claim to possess the practical agencies for ensuring the attainment of final good by men who accept the truths they declare."[28]

Dewey's critique of Ayer's argument in *Theory of Valuation* took the form of demonstrating that, if one took into account the context in which emotive "ejaculations" of all sorts were made (not only those using moral terms or, indeed, words at all), most were in fact propositional value judgments of a predictive sort. Thus, even if one granted the positivist assumption that value statements were merely emotive ejaculations, one need not deny that they were propositional or subject to at least some empirical tests.

An ejaculation that evinced feelings, Dewey noted, was a component of a larger organic situation. A baby's cry, for example, was constituent of a situation involving hunger, pain, or some other such experience. As such, it was not a value expression or even linguistic behavior. But within the social context of interpersonal relationships in which such ejaculations occurred, they could be (and usually were) taken and/or intended as signs: the mother took the baby's cry to mean that the baby was hungry or hurt, and eventually the baby learned to cry as a sign designed to evoke a response from the mother. Taken and used as signs, such expressions were linguistic symbols that said something propositional ("I am hungry") that was subject to empirical verification or refutation. Thus at least some emotive expressions were propositional. One might argue that, though both moral judgments and propositions such as this were emotive expressions, only the former were value expressions and that something special about value expressions rendered them nonpropositional. But, Dewey observed, the latter were also value propositions because, when unpacked, they could be seen to refer indirectly to an existing situation to which a relatively negative value was attached and indirectly to a more desirable future situation that the proposition was intended to help produce. Moreover, they advanced "a specifiable and testable relation between the latter as an

28. "Introduction: The Problems of Men and the Present State of Philosophy" (1946), *Later Works* 15:159–160; "Some Questions about Value" (1944), *Later Works* 15:107. See also the exchange between JD and logical positivist Hans Reichenbach in Schilpp, *Philosophy of John Dewey*, pp. 178–182, 540–543.

end and certain activities as means for accomplishing it." For example, the baby's cry, when intended as a sign, said something like the following: "I am hungry, which is an unappealing situation, and I cannot do anything about it myself. If you read my cry correctly, mother, and get me something to eat, I will be satisfied and no longer in pain, which is a good thing." If the baby is fed, and the prediction is born out, then the cry could be said to have articulated a true, value-laden proposition. Ayer, Dewey concluded, was correct in pointing out similarities between value judgments using moral terms with emotive expressions like a baby's cry. Indeed, they were even more tightly linked than he indicated since the latter were, when their context was considered, also value expressions. But he was mistaken to believe that neither were empirically testable propositions.[29]

The shortcomings of Ayer's analysis, Dewey asserted, could be traced to a failing common in many theories about value judgments: failure to consider the experiential context in which such judgments were made. This context, as was the case for all judgments, was the problematic situation. Valuation involved desiring, and desires arose only in problematic existential contexts, situations "in which some lack prevents the immediate execution of an active tendency" (*TV*, 205):

> Desires arise only when "there is something the matter," when there is some "trouble" in an existing situation. When analyzed, this "some-

29. *Theory of Valuation* (1939), *Later Works* 13:196–202. Page numbers for further references (*TV*) appear in the text. At least two commentaries on the Ayer-Dewey debate suggest that the two philosophers were talking past one another in that Ayer was chiefly making a point about nondescriptive uses of moral language which Dewey could have accepted without undercutting his own analysis of moral experience and in that Dewey was talking about a descriptive use of moral language which Ayer did not regard as properly ethical and hence simply ignored. See Stanley Cavell and Alexander Sesonske, "Logical Empiricism and Pragmatism in Ethics," *Journal of Philosophy* 48 (1951): 5–17, and Gouinlock, *Dewey's Philosophy of Value*, pp. 188–197. Dewey took up the second of the positivist claims about value judgments, that they not only evinced feelings but were imperatives designed to move others to particular actions, in a critical comment on the work of Charles Stevenson, a prominent American emotivist who focused on this aspect of moral language in his widely discussed book *Ethics and Language* (1944). Dewey did not doubt the obvious fact that sentences with ethical terms were often used to encourage, alter, or redirect conduct, but he did deny that this function was "legitimately ethical" unless it was a matter of giving good reasons for acting one way or another. "*Evaluative* statements concern or have reference to what ends are to-be-chosen, what lines of conduct are to be followed, what policies are to-be-adopted. But it is morally necessary to state grounds or reasons for the course advised and recommended. Insofar as noncognitive or extracognitive factors were at work in ethical sentences, "those sentences are by just that much deprived of the properties sentences should have in order to be genuinely *ethical*" ("Ethical Subject-Matter and Language," [1945], *Later Works*, 15:139, 137). On Dewey and Stevenson see Gouinlock, *Dewey's Philosophy of Value*, pp. 198–201, and Sidney

thing the matter" is found to spring from the fact that there is something lacking, wanting, in the existing situation as it stands, an absence which produces conflict in the elements that do exist. When things are going completely smoothly, desires do not arise, and there is no occasion to project ends-in-view, for "going smoothly" signifies that there is no need for effort and struggle. It suffices to let things take their "natural" course. (*TV*, 220)

As responses to such problematic situations, desires were not prerational impulses (though such impulses might be said to be an element of desire) because they had an inherent intellectual component to them. "Vital impulses are doubtless conditions *sine qua non* for the existence of desires and interests. But the latter include foreseen consequences along with ideas in the form of signs of the measures (involving expenditure of energy) required to bring the ends into existence" (*TV*, 207). A desire was not then a noncognitive feeling but a prizing of a particular object or end-in-view because that object was thought to be a means to the solution to the troubles that provoked the desire. Hence desiring was not an "affective-motor" but an "affective-*ideational*-motor" activity and contained predictive judgments (*TV*, 218). To desire an object was, in effect, to argue that that object as an end-in-view would, when actively pursued and achieved, resolve the troubled situation in which the agent currently found himself. Because all such judgments were subject to empirical test by measuring the consequences of the end-achieved against the consequences predicted by the end-in-view, they were subject to verification or refutation and could be then said to be warranted or unwarranted.[30]

The key to this argument was the treatment of all ends as means. That is, within the concrete context of particular value judgments, ends were initially the ends-in-view of particular desires, which were means to the resolution of particular problems and were to be assessed as such. One could test the judgments that one's desires entailed simply by acting on them without further reflection, and thereby often learn the hard way that uninterrogated desires often embodied unwarranted predictive judgments. *Appraisal* took place when one subjected desires

---

Hook, "The Desirable and Emotive in Dewey's Ethics," in Hook, ed., *John Dewey*, pp. 207–216.

30. For an astute discussion of the centrality of this contention that desires have an intellectual component to Dewey's theory of valuation and to his claim to have transcended traditional empiricist and rationalist theories of value see Paul E. Hurley, "Dewey on Desires: The Lost Argument," *Transactions of the Charles S. Peirce Society* 24 (1988): 509–519.

(prizings) to critical scrutiny by investigating the conditions under which they arose and, especially, by estimating the consequences of acting on them. These estimates were a matter of considering the efficacy of the end-in-view for reconstructing the problematic situation. This involved foreseeing the consequences of utilizing the means necessary to achieve the desired end and the consequences achieving it might have for the whole range of one's interests (that is, the way the end would itself function in subsequent experience as a resource or obstacle). "The more overtly and emphatically the valuation of objects as ends is connected with desire and interest, the more evident it should be that, since desire and interest are ineffectual save as they cooperatively interact with environing conditions, valuation of desire and interest, as means correlated with other means, is the sole condition for valid appraisal of objects as ends" (*TV*, 216). The net outcome of investigation of the ways in which people actually made value judgments indicated "(i) that the problem of valuation in general as well as in particular cases concerns things that sustain to one another the relation of means-ends; that (ii) ends are determinable only on the ground of the means that are involved in bringing them about; and that (iii) desires and interests must themselves be evaluated as means in their interaction with external or environing conditions. Ends-in-view, as distinct from ends as accomplished results, themselves function as directive means; or, in ordinary language, as *plans*" (*TV*, 238).

The role of intelligence in value judgments on this account was to ensure that desires reflected a full consideration of the consequences of realizing their ends-in-view. A value judgment was adequate "in just the degree in which the end is constituted in terms of the conditions of its actualization" (*TV*, 218). Desires were more or less intelligent depending on "the adequacy with which inquiry into lacks and conflicts of the existing situation has been carried on" and "the adequacy of the inquiry into the likelihood that the particular end-in-view which is set up will, if acted upon, actually fill the existing need and do away with conflict by directing activity so as to institute a unified state of affairs" (*TV*, 221–222). The end-in-view that emerged from this sort of appraisal was not merely desired but desirable:

The "desirable," or the object which *should* be desired (valued), do not descend out of the a priori blue nor descend as an imperative from a moral Mount Sinai. It presents itself because past experience has shown that hasty action upon uncriticized desire leads to defeat and possibly to catastrophe. The "desirable" as distinct from the "desired" does not then designate something at large or a priori. It points to the difference between the operation and consequences of unexamined impulses and those of desires and interests that are the product of investigation of conditions and consequences. (*TV*, 219)

Few denied that propositions about means could have evidential warrant and be subject to experimental test. And if on close examination value judgments were at bottom appraisals of means (and means to means), if distinguishing the desired from the desirable was a matter of critical inquiry into conditions and consequences, then scientific inquiry and the scientific attitude were essential to sound value judgments.[31]

Objections to this argument, Dewey noted, were bound to come from those who felt it neglected the preeminence in value judgments of "ends-in-themselves." Dewey, such critics would say, was dealing with *mere* means, an important yet secondary and technical affair, and not "real" ends, which were not subject to scientific evaluation but could only be felt (the traditional empiricist position) or discovered by a higher reason (the traditional rationalist position). But, Dewey countered, the advocates of ends-in-themselves ignored the way in which ends actually functioned in value-laden experience, which was as means (as plans), and their position was indefensible apart from the bald assertion that "real" ends should not also be means. Ironically, it was this position and not Dewey's means-focused theory of valuation which reduced the role of scientific intelligence in the moral life to technical reason, for it protected a select group of ends-in-view from the critical scrutiny that his theory sought to put at the heart of ethical deliberation. The affirmation of ends-in-themselves led to a defense of the dubious maxim that "the end justifies the means," which posited a unilateral rather than a reciprocal relationship between ends and means. This unilateral relationship shielded the end from criticism occasioned by any untoward consequences of the means used to achieve it or by any adverse effects it might have as a means to further consequences. This faulty maxim was perhaps the best evidence (albeit negative) that "the distinction between ends and means is temporal and relational. Every condition that has to be brought into existence in order to serve as means is, *in that connection*, an object of desire and an end-in-view, while the end actually reached is a means to future ends as

---

31. This important distinction between the desired and the desirable was first (and less adequately) formulated in *The Quest for Certainty* (1929), *Later Works* 4:203–228. See also *Logic: The Theory of Inquiry* (1938), *Later Works* 12:161–181.

well as a test of valuations previously made. Since the end attained is a condition of further existential occurrences, it must be appraised as a potential obstacle and potential resource" (*TV*, 229). If the fallacy of the ends-in-themselves position were abandoned, Dewey concluded, "human beings would for the first time in history be in a position to frame ends-in-view and form desires on the basis of empirically grounded propositions of the temporal relations of events to one another" (*TV*, 229).[32]

Dewey argued that responsibility for the failure of the ends-in-themselves school to close down in the face of an empirical analysis of value judgments had, in part, to be laid at the feet of empiricists (such as Ayer) who had advanced an empirical yet false description of this crucial feature of human experience. Most empiricists treated desires apart from the contextual situations in which they arose and thus ignored the intellectual factor in every desire (its character as a prediction). Taken at large in this fashion, desires became ultimate for Hobbes, Hume, and their positivist successors and thereby inaccessible to empirical test. As a result, valuation became arbitrary: "any desire is just as 'good' as any other in respect to the value it institutes." As I noted, the most troubling thing for Dewey about this theory was not the anarchy that threatened in the unlikely event that people tried to live by this theory but the credence its failures lent to the theories of transcendental rationalists, the principal defenders of ends-in-themselves. Such rationalism severed the connection between desire and values and tried to subject desires to the control of a priori standards and ideals, and "in its endeavor to escape from the frying pan of disordered valuations, jumps into the fire of absolutism. It confers the simulation of final and complete rational authority upon certain interests of certain persons or groups at the expense of all others: a view which, in turn, because of the consequences it entails, strengthens the notion that no intellectual and empirically reasonable control of desires, and hence of valuations and value-properties, is possible" (*TV*, 241).

To say that there were no ends-in-themselves was not to deny the existence or importance in value judgments of "generalized ideas of ends and values" such as health, justice, happiness, or freedom. But

---

32. As Dewey said, there was a sense in which "the end justifies the means" was a solid maxim, that is, in the sense that actual consequences provided warrant for the means employed to reach them. But as it was usually employed, the maxim defended the singling out of a fragment of the consequences of the use of certain means as the authority for their use while dismissing the need to consider the implications of the rest of those consequences (*TV*, 228–229).

there was no need to look beyond empirical explanations for them, Dewey contended. They were not transcendent absolutes but generalizations grounded in prior experience. They were in origin and function akin to the principles that guided all scientific investigation. "Experience has shown that problems for the most part fall into certain recurrent kinds so that there are general principles which, it is believed, proposed solutions must satisfy in a particular case. There thus develops a sort of framework of conditions to be satisfied—a framework of reference which operates in an *empirically* regulative way in given cases" (*TV*, 233). General principles of this sort were "abstract" not because they stood apart from all empirical cases but because they were not directly connected with any particular empirical case. They served as "intellectual instrumentalities in judgment of particular cases as the latter arise; they are, in effect, tools that direct and facilitate examination of things in the concrete while they are also developed by the results of their application in these cases" (*TV*, 230). They were not ends-in-themselves but standards by which to measure the effectiveness of ends-in-view as means to the resolution of particular problems, progressively self-corrective criteria of judging which agents had developed in the course of innumerable, definite, empirical instances of judgment.

This argument raised the question of which tools of this sort *should* guide judgment in 1939, that is, what sort of criteria did past experience indicate an agent ought to use in evaluating the foreseen conditions and consequences of establishing a particular end-in-view. Which standards of judgment promised on the basis of past performance to most effectively secure and extend the goods of experience? This was a question Dewey posed but did not answer in his *Theory of Valuation*, leading one reviewer, Herbert Marcuse, to charge that Dewey's ethical theory was bereft of the most important resource required to challenge fascism, a standard of judgment by which to condemn cultures that were forging an "escape from freedom."[33]

If lack of this guidance was a shortcoming of this brief monograph, it was explicitly remedied elsewhere (and earlier) in Dewey's work. He

33. Herbert Marcuse, "Review of *Theory of Valuation*," *Studies in Philosophy and Social Sciences* 9 (1941): 144–148. Marcuse characterized Dewey's philosophy throughout this review as "positivist," by which he seems to have meant empirical (which was true) or outside the tradition of German idealism (which was not). The charge that Dewey and pragmatism had helped foster the moral disarmament of Western democracies in the face of the fascist threat was widespread in the late thirties and early forties, and I consider it at length in Chapter 14.

had since his very first essays on the logic of moral judgments acknowledged that such judgments were distinguished by the shaping influence of the character of the agent, and he reiterated this point in the thirties. "A set and disposition of character," he said, "leads to anticipation of certain kinds of consequences and to passing over other effects of action without notice. A careless man will not be aware of consequences that occur to a prudent man; if they do present themselves to thought, he will not attach the force to them which the careful man does." Ethical theorists had not fully discharged their responsibility until they had distinguished good character. A reflective morality "wants to discover what *should* be esteemed so that approbation will follow what is decided to be *worth* approving." Dewey had long believed that philosophers, as cultural critics, should critically assess the standards of moral judgment which had thus far been fashioned by human beings (including philosophers). He had made this assessment most thoroughly in the *Ethics* he wrote with James Tufts in 1908, and in a heavily revised edition of this text published in 1932, they had again taken up this task.[34]

Dewey's reiterated there (albeit more concisely and elegantly) his criticisms of utilitarian and Kantian ethics and argued for a synthetic conception of the moral life which stripped the former of its hedonistic psychology, made explicit the substantive claims of the latter's formalism, and added a good measure of neo-Aristotelian virtue ethics. As before, he pointed to an ideal of good character as "sympathetic character" that found happiness in "the objects and purposes which bring happiness to others" (*2E*, 243).

This ideal of good character, Dewey emphasized, did not prescribe any particular end but rather provided "a conception of the *way* in which ends that are adopted *should* be formed; namely, that they should be such as to merit approbation because their execution will conduce to the general well-being" (*2E*, 246). To aim at the general good did not mean to cultivate a desire for the general good, an indeterminate and vague end-in-view that "would only arouse a diffused sentimental state, without indicating just how and where conduct should be directed" (*2E*, 247). Rather it required that desires that did aim at definite and concrete ends-in-view should be evaluated in terms of their consequences for the well-being of all concerned. Here again Dewey was focusing on means, but the implications of the means he was examining were so

34. *Ethics* (1932), *Later Works* 7:175, 237. Page numbers for further references to this edition (*2E*) appear in the text.

significant that one would be hard pressed to describe them as *mere* means. In this case, a standard as means functioned "to discriminate between the various kinds of satisfaction so as to determine which kind of happiness is truly moral; that is, approvable":

> It says that among the different kinds that one is to be approved which at the same time brings satisfaction to others, or which at least harmonizes with their well-being in that it does not inflict suffering upon them. It does not tell what things should be specifically aimed at. It does tell us how to proceed in passing condemnation or giving approval to those ends and purposes which occur to the mind independently because of our desires. . . . The standard says that we should desire those objects and find our satisfaction in the things which also bring good to those with whom we are associated in friendship, comradeship, citizenship, the pursuit of science, art, and so on. (*2E*, 247–248)[35]

Dewey was once more quick to distinguish his advocacy of sympathetic character from the ethic of benevolence which guided so many reformers, an ethic he believed Thomas Carlyle had rightly termed "a universal syllabub of sentimental twaddle" (*2E*, 251). The sympathetic character was not one that gave way to sentiments of sympathy and pity in direct action. Rather it was one in which sympathy functioned as a principle of insight and reflection. "Intelligent sympathy widens and deepens concerns for consequences. To put ourselves in the place of another, to see things from the standpoint of his aims and values, to humble our estimate of our own pretensions to the level they assume in the eyes of an impartial observer, is the surest way to appreciate what justice demands in concrete cases. The real defect of sentimentalism is that it fails to consider the consequences of acting upon objective well-being; it makes the immediate indulgence of a dominant emotion more important than results" (*2E*, 251). Sympathy was the "animating mold" of moral judgment not because it had precedent over other impulses but because it furnished the best intellectual standpoint for evaluation. "The only truly *general* thought," Dewey concluded, "is the *generous* thought" (*2E*, 270).

Dewey again criticized the distinctions between self-interest and so-

---

35. This standard of appraisal was implicit in some of the examples of good moral judgment Dewey offered in *Theory of Valuation*, which led Marcuse to admit that he clearly displayed a "preference" for freedom. But absent the arguments he offered for freedom in other writings, it did appear to be little more than a bare, even arbitrary, preference. See *TV*, p. 244, and Marcuse, "Review of *Theory of Valuation*," pp. 147–148.

cial interest, selfishness and selflessness as false dichotomies traceable to exploded theories positing presocial individuals. Interest in self and community were reciprocal. The good was to be found in a reconstruction of individual desire "after a definite pattern" that took account of the desires of others; thereby one achieved "a *kind* of happiness which is harmonious with the happiness of others" (*2E*, 248). At the same time, demands to do the right thing, which were essentially the claims of others on an individual, were legitimate only so far as the obligations imposed "actually contribute to a good in which the one from whom an act is demanded will *share*" (*2E*, 230).

Again Dewey stressed that social life had intrinsic moral significance because it entered "intimately into the formation and the substance of the desires, motives, and choices which make up character" (*2E*, 340). Social institutions and practices determined the opportunities and choices available to individuals, stimulated and evoked different powers in them, and defined their obligations. Sympathetic character could not develop apart from a social context that fostered it. "Only when individuals have initiative, independence of judgment, flexibility, fullness of experience, can they act so as to enrich the lives of others, and only in this way can a truly common welfare be built up. The other side of this statement, and of the moral criterion, is that individuals are free to develop, to contribute and to share, only as social conditions break down walls of privilege and of monopolistic possession" (*2E*, 348). The social ideal of reflective morality was thus, in brief (and as always), the democratic ideal. Just as sympathetic character was essential to individual moral judgment at its best, so democracy best embodied moral intelligence in social life. Ideally, democratic society institutionalized free inquiry into the conditions and consequences of social action and afforded the opportunity for every individual to "share in the duties and rights belonging to control of social affairs" while at the same time eliminating "those external arrangements of status, birth, wealth, sex, etc., which restrict the opportunity of each individual for full development of himself" (*2E*, 349).

Throughout the thirties Dewey's ethics was buttressed by the analysis of experience he had offered in *Experience and Nature* and *Art as Experience* and, in particular, by the conceptions of growth and consummatory experience he had offered there. As a result, the essentially aesthetic criteria for measuring the moral life which had always been a characteristic of his ethics became far more explicit. Sympathetic character provided the standpoint for moral judgment because it afforded the greatest opportunity for growth and consummatory conduct. That is, it took self-realization of an essentially aesthetic sort as its ideal, an organic unity of competing forces like that characteristic of great art. Desires were to be judged on how "inclusive" they were; sound judgment was "the ability to foresee consequences in such a way that we form ends which grow into one another and reinforce one another" (2E, 189–190, 210). The moral self was the growing self, and it was "in the *quality* of becoming that virtue resides." The good person was the one "most concerned to find openings for the newly forming or growing self; since no matter how 'good' he has been, he becomes 'bad' (even though acting upon a relatively high plane of attainment) as soon as he fails to respond to the demand for growth." A bad self was mired in mere subsistence while "the growing, enlarging, liberated self, on the other hand, goes forth to met new demands and occasions, and re-adapts and remakes itself in the process." A bad self was a hopelessly divided self or a static and isolated whole. But the good self was constantly refashioning itself into a more complex, internally differentiated yet harmonious unity, into a work of art. Ends came and went but "*the* end is growth itself" (2E, 306–307). Democracy was the social ideal not only because it nurtured individual growth but because it envisioned a growing community that would itself be a complex, organic work of art, harmonizing "the development of each individual with the maintenance of a social state in which the activities of one will contribute to the good of all the others" (2E, 350).

If the animating ideals of Dewey's ethics remained largely unchanged since 1908, there had crept into his work a considerably more chastened, even occasionally tragic, view of experience and a more explicitly modest estimate of the reach of moral philosophy. The value he had attributed to consummatory experience and growth was now enhanced by a greater willingness to acknowledge its rarity. Philosophers, he said, should frankly admit that "uncertainty and conflict are inherent in morals" and that the most an agent could do in any moral conflict was "make the best adjustment he can among forces which are genuinely disparate."[36] All philosophers could do to help these agents, Dewey argued, was to provide tools, not solutions, and even with these tools there were no guarantees that agents would find a satisfactory solution to the toughest moral choices or avoid conflict among themselves about what those choices should be. Moral theory could not "offer a table of commandments in a catechism in which answers are as definite as are the questions which are asked. It can render personal

36. "Three Independent Factors in Morals" (1930), *Later Works* 5:280, 288.

choice more intelligent, but it cannot take the place of personal decision, which must be made in every case of moral perplexity" (2E, 166).

It is perhaps worth summarizing briefly what Dewey did and did not
attempt to do as a moral theorist. He did not prescribe ends-in-
themselves; rather, he attacked the notion that there were such things.
Nor did he offer his readers a "hierarchised" set of values. Indeed, he
offered no substantive prescriptions, for he believed the good of every
situation was unique. "The business of reflection in determining the
true good cannot be done once for all," he said. "It needs to be done,
and done over and over and over again, in terms of the conditions of
concrete situations as they arise" (2E, 212). He confined his attention to
ends-as-means and to the methods and criteria of judgment with which
agents might evaluate them as such, but in the process he managed to
argue for a conception of good character and a social ideal. He did not
attempt to derive values from facts, for, as he saw it, only those who
believed science had denuded nature of qualities found a need to do so.
Values were facts, hence there was no need to worry about how to find
them, only about how to secure and extend them. Nor, as Morton
White claimed, was the distinction he drew between the desired and the
desirable an effort to derive an "ought" proposition from an "is" proposition; rather, his was a concern to separate from one another the
more or less intelligent predictive judgments inherent in our desires.[37]

If Dewey limited the scope of moral theory, he did not limit the range
of resources on which agents might draw to those of moral theory or
science. Although he was convinced that "if valuing consists *wholly* and
exclusively of something inherently recalcitrant to inquiry and adjudication, then it must be admitted that it can not rise above the brute-
animal level," he readily acknowledged that the moral life required
much that science or philosophy could not offer. There was more to
the pursuit of happiness, justice, and virtue than good judgment,
which could draw only on past experience. If valuing consisted wholly
of inquiry and adjudication then it would be cut off from the untried
possibilities of experience, which could only be imagined. Imagination
was the chief instrument of the good, and Dewey believed that artists,

37. For White's influential criticism see his "Value and Obligation in Dewey and
Lewis," *Philosophical Review* 58 (1949): 321–330, and *Social Thought in America*, 3d ed.
(Boston: Beacon Press, 1976), chap. 13. And for some penetrating criticisms of his argument see Hook, "Desirable and Emotive in Dewey's Ethics," pp. 200–207; R. W. Sleeper,
"Dewey's Metaphysical Perspective: A Note on White, Geiger, and the Problem of Obligation," *Journal of Philosophy* 57 (1960):100–108; Gouinlock, *Dewey's Philosophy of Value*, pp.
137–140; and Gouinlock, "Dewey's Theory of Moral Deliberation," *Ethics* 88 (1978):
218–228.

not philosophers, were the most significant, if often unconscious, trustees of the moral imagination. Moreover, by the thirties he was arguing that, at its most visionary, the moral imagination projected inclusive ends eliciting a faith that could only be termed religious.[38]

A COMMON FAITH

"What does John Dewey think about God?" asked the editors of the *Christian Century* in 1933. "That question has been asked a thousand times by those who have come under the spell of his mind. To it Mr. Dewey has responded with profound silence. His writings have never come to grips with the concept of God, except in more or less casual rejection of the authoritarian or supernaturalistic conception. One turns the pages of his books in vain to find any treatment of the idea of God which recognizes the attempts of many modern theologians to state their theistic belief in terms consistent with the best modern thinking."[39]

The editors were more or less correct in noting Dewey's silence for over forty years on religious questions. He had had little to say about religion and nothing about God since he left Michigan and the Congregational church. In one of the few articles he did write on religious matters, a brief 1908 piece "Religion and Our Schools," he called for a moratorium on religious instruction in the public schools for reasons that suggest what lay behind his long-term suspension of discussion of religion. There were, he said, "types of religious feeling and thought which are consistent with modern democracy and modern science," that is, ways of thinking about religion that precluded supernaturalism. But, he believed, "lucidity, sincerity, and the sense of reality" demanded that "until the non-supernatural view is more completely elaborated in all its implications and is more completely in possession of the machinery of education, the schools shall keep hands off and shall do as little as possible." By the same token, Dewey kept his hands off religion and said as little as possible until he had fully elaborated his naturalism in the twenties.[40]

38. "Some Questions about Value," p. 108.
39. "Dewey and Wieman," *Christian Century*, 5 April 1933: 449.
40. "Religion and Our Schools" (1908), *Middle Works* 4:167–168. Of late, Dewey has proved something of an embarrassment to secular humanists in their battles with religious fundamentalists over the place of religion in the public schools. Because Dewey regarded his own humanism as religious and argued that this religious perspective

This done, Dewey did venture some brief remarks on nonsupernatural religion. As he saw it, his argument in his major books of the twenties for continuity between man and nature, his attempt to supplant philosophies that made man "an unnaturalized and unnaturalizable alien in the world," had religious implications. An appreciation of this continuity, he believed, should engender both a pious sense of human dependence on nature and a faith in those artful interactions with nature which were "the stay and support of all reasonable hopes." Dewey's naturalism argued for a world full of peril, yet one that would sustain if not guarantee human aspirations, a world in which one might be hopeful if not optimistic. In the human search for the means to secure and extend the valued qualities of experience, men and women were often rightly gripped by a religious sense of "a community of life in which continuities of existence are consummated." Religious experience of this sort liberated man from the "conceit of carrying the load of the universe" and generated a feeling that "within the flickering inconsequential acts of separate selves dwells a sense of the whole which claims and dignifies them."[41]

Before the thirties Dewey's fullest discussion of religious experience came in the concluding chapter of *The Quest for Certainty*. Feeling compelled perhaps by the charge of the Gifford Lectures on which the book was based to say something about the "true knowledge of God," he concluded this book by indicating that, though the quest for certainty he had attempted to quash in the preceding pages was closely tied historically to religious belief, the connection was not a necessary one. Religious conviction might detach itself from belief in an independent and antecedent realm of Reality or Being and take the form of a "natural piety" that placed its faith in the unrealized possibilities of nature which might lie ahead:

Religious faith which attaches itself to the possibilities of nature and associated living would, with its devotion to the ideal, manifest piety

---

should be "in possession of the machinery of education," he appears in legal briefs and court decisions in cases involving such matters as the content of school textbooks as a star witness for fundamentalist plaintiffs, who argue that what the humanists are attempting to do is not separate church and state in the schools but assure that a particular religious perspective has hegemony over all others. See the nicely argued ruling for such plaintiffs of Judge W. Brevard Hand of the U.S. District Court for the Southern District of Alabama in *Douglas T. Smith vs. Board of School Commissioners of Mobile County* (1987). I am grateful to Eugene Genovese for bringing this document to my attention.

41. *Experience and Nature*, pp. 314, 325–326; *Human Nature and Conduct*, p. 226.

toward the actual. It would not be querulous with respect to the defects and hardships of the latter. Respect and esteem would be given to that which is the means of realization of possibilities, and that in which the ideal is embodied if it ever finds embodiment. Aspiration and endeavor are not ends in themselves; value is not in them in isolation but in them as means to that reorganization of the existent in which approved meanings are attained. Nature and society include within themselves projection of ideal possibilities and contain the operations by which they are actualized. Nature may not be worshiped as divine even in the sense of the intellectual love of Spinoza. But nature, including humanity, with all its defects and imperfections, may evoke heartfelt piety as the source of ideals, of possibilities, of aspiration in their behalf, and as the eventual abode of all attained goods and excellencies.

Faith of this sort fostered a "sense of dependence" on nature and deflected the sin of pride which isolated men and women from nature and from one another, and, for this reason it nourished "a sense of common participation in the inevitable uncertainties of existence . . . coeval with a sense of common effort and shared destiny."[42]

Were it not for the eagerness of editors of the *Christian Century* to find out more of what Dewey thought about religion, he might not have said anything more on the subject. But in 1933 he acceded to their request to review a book titled *Is There a God?*, a reprinting of an extended, three-way "conversation" on the question that had taken place in the pages of the magazine the previous year between liberal theologians Douglas Macintosh and Henry Wieman and philosopher Max Otto, a friend of Dewey's who had argued the negative. The magazine heralded Dewey's forthcoming review in a full-page ad as "a Journalistic Event of the First Importance," and it set in motion a train of controversy which a number of Dewey's followers, if not Dewey himself, found regrettable. As events proceeded, Otto wrote Dewey that "in the back of my consciousness there has been a smile, most of the time, as I

---

42. *Quest for Certainty*, pp. 244–246. Dewey's encounter with China and Chinese philosophy appears to have influenced the development of his own natural piety. *Reconstruction in Philosophy*, the Japanese lectures, contains a striking and strikingly uncritical or even ironic account of Francis Bacon's conception of experimental science as a "torture" of nature designed to establish an "Empire of Man over Nature" (*Reconstruction in Philosophy* [1920], *Middle Works* 12:95–100). A few years later, after his stay in China, Dewey was condemning this perspective in *Experience and Nature* as that of the "ruthless overlord" (314). For evidence that the Chinese had something to do with this shift of perspective see "As the Chinese Think" (1922), *Middle Works* 13:217–227.

have said to myself: I'll bet he didn't know what he was letting himself in for when he agreed to review the debate."[43]

Dewey's review focused on Wieman's position, which struck him as the most interesting because it defined the outer limits of liberal theism. Macintosh clearly believed God was a "superhuman spiritual being" whose existence could be established on empirical grounds, and Otto had contested these grounds with arguments Dewey found persuasive. Wieman, on the other hand, seemed to Dewey to cross the line dividing theism and nontheistic naturalism as he himself had in the 1890s, yet to be unwilling to admit he had done so. And as is often the case in exchanges of this sort, Dewey reserved his sharpest knife for the opponent whose beliefs were closest to his own. Although he bridled at Macintosh's suggestion that his arguments were "probably colored by some untoward happening in my own personal history," there was more than a little of the apostate's fervor in his critique of liberal theology.[44]

Unlike Macintosh, Dewey observed, Wieman did not look for empirical evidence to sustain a belief in God; rather, he looked to nature to see if there was not something there to which the term "God" might be applied. He found what he was looking for in the "conditions and forces in existence which generate and sustain the goods of living." Dewey had no objection to this and indicated that he would himself be willing to use the word "God" to designate a collective noun referring to these conditions and forces having a similar functional effect in experience. But, he said, Wieman went further than this when he asserted that these things comprised "a unified and single object." This was to "shift from something which we may be said intelligibly to find in experience, namely, forces making for the production and extension of goods, to something which we do *not* find," and, without this shift, he did not see that there was "a shred of theism in Mr. Wieman's position." As a result, he concluded, "I can but think that Mr. Wieman's God rests upon hypostatization of an undeniable fact, experience of things, persons, causes, found to be good and worth cherishing, into a single objective existence, *a* God."[45]

Dewey's review and subsequent exchanges with Wieman and Macin-

43. Henry Wieman et al., *Is There a God?* (Chicago: Willett, Clark, 1932); Advertisement in *The Christian Century*, 18 January 1933: 101; Max Otto to JD, 5 April 1933, Max Otto Papers, State Historical Society of Wisconsin, Madison.

44. JD, "A God or the God?" (1933), *Later Works* 9:214; "Mr. Wieman and Mr. Macintosh 'Converse' with Mr. Dewey" (1933), *Later Works* 9:421–422; "Dr. Dewey Replies" (1933), *Later Works* 9:223.

45. "A God or the God?" pp. 219–220.

tosh created a stir among liberal Christians and led to an invitation to Dewey to deliver the Terry Lectures at Yale, lectures endowed for the purpose of considering "religion in the light of science and philosophy." In these lectures, subsequently published as *A Common Faith* (1934), Dewey elaborated on his critique of liberal theology and offered a fuller discussion of his own religious views.

The central proposition against which Dewey contended in his lectures was the belief, held by the friends and critics of religion alike, that "nothing worthy of being called religious is possible apart from the supernatural." Over against this commonplace, he hoped to develop another conception of the "religious aspect of experience" which separated it from the "encumbrances" of the supernatural and thereby enabled it to "develop freely on its own account."[46]

He began his discussion with a distinction between *religion* and *religious*. Religion, as a noun substantive, was a strictly collective term, referring to a "miscellaneous aggregate." Once could not have religion without having *a* religion, and a religion always entailed a special body of institutionalized beliefs, practices, and organization. In contrast, religious, as an adjective, denoted no specific entity but rather a quality of experience. Dewey was not, he said, proposing a new religion but rather the "emancipation" of experience with religious qualities from the grip of religions (*CF*, 8).

A religious attitude, Dewey argued, was achieved by an imaginative "intervention" in experience which produced "a composing and harmonizing of the various elements of our being such that, in spite of changes in the special conditions that surround us, these conditions are also arranged, settled, in relation to us"—a change *of* will rather than a mere change *in* will. It was crucial to Dewey's argument that this "harmonizing of the self" be seen as an act of *imagination*. "Neither observation, thought, nor practical activity can attain that complete unification of the self which is called a whole. The *whole* self is an ideal, an imaginative projection. Hence the idea of a thoroughgoing and deep-seated harmonizing of the self with the Universe (as a name for the totality of conditions with which the self is connected) operates only through imagination" (*CF*, 14).

Such acts of imagination produced a conviction that "some end should be supreme over conduct," and when such ends were "so inclu-

---

46. *A Common Faith* (1934), *Later Works* 9:3–4. Page numbers for further references (*CF*) appear in the text.

sive that they unify the self" one could speak of a conviction that was religious in quality (*CF*, 15, 16). Religious quality was thus present in experience when there was "the unification of the self through allegiance to inclusive ideal ends, which imagination presents to us and to which the human will responds as worthy of controlling our desires and choices" (*CF*, 23). Religious conviction or belief was not a matter of knowledge but of moral faith. "Conviction in the moral sense signifies being conquered, vanquished, in our active nature by an ideal end; it signifies acknowledgment of its rightful claim over our desires and purposes. Such acknowledgment is practical, not primarily intellectual. It goes beyond evidence that can be presented to *any* possible observer" (*CF*, 15). Indeed, the effort to convert moral convictions into propositions for intellectual assent was evidence of a lack of faith, for in so doing "faith that something should be in existence as far as lies in our power is changed into the intellectual belief that it is already in existence" (*CF*, 16). This led to the quest for certainty and to supernaturalism. Moral faith carried no guarantees; it was a faith in the possible not the actual or the necessary or the inevitable. "The authority of the object to determine our attitude and conduct, the right that is given to claim our allegiance and devotion is based on the intrinsic nature of the ideal. The outcome, given our best endeavor, is not with us" (*CF*, 17).

This latter argument pointed to the notion of "natural piety" Dewey had briefly outlined in *The Quest for Certainty*. Human destiny was so interwoven with forces beyond human control that humility and dependence were essential aspects of an inclusive, religious ideal:

Our dependence is manifested in those relations to the environment that support our undertakings and aspirations as much as it is in the defeats inflicted upon us. The essentially unreligious attitude is that which attributes human achievement and purpose to man in isolation from the world of physical nature and his fellows. Our successes are dependent upon the cooperation of nature. The sense of dignity of human nature is as religious as is the sense of awe and reverence when it rests upon a sense of human nature as a cooperating part of a larger whole. Natural piety is not of necessity either a fatalistic acquiescence in natural happenings or a romantic idealization of the world. It may rest upon a just sense of nature as the whole of which we are parts, while it also recognizes that we are parts that are marked by intelligence and purpose, having the capacity to strive by their aid to bring conditions into greater consonance with what is humanly desirable.

Such piety is an inherent constituent of a just perspective in life. (*CF*, 18)

Dewey admitted that lives inspired by loyalty to inclusive ideals of the sort he described were rare. But he argued that this rarity, in part at least, could be attributed to "the fact that the religious factors of experience have been drafted into supernatural channels and thereby loaded with irrelevant incumbrances." Religion had set the religious apart from "the common and natural relations of mankind" and thereby served to "weaken and sap the force of the possibilities inherent in such relations" (*CF*, 19). What better argument, he asked, could be offered for liberating the religious from religion?

The crisis of religion, Dewey contended, stemmed principally from the insistence of theologians on making cognitive claims, claims that science alone had earned the right to make. Fundamentalists seemed to understand this better than liberals, for the former realized that once any cognitive territory was ceded to science all was lost. Unless one wanted to join the fundamentalists and deny the relative fruitfulness of science in fixing knowledge, he chided liberals, one had to see that religious faith was noncognitive and could not be made scientific. "The religious function in experience can be emancipated only through surrender of the whole notion of special truths that are religious by their own nature, together with the idea of peculiar avenues of access to such truths" (*CF*, 23).[47]

Once again Dewey's insistence that the real and the known were not one and the same enabled him simultaneously to assert the cognitive hegemony of science without vaporizing noncognitive—in this case, religious—experience. To say that the inclusive ideals of religious faith were not known did not mean they were not real. "The reality of ideal ends as ideals is vouched for by their undeniable power in action. An ideal is not an illusion because imagination is the organ through which it is apprehended, for *all* possibilities reach us through the imagination" (*CF*, 30). Ideals were generated by the imagination but they were "not made out of imaginary stuff. They are made out of the hard stuff of the world of physical and social experience." Religious imagination was, in effect, a more expansive aesthetic imagination, for, as in art, a new vision emerged through seeing "old things in new relations serving

47. For a superb demonstration of the disaster for liberal religion of its attempt to make cognitive claims and thereby compete with science on the terms of science see James Turner, *Without God, without Creed: The Origins of Unbelief in America* (Baltimore: Johns Hopkins University Press, 1985).

a new end which the new end aids in creating" (*CF*, 34). Once admit that ideals were linked to existence and existed themselves as forces and there was no need to seek authority and value for them in some "prior complete embodiment." It was unnecessary and counterproductive to believe that "the efforts of human beings in behalf of justice, or knowledge or beauty, depended for their effectiveness and validity upon assurance that there already existed in some spiritual region a place where criminals are humanely treated, where there is no serfdom or slavery, where all facts and truths are already discovered and possessed, and all beauty is eternally displayed in actualized form" (*CF*, 33).

The controversy that swirled around *A Common Faith* centered primarily on the notion of "God" which Dewey offered his readers within this larger conception of the religious as imaginative moral faith. Because our most inclusive moral convictions were imaginative, they were neither completely embodied in existence nor "mere rootless ideals, fantasies, utopias," he said. They were generated and supported by forces at work in nature and society and were unified by human action that made use of these forces. This "*active* relation between ideal and actual" was what Dewey thought merited the name "God"—though he did not insist on the term. Such a God was not a Being or an antecedent existence; rather it was a process and usually an incomplete one at that. The union of actual and ideal was "a *uniting*, not something given" (*CF*, 34–35).

Dewey cautioned that this God was not omnipresent. "It selects those factors in existence that generate and support our idea of good as an end to be striven for. It excludes a multitude of forces that at any given time are irrelevant to this function. Nature produces whatever gives reinforcement and direction but also what occasions discord and confusion" (*CF*, 36). But if God was not everywhere, neither was He merely in church, and Dewey concluded his lectures by rounding back to his indictment of religions for claiming the religious for themselves alone. His conception of the religious and of God obliterated the distinction between the sacred and the profane, and he argued that the natural place of the religious was "in every aspect of human experience that is concerned with estimate of possibilities, with emotional stir by possibilities as yet unrealized, and with all action in behalf of their realization. All that is significant in human experience falls within this frame" (*CF*, 39). He was more charitable toward religious institutions than he had been in the early 1890s when he had called upon the church to universalize itself and pass out of existence. Now he merely asserted that "the fund of human values that are prized and that need to be cherished, values that are satisfied and rectified by *all* human concerns and arrangements, could be celebrated and reinforced, in different ways and with differing symbols, by the churches. In that way the churches would indeed become catholic" (*CF*, 54–55).

Reviewing *A Common Faith* for the *Christian Century*, Wieman pounced on it as conclusive evidence that he and Dewey were soulmates after all. Dewey's invocation of piety toward the forces in nature which generated and supported ideals and his conception of God as that activity which unites the actual and the ideal indicated to Wieman that Dewey believed in a superhuman if not supernatural process of progressive integration, a divine "operative reality" at work in the cosmos. Wieman took natural piety considerably further than Dewey had done, transforming it into the worship of nature against which Dewey had warned. Wieman misunderstood Dewey's union of actual and ideal in an interaction between "the aim of conscious intelligent effort and those existent conditions that are relevant to that aim" to be one in which agency could be attributed to the ("superhuman") interaction rather than to the human beings who participated in it. In calling this interaction "God," Wieman concluded, Dewey had separated himself from those who would vest the union of ideal and actual in "merely the conscious, intelligent effort of men" and had thereby pronounced "non-theistic humanism as futile and mistaken."[48]

Before Dewey could respond to Wieman's review, another reader, Edwin Ewart Aubrey, leaped into the breach and produced a wealth of textual evidence demonstrating that Dewey remained a "non-theistic humanist" insofar as "the integrative power binding actual and ideal is still restricted, in Mr. Dewey's thought, to human imaginative intelligence" and not to some "trans-human power or principle of integration." Dewey followed with "complete approval of Mr. Aubrey's statement of my position." Although he had indeed said that many different forces and conditions generate and sustain human ideals and that as such they were worthy of natural piety, he had explicitly described the conscious unification of these forces and conditions as "the work of human imagination and will." Wieman's review confirmed Dewey's earlier suspicion that what divided them was Wieman's inclination to look for a singular integrative force at work in the universe (an operative reality rather than operative realities) and his worship of a superhuman if natural God that was in fact a human artifact—an organic unity of ideals which, Dewey said, "is something which *should*

48. Henry Wieman, "John Dewey's Common Faith" (1934), *Later Works* 9:426–434.

exist, or as far as it is already exemplified in existence, is something effected through the mediation of past generations of human devotion and energy."[49]

To a number of Dewey's fellow "non-theistic humanists," especially those who were Marxists, this debate amounted to hairsplitting that Dewey could have avoided if he had followed his own warnings about the misconceptions likely to attend any use of the word "God" (CF, 35). One such critic, Corliss Lamont, devoted two articles in the New Masses to an attack on Dewey's religious thinking. Quoting Lenin approvingly to the effect that "every defence or justification of the idea of God, even the most refined and well-intentioned, is a justification of reaction," Lamont declared that "nothing that John Dewey has ever done or said shows more clearly, in my opinion, both his actual class allegiances, and the necessity for honest and uncompromising minds to repudiate his leadership." Dewey's distinction between religion and the religious was "as if someone renounced all the existing forms of Fascism as evil, but claimed that the adjective *fascist* meant the true, the good, and the beautiful."[50]

Dewey told Hook, an equally puzzled if more sympathetic Marxist, that he had used the word "God" because "there are so many people who would feel bewildered if not hurt were they denied the intellectual right to use the term 'God.' They are not in the churches, they believe what I believe, they would feel a loss if they could not speak of God. Why then shouldn't I use the term?"[51] In 1934 "God" was also a useful ally in the democratic politics of uniting the actual and the ideal to which Dewey had committed himself. "Human beings have impulses toward affection, compassion and justice, equality and freedom," he said. "It remains to weld all these things together." Whether one termed this welding "God" or not was a matter of personal predilection, but the function of a "working union of the ideal and the actual" was one with "the force that has been attached to the conception of God in all the religions that have a spiritual content; and a clear idea of that function seems to me urgently needed at the present time" (CF, 35).

What Dewey desired above all was a revitalized civic religion, a "re-

49. Edwin Ewart Aubrey, "Is John Dewey a Theist?" (1934), *Later Works* 9:435–437; JD, "Reply to Aubrey and Wieman in 'Is John Dewey a Theist?'" (1934), *Later Works* 9:294–295; "Dr. Dewey Replies" (1933), *Later Works* 9:226.

50. Corliss Lamont, "John Dewey Capitulates to 'God,'" *New Masses*, 31 July 1934: 23, and "The Right Reverend Re-Definer," *New Masses*, 2 October 1934: 38.

51. Dewey quoted in Hook, *Pragmatism and the Tragic Sense of Life*, p. 114. Dewey offered a similar explanation for his use of "God" to Lamont. See Corliss Lamont, "New Light on Dewey's *Common Faith*," *Journal of Philosophy* 58 (1961): 21–28.

ligion of shared experience." If "God" would assist its growth, he would use the word. Democracy was his own inclusive ideal, the ideal that fired his moral faith and lent unity to his work. It was for him the "clear and intense conception of a union of ideal ends with actual conditions" most "capable of arousing steady emotion" (*CF*, 35). It was not, he insisted, a utopian ideal but a vision of possibilities in experience: "it simply projects to their logical and practical limit forces inherent in human nature and already embodied to some extent in human nature. It serves accordingly as basis for criticism of institutions as they exist and of plans of betterment" (*2E*, 349).[52]

Dewey admitted that as an inclusive, unifying end democracy seemed to pose an intractable difficulty: "how to harmonize the development of each individual with the maintenance of a social state in which the activities of the one will contribute to the good of all others." But the only way to test the power of the democratic imagination was to act on it with the conviction that this difficulty was not intractable (this much of "the will to believe" Dewey accepted). As he had argued since the 1890s, the democratic ideal "expressed a postulate in the sense of a demand to be realized," for like every ideal it was not "something ready-made" but "something to be done" (*2E*, 350). In it were all the elements for "a religious faith that shall not be confined to sect, class, or race." It remained only for democrats to make this faith "explicit and militant" (*CF*, 58). And though he was one of its more aged communicants, few made the democratic faith more explicit or served it more militantly in the 1930s than Dewey.

52. J. H. Randall, Jr., offered an insightful discussion of democracy as Dewey's religion in "The Religion of Shared Experience," in Ratner, ed., *The Philosopher of the Common Man*, pp. 106–145.

CHAPTER 12

Socialist Democracy

✳

By the end of the twenties John Dewey would admit, if pressed, that he was a socialist, for he was convinced that democracy required an end to private control of the commanding heights of the means of production. But he remained cool to much of the theory and practice that laid claim to this ideological label, even in the midst of the Great Depression. He avoided the word "socialism" if he could, and when he could not he was careful to discriminate between his own peculiar socialist vision and the one he identified with the common usage of the word, between "liberal" or "democratic" socialism and authoritarian, bureaucratic, or, as he most often characterized it, "state" socialism.[1]

This wariness puzzled some of Dewey's radical admirers. Preparing a study in the late forties of Dewey and Marxist humanism, Jim Cork, a trade-union activist and intellectual, wrote to Dewey asking him to clarify his ambivalent position toward socialism in general and democratic socialism in particular. Dewey replied that no "existing brand of socialism has worked out an adequate answer to the question of *how* industry and finance can progressively be conducted in the widest possible human interest and not for the benefit of one class." Yet despite this reservation, he claimed: "I can be classified as a democratic socialist. If I were permitted to define 'socialism' and 'socialist' I would so

---

1. *Individualism Old and New* (1930), *Later Works* 5:98. Page numbers for further references (*ION*) appear in the text.

classify myself today." Reflecting later on his reply to Cork, Dewey indicated to both Sidney Hook and James Farrell the problem of definition which troubled him. "My real uncertainty," he told Hook, "came from the fact that in 'democratic socialism' democratic should apply to socialism when attained not merely to the method of attaining it and the weak point in socialism as an *ism* is a lack of definiteness on that point." Democratic socialism for Dewey was more than a matter of socialist politicians' winning power at the polls, and he wondered about the depth of the commitment to democracy of those who called themselves democratic socialists. "What is Democratic Socialism?" he asked Farrell. "I read considerable talk about 'the democratic' as applying to the process of getting socialism; damn little about it as an adjective applying to socialism when you get it."[2]

Hook argued in 1939 that "it requires no exegesis whatsoever to show that Dewey's present position is one that differs from democratic socialism only in name," but as Dewey's own remarks suggest, this is not the case. Considerable exegesis is required if Dewey is not to be mistakenly lumped with those with whom he had little sympathy. He is perhaps best characterized as a socialist democrat rather than a democratic socialist, for socialism was a proximate end to which he became committed in his search for the means to the more inclusive end of "democracy as a way of life." Dewey's socialism, like the democratic theory from which it flowed, was unique and confronted its own particular dilemmas in the thirties and forties.[3]

Reconstructing Liberalism

Dewey's greatest concern was that socialists would lose touch with the values of liberalism which remained essential to a democratic politics. Thus his argument for democratic socialism took the form of an effort to revitalize and reconstruct the Anglo-American liberal tradition. This roundabout way of arguing for socialism proved remarkably powerful. Dewey's socialism followed, as he saw it, from reflection on the implications in the twentieth century of holding to what he took to be the

2. JD to Jim Cork as quoted in Cork, "John Dewey and Karl Marx," in Sidney Hook, ed., *John Dewey: Philosopher of Science and Freedom* (New York: Dial Press, 1950), pp. 348–349; JD to Sidney Hook, 5 November 1948, Hook Collection; JD to James Farrell, 8 November 1948, Dewey Papers.

3. Sidney Hook, *John Dewey: An Intellectual Portrait* (New York: John Day, 1939), p. 161.

central tenets of liberalism. This argument was consistent with his conception of the role of philosophers, which centered on their responsibility to undertake a critical examination of the values and traditions that guided social life in their culture. In modern America, these were, above all, the values of the liberal tradition.

The standing of liberalism in the thirties, especially in the American left, was not to be envied. "In the minds of many persons," Dewey observed in *Liberalism and Social Action* (1935), "liberalism has fallen between two stools, so that it is conceived as the refuge of those unwilling to take a decided stand in the social conflicts going on. It is called mealy-mouthed, a milk-and-water doctrine and so on." Nonetheless, he averred, "I have wanted to find out whether it is possible for a person to continue, honestly and intelligently, to be a liberal, and if the answer be in the affirmative, what kind of liberal faith should be asserted today."[4]

The first step in this inquiry was to separate the wheat from the chaff in the liberal tradition. The wheat, Dewey argued, lay in three values central to liberalism: liberty, individuality, and the freedom of inquiry, discussion, and expression. The chaff lay in the adventitious connection between liberalism and the legitimation of capitalism. Dewey admitted that much could be said for the characterization of liberal democracy as "bourgeois" democracy. Historically, the rise of democracy had accompanied the transfer of power from the landed aristocracy to the industrial bourgeoisie. In most so-called democracies, "power rests finally in the hands of finance capital, no matter what claims are made for government of, by, and for all the people." Liberalism was undeniably the ideology of the bourgeoisie, and "the movement for which it stood gave power to a few over the lives and thoughts of the many." While it would be foolish to deny that a change of masters and the rule of the bourgeoisie had not brought some benefits to the masses, the "distortion and stultification of human personality by the existing pecuniary and competitive regime give the lie to the claim that the present social system is one of freedom and individualism in any sense in which liberty and individuality exist for all." But it was in this very gap between liberal ideals and the reality of capitalist society that Dewey saw the radical potential of liberalism. Liberal ideals, he felt, no longer legitimated capitalist society but were a potent force for its delegitimation. Rightly understood, these ideals could serve as the basis for a liberalism that was not mealy-mouthed but radical, a liberalism that

4. *Liberalism and Social Action* (1935), *Later Works* 11:5–6. Page numbers for further references (*LSA*) appear in the text.

attempted to "realize democratic modes of life in their full meaning and far-reaching scope."[5]

If liberal values were to be revitalized and made the basis of a democratic society, Dewey argued, liberals had to be alert to the historical circumstances in which their philosophy had developed. Nineteenth-century liberals were often blind to the historically conditioned nature of their interpretations of liberty and individuality, and as a consequence they had interpreted these ideals as immutable and absolute truths. The result was the identification of liberty and individuality with the negative liberty of laissez-faire capitalism and the possessive individualism of the entrepreneur. In the twentieth century, this absolutizing of a contingent relationship between liberalism and capitalism had transformed liberalism into a conservative ideology. Values that had once liberated the bourgeoisie from the arbitrary authority of church and state were now called upon by men of wealth and power to defend the inequities of a new system of class power. Liberalism, Dewey said, had degenerated into "pseudo-liberalism" that "ossified and narrowed generous ideas and aspirations." Liberalism had once been a call for freedom, but it was now—as pseudo-liberalism—a justification for the limitation of the freedoms of most men and women. "Even when the words remain the same," Dewey noted, "they mean something very different when they are uttered by a minority struggling against repressive measures and when expressed by a group that has attained power and then uses ideas that were once weapons of emancipation as instruments for keeping the power and wealth they have obtained. Ideas that at one time are means of producing social change assume another guise when they are used as means of preventing social change." If liberal values were to serve democracy, Dewey argued, their interpretation had to undergo radical surgery. They had to be adapted to the vast changes American society had undergone since the nineteenth century. Hence, Dewey offered up-to-date interpretations of liberal values, interpretations grounded in his own social philosophy.[6]

5. "Democracy Is Radical" (1937), *Later Works* 11:296–299.
6. "The Future of Liberalism" (1935), *Later Works* 11:291. It is important to keep in mind that in 1935 in the United States "liberalism" was a highly contested term and that, as Dewey's argument suggests, those we would now call "conservatives" (such as Herbert Hoover) were most unwilling to relinquish the "liberal" label in the thirties to the likes of Franklin Roosevelt, let alone Dewey. Dewey's position was more radically democratic than any taken by others battling to capture the term in the thirties, a position with more in common with Roosevelt's than with Hoover's yet distinctive from welfare-state liberalism in important respects. Two penetrating accounts of this debate are Ronald D. Rotunda, *The Politics of Language: Liberalism as Word and Symbol* (Iowa City: University of Iowa Press,

The key value was individuality; liberty and the freedom of "intelligence" were conditions for individual self-development. "Individuals," Dewey declared, "are the finally decisive factors of the nature and movement of associated life." But, as he had long argued, individuality was not something preformed and standing over against society, as most nineteenth-century liberals and many contemporary liberals held. The "individual" and the "social" were not nouns but adjectives standing for what was intrinsic in the constitution and development of human beings. Individuality was the product of an ongoing interaction of the capacities of a human being and an environment made up, in part, of other human beings. Hence the development of individuality rested in large measure on the nature of social life: "Individuals will always be the center and consummation of experience, but what the individual actually *is* in his life experience depends upon the nature and movement of associated life."[7]

Democracy was the form of associated life which provided the opportunity for the full flowering of individuality, and the "keynote of democracy" was "the necessity for the participation of every mature human being in the formation of the values that regulate the living of men together." Because associated life was essential for the development of individuality, the individual must have the opportunity to participate in the direction of this life. "All those who are affected by social institutions must have a share in producing and managing them. The two facts that each one is influenced in what he does and enjoys and in what he becomes by the institutions under which he lives, and that therefore he shall have, in a democracy, a voice in shaping them, are the passive and active sides of the same fact."[8]

Limitation on full democratic participation in social life was, Dewey observed, a subtle way of suppressing individuality:

It gives individuals no opportunity to reflect and decide upon what is good for them. Others who are supposed to be wiser and who in any case have more power decide the question for them and also decide the methods and means by which subjects may arrive at the enjoyment of

1986), chap. 4, and David Green, *Shaping Political Consciousness: The Language of Politics in America from McKinley to Reagan* (Ithaca: Cornell University Press, 1987), pp. 86–163. For a solid analysis of Dewey's liberalism close to my own see Alfonso J. Damico, *Individuality and Community: The Social and Political Thought of John Dewey* (Gainesville: University Presses of Florida, 1978).

7. "I Believe" (1939), *Later Works* 14:91. See also "The Crisis in Human History: The Danger of the Retreat to Individualism" (1946), *Later Works* 15:210–223.

8. "Democracy and Educational Administration" (1937), *Later Works* 11:217–218.

what is good for them. This form of coercion and suppression is more subtle and more effective than is overt intimidation and restraint. When it is habitual and embodied in social institutions, it seems the normal and natural state of affairs. The mass usually become unaware that they have a claim to a development of their own powers. Their experience is so restricted that they are not conscious of restriction. It is part of the democratic conception that they as individuals are not the only sufferers, but that the whole social body is deprived of the potential resources that should be at its service.[9]

In capitalist society, Dewey argued in *Individualism Old and New* (1930), associated life and participatory democracy were stunted and underdeveloped, and as a consequence this society produced stunted, underdeveloped, "lost" individuals. The capitalist Great Society was not a democratic Great Community, and Dewey placed the blame squarely at the door of the political economy. "The chief obstacle to the creation of a type of individual whose pattern of thought and desire is enduringly marked by consensus with others, and in whom sociability is one with cooperation in all regular human associations," he declared, "is the persistence of that feature of the earlier individualism which defines industry and commerce by ideas of private pecuniary profit" (*ION*, 84). The pursuit of private gain isolated individuals from one another, and the exploitative possessive individualism fostered by capitalism inhibited the formation of the participatory communities of democratic action essential to self-development and social welfare.

As these remarks suggest, Dewey continued to regard political democracy, narrowly conceived, as an insufficient guarantee of individuality. The development of individuality required the democratization of all social institutions—pluralism, to be sure, but pluralism constrained by democracy. "If the methods of regulation and administration in vogue in the conduct of secondary social groups are nondemocratic," he said, "whether directly or indirectly or both, there is bound to be an unfavorable reaction back into the habits and feeling, thought and action of citizenship in the broadest sense of that word."[10] He remained particularly critical of the effects on the development of individuality of alienating work and the authoritarian social relations of capitalist production. As we have seen, this concern animated *Art as Experience*, and it often found expression in his popular journalism as well. "Most of those who are engaged in the outward work of produc-

9. Ibid., pp. 218–219.
10. Ibid., pp. 221.

tion and distribution of economic commodities," he observed in 1930, "have no share—imaginative, intellectual, emotional—in directing the activities in which they physically participate." Workers did not share in management and were often nothing more than "hands," their intellect and imagination deadened by their work. "The philosopher's idea of a complete separation of mind and body is realized in thousands of industrial workers, and the result is a depressed body and an empty and distorted mind" (*ION*, 104).

Liberty had always been the liberal value Dewey was most eager to reconstruct, and it remained so in the thirties. He was disturbed by the continued association of liberty with negative liberty and the threat this association posed to democracy. "Today there is no word more bandied about than liberty," he noted in "Liberty and Social Control" (1935). "Every effort at planned control of economic forces is resisted and attacked, by a certain group, in the name of liberty. The slightest observation shows that the group is made up of those who are interested, from causes that are evident, in the preservation of the economic status quo; that is to say, in the maintenance of the customary privileges and legal rights they already possess."[11]

Properly understood, Dewey argued, liberty was not just an abstract principle but *power*, the "effective power to do specific things." There was no such thing as liberty in general. The demand for liberty was a demand for power, either for the retention of power already possessed or for the possession of new powers of action. "The present ado in behalf of liberty by the managers and beneficiaries of the existing economic system," he remarked, "is immediately explicable if one views it as a demand for preservation of the powers they already possess. Since it is the existing system that gives them these powers, liberty is thus inevitably identified with the perpetuation of that system." Questions about liberty were questions about the *distribution* of power, for power was a relative concept. "There is no such thing as the liberty or effective power of an individual, group, or class, except in relation to the liberties, the effective powers, of *other* individuals, groups and classes." The ruling class demanded liberty to sustain the prevailing distribution of power; the subordinate classes demanded increased liberty in order to redistribute power. "The system of liberties that exists at any time is always the system of restraints or controls that exists at

11. "Liberty and Social Control" (1935), *Later Works* 11:360. Page numbers for further references (LSC) appear in the text.

that time. No one can *do* anything except in relation to what others can do and cannot do" (LSC, 360–361).

Putting this conception into the context of the struggle for the control of the political economy, Dewey observed that the issue at hand was not that of liberty versus social control but "simply that of one system of control of the social forces upon which the distribution of liberties depends, versus some other system of social control which would bring about another distribution of liberties." It was nonsense to suppose that the prevailing order acclaimed by its defenders in the name of liberty was not a system of social control filled with restraints on the relative liberties of individuals. Indeed, the problem with capitalism lay in its character as a form of social control "exercised by the few who have economic power, at the expense of the liberties of the many and at the cost of increasing disorder, culminating in that chaos of war which the representatives of the possessing class identify with true discipline." Dewey warned radical democrats "not to be jockeyed into the position of supporting social control at the expense of liberty, when what they want is another method of social control than the one that now exists, one that will increase significant human liberties" (LSC, 362–363).

Dewey disputed the claim that liberty and equality were incompatible values. Equality was simply the demand for a distribution of liberty (power) which was conducive to the full development of the individuality of everyone in a society. It was the demand for a system of social control which would maximize the opportunity for every individual "to be socially useful and to develop personal powers in the only way they can be developed, through some form of creative activity." Equality was not opposed to liberty but was a democratic distribution of liberties. At the same time, "the tragic breakdown of democracy is due to the fact that the identification of liberty with the maximum of unrestrained individualistic action in the economic sphere, under the institutions of capitalistic finance, is as fatal to the realization of liberty for all as it is to the realization of equality."[12]

True to a long-standing theme of his democratic theory, Dewey repeated in the thirties his conviction that an egalitarian distribution of knowledge was a crucial component of a democratic community. The liberal values of free inquiry, free discussion, and free expression must remain essential ideals for democratic socialists. A community was not fully democratic until it had "socialized intelligence."

As he had in the past, Dewey argued that free intelligence was best

---

12. "Liberalism and Equality" (1936), *Later Works* 11:370.

exemplified in science and that the modern scientific community provided the model of a community committed to the socialization of intelligence. "Consideration of the full application of science," he declared, must be "prophetic," looking forward to "a time when all individuals may share in the discoveries and thoughts of others, to the liberation and enrichment of their own experience":

> No scientific inquirer can keep what he finds to himself or turn it to merely private account without losing his scientific standing. Everything discovered belongs to the community of workers. Every new idea and theory has to be submitted to this community for confirmation and test. There is an expanding community of cooperative effort and of truth. It is true enough that these traits are now limited to small groups having a somewhat technical activity. But the existence of such groups reveals a possibility of the present—one of the many possibilities that are a challenge to expansion, and not a ground for retreat and contraction. (*ION*, 115)

The liberation of individuality and the expansion of effective liberty required the diffusion throughout society of scientific intelligence and the institution of democratic planning. "The crisis in democracy," Dewey declared, "demands the substitution of intelligence that is exemplified in scientific procedure for the kind of intelligence that is now accepted" (*LSA*, 51).

The kind of social reorganization his reconstruction of liberal ideals suggested would require, Dewey acknowledged, a radical change in public education, the kind of change he had been advocating since the 1890s. Education would have to be geared to providing every individual with the knowledge and skill to enable him participate to the best of his abilities in the planning process as a worker, consumer, and citizen. Dewey discounted the objection that such knowledge and skill were beyond the reach of the average individual, and again he laid the blame for the existing incapacities of the individual on the inequities of capitalist society:

> The indictments that are drawn against the intelligence of individuals are in truth indictments of a social order that does not permit the average individual to have access to the rich store of the accumulated wealth of mankind in knowledge, ideas, and purposes. There does not now exist the kind of social organization that even permits the average human being to share the potentially available social intelligence. Still less is there a social order that has for one of its chief purposes the

establishment of conditions that will move the mass of individuals to appropriate and use what is at hand. Back of the appropriation by the few of the material resources of society lies the appropriation by the few in behalf of their own ends of the cultural, the spiritual, resources that are the product not of the individuals who have taken possession but of the cooperative work of humanity. It is useless to talk about the failure of democracy until the source of its failure has been grasped and steps are taken to bring about that type of social organization that will encourage the socialized extension of intelligence. (*LSA*, 38–39)

By reconstructing the ideals of liberal democracy, Dewey thus arrived by the mid-thirties at a thoroughgoing critique of capitalism and the theoretical foundations of a democratic-socialist alternative. From the tradition of Locke, Jefferson, John Stuart Mill, and T. H. Green, he winnowed that strain in Anglo-American liberal-democratic thought which, as C. B. Macpherson said, was "based on a view of man's essence not as a consumer of utilities but as a doer, a creator, an enjoyer of his human attributes," a view that sought to maximize the potential of all "for using and developing their uniquely human capacities." This strain of thought, when freed from the accretions and contradictions of efforts to provide an ideological defense of capitalism, stood as an indictment of modern capitalist society, a society in which, Dewey asserted, "servility and regimentation are the result of the control by the few of access to the means of productive labor on the part of the many" (*LSA*, 29).[13]

Liberalism properly understood, Dewey concluded, was "committed to an end that is at once enduring and flexible: the liberation of individuals so that realization of their capacities may be the law of their life" and to the creation of "a social organization that will make possible effective liberty and opportunity for personal growth in mind and spirit in all individuals" (*LSA*, 41). A liberalism true to these ideals "must now become radical, meaning by 'radical' perception of the necessity of thoroughgoing changes in the set-up of institutions and corresponding activity to bring them to pass. For the gulf between what the actual situation makes possible and the actual state itself is so great that it cannot be bridged by piecemeal policies taken *ad hoc*" (*LSA*, 45). The cause of liberalism was doomed unless it was prepared to "socialize the forces of production, now at hand, so that the liberty of individuals

13. C. B. Macpherson, "The Maximization of Democracy," in Macpherson, *Democratic Theory: Essays in Retrieval* (Oxford: Oxford University Press, 1973), p. 4. Macpherson does not discuss Dewey in these essays, but his arguments resemble Dewey's in many respects.

will be supported by the very structure of economic organization" (*LSA*, 62).

AGAINST STATE CAPITALISM

Given his radical reconstruction of liberal-democratic principles, the key difficulty for Dewey in the thirties became the practical one of envisioning the "democratic forms" that could control the productive forces of an advanced industrial economy and provide for both economic security and the development of individuality. "The problem of democracy," he concluded, "becomes the problem of that form of social organization, extending to all the areas and ways of living, in which the powers of individuals shall not be merely released from mechanical external constraint but shall be fed, sustained, and directed" (*LSA*, 25).

Despite the ethical power of Dewey's argument for democratic socialism, his thinking remained bedeviled by the lack of a clear program of action. Radicalism of the sort he called for demanded "a social goal based upon an inclusive plan," but his efforts to formulate such a plan were beset with dilemmas (*LSA*, 45). Particularly troubling was the fact that the destruction of corporate capitalism and the institution of social planning seemed, in the minds of both their proponents and opponents, to mean the establishment of a powerful state that itself posed a threat to democracy. "The danger at present," Dewey remarked in 1939, "is that in order to get away from the evils of private economic collectivism we shall plunge into political economic collectivism. . . . Earlier events proved that private economic collectivism produced social anarchy, mitigated by the control exercised by an oligarchic group. Recent events have shown that state socialism or public collectivism leads to suppression of everything individuality stands for." Dewey continued to maintain that it was not simply a matter of either/or. "There is, however, a socialism which is not state socialism," he insisted. But it was unclear just what he thought such a socialism would look like or how one went about building it.[14]

Throughout the twenties, Dewey held to the belief he had articulated at the end of the war that state capitalism might be a transitional stage on the way to democratic socialism. In early 1930 he even argued that the first step toward democratic control of the economy might lie in the kind of corporatism he saw as implicit in Herbert Hoover's efforts to

14. "I Believe," pp. 94–95.

meet the crisis of the Depression. Out of the industrial conferences that Hoover convened in the face of a collapsing economy, Dewey suggested, might grow a permanent, representative "Economic Council," a "coordinating and directive council in which captains of industry and finance would meet with representatives of labor and public officials to plan the regulation of industrial activity." This development, Dewey believed, "would signify that we had entered constructively and voluntarily upon the road which Soviet Russia is traveling with so much attendant destruction and coercion" (ION, 97–98).[15]

By the early thirties, Dewey had abandoned this argument. As far as the United States was concerned, he observed, the corporatism of state capitalism had proved to be a means employed, with limited success, to stabilize and protect private control of the economy and deflect radicalism. It was a "half-way house" that was inadequate and counterproductive. As he put it, "The magic of eating a hair of the dog which bit you in order to cure hydrophobia is as nothing to the magic involved in the belief that those who have privilege and power will remedy the breakdown they have created. As long as politics is the shadow cast on society by big business, the attenuation of the shadow will not change the substance."[16]

This altered perspective was reflected in Dewey's criticism of the early New Deal in which he argued that voluntary corporatism of the sort Roosevelt was fostering without a prior removal of the prerogatives of capital was destined not to evolve into democratic socialism but into a more tightly organized form of state capitalism or even fascism. Such state capitalism might be capable of weathering the immediate economic crisis but was in no way conducive to industrial democracy or long-term economic security. Labor would be admitted into such an order with a view not toward workers' control but toward controlling workers. This inevitable result was apparent, he argued, in the National Recovery Administration (NRA), which "had a glimpse of self-governing industrial groups, but, quite apart from its conflict with the existing legal system . . . loaded the dice in favor of the existing system of control of industry—with a few sops thrown in to 'labor.' At best it could not have worked out in the direction of freely functioning occupational groups." The consumer was sacrificed in state capitalist society as well, for capitalist collectivism restricted production at the very moment when

15. The development of Dewey's attitudes toward the Soviet Union is analyzed at length in Chapter 13.
16. "The Need for a New Party" (1931), Later Works 6:163.

consumers desperately needed an expansion of goods and services. The New Deal had defined the economic problem as overproduction rather than underconsumption and, in so doing, had placed itself on the side of big business and big agriculture and in opposition to the best interests of the consumer.[17]

In the wake of the shift in his thinking about state capitalism as a transitional stage, Dewey called for the socialization of the "commanding heights" of the economy. "There is no way out for America," he declared, "except to recognize that labor has prior claims upon production which take precedence of current return upon property, even when property ownership is due to investment of savings from labor income. . . . We cannot achieve a decent standard of living for more than a fraction of the American people by any other method than that to which the British Labor Party and the Social Democratic Parties of Europe are committed—the socialization of all natural resources and natural monopolies, of ground rent, and of basic industries." The immediate steps in the program of socialization Dewey proposed were a massive program of public works, particularly in housing; a thorough redistribution of wealth through taxation; and the nationalization of banking, public utilities, natural resources, transportation, and communication.[18]

17. "I Believe," pp. 95–96. See also "The Economic Basis of the New Society" (1939), *Later Works* 13:319–320. Dewey's criticism of the New Deal has been difficult to swallow for liberal defenders of the Roosevelt administration who see it as the institutionalization of "pragmatism." Why, they ask, would the leading pragmatist in America attack the public embodiment of this philosophy? This puzzlement has produced such oddities as the lecture delivered to Deweyans by Arthur Schlesinger, Jr., on the proper meaning of experimentalism. "What was for a moment puzzling," Schlesinger writes, "was to reconcile Dewey's longtime advocacy of the experimental method in public affairs with his flat rejection of the New Deal. But it became apparent in the thirties that Dewey advocated experimentalism in a restricted and special sense. 'Experimental method,' Dewey wrote in 1935, 'is not just messing around nor doing a little of this and a little of that in the hope that things will improve. Just as in the physical sciences, it implies a coherent body of ideas, a theory, that gives direction of effort.' Experimentalism for Dewey did not mean trial-and-error pragmatism; it meant action according to systematic hypothesis. For all his nominal dislike of absolutism, he held social policy to the requirements of ideology. Paradoxically, the New Deal, preferring experiment to abstraction, became repugnant to this theoretical experimentalist." Schlesinger, of course, resolved his own paradox. The New Deal, as he defined it, simply did not fit a scientific definition of experimental, a point Dewey often made. Insofar as Roosevelt's policies embodied "trial-and-error pragmatism," they were what Dewey called "vulgar" empiricism, but Dewey was more inclined to believe that the New Deal was itself an enterprise guided by a very obvious ideological commitment, "trying to save the profit system from itself." See Arthur Schlesinger, Jr., *The Age of Roosevelt: The Politics of Upheaval* (Boston: Little, Brown, 1960), p. 155; JD, "No Half Way House for America" (1934), *Later Works* 9:289. On "vulgar empiricism" see *Logic* (1938), *Later Works* 12:490–492, and *Freedom and Culture* (1939), *Later Works* 13:131.

18. "No Half Way House for America," pp. 289–290.

Democratization remained at bottom a question of power for Dewey, and the redistribution of power was the first priority of the social-democratic proposals he advanced:

> Power today resides in control of the means of production, exchange, publicity, transportation and communication. Whoever owns them rules the life of the country, not necessarily by intention, not necessarily by deliberate corruption of the nominal government, but by necessity. Power is power and must act, and it must act according to the nature of the machinery through which it operates. In this case, the machinery is business for private profit through private control of banking, land, industry, reinforced by command of the press, press agents and other means of publicity and propaganda. In order to restore democracy, one thing and one thing only is essential. The people will rule when they have power, and they will have power in the degree they own and control the land, the banks, the producing and distributing agencies of the nation. Ravings about Bolshevism, Communism, Socialism are irrelevant to the axiomatic truth of this statement. They come either from complaisant ignorance or from the deliberate desire of those in possession, power and rule to perpetuate their privilege.[19]

Dewey readily acknowledged that a significant redistribution of power would not come easily. "Radical political action is necessary," he observed, for the economy to be publicly controlled so that the "divisions of labor may be free where they are now coercive."[20]

Dewey's longtime defense of "organized intelligence," his previous neglect of political action, and his critique of violence led such hard-boiled critics as Reinhold Niebuhr to the conclusion in the thirties that he neglected or repudiated politics and a struggle for power in favor of an "appeal to reason." But by the onset of the Depression, Dewey had come to conceive of politics as among the most significant forms of organized intelligence, one in which social ends were articulated and analyzed and forceful action was taken to secure these ends. Political activity in a democracy was in the broadest sense an educational enterprise, but this function did not rule out the exercise of power. True education was not "a cloistered withdrawal from the scene of action," for "there is no education when ideas and knowledge are not translated into emotion, interest, and volition. There must be constant accom-

---

19. "Imperative Need: A New Radical Party" (1934), *Later Works* 9:76–77.
20. "Liberalism in a Vacuum: A Critique of Walter Lippmann's Social Philosophy" (1937), *Later Works* 11:493.

panying organization and direction of organized action and practical work. 'Ideas' must be linked to the practical situation, however hurly-burly that is."[21]

A NEW PARTY

Electoral politics, Dewey believed, was the best political weapon for American radicals because it was the most democratic means to their ends. He also maintained that in a formal democracy like the United States the power of the dominant interests rested in large measure on ignorance and ideology, obstacles to change which were susceptible to the education that political campaigns could provide. "There is a general tendency," he remarked to Horace M. Kallen, "to think that certain social tendencies are inevitable because they exist with a certain amount of power, when in reality their existence depends upon the attitude of acceptance by individuals. Powers that be reign only by the complicity of those whom they rule, and accordingly never really have the strength they seem to have."[22]

But for Dewey the decision to pursue an electoral strategy for radical ends did not entail "boring from within" the Democratic or Republican party but the creation of a new, third party. In American partisan politics in the early thirties, he said, "democracy has joined the unemployed." Both major parties were but "errand boys" of big business—hence the need for a new party that would take up "the business of educating the people until the dullest and the most partisan see the connection between economic life and politics. Its business is to make the connection between political democracy and industrial democracy as clear as the noon-day sun."[23]

Two major strategic principles guided Dewey in his efforts to foster a third party. The first was finding common ground for the political cooperation of farmers, blue- and white-collar workers, small business-men, and professionals. Labor was essential to this coalition, but it was the allegiance of the middle class which that would make or break a

21. "Is There Hope for Politics?" (1931), *Later Works* 6:188. For further consideration of Niebuhr's criticisms of Dewey's social philosophy see Chapter 14.

22. JD to Horace Kallen, 5 March 1932, Horace M. Kallen Collection, American Jewish Archives, Hebrew Union College, Cincinnati.

23. "Democracy Joins the Unemployed," speech delivered at the annual conference of the League for Independent Political Action, Cleveland, 9 July 1932, copy in Sabino Dewey Papers, Special Collections, Morris Library, Southern Illinois University, Carbondale. See also "John Dewey Assails the Major Parties" (1929), *Later Works* 5:442.

third-party effort. For this reason, he argued, "the first appeal of a new party must be to what is called the middle class: to professional people, including, of course, teachers, the average retail merchant, the fairly well-to-do householder, the struggling white-collar worker, including his feminine counterpart, and the farmer—even the farmer who has not as yet reached the ragged edge of despair." One senses that Dewey's prototype of the party member was the public school teacher: educated and imbued with a professional service ethic, frustrated by low pay, low status, and sexual discrimination, and familiar with the advantages of collective action. The petty bourgeoisie as a whole, he believed, retained a devotion to ideals of independence and decentralized power that were indispensable to democracy. This class need not, as many believed it had, provide the shock troops of fascism. The task was to convince its members that the connection between some of their most deeply held ideals and capitalism had been destroyed by the historical development of industrial society and that they could be preserved only by the radical reconstruction of capitalist civilization along democratic socialist lines.[24]

Dewey's concern with the political education of the middle class led him to a second strategic principle. Socialism, he argued, could not come to the United States under that name, a name that signaled to the middle class a deep threat to its values. "I think," Dewey said, "a new party will have to adopt many measures which are now labeled socialistic—measures which are discounted and condemned because of that tag. . . . The greatest handicap from which special measures favored by the Socialists suffer is that they are advanced by the Socialist party as Socialism. The prejudice against the name may be a regrettable prejudice but its influence is so powerful that it is much more reasonable to imagine all but the most dogmatic Socialists joining a new party than to imagine any considerable part of the American people

24. "The Need for a New Party" (1931), *Later Works* 6:171. The politics of the petty bourgeoisie remains a subject of important debate among historians, some of whom have come to think Dewey may have had a point. See Arno Mayer, "The Lower Middle Class as a Historical Problem," *Journal of Modern History* 47 (1975): 409–436; Frank Bechoffer and Brian Elliott, "Persistence and Change: The Petite Bourgeoisie in Industrial Society," *Archives européenes de sociologie* 17 (1976): 74–99; Jonathan M. Wiener, "Marxism and the Lower Middle Class," *Journal of Modern History* 49 (1977): 666–671; and Philip Nord, *Paris Shopkeepers and the Politics of Resentment* (Princeton: Princeton University Press, 1986), pp. 3–18. Catherine M. Stock, *Main Street in Crisis: The Old Middle Class on the Northern Plains, 1925–1938* (Chapel Hill: University of North Carolina Press, forthcoming), is a superb case study of petty-bourgeois culture in the Dakotas in the thirties which highlights its ambivalences and effectively complicates the conventional, often condescending, view of this class.

going over to them." As he wrote Clarence Senior, the Socialist party national secretary:

> I crave a long talk with you—[Norman Thomas, the Socialist Party leader] is not—in my judgment doing anybody any good by appearing to scoff at what is a perfectly earnest and honest—and *troubled* question in our minds concerning the SP and the necessary power strategy. We don't see how power can be won with the socialist name or without the socialist forces. This isn't "bourgeois"—or an evidence of lily fingers or anything of the kind. We know full well that any movement for socialization will be heaped with abuse, but feel that the evidence is clearer all the time that the real ground swell, if it comes, will produce a movement that cannot be persuaded to call itself socialist. . . . I'm tremendously impressed by the overwhelming conviction among the people I talk with—or rather hear talk—that the notion of the name handicap is not a fiction but something deadly real. I'm a socialist in everything except my dislike for [Morris] Hillquit dogmatism—a type that carries me back painfully to my church days—and shall work and vote SP unless and until a larger body similarly committed can be formed.

The leaders of the Socialist party did not find Dewey's arguments convincing, and the failure of the Socialists to join the effort to build a new party on anything but their own terms frustrated Dewey, who regarded their participation as essential.[25]

In the early thirties Dewey's political activism was centered in the work of two organizations he served as president: the League for Independent Political Action (LIPA) and the People's Lobby—groups committed to the organization of a radical third party built on a coalition of labor, farmers, and the middle class. The People's Lobby traced its origins to the People's Reconstruction League, formed shortly after World War I to lobby on behalf of unions. This group broadened its operations in the twenties and changed its name to the Anti-Monopoly League. In 1929 the executive secretary of the League, Benjamin Marsh, invited Dewey to become its president. Dewey agreed to do so if the group again changed its name to the People's Lobby to better accord with its slogan: "We fight for the people. We get and give the facts." Marsh handled the day-to-day operations of the Lobby, and Dewey's role consisted principally of issuing press releases to the *New*

25. "The Need for a New Party," p. 170; JD to Clarence Senior, 15 March 1933, Socialist Party of America Papers, Duke University.

York Times (many of them coauthored with Marsh) until 1931, when the group began publishing the *People's Lobby Bulletin*, to which he was a major contributor. During the early years of the Depression, the People's Lobby called for massive increases in relief funds for the unemployed, farmers, and children and for federal unemployment insurance, reconstruction of the tax system to redistribute wealth, and other substantial reforms. As the economic crisis deepened, Lobby demands escalated to government ownership of "the basic agencies upon which industry and commerce depend." Dewey served as president of the Lobby until 1936, often coordinating its work with that of the LIPA.[26]

The League for Independent Political Action and its immediate successors were the single most important political organizations in which Dewey ever participated. The group was organized at a New York meeting of some fifty leading progressive intellectuals on 15 December 1928. These men and women were veterans of a decade of frustration and failure in popular politics, and chastened by this experience, many in attendance believed it was time to retrench and opt for a strategy akin to that of the British Fabians, in which the LIPA would, for the moment, rest content to remain an elite cadre of experts. "I want to start with a small nucleus representing intellectual ability and technical knowledge," wrote one member to meeting organizer Paul H. Douglas, "and let the work they do attract its own following because of its incontrovertible accuracy and vision and importance." But Douglas and other leaders of the LIPA hoped to move more quickly to organize a radical third party, though they too looked to England for inspiration, taking the British Labour party as the model of the sort of party needed in the United States.[27]

In the spring of 1929 Dewey agreed to serve as LIPA national chairman. Douglas, W. E. B. DuBois, editor of the NAACP's *Crisis*, Zona Gale of the American Union against Militarism, and James H. Maurer,

26. Dykhuizen, pp. 229–230. The press releases and bulletins of the People's Lobby are in *Later Works* 5:427–450, 6:335–400, 9:247–290.
27. Constance Todd to Paul Douglas, 21 October 1928, as quoted in Eugene M. Tobin, *Organize or Perish: America's Independent Progressives, 1913–1933* (Westport, Conn.: Greenwood Press, 1986), pp. 196–197. Tobin's is the best account of LIPA activities through 1932, and I follow it closely here. See also Karl Denis Bicha, "Liberalism Frustrated: The League for Independent Political Action, 1928–1933," *Mid-America* 48 (1968): 19–28; Edward J. Bordeau, "John Dewey's Ideas about the Great Depression," *Journal of the History of Ideas* 32 (1971): 67–84; Richard J. Brown, "John Dewey and the League for Independent Political Action," *Social Studies* 59 (1968): 156–161; Bernard Johnpoll, *Pacifist's Progress: Norman Thomas and the Decline of American Socialism* (Chicago: Quadrangle, 1970), pp. 70–73; and R. Alan Lawson, *The Failure of Independent Liberalism* (New York: G. P. Putnam's Sons, 1971), passim.

a leading Socialist, were named vice chairmen, and Howard Y. Williams, a Unitarian minister and social activist from St. Paul, was appointed executive director. Others in the group's leadership included liberal editor Oswald G. Villard, Socialist party leader Norman Thomas, Devere Allen, an associate editor of the *Nation*, Harry Laidler, the executive director of the League for Industrial Democracy, and radical minister Reinhold Niebuhr. In the late fall of 1929 on the heels of the stock market crash the LIPA finally announced its program, calling for a realignment of American politics and a new party committed to a program that included demands for unemployment, old-age, and health insurance, substantial public-works spending, farm credit, guarantees of civil liberties, consumer and producer cooperatives, democratic control of industry, income redistribution, and the outlawry of war.

From the outset, the LIPA was plagued by tensions within its ranks. Chief among these was a division between the Socialist party members in the group and other activists. Norman Thomas and other Socialists hoped to make the LIPA an instrument of their party, while many non-Socialists shared Dewey's conviction that the Socialist party could never be the third party the nation required and his belief that the very word "socialism" was a hindrance to effective radical politics. These differences remained under control through 1930. The LIPA program largely mirrored that of the Socialist party, and in the elections that fall the LIPA lent its support to a number of Socialist candidates in what was (for the Socialists) a relatively successful campaign. But as the economic crisis deepened and national third-party organization made little headway, Dewey decided the time had come for a bold move, a move that outraged the Socialists.

On Christmas Day 1930 Dewey made public a letter he had written to a leading Republican insurgent, Senator George W. Norris of Nebraska, urging Norris to abandon the GOP and assume a leading role in the organization of a new party more in tune with his convictions. Agreeing with the executive director of the Republican National Committee that Norris had no place in the party, Dewey observed that "the Republican Party stands for 'rugged' individualism. You stand for social planning and social control. Republican leaders believe that by giving free rein to private competition somehow they will build a better world. You believe that in this complicated age that method is impossible, but that society must plan for its production and consumption. The controlling wing of the Republican party places property rights first. You place human rights first." Telling Norris that "we could win the Presi-

dency by 1940," Dewey urged the senator to help produce a realignment that would bring to American politics "a real conflict of ideas"
and thereby "give desperate workers and farmers a constructive vehicle
of political expression." The capstone of his appeal showed that, although no Christian, he was well aware of the secure place of Christianity in American public life. "At this Christmas season," he asked
Norris, "will you not renounce both of these old parties and help give
birth to a new party based upon the principle of planning and control
for the purpose of building happier lives, a more just society and that
peaceful world which was the dream of Him whose birthday we celebrate this Christmas Day?"[28]

Dewey's proposal, the *New York Times* editorialized, had about it the
"smell of the lamp" and could not have been composed by "a man in
close touch with the hard realities of political life." A day later Norris
respectfully declined Dewey's invitation, arguing in a letter published
in the *Times* that "experience has shown that the people will not respond to a demand for a new party except in case of a great emergency,
when there is practically a political revolution." A better strategy, Norris
said, would be to press for the abolition of the Electoral College (a pet
project of his), which he believed would loosen the grip of parties on
national elections and allow independent voters to vote independently.[29]

Norris's demurrer was far more polite than the response Dewey's
letter received from his Socialist colleagues in the LIPA. Already uncomfortable with Dewey's appeals to the middle class, many Socialists
saw the letter to Norris as compelling evidence that he and the LIPA
were insufficiently militant and not, after all, a group with which their
party should work closely. "A loosely constructed party with a nice
program, built around a few prominent individuals will get us nowhere," remarked A. J. Muste, who was advocating a strictly working-
class Labor party. Dewey, he charged, was "seeking after Messiahs who
are to bring down a third party from out of the political heavens." Some
called for a mass exodus of Socialist party members from the LIPA, and
many Socialists, including Thomas, did depart over the next several
months. Thus the consequences of Dewey's escalation of LIPA efforts
to enlist support for a third party from leaders of the left wings of the
existing parties were disastrous. Not only did he fail to win the support

28. "Dewey Asks Norris to Lead a New Party" (1930), *Later Works* 5:444–446.
29. *New York Times*, 27 December 1930; "Insurgents Back Norris in Refusing to Quit
Republicans" (1930), *Later Works* 5:504–505.

of congressional progressives, he alienated the Socialists in the LIPA and thereby further weakened the struggling organization.[30]

Undaunted, Dewey and the LIPA continued their efforts at third-party organization over the next two years. He published several articles advancing the arguments for realignment, and at the LIPA's national conference on the economy in January 1932 the group laid out a "Four-Year Presidential" plan, more or less a recapitulation of the program it had been advocating since its inception. When no alternative had emerged by the summer of 1932, the LIPA limped back to the Socialist party and supported Thomas for president, though some Socialists (probably correctly) suspected that many of its members voted for Franklin Roosevelt. Ever ready to find a silver lining in the darkest cloud, Dewey and other LIPA leaders took Roosevelt's victory and Thomas's disappointing showing as evidence of widespread sentiment for substantial social reform. Certain that Roosevelt would fail to meet the challenge of the Depression, the LIPA resumed its third-party organizing after the election, confident that its hour would come in 1936.[31]

In the spring of 1933 the LIPA merged its third-party organizing efforts with those of activists gathered around a new radical magazine, *Common Sense*, edited by two wealthy young Yale graduates, Alfred Bingham and Selden Rodman. Dewey and Bingham agreed to cooperate to build a United People's party, and *Common Sense* became the unofficial organ of the LIPA, carrying its "News Bulletin" as a regular feature. Their political strategy centered on the establishment of farmer-labor parties in the Midwest, where third-party sentiment was strong and an effective Farmer-Labor party had already become a going concern in Minnesota. In the summer of 1933 this coalition initiated a United Action Campaign, and at a United Conference for Progressive Political Action held in Chicago in September, the delegates—mostly agrarian radicals—established a national Farmer-Labor Political Federation (FLPF) to aid the establishment of state farmer-labor parties. The LIPA was relegated to purely educational functions,

---

30. A. J. Muste as quoted in Tobin, *Organize or Perish*, p. 212.
31. "The Need for a New Party," pp. 156–181; "Is There Hope for Politics?" (1931), *Later Works* 6:182–189; "Prospects for a Third Party" (1932), *Later Works* 6:246–252; "After the Election—What?" (1932), *Later Works* 6:253–255. The bible of the LIPA was Paul H. Douglas, *The Coming of a New Party* (New York: McGraw-Hill, 1932), for which Dewey wrote a foreword. The LIPA's "Four Year Presidential Plan" is reproduced in the *American Labor Year Book* (New York: Rand School of Social Science, 1916–32), 13:102–112.

and it disbanded in a matter of months. Wisconsin radical Thomas Amlie was named chair of the FLPF, Bingham was made executive secretary, and Williams left his post in the LIPA to become its national organizer. Dewey was named honorary chairman of the group, and for the next three years he followed the lead of Bingham, who shared his commitment to a thoroughly democratic socialism and to a radical politics respectful of the values and aspirations of the middle class.[32]

The program of the FLPF was more openly socialist in program if not in name than that of the LIPA, and the polemics that Bingham, Dewey, and other intellectuals ventured on its behalf were aimed primarily at the New Deal for falling short of the measures necessary to end the Great Depression and prevent another. It worked to promote state farmer-labor parties where they did not exist, to radicalize such parties where they did exist, and to prepare the ground for a national party that could wage a campaign for "production for use" in 1936. The principal targets of Amlie, Williams, and other FLPF organizers were Wisconsin, Minnesota, Iowa, and the Dakotas, though some work was done in the East and Far West.[33]

In the end, the hopes of the FLPF hinged on events in Wisconsin and, especially, Minnesota. In Wisconsin, following the break of the La Follette Progressive machine with the Republicans in 1934, Amlie succeeded in exerting some influence on Governor Philip La Follette and Senator Robert La Follette, Jr., and won a congressional seat for himself, but he could not get Fighting Bob's sons to commit themselves to a national third party. They, like most farmer-labor radicals, looked to Minnesota for leadership in this regard. Thus, as Amlie, Bingham,

32. I follow here the excellent, detailed account of Bingham and Amlie's politics in Donald L. Miller, *The New American Radicalism: Alfred M. Bingham and Non-Marxian Insurgency in the New Deal Era* (Port Washington, N.Y.: Kennikat Press, 1979), pp. 68–136. For Bingham's socialist vision see his series of articles called "The New Society" published in *Common Sense* from 30 March to 8 June 1933. Bingham's program for a "100% American radicalism" that would appeal to the middle class was outlined in his *Insurgent America: Revolt of the Middle Classes* (New York: Harpers, 1935). Miller usefully contrasts Bingham's work with that of such American Marxists as Leon Samson and Lewis Corey who awoke at about the same time to the fact that the middle class was not disappearing but, indeed, growing and so had to be accounted for in radical theory and politics. Crudely, the difference turned on the question of whether white-collar workers were best seen as a new middle class to which the working class aspired or a new working class into which the middle class had fallen (Miller, pp. 88–111). See also Frank A. Warren, *An Alternative Vision: The Socialist Party in the 1930s* (Bloomington: Indiana University Press, 1974), pp. 49–68.

33. For a collection of writings from *Common Sense* critical of the New Deal see Alfred Bingham and Selden Rodman, eds., *Challenge to the New Deal* (New York: Falcon Press, 1934). Dewey wrote the introduction to this volume.

Williams, and Dewey had anticipated, the success of their third-party dreams depended heavily on winning the allegiance of the Minnesota Farmer-Labor party (FLP), the most powerful radical party in the country, and its leader, Governor Floyd Olson. Their hopes that the Minnesotans would serve as the vanguard of their political revolution were raised when Olson seemed receptive to their overtures and accepted the position of honorary vice chairman of the FLPF.[34]

Despite the limited success of their organizing efforts outside of the upper Midwest, Amlie and Bingham were eager to take advantage of growing discontent with the New Deal following the initial burst of enthusiasm for the reforms of FDR's first hundred days. They called for a convention of third-party enthusiasts in Chicago in July 1935 to prepare for a national campaign the following year. There the FLPF was replaced by the American Commonwealth Political Federation (ACPF), which was essentially the FLPF in a new dress designed to appeal to voters outside of the group's strongholds. The officers of the ACPF were the same as those of the FLPF, with Dewey once again serving as honorary chair.

Throughout the remainder of 1935 and into 1936, the ACPF joined Huey Long, Father Charles E. Coughlin, Francis Townsend, and others in attacking Roosevelt and the New Deal, while Amlie and Bingham waited for Olson to champion a national third party and put the Minnesota FLP and himself in the vanguard of the movement. But Olson (who was dying of pancreatic cancer) was a far more practical and cautious politician than his radical rhetoric suggested. He had decided to back Roosevelt in 1936, and he offered only lukewarm, noncommittal support to the ACPF, and consequently its national campaign collapsed. Bingham reluctantly advised *Common Sense* readers in October to vote for Roosevelt as the only realistic choice, and Dewey once again cast his ballot for Thomas.[35]

Roosevelt's landslide victory in 1936 brought an end to serious third-party threats to the Democrats for the remainder of his presidency. It also brought an end to the most intense years of political activism of Dewey's life. Although this activity was not blessed with success, and indeed often showed the philosopher to be an inept practitioner of the

34. On the Minnesota Farmer-Labor party see Millard L. Gieske, *Minnesota Farmer-Laborism: The Third-Party Alternative* (Minneapolis: University of Minnesota Press, 1979), and Richard M. Valelly, *Radicalism in the States: The Minnesota Farmer-Labor Party and the American Political Economy* (Chicago: University of Chicago Press, 1989).

35. Miller, *New American Radicalism*, pp. 126–136; "How They Are Voting: 2" (1936), *Later Works* 11:526.

"hurly-burly" political arts, it did mark an important turning point in his career, for he had finally committed himself to the politics that his ideals and his political theory demanded. In the People's Lobby, the LIPA, and the FLPF he had helped build and lead organizations of the sort he had argued were required to educate and organize inchoate publics and invest them with the power to define their interests and reconstruct the state. The failure of third-party politics in the early thirties had also, unhappily, confirmed his contention that the organization of new publics would always be extremely difficult because of the obstructions of "inherited political agencies."

AGAINST STATE SOCIALISM

If his activism on behalf of a new party did little to dent the armor of the New Deal, Dewey's call for the socialization of the "commanding heights" of the economy in the mid–1930s solved in theory the problem of transcending state capitalism. But it raised other problems that became increasingly obvious to him as he viewed with alarm the development of authoritarian collectivism at home and abroad. In the Soviet Union, "the withering away of the state which was supposed to take place is not in evidence. On the contrary, seizure of political power as the means to the ultimate end of free individuals organized in functional occupational groups has led to the production of one more autocratic political state." In Germany and Italy, "the Fascists also proclaim the idea of a corporate state, but again there is reliance upon uncontrolled and irresponsible political power. Instead of a corporate society of functional groups there is complete suppression of every formal voluntary association of individuals." In the United States, the same problem was evident among technocratic progressives who "had a glimpse of the potentialities inherent in self-directed activities of autonomous groups performing necessarily social functions" but who "ruined their vision when they fell into the pit dug by Wells and Shaw, that of rule from above by an elite of experts." A corporatism dominated by a bureaucratic state was no more satisfactory to Dewey than a corporatism dominated by big business.[36]

Dewey had difficulty with the thinking of many radicals who, though they proclaimed themselves democrats, seldom gave evidence that democracy was their most inclusive end or considered the effects that the

36. "I Believe," pp. 95–96.

means by which they hoped to effect the good society would have on democracy. This, he said, was "the great tragedy of democracy in the world today." He insisted that the democratic ends of social security for all and equal opportunity for self-development dictated democratic means of consent, voluntarism, nonviolence, and organization from below. "The fundamental principle of democracy," he declared, "is that the ends of freedom and individuality for all can be attained only by means that accord with these ends."[37]

The specter of bureaucratic collectivism forced Dewey to define socialism and socialization more carefully in order to avoid the pitfalls of radical authoritarianism. "I should want to see politics used to forward the formation of a genuinely cooperative society," he said, "where workers are in control of industry and finance as directly as possible through the economic organization of society itself rather than through any superimposed state socialism, and where work ensures not only security, leisure, and opportunity for cultural development but also such a share in control as will contribute directly to intellectual and moral realization of personality." Dewey had established to his satisfaction that capitalism was inimical to both economic security and participatory democracy; he had now to deal with a collectivism that promised the first at the expense of the second. "The ultimate problem of production," he commented, "is the production of human beings. To this end, the production of goods is intermediate and auxiliary. It is by this standard that the present system stands condemned. 'Security' is a means, and although an indispensable social means, is not the end. . . . The means have to be implemented by a social-economic system that establishes and uses the means for the production of free human beings associating with one another on terms of equality. Then and only then will these means be an integral part of the end, not frustrated and self-defeating, bringing new evils and generating new problems."[38]

The state had an important instrumental role in the creation and maintenance of a democratic society, but it was essential that the state be subject to democratic controls. Dewey was adamant about the "absolute importance of democratic action in determining the policies of the government—for only by means of 'government by the people' can government *for* the people be made secure." Given such democratic controls, the state was "a powerful instrumentality for ends as valuable

37. "Democracy Is Radical," pp. 298.
38. "Unity and Progress" (1933), *Later Works* 9:72; "Economic Basis of the New Society," p. 320.

as they are far-reaching." But without these controls the instrumentality itself could become an end.[39]

Dewey's apprehensions about such abuse of state power manifested itself in a concern that American radicals would cut themselves off from the legacy of a native tradition of thought at once critical of corporate capitalism and worried about an authoritarian state. Although he shared the enthusiasm of many radicals of his day for the utopian imagination of Edward Bellamy, whom he called "a great American prophet," Dewey much preferred Bellamy's second book, the more populist and democratic *Equality* (1897), to the more popular and authoritarian *Looking Backward* (1888). Moreover, he displayed far greater enthusiasm for the reform program of Bellamy's contemporary Henry George, which was designed to secure a democratic distribution of wealth and power without establishing an all-powerful, bureaucratic state. Although Dewey did not hold with some of the Georgian true believers that the single tax on rentiers was a sufficient measure of reform, he did believe it a necessary one. "Henry George was right," he declared, "when he said that while socialization of natural opportunities, the land and the materials and power that come from it, is not a panacea, it is the foundation measure."[40]

But perhaps the most telling indicator of Dewey's search for a nonstatist radicalism was his effort to ensure that the influence of Thomas Jefferson was not completely eclipsed in the American left. In 1939 Dewey edited a volume of Jefferson's writings in the "Living Thoughts Library" and offered readers a Deweyan Jefferson for their times. Jefferson, Dewey wrote in his introduction, was "a character of singular consistency and charm" and "our first great democrat." Jefferson believed, as he said, that "we of the United States are constitutionally and conscientiously democrats," and, like Dewey, he emphasized the moral meaning of democracy. He argued, Dewey said, that "man is created with a want for society and with the powers to satisfy that want in concurrence with others. When he has procured that satisfaction by institution of a society, the latter is a product which man has a right to regulate 'jointly with all those who have concurred in its procurement.'" Jefferson had a "deep-seated faith in the people," believing "they might be fooled and misled for a time, but give them light and in

---

39. JD to Hu Shih, 27 October 1939, Dewey Papers.
40. "A Great American Prophet," *Later Works* 9:102–106; "Socialization of Ground Rent" (1935), *Later Works* 11:256–257. See also "An Appreciation of Henry George" (1928), *Later Works* 3:359–360, and "Foreword to *The Philosophy of Henry George*" (1933), *Later Works* 9:299–302.

the long run their oscillations this way and that will describe what in effect is a straight course ahead." Dewey emphasized the importance Jefferson attached to small, self-governing communities, to his injunction (never followed) to "divide the counties into wards." Jefferson's proposed ward system, Dewey said, was "the heart of his philosophy of politics," for, were it instituted, "every man would then share in the government of affairs not merely on election day but every day."[41]

A "Jeffersonian socialist" critique of state socialism required a conception of socioeconomic planning which offered an alternative to both the anarchy of unregulated capitalism and the authoritarianism of bureaucratic collectivism or technocracy. Dewey's call for scientific planning has often been confused with a call for thoroughly centralized planning controlled by a scientific elite, clearly a misreading of his intentions. But there is no denying that this is what planning meant to many intellectuals in the thirties, many of them participants in the same political organizations and contributors to the same journals as Dewey. Advocates of planning ranged in their commitment to democracy across a broad spectrum of opinion from the openly antidemocratic Technocracy movement led by Howard Scott to American guild socialists like Dewey and Bingham. Nowhere was a preoccupation with the opportunities that planning afforded for the expansion of the authority of the intelligentsia more evident than among the neoprogressive intellectuals who controlled the command posts of liberal opinion in the thirties. From such platforms as the *New Republic*, the *Nation*, *Common Sense*, and *Plan Age*, technocratic progressives including Thurman Arnold, Adolph Berle, Bruce Bliven, Stuart Chase, Morris L. Cooke, Paul Douglas, Freda Kirchway, Max Lerner, Harold Loeb, Lewis Lorwin, Robert Lynd, Gardiner Means, George Soule, and Rexford Tugwell argued for the identification of the good society with the rationalized society, which to them meant a society managed by an elite of far-sighted planners. They called for the creation of a new social order guided by "experts who are not representatives of the capitalists but of the public interest."[42]

Dewey was deeply critical of this proposed rule of experts, and he

41. "Presenting Thomas Jefferson" (1940), *Later Works* 14:202, 213–218.
42. "What We Hope For," *New Republic*, 10 February 1932: 337. The closest thing to a manifesto of technocratic progressivism is George Soule, "Hard-Boiled Radicalism," *New Republic*, 21 January 1931: 261–265. The literature on these intellectuals is quite thin, but see William E. Akin, *Technocracy and the American Dream* (Berkeley: University of California Press, 1977); Douglas Ayer, "In Quest of Efficiency: The Ideological Journey of Thurman Arnold in the Interwar Period," *Stanford Law Review* 23 (1970/71): 1049–1086; Lawson, *Failure of Independent Liberalism*, passim; Miller, *New American Radicalism*, pp. 50–66; and my "Tribune of the Technostructure: The Popular Economics of Stuart Chase,"

tried to envision a method of planning compatible with participatory democracy. This, he felt, was possible, and he had little patience with those like Walter Lippmann who, moving steadily rightward, had by the mid-thirties come to identify all forms of socialist planning with the authoritarianism of state socialism. Reviewing Lippmann's *Good Society* (1937), Dewey complained that "for a writer who at times shows a wide acquaintance with the history of social thought, [Lippmann] strangely identifies every form of socialism and collectivism with state or governmental socialism, and hence with overhead control of the activities of groups and individuals by bureaucratic officialdom."[43]

Dewey's efforts to conceptualize democratic planning rested on his distinction between the "planned" and the "planning" society. The former entailed the imposition of plans—fixed blueprints—from the top down. The latter entailed the formulation of ends and control of means by the public and by association, discussion, and contention within and among voluntary, functional groups of producers and consumers. The planned society left the choice of ends to the powerful who used "physical and psychological force" to secure conformity and left the choice of means to technicians who asked how but not why. The mass of men remained "hands," gaining economic security at the price of individual growth. In the planning society all citizens contributed to the limits of their capacities to the formation of social ends and the choice and control of the means to attain these ends. Here all individuals had the opportunity to maximize their powers of self-development through participation in the decisions shaping their lives and those of their communities. In the planning society the individual was not provided for; he provided for himself. It valued process as well as product—a society of "ing" words. Creating such a society, Dewey warned, required "remaking a profit system into a system conducted not just, as is sometimes said, in the interest of consumption, important as that is, but also in the interest of positive and enduring opportunity for productive and creative activity and all that signifies for the development of the potentialities of human nature."[44]

American Quarterly 32 (1980): 387–408. Lawson's account, perhaps the most familiar, is largely uncritical and, ignoring the issue of democracy and planning, lumps Dewey with Chase and Soule as "pragmatic rationalists."

43. "Liberalism in a Vacuum," pp. 489–490. For a good discussion of the differences between Dewey's idea of planning and that prevalent in the technocratic "policy sciences" see Timothy V. Kaufman-Osborn, "Pragmatism, Policy Science, and the State," *American Journal of Political Science* 29 (1985): 827–849.

44. "Economic Basis of the New Society," pp. 321–322, 318.

Dewey did not go much beyond these abstractions in envisioning the nature of democratic planning. Clearly he favored the decentralization of authority, democratization of the workplace, redistribution of wealth, and strengthening civil liberties and the representative institutions essential to dissent and the diffusion of power, but what form these measures and institutions might take Dewey did not say. This omission rendered his conception of a planning society vague and a rather poor hypothesis for experimental social action despite its stirring quality as an ideal. Dewey's complaints about the "lack of definiteness" in socialist ideology about what democracy would look like in "socialism when attained" could well have been directed at his own thinking.[45]

Guild socialism had long served Dewey as the model of "a socialism that is not state socialism." But by the thirties important criticisms had been made of guild socialism, many by guild socialists themselves, including G. D. H. Cole, its leading proponent. One had to take seriously, Cole warned, the possibility that socialist economic planning involved substantial centralization of decision-making power by its very nature and hence involved limitations on participatory democracy not foreseen by guild socialists. A powerful state was necessary not only to foster the foundation of voluntary associations of producers and consumers but also to control their interaction in the interests of prosperity and stability. The governmental authority necessary to maintain the rules of the game and handle the indirect consequences of voluntary action could be more considerable than Dewey envisioned. By the late forties, he had to admit with Cole that "the so-called guild socialists once started something, but events have left them nearly as much behind as it has the 'old-fashioned' socialists."[46]

This is not to say that Cole was right in every respect, or that Dewey's notion of planning was incompatible with Cole's later postguild conception of industrial democracy (which, in any case, was still more radically democratic than any existing socialist society). It is but to observe that

45. I believe that, if Dewey had given a clearer indication of what a planning society might look like, it probably would have been close to Bingham's 1933 vision of the "New Society" (see note 32).

46. JD to James Farrell, 8 November 1948, Dewey Papers. The shifts in Cole's thinking can be traced in *Self-Government in Industry* (1917), *Guild Socialism Re-Stated* (1920), *Principles of Economic Planning* (1935), and *The Machinery of Socialist Planning* (1938). Cole's work has been examined in detail by two very good intellectual biographies: Luther P. Carpenter, *G. D. H. Cole* (Cambridge: Cambridge University Press, 1973), and A. W. Wright, *G. D. H. Cole and Socialist Democracy* (Oxford: Oxford University Press, 1979). See also Carole Pateman, *Participation and Democratic Theory* (Cambridge: Cambridge University Press, 1970), pp. 35–44.

Dewey tended to resolve the difficulties that troubled Cole by assertion. His distinction between the planned and the planning society rested on an abstract argument that left untouched the important particulars essential to the kind of concrete, experimental social inquiry he himself advocated. He never formulated the "inclusive plan" for democratic socialism he had called for, and consequently his social and political theory proved least useful at those points where the questions about democratic planning were the toughest.

THE LONG RUN

Dewey's radical convictions remained intact until his death, despite the political defeats of the mid-thirties. Unlike many socialists who began to offer critical support for Roosevelt after 1936, he continued to keep his distance from the New Deal. Although his own political writing tailed off in the forties, his enthusiasm for the work of other democratic social critics, especially those writing for a new magazine, *Commentary*, indicated that his commitment to socialist democracy had not waned.

Commentary, which began publication in 1946, quickly established itself in Dewey's mind as "the most rewarding of all the liberal journals I see," and the magazine received his especially hearty praise for its regular feature "The Study of Man," which sought to provide the layman with a critical guide to research in the social sciences. Dewey wrote young friends that the *Commentary* articles were "dealing with sociology much more critically and fundamentally than I know of elsewhere." In one of his own contributions to the series, he noted that the articles were linked by "a troubled awareness of a narrowness, a restraint, a constriction imposed upon the social sciences by their present 'frame of reference,' ie. the axioms, terms, and boundaries under which they function today." The *Commentary* critics had established that social scientists too often identified the prevailing social order with "society" as such, a practice Dewey charged was both unscientific as to method and untrue to the possibilities that social scientific inquiry held for human freedom. "Instead of resulting in liberation from conditions previously fixed (which is the fruit of genuine scientific inquiry)," contemporary social science tended "to give scientific warrant, barring minor changes, to the *status quo*—or the established order—a matter especially injurious in the case of economic inquiry."[47]

47. *"Commentary* and Liberalism" (1948), *Later Works* 15:362; JD to Jack Lamb, 2 March 1947, Dewey Papers; JD to Robert Daniels, 15 February 1947, in "Letters of John Dewey

In light of Dewey's long-standing call for the democratization of the workplace, it is not surprising that his favorite study in the "Study of Man" series was Daniel Bell's "Adjusting Men to Machines," a sharp critique of industrial sociology which Dewey hailed as "virtually epoch-making." In this piece Bell noted the growth of extensive cooperation between big business and the universities in the study of industrial sociology. He attributed this cooperation to the fact that corporate executives used universities' trained research personnel to lend prestige to public-relations campaigns or to sell their management programs to unions. The professors, moreover, had an ideology geared to corporate needs. "Being scientists," Bell observed, "they are concerned with 'what is' and are not inclined to involve themselves in questions of moral values or larger social issues. They operate as technicians, approaching the problem as it is given to them and keeping within the framework set by those who hire them. . . . And almost none among them seems to be interested in the possibility that one of the functions of social science may be to explore *alternative* (and better, ie., more human) modes of human combinations, not merely to make more effective those that already exist."[48]

Critically reviewing the work of these sociologists, Bell showed that they lacked any conception of the class relationships between managers and workers and accepted the prevailing organization of industrial production as an "inalterable given." Their research rested on the assumption they took from their employers that "mechanical efficiency and high output are the sole tests of achievement—of 'good' results." Most industrial sociologists saw their job as one of adjusting men to machines and the social relations of capitalist production rather than as one of critically assessing the impact of managerial "rationalization" on workers. "The gravest charge that can be leveled against these researches," Bell concluded, "is that they uncritically adopt industry's own conception of workers as *means* to be manipulated or adjusted to impersonal ends. The belief in man as an end in himself has been ground under by the machine, and the social science of the factory researchers is not a science of man but a cow-sociology."[49]

to Robert V. Daniels, 1946–1950," *Journal of the History of Ideas* 20 (1959): 571; "Liberating the Social Scientist" (1947), *Later Works* 15:225–226.

48. "Comment on Bell and Polanyi" (1947), *Later Works* 15:361; Daniel Bell, "Adjusting Men to Machines: Social Scientists Explore the World of the Factory," *Commentary*, January 1947: 80. A fine study of Bell's work in the forties is Howard Brick, *Daniel Bell and the Decline of Intellectual Radicalism: Social Theory and Political Reconciliation in the 1940s* (Madison: University of Wisconsin Press, 1986).

49. Bell, "Adjusting Men to Machines," pp. 87–88.

Much as he liked Bell's article, Dewey reserved his greatest praise in the last years of his life for the work of Karl Polanyi, the Hungarian-born economic anthropologist who emigrated to the United States in the early forties. Polanyi's *Great Transformation* (1944), a sharply critical study of the origins and development of capitalist market society, made a profound impression on Dewey, who found it "intensely exciting" and "a wonder," and he was delighted when Polanyi found his way into *Commentary* alongside Bell and other critics of the social sciences.[50]

Polanyi argued that the full-blown capitalist market society that emerged with the transformation of land and labor into commodities was a historical and anthropological aberration. No other civilization had ever so totally subordinated social and political relations to market relations. Many societies had markets, but there had been but one market society, the society of nineteenth-century liberal capitalism. "Aristotle was right," Polanyi said, "man is not an economic, but a social being": "He does not aim at safeguarding his individual interest in the acquisition of material possessions, but rather at ensuring social good-will, social status, social assets. He values possessions primarily as a means to that end. His incentives are of that 'mixed' character which we associate with the endeavor to gain social approval—productive efforts are no more than incidental to this. *Man's economy is, as a rule, submerged in his social relations.* The change from this to a society which was, on the contrary, submerged in the economic system was an entirely novel development." This aberration, Polanyi observed, could not sustain itself for long. In the twentieth century, liberal capitalism had crumbled, and the laissez-faire economy was in the process of being replaced by various forms of political control. The difficulty now was one of bringing industrial society under control without sacrificing the genuine freedoms liberalism had instituted. This was a problem that socialists had to confront. As Polanyi concluded, "The search for industrial democracy is not merely the search for a solution to the problem of capitalism, as most people imagine. It is a search for an answer to industry itself."[51]

Polanyi, Dewey wrote Hook, "gives the best interpretation of general trends in 19th century history and 20th century up to date that I have ever seen. Without his using the phrase the net outcome is an argument, stated in factual concrete terms, for humanistic socialism." He

50. JD to Sidney Hook, 28 June 1945, Hook Collection; JD to Jack Lamb, 2 March 1947, Dewey Papers.

51. Karl Polanyi, "Our Obsolete Market Mentality," *Commentary*, February 1947: 112, 109. This article is a convenient summary of the major themes of *The Great Transformation*.

had, Dewey felt, completely routed the argument of Friedrich von Hayek's *Road to Serfdom* (1944), a book that had, much to Dewey's chagrin, generated a resurgence of enthusiasm for laissez-faire individualism. "If Hayek had ever read one chapter of [*The Great Transformation*]," he said, "I think that he would have been ashamed to write his book—for it is a convincing proof that all the evils and objectionable problems Hayek builds on are the products of the necessity of social protections against a market economy, but taken piecemeal and rather blindly, because without repudiation of the basic tenets and practices of the market economy and without having a social system developed even in principle to replace the market economy."[52]

Dewey's activism slowed in the forties, yet he remained remarkably involved in practical politics for a man approaching ninety. He continued to push nationally and in New York for a radical third party committed to democratic socialism, although by the end of the decade his political prognostications became increasingly wistful. On the eve of what would be his final presidential election in the fall of 1948, he was undecided whether to cast yet another vote for Norman Thomas or return to the Democratic fold. Perhaps, he suggested to James Farrell, the loss of the election would bring on the fragmentation of the Democratic party, purging the Communists and Southern Bourbons and leaving a coalition centered around the major industrial unions which could serve as "the nucleus of the kind of party that is needed." Applying a rather inexact analogy, he wrote Farrell that the situation in 1948 "seems to me much like that of 1856; the republican party was defeated as the dem party will be this time. But it came back in '60, and [while] its postwar record is nothing to brag about, it did a useful work under Lincoln even if not quite that of Saving the Union." On these grounds, he unwittingly voted for a winner. Truman's victory took him (and many others) by complete surprise and left a Democratic party that was, he admitted, "more than a nucleus."[53]

But such setbacks did not dull Dewey's faith in democratic political action. Radical politics was a matter of the long run, he advised, and he calculated in 1932 that the transformation of American society he envisioned would entail "at least a thirty years war." Sometimes his own best critic, he admitted after the war that neither he nor anyone else had

52. JD to Sidney Hook, 28 June 1945, Hook Collection.
53. JD to James Farrell, 11 October, 24 October, and 9 November 1948, Dewey Papers. See also "American Youth, Beware of Wallace Bearing Gifts" (1948), *Later Works* 15:242–247.

provided an adequate program for democratic socialism. "To get out of [their] ruts," he said, "socialists have to do a lot of critical inquiry— including that into their own ideas." He called for the kind of investigation of the conditions and consequences of democratic planning which his own work had failed to provide. "It is at the furthest remove from endorsement of the arguments which claim that organized social intervention and planning is a return to serfdom," he remarked in 1948, "to say that the problem of working out the specific means and agencies by which organized planning and intervention will result in promotion of freedom is a deeply serious one."[54]

Dewey knew how to frame the agenda for democratic socialism, if not how to fill it. He was not blind to the obstacles radical democrats faced, only deaf to the protestations that these obstacles were immovable. As he neared the end of his own long run, he continued to counsel the virtue of persistence. "Forty years spent wandering in a wilderness like that of the present is not a sad fate," he had remarked in his autobiographical sketch of 1930, "unless one attempts to make himself believe that the wilderness is after all itself the promised land."[55] Twenty more years of wandering in the wilderness did nothing to dim this conviction, and unlike many liberal intellectuals, Dewey never believed that American democracy was out of the woods.

54. "Prospects for a Third Party" (1932), *Later Works* 6:246; JD to James Farrell, 8 November 1948, Dewey Papers; "How to Anchor Liberalism" (1948), *Later Works* 15:249– 250.
55. "From Absolutism to Experimentalism" (1930), *Later Works* 5:160.

CHAPTER 13

Their Morals and Ours

*

JOHN DEWEY's *Liberalism and Social Action*, wrote Sidney Hook in 1939, "may very well be to the twentieth century what Marx and Engels' *Communist Manifesto* was to the nineteenth." This judgment was less the prediction of a dispassionate observer than the dream of a devoted disciple, yet Hook's explicit comparison of Deweyan liberalism to Marxism suggests a context essential to an understanding of Dewey's social thought in the thirties and forties. The commitment to participatory democracy that led Dewey to his peculiar brand of libertarian socialism led as well to his critical assessment of Marxism and Stalinism. The character of his democratic theory in these years is not fully explicable without reference to the ideology and politics of left-wing anti-communism.[1]

The close relationship that developed between Dewey and anti-Stalinist radicals in the interwar period is yet another feature of his career which distinguishes him from the progressives and liberals with whom he is sometimes grouped. Unlike many liberals who eventually reached a rapprochement with the New Deal in the thirties, Dewey continued to question the capacity of capitalism—even a reformed capitalism—to promote democratic values. At the same time, he warned of the threat of Soviet collectivism to these same values. After

1. Sidney Hook, *John Dewey: An Intellectual Portrait* (New York: John Day, 1939), p. 158.

463

breaking bitterly with the "totalitarian liberalism" of the Popular Front progressives at the *New Republic* during the Moscow Trials, Dewey was able to find a congenial home among anti-Stalinist misfits including Sidney Hook, James T. Farrell, and Jim Cork—"New York intellectuals" who shared his antipathy to antidemocratic ideologies of all stripes.[2]

For Dewey, his former student Sidney Hook was the most important of these young radicals, and Hook exerted considerable influence on the development of Dewey's anticommunism. Often Hook was Virgil to Dewey's Dante, pointing out the horrors of Stalin's hell, guiding him through the labyrinths of Marxism, protecting Dewey's philosophy from the slanders of the priests of dialectical materialism, and encouraging him to undertake confrontations with communist demons who threatened the democratic faith. It is difficult in an assessment of this relationship of deep mutual respect and affection to determine exactly who was the teacher and who the student on anticommunist issues. Dewey and Hook did not always agree on such matters, and perhaps Dewey would have reached many of his anticommunist conclusions without Hook's help, but it was usually Hook who kept his professor on his toes concerning totalitarian matters. For Hook, as well as for many other anti-Stalinist radicals, Dewey was a beloved mentor, and they warmly welcomed him to their cause. "How fortifying it is to have Dewey return to the attack, at his age, with the wonderful spirit and freshness he displays," Newton Arvin remarked in 1943. "At such times, as Emerson said of Channing, we remember that he is our bishop, and that we have not done with him yet."[3]

In the mid-thirties, Dewey and other anti-Stalinist radicals saw themselves as part of a "third camp," waging a two-front war on American capitalism and Russian state socialism, on New Deal liberalism and Soviet Marxism. Their attitude was succinctly summarized in Dewey's

2. A useful survey of the attitudes of liberal intellectuals toward communism in the thirties which does make the appropriate distinctions is Frank Warren, *Liberals and Communism* (Bloomington: Indiana University Press, 1966). Three major studies of the "New York intellectuals" have recently been published: Alexander Bloom, *Prodigal Sons: The New York Intellectuals and Their World* (Oxford: Oxford University Press, 1986); Terry A. Cooney, *The Rise of the New York Intellectuals: "Partisan Review" and Its Circle, 1934–1945* (Madison: University of Wisconsin Press, 1986); and Alan Wald, *The New York Intellectuals: The Rise and Decline of the Anti-Stalinist Left from the 1930s to the 1980s* (Chapel Hill: University of North Carolina Press, 1987). Of the flood of memoirs by these intellectuals the most relevant here is Sidney Hook, *Out of Step: An Unquiet Life in the Twentieth Century* (New York: Harper and Row, 1987).

3. Newton Arvin, "A Trench Defended," *Partisan Review* 10 (1943): 208. For Hook's perspective on his relationship to Dewey see "Some Memories of John Dewey," in Hook, *Pragmatism and the Tragic Sense of Life* (New York: Basic Books, 1974), chap. 6, and *Out of Step*, chap. 7.

contention that there was a socialism that was not state socialism. This alternative socialism was clear about its ideal: democratic means to radically democratic ends. Democratic means, however, proved difficult to conceptualize, let alone organize, and the dreams of democratic socialists came to rest on a soft foundation of hopes for a radical third party.

The temptation in this situation of meager political resources was to retreat to secure but ineffectual ideological purity by defending democratic socialism in purely negative terms as anticapitalist liberalism and anti-Stalinist socialism without offering any positive program for social reconstruction or, alternatively, to give up the two-front war and risk dissolution in an alliance with liberal capitalism against Stalinism, the greater of the two evils. It was to the blandishments of this second temptation that many anti-Stalinist radicals succumbed in the late forties and early fifties.

Dewey, for his part, never ceased to call for a radical, democratic politics and the reconstruction of American society, but the tensions of the Cold War were not without their effect on his thinking. He was in his last years once again a wary and, occasionally, a stridently defensive democrat. The threat of domestic anticommunism to civil liberties did alert him to the ironies of a socialist anti-Stalinism that was by the late forties finding itself with ever-stranger bedfellows, but he could do little to thwart the unintended consequences for democracy of a politics he had helped initiate in its defense.

PRAGMATISM AND MARXISM

Dewey was a unique anti-Stalinist radical in that he did not care much for Marx. This was not a particularly informed judgment on his part, for he had read little of Marx's work despite the exhortations of Hook and others to do so. He admitted his ignorance freely, telling Max Eastman, for example, that he knew too little Marx to judge intelligently whether Eastman or Hook had the better of the seemingly interminable debate the two waged in the late twenties and early thirties over the meaning of Marxism. He informed V. F. Calverton, the editor of the *Modern Quarterly*, that he had no "great familiarity with socialist literature," yet he nonetheless contributed to the symposium "Marx and Social Change" on the basis of his understanding of what contemporary Marxists said Marx had said. This foray reflected Dewey's feeling that not Marx but Marx*ism*, particularly Soviet Marxism, was the antagonist. Unlike the thought of the "real Marx," whatever that was, Soviet dialectical materialism was an important ideological force exercising immediate influence on his own experience and on the larger world. It was, he believed, a pernicious philosophy, and he was confident in attacking it from his own point of view without forming any entangling alliances with a nineteenth-century German who seemed on the face of it to have been less successful than he had been in recovering from the Hegelian virus. As Hook put it, "Marxism for Dewey was what those who call themselves Marxists made of it; just as Marxists would say that Christianity is what those who call themselves Christian live by."[4]

Both Hook and Jim Cork tried to bring Dewey's philosophy together with that of Marx. Cork pointed out the manifest similarities in logic, metaphysics, epistemology, psychology, ethics, and aesthetics between Marxism, properly understood, and Deweyan naturalism. Both Dewey and Marx, he argued, were democratic humanists whose social philosophies were compatible. He applauded Dewey's critique of "vulgar Marxism" but urged him to distinguish between Marx and Marxism and to consider the value of Marxian class analysis and the praxis of class struggle. "If," Cork concluded, "the pragmatists would stop confusing Marx with some Marxists, recognize the hard, ineradicable, humanist-democratic core of Marx's thinking as akin to their own, and implement their praiseworthy, general value judgments with concrete instrumentalities applied to political and social questions; and if the socialists, on their part, would drop overboard the ludicrous excess baggage of the dialectic, rid themselves of the remaining shreds of inevitabilism, abandon their narrow class conception of democratic values, and learn to think experimentally in politics . . . their positions would converge on a set of common hypotheses leading to common activities."[5]

Hook's efforts to link Dewey and Marx were more extensive and more important. Already a battle-scarred veteran of New York socialist politics by the time he finished high school, Hook began his training in philosophy in the early twenties at City College under the tutelage of

4. JD to Max Eastman, 10 May 1933, Max Eastman Papers, Lilly Library, University of Indiana; V. F. Calverton to JD, 18 April 1930, and JD to V. F. Calverton, 21 April 1930, V. F. Calverton Papers, New York Public Library; JD to Sidney Hook, 9 October 1931, Hook Collection; "Social Change and Its Human Direction" (1930), *Later Works* 5:363–367; Hook, *John Dewey*, p. 162. An insightful account of the Hook-Eastman debate is John Diggins, "Getting Hegel out of History: Max Eastman's Quarrel with Marxism," *American Historical Review* 79 (1974): 52–57.

5. Jim Cork, "John Dewey and Karl Marx," in Sidney Hook, ed., *John Dewey: Philosopher of Science and Freedom* (New York: Dial Press, 1950), p. 350.

one of Dewey's most implacable intellectual foes, Morris Raphael Cohen. He then went on to Columbia, where his efforts to refute pragmatism resulted instead in his conversion to it (much to Cohen's chagrin), and he earned his doctorate in 1927 with a dissertation titled "The Metaphysics of Pragmatism." There followed a year in Germany researching post-Hegelian philosophy on a Guggenheim fellowship and a summer in Moscow, where he was among the first Western scholars to exploit the vast archival resources of the Marx-Engels Institute.[6]

Hook returned to the United States with the onset of the Depression and quickly established himself as the nation's most formidable Marxist theoretician. In 1933 he published his extraordinary book *Towards the Understanding of Karl Marx*, which was, in his words, an attempt "to develop a kind of Americanized Marxism, strengthened by John Dewey's activist theory of mind and knowledge, as well as his philosophy of education and naturalistic humanism, that would be in consonance with the American revolutionary tradition." Like his fellow "Western Marxists" George Lukács and Karl Korsch, whose work he had read and critically absorbed, Hook offered a fresh and heretical reading of Marx which owed a substantial debt to the insights of "bourgeois" philosophy, in this case, Deweyan pragmatism. Drawing on Dewey's conception of science as an experimental, fallible enterprise and identifying it with Marx's dialectic, Hook's pragmatic Marxism posed a challenge to the dialectical materialism of both orthodox social democrats and orthodox communists. On the one hand, he rejected as unscientific the determinism, faith in inevitable progress, and reformism of the social democrats in favor of a politics of revolutionary praxis. On the other hand, the link he discovered between science and radical democracy in the philosophy of Dewey and Marx raised uncomfortable questions about the authoritarian social engineering the Soviet Union had launched in Marx's name.[7]

Politically, Hook flirted with the American Communist party for several years before his philosophical heresies and democratic inclinations put him permanently at loggerheads with the party leadership. Denounced by them as a "counterrevolutionary reptile," he became active in 1934 in the organization of the short-lived American Workers party, led by A. J. Muste, which put Hook's conception of "workers' democra-

6. *Out of Step*, chaps. 1–10. The account here of Hook's early career and thought draws on my review of his autobiography, "Stream of Contentiousness," *Nation*, 30 May 1987: 726–730.

7. *Out of Step*, chaps. 11–12, 14; Hook, *Towards the Understanding of Karl Marx* (New York: John Day, 1933).

cy" at the heart of its platform. This idea, which represented the full flowering of Hook's libertarian Marxism and influenced Dewey's thinking about Russian society, was an effort to reinterpret the dictatorship of the proletariat as the rule of workers' democratic councils and distinguish it from the rule of the Communist bureaucracy in the Soviet Union, which Hook characterized as "dictatorship *over* the proletariat."[8]

In their efforts to join Marxism and pragmatism, Hook and Cork were asking a great deal of orthodox Marxists and very little of Dewey. Dewey had, after all, admitted Marx's considerable virtues as a sociologist and historian. Passages of *Liberalism and Social Action* in which he argued that the root of the crisis of contemporary society lay in the inappropriateness of the social relations of production to the forces of production developed by modern science sound very Marxian. What Dewey's friendly radical critics objected to most was that in the crisis of the thirties he eschewed revolutionary politics yet offered little guidance to the specific kinds of political action which might serve as the means to a democratic socialist society. But Dewey was not without ideas on the subject, centering his proposals, as we have seen, on third-party politics, and the problem both Dewey and his Marxist critics faced was less one of prescription than of power. Class analysis, no matter how acute, could not guarantee class politics. In retrospect, Dewey's call for a broad coalition of farmers, labor, and the lower middle class seems no less realistic than the Marxists' advocacy of working-class revolt; the failures of the League for Independent Political Action were certainly no greater than those of the American Workers party. At the very least, Dewey's tactical flexibility buffered him against undue political disappointment, despair, and resignation. Thus it is not surprising that Dewey believed that much of what Marx was said to offer him he already had and that what he did not have was not particularly attractive to him.

Dewey was not as indifferent to Soviet Marxism, be it of the Stalinist or Trotskyist variety. To him, communism posed at least as great a threat to democratic values as did corporate liberalism. Moreover, this was an ideology wielded by intellectuals in the American Communist party and among its fellow travelers who distorted and attacked his own philosophy, wrecked some of the organizations in which he placed his

8. *Out of Step*, chaps. 12–15. On "workers' democracy" see Hook, "On Workers' Democracy," *Modern Monthly* 8 (1934): 529–544, and "The Democratic and Dictatorial Aspects of Communism," *International Conciliation* 305 (December 1934): 452–464.

political hopes, and defamed his character. Small wonder that the communists who assaulted Dewey from the left found as little favor as conservatives who besieged him from the right. The marvel is that Dewey retained some measure of tolerance.

Dewey listed his fundamental objections to what he termed "Communism, official Communism, spelt with a capital letter" in his contribution to a *Modern Quarterly* symposium in 1934 in which he, Bertrand Russell, and Morris Cohen were asked to reveal "Why I Am Not a Communist." These objections, confirmed and strengthened by subsequent polemics and political experience, were the foundation of his anticommunism. First, Dewey registered his opposition to the dogmatism of a philosophy that "has made the practical traits of the dictatorship *of* the proletariat and *over* the proletariat, the suppression of the civil liberties of all non-proletarian minorities, integral parts of the standard communist faith and dogma." He also complained of the determinism of the Communist philosophy of history and its strategic and tactical monism, and he objected to the assertion of the inevitability of class war and violent revolution. Finally, he noted:

> It is not irrelevant to add that one of the reasons I am not a Communist is that the emotional tone and methods of dispute which seem to accompany Communism at present are extremely repugnant to me. Fair play, elementary honesty in the representation of facts and especially of the opinions of others, are something more than "bourgeois virtues." They are traits that have been won only after long struggle. They are not deep-seated in human nature even now—witness the methods that brought Hitlerism to power. The systematic, persistent and seemingly intentional disregard of these things by Communist spokesmen in speech and press, the hysteria of their denunciations, their attempts at character assassination of their opponents, their misrepresentation of the views of the "liberals" to whom they also appeal for aid in their defense campaigns, their policy of "rule or ruin" in their so-called united front activities, their apparent conviction that what they take to be the end justifies the use of *any* means if only those means promise to be successful—all these, in my judgment, are fatal to the very end which official Communists profess to have at heart.[9]

The issue of the inevitability of class struggle and violence was one to which Dewey returned in 1935 in *Liberalism and Social Action*. There he

9. "Why I Am Not a Communist" (1934), *Later Works* 9:91–95. See also Paul Slater and Jack Libronne, "Dewey, Russell, and Cohen: Why They Are Anti-Communist," *New Masses*, 17 July 1934: 24–27, and 24 July 1934: 22–23.

argued that he did not rule out the use of force in the task of socializing the economy, only the supposed necessity of its use. He was perfectly willing to consider class conflict as a possible means to democratic ends in particular situations; he objected only to the conclusion that some "law of history" made such conflict, especially violent conflict, the *inevitable* means to these ends. "The issue," Dewey argued, "is not whether some amount of violence will accompany the effectuation of radical change of institutions. The question is whether force or intelligence is to be the method upon which we consistently rely and to whose promotion we devote our energies . . . . Moreover, acceptance in advance of the inevitability of violence tends to produce the use of violence in cases where peaceful methods might otherwise avail." The fact that the means of violence were centralized in the United States within a formally democratic polity suggested to Dewey both the foolishness of violent radical tactics and the potential efficacy of nonviolent political revolution. In any case, he concluded, "it is sheer defeatism to assume in advance of actual trial that democratic political institutions are incapable either of further development or of constructive social application."[10]

The one exception to a nonviolent strategy which Dewey was willing to admit as prima facie reasonable, if not inevitable, found him making a version of the argument about the limits of toleration "after the revolution" which he had criticized in the *Modern Quarterly* symposium the year before: "The one exception—and that apparent rather than real—to dependence upon organized intelligence as the method for directing social change is found when society through an authorized majority has entered upon the path of social experimentation leading to great social change, and a minority refuses by force to permit the method of intelligent action to go into effect. Then force may be intelligently employed to subdue and disarm the recalcitrant minority." Full membership in the good society could be extended only to those willing to join a democratic community on its own terms, not to those who refused to play by the rules of democracy and attempted to disrupt its workings. Dewey's procedural absolute, his intolerance for antidemocratic intolerance, was thus his first principle of public order. Despite this concession to revolutionary repression in defense of democracy, one can see why by the thirties Dewey regarded the Soviet Union as an unsuccessful revolutionary society and why he viewed its defenders as a

---

10. *Liberalism and Social Action* (1935), *Later Works* 11:55, 60. Dewey cited Marx's own suggestion that "change might occur in Great Britain and the United States, possibly Holland, by peaceful means" (59).

threat to his democratic ideals. Drawing on Hook's arguments, he now argued that because Russia was not a "workers' democracy" (dictatorship *of* the proletariat) but a bureaucratic tyranny (dictatorship *over* the proletariat), Stalinist repression could scarcely be legitimated as protection for democracy.[11]

Dewey put his reflections on violence and class struggle in a broader philosophical context in a debate with Leon Trotsky over revolutionary means and ends in the pages of the American Trotskyist journal, the *New International*, in 1938. Replying to the conception of revolutionary ethics Trotsky articulated in an article titled "Their Morals and Ours," Dewey noted in "Means and Ends" that the controversy over the Soviet purge trials "has had at least one useful theoretical result. It has brought out into the open for the first time . . . an explicit discussion by a consistent Marxian on the relation of means and ends in social action." Dewey believed, as he told one correspondent in 1946, that "Trotsky was a fanatic and in power would probably have disposed of dissidents as ruthlessly as did Stalin," but at the same time he regarded his series of encounters with the Bolshevik leader in the late thirties as "the most interesting single intellectual experience of my life."[12]

In responding to Trotsky's polemic, which denounced the ethics of petty-bourgeois intellectuals "who wish that history would leave them in peace with their little books, little magazines, subscribers, common sense, and moral copybooks," Dewey agreed with his adversary on a number of important points. Both rejected absolutist and supernatural ethics, both regarded the liberation of mankind as the inclusive end against which other ends were measured as means, and both shared the belief that "the end in the sense of consequences provides the only basis for moral ideas and action, and therefore provides the only basis for moral ideas and action, and therefore provides the only justification that can be found for means employed" (ME, 350). Dewey commended Trotsky's rendering of this principle as one which justified those means "which really lead to the liberation of mankind" (ME, 350). If one

11. Ibid., p. 61. Dewey applied this argument explicitly to the case of the Spanish Civil War ("Aid for the Spanish Government," *Christian Century* [3 March 1937]: 292). This defense of the use of force to put down a reactionary threat to a democratic revolution was an aspect of Dewey's thinking which his radical critics often overlooked. Dwight Macdonald, for example, chided Dewey for not having an answer for situations such as Spain. See "An Open Letter to Dr. John Dewey," ms. in Dwight Macdonald Papers, Sterling Library, Yale University. This letter was apparently never sent; I am indebted to Robert Cummings for bringing it to my attention.

12. "Means and Ends" (1938), *Later Works* 13:349; JD to [W. R. Houston], 22 April 1946, Dewey Papers; JD to Max Eastman, 12 May 1937, Max Eastman Papers. Page numbers for further references to "Means and Ends" (ME) appear in the text.

reasoned in accordance with this principle, Dewey continued (in a vein familiar to those who knew his ethics), the end should serve to direct action and the choice of means. It should, that is, mean an "examination of *all* means that are likely to attain this end without any fixed preconception as to what they *must* be, and that every suggested means would be weighed and judged on the express ground of the consequences it is likely to produce" (ME, 351).[13]

At this point Dewey and Trotsky parted company, for rather than engage in the kind of inquiry Dewey suggested, Trotsky deduced his means, the class struggle, from a "law" of historical development standing outside of any critical examination of the means-end relationship. "The professed end—the end-in-view—the liberation of mankind," Dewey remarked, "is thus subordinated to the class struggle as the means by which it is to be attained" (ME, 352). Establishing the class struggle deductively as the only means to the liberation of mankind, Trotsky had freed his means from the test of means-ends interdependence, and his defense of class conflict was "automatically absolved from all need for critical examination" (ME, 352).

Dewey was careful to point out that his own position did not rule out class struggle as a means to human freedom, only that it refused to accept this proposition as a deduction from the assumption of a fixed law of social development. Trotsky was operating with a fallacious conception of science which treated theory as absolute law rather than as fruitful empirical generalization and, in deducing his means from such a law, was providing history with a moral purpose, something science, rightly conceived, could not do. Dewey observed further that "the belief that a law of history determines the particular way in which the struggle is to be carried on certainly seems to tend toward a fanatical and even mystical devotion to the use of certain ways of conducting the class struggle to the exclusion of all other ways of conducting it" (ME, 353). Hitting Trotsky where he lived, he suggested that "it is conceivable that the course actually taken by the revolution in the U.S.S.R. becomes more explicable when it is noted that means were deduced from a supposed scientific law instead of being searched for and adopted on the ground of their relation to the moral end of the liberation of mankind" (ME, 353–354).

13. Leon Trotsky, "Their Morals and Ours" (1938), in *Their Morals and Ours: Marxist versus Liberal Views on Morality*, ed. George Novack (New York: Pathfinder Press, 1969), p. 10. Perhaps because he did not address Dewey directly, Trotsky's essay is not reprinted in Dewey's *Later Works*. Dewey's essay in response to Trotsky can, however, be found in *Their Morals and Ours*.

Dewey concluded that Trotsky was avoiding absolutist ethics of one sort only to pick up those of another sort. Morality was meaningless without human choice; science could make such choices more intelligent but it could not preclude them. "To be scientific about ends does not mean to read them out of laws, whether the laws are natural or social," Dewey avowed. "Orthodox Marxism shares with orthodox religionism and with traditional idealism the belief that human ends are interwoven into the very texture and structure of existence—a conception presumably from its Hegelian origin" (ME, 354).[14]

In *Freedom and Culture*, published a year later, Dewey offered his most extended treatment of Marxist philosophy, once again blasting its pretensions to scientific status. He did this in the context of his larger argument about culture as a concept that pointed to human experience as an ongoing series of interactions between individual human nature and the social environment. He pointed critically to Marxism as "the type of social theory which reduces the human factor as nearly as possible to zero; since it explains events and forms policies exclusively in terms of conditions provided by the environment." Noting the tendency of orthodox Marxists to brand their opponents as "pro-Fascist," Dewey began his critique with a statement of his own radical bona fides: "One may hold that if there is to be genuine and adequate democracy there must be a radical transformation of the present controls of production and distribution of goods and services, and may nevertheless accept the criticisms to be made [of Marxism]—indeed may make or accept the criticisms *because* one believes the transformation is required."[15]

Dewey began by offering Marxists a way out, acknowledging that Marx had allowed for the influence of the noneconomic superstructure, once formed, back upon the mode of production. This theory would entail the recognition of a complex, pluralistic set of interactions between variables requiring that social action be predicated on empirical generalizations based on historical and sociological research. This kind of sophisticated Marxism Dewey found very congenial and very scarce, and he focused his attention on the "extremists" who were neither sophisticated nor rare. Here again the villain was the dialectic,

14. For two different views of this debate from Trotsky's perspective see Isaac Deutscher, *The Prophet Outcast* (New York: Vintage Books, 1963), pp. 438–444, and Baruch Knei-Paz, *The Social and Political Thought of Leon Trotsky* (Oxford: Oxford University Press, 1978), pp. 556–567. Steven Lukes has recently made good use of this debate in *Marxism and Morality* (Oxford: Oxford University Press, 1985), chap. 6.

15. *Freedom and Culture* (1939), *Later Works* 13:117–118. Page numbers for further references (*FC*) appear in the text.

the all-embracing law of historical change with its dynamic of inevitable class struggle. This law, for the orthodox Marxist, was not an empirical generalization but a metaphysical faith, derived from Hegelian idealism yet aggressively materialistic in its denial of power to human valuation. "In lieu of one type of romantic absolutism," Dewey contended, Marxism "developed another type more in harmony with the prestige which science and scientific law were gaining" (FC, 120).

Perhaps the most important feature of Dewey's critique was his challenge to Marxism's scientific pretensions. Dialectical materialism, he argued, was based on an outmoded, nineteenth-century conception of scientific law and causality. Science had since retreated from a search for forces and laws lying behind events to a more modest quest for nonmetaphysical empirical generalizations that could make sense of observed relationships between events. Marxism was dated, Dewey argued, "for just as *necessity* and search for *single* all-comprehensive law was typical of the intellectual atmosphere of the forties of the last century, so *probability* and *pluralism* are the characteristics of the present state of science" (FC, 123). Marxism thus bore the mark of a period in which science was battling religion on religion's terms, searching for the Force that would tie phenomena together. This was a competition that science—but not Marxism—eventually abandoned. As a result, Marxism's potential contribution to social science was obscured by metaphysical mumbo-jumbo:

> The criticism made is not directed then to any generalization made by Marx on the basis of observation of actual conditions. On the contrary, the implication of the criticism is the necessity for *continued* observation of actual conditions, with testing and revision of all earlier generalization on the basis of what is now observed. The inherent theoretical weakness of Marxism is that it supposed a generalization that was made at a particular date and place (and made even then only by bringing observed facts under a premise drawn from a metaphysical source) can obviate the need for continued resort to observation, and to continual revision of generalizations in their office of working hypotheses. In the name of science, a thoroughly anti-scientific procedure was formulated, in accord with which a generalization is made having the nature of ultimate "truth," and hence holding good at all times and places. (FC, 125)

Dialectical materialism was, as far as Dewey was concerned, not science but philosophical absolutism. "There is no better evidence of the intellectual backwardness of Communist theory," he later remarked, "than their hanging onto 'materialism' after any ground for it has dropped out of physical science."[16]

Dewey turned to the Soviet Union for evidence of the disastrous social and political consequences of the institutionalization of this philosophical absolutism. The defense of absolute truth, unlike that of "warranted assertability," generated fanaticism and intolerance of dissent, which was regarded as the product of a malevolent will. Repressive structures of authority were established to defend "the Truth" and apply it to particular situations: "arbitrary irresponsibility varies in direct ratio to the claim for absoluteness on the part of the principle in behalf of which power is exercised." Particularly vulnerable were "heretics" like Trotsky who accepted the Truth yet resisted its orthodox interpretation and application. Such heretics were considered much worse than the outright defenders of capitalism who "like pagans, as distinct from heretics, do not know any better." In the United States, Dewey could not resist saying, Communists lacked the power necessary to enforce their absolute principles and were reduced to using verbal abuse, "the mildest epithet being that of Fascist or friend of Fascism" (FC, 128, 129).

The moral of Dewey's consideration of Marxist theory was, not surprisingly, the need to put scientific method, rightly understood, at the heart of democratic social action. By this, he repeated, he did not mean New Deal pragmatism, but he also most emphatically did not mean Marxist "science": "The experimental method of science is the exemplification of empirical method when experience has reached maturity. It is opposed equally to 'vulgar' empiricism which recognizes only rule-of-thumb action, depending upon a succession of trial-and-error acts that are unregulated by connection with an idea which is both expressed and tested, and to that absolutism which insists there is but one Truth and that truth one already revealed and possessed by some group or party" (FC, 131). Quoting the statement by John Strachey, an English Marxist, that Communist parties in their "refusal to tolerate the existence of incompatible opinions . . . are simply asserting the claim that Socialism is scientific," Dewey remarked that "it would be difficult, probably impossible, to find a more direct and elegantly finished denial of all the qualities that make ideas and theories either scientific or democratic than is contained in this statement" (FC, 131). Thus the great irony of Marxism in Dewey's mind was that "the theory

16. JD to Edwin Wilson, 28 March 1947, Dewey Papers. See also JD to Robert Daniels, 25 February 1950, in Daniels, ed., "Letters of John Dewey to Robert V. Daniels, 1946–1950," *Journal of the History of Ideas* 20 (1959): 576.

which has made the most display and the greatest pretense of having a scientific foundation should be the one which has violated most systematically every principle of scientific method" (*FC*, 135).

Dewey concluded his argument with a call for a recognition of the interaction between human consciousness and will and the external social world. Orthodox Marxism ignored this interaction in its insistence on the determination of consciousness by material conditions. Class consciousness, he insisted, was a psychological development that could not simply be predicted on the basis of material facts, and "overt recognition of the psychological factors entails introduction of values and judgments of valuation into a theory of social movement" (*FC*, 134).

Stripping Soviet Marxism of its scientific credentials, enabled Dewey to maintain his identification of scientific and democratic method. The vitality of Dewey's democratic ideal rested on dissent and diversity of opinion cast within the discipline of a truly scientific method. What this democracy could not tolerate was dissent in the name of some absolute principle against the authority of this method. When democracy became truly scientific, Dewey prophesied with ill-disguised glee, "it will relegate political groups that pride themselves upon refusing to admit incompatible opinions to the obscurity which already is the fate of similar groups in science" (*FC*, 135). After a Deweyan revolution, dialectical materialists, particularly those who resorted to violence, would find little comfort in the Great Community.

ANTI-STALINIST POLITICS

Soviet society was widely hailed by its defenders in the United States as a great moral experiment. Dewey took them at their word, and subjected this experiment to the test of means-ends interdependence. Was communism, as embodied in Russian practice, he asked, an appropriate means to the liberation of mankind? Was the Soviet Union embarked on an experiment that would lead to Trotsky's professed end of "increasing the power of man over nature and abolishing the power of man over man?" Dewey's answers to these questions made him few friends in the Soviet Union or among Stalinists in the United States. More significantly, his criticisms of communist practice put him at odds with those liberals to whom, as Max Eastman put it, "while not perhaps a promised land, Russia seems at least a promising land."[17]

Addressing himself to the problems of Stalinist terror, Soviet-Ameri-

17. Max Eastman, "Motive-Patterns of Socialism," *Modern Quarterly* 11 (1939): 46.

can relations, and domestic Communism, Dewey confronted these opponents in a series of controversies in the thirties and forties. It was on these occasions that he developed the antipathy to the Communist style of "debate" he expressed in the remarks I quoted earlier, and again showed that as a polemicist he was no piker himself.

Dewey's initial impressions of the Soviet Union had been quite favorable. Traveling to that country in 1928 with a delegation of American educators, he filed an account of his trip in a series of articles in the *New Republic*. He characterized Russian culture as "a vast human revolution that has brought with it—or rather that consists of—an outburst of vitality, courage, confidence in life . . . . the outstanding fact in Russia is a revolution, involving a release of human powers on such an unprecedented scale that it is of incalculable significance not only for that country, but for the world." Writing from Berlin, Hook (who described himself at the time as "a communist with a small c") congratulated Dewey on doing "the series well enough to earn the gratitude of every lover of truth and friend of Russia." Dewey's reputation in the Soviet Union itself soared to lofty heights from which it would soon fall precipitously, and he was branded a communist by the American right.[18]

As we examine this glowing report on Soviet society it is important to note what it was Dewey was glowing about. An old friend from the Chicago years informed him that her brother had remarked that the report "was 99% John Dewey and 1% Russia." Indeed, what Dewey liked about the Soviet Union were those features of the society which indicated to him that it was moving toward the democracy he had envisioned in *The Public and Its Problems*. He applauded the cooperatives, the art museums for the proletariat, and, most especially, the educational experimentation that tied cultural and vocational education to "a single and comprehensive purpose." He argued that beneath Marxist dogma he could see a society with the twin goals of economic security and participatory democracy. "In its ulterior reaches," Dewey concluded, "it is an experiment to discover whether the familiar democratic ideals—familiar in words, at least—of liberty, equality and brotherhood will not be most completely realized in a social regime based on voluntary cooperation, on conjoint workers' control and management of industry, with an accompanying abolition of private property as a fixed institution." Dewey said nothing about Russian politics, and his comments about Marxist ideology were uniformly critical. The revolu-

18. "Leningrad Gives the Clue" (1928), *Later Works* 3:207; Sidney Hook to JD, 9 January 1929, Dewey Papers. See also Sidney Hook, "Why I Am a Communist (Communism without Dogmas)," *Modern Monthly* 8 (April 1934): 143–165. I am grateful to Ernest B. Hook for permission to quote from his father's unpublished correspondence.

tion he saw in Russia was in the minds and hearts of the people, and it was, he argued, going on behind the back of the party leadership and could not be understood with Marxist catagories. "However rigid and dogmatic the Marxian symbols may be," he contended, "actual practices are affected by an experimental factor that is flexible, vital, creative." Though he was wary of prophecy, Dewey suggested that the Soviet Union had the potential to become a Deweyan democracy:

> If I venture in the direction of a prediction, it is only by way of calling attention to two movements already going on. The factor of greatest importance seems to me to be the growth of voluntary cooperative groups. In the orthodox theory, these form a transition stage on the road to the predestined end of Marxian Communism. Just why the means should not also be the end, and the alleged transitory stage define the goal, is not clear to me. The place occupied by the peasant in Russian life, the necessity of consulting his interests and desires, however disagreeable that consultation is, the constant concessions made to him in spite of official preference for the factory city worker, strengthens belief in the probability of cooperative rather than a strictly communistic outcome. Side by side with this factor, though of less immediate practical force, I should place the experimental aspect of the educational system. There is, of course, an immense amount of indoctrination and propaganda in the schools. But if the existing tendency develops, it seems fairly safe to predict that in the end this indoctrination will be subordinate to the awakening of initiative and power of independent judgment, while cooperative mentality will be evolved.[19]

Dewey's dismal record as a prophet was not enhanced by these predictions. Stalin smashed the cooperatives, murdered millions of peasants, and brought experimental education to an abrupt halt. After Stalin's "revolution from above," Dewey chastised himself for not having explored the dynamics of Soviet politics in the late twenties. "My ignorance of the whole factional controversy," he wrote in 1937, "was rather shameful as I now look back on it." Nonetheless, he retained a great deal of respect for the energy of the Russian people, who had, he felt, been betrayed by their leadership. As late as 1946, he remembered from his visit "the sense of new lives, of having a future, especially strong with young people—a kind of atmosphere of being in a new world when and where anything might happen. That was before the

19. Kate Crane-Gartz to JD, 24 August 1929, Dewey Papers; "The Great Experiment and the Future" (1928), *Later Works* 3:244, 248–249. See also "Religion in the Soviet Union" (1930), *Later Works* 5:355–362, and "Surpassing America" (1931), *Later Works* 6:263–267.

purges, but I have no doubt a lot of the good things persisted; the Russians are and will be a great people—when they get the chance."[20]

Dewey's anticommunism in the early thirties was marked by a continuing antipathy to Marxist theory and a growing irritation at the disruptive political tactics employed by American Communists, particularly those who were making an effort to take over control of his own union, Local No. 5 of the American Federation of Teachers. His comments in the *Modern Quarterly* symposium about the deceit and calumny of American Communists quoted earlier were part of his commentary on this experience. Employing the tactics of "rule or ruin" in the early thirties, Communist members of the union had engaged in obstruction, browbeating, and name calling to bring the effective working of Local 5 to a halt by 1933. When efforts to control the Communists failed, Dewey joined the leadership in resigning from the union and forming the independent New York Teachers Guild. These events affected him deeply, for he was a founding member of the union and a long-time advocate of the unionization of educators. He later attributed the occasional extremity of his anticommunist rhetoric in part to the memory of "the disruptive work, largely by means of lies and character assassinations by a group of NY communists in wrecking the original Teachers Union there." He was convinced that

> there was an active minority group who wished to use the union for purposes foreign to its object, that they wished to subordinate its activities to their own partisan political ends, and would not stop at any measures to accomplish their object—even wrecking the union. While they engaged in the most extreme and lying abuse of others . . . they tried to shelter themselves from any criticism by the baby-act, calling it redbaiting. . . . The greatest enemy to the organization of teachers in connection with the labor movement is in my opinion the activities of the CP in trying to use the organizations. There won't be any general headway for the movement in the country at large until it has got clear of this harmful element.

Events such as this led Dewey to the opinion that the American Communist party "is almost incredibly stupid—its nearest rival as a group is some of our official spokesmen of Chambers of Commerce."[21]

20. JD to Alexander Gumberg, 12 May 1937, Alexander Gumberg Papers, State Historical Society of Wisconsin, Madison, Wisconsin; JD to W. R. Huston, 22 April 1946; JD to Robert Daniels, 28 October 1949, in Daniels, "Letters," p. 573.

21. JD to W. R. Huston, 23 March 1946, Dewey Papers; JD to George Geiger, 20 November 1940, Joseph Ratner Papers, Morris Library, Southern Illinois University; JD

It was, above all, the Moscow purge trials and the equivocal attitude toward the trials of Popular Front liberals that intensified Dewey's anti-communism to the point where he burdened himself in his mid-seventies with a major role in the anti-Stalinist opposition. This cost him friendships and long-term institutional associations and brought a rain of opprobrium from those who accused him of aiding fascism by taking an unduly critical attitude toward Stalin's regime. Most important, it committed him to the two-front war, which held special perils for his democratic hopes, for the temptation in a battle with those who had little regard for democratic means was to reach for weapons that would vanquish the opponent while at the same time wound democratic ends.

Dewey's most significant act of opposition to the purges was to serve as chairman of the Commission of Inquiry into the Charges Made against Leon Trotsky in the Moscow Trials, which came to be known as the Dewey Commission. This commission was put together in March 1937 by the American Committee for the Defense of Leon Trotsky, of which Dewey was the honorary chairman. This committee consisted of American liberals and radicals, including such leading American Trotskyists as George Novack, who served as secretary. Its membership list was a virtual roster of the American anti-Stalinist left, including James Burnham, V. F. Calverton, John Dos Passos, Max Eastman, James T. Farrell, Sidney Hook, Horace M. Kallen, Dwight Macdonald, Mary McCarthy, Reinhold Niebuhr, Herbert Solow, Norman Thomas, Lionel Trilling, and Edmund Wilson.

The Trotskyists' role in this effort concerned Dewey, for he feared that the committee would be seen (as it was) as a Trotskyist front acting in the service of Trotsky's political aims rather than as an impartial inquiry into the charges made against him in Moscow. Dewey made it clear that he was defending "Trotsky's right to a public trial, although I have no sympathy with what seems to me to be his abstract ideological fanaticism," and he made every effort to control the use of the commission's findings for Trotskyist propaganda. As he wrote to Hook: "Of course

to Agnes Meyer, 11 November 1935, Agnes Meyer Papers, Library of Congress; JD, "On the Grievance Committee Report" (1933), and *The Report of the Special Grievance Committee of the Teachers Union* (1933), *Later Works* 9:315–345; William E. Eaton, *The American Federation of Teachers, 1916–1961* (Carbondale: Southern Illinois University Press, 1975), pp. 79–121. See also JD to Harry Ward, 20 April 1933, Harry Ward Papers, Union Theological Seminary, New York City; JD to Arthur Bentley, 7 April 1948, in *John Dewey and Arthur F. Bentley: A Philosophical Correspondence, 1932–1951*, ed. Sidney Ratner and Jules Altman (New Brunswick, N.J.: Rutgers University Press, 1964), p. 589; and JD to Edwin Wilson, 2 September 1950, Dewey Papers.

Defense Committee is the usual name for all Committees that are trying to enable a fair defense to be instituted. But in this case, [critics] are insisting that the name means that *we* are engaged in the defense of Trotsky that assumes his innocence—it is probable that aside from those who want to discredit the Com. this appearance has caused misunderstanding among those who are otherwise fairminded. . . . I don't suppose this can be helped. But it might be well to have an article pointing out that it was not *we* who created the issue but the methods by which Trotsky had been condemned." For Dewey, the commission provided an opportunity to display the methods of scientific inquiry in action and, once again, to contrast these methods with the "scientific socialism" of Stalin (and Trotsky himself). Addressing himself to the commission's activities, Soviet ambassador Troyanovsky had requested that, in assessing the Moscow trials, the American public not "be too cautious or too skeptical in recognition of the contemporary situation," by which he meant the struggle against fascism. Dewey replied that "for while we are not all from Missouri, most American citizens are close enough to its border to want to be shown when elementary human decency, justice, and historic truth are at stake."[22]

Amid growing abuse in the radical press and fears of his family for his life, Dewey put aside work on his *Logic* and journeyed to Mexico with the commission in April 1937 to hear Trotsky's testimony. Trotsky worried that the aged philosopher would not be able to stay awake during the hearings, but Dewey proved to be an alert, patient, and thorough chairman whose energy and devotion to the task at hand impressed observers as well as Trotsky himself. In December 1937 the commission published its findings, declaring that a fair assessment of the evidence indicated that Trotsky and his son were not guilty of Stalin's charges of treason and murder and characterizing the Moscow Trials as a farcical travesty of justice.[23]

Dewey was quick to draw conclusions from the investigation. In a long interview in the *Washington Post* in December 1937 he asserted: "The great lesson to be derived from these amazing revelations is the complete breakdown of revolutionary Marxianism. . . . The Russian

22. JD to Sidney Hook, 16 November 1936, 12 March 1937, Hook Collection; *Truth Is on the March* (1937), *Later Works* 11:320. For a succinct account of the work of the Dewey Commission see Alan Wald, *James T. Farrell: The Revolutionary Socialist Years* (New York: New York University Press, 1978), pp. 60–75.
23. See the reports issued by the commission: *The Case of Leon Trotsky* (New York: Harper, 1937) and *Not Guilty* (New York: Harper, 1938) and Leon Trotsky to JD, 15 July 1938, Dewey Papers.

experiment proves conclusively that when violence is used to bring about economic and political reform, the method of force must be employed to keep the new government in power. . . . The idea of democracy is an exacting master. The limitation of it to a small group involves such a contradiction that in the end democracy even within the party is bound to be destroyed."

Dewey also touched briefly on a theme he would elaborate on in his *New International* debate with Trotsky, the relationship of means and ends in politics and "the necessity of surveying our situation with a view to attaining democratic means to achieve our democratic ends." In addition he adumbrated another idea to which he would later return, the similarities between the totalitarian regimes of Hitler and Stalin. "The essence of fascism," he remarked, "is no sweeter if called by some other name." The lesson for Americans, Dewey concluded, was that they "must stop looking to the Soviet Union as a model for solving our own economic difficulties and as a source of defense for democracy against fascism."[24]

The commission's findings and Dewey's conclusions did not sit well with the Stalinist community. The American Communist press showed its skill in *ad hominem* argument, characterizing Dewey as "a Fascist," "a tool of reaction," and "a Charlie McCarthy for the Trotskyites." "Liberals like Dr. Dewey," intoned the *Daily Worker*, "who in the face of the overwhelming evidence of Trotsky's guilt persist in stooging for this enemy of everything liberal and progressive, not only cover themselves with shame, but injure the cause of genuine liberalism and democracy." His most prominent critics were fifty writers, artists, and editors including Lillian Wald, Heywood Broun, Max Lerner, Louis Fischer, Corliss Lamont, Robert Lynd, Theodore Dreiser, and Lillian Hellman who warned in a letter to the *New Masses* that Dewey and other liberals were being used by the Trotskyists. Not surprisingly, Dewey's stock also dropped quickly in the Soviet Union. The relatively accurate rendering of his philosophy within the limits of the jargon of dialectical materialism in the 1931 edition of the *Large Soviet Encyclopedia* gave way to charges by Soviet philosophers that "the philosophy of Dewey is a philosophy of war and fascism" and that "Dewey is the mouthpiece of modern imperialistic reaction, the ideologist of American imperialism."[25]

24. Quoted in "Significance of the Trotsky Inquiry" (1937), *Later Works* 11:330–336. See also "The Moscow Trials" (1937), *Later Works* 11:326–329.

25. *Daily Worker*, 3 April 1937, as quoted in Dykhuizen, p. 282; the signers of the *New Masses* letter and the circumstances surrounding it are discussed in Eugene Lyons, *The*

These attacks Dewey expected. What he did not anticipate was the equivocal stance taken by many liberals and progressives who took a "know nothing" attitude toward the purge trials and criticized the Dewey Commission for threatening the unity of the popular front against fascism. "I find it disheartening," he told the *Washington Post*, "when in our country, some professed liberals have come to believe that for reasons of expediency our own people should be kept in the dark as to the actual situation in Russia. For truth, instead of being a bourgeois virtue, is the mainspring of all human progress." In attacking the Dewey Commission, he argued elsewhere, liberals were abandoning one of the central values of liberalism, the commitment to free inquiry. The willingness of these liberals to hedge on the issue of the Moscow Trials, he angrily observed, "marks an intellectual shirking that is close to intellectual dishonesty. More than that it is treachery to the very cause of liberalism. For if liberalism means anything, it means complete and courageous devotion to freedom of inquiry."[26]

Popular Front liberals were operating with a more short-range end-in-view than Dewey: the defeat of fascism. They feared the consequences of action that would threaten the alliance with the Communists against Hitler. As Alexander Gumberg wrote to Dewey, the "total effect" of the philosopher's anti-Stalinism was believed by these liberals to be "that of allying you with the enemies of the Soviet Union and that includes not only . . . the unknown and irresponsible personalities called 'Trotskyites,' but everybody who is engaged in the struggle on the side of Fascism. . . . The social significance of your present activity seems of much greater importance than the *possible temporary* injustice to one individual." Malcolm Cowley expressed similar sentiments to Dewey, remarking that "as for the Soviet Union, I certainly would not defend, and have not defended, everything that has been done there. There is too much repression and too much mass worship of one leader. But I also feel that in general the Soviet Union has been moving in the right direction and that it has to be defended against the fascist nations. . . . I think American progressives of all shades of opinion

Red Decade (New York: Bobbs-Merrill, 1970), pp. 250–256; *Large Soviet Encyclopedia* quoted in Martin Levit, "Soviet Version of John Dewey and Pragmatism," *History of Education Journal* 4 (1953): 135–141.

26. "Significance of Trotsky Inquiry," p. 336; *Truth Is on the March*, p. 318. See also JD, "Pravda on Trotsky" (1937), *New Republic*, 24 March 1937: 212–213, and "In Defense of the Mexican Hearings" (1938), *Later Works* 13:347–348. The latter is a response to *Common Sense* editor Selden Rodman's article "Trotsky in the Kremlin" (1937), *Later Works* 13:391–400.

should be working together (they will have to hang together or hang some other way)."[27]

Dewey disagreed with these liberals that the alliance with the Communists was essential to the defeat of fascism, but he did not base his fundamental objections to their position on this argument. Rather, he attacked the Popular Front as an inappropriate means to the defeat of fascism if it required that liberals sacrifice their allegiance to the more inclusive ends of the search for truth and justice, asking them to wink at acts that were perilously close to if not congruent with the fascism they were presumably out to defeat. If expediency dictated an alliance with the Communists against fascism, it did not dictate an alliance that required an equivocal attitude toward Soviet repression or the value of scientific inquiry. The Soviet Union was *not* moving in the right direction, and it was the ideological concession required by the Popular Front on this point which most infuriated Dewey. As he replied to Cowley, "With Russia and Soviet methods so constantly held up to us as a model for America, I think it is necessary for the clarification of American political thought and action that an honest effort be made to get at the truth. . . . *If* the charges [against Trotsky] should turn out to be false it is pretty hard to believe that the Soviet Union 'is moving in the right direction.'" For Dewey, a successful defeat of fascism at the cost of the value of inquiry and blindness to injustice was a Pyrrhic victory.[28]

Perhaps the most painful consequence for Dewey of his split with the Popular Front was the break it forced with the *New Republic*, which had been his political home for over twenty years. In his letter of resignation in 1937 from the editorial board, Dewey explained that he was leaving the journal because its handling of the purge trials had evidenced a persistent failure to live up to "the democratic practice of submitting conflicts to full and fair discussion." He cited the tendency of the *New Republic* to argue that the trials were irrelevant to Americans while elsewhere commenting freely on their significance. He also noted the magazine's habit of accompanying a statement pleading lack of evidence on the trials with an implicit argument for the guilt of the

27. Alexander Gumberg to JD, 11 May 1937, Gumberg Papers; Malcolm Cowley to JD, 4 June 1937, Hook Collection. See also Raymond Robins to JD, 21 May 1937, Raymond Robins Papers, State Historical Society of Wisconsin, Madison. For Cowley's second thoughts on these issues see "Echoes from Moscow: 1937–1938," *Southern Review* 20 (1984): 1–11. I am grateful to Robert Cowley for permission to quote from his father's letter to Dewey.

28. JD to Malcolm Cowley, [June 1937], Hook Collection. See also JD to Sidney Hook, 16 March 1938, Hook Collection; JD to James Farrell, 22 February 1939, Dewey Papers; JD to Max Otto, 28 November 1939, Max Otto Papers, State Historical Society of Wisconsin, Madison.

defendants, and its assumption before the fact that the Dewey Commission could establish nothing of consequence and hence was not worth supporting. It was thus not so much the positions that the editors took to which Dewey objected (although he did not agree with them) as the method by which these positions had been formulated. "I am not questioning of course the right of the New Republic to take sides and stick to the side it selects," he wrote them, "but a long series of logical inconsistencies with pretty systematic blurring and obscuring of one side cannot but make one ask what is back of them, even if each one taken by itself is of no great importance." Henceforth, Dewey referred to the *New Republic* to which he had contributed before his resignation as the "old" *New Republic*.[29]

Dewey continued his attack on Soviet repression and the Popular Front in 1939 as the honorary chairman of the newly organized Committee for Cultural Freedom (CCF). The manifesto of this group, published in the *Nation* in May 1939, made more explicit the connection Dewey and others had drawn earlier between the totalitarian societies of the fascist and communist states: "The tide of totalitarianism is rising throughout the world. It is washing away cultural and creative freedom along with all other expressions of independent human reason. . . . Under varying labels and colors but with an unvarying hatred for the free mind, the totalitarian idea is already enthroned in Germany, Italy, Russia, Japan, and Spain. There intellectual and creative independence is suppressed and punished as a form of treason. Art, science, and education have been forcibly turned into lackeys for a supreme state, a deified leader, and an official pseudo-philosophy." The manifesto went on to call on intellectuals to defend cultural freedom both at home and abroad and took a swipe at Popular Front intellectuals who "hasten to exalt one brand of intellectual servitude over another; to make fine distinctions between various methods of humiliating the human spirit and outlawing intellectual integrity." The CCF followed Dewey in arguing for the establishment of the freedom for unconstrained thought and inquiry as "the fundamental criteria for evaluating all social philosophies today."[30]

29. JD to Bruce Bliven, 26 May 1937, Hook Collection. See also JD to Max Otto, 29 April 1941, Max Otto Papers; JD to [W. R. Huston], 22 April 1946. For the *New Republic*'s position on the Moscow trials see "Editorial," 9 January 1935: 233; "The Conditions of Civil Liberties," 27 February 1935: 60–62; "Another Russian Trial," 3 February 1937: 399–400; "Trotsky and the Russian Trials," 17 March 1937: 169–170; and "Agnosticism in the Moscow Trials," 19 May 1937: 33–34.

30. *Nation*, 27 May 1939: 626. See also the editorial "Liberty and Common Sense," *New Republic*, 31 May 1939: 89–90, and JD, "The Committee for Cultural Freedom" (1939), *Later Works* 14:365–366.

In August 1939 in a letter to the *Nation* a group of four hundred "fellow travelers" responded to the manifesto with a familiar argument. The contention that the Soviet Union was similar in any sense to the fascist states and hence an equal totalitarian menace to democratic values was, they declared, fascist propaganda designed to split the united forces of antifascism. The liberals of the CCF had fallen victim to this fascist trap and to the ministrations of those of its members "who have for years had as their chief political objective the maligning of the Soviet people and their government." Unfortunately for the signers of this letter, it was published two days after the signing of the Nazi-Soviet nonaggression pact. This alliance, however expedient, created severe difficulties for the argument that the USSR was the main bulwark against fascism, difficulties that only the most dedicated fellow travelers would attempt to resolve.[31]

Following the pact, Dewey resigned as honorary chairman of the CCF. In resigning he indicated that he believed that "the effect of the Stalinite-Nazi axis has been such as to make a marked change in the situation as far as the great number of liberals who had been honestly misled by the Russian policies are concerned. The particular pressure from that quarter has been so reduced that that phase of the emergency has it seems to me largely passed, and the strain is now centered elsewhere, requiring a somewhat different line of approach." He explained this last allusive statement in a letter to Hook:

It is one of the ironies of history that just at the time when the Stalinites have exposed and discredited themselves, everybody pretty nearly has begun to jump upon them, and there is real danger to my mind that not only will the CP be driven underground but that danger to cultural freedom, freedom of thought etc now comes from quite a different quarter—you perhaps noted the action of the NJ senate in passing a bill unanimously requiring registration of all aliens. This is the sort of thing which seems to me likely, along with the self-discrediting of the CPs, to demand the most attention in the future, a situation which may demand some shift in the strategy as well as tactics of the CCF.

Dewey here sensed the need for anti-Stalinists to keep their more inclusive ends in view as the antifascists had not. There was a danger that the anticommunist campaign, like that against fascism, would enlist allies who threatened not only communism but also democracy. This was a

31. *Nation*, 26 August 1939: 228. See also "A Letter to the L.A.W. [League of American Writers]," *Partisan Review* 6 (Fall 1939): 127–128.

prescient observation, but perhaps even more noteworthy was Dewey's confidence that this difficulty could be handled relatively easily. What he had yet to foresee were the ironies that loomed for intellectuals who would engage in an anticommunist defense of cultural freedom without the power to control the unintended consequences of their action.[32]

COLD WAR SOCIALISM

After Hitler invaded the Soviet Union in June 1941 the ideology of the Popular Front was revived, and Dewey returned to the fray in 1942 "to offer a few observations which are none the less pertinent for being unfashionable now." The focus of his concern was the wartime alliance with the Soviet Union and the fear that the price of this alliance would again be a lack of realism about Soviet society and politics.[33]

In January 1942 Dewey wrote a scathing letter to the *New York Times* denouncing Ambassador Joseph Davies's whitewash of the Moscow Trials in his best-selling memoirs, *Mission to Moscow*. Dewey acknowledged that the United States should give the Russians every possible aid against the Nazi invasion, but this aid, he remarked, did not entail shutting one's eyes to Stalin's repression or entertaining any illusions of Russian benevolence. The best policy was instead to emulate Stalin himself: "He recognizes a common interest with us. He accepts what aid we can provide him. But he does not trust us. . . . For Stalin knows what his apologists here apparently do not know—totalitarianism and democracy will not mix. Our future would be much more secure than it now appears if we were to emulate his circumspection instead of indulging in the fatuous one-sided love feast now going on in this country."[34]

When the Davies book was made into a movie in 1943 which was an even more glaring apologia for Stalinism, Dewey was reluctant to do battle again, yet eventually he decided to lend his name to another letter to the *New York Times* pointing out the deficiencies of the film. The letter, written by Suzanne La Follette, drew a vigorous response

32. JD to Frank Trager, 16 November 1939, 22 November 1939; JD to Sidney Hook, 16 November 1939, Hook Collection.

33. "Russia's Position" (1942), *Later Works* 15:338. On debates over Stalinism among American intellectuals during the war and immediate postwar years see William L. O'Neill, *A Better World: The Great Schism—Stalinism and the American Intellectuals* (New York: Simon and Schuster, 1982).

34. "Russia's Position," p. 341. See also "*Mission to Moscow* Reveals No New Evidence on Soviet Trials" (1942), *Later Works* 15:289–294.

from Arthur Upham Pope, director of the Committee for National Morale, who defended the movie and warned that, in the interest of the war effort, "the public mind should not be unduly agitated." This latter defense of the film, Dewey and La Follette observed in their parting shot, "is equivalent to the suggestion that democracy take a vacation for the duration."[35]

Commenting on Dewey's criticism of Davies, John L. Childs, a leading progressive educator, expressed the wish, despite his agreement with the bulk of the philosopher's critique, that Dewey had considered the value of postwar cooperation with Stalin. Dewey responded that postwar policy should aim not at cooperation with Stalin but at an approach "which will eliminate the dangers inhering in Stalinist supremacy and establish the basis for helpful relations after the peace between a Russia freed from totalitarian menace and Great Britain and this country: relations in which we can learn from whatever of good Russia has accomplished and that country can be assisted forward on a genuinely democratic path." Stalinism and bureaucratic communism, in short, had to go before cooperation with Russia could be initiated.[36]

As the war moved to a successful conclusion, Dewey worried even more about the shape of the postwar world and the Russian threat. "The failure of nerve persists and intensifies," he wrote Hook in March 1945. "Its wonderful how the persons who were very critical of British appeasement of Hitler, pointing out it is more likely to produce war than the other course now urge the same course with Stalin—as the way this time of *avoiding* war." The way to avoid war, he suggested, was to get tough with the Russians. "Talking or planning war with Russia is criminal," he wrote his young friend Jack Lamb, yet, short of war, he was unclear about how to put the Soviet Union in what he termed "a

35. JD and Suzanne La Follette, "Several Faults Are Found in 'Mission to Moscow' Film"; Arthur Upham Pope, "'Mission to Moscow' Film Viewed as Historical Realism"; JD and La Follette, "Moscow Film Again Attacked"; Pope, "Merit Seen in Moscow Film"; JD and La Follette, "More on 'Mission to Moscow'" (1943), *Later Works* 15:345–355, 492–501. See also JD to Sidney Hook, 21 April 1943, Hook Collection; JD to Belinda Jeliffe, 31 May 1943, Dewey Papers; and JD to Robert Daniels, 17 November 1947, in Daniels, "Letters," p. 572. The movie screenplay has been republished with a useful introduction detailing the controversy that swirled around the film in David Culbert, *Mission to Moscow* (Madison: University of Wisconsin Press, 1980). For the wider context of this film see Melvin Small, "Buffoons and Brave Hearts: Hollywood Portrays the Russians, 1939–1944," *California Historical Quarterly* 52 (1973): 326–337, and "How We Learned to Love the Russians: American Media and the Soviet Union during World War II," *Historian* 36 (1973/74): 455–478; and Clayton Koppes and Gregory Black, *Hollywood Goes to War* (New York: Free Press, 1987), pp. 185–209.

36. "Comments by John L. Child on Dr. Dewey's Letter" (1942); "Dr. Dewey on Our Relations with Russia" (1942), *Later Works* 15:487–491, 342–344.

more reasonable state." There can be no doubt, however, that Dewey was hardening in his attitudes as he became increasingly angry at the Soviets' ideological appropriation of his most sacred ideals: "It seems to me a part of the degradation of language that has been going on now for over ten years that Russian leaders talk about their 'democracy' because of economic conditions. There is a democracy that is neither economic nor yet definitely political, though its existence depends more or less on political conditions and then reacts back on them. I refer to such things as are found in our Bill of Rights. Lenin was honest enough to denounce democracy as played out. The present adoption of the word, to say nothing of the claim to be THE democratic nation is disgusting to me in its hypocrisy."[37]

Of course, a thoroughly critical perspective on this issue demanded that some note be taken of the ideological use made of democracy in the prosecution of American foreign policy, which linked it in a marriage with free enterprise, a link Dewey had himself long before attempted to annul, but Dewey offered no such criticism. By the late forties he was uncritically defending American foreign policy, viewing it simply as the bulwark against what he saw as an expansionist Soviet threat to social democracy in western Europe. The Russians, he argued, did not want war and were too weak in any case to wage war. However, "Russia does want to see the world Bolshevized and is systematically working toward that end." Its strategy was that of infiltration and subversion of the polities of the states of the West. The Soviet Union had since the revolution moved from a policy of internationalism to one of "multi-national Bolshevism," which required in turn an American policy of containment and a strong military position as a defensive measure. Dewey vigorously defended the Truman Doctrine and the Marshall Plan, and in 1950 he wrote to the *New York Times* calling for the cessation of criticism of the foreign policy of Dean Acheson, characterizing such criticism as "our free gift to the Communist cause."[38]

By the late forties, Dewey's two-front war had become, at least on foreign-policy issues, confined to a single front. His position here was indistinguishable from that of liberals in the State Department, and he

37. JD to Sidney Hook, 8 March 1945, Hook Collection; JD to Jack Lamb, 12 December 1945, Dewey Papers. See also Dewey's contribution to the UNESCO symposium *Democracy in a World of Tensions*, ed. Richard McKeon and Stein Rokkan (Chicago: University of Chicago Press, 1951), pp. 62–68.

38. JD to Jack Lamb, 15 March 1947, Dewey Papers; "Mr. Acheson's Critics: Their Attacks Feared Damaging to Our World Prestige," *New York Times*, 19 November 1950. See also Dean Acheson to Roberta L. Dewey, 14 March 1961, copy in Hook Collection.

failed to subject the thought and practice of his allies of expedience to the sort of criticism he had demanded of Popular Front liberals. One can appreciate the difficulties of the situation and the problems posed by the apparent lack of alternatives and still be struck by Dewey's seeming lack of anguish over the position he had taken. The threat of Stalinism had become so great in his mind that he had converted what his democratic radicalism taught was a lesser evil into a positive good. Demanding that cooperation with the Soviets be predicated on its abandoning its repressive social system and moving to institute genuine democracy, he at the same time uncritically defended an American foreign policy with its own pretensions to international hegemony.

The emotional pitch of Dewey's anticommunism reached its peak in his blast in the *New Leader* against the Progressive party presidential campaign of Henry Wallace in 1948. The *New Leader* was a hotbed of anticommunist emotionalism, Dewey had admitted in 1946, but he attributed this to the constant contact its contributors had with "NY communists and fellow travelers, and sentimentalists." He also noted the presence among those who wrote for the journal of many former Communists, commenting perceptively to one correspondent on their mentality:

> Its a shock to be forced to lose one's religion when the loss is forced by those who had been set up as heads of the Church. I don't suppose you've read Barmines, ONE WHO SURVIVED—he is one of the men who probably won't ever recover from the moral-psychiatric shock, having been a devotee of the active working kind from the time he was 16 or 17 years old. You wouldn't enjoy reading the book in all probability. But the photographs of groups of old Bolsheviks found at the end of the book, with the captions of what has become of them, "purged" or "unknown," are sufficiently revealing as the cause of the present attitude of men who shared their faith and their work. With some exaggeration they feel as the friends of the apostles might have felt if Judas Iscariot had them all purged and all in the name of their master.[39]

Dewey's attack on Wallace in 1948 was vintage *New Leader*. He characterized the Progressives as "the party of illiberalism, the spokesmen for the slaveholders of the 20th century," arguing that the Progressive party had "its deepest roots in the sub-soil of Soviet totalitarianism." Like the Soviets, he declared, the former vice president's "use of the language and idealism that is democracy can only lead to debasement

39. JD to W. R. Huston, 23 March 1946.

of that language and to cynicism about its ultimate meaning." Dewey failed to see any merit in Wallace's criticisms of American foreign policy and characterized him as "the willing colporteur of a dictatorship which has overswept the great part of the European land-mass and which has its legions posted in Western Europe awaiting The Day." He pointed to the prominence of Communists in Wallace's party and remarked that "it is not mere negativism to say that a political party which willingly accepts and welcomes support of Communist leaders has no more place in the liberal growth of our country than a political party which welcomes support from Ku Klux Klansmen or from leaders of the Nazi Bund." Worst of all, Dewey concluded, Wallace threatened to stall the development of a truly radical third-party movement "rooted in the trade union movement" which might offer "a genuinely NEW position in the extension and enrichment of democracy." Dewey was anxious to establish that Communists had no place in the political organizations that might reconstruct American democracy, and his articles aimed to distinguish the as-yet-unclear political strategy of the anti-Stalinist democratic socialists from that of Henry Wallace. They served this purpose, but they also served those of Harry Truman. Denouncing the second camp in the name of the third, Dewey and other anti-Stalinist radicals helped the first camp to victory as the ironies of anticommunist politics sprouted in the fertile soil of the Cold War.[40]

Dewey's anticommunism, even in its most extreme moments, was cast consistently within the framework of his ethical theory, which held open the possibility of a retreat from a militant anticommunist stance if its consequences were deemed subversive of a more inclusive end, particularly if it threatened the "democratic form" itself. Dewey attempted a partial retreat of this sort in 1949 in addressing himself to the issue of whether or not members of the Communist party should be allowed to teach in universities. In a letter to the *New York Times*, he registered his "serious doubts" about such a restriction, noting that he had not spoken out earlier "due to my great respect for the university men who advocated the contrary view." Dewey agreed that, in the abstract, there was good reason to question the professional ethics of Communist teachers, given the party's commitment to unquestioning dogmatism. A good Deweyan, however, never reasoned from abstraction alone. "Aversion to deciding important matters on abstract grounds without reference to

<hr/>

40. "Henry Wallace and the 1948 Elections" (1947), *Later Works* 15:239–241; "American Youth, Beware of Wallace Bearing Gifts" (1948), *Later Works* 15:242–247. See also JD to Albert Barnes, 29 April 1947, and Joseph Ratner to JD, 26 May 1948, Dewey Papers.

concrete conditions and probable consequences," he said, "prevented me from giving ready assent to the proposition that this commitment [to the Communist party] is of itself alone, without evidence of bias in conduct of work, a sufficient ground for dismissal." As Dewey saw it, making such a categorical prohibition could have two unfortunate consequences. It might drive existing Communists deeper into duplicity and fanaticism, but more important and more likely, a movement to institute this principle might also get "taken up into a larger movement where it goes far beyond the point that was intended by the scholarly leaders who proposed something which in abstract logic was justified. It acts as a provocation to those who are much more emotional than scholarly; who are more given to following a crowd than to engaging in careful discrimination; it stimulates a campaign to the point where the university presidents and professors who endorsed a limited move will be the first to disapprove." Citing an investigation of college textbooks by the House Committee on Un-American Activities, he observed that current developments indicated that this was a probable consequence. "It is to be hoped," he concluded, "that the public response to the very great error of the committee will check the hysterical wave. I do not see, however, how the original proposal, coming as it did from university leaders, did anything, to put it as mildly as possible, to discourage the sort of thing which has been going on."[41]

In taking this position, Dewey was unaware that he was implicitly critical of the position on this issue which Hook had taken a brief time before in the Sunday *Times Magazine*. Hook had argued, primarily on evidence drawn from official prescriptions of the Communist party, that a teacher who was a member of that party was required by virtue of this membership to "inject" the party line into the classroom and thereby to subvert free and independent inquiry. On the basis of such prescriptions, he concluded that membership in the party was prima facie evidence of an individual's unfitness to teach. Hook argued further that any attempt to assess the actual behavior of such teachers would be inconclusive and that efforts to monitor classroom activities posed a greater threat to academic freedom than the assumption of the unfitness of Communists. A policy built along the lines of Hook's argument thus would leave Communist teachers with little defense, for the case against them would be not only prima facie but steeled against empirical disproof.[42]

41. "Communists as Teachers," *New York Times*, 21 June 1949.
42. Sidney Hook, "Should Communists Be Permitted to Teach?" *New York Times Magazine*, 27 February 1949: 7, 22–29. See also Sidney Hook to JD, 27 June 1949, Hook Collection. Hook was, it should be said, not insensitive to questions of means and ends in

Upon reading Dewey's letter to the *Times*, Hook dashed off a letter of wounded surprise to his mentor, telling him, "I know what hysteria is and we certainly are not suffering from it," and expressing grief that he would have to make a public reply to Dewey's statement. This internecine disagreement never did get into the newspapers, but it is still important because it reveals that Hook, the anti-Stalinist spokesman on matters of academic freedom, was making, for a Deweyan, a curiously abstract argument that Dewey himself found difficult to swallow.[43]

The debate turned on Hook's defense of the principle of membership in the Communist party as prima facie grounds for dismissal from a university teaching position, which Dewey challenged, and Dewey's contention that there was real potential for hysteria over this issue, which Hook discounted. Dewey was troubled by Hook's grounding of his argument in a judgment about what each individual member of the Communist party in academia was likely to be doing based not on empirical examination of the behavior of particular individuals but on a prediction of their action derived simply from the fact of their party membership. Hook was, that is, imputing behavior to individuals on the basis of a generalization about Communism (drawn, to be sure, from a wealth of prescriptive evidence), while at the same time dismissing the need for and desirability of testing such generalizations in each concrete instance. Communist teachers, he said, would act as the Communist party instructed them to act or they would no longer be allowed to remain in the party. Dewey, who agreed that Communist prescriptions were at odds with the ideals of free inquiry and good teaching, was nonetheless wary of judging any individual Communist to be professionally unethical solely on the grounds of party membership. He believed that "to assume without evidence that every teacher who had taken the pledge was *therefore* unfit to teach seemed—and still seems— to me to be entering upon a dangerous policy."[44]

Dewey agreed with Hook that "one shouldn't be dogmatic about the amount of hysteria there is or there isn't," but he believed that such developments as New York's Feinberg Law showed that "in some cases the danger line has been passed." This law, which went into effect in

---

the application of his argument. He carefully distinguished between teachers who held heretical ideas (including communism) and those who were subversive conspirators by virtue of their party membership, and he urged that application of the principle he articulated be tempered lest it create a climate conducive to purges that extended to the ideas teachers held and hence threatened not only communists but radicals and liberals as well. For this same reason, he urged that teachers be allowed to police themselves free of the political meddling of interested politicians and other outsiders.

43. Sidney Hook to JD, 22 June 1949, Hook Collection.
44. JD to Sidney Hook, 21 July 1949, Hook Collection.

July 1949, provided for a checkup on the politics of every teacher in the state. Current membership in subversive organizations was prima facie grounds for dismissal, and past membership in such organizations was taken, without the provision of counterevidence by the teacher, as presumption of present membership. The burden of proof resided wholly with the teacher. Such legislation convinced Dewey that his fear of hysteria was not unfounded. "When feelings get greatly stirred up," he observed to Hook, "the reactionaries are practically sure to use the feeling against what *they* think is dangerous to their own privileges."[45]

Despite his sensitivity to the dangers of obsessive anticommunism on this issue, Dewey's contribution to the Cold War climate of fear cannot be dismissed. He, like Hook, played a role in the escalation of rhetoric which prepared the ground emotionally, if not logically, for the reactionary attack against radicalism by Senator Joseph McCarthy and others for whom a democratic socialist was as red as a Soviet agent. Perhaps the most even-handed criticism of Dewey's anticommunism in the Cold War years is that which, from his own point of view, questions its intelligence while recognizing what a difficult thing it was to be an intelligent anticommunist in the early Cold War. Anti-Stalinist radicalism called for a careful, skeptical temperament, one suspicious of a loose rhetoric of freedom and tyranny. It required, as Irving Howe later remarked, "a very considerable degree of political sophistication, the capacity for seeing two enemies at the same time and trying to make relative judgments of which at a given moment is the greater enemy—and there's no sure-fire way of doing it because you're dealing with an historically unprecedented situation in the age of totalitarianism; and it also requires considerable moral poise." This kind of political sophistication and moral poise was difficult for American intellectuals to

45. Ibid. Hook's further thoughts on this issue are collected in *Heresy, Yes—Conspiracy, No* (New York: John Day, 1953). See also the debate in the *Journal of Philosophy* between Hook and Arthur Lovejoy and Victor Lowe in which Lowe took a position similar to Dewey's: Lowe, "A Resurgence of 'Vicious Intellectualism'," *Journal of Philosophy* 48 (1951): 435–447; Lovejoy, "On a Supposed Resurgence of Vicious Intellectualism"; Hook, "Mindless Empiricism"; Lowe, "In Defense of Individualistic Empiricism"; Lovejoy, "Rejoinder to Mr. Lowe"; and Hook, "Not Mindful Enough," *Journal of Philosophy* 49 (1952): 85–121. See also Victor Lowe to JD, 3 August 1951, Dewey Papers; Arthur Bentley to JD, 26 June 1949, in *Dewey and Bentley*, p. 603. Ellen Schrecker, *No Ivory Tower* (New York: Oxford, 1976), is a recent study of the issue of universities and anticommunism during the Cold War. Dewey was himself under FBI surveillance during part of this period. See Fred Zimring, "Cold War Compromises: Albert Barnes, John Dewey, and the Federal Bureau of Investigation," *Pennsylvania Magazine of History and Biography* 108 (1984): 87–100, and John A. Beineke, "The Investigation of John Dewey by the FBI," *Educational Theory* 37 (1987): 43–52.

sustain in the late forties and early fifties, and Dewey was no exception.[46]

Dewey's anticommunism was nonetheless an important element in his democratic thought. In attacking Stalinism and orthodox Marxism, he provided a nice illustration of what he meant (and did not mean) by a "scientific" democracy. In his favorable comments on Soviet society in 1928, wrongheaded as they were in many respects, he gave an inkling of the kind of democratic institutions he envisioned in America. He also more firmly established, both here and in his subsequent criticism of Stalin's regime, the distinction between an antidemocratic planned society and a planning society in which authority, social goals, and political action flowed from a democratic public. Dewey's anticommunist politics also illustrated once more the frustrations of a democratic activism bereft of power. Dewey correctly perceived that orthodox Marxism and Communist politics were a threat to his most cherished end of participatory democratic community. He was periodically undone, however, by the difficulties of attacking Communists in a polity in which such action by the democratic left more often than not served best the interests of those who were nearly as hostile as the Communist party to Dewey's conception of the democratic way of life.

46. Irving Howe, Morris Dickstein, and Hilton Kramer, "New York and the National Culture: An Exchange," *Partisan Review* 44 (1977): 201.

CHAPTER 14

Keeping the Common Faith

✷

In 1939 John Dewey was honored to be chosen the first subject for a series of volumes in the "Library of Living Philosophers" edited by Northwestern University philosopher Paul Schilpp. Each volume in the series (still ongoing) was to consist of a brief intellectual autobiography or biography of an eminent contemporary philosopher, a series of commentaries and critical articles on that philosopher's work, and a full bibliography of the philosopher's writings. Although this book was planned to coincide with Dewey's eightieth birthday, it was hardly a celebration. As I noted, none of the several collections of commemorative essays published in the last decades of Dewey's life was wholly uncritical, but this volume stood out by virtue of the near-total disagreements that divided Dewey from some contributors who, he said privately, "think that if I have ever had two ideas that hung together it was a piece of good luck." The book afforded a useful measure of the obstinate resistance to the "Copernican revolution" in philosophy he hoped to foster and serves as a useful reminder lest we exaggerate Dewey's influence on his contemporaries at the end of his career.[1]

Perhaps because it was published close on the heels of Dewey's *Logic* (1938), a magisterial summing up and refinement of some forty years

---

1. Paul A. Schilpp, ed., *The Philosophy of John Dewey*, 2d ed. (New York: Tudor, 1951), pp. vii–xv. JD to Corrinne Chisholm Frost, 22 July 1939, in "Reflections of John Dewey: Excerpts from Unpublished Correspondence," *Daedulus* 88 (1959): 552.

of his work in the theory of knowledge, the bulk of the critical essays in the Schilpp book (even Henry W. Stuart's essay on Dewey's ethics) focused on his logic and metaphysics. The adversarial intent of the volume was clearly signaled by the contribution from George Santayana, a virtual reprint of his highly critical 1925 review of *Experience and Nature*, as well as by a very funny but hackneyed essay by Bertrand Russell which repeated the criticisms of pragmatism that had angered Dewey ever since Russell had first advanced them before World War I. Dewey patiently reiterated the responses he had made to both Santayana and Russell years earlier, indicating that in both these instances (and in others) his critics had failed to understand or appreciate his arguments because of their inattentiveness to the centrality in his thinking of the notion of experience as a transactional *situation* involving an organism and its environment in which distinctions between subjects and objects were functional and not ontological. Thus Russell's reading of pragmatism as a theory of truth grounded in the satisfaction of personal desire rested on a misinterpretation of Dewey's idea of the "problematic" situation as one of *subjective* doubt or *personal* problems. This misreading led Russell, with impeccable logic and a snicker, to the conclusion that Dewey's conception of a "warranted assertion" as that which resolved problematic situations entailed the taking of "generalized wishful thinking as a definition of truth." As Dewey said:

> Mr. Russell proceeds first by converting a doubtful *situation* into a personal doubt, although the difference between the two things is repeatedly pointed out by me. I have even explicitly stated that a personal doubt is pathological unless it is a reflection of a *situation* which is problematic. Then by changing doubt into private discomfort, truth is identified with removal of this discomfort. The only desire that enters, according to my view, is desire to resolve as honestly and impartially as possible the problem involved in the situation. "Satisfaction" is satisfaction of the conditions prescribed by the problem. Personal satisfaction may enter in as it arises when any job is well done according to the requirements of the job itself; but it does not enter in any way into the determination of validity, because, on the contrary, it is conditioned by that determination.

The rehashing of these ancient disputes lent credence to Dewey's conviction that unless and until his critics accepted his "biological-anthropological method of approach to experience" debate would be interminable. In this Russell concurred. "Reading Dr. Dewey," he said, "makes me aware of my own unconscious metaphysic as well as of his. Where they differ, I find it hard to imagine any arguments on either side which do not beg the question."[2]

Perhaps the most interesting feature of the Schilpp volume was the exchange on Dewey's theory of science between Dewey and Hans Reichenbach, a leading logical positivist. Like other emigrés in this school, Reichenbach was eager for a meeting of minds with Dewey, and his essay was clearly part of the abortive effort of the logical positivists to forge an alliance with the doyen of American pragmatism. As we have seen, Dewey had contributed to the positivists' *International Encyclopedia of Unified Science*, but he had made a point there of sharply distinguishing his value theory from that of his hosts. Other substantial differences emerged in his friendly but wary exchange with Reichenbach which further suggest why this initiative met with so little success.

Reichenbach, who was the sort of "scientistic" thinker which Dewey was often accused of being, was most troubled by Dewey's unwillingness to admit that only scientific objects could be said to be really real. He worried, on the one hand, that Dewey's conception of such objects as known relations between things rendered them unreal and, on the other, that Dewey's insistence that things like tertiary qualities and dreams were not simply subjective feelings but very real aspects of primary experience was to grant reality to mere "appearances." He urged Dewey to drop such fallacious notions as a service to the empiricist cause he had, in other respects, done so much to advance.[3]

Dewey responded that, though he would like to agree with Reichenbach that the differences between himself and the logical positivists were minor disagreements between fellow empiricists, the way that Reichenbach threw around such terms as "subjective," "objective," "appearance," and "real" indicated that their differences were more deeply rooted and, at bottom, metaphysical. He noted that taking scientific objects to be relations did not render them less real, unless one clung (as he continued to suspect the positivists did) to an atomistic meta-

2. George Santayana, "Dewey's Naturalistic Metaphysics," Bertrand Russell, "Dewey's New *Logic*," JD, "Experience, Knowledge and Value: A Rejoinder," in Schilpp, *Philosophy of John Dewey*, pp. 243–261, 135–156, 530–534, 544–549, 568–574. Other highly critical essays in the book were those by Arthur Murphy on Dewey's epistemology and metaphysics, Stephen Pepper on his aesthetics, Henry Stuart on his ethical theory, and Edward Schaub on his interpretation of religion. I depart here from my practice of citing strictly from Dewey's collected works because it is difficult to follow Dewey's rejoinder without moving back and forth between it and the essays of his critics, which, given their length, are understandably not reprinted in the collected works. Dewey's rejoinder can be found in *Later Works* 14:3–90.

3. Hans Reichenbach, "Dewey's Theory of Science," in Schilpp, *Philosophy of John Dewey*, pp. 157–192.

physics that denied the basic contention of *radical* empiricists like himself and William James that relations were as real as the things and qualities they related. Reichenbach's use of the terms "real" and "apparent" to distinguish scientific objects from noncognitive competitors suggested further that logical positivists were among those held in the grip of the pernicious privileging of the reality of cognitive experience. Dewey acknowledged that, for purposes of knowing, distinctions could be made between real and apparent things as a way of distinguishing their *evidential* value, but this was not to deny the existential reality of noncognitive experience. "What to me is a difference [between appearance and reality] arising *within* the reflective or cognitive use of primary experiential material, is to Mr. Reichenbach a difference between that primary material itself, which is inherently only 'apparent,' and the material of cognition as 'real.'"[4]

At one point in his essay, Reichenbach suggested that an ethical motive lay behind Dewey's insistence on the reality of qualitative experience and that this motive, more than anything else, stood in the way of a rapprochement between Dewey and his positivist critics. "If the pragmatist considers secondary and tertiary qualities as real," he said, "he does so because he wants to establish esthetics and ethics as aspects of reality comparable to physics." If one makes allowances for the differences separating Dewey and Reichenbach over what physics was all about, this was, as Dewey acknowledged both in his reply to Reichenbach and in his contributions to the *Encyclopedia*, an astute insight into the principal reason why he opposed the logical positivists. Dewey, in granting science a relatively modest portion of existential reality but enormous functional power, had extended its range of operations across the whole spectrum of human experience. The positivists, in granting science the whole of the real and confining its functional power to investigation of this "objective" realm apart from the mere appearances of "subjective" qualities, had rendered it largely irrelevant to judgments of value and relegated "all moral affairs, personal and social, to the status of private desires or else to the use of coercive force."[5]

Unfortunately, matters such as this and their place in Dewey's overriding commitment to democracy got short shrift in the Schilpp collection. If the book nicely displayed the deeply contested issues in meta-

4. JD, "Experience, Knowledge and Value," pp. 534–543, 574–575.
5. Reichenbach, "Dewey's Theory of Science," p. 178; JD, "Experience, Knowledge and Value," pp. 543, 567. See also JD, "Introduction to *Problems of Men*: The Problems of Men and the Present State of Philosophy" (1946), *Later Works* 15:158–160.

physics and logic dividing Dewey from other philosophers, it was far less useful as a guide to the debates engendered by his social and political philosophy. His friends, students, and colleagues wrote the essays on these topics, and, at best, they gently raised gentle objections. This treatment was quite misleading, because in 1939 Dewey was surrounded not only by skeptical metaphysicians and epistemologists but by sharp critics of his social theory, his politics, his vision of progressive education, and his position on American intervention in World War II, which began in September of that year.[6]

PROGRESSIVE EDUCATION

Dewey continued to be an important voice in debates among American educators in the interwar decades, and he persistently hammered away at the failures of the nation's schools. Significant changes had taken place in American education since the early years of the century,

6. A piece highly critical of Dewey's social and political philosophy by Communist party intellectual V. J. McGill was dropped from the collection after Sidney Hook launched an aggressive effort to have it excluded. On learning that McGill was to be a contributor, Hook wrote to Schilpp informing him that in addition to a serious if wrongheaded piece on Dewey published under his own name (an essay that led Schilpp to solicit his participation in the book) McGill had also written an "underhanded abusive tirade" against Dewey under his assumed party name, "Philip Carter." This "double-dealing," he argued, made McGill an unfit contributor. Schilpp, in reply, charged Hook with attempting to abridge the very cultural freedom he was defending in his battles with the Stalinists and contended it would be valuable to have Dewey respond to the criticism McGill was advancing. Dewey's correspondence does not comment on Hook's assertion that McGill's "Carter" article had rendered him an unfit contributor. But he did indicate that he did not find McGill's criticisms worthy of more than a perfunctory reply. "I can hardly do more, in addition to correcting false impressions and erroneous statements," he wrote Schilpp, "than point to the fact that he invites readers to make a choice between a democratic philosophy as expressed in my writings and a totalitarian one as practiced in Russia under the Stalin bureaucracy." Schilpp dropped McGill's essay on the grounds that the principal reason for using it would have been to evoke an extended reflection from Dewey on the differences separating him from his Marxist critics. This justification may just have been a convenient way for Schilpp to avoid Hook's threats to make a public issue of the matter, but I doubt it. Schilpp strongly stood his ground in his exchanges with Hook, and, had Dewey been willing to offer the kind of reply to McGill that Schilpp wanted, the essay would probably have been included. Although I have no evidence to support this conclusion, I think it reasonable to suppose that Dewey refused because he wished to avoid participating in the suppression of McGill's article on partisan grounds while at the same time to put as little strain as possible on his friendship with Hook. See the extensive correspondence on this matter in June 1939 in the Hook Collection and the Paul A. Schilpp Papers, Special Collections, Morris Library, Southern Illinois University. For McGill's views of Dewey's philosophy see V. J. McGill, "Pragmatism Reconsidered: An Aspect of John Dewey's Philosophy," *Science and Society* 3 (1939): 289–322, and Philip Carter, "Pitfalls of Pragmatic Logic," *Communist* 18 (1939): 163–169.

he conceded, but these changes were piecemeal, and many schools, particularly those in the large cities and rural areas, were "still in a condition that should be a public scandal." Methods of instruction were still often mechanical, and "the worst thing is that, even in the schools where pupils are not treated as intellectual robots, their individual traits are stimulated more or less at haphazard, rather than directed." Students spent much of their time and energy accumulating, memorizing, and largely forgetting a mass of disconnected information and acquiring mechanical skills. Little attempt had been made to change this situation, and as a result "too large a part of our citizens has left our schools without power of critical discrimination, at the mercy of special propaganda, and drifting from one plan and scheme to another according to the loudest clamor of the moment."[7]

Dewey saluted those who struggled to remedy this public scandal, but at the same time he criticized educational reformers as much as their opponents, for since responsibility for "progressive education" was often laid at his doorstep, he was anxious to distinguish his thinking from that of other reformers with whom he often profoundly disagreed. After World War I educational reform had splintered into warring camps as advocates of "scientific efficiency" battled with romantic proponents of "child-centered" education, and in the thirties "social reconstructionists" challenged both. Dewey was, to a greater or lesser degree, critical of them all.[8]

Dewey sustained his critique of the "gospel of efficiency" and "administrative progressivism" beyond the vocational education debate that had initially provoked it, broadening his objections into a condemnation of a complacent scientism rife among educational reformers. The scientific study of education, he argued, had too often fueled a deeply conservative impulse to construct a system of education which

7. "Need for Orientation" (1935), *Later Works* 11:163–165.
8. The opinion of H. L. Mencken was characteristic of the sort of attribution of influence Dewey was up against. "I am convinced," Mencken wrote, "that Teachers College Columbia has done more harm in the United States than any other educational agency, save maybe the public schools. It has been dominated by quacks since the beginning, and their quackeries are now in full blast everywhere. They have not only seized the public schools, but nearly all the private schools. The man primarily responsible is probably John Dewey, though he doesn't go the whole way with the rest of the brethren. I believe he is the worst writer ever heard of in America, and probably the worst philosopher known to history. All the while, of course, he remains an extremely amiable and honest man. This is a familiar combination." H. L. Mencken to A. G. Keller, 22 April 1940, in Carl Bode, ed., *New Mencken Letters* (New York: Dial Press, 1977), p. 462. A useful corrective is Joe R. Burnett, "Whatever Happened to John Dewey?" *Teachers College Record* 81 (1979): 192–210.

would simply (if efficiently) reproduce the prevailing social order by preparing students for roles determined largely by their class, race, sex, and ethnicity. "If we are satisfied upon the whole with the aims and processes of existing society," he said, then the current science of efficiency advocates such as David Snedden, Franklin Bobbitt, and Werrett Wallace Charters was most appropriate. "If you want schools to perpetuate the present order, with at most an elimination of waste and with such additions as enable it to do better what it is already doing, then one type of intellectual method or 'science' is indicated. But if one conceives that a social order different in quality and direction from the present is desirable and that schools should strive to educate with social change in view by producing individuals not complacent about what already exists, and equipped with desires and abilities to assist in transforming it, quite a different method and content is indicated for educational science."[9]

Dewey devoted the greatest energy to distinguishing his position from that of the "child-centered" progressives with whom he was most often mistakenly identified. These romantic reformers had gathered together to form the Progressive Education Association (PEA) in 1919, and theirs was the predominant voice in the PEA until the mid-thirties. When commonly employed, the term "progressive education" referred to their theory and practice. Although Dewey applauded their criticisms of conventional education, he took every available opportunity (including his installation as honorary president of the PEA in 1928) to question the wisdom of the ideology and programs that child-centered reformers offered in its stead. And though Dewey was widely regarded as the father of progressive education of this sort, the centerpiece of his last book on education, *Experience and Education* (1938), was a sharp indictment of much that marched under this banner.[10]

The child-centered romantics, Dewey argued, had responded to the defects of traditional educational practice with methods of instruction that simply negated those traditionally employed without establishing a positive pedagogy of their own. "The problems are not even recog-

9. "Progressive Education and the Science of Education" (1928), *Later Works* 3:262. On the party of efficiency in educational thought after World War I see Lawrence A. Cremin, *The Transformation of the School: Progressivism in American Education, 1876–1957* (New York: Vintage, 1964), pp. 192–200. For a full accounting of Dewey's critique of this position see Carmine A. Yengo, "John Dewey and the Cult of Efficiency," *Harvard Educational Review* 34 (1964): 33–53.

10. On the Progressive Education Association and child-centered progressivism see Patricia A. Graham, *Progressive Education: From Arcady to Academe* (New York: Teachers College Press, 1967), and Cremin, *Transformation of the School*, pp. 201–215, 240–347.

nized, to say nothing of being solved," he said, "when it is assumed that it suffices to reject the ideas and practices of the old education and then go to the opposite extreme." The line of the party of "freedom" went something like this: "Let us surround pupils with certain materials, tools, appliances, etc., and then let pupils respond to these things according to their own desires. Above all, let us not suggest any end or plan to the students; let us not suggest to them what they should do, for that is an unwarranted trespass upon their sacred intellectual individuality since the essence of such individuality is to set up ends and aims." Dewey's judgment on this sort of pedagogy was uncharacteristically blunt. "Such a method," he said, "is really stupid." It was stupid because "it attempts the impossible, which is always stupid; and it misconceives the conditions of independent thinking. There are a multitude of ways of reacting to surrounding conditions, and without some guidance from experience these reactions are almost sure to be casual, sporadic, and ultimately fatiguing, accompanied by nervous strain." Because teachers were more experienced than their students they had a right, indeed an obligation, to suggest to their students what to do (and romantics ignored the extent to which such direction was already implicit in the materials with which they surrounded children). The suggestions, which was not to say the dictations, of a teacher "will presumably do more to getting something started which will really secure and increase the development of strictly individual capacities than will suggestions springing from uncontrolled haphazard sources."[11]

Romantic progressivism was, in effect, a celebration of negative freedom, in this case freedom from the restrictions of the traditional classroom. But it offered children little guidance and left them at the mercy of their spontaneous impulses (a failing of progressive schools nicely captured in a famous *New Yorker* cartoon in which a gloomy child in such a school asks her teacher: "Do we have to do what we want today?"). For Dewey, here as elsewhere, negative freedom was to be valued not in itself but as an opportunity to develop "effective freedom." Freedom from restrictions was to be prized "only as a means to freedom which is power: power to frame purposes, to judge wisely, to evaluate desires by the consequences which will result from acting upon them; power to select and order means to carry chosen ends into operation." The task of the teacher was not to permit the natural impulses of the child to express themselves spontaneously but to provide the guid-

11. *Experience and Education* (1938), *Later Works* 13:8–9; "Individuality and Experience" (1926), *Later Works* 2:58–59.

ance that would enable the child to subject these impulses to intelligent direction. "The ideal aim of education is creation of power of self-control."[12]

Though Dewey rarely named names in his criticisms of progressive reform, one of his principal targets was William H. Kilpatrick, his colleague at Columbia Teachers College, whose "project method" was perhaps the single most influential practical curricular reform to emerge from child-centered progressivism. The *Teachers College Record* distributed some sixty thousand reprints of the 1918 article in which Kilpatrick first described the project method, and by the twenties Kilpatrick was the dominant figure at the leading school of education in the country and probably the nation's most influential teacher of teachers (he is said to have taught over 35,000 students in his career). Kilpatrick thought of himself as Dewey's disciple, and like Dewey he argued for a psychological organization of the curriculum which built on the existing interests and activities of the child and treated thinking as problem solving. A "project," as Kilpatrick defined it, was a "wholehearted purposeful activity proceeding in a social environment," and he argued for an "activity curriculum" built around a succession of such projects. In this curriculum, he emphasized, the purposes and plans guiding such projects would be those of children and not those of their teachers. Subject matter would take a back seat to the accomplishment of the child's goals. What children thought about was up to them; the aim of the school was to teach them how to think about whatever this might be.[13]

It was this privileging of the child's purposes and the thorough subordination of subject matter to them that tipped Kilpatrick's thinking toward the sort of romanticism which troubled Dewey and made Kilpatrick's program, to a significant degree, little more than an updated version of the child-centered pedagogy Dewey had been criticizing since the 1890s. Dewey agreed with Kilpatrick that learning had to begin with the child's interests, but the simple pursuit of these interests, which were often vague and chaotic, would produce only projects that "were too trivial to be educative." Dewey had no objections to the "project method" as such (indeed, it bore considerable resemblance to the "occupational" pedagogy of his Laboratory School), nor did he deny that use of such a method would require considerable reorganization

12. *Experience and Education*, p. 41.
13. William H. Kilpatrick, "The Project Method," *Teachers College Record* 19 (1918): 329–335. This method was more fully elaborated in his *Foundations of Method* (New York: Macmillan, 1925).

of subject matter. But he insisted that projects must have as one of their goals the child's mastery of organized subjects. As Herbert Kliebard has said, in Kilpatrick's hands the project or occupation became "not simply a way of reorganizing the teaching of, say, science; it became, contrary to Dewey's position, a substitute for science." And much of what critics (then and now) attacked as aimless, contentless "Deweyism" was in fact aimless, contentless "Kilpatrickism."[14]

As his criticism of the project method suggests, Dewey continued to try to define a position between child-centered and teacher-centered, learner-centered and subject-matter-centered, education. Perhaps the best way to characterize his position, he said, was to think of it as one that sought to model learning on the sort of education that went on in apprenticeship to a calling such as carpentry:

> The customs, methods and *working* standards of the calling constitute a "tradition," and initiation into the tradition is the means by which the powers of learners are released and directed. But we should also have to say that the urge or need of an individual to join in an undertaking is a necessary prerequisite of the tradition's being a factor in his personal growth in power and freedom; and also that he has to *see* on his own behalf and in his own way the relations between means and methods employed and results achieved. Nobody else can see for him, and he can't see just by being "told," although the right kind of telling may guide his seeing and thus help him see what he needs to see.

This notion of teachers as master conveyers of a tradition (which, it should be said, Dewey conceived as a growing and changing body of knowledge and practice to be contrasted with "fixed and absolute convention") pointed again to a notion of children's freedom not as an original possession but as a power that had to be "wrought out" in the context of a critical engagement with the accumulated knowledge of mankind.[15]

Dewey also objected that child-centered progressivism almost wholly evaded consideration of the "social potentialities" of education. The

14. *The Way out of Educational Confusion* (1931), *Later Works* 6:86; Herbert M. Kliebard, *The Struggle for the American Curriculum, 1893–1958* (Boston: Routledge and Kegan Paul, 1986), p. 166. See also Cremin, *Transformation of the School*, pp. 215–220. As both Cremin and Kliebard suggest, the progressive educator closest to Dewey in his thinking was not Kilpatrick but Boyd Bode, the leading figure at Ohio State, a principal rival of Teachers College for preeminence among schools of education. See especially Bode's *Modern Educational Theories* (New York: Macmillan, 1927) and *Progressive Education at the Crossroads* (New York: Newson, 1938).

15. "Individuality and Experience," p. 57.

tendency of progressive schools had been to "put emphasis upon things that make schooling more immediately enjoyable to pupils rather than upon things that will give them the understanding and capacity that are relevant to contemporary social life." An education that supplied "additions to the resources of the inner life of pupils" was important, but "surely the problem of progressive education demands that this result be not effected in such a way as to ignore or obscure preparation for the social realities—including the evils—of industrial and political civilization." Romantic progressivism, he remarked ruefully, had done something to sharpen the aesthetic sensibilities of the upper middle class but had done little to provide students with "insight into the basic forces of industrial and urban civilization." Only schools that did so could claim to be "progressive in any socially significant sense."[16]

In the thirties, Dewey joined other leading educators—including John L. Childs, George Counts, Kilpatrick (ever alert to shifting trends), Bruce Raup, Harold Rugg, and Goodwin Watson—who shared his critique of the individualism of child-centered progressivism and sought to join educational reform to radical politics. These "social reconstructionists," most of them Teachers College professors, challenged the leaders of the PEA for control of that organization and launched a lively journal, *Social Frontier*, which for the five years of its existence published a wide-ranging critique of American capitalism and the New Deal and urged American teachers to join the democratic left. Dewey was the elder statesman of this group, and "John Dewey's Page" was a regular monthly feature of the *Social Frontier* from 1935 to 1937.[17]

Although Dewey clearly felt most at home among this group, he differed with some of its members on the question of whether radicals should "indoctrinate" students with adversarial beliefs, an issue that produced heated discussion in the pages of the *Social Frontier* and elsewhere in the mid-thirties. Some radical educators, led by George Counts, argued that capitalism could not be reconstructed into a more humane social order unless the conservative indoctrination to which students were subjected was challenged by radical counterindoctrination. Counts urged teachers to be undeterred by "the bogies of *imposition and indoctrination*" and to seize the power they had to shape young minds. In his widely discussed pamphlet *Dare the School Build a New Social Order?*, he declared he was "prepared to defend the thesis that all

16. "How Much Freedom in New Schools?" (1930), *Later Works* 5:324–325.
17. The group also published a collection of essays articulating their general point of view: William H. Kilpatrick, ed., *The Educational Frontier* (New York: Century, 1933). C. A. Bowers, *The Progressive Educator and the Depression: The Radical Years* (New York: Random House, 1969), is the only study of the "social reconstructionists."

education contains a large element of imposition, that in the very nature of the case this is inevitable, that the existence and evolution of society depend upon it, that it is consequently eminently desirable, and that the frank acceptance of this fact by the educator is a major professional obligation."[18]

Dewey agreed that much of the education in American schools was little more than indoctrination, "especially with reference to narrow nationalism under the name of patriotism, and with reference to the dominant economic regime." He was disturbed as well by the views of such prominent figures in higher education as University of Chicago president Robert Hutchins, who called for a radically revamped college curriculum grounded in the absolute values of a transcendental metaphysics. But these threats to democracy, Dewey argued in 1935, did not justify counterindoctrination as a means to promote democratic ends, a means he found counterproductive. Moreover, for radicals to engage in such counterpropaganda was to demonstrate a lack of confidence in the power of the convictions they held and the means by which they themselves had presumably arrived at these convictions. They had not been indoctrinated into the conclusions they had reached about the shortcomings of capitalist society but had reached these conclusions by means of "an intelligent study of historical and existing forces and conditions." Radical democrats had to credit their students with the capability to reach the same conclusions by the same means, not only because this method was more democratic but also because these conclusions should be subjected to the continuous scrutiny such education would provide. "If the method of intelligence has worked in our own case," he asked, "how can we assume that the method will not work with our students, and that it will not with them generate ardor and practical energy?" Dewey was not, of course, advocating "value-neutral" education, but he was confident that if teachers cultivated democratic character and intelligent judgment in their students—the "standpoint" that his ethics authorized—then they could be confident that the existing social order would not prove immune to sharp criticism from its children.[19]

Dewey's criticisms of other reformers were usually politely received

---

18. George S. Counts, "Dare Progressive Education Be Progressive?" *Progressive Education* 9 (1932): 259, and *Dare the School Build a New Social Order?* (New York: John Day, 1932), p. 9.

19. "Education and Social Change" (1937), *Later Works* 11:415; "The Crucial Role of Intelligence" (1935), *Later Works* 11:343. See also "President Hutchins' Proposals to Remake Higher Education" (1937), *Later Works* 11:397–401; "Discussion of 'Freedom, in Relation to Culture, Social Planning, and Leadership'" (1932), *Later Works* 6:142–145. For an excellent discussion of the indoctrination debate see Mary Anne Raywid, "The Discovery and Rejection of Indoctrination," *Educational Theory* 30 (1980): 1–10.

but they changed few minds, and, perhaps because many of his criticisms were so politely made, some (like Kilpatrick) continued to think of themselves as Deweyans. Few followed the "way out of educational confusion" that Dewey proposed. For most educators, it posed too great a threat to traditional methods and subject matter. At the same time, its social implications were too radical for advocates of scientific efficiency and not radical enough for some proponents of social reconstruction. And, though it called for a reconstruction of the curriculum that would build on the impulses and interests of children, it was too respectful of tradition and subject matter to satisfy romantics. Thus, as Kliebard has said, "his intellectual stature, his international reputation and his many honors notwithstanding, Dewey did not have enough of a true following in the world of educational practice to make his impact felt."[20]

This marginality, of course, was nothing new, and had Dewey still believed that the teacher was "the usherer in of the true kingdom of God," he might have been more distressed than he seemed that his arguments so often fell on deaf ears. But the philosophy of education was no longer the focus of his concern as it had been in the years immediately preceding World War I. In part, this shift reflected a less naive estimate of the place of the school in social reconstruction, a substantial displacement of the classroom from the center of his reform vision. What had once been to his mind *the* critical means for the democratization of American life became one of a number of critical means, and one clearly secondary to more overtly political institutions for public education. "It is unrealistic, in my opinion," he wrote in 1937, "to suppose that the schools can be a *main* agency in producing the intellectual and moral changes, the changes in attitudes and disposition of thought and purpose, which are necessary for the creation of a new social order. Any such view ignores the constant operation of powerful forces outside the school which shape mind and character. It ignores the fact that school education is but one educational agency out of many, and at the best is in some respects a minor educational force."[21]

This more modest estimate of the role of institutions of formal education in radical social change did not mean Dewey doubted that the school was a necessary if not a sufficient medium for "forming the understanding and the dispositions that are required to maintain a genuinely changed social order." Thinking about the predicament of

20. Kliebard, *Struggle for the American Curriculum*, p. 179.
21. "Education and Social Change," p. 414

American education could still evoke some of his most powerful flights of rhetoric. But the militant tone of many of his speeches to educators disclosed an insistence, often absent before World War I, that the school was itself a political arena, a contested site of struggle:

> How often in the past have we depended upon war to bring out the supreme loyalties of mankind. Its life and death struggles are obvious and dramatic; it results in changing the course of history are evident and striking. When shall we realize that in every school-building in the land a struggle is also being waged against all that hems in and distorts human life? The struggle is not with arms and violence; its consequences cannot be recorded in statistics of the physically killed and wounded, nor set forth in terms of territorial changes. But in its slow and imperceptible processes, the real battles for human freedom and for the pushing back of the boundaries that restrict human life are ultimately won. We need to pledge ourselves to engage anew and with renewed faith in the greatest of all battles in the cause of human liberation, to the end that all human beings may lead the life that is alone worthy of being entitled wholly human.[22]

Dewey now more openly acknowledged that schools were inextricably tied to prevailing structures of power and therefore extremely difficult to transform into agencies of democratic reform. Efforts to do so, he observed in 1935, repeatedly ran afoul of interests anxious to preserve the existing social order. School boards as the representatives of these dominant interests "regard themselves after the analogy of private employers of labor and the teaching staff as their hired men and women." Teachers had very little control over their work. Administrators made out the course of study, prepared syllabuses for instruction, and established methods of teaching. The teacher simply took orders. The administrator, in turn, was dependent for his job on "undue conformity to the desires of the economic class that is dominant in school boards as the agents of social control." Teachers, Dewey argued elsewhere that same year, should recognize that they were as much "workers" as farmers and factory laborers and as such were subject to the control of "the small and powerful class that is economically privileged." Their job security and advancement "depended largely upon conformity with the desires and plans of this class." He encouraged teachers to struggle to gain control over their work and to ally themselves with other workers "against their common foe, the privileged

22. Ibid.; "Philosophy and Education" (1930), *Later Works* 5:297–298.

class, and in the alliance develop the character, skill, and intelligence that are necessary to make a democratic social order a fact."[23]

In short, the defects of schools mirrored and sustained the defects of the larger society and these defects could not be remedied apart from a struggle for democracy throughout that larger society. Schools would take part in the democratic social change only "as they ally themselves with this or that movement of existing social forces." They could not be viewed, as Dewey had once been prone to see them, as the vehicle for an end run around politics. "Dare the school build a new social order?" was no longer a question he would ask.[24]

PRAGMATISM AND BARBARISM

Dewey played but a minor role in the controversies over American foreign policy engendered by the rise of fascism in Europe. The Foreign Policy Association debate in 1932 over the United States' response to the Manchurian crisis marked the last occasion in which he would actively participate in public discussions of foreign policy. Now firmly convinced that Randolph Bourne was correct in his contention that war was a means of social action which set its own agenda apart from the best intentions of the honorable men and women who might attempt to use it to further justice and democracy, Dewey took a near-absolute position in the thirties in opposing American involvement in another world war. As a result, he found himself struggling until the very day the Japanese bombed Pearl Harbor to figure out a way both to oppose fascism and to argue that such opposition must stop short of war with the fascist powers.

In 1935 the editors of the *Modern Monthly* convened a symposium called "When America Goes to War." They asked leading intellectuals what they would do "when America goes to war" and whether that decision would be altered if the Soviet Union were to ally with the United States in a war with Japan or if a German victory over most of Europe seemed likely. Dewey's reply was among the briefest of all respondents: he would "do my best first to keep the country out and then if it happens to keep out myself." To the other two questions he simply replied "No" and "No, as at present informed."[25]

23. "Need for Orientation," p. 165; "The Teacher and the Public" (1935), *Later Works* 11:161.
24. "Can Education Share in Social Reconstruction?" (1934), *Later Works* 9:207.
25. "When America Goes to War: A Symposium," *Modern Monthly* 9 (1935): 200.

The brevity of Dewey's response left it to the reader to guess why he felt as he did, but his positions on particular issues in the late thirties indicated that he was under no illusions about the threat fascism posed to his most deeply held values but that at the same time he was convinced that war with fascism would only make matters worse. This tension between his antifascist and antiwar convictions led him to make some fine distinctions between the sort of antifascist policies he would or would not support. For example, in 1937 Dewey criticized pacifists for calling for the curtailment of American aid to the Republican government during the Spanish Civil War. The situation, he said, called simply for the maintenance of normal commercial relations with an established government, which would permit the Spanish government "to buy here whatever supplies it desires, and the full denial to the rebels of any such right." The Spanish people were entitled to "progress peacefully under an elected government of their own choosing," and if they were denied this opportunity, "democracy as a force for social progress is finished." But, he argued, to aid a democratically elected government in the suppression of an armed revolt was one thing, for the United States itself to wage war on fascism was quite another. "Between fascist and democratic states," he declared, "any international war at present is bound to be a struggle between rival capitalisms. Civil war like the one in Spain may be the means of defending and continuing the democratic method and checking fascism." What should be done if fascist states turned from supporting the likes of Franco to acting aggressively across national boundaries Dewey did not say, but his argument implied that even in such cases the United States should continue to seek out methods short of war which would protect democracy. He would remain perched in this position, between isolation and intervention, until events rendered it no longer available in 1941.[26]

Dewey's opposition to American participation in another world war was not grounded, as some of his critics contended, in confidence in the essential goodness of human nature and the power of rational discourse to resolve conflicts of interest with the fascist powers but rather in deep-seated fears about the consequences for democracy in the United States of another war. On the eve of World War II in an article titled "No Matter What Happens—Stay Out," Dewey warned that "it is quite conceivable that after the next war we should have in this country a semi-military, semi-financial autocracy, which would fash-

26. "Aid for the Spanish Government" (1937), *Later Works* 11:527–528.

ion class divisions on this country for untold years. In any case we should have the suppression of all the democratic values for the sake of which we professedly went to war." The war would be "the greatest social catastrophe that could overtake us, the destruction of all the foundations upon which to erect a socialized democracy." For Americans to resort to war, he warned soon after the war in Europe began, would be "a first sure sign that we are giving up the struggle for the democratic way of life, and that the Old World has conquered morally as well as geographically." As the country drifted toward war it was not naive hope but deep pessimism that gripped Dewey, and, for one of the few times in the latter years of his long life, he considered the possibility that he had outlived his usefulness as a social critic. "An epoch has come to an end, I think," he wrote Max Otto in 1941, "but what is beginning is too much for me."[27]

Dewey's fears about the domestic consequences of another war were fueled during the "defense period" by several incidents close to home which suggested to him the abridgments of freedom which might be in store for Americans should the nation commit itself to military intervention. As I noted, Dewey cautioned his colleagues in the Committee for Cultural Freedom in 1939 that their right flank was unprotected, and in the following year events heightened this concern. Government campaigns against "subversion" in the schools, especially an attack on the social-studies textbooks of his fellow social reconstructionist Harold Rugg, elicited Dewey's sharp protest, as did the efforts of Columbia president Nicholas Murray Butler once again to crank up the machinery for suppressing academic freedom in the national interest. But nothing disturbed Dewey more than the successful effort by conservative religious and civic groups in New York City to annul the appointment of Bertrand Russell to a chair of philosophy at City College on the grounds that his writings on marriage and sex were, as one lawyer put it, "lecherous, salacious, libidinous, lustful, venerous, erotomaniac, aphrodisiac, atheistic, irreverent, narrow-minded, untruthful, and bereft of moral fiber." Although Dewey had little love for Russell or his work, he led the protest against the court decision denying the British philosopher his appointment, and when this was unavailing, he persuaded Albert Barnes to hire Russell to teach at the Barnes Foundation.[28]

27. "No Matter What Happens—Stay Out" (1939), *Later Works* 14:364; *Freedom and Culture* (1939), *Later Works* 13:187; JD to Max Otto, 7 July 1941, Max Otto Papers.

28. See "Higher Learning and War" (1939), *Later Works* 14:272–274; "Investigating Education" (1940) and "Censorship Not Wanted" (1940), *Later Works* 14:371–373; "State-

During the defense period, Dewey remained in the opposition to both direct American involvement in the war and simple isolationism. Having backed the Keep America Out of War Congress organized by Norman Thomas in 1938, he headed a committee of intellectuals supporting Thomas's presidential candidacy in 1940, a candidacy grounded in little more than opposition to American participation in the conflict. In 1941 he criticized the isolationists in the America First Committee and defended Lend-Lease to Great Britain as a policy designed to defeat fascism without direct American military intervention. After Pearl Harbor when his antiwar interventionism became untenable, his resistance to American participation in the war ceased—he was never an absolute pacifist and had never questioned the necessity and justice of national self-defense in the face of overt aggression. He devoted his efforts as an activist during the war to preserving civil liberties and combating the widespread mystification of the Soviet alliance. During World War II, there would be no reprise of the lectures Dewey had offered during World War I on the "social possibilities of war." The most one could hope for, he said, was that after this war no one would again think to give such lectures. "In that case, if destructive wars continue to be resorted to—as they may be—it will be because of outright relapse into barbarism and not as an agency for advancing civilization and culture."[29]

Had he been allowed to do so, Dewey probably would have remained as distant from the war as he had predicted in his brief 1935 statement. But if he would not defend the war as anything more than a necessary evil, he would defend himself more aggressively, and when a coterie of critics tried to blame him and his philosophy for weakening the will of

---

ment on Academic Freedom" (1940), *Later Works* 14:374; "The Case for Bertrand Russell" (1940), *Later Works* 14:231–234; and JD and Horace Kallen, eds., *The Bertrand Russell Case* (New York: Viking, 1941). The lawyer quoted is Joseph Goldstein, attorney for Jean Kay, who brought suit to vacate Russell's appointment on the grounds that he posed a moral threat to her daughter, a student at City College (*Bertrand Russell Case*, p. 58). While at the Barnes Foundation, Russell crafted the lectures that were to become his *History of Western Philosophy*, including one on Dewey which again retailed his interpretation of pragmatism as a manifestation of American industrialism. Russell's experience with Barnes was more typical than Dewey's, and he left Merion in the wake of an acrimonious dispute with Barnes over the right of his wife to knit while attending his classes. See Russell, *A History of Western Philosophy* (New York: Simon and Schuster, 1945), pp. 819–828, and Howard Greenfield, *The Devil and Dr. Barnes* (New York: Viking, 1987), pp. 199–230.

29. Bernard K. Johnpoll, *Pacifist's Progress: Norman Thomas and the Decline of American Socialism* (Chicago: Quadrangle, 1970), chap. 7; Charles Howlett, *Troubled Philosopher: John Dewey and the Struggle for World Peace* (Port Washington, N.Y.: Kennikat Press, 1977), chaps. 9–10; "The Basis for Hope" (1939), *Later Works* 14:251, 249.

democrats to resist fascism, he could not let such charges go unanswered.

The leader among Dewey's critics was his old nemesis Lewis Mumford. As total war descended on the world in the late thirties, Mumford denounced liberal acquiescence in the triumphs of fascism in an outpouring of fiery articles and books. Although Mumford seldom mentioned Dewey by name, he drew directly on the language and arguments of his earlier criticisms of the philosopher, and few doubted that Dewey was among Mumford's principal targets.[30]

In "The Corruption of Liberalism" (1940), the essay that firmly established Mumford's standing as a leading "war intellectual," he argued that the record of liberalism in the thirties was one of "shameful evasion and inept retreat." Either bereft of convictions or lacking the courage to defend them, liberals had capitulated to Stalinism by allying themselves in popular-front politics with the Communist party and were now rapidly giving ground to fascism by resorting to "passivist" appeasement and "isolationism" in the face of Hitler's aggression. They had committed themselves to a self-destructive "peace" that entailed the victory of forces fundamentally opposed to the liberal ideals of objective reason, freedom of thought, and human dignity.[31]

The concessions that liberalism had made to barbarism, Mumford argued, were not mere strategic errors but were traceable to "fatal deficiencies that go to the very roots of liberal philosophy" (CL, 568). Liberalism was a very mixed doctrine. On the one hand, it was wedded to the "humanist traditions of personal responsibility, personal freedom, and personal expression" that were threatened by fascism (CL, 569). On the other hand, the humanism of this "ideal liberalism" had been loosely joined since the eighteenth century to a quite different sort of liberalism, what Mumford termed "pragmatic liberalism," which had left liberals impotent in the face of this threat. Pragmatic liberalism was but a fresh alias for Mumford's old *bête noire*, utilitarianism, and echoes of his critique of Dewey in *The Golden Day* sounded through this and Mumford's other war essays.

---

30. For a fuller discussion of Mumford's criticisms of Dewey in the late thirties and forties than I offer here see my "Lewis Mumford, John Dewey, and the 'Pragmatic Acquiescence'" in Agatha Hughes and Thomas Hughes, eds., *Lewis Mumford: Public Intellectual* (New York: Oxford University Press, 1990), from which I am drawing.

31. Mumford, "The Corruption of Liberalism," *New Republic*, 29 April 1940: 568. Page numbers for further references (CL) appear in the text. For an extended version of the argument of this essay see Mumford, *Faith for Living* (New York: Harcourt Brace, 1940), pp. 44–126.

Pragmatic liberalism, he asserted, was "vastly preoccupied with the machinery of life," and "the only type of human character it could understand was the utilitarian one," believing that "the emotional and spiritual life of man needs no other foundation than the rational, utilitarian activities associated with the getting of a living" (CL, 569). The pragmatic liberal was color-blind to moral values and had taken "values, feelings, emotions, wishes, purposes, for granted. He assumed either that this world did not exist or that it was relatively unimportant; at all events, if it did exist, it could be safely left to itself without cultivation" (CL, 570). Science "would eventually supply all the guidance necessary for human conduct" and the evils of life would be solved by "extending the blessings of the machine" (CL, 570). All this rendered pragmatic liberals incapable of understanding the barbarism of Hitler and Stalin and of mustering the courage to resist it with coercive force. "The isolation that is preached by our liberals today," Mumford warned, "means fascism tomorrow" (CL, 573).

Once again Mumford was wide of the mark where Dewey (if not many liberals) was concerned. Dewey was a relatively early and vigorous opponent of Stalinism (and his record here was far superior to Mumford's), and the charge that he was purblind to values, feelings, emotions, wishes, and purposes was no more accurate in 1940 than it had been in 1926. But Dewey did oppose American military intervention in World War II and, in the end, "pragmatic liberalism" was little more than a catch-all term under which Mumford grouped everyone who he believed had contributed to a "spineless" response to fascism. As James T. Farrell said, the pragmatic liberal became for Mumford "a grouping which includes just about everyone, living or dead, with whom he disagrees."[32]

In 1935 Mumford had shared Dewey's fears about the consequences for democracy of another world war. Although he did not agree with

32. James T. Farrell, "Faith of Lewis Mumford," *Southern Review* 6 (1940/41): 432. See also Sidney Hook, "Metaphysics, War and the Intellectuals," *Menorah Journal* 28 (1940): 326–337. Mumford recognized the difficulties his late arrival as an anti-Stalinist created for him. He told Brooks in 1939, "I reproach myself for having remained so long indifferent to the fate of Communism in Russia and so silent about the villainies of its dictatorship: the period of suspended judgment lasted too long, and the suspense has now proved almost a noose around our own necks." A few months later he revealed, "I feel deeply my own guilt during the past twenty years, when, despite my extreme skepticism of the totalitarian tyranny that was being built up in Russia, I said nothing and did nothing to counteract it" (Mumford to Brooks, 3 November 1939, 10 February 1940, *Brooks-Mumford Letters*, pp. 167, 181). He may also have regretted his cheerful estimate of the future of Germany in the early thirties and his discounting of the "childishness and insanity" of the Nazis ("Notes on Germany," *New Republic*, 26 October 1932: 279–281).

Dewey that such fears necessarily entailed an antiwar stance, he did declare in the *Modern Monthly* symposium his general opposition to war "because of its imbecility, its absence of human purpose, its brutalization of life, its abject failure to achieve reasonable goods, and its futile simplification of all the conflicts and real issues involved in life in communities." He committed himself to fight the "war animus" in time of peace, and though he could imagine supporting a war as a lesser evil, he avowed that, in this event, his principal duty as a writer would be to continue this fight and do what he could to prevent the pressures of war from engendering fascism in America. "*By reason of the very technique of fighting and its special behavior patterns—no matter how just and rational the cause seems at the outset,*" Mumford warned, "war is always a losing fight even when it is a just one."[33]

By the end of the thirties, Mumford was promoting rather than fighting the war animus, convinced that the need to defeat fascism abroad outweighed any temporary damage to democratic values and institutions at home. "We cannot preserve ourselves against this barbarism and worry about the cost of our effort," he said. He admitted that there were dangers in going to war, for the tasks of war were "of their nature brutal and self-deadening ones. . . . The very process of attacking and killing a remorseless enemy inevitably coarsens the human fiber; and the more base that enemy, the more violent his attack, the more terrible to oneself become the consequences of resisting him." A "totalitarian element" in mobilization for war "will be inescapable," Mumford said, yet he was confident that any curtailment of democracy at home would not outlive the conflict. He was particularly contemptuous of liberals who worried about the effect of war on civil liberties. "Facing a war waged mercilessly by fascism against all his ideals and hopes," he scornfully remarked, "the liberal shows himself more concerned over minor curtailments of private liberties, necessary for an effective defense against fascism, than he is over the far more ghastly prospect of permanent servitude if fascism finally covers the earth." Fascism at home, he contended, was more likely to come about as a result of the economic crisis and psychological security brought on by isolation from a fascist-dominated world order than from armed conflict aimed at preventing the establishment of such barbarism in the rest of the world. Indeed, he argued, the crisis of war against the radical evil of fascism might even engender a "large-scale conversion"

33. Mumford in "When America Goes to War: A Symposium," *Modern Monthly* 9 (1935): 203–204.

of Americans to the moral values necessary for the construction of a more thoroughly democratic and life-enhancing society in the United States.[34]

No doubt, most would agree that Mumford had the better of this argument. Particularly in retrospect, it is clear that the Nazis were barbarians to a degree even Mumford did not suspect, and American arms were essential to their defeat. Moreover, the American war effort did not create a fascist regime at home. Even without the advantages of hindsight, Mumford's fears of fascism abroad were better placed than Dewey's dread of Thermidor at home. But though the consequences of the American war effort were worth the costs, there *were* costs and of the sort Dewey feared: unprecedented abuse of civil liberties in the treatment of Japanese-Americans, the ebbing of social reform, the consolidation of the dominant position of large corporations in the political economy, the centralization of state power in the hands of executive elites, and, in general, the constriction of democracy in the United States. In addition, the targeting of civilian populations by all sides in the conflict, which culminated in the dropping of atomic bombs on Hiroshima and Nagasaki, recalled Mumford's remark in 1935 that even just wars may be unjustly fought and Bourne's earlier warnings of the impotence of moral reason in the face of the demiurge of "military necessity."[35]

Ironies abound in this last act of the stormy relationship between Mumford and Dewey. Damned by Mumford in the twenties with Bourne's words for embracing World War I, Dewey was now condemned by Mumford for accepting the sort of "romantic defeatism that Bourne had preached in 1917." Mumford thus continued to cling to a Bourne-inspired misreading of Dewey's philosophy, while at the same time arguing that Bourne's opposition to Dewey's support for World War I, which had provoked this interpretation, was mistaken and that "perhaps the greatest catastrophe" of the Great War was that many of his generation, including himself for some time, had adopted Bourne's perspective. In the late thirties and early forties, it was Mumford (whom Van Wyck Brooks had invested with the mantle of

34. Mumford, *Faith for Living*, pp. 307, 232, 106, 57, 191, 194. See also Mumford, *Men Must Act* (New York, Harcourt Brace, 1939).

35. For a consideration of the radical antiwar argument attuned to its insights as well as its substantial defects see Frank A. Warren, *An Alternative Vision: The Socialist Party in the 1930's* (Bloomington: Indiana University Press, 1974), chap. 9. Mumford, it should be said, later emerged as a leading student of the moral disasters of the "Good War." See especially "The Morals of Extermination," *Atlantic*, October 1959: 38–44.

Bourne's heir apparent) who, as Dewey once had, waxed eloquent about the possibilities that war afforded for democratic reconstruction at home and abroad, defended the use of war technique as an efficient ethical means ("a surgeon's knife"), and excoriated "passivist" opponents unduly squeamish about the use of force. At the same time, Dewey emerged from the twilight of idols to echo Bourne's conviction that war was the health of the antidemocratic state.[36]

Even more ironic was the manner in which Mumford and, to a greater extent, his close ally Waldo Frank (who did attack Dewey by name), couched their criticisms of Dewey in language perilously close to that of fascist intellectuals. Fascist ideology, as John Diggins has said, had little in common with Dewey's empirical naturalism, which Mumford and Frank saw as the "bitch-goddess of twentieth century totalitarianism." But it had a good deal in common with the alternatives recommended by Mumford and Frank, particularly with Frank's effusions about "the intuitive conduit to the organic real, the dynamic indwelling of man's spirit with the universe whereby alone man touches the realm of freedom that dwells within necessity." As Diggins notes, "Biological vitalism, the mystical idea of transcendence, the purity of the soil and its elemental union with nature, the theory of the organic state and the quest for community, the power of intuition and emotion, and the ultimate realization of authentic consciousness—such were the metaphysical tenets of the European Right."[37]

Dewey did not respond directly to Mumford and Frank, leaving that task to such friends as Farrell and Hook, but a reply to them was implicit in his response to Mortimer Adler, a critic who, like Mumford and Frank, charged Dewey with the moral disarmament of American culture in the face of the fascist threat. Adler was one of the few individuals whom Dewey might be said to have intensely disliked. A student of Dewey's at Columbia in the twenties, Adler had developed an immediate aversion to pragmatism and was, by his own admission, "an objectionable student, in some respects perhaps repulsive." In the thirties Adler moved on to the University of Chicago, where he served as President Hutchins's right-hand man in his controversial crusade to reorganize the college curriculum around the study of the "Great

---

36. Mumford, "The Aftermath of Utopianism" (1941), in Mumford, *Values for Survival* (New York: Harcourt Brace, 1946), p. 63.

37. John P. Diggins, *Mussolini and Fascism: The View from America* (Princeton: Princeton University Press, 1972), p. 448; Waldo Frank, "Our Guilt in Fascism," *New Republic*, 6 May 1940: 606. See also Archibald MacLeish, "The Irresponsibles," *Nation*, 18 May 1940: 618–623.

Books." Hutchins and Adler singled out empirical naturalism, of both the pragmatic and positivist varieties, as the principal enemy of their program, which was grounded in a metaphysical absolutism often termed "neo-Aristotelian" but which owed more to Saint Thomas Aquinas than to Aristotle.[38]

In his review of Hutchins's *Higher Learning in America* (1936), Dewey had applauded his criticisms of the disarray of American higher education but had taken issue with his reform program principally because it was rooted in a potentially authoritarian metaphysics positing "ultimate first principles" that would be imparted to students via the classic texts of Western philosophy. "There is implicit in every assertion of fixed and eternal first truths," Dewey said, "the necessity for some *human* authority to decide, in this world of conflicts, just what these truths are and how they shall be taught," and in his book Hutchins had "completely evaded the problem of who is to determine the definite truths that constitute the hierarchy." While he would not want to say Hutchins had "any sympathy with fascism," Dewey concluded nonetheless that "his idea as to the proper course to be taken is akin to the distrust of freedom and the consequent appeal to *some* fixed authority that is now overrunning the world."[39]

Hutchins responded to Dewey's review with a lawyerlike brief that again evaded the central issue Dewey had raised about his thinking, a response that led Dewey to ask Hutchins's forgiveness "if I took his book too seriously." But there were serious issues at stake here, and in 1940 Adler, who did not doubt his ability to enlighten others about where absolute truth lay, revitalized the debate Dewey had tried to initiate in 1937 by turning the tables on Dewey and arguing that it was not Hutchins but Dewey who was giving aid and comfort to fascism. In a widely publicized speech titled "God and the Professors," delivered at a Conference on Science, Philosophy, and Religion in New York in September 1940, Adler charged that Dewey and other "positivists" had left Western civilization bereft of the absolute values it required to mount resistance to the Nazis. "The most serious threat to Democracy," he intoned, "is the positivism of the professors, which dominates every

38. Mortimer J. Adler, *Philosopher at Large: An Intellectual Autobiography* (New York: Macmillan, 1977), pp. 25, 27–29, 49. See the excellent discussion of the collaboration of Hutchins and Adler in James Sloan Allen, *The Romance of Commerce and Culture: Capitalism, Modernism, and the Chicago-Aspen Crusade for Cultural Reform* (Chicago: University of Chicago Press, 1983), pp. 78–109. On Dewey's dislike of Adler see Sidney Hook, *Pragmatism and the Tragic Sense of Life* (New York: Basic Books, 1974), pp. 105–106.

39. "President Hutchins' Proposals to Remake Higher Education," p. 400.

aspect of modern education and is the central corruption of modern culture. Democracy has much more to fear from the mentality of its teachers than from the nihilism of Hitler." Until Dewey and his ilk were "liquidated," Adler advised, "the resolution of modern problems—a resolution which history demands shall be made—will not even begin."[40]

Dewey let Hook, who was a commentator at the conference, shoulder the burden of an immediate response to Adler, but the charges were so inflammatory that he could not himself remain silent despite his weariness and a rare bout of ill health. He took up the polemic and the broader issues it raised more than a year later in a speech at Cooper Union in New York, a speech delivered, as it happened, on 7 December 1941.[41]

In this address, "Lessons from the War—in Philosophy," Dewey argued that the chief lesson of the war for philosophers was not that empirical naturalism was morally bankrupt but that the world had suffered from the inability of empirical naturalism to extend its influence beyond the natural sciences and make its riches more broadly available. Because naturalism had yet to win the terrain of ethics as well as that of science from transcendental absolutism the door was open to totalitarian amalgams that conjoined premodern moral absolutism to the technical and technological accomplishments of science. Modern philosophy had "been modern in only a half-hearted way," and what was required was not a return to medieval ways of thinking, as Adler proposed, but a wholehearted modernism that would render judgments of value scientific in the fashion Dewey had outlined over the course of his career.[42]

Such a philosophy, Dewey noted, would be content with what Adler sneeringly termed "merely the certainty that now exists in physics and chemistry." To ask for more was to risk the authoritarianism of which fascism was but the most recent example:

The claim to possession of absolute truths, and of final, unalterable standards might be practically harmless, it might conceivably be even a

40. Robert Hutchins, "Grammar, Rhetoric, and Mr. Dewey" (1937), *Later Works* 11:592–597; JD, "The Higher Learning in America" (1937), *Later Works* 11:402–407; Mortimer J. Adler, "God and the Professors," *Vital Speeches*, 1 December 1940: 100, 102. See also Adler, "This Pre-War Generation," *Harper's*, October 1940: 524–534, and "The Chicago School," *Harper's*, September 1941: 377–388.

41. See Sidney Hook, "The New Medievalism," *New Republic*, 28 October 1940: 602–606.

42. "Lessons from the War—in Philosophy" (1941), *Later Works* 14:327.

boon, if everybody had the same set of absolute truths and standards, or if there were in existence some method by which differences could be amicably ironed out and men brought to agreement. What upholders of absolute principles always forget is the vulnerability of their implicit assumption that the principles which *they* advance are *the* absolute principles which any can accept. The claim to possession of first and final truths is, in short, an appeal to final arbitrament by force. For when the claim to possession of the truths by which life should be directed is asserted to have its origin outside of anything in actual experience, and when the claim is asserted to be incapable of being tested by anything in experience, and nevertheless different systems are asserted to possess ultimate truth, there is no reasonable, no practicable way of negotiating their differences. Stark and absolute opposition and conflict covers the whole situation. The only way out is trial by force, the result of which will give the side having superior force the ability to impose acceptance of its dogmas, at least for as long a time as it has superior forces.

Absolutism bred a head-bashing ethics. If an American like Adler could call for the liquidation of those who had abandoned absolute truth, Dewey wryly observed, then "I don't know why Germans shouldn't feel that as the great representatives of idealism that they should be entitled to bring it, rather forcibly if need be, to the attention of people who had gone off for lower things."[43]

But if Dewey reserved his sharpest barbs for Adler and other absolutists, he did not go lightly on his fellow empirical naturalists, particularly the positivists with whom Adler and others insisted on lumping him. For, as he had warned, Adler and his allies could be said to have filled a vacuum for which the positivists, with their repudiation of a role for science in ethical judgment, could be held partially responsible. In positivism "the difficult but urgent problem, of whether emotional charges that are not warranted can possibly be replaced by desires that are linked up with our best knowledge is evaded." Yet there was no more important problem for philosophers to confront, for "this is the problem which we are compelled to face if we ask whether human behavior is capable of being directed by other means than either superior force, external authority, uncriticized customs, or sheer emotional outbursts not controlled by authenticated ideas."[44]

Dewey reiterated his critique of moral absolutism and renewed his

43. Ibid., pp. 321–322, 332. See also "Challenge to Liberal Thought" (1944), *Later Works* 15:261–275.
44. Ibid., p. 325.

call for a "modern" response to fascism in 1942 in "The One-World of Hitler's National Socialism," a lengthy introduction to a new edition of *German Philosophy and Politics*, and also provided there his most extended discussion of German fascism. The point of this discussion, while not minimizing the distinctiveness of Hitler's ideology, was to link Nazism to the idealist tradition Dewey had held substantially accountable for German militarism during World War I. "Only a prepared soil and a highly favorable climate of opinion could have brought to fruition the seeds which Hitler sowed," he said. "It is reasonable to hold that absence of direct channels of influence [of the established philosophical tradition of Germany] but points the more unerringly to a kind of preestablished harmony between the attitudes of belief in which Germans had been indoctrinated and the terms of the Hitler appeal:—terms whose adaptation to the state of German mentality must be judged by the triumph they speedily achieved." Hitler was a brilliant opportunist, who had "aroused hopes and desires that accorded with the basic beliefs of every section of the German people, without display of ideas of an openly philosophical kind."[45]

Although Hitler glorified brute force and one could not overlook this aspect of his regime, Dewey stressed Hitler's own emphasis on the need to subordinate force to "spiritual" ideals. "Hitler has a truly Germanic devotion to a *Weltanschauung*" (OW, 426). He was like Hegel (though in a profoundly different fashion) trying to overcome the Kantian dualism of real and ideal. "Hitler's philosophy, or world-outlook, is that the identity of the ideal with hard fact may be effected here and now, by means of combining faith in the ideal to which destiny has called the German people with force which is thoroughly organized to control every aspect of life, economic, cultural, artistic, educational, as well as military and political" (OW, 430).

Hitler's *Weltanschauung* posed an especially difficult challenge for democrats. The German dictator had taken the democratic ideals of "personality" and "community" and made them the basis of an authoritarian state. The perverse mass politics of fascism, Dewey observed (drawing on the work of Karl Mannheim), gave "the democratic way of life a significance it never had before." Hitler had "inverted democracy" by brutally imposing social unity from above, a method that stood in dramatic contrast to the methods of democratic consensus building from below (OW, 440). Those committed to democracy, he advised,

45. "The One-World of Hitler's National Socialism" (1942), *Middle Works* 8:421–422, 423. Page numbers for further references (OW) appear in the text.

"now have to demonstrate that its method of attaining social unity, both within the nation and between nations, is as superior to the Hitlerian method of violent suppression as the better elements of human nature are superior to the baser elements which Hitler first appealed to and then organized with true German thoroughness."[46]

Americans who, like Adler, sought to fight Hitler by grounding democracy in a competing set of moral absolutes were playing Hitler's game and could only hope their battalions were stronger. Positivists who retired from the field of battle without a fight were indeed, as Archibald MacLeish charged, "irresponsibles." But Dewey believed these were not the only alternatives. "As yet," he said, "we have no adequately developed American philosophy, because we have not as yet made articulate the methods and aims of the democratic way of life" (OW, 444). A philosophy that formulated those methods and aims would be one that "acknowledges the primacy of communication in alliance with those processes of patient extensive observation and constant experimental test which are the human and social significance of science" (OW, 444). Such a philosophy would root democracy in reasonable conviction if not rational certainty. It would, moreover, commit Americans and others willing to venture this uncommon reading of the American way to "unceasing effort to break down the walls of class, of unequal opportunity, of color, race, sect, and nationality, which estrange human beings from one another" (OW, 446). This philosophy, of course, was the one for which Dewey had been arguing since well before the last time the civilized world had plunged into the slaughter of world war.

THE CHALLENGE OF REINHOLD NIEBUHR

By the early forties it was already clear not only that *Liberalism and Social Action* would not mean to the twentieth century what *The Communist Manifesto* had meant to the nineteenth but also that Dewey was steadily losing ground in his effort to lead merely the reconstruction of modern American liberalism to a charismatic competitor from a few blocks uptown: Reinhold Niebuhr. Niebuhr's rise to preeminence among American liberals was, to a considerable degree, built on his

46. "Foreword to Revised Edition," *German Philosophy and Politics* (New York: G. P. Putnam's Sons, 1942), p. 6. For an elaboration Dewey's appreciative response to Mannheim's work (pp. 5–6) see "The Techniques of Reconstruction, Review of Karl Mannheim's *Man and Society in an Age of Reconstruction*" (1940), *Later Works* 14:293–294.

criticisms of Dewey, who served as the principal foil to his "liberal realism" in its formative stages.

Like the Bourne-Dewey confrontation, the Niebuhr-Dewey clash (which was also absent much direct engagement between the principals) has become a staple in the textbook diet of recent intellectual history, providing, it is often said, a sharp contrast of perspectives by which to define a critical moment in the course of American social thought. Just as radicals have taken Bourne's break with Dewey as a pivotal moment in the history of their critique of the merely technical rationality of corporate liberalism, so liberals have taken Niebuhr's scornful repudiation of Deweyan "optimism" as a decisive contribution to the maturation of a responsible liberal world view. But what is often overlooked in the latter instance, as in the former, is the degree to which Niebuhr's criticisms were advanced from within a set of assumptions and commitments he shared with Dewey. (Common ground, it should be said, overlooked not only by many historians but, usually, by Niebuhr and Dewey themselves). Many, if not all, of the supposedly irreconcilable differences between Niebuhr and Dewey were differences of emphasis. In the end, these mattered a great deal in the development of liberal-democratic thought, but this importance should not obscure their nature.[47]

Niebuhr first forcefully broached his disagreements with Dewey in *Moral Man and Immoral Society* (1932), and this critique may well have come as something of a surprise to the philosopher, for the two men had marched through the twenties pretty much in lockstep. Dewey and the young rising star among liberal Protestant intellectuals supported many of the same causes, wrote for many of the same journals, joined the same organizations, shared similar hopes for an "American" socialism, and found friends and political allies in the same network of activists. As pastor of Bethel Church in Detroit, Niebuhr had captured national attention with his sharp criticisms of Henry Ford, and when he left his pulpit there in 1928 for a professorship of Christian ethics at Union Theological Seminary, Dewey had every reason to believe that he had acquired a neighbor with whom he could make common cause.

47. Arthur Schlesinger, Jr., has done more than anyone else to establish the conventional view of Niebuhr's criticisms of Dewey and to claim for him a crucial role in the development of a more realistic American liberalism. See especially his "Reinhold Niebuhr's Role in American Political Thought and Life," in Charles W. Kegley and Robert W. Bretall, *Reinhold Niebuhr: His Religious, Social, and Political Thought* (New York: Macmillan, 1956), pp. 124–150. For a typical textbook account of the Niebuhr-Dewey debate see Bernard Bailyn et al., *The Great Republic* (Lexington, Mass.: D. C. Heath, 1974), pp. 1151–1152. The work of Richard W. Fox cited below is the best corrective.

Indeed, shortly before the appearance of *Moral Man and Immoral Society* in the fall of 1932, Dewey was a featured speaker at a campaign banquet for supporters of Niebuhr's candidacy for Congress on the Socialist party ticket.[48]

Moral Man and Immoral Society, Niebuhr's sharp indictment of the sentimentalism of both secular and religious liberalism, set the mold for his treatment of Dewey, a mold that, despite Dewey's protests, would never be broken. The book, Niebuhr said, was a polemic against moralists "who imagine that the egoism of individuals is being progressively checked by the development of rationality or the growth of a religiously inspired goodwill and that nothing but the continuance of this process is necessary to establish social harmony between all the human societies and collectivities." Dewey was singled out as a leader of such moralists, a sunny exponent of the inevitable triumph of human intelligence who lacked any appreciation of "predatory self-interest" and who attributed social conservatism solely to ignorance. Dewey, Niebuhr charged, had failed to understand "the brutal character of the behavior of all human collectives, and the power of self-interest and collective egoism in all intergroup relations." Consequently, he could not appreciate that "relations between groups must therefore always be predominantly political rather than ethical, that is, they will be determined by the proportion of power which each group possesses at least as much as by any rational and moral appraisal of the comparative needs and claims of each group." Conscience and reason could qualify a struggle for power but they could not abolish it. "Conflict is inevitable, and in this conflict power must be challenged by power."[49]

Flexing the muscular, Marxist-sounding rhetoric he favored in the early thirties, Niebuhr declared that capitalism was dying and the only remaining question was how it would finally expire. One thing certain was that capitalists would not commit suicide as he claimed Dewey and other liberals believed. "Those who still regard this as possible are rationalists and moralists who have only a slight understanding of the stubborn inertia and blindness of collective egoism." In a thinly veiled swipe at what he now regarded as the hopelessly bourgeois League for Independent Political Action, Niebuhr declared that "liberalism in politics is a spent force" and "futile will be the efforts of liberals who stand to the left of Mr. Roosevelt and who hope to organize a party which will give the feverish American patient pills of diluted socialism coated with

48. Richard Fox, *Reinhold Niebuhr: A Biography* (New York: Pantheon, 1985), p. 135.
49. Reinhold Niebuhr, *Moral Man and Immoral Society* (New York: Scribners, 1932), pp. xii–xv, xx, xxiii.

liberalism, in the hope that his aversion to bitter pills will thus be cir-
cumvented." What American workers required was less the disinterested social intelligence Dewey advocated than morale, and "morale
is created by the right dogmas, symbols, and emotionally potent
oversimplifications."[50]

In his only public response to Niebuhr, Dewey objected vigorously in
a couple of articles published in 1933 and 1934 to Niebuhr's caricature
of his thinking in *Moral Man and Immoral Society* and elsewhere. He
readily admitted that intelligence in itself was powerless; he had never
claimed otherwise. "Intelligence has no power *per se*." It became powerful "only as it is integrated into some system of wants, of effective
demands." Dewey was not the sort of rationalist Niebuhr was attacking,
the sort of rationalist who rested his hopes on self-sufficient reason.
Indeed, he had himself long been a critic of such rationalism, which
separated intelligence and action and conceived of action as "a merely
external expression" of reason. "If I held that notion of intelligence,"
he said, "I should more than agree with the critics who doubt that
intelligence has any particular role in bringing about needed social
change." This notion held that knowledge came first, a notion completely at odds with Dewey's conception of the mediating function of
thought in both individual and social experience and contrary to his
notion of human beings as "thinking desire." Niebuhr, he contended,
had criticized him "on the basis of attributing to me the very idea that I
have been concerned to overthrow."[51]

By the thirties, Dewey was not arguing for "social intelligence" as an
alternative to politics but for a radical politics that incorporated social
intelligence into its practice. Although at an earlier stage in Dewey's
career Niebuhr's contention that he hoped to persuade the powerful to
admit the injustice of their rule and to relinquish their power might
have had some force, by the early thirties it was misplaced. Dewey's call
for an "intelligent" politics was not a plea to the oppressed to abandon
the effort to match power with power in favor of reasoning with the
"dominant economic interests" but rather an appeal to them to wage

50. Niebuhr, "After Capitalism—What?" *World Tomorrow*, 1 March 1933: 203–205;
Moral Man, p. xv.
51. "Intelligence and Power" (1934), *Later Works* 9:109–110. Here Dewey noted that
the only textual evidence of his thinking Niebuhr offered in *Moral Man and Immoral
Society* (xiii) was a very poor reading of a 1931 essay on "Science and Society" (*Later Works*
6:53–63), but he might also have complained that Niebuhr's quotation from this article
was an ellipse-filled, cobbled affair to which Niebuhr had added words like "then" to
make it appear that one phrase followed another in a fashion decidedly at odds with
Dewey's meaning.

their struggles intelligently. It was not disinterested intelligence but "interested" intelligence, tied to democratic interests, that he hoped to foster. "Dominant interest is never the exclusive interest that exists—not when there is a struggle taking place," he observed. "The real problem is whether there are strong interests now active which can best succeed by adopting the method of experimental intelligence into their struggles, or whether they too should rely upon the use of methods that have brought the world to its present estate, only using them the other way around." Intelligent politics entailed "the method of considering, on the one hand, urgent needs and ills and measures which will cope with them, and, on the other hand, of forming an idea of the kind of society we desire to bring into existence, which will give continuity of direction to political effort." As the latter suggests, Dewey advocated a politics guided by moral conviction—inclusive ideal ends that "vanquished" the self—as well as intelligence. Moreover, as he said, even if his faith in intelligent method was an illusion, it might be partially realized if resolutely believed (as Niebuhr said such illusions often were) and "illusion for illusion, this particular one may be better than those upon which humanity has usually depended."[52]

Dewey's protests were unavailing. Niebuhr continued to view him as a rationalist squeamish about power and unwilling to face up to the need for a realistic politics if the socialist vision they shared was to be realized. Reviewing *Liberalism and Social Action* in 1935, Niebuhr approvingly cited Dewey's worries about violent means to social change but at the same time criticized him for seeing "violence only as a consequence of a social ignorance which a more perfect intelligence will be able to eliminate." As Niebuhr read him, Dewey expected to "soothe the savage breast of an imperiled and frantic oligarchy" by means of sweet reason. But if violence was to be avoided, Niebuhr declared, radicals must rely less on intelligence and more on "securing some modicum of political cooperation between the industrial workers, the farmers, and the lower middle classes." This, of course, was precisely Dewey's politics, and in 1935 he remained a good deal more committed to it than Niebuhr.[53]

After 1935 Niebuhr's political concerns shifted with the growing menace of fascism, and his thinking and activism focused less on securing justice for the working class within industrial capitalist societies and more on defending more or less democratic societies from the total-

---

52. Ibid., pp. 109, 108; "Unity and Progress" (1933), *Later Works* 9:73.
53. Niebuhr, "The Pathos of Liberalism," *Nation*, 11 September 1935: 304.

itarian threat. He abandoned Marxist formulations and began to center his attention on conflicts between nations and on the social cohesion necessary for democratic nations to protect their interests. Having once declared that liberalism was spent, he now called for a new liberalism, revitalized by a stiff dose of "political realism." In the late thirties, he joined Mumford and Frank in the leadership of interventionist intellectuals, though he was critical of what he regarded as their nostalgic quest for a more organic culture. In this context, he renewed his tendentious attack on Dewey. Delivering his Gifford Lectures as Nazi bombs fell on nearby Edinburgh neighborhoods, Niebuhr sharply rebuked Dewey for naively seeking "a secure place for disinterested intelligence above the flux of process"—a thorough misunderstanding of Dewey's work which might have been easily corrected by a cursory reading of *his* Gifford Lectures.[54]

If Niebuhr continued to use Dewey as a whipping boy, Dewey more or less ignored Niebuhr after 1935, particularly after the latter's work took a theological turn in the mid-thirties. He turned the chores of defending Deweyan pragmatism from Niebuhr's distortions to others, principally Hook, and contented himself with general indictments of various practitioners of "anti-naturalism in extremis," among whom he apparently included Niebuhr. This delegation was unfortunate because Hook, a considerably more "scientistic" thinker than his mentor, was not as alert as he might have been to the affinities between Niebuhr's theology and Dewey's metaphysics.[55]

Niebuhr himself had suggested such affinities in his brief review of Dewey's *A Common Faith*, though he did not do much himself to explore them further. Dewey's faith, his natural piety, Niebuhr said, was "the kind of faith which prophetic religion has tried to express mythically and symbolically." Niebuhr was no supernaturalist. "God is not a separate existence," he said, "but the ground of existence." Despite the neo-

---

54. Niebuhr, *The Nature and Destiny of Man* (New York: Scribners, 1946), 1:111. On Niebuhr's political trajectory see Richard W. Fox, "Reinhold Niebuhr and the Emergence of the Liberal Realist Faith, 1930–1945," *Review of Politics* 38 (1976): 250, 256, and Fox, *Reinhold Niebuhr*, pp. 193–223. It is exhausting just to read in Fox's biography about Niebuhr's burdensome schedule of teaching, traveling, lecturing, and other public appearances and activities, and it is little wonder that he rarely found the time for careful reading of the work of others, though, in Dewey's case at least, this did not deter him from making pronouncements about its shortcomings.

55. See Sidney Hook, "Social Change and Original Sin: Answer to Niebuhr," *New Leader*, 8 November 1941: 5, 7; Hook, "The New Failure of Nerve," *Partisan Review* 10 (January-February 1943): 2–23; "Anti-Naturalism in Extremis" (1943), *Later Works* 15:46–62; JD to Robert Daniels, 17 November 1947, in "Letters of John Dewey to Robert V. Daniels, 1946–1950," *Journal of the History of Ideas* 20 (1959): 571.

orthodox label that was attached to him, Niebuhr remained, for all his criticisms of liberal sentimentalism, a liberal theologian. No one recognized this better than H. Richard Niebuhr, one of his severest critics. "You think of religion as a power—dangerous sometimes, helpful sometimes," he wrote his brother. "That's liberal. . . . You're speaking of humanistic religion so far as I can see. You come close to breaking with it at times but you don't quite do it." Despite his insistence on a suprahuman God, Reinhold Niebuhr was nearly as anthropocentric in his concerns as Dewey. Both were fixated on the "nature and destiny of man," and, for Niebuhr, Christian beliefs were not literal but "mythic" truths that offered profound insight into the human condition. Moreover, though Niebuhr believed in absolute truth, this was God's truth and was not available to man. "The truth, as it is contained in the Christian revelation, includes the recognition that it is neither possible for man to know the truth fully nor to avoid the error of pretending that he does." Niebuhr had as much contempt as Dewey for the pretense of those who claimed access to divine truth, and when it came to human knowledge, he was as certain as Dewey of its uncertainty. Niebuhr had cut his teeth intellectually at Yale Divinity School on William James, and though Edward Purcell may go too far in saying that Niebuhr's theology was "a Christian restatement of William James's pragmatism," Niebuhr shared far more with James and Dewey and other naturalists than with the antinaturalists Dewey and Hook attacked for their "failure of nerve." Although Dewey's thinking could never be wholly reconciled with that of any theologian, the differences that divided Dewey and Niebuhr were far more akin to those that separated Dewey and James than those that set Dewey at odds with the likes of Mortimer Adler.[56]

Dewey was not an optimist and Niebuhr was not a pessimist. Both made a point of distinguishing their position from each of these views of human destiny. Each, albeit in very different language, advanced a view of experience and nature which warned against both the pride and arrogance of optimism and the despair and abasement of pessim-

56. Niebuhr, "A Footnote on Religion," *Nation*, 26 September 1934: 358; Niebuhr, *Nature and Destiny of Man*, 2:217; Edward A. Purcell, Jr., *The Crisis of Democratic Theory: Scientific Naturalism and the Problem of Value* (Lexington: University of Kentucky Press, 1973), p. 243. Richard Niebuhr's letter to his brother is quoted in Fox, *Reinhold Niebuhr*, p. 145. One of the best things about this remarkable biography is its exploration of the complex relationship between the Niebuhr brothers. See also Fox, "The Niebuhr Brothers and the Liberal Protestant Heritage," in Michael Lacey, ed., *Religion and Twentieth-Century American Intellectual Life* (New York: Cambridge University Press, 1989), pp. 94–115.

ism. Both were members of the party of humility and faith. Dewey no less than Niebuhr could caution that "humility is more demanded at our moments of triumph than at those of failure" and advise "a sense of our dependence upon forces that go their way without our wish and plan." And Niebuhr no less than Dewey could declare his faith in an ethical ideal that tightly wedded self-realization and community. "By the responsibilities which men have to their family and community and to many common enterprises," he said, "they are drawn out of themselves to become their true selves."[57]

At bottom, the most significant difference between Dewey and Niebuhr was the difference of emphasis each placed on the various elements of this common view of the possibilities and limits of the moral life and of a shared understanding of the task of cultural criticism and politics. As Niebuhr defined this understanding, the task was one of

> analysing the moral resources and limitations of human nature, of tracing their consequences and cumulative effect in the life of human groups and of weighing political strategies in the light of the ascertained facts. The ultimate purpose of this task is to find political methods which will offer the most promise of achieving an ethical social goal for society. Such methods must always be judged by two criteria: 1. Do they do justice to the moral resources and possibilities in human nature and provide for the exploitation of every latent moral capacity in man? 2. Do they take account of the limitations of human nature, particularly those which manifest themselves in man's collective behavior?

By these lights, Dewey's philosophy emphasized the moral resources and slighted the limitations of human nature, and Niebuhr's philosophy was weighted in the opposite fashion. Niebuhr found that man "constitutionally corrupts his purest visions of disinterested justice," while Dewey asked why he had "to believe that every man is born a sonofabitch even before he acts like one, and regardless of why and how he becomes one?" Dewey worried more about despair than arrogance and Niebuhr more about arrogance than despair. Dewey spoke of God to comfort his readers; Niebuhr spoke of God to discomfort his. If Dewey flirted with sentimentalism about what might be, Niebuhr flirted with complacency about what must be, and neither, at his best, succumbed to these temptations.[58]

57. *Human Nature and Conduct* (1922), *Middle Works* 14:200; Niebuhr, *The Children of Light and the Children of Darkness* (New York: Scribners, 1944), p. 56.
58. Niebuhr, *Moral Man and Immoral Society*, pp. xxiv–xxv; Niebuhr, *Nature and Destiny*

But these differences, though less momentous than those posited in the conventional accounts of Niebuhr's slaying of Dewey, were nonetheless of considerable moment for American democratic theory. For Dewey and Niebuhr were not always at their best, and nowhere was Niebuhr's flirtation with complacency more evident than in the democratic ideal he began to advance in the mid-forties, an ideal not only less expansive than Dewey's but one that, as Richard Fox has said, expunged from his own thought "the prophetic, critical, and self-critical element that had been one of its central features in the thirties." Concerned during the war about what he termed "the excessively optimistic estimates of human nature and of human history with which the democratic credo has been historically associated," Niebuhr offered a more "realistic" reading of the virtues of democracy which neglected any connection it might have with the "moral resources and possibilities of human nature" and recommended it principally as a prophylactic against the abuse of power. The best thing that could be said about democracy in this view, he said, was that it placed "checks upon the power of the ruler and administrator and thus prevent it from becoming vexatious." In a judgment that, as Fox says, would have appalled the author of *Moral Man and Immoral Society*, Niebuhr declared in 1943 that in democracies like that of the United States "there is such a constant shift in the oligarchy, both in the political and economic sphere, through pressure from below that the oligarchy is kept fluid," so fluid that the "concept of elite does not really apply." Moreover, justice was secured in democratic societies not only by the circulation of elites but by competition between them, "by tension between various oligarchies." By the mid-forties the radical prophet had become a liberal pluralist, lending his support to the corporate order of countervailing powers which was crystallizing during World War II.[59]

The striking thing about Niebuhr's argument for democracy in such books as *The Children of Light and the Children of Darkness* (which established him as an early member of the club C. Wright Mills would term the "balancing boys") was not only that it was shortsighted as a description of American society, but that, as an ideal, it stripped democracy of most of its moral implications and reduced it to little more than a mechanical equilibrium of power. Moreover, by implicitly identifying

---

of Man, 1:110; Dewey quoted in Sidney Hook, *Out of Step: An Unquiet Life in the Twentieth Century* (New York: Harper and Row, 1987), p. 66.

59. Fox, "Niebuhr and the Emergence of the Liberal Realist Faith," p. 246; Niebuhr, *Children of Light*, pp. xii, xiv; Niebuhr, "Study in Cynicism," *Nation*, 1 May 1943: 638; Fox, *Reinhold Niebuhr*, pp. 220–221.

democracy with what he took to be the prevailing character of social and political life in the United States, Niebuhr elided description and prescription, a move that, with the onset of the Cold War, would become increasingly commonplace among American democratic theorists. Niebuhr made no small contribution to this development, for what Arthur Schlesinger, Jr., celebrated as his "penetrating reconstruction of the democratic faith" denuded that faith of much of the critical power with which Dewey had tried to clothe it. Ironically, it was Niebuhr, who constantly warned of the sin of pride, and not Dewey, the supposed innocent, who proved less reluctant to declare American democracy a sufficient success.[60]

The Task before Us

Niebuhr's growing influence among liberal intellectuals in the late forties was for Dewey but one sign of the ground he had lost or, more often, never gained. In the last years of his life, he was, as a pragmatist and a radical democrat, decidedly on the defensive, and, after World War II, his work took on much the same embattled tone it had had after the first Great War. Both among philosophers and in the larger society, he had become a figure widely honored and broadly ignored.

Commenting in 1946 on a report of the American Philosophical Association titled *Philosophy in American Education*, Dewey observed ruefully that the epistemology industry remained a healthy enterprise in his profession. Most philosophers still clung to the view that "the primary aim of philosophy is knowledge of Being or 'Reality' which is more comprehensive, fundamental, and ultimate than the knowledge which can be provided by the organs and methods at the disposal of the 'special' sciences." This was true, he noted, despite the inroads science had made in philosophy and, indeed, was often most true of those philosophers who prided themselves on the scientific character of their thinking. "The most striking fact about these modern philosophies," Dewey said, "is the extent in which they exhibit the influence of the postmedieval movements in politics, industry, and science, but without having surrendered the old, the classic view that the chief business of philosophy is search for a kind of Reality that is more fundamental and

60. C. Wright Mills, *The Power Elite* (New York: Oxford University Press, 1956), pp. 242–268; Schlesinger, "Niebuhr's Role," p. 150. On Niebuhr's impact on postwar democratic theory see Purcell, *Crisis of Democratic Theory*, pp. 243–247.

more ultimate than are or than can be the facts disclosed by the sciences." Not content with wisdom or the role as cultural critics which wisdom would afford them, philosophers continued what Dewey had long ago decided was a futile and increasingly hermetic quest for the foundations of knowledge.[61]

The forties was, as well, no time for cheery political pronouncements by radical democrats, though the situation was still fluid enough before the calcification of the Cold War to sustain a flickering hope ("I became a socialist in 1948," Michael Harrington wrote, "the last year of the thirties"). As I noted, Dewey did his best to nourish this hope. As long as he continued to live and as long as liberals and democratic socialists felt the need to memorialize his longevity, he used these birthday parties, banquets, and other such occasions to remind them of the long road to participatory democracy which remained ahead. People showed up at these affairs, *New Republic* editor Bruce Bliven remarked, expecting to comfortably salute an aged monument, only to have Dewey dress them down with a stern reminder of the evils of complacency in the face of a society still crying out for reconstruction.[62]

At one of his eightieth-birthday-party celebrations in 1939, Dewey established the pattern for the speeches he would give on similar occasions for the next decade. He admonished his audience to remember that "creative democracy" remained an ideal and not a fact of life in the United States—a "task before us." Surveying the events of his long lifetime, he noted that Americans could no longer rely on the frontier to regenerate democracy as they had in his childhood. "At the present time, the frontier is moral, not physical," he said. "The period of free lands that seemed boundless in extent has vanished. Unused resources are now human rather than material. They are found in the waste of grown men and women who are without the chance to work, and in the young men and women who find doors closed where there was once opportunity. The crisis that one hundred and fifty years ago called out social and political inventiveness is with us in a form which puts a heavier demand on human creativeness."

Reiterating the familiar themes of his social philosophy, Dewey cautioned that democracy must not be conceived narrowly as external political machinery. Rather, it must be understood to be a way of life

---

61. "Introduction to *Problems of Men*: The Problems of Men and the Present State of Philosophy" (1946), *Later Works* 15:156–157.

62. Michael Harrington, *Fragments of the Century* (New York: Simon and Schuster, 1977), p. 64; Bruce Bliven interview, spring 1975.

deep-seated in the character of individual human beings. Democracy was shaped by a "working faith in the possibilities of human nature," a belief in human equality, and a commitment to provide the conditions for the growth of every individual in a society. He pled guilty to a faith in the capacity of the "common man" for intelligent social action. He could not, as a democrat, believe otherwise:

> Democracy is a way of personal life controlled not merely by faith in human nature in general but by faith in the capacity of human beings for intelligent judgment and action if proper conditions are furnished. I have been accused more than once and from opposed quarters of an undue, a utopian, faith in the possibilities of intelligence and in education as a correlate of intelligence. At all events, I did not invent this faith. I acquired it from my surroundings as far as those surroundings were animated by the democratic spirit. . . . I am willing to leave to upholders of totalitarian states of the right and the left the view that faith in the capacities of intelligence is utopian. For the faith is so deeply embedded in the methods which are intrinsic to democracy that when a professed democrat denies the faith he convicts himself of treachery to his profession.

Admitting that much of what he had to say was little more than a set of moral commonplaces, Dewey observed that this was precisely the point. Democracy's greatest power was as a moral ideal, something obscured by the narrow conceptions of its meaning which all too often prevailed. "To get rid of the habit of thinking of democracy as something institutional and external and to acquire the habit of treating it as a way of personal life is to realize that democracy is a moral ideal and so far as it becomes a fact is a moral fact."[63]

Dewey admitted that it was difficult to conceive of the world as "homelike" after World War II. Alienation was the more ready response to the events of the recent past, and "in most practical matters there is no more widespread sense than that of insecurity." Nonetheless, it was hope not optimism that he had always counseled, and nothing had deterred his conviction that hope remained a live option. He urged philosophers to come out of their professional shell and "turn to the projection of large generous hypotheses which, if used as plans of action, will give intelligent direction to men to search for ways to make

---

63. "Creative Democracy—The Task before Us" (1939), *Later Works* 14:224–230. See also "John Dewey Responds," in Harry Laidler, ed., *John Dewey at Ninety* (New York: League for Industrial Democracy, 1950).

the world more one of worth and significance, more homelike, in fact."[64]

Dewey's own hope and energies remained unquenchable. Acknowledging that the "linguistic turn" Anglo-American philosophy had made was not without its talking points, he worked with a longtime correspondent, social philosopher Arthur Bentley, to clear up the confusions of language they believed plagued logic and the theory of knowledge, and in 1949 the fruits of their researches were published as *Knowing and the Known*. At the same time, he worked on the manuscript for a long book that was to summarize the whole of his philosophy. This manuscript was never completed, and the only copy of a near-complete draft was lost one summer in transit between the Dewey's home in Hubbards, Nova Scotia, and New York. For a couple of days thereafter Dewey was devastated by this loss, but he bounced back in typical fashion. "You know," he told a reporter, "in a way this has given me new ideas, starting over fresh again. I think I have better ideas now."[65]

As ever, Dewey did not let more abstruse philosophical matters absorb all his intelligence. He continued to rush to the defense of pragmatism from its cultured despisers, criticizing one of these, Julian Benda, for linking William James (and by implication himself) with all the unsavory figures who found it convenient to call themselves pragmatists. Like "all the large words and abstractions of our time," he noted, "pragmatism" had been abused. "After all, Hitler called himself a 'socialist,' Stalin calls himself a 'democrat,' clerical authoritarians call themselves 'humanists,' and Franco calls himself a 'Christian.'" He also remained unwavering in his support of science in the face of charges that Hiroshima gave clear evidence of its inherent evil rather than of the evil to which it might be turned. The use to which the splitting of the atom was put in the war was the product, he argued, of the more long-standing split between the "material" and the "spiritual," between science and morality against which he had contended for decades.

---

64. "Introduction to *The Problems of Men*," p. 20.

65. JD and Arthur F. Bentley, *Knowing and the Known* (Boston: Beacon Press, 1949); *New York Times*, 19 October 1949. See also *John Dewey and Arthur F. Bentley: A Philosophical Correspondence, 1932–1951*, ed. Sidney Ratner, Jules Altman, and James E. Wheeler (New Brunswick, N.J.: Rutgers University Press, 1964). Dewey also took great interest in the postwar years in the research on visual perception of Adelbert Ames, Jr., a Dartmouth physiologist, which lent empirical support to the "transactional" conception of experience which he and Bentley were articulating. See *The Morning Notes of Adelbert Ames, Jr., Including a Correspondence with John Dewey*, ed. Hadley Cantril (New Brunswick, N.J.: Rutgers University Press, 1960), pp. 171–231, and JD to Robert Daniels, 19 November 1946, in "Letters of Dewey to Daniels," p. 570.

Hence the way out of the dilemmas posed by the Bomb lay not, as some asserted, in the subjugation of science to "higher values" certified by "externally imposed authority" but rather in the "application of our best scientific procedures and results so that they will operate within, not just outside of and against, the moral values and concerns of humanity." And finally, as we have seen, Dewey remained tireless in his efforts on behalf of democratic education and the tricky task of fashioning an anticommunist socialism.[66]

But perhaps the most striking manifestations of Dewey's hope in the postwar period were his efforts to make the last years of his own life literally more homelike. In December 1946 he married Roberta Grant Lowitz, a women some forty-five years his junior whom he had known since she was a young girl, and soon thereafter the couple adopted two Belgian war orphans, John and Adrienne. Thus in his late eighties Dewey once again found himself working amid noisy, curious children (who called him "Grandpa"), a situation he had always found to favor an appreciation of the richest possibilities of human experience.

66. "William James' Morals and Julian Benda's: It Is Not Pragmatism That Is Opportunist" (1948), *Later Works* 15:19–26; "Dualism and the Split Atom" (1945), *Later Works* 15:199–203. See also "The Revolt against Science" (1945), *Later Works* 15:188–191, and "Philosophy's Future in Our Scientific Age: Never Was Its Role More Crucial," *Commentary*, October 1949: 388–394. The article on Benda and James was a response to Benda, "The Attack on Western Morality" (1947), *Later Works* 15:381–392. The exchange took place in *Commentary*.

The Wilderness and
the Promised Land

✳

JOHN DEWEY died of pneumonia on June 1, 1952, at the age of ninety-two. Although he was slowed in his last months by a broken hip—suffered while playing with his children—he remained intellectually active to the very end of his life. Only death could still his illegible typing. Dewey had not been a church member since the early 1890s, but by his own lights his faith in democracy was religious. Realizing this, Roberta Dewey held the funeral services in the nondenominational Community Church in New York City, which maintained that "the core of its faith and the purpose of its life are the realization on earth of the Beloved Community."[1]

At the time of his death, Dewey's influence as a philosopher, educator, and democrat was approaching its nadir. By the early fifties, most American philosophers had abandoned Dewey's larger ethical, social, and political concerns for narrower, more rigorous and professional puzzles of symbolic logic and language analysis. If philosophers took an interest in the "problems of men" it was not in the problems themselves but in the ways people talked about them. As one anonymous young Harvard scholar commented in 1948, philosophy had become "more and more a detailed, isolated, academic discipline." Among analytic

1. Dykhuizen, pp. 320–321. Anyone who has worked with Dewey manuscripts will testify to the accuracy of my characterization of his typing.

philosophers, as James Gouinlock has said, Dewey came to be regarded as "a nice old man who hadn't the vaguest conception of real philosophical rigor or the nature of a real philosophical problem." Not the least of Dewey's sins in this regard was his resistance to insular professionalism and his insistence that philosophy could not be and should not be conceived as a specialized body of knowledge. His postwar eclipse was forecast in a genially condescending tribute by positivist Hans Reichenbach in 1939. Dewey, Reichenbach said, had had an admirably "progressive" influence on philosophy, but "the early period of empiricism in which an all-round philosopher could dominate at the same time the fields of scientific method, of history of philosophy, of education and social philosophy, has passed. We enter into the second phase in which highly technical investigations form the indispensable instrument of research, splitting the philosophical campus into specialists of its various branches."[2]

In the last three decades, the grip of positivism and analytical philosophy on American philosophy departments has eased. The dominance of the kind of scientific philosophy Reichenbach espoused fell victim by the sixties to its own inability to explain how science worked. At the same time, some analytical philosophers, led by W. V. O. Quine, Nelson Goodman, and Wilfred Sellars (all thinkers tinged with pragmatism), began to raise troubling questions about its root dogmas. Of late, bridges have been built to various schools of Continental philosophy previously regarded as unacceptably "soft," and analytical philosophers themselves have extended the range of what they consider important problems to include substantive matters of ethics and politics. These developments have allowed those benighted souls interested in the American philosophical tradition to go about their work in an atmosphere of greater tolerance if not appreciation. Recently as well, social theorists in the United States who once felt compelled by the hegemony of positivism and analytic philosophy to look to Western Marxism for philosophical sustenance have shown some signs of returning home to give not only Dewey but other American thinkers another look, ironically joining those Europeans like Jürgen Habermas who have profitably mined the democratic vein of American pragmatism for years. The editors of *Telos*—perhaps the most slavishly Euro-

2. Bruce Kuklick, *The Rise of American Philosophy: Cambridge, Massachusetts, 1860–1930* (New Haven: Yale University Press, 1977), p. 572; James Gouinlock, *John Dewey's Philosophy of Value* (New York: Humanities Press, 1972), p. xi; Hans Reichenbach, "Dewey's Theory of Science," in Paul Schilpp, ed., *The Philosophy of John Dewey*, 2d ed. (New York: Tudor, 1951), p. 192.

centric journal of radical social thought in the United States—recently remarked that "when all is said and done, if recent chatter about civil society, liberalism, democracy and autonomy is stripped of its mystifying jargon and foreign accents, one is left with a warmed-over version of that pragmatist discourse that engaged Left American intellectuals in the 1930s. . . . Thus the intellectual task is clear. Radical thought in the U.S. has to rediscover its American roots and take it from there."[3]

No one has done more to revive interest in Dewey among American academics than Richard Rorty, "the red-white-and-blue Nietzsche," who opened *Philosophy and the Mirror of Nature* (1979), his bold dismantling of the Western philosophical tradition since Descartes, with the blunt assertion that Dewey along with Wittgenstein and Heidegger were "the three most important philosophers of our century." Since that time he has published a steady stream of essays laying out a radically historicist, "postphilosophical" position that he labels "Deweyan." This is not the place to consider fully Rorty's appropriation of Dewey, but it is worth pointing out that it is a controversial one. Positions Rorty calls "Deweyan" are often at odds with what most take to be Dewey's positions on philosophical questions, and Rorty himself sometimes openly admits that his use of "Deweyan" for purposes of self-identification is distorting if taken too literally. "Sometimes," he says, "when we think we are rediscovering the mighty dead, we are just inventing imaginary playmates."[4]

3. Juan Corradi and Paul Piccone, "Introduction," *Telos* 66 (Winter 1985–86): 3. On the recent history of American philosophy see Frederick Suppe, "The Search for Philosophic Understanding of Scientific Theories," in Suppe, ed., *The Structure of Scientific Theories*, 2d ed. (Urbana: University of Illinois Press, 1977), pp. 3–241; John Rajchman, "Philosophy in America," in Rajchman and Cornel West, eds., *Post-Analytic Philosophy* (New York: Columbia University Press, 1985), pp. ix–xxx; Cornel West, *The American Evasion of Philosophy: A Genealogy of Pragmatism* (Madison: University of Wisconsin Press, 1989), pp. 182–193. For a good overview of recent work on American philosophy see John J. McDermott, "The Renascence of Classical American Philosophy," in *Streams of Experience* (Amherst: University of Massachusetts Press, 1986), pp. 223–234. J. E. Tiles, *Dewey* (London: Routledge, 1988), provides an insightful discussion of the differences separating Dewey's thinking from that of analytic philosophers. In a recent interview Habermas remarked that, from the outset of his career, he has "viewed American pragmatism as the third productive reply to Hegel, after Marx and Kierkegaard, as the radical-democratic branch of Young Hegelianism, so to speak. Ever since, I have relied on this American version of the philosophy of praxis when the problem arises of compensating for the weaknesses of Marxism with respect to democratic theory" (*Autonomy and Solidarity: Interviews with Jürgen Habermas*, ed. Peter Dews [London: Verso, 1986], p. 151).

4. Carlin Romano, "Naughty, Naughty: Richard Rorty Makes Philosophers Squirm," *Voice Literary Supplement*, June 1987: 14; Richard Rorty, *Philosophy and the Mirror of Nature* (Princeton: Princeton University Press, 1979), p. 5; Rorty, "Dewey's Metaphysics," in *The Consequences of Pragmatism* (Minneapolis: University of Minnesota Press, 1982), chap. 5; Rorty, "Philosophy of the Oddball," *New Republic*, 19 June 1989: 38.

What Rorty likes most in Dewey's philosophy is his polemical attempt at "overcoming of the tradition," his efforts to close down the epistemology industry. What he finds peculiar or misguided are Dewey's metaphysics, logic of inquiry, and theory of valuation—his efforts to construct a persuasive naturalism on the ground he cleared as an intellectual historian. As Rorty sees it, it is thumbs up for *Reconstruction in Philosophy*, thumbs down for *Experience and Nature*. Rorty would have philosophers simply be "people who work with the history of philosophy and the contemporary effects of those ideas called 'philosophic' upon the rest of culture." Dewey thought they should be this and more. Rorty urges philosophers to abandon claims to knowledge and rest content with "edifying," "therapeutic" criticism; Dewey, while also warning sternly of the "conceit of knowledge," worried as well that philosophy that was *merely* edifying would degenerate into little more than an expression of "cloudy desire." Rorty sees philosophy as playful; Dewey insisted it was, as an *intellectualized* wish, hard work. Rorty argues that there is no need for social theorists to consider such topics as "the nature of selfhood, the motive of moral behavior, and the meaning of human life." Dewey thought that as a social theorist he had to say something about such things. "On the Deweyan view," Rorty says, "no such discipline as 'philosophical anthropology' is required as a preface to politics"; Dewey's view was quite otherwise. Rorty seeks to deconstruct philosophy; Dewey sought to reconstruct it. As Richard Bernstein has said, what Rorty slights or dismisses as "trivial" or "mistaken" in Dewey's thought is his primary concern with "the role that philosophy might play *after* one had been liberated from the obsessions and tyrannies of the 'problems of philosophy.'" Perhaps the best way to sum up briefly the differences separating Dewey and Rorty as philosophers is to say that, while both ruthlessly undercut the quest for certainty, Dewey believed effective cultural criticism still might profit from the general "ground-maps" that philosophers could provide. Finding such maps useless and unnecessary, Rorty argues for cultural criticism that flies entirely by the seat of its pants.[5]

5. Rorty, "Dewey's Metaphysics," p. 87; Rorty, "The Priority of Democracy to Philosophy," in Merrill D. Peterson and Robert C. Vaughan, eds., *The Virginia Statute for Religious Freedom* (New York: Cambridge University Press, 1988), pp. 261–262; Richard Bernstein, "Philosophy in the Conversation of Mankind" in *Philosophical Profiles* (Philadelphia: University of Pennsylvania Press, 1986), p. 48. See also Rorty, *The Consequences of Pragmatism*, Introd. and chaps. 3, 9, 11; Rorty, "Pragmatism without Method," in Paul Kurtz, ed., *Sidney Hook: Philosopher of Democracy and Humanism* (Buffalo: Prometheus Books, 1983), pp. 259–273; Rorty, "Solidarity or Objectivity?" in Rajchman and West, *Post-Analytic Philosophy*, pp. 3–19; Rorty, "Science as Solidarity," in John S. Nelson et al., eds., *The*

Pressed by critics to make clearer his moral and political commitments, Rorty has said enough of late to suggest that his "social hope" as well as his view of the responsibilities of philosophy differs significantly from Dewey's. Refusing to accept the ethical postulate conjoining self-realization and the social good which was at the heart of Dewey's ethics throughout his career, Rorty has argued for a "liberal utopia" in which there prevails a rigid division between a rich, autonomous private sphere that will enable elite "ironists" like himself to create freely the self they wish—even if that be a cruel, antidemocratic self—and a lean, egalitarian, "democratic" public life confined to the task of preventing cruelty (including that of elite ironists). For Dewey, of course, democracy was a "way of life" not merely a way of public life—an ideal that "must affect all modes of human association"—and he would not have accepted Rorty's contention that "there is no way to bring self-creation together with justice at the level of theory" for that would have required him to give up a principle article of his democratic faith. Rorty contends that the belief that "the springs of private fulfillment and of human solidarity are the same" is a bothersome Platonic or Christian hangover. If so, Dewey suffered from it.[6]

But even if we grant Rorty a halfway covenant with Dewey, what little he has said about the norms he would have guide public life suggests that he is far too enamored of a strictly negative conception of liberty and too deaf to the appeal of fraternity to claim the Deweyan label even in this sphere. For Rorty, liberal-democratic politics involves little more than making sure that individuals hurt one another as little as possible and interfere minimally in the private life of each. There is little in his social or political vision of the communitarian side of Dewey's thinking, noth-

Rhetoric of the Human Sciences: Language and Argument in Scholarship and Public Affairs (Madison: University of Wisconsin Press, 1988), pp. 38–52. Other critical responses to Rorty's interpretation and use of Dewey include Garry Brodsky, "Rorty's Interpretation of Pragmatism," *Transactions of the Charles S. Peirce Society* 18 (1982): 311–337; James Campbell, "Rorty's Use of Dewey," *Southern Journal of Philosophy* 22 (1984): 175–187; Thomas M. Jeannot, "On Co-opting Pragmatism in the Debate about Foundations: Dewey, Rorty and Whitehead," *Transactions of the Charles S. Peirce Society* 23 (1987): 263–288; Konstantin Kolenda, "Rorty's Dewey," *Journal of Value Inquiry* 20 (1986): 57–62; John J. McDermott, R. W. Sleeper, Abraham Edel, and Richard Rorty, "Symposium on Rorty's *Consequences of Pragmatism*," *Transactions of the Charles S. Peirce Society* 21 (1985): 1–48; R. W. Sleeper, *The Necessity of Pragmatism: John Dewey's Conception of Philosophy* (New Haven: Yale University Press, 1986), pp. 1–2, 7–8, 107–109, 132–133, 189; West, *American Evasion of Philosophy*, pp. 194–210, and James Gouinlock, "What Is the Legacy of Instrumentalism? Rorty's Interpretation of Dewey," *Journal of the History of Philosophy* 28 (1990): 251–269.

6. Rorty, *Contingency, Irony, Solidarity* (New York: Cambridge University Press, 1989), pp. xiii–xiv, 73–95, 120.

ing of Dewey's veneration of *shared* experience. Rorty argues for the centrality of solidarity in public life, but his is an extremely thin solidarity, amounting to little more than a common aversion to pain and humiliation and explicitly not "a common possession or a shared power." It is simply dead wrong to read Dewey's liberalism, as Rorty has done, as celebrating a politics centered on "our ability to leave people alone." Rorty—the self-proclaimed "postmodernist bourgeois liberal"—seems not to have fully grasped the essentials of Dewey's social philosophy, for, had he done so, it is difficult to see how he could arrive at the conclusion that a Deweyan liberalism could be either postmodernist or bourgeois. Yet here his identification of his views with those of Dewey has been even more unqualified than in his critique of the conventional epistemological concerns of philosophers. All this is not to gainsay the salutary influence Rorty has had in bringing Dewey back into view. Nor is it to deny the rich rewards that reading Rorty can bring. But it is to worry that Rorty will convince his readers that Deweyan and Rortyean philosophy amount to pretty much the same thing.[7]

If philosophers largely ignored Dewey's work after World War II, others were even less charitable. Dewey's philosophy of education came under heavy attack in the fifties from the opponents of progressive education, who took him to task for virtually everything that was wrong with the American public school system. Although his actual impact on American schools was quite limited, Dewey proved a convenient symbol of opprobrium for "fundamentalists" worried about the decline of intellectual standards in the schools and the threat this posed to a nation at Cold War with communism. Following the launching of the Russian

---

7. See Rorty, *Contingency, Irony, and Solidarity*, p. 91; "Priority of Democracy to Philosophy," p. 273; Rorty, "Postmodernist Bourgeois Liberalism" in Robert Hollinger, ed., *Hermeneutics and Praxis* (Notre Dame, Ind.: University of Notre Dame Press, 1985), pp. 214–221; Rorty, "On Ethnocentrism: A Reply to Clifford Geertz," *Michigan Quarterly Review* 25 (1986): 525–534; Rorty, "That Old-Time Philosophy," *New Republic*, 4 April 1988: 28–33; Rorty, "Education without Dogma," *Dissent*, Spring 1989: 198–204. Richard Bernstein has countered Rorty's understanding of "Deweyan" politics with an alternative close to my own. See "John Dewey on Democracy: The Task before Us," in *Philosophical Profiles*, pp. 260–272; "Rorty's Liberal Utopia," *Social Research* 57 (1990): 31–72; and the exchange between him and Rorty in the symposium "Liberalism and Philosophy," in *Political Theory* 15 (1987): 538–580. Three other sharply critical recent assessments of Rorty's political thinking are Nancy Fraser, "Solidarity or Singularity?: Richard Rorty between Romanticism and Technocracy," *Praxis International* 8 (1988): 257–272; Sheldon Wolin, "Democracy in the Discourse of Postmodernism," *Social Research* 57 (1990): 5–30; and Thomas McCarthy, "Private Irony and Public Decency: Richard Rorty's New Pragmatism," *Critical Inquiry* 16 (1990): 355–370. See also the "Exchange on Truth, Freedom, and Politics" between McCarthy and Rorty in *Critical Inquiry* 16 (1990): 633–655.

space satellite Sputnik, as two historians of the fifties have said, "the already swelling outcry against the educational system became a deafening roar. Everyone joined in—the President, the Vice-President, admirals, generals, morticians, grocers, bootblacks, bootleggers, realtors, racketeers—all lamenting the fact that *we* didn't have a hunk of metal orbiting the earth and blaming this tragedy on the sinister Deweyites who had plotted to keep little Johnny from learning to read." Since the fifties, variations on this theme have become a regular, periodic feature of debate about the condition of American public education, and each new call for a return to the "basics" has brought with it some predictable Dewey-bashing. Although perhaps every public school district has at least one teacher who has read Dewey and tried to teach as he would have had her or him teach, his critics have vastly overestimated his influence. American schools remain far from the interesting and dangerous outposts of a humane civilization he would have had them be.[8]

The fifties also marked the consolidation of the triumph of realism in American democratic theory. The effort that began in the twenties to transform the meaning of democracy by constricting its participatory dimension had by the fifties succeeded in establishing the hegemony of "democratic elitism" among American liberals. Some realists attacked Dewey's social philosophy directly, but most neglected him and went straight to the task of constructing an "empirical" democratic theory in tune with what were taken to be the facts of life in a complex industrial society. In so doing, they offered, as the best of all possible worlds, a much more limited democratic ideal than Dewey would ever have been able to accept.[9]

8. Douglas T. Miller and Marion Nowak, *The Fifties* (Garden City, N.Y.: Doubleday, 1977), p. 254. On the criticism of Dewey and progressive education in the fifties see Lawrence Cremin, *The Transformation of the School* (New York: Vintage, 1961), pp. 328–353; Patricia A. Graham, *Progressive Education from Arcady to Academe: A History of the Progressive Education Association* (New York: Teachers College Press, 1967), pp. 102–127; and Robert Church and Michael Sedlak, *Education in the United States: An Interpretive History* (New York: Free Press, 1976), chap. 13. For a recent example of Dewey-bashing see Paul Q. Beeching, "Our Schools: Why They Don't Teach," *New York Times*, 25 April 1982. Dewey also takes his licks in the best-sellers of the most recent revival of concern about the sorry condition of American schools. See Allan Bloom, *The Closing of the American Mind* (New York: Simon and Schuster, 1987), pp. 56, 195; and E. D. Hirsch, Jr., *Cultural Literacy* (Boston: Houghton Mifflin, 1987), pp. xv–xvii, 19, 118–126. A good summary of the case against imputing much influence to Dewey on the practice of American education is Joe R. Burnett, "Whatever Happened to John Dewey?" *Teachers College Record* 81 (1979): 192–210.

9. For realist postmortems on Dewey's democratic theory see Arthur Bestor, "John Dewey and American Liberalism," *New Republic*, 29 August 1955: 18–19; Arthur F. Murphy, "John Dewey and American Liberalism," *Journal of Philosophy* 57 (1960): 420–

Unlike Dewey, who believed that "the world has suffered more from leaders and authorities than from the masses," realists continued to fear most the threat they believed an ignorant and irrational public posed to stable and efficient government. Unable to believe, as Dewey did, that most men and women could become active participants in the decisions shaping their lives, realists argued that decision-making power should be vested in elites who possessed the knowledge and skills to govern effectively. Societies that did so would remain democratic in that political leaders would be subject to periodic elections, at which time the masses could decide whether or not they wished to continue to be ruled by the same elites.[10]

As these comments suggest, later realists joined Walter Lippmann in conceiving of democracy in narrowly political and strictly procedural terms. For them, the power of average citizens should lie not in their direct participation in public life but in the indirect effect their votes would have on those who made policy. To remain in power, elites in a democracy had to remain responsible to the opinions of the citizenry, and hence citizens as voters retained a measure of influence without any direct participation in policy making and usually without even any direct communication with policy makers. There was a difficulty with this argument, for the realists themselves had demonstrated the effectiveness with which elites could manipulate the public opinion to which they were supposed to be responding, thereby negating the power of public desires and interests to act as independent variables in policy making. But realists attempted to avoid this difficulty by arguing that competition between elites for public support would be sufficient to prevent any one group from engineering consent. The essence of popular government, to repeat Lippmann's formulation, was "to support the Ins when things are going well; to support the Outs when things are going badly." This much, if no more, the realists believed the average citizen could handle.[11]

436; and Howard White, "The Political Faith of John Dewey," *Journal of Politics* 20 (1958): 353–367. Important contributions to democratic realism include Bernard Berelson et al., *Voting* (Chicago: University of Chicago Press, 1954); Robert Dahl, *A Preface to Democratic Theory* (Chicago: University of Chicago Press, 1956) and *Who Governs?* (New Haven: Yale University Press, 1961); V. O. Key, *Public Opinion and American Democracy* (New York: Knopf, 1961); Seymour Martin Lipset, *Political Man* (Garden City, N.Y.: Doubleday, 1960); and Henry Mayo, *An Introduction to Democratic Theory* (New York: Oxford University Press, 1960).

10. *The Public and Its Problems* (1927), *Later Works* 2:365.

11. Walter Lippmann, *The Phantom Public* (New York: Macmillan, 1925), p. 126. For a critical assessment of modern American elections as instruments of even this modest measure of democracy see my "Politics as Consumption: Managing the Modern Ameri-

For the realists, widespread political participation was not only not a necessary feature of democracy, it was also not a desirable feature. They argued that increased political participation by incompetent citizens might undermine the stability of liberal-democratic regimes by unleashing irrational passions and encouraging demagoguery, thereby destroying the peaceful competition of responsible elites which was at the heart of a realistic democracy. Widespread apathy was thus seen by some as a *functional* feature of an effective democratic polity. Participatory ideals were useful primarily for purposes of legitimation and for ensuring elite responsibility but were not to be taken seriously as ideals. As one political scientist remarked, "It is important to continue moral admonishment for citizens to become active in politics, not because we want or expect great masses of them to become active, but rather because the admonishment helps keep the system open and sustains a belief in the right of all to participate, which is an important norm governing the behavior of political elites."[12]

The realism of the late forties and fifties was different from earlier forms in its tendency to conflate description and prescription. All too often, a description of the way politics worked in the United States provided realists with their normative conception of what democracy should be. Whereas Lippmann and other realists of the twenties had been mainly concerned to open to view the gap between the reality of American politics and democratic ideals, the realists of the postwar period took this analysis one step further and, more or less consciously, tried to establish the reality of American politics as a new ideal. This conflation of the real and the ideal was most apparent in the work of students of comparative politics who used the United States as a model against which to measure the political development of other nations. This use of America as a normative concept was born of the struggle against fascism and communism, for the government of the United

---

can Election," in Richard W. Fox and T. J. Jackson Lears, eds., *The Culture of Consumption* (New York: Pantheon, 1983), pp. 143–173.

12. Lester W. Milbrath, *Political Participation* (Chicago: Rand McNally, 1965). This argument for the convenient uses of the myth of popular participation is a very old one in liberal thought. For an account of its origins see Edmund S. Morgan, *Inventing the People: The Rise of Popular Sovereignty in England and America* (New York: Norton, 1988). The notion that the masses rather than elites were the source of potential instability in democratic regimes was central to the liberal interpretation of McCarthyism, and this interpretation in turn animated democratic realism. See especially the essays in Daniel Bell, ed., *The Radical Right* (Garden City, N.Y.: Doubleday, 1964). Later studies have argued that McCarthyism was not a mass movement but an affair involving the very competing elites upon whom realists depend for stability. See Michael P. Rogin, *The Intellectuals and McCarthy: The Radical Specter* (Cambridge: M.I.T. Press, 1967).

States was the closest thing to a democratic system that liberals could find in a world beset by totalitarianism. The existing American polity became a regulative ideal for policy makers and intellectuals alike, and as such it dampened reform at home and fueled an aggressive foreign policy to make the world safe for democratic elitism. It also revealed the ease with which Americans could fall prey to the confusion of the wilderness and the promised land.[13]

Perhaps the most significant revision that democratic realists made in democratic theory was an ethical one. Not only did they narrow the issues of democracy to those of political machinery, they also continued to argue, explicitly or implicitly, that self-government was but a means to other ends. It had no value in itself, and, as means, it was to be measured against other means strictly on the grounds of efficiency. Realists were less concerned with fostering individual growth than in securing social stability, and they were willing to sacrifice a large measure of self-government to achieve this goal. The central political imperative for Dewey was to develop a society that provided the conditions for growth through participation in community life, participation he believed essential to self-realization. The central political imperative for the realists was to develop a system that was governed effectively and efficiently and retained enough participation to be relatively democratic in a world of more or less authoritarian regimes. For the realists, participatory democracy was not essential to the welfare of the public. For Dewey, it was indispensable.

During the fifties, Dewey's democratic ideals found few spokesmen. Sidney Hook remained a visible and articulate defender of his mentor, but Hook was so obsessed with the struggle against communism that he rarely turned his attention to the shortcomings of American society. Those few intellectuals who did vigorously contest democratic realism and advance a radical-democratic critique of American culture were angry outsiders such as C. Wright Mills (whose work clearly bore the stamp of Dewey's influence).[14]

13. On the conflation of description and prescription in postwar democratic theory see Edward A. Purcell, Jr., *The Crisis of Democratic Theory: Scientific Naturalism and the Problem of Value* (Lexington: University of Kentucky Press, 1973), pp. 235–272, and Raymond Seidelman, *Disenchanted Realists: Political Science and the American Crisis, 1884–1984* (Albany: State University of New York Press, 1985), chap. 5. A good guide to the theory and practice of political development is Robert A. Packenham, *Liberal America and the Third World: Political Development Ideas in Foreign Aid and Social Science* (Princeton: Princeton University Press, 1973).

14. In his doctoral thesis, *Sociology and Pragmatism* (New York: Oxford University Press, 1966), Mills was quite critical of Dewey, but nevertheless he had absorbed more of

But in the sixties a number of critics of democratic realism emerged, many of them unknowingly advancing decidedly Deweyan arguments for the revitalization of democracy as a way of life. Criticisms of the revisions the realists had made in democratic ideals and a call for a more participatory conception of democracy were heard both within the social sciences and in the larger arena of American politics. Several younger political scientists and sociologists, many of them influenced by the return of radical politics in the sixties, attacked democratic realism as a conservative ideology lending legitimacy to societies that fell far short of "moral democracy." Few statements better captured the gulf separating democratic realists and democratic radicals in the sixties than these comments by radical Jack L. Walker in an exchange with realist Robert Dahl:

> Perhaps the most significant point upon which Professor Dahl and I differ is this final question of the criteria to be used in evaluating the performance of democratic political systems. Professor Dahl places great value on the capacities of a system "for reinforcing agreement, encouraging moderation, and maintaining social peace." . . . He is part of a generation which has experienced a series of savage attacks on political democracy and his concern with political stability, in light of all that has happened, is certainly understandable. Political stability is indeed a precious commodity; I do not wish to create the impression that I reject its obvious importance. But I do think that both the discipline of political science and American society have suffered from our excessive concern with the protection and maintenance of our political system. I believe that the time has come to direct our attention to the infinitely more difficult task of involving larger and larger numbers of people in the process of government. The theory of democracy beckons us toward an ancient ideal: the liberation of the energies of all our citizens in the common pursuit of the good society.

By the end of the sixties radical democratic theory was showing signs of life in the academy. Although John Rawls's *Theory of Justice* (1971), the masterpiece that brought American political philosophy back from its deathbed, had little to say about political participation, the revival of

---

Dewey's philosophy than he perhaps cared to admit. See, for example, the discussion of masses and publics in *The Power Elite* (New York: Oxford University Press, 1956), pp. 298–324. A useful corrective in this regard is J. L. Simich and Rick Tilman, "Radicalism vs. Liberalism: C. Wright Mills' Critique of John Dewey's Ideas," *American Journal of Economics and Sociology* 37 (1978): 412–430. See also Jim Miller, "Democracy and the Intellectual: C. Wright Mills Reconsidered," *Salmagundi* 70–71 (1986): 82–101.

normative argument it initiated boded well for participatory democratic theory.[15]

Disputes over the meaning of democracy were not confined to the
academy in the sixties. Political activists from the black civil rights movement in the early sixties to the incipient feminist movement at the end
of the decade called for a more fully participatory democracy in America. In the rhetoric of some of these movements Dewey would have no
doubt heard phrases that echoed his own hopes and fears. Although
one would be hard pressed to claim for Dewey much direct influence
on the New Left, his work—especially *The Public and Its Problems*—did
appear on its reading lists, and occasionally it was read. Timothy
Kaufman-Osborn, for one, has recently recalled:

> In 1969, at the age of sixteen, I discovered [*The Public and Its Problems*] on
> a bookshelf in the home of my parents, pressed between John Calvin's
> "On Civil Government" and Sigmund Freud's *Civilization and Its Discon-
> tents.* I read each of these, but it was Dewey who spoke most directly to
> my everyday experience. . . . Dewey insisted, although the nation was
> now joined together by the division of labor into an interdependent
> whole, this society was no community; for the vast majority of men and
> women, the democratic public, could neither appreciate nor com-
> prehend the ties which bound them to their fellow citizens. . . . The
> problem of the democratic public was that its political institutions were
> no longer its own. I first read this analysis of American politics at a
> moment when the citizenry of the United States appeared unable to
> bring to a halt a war whose initiation it had only tacitly condoned and
> which it now sought to end. The parallel between this situation and that
> which had stimulated Dewey's analysis of the 1920s was acute and
> provocative; for it suggested that now, as then, the future of democratic
> politics turns upon the ability of the democratic public to restore to itself
> its capacity for autonomous action.

I suspect that this is not a typical story, but if few young radicals could
be found with a copy of *The Public and Its Problems* in their hip pockets,

15. Jack L. Walker, "A Reply," *American Political Science Review* 60 (1966): 392. A good
reader on the controversy between democratic realists and radicals is Henry S. Kariel,
ed., *Frontiers of Democratic Theory* (New York: Random House, 1970). See also Peter
Bachrach, *The Theory of Democratic Elitism* (Boston: Little, Brown, 1967), and Carole Pateman, *Participation and Democratic Theory* (Cambridge: Cambridge University Press, 1970).
Amy Gutmann has argued that Rawls's theory of justice might and should include participatory democracy among its requirements (*Liberal Democracy* [Cambridge: Cambridge
University Press, 1980]).

many did get a dose of Dewey secondhand from Mills, Paul Goodman, and others [16]

Perhaps nowhere did Dewey's ideals echo more resoundingly than in the "Port Huron Statement" (1962) of the Students for a Democratic Society. As James Miller has shown, in its early years SDS activists put the concept of participatory democracy at the heart of their ideology and activism, seeking, as they put it at Port Huron, "the establishment of a democracy of individual participation, governed by two central aims: that the individual share in those social decisions determining the quality and direction of his life; that society be organized to encourage independence in men and provide the media for their common participation." While he was drafting this pivotal document in the history of the politics of the sixties, Tom Hayden—who was heavily influenced by Mills and other intellectuals shaped by Dewey's ideas such as Arnold Kaufman and Harold Taylor—wrestled with the same issues that had been posed in the twenties in the face-off between Dewey and Lippmann. And, like Dewey, he fudged the difficulties of the means to and the forms of participatory democracy, leaving them to be worked out in practice—which they never were. At first Hayden and others in SDS did not intend that participatory democracy replace representative democracy; like Dewey they saw participatory and representative institutions as supplementary and mutually enhancing. But the exacting task of formulating a workable vision of this sort of democracy never got under way. Within SDS participatory democracy quickly came to designate the impossible ideal of an exclusively face-to-face, consensual politics, and SDS groups seeking to prefigure such politics in their own organization found themselves locked in all-night meetings trying to decide such things as whether to take a day off to go to the beach. Finally, in the late sixties, amid growing repression and the romanticization of peasant revolutionaries, the ideals of participatory democracy were sacrificed to an existentialist politics of (often violent) self-assertion in the streets. As Miller says, "In the mounting enthusiasm for 'breakaway experiences,' the original vision of democracy was all but forgotten."[17]

16. Timothy V. Kaufman-Osborn, "John Dewey," in Sohnya Sayres et al., eds., *The Sixties without Apology* (Minneapolis: University of Minnesota Press, 1984), pp. 289–290. Dewey's influence on Goodman is manifest in *Growing Up Absurd* (New York: Vintage, 1960) and *Compulsory Mis-Education/The Community of Scholars* (New York: Vintage, 1962). See also Marcus Raskin, *Being and Doing* (New York: Random House, 1971), pp. 169–264.
17. James Miller, *"Democracy Is in the Streets": From Port Huron to the Siege of Chicago*

The ideological impact of the radicalism of the sixties is still being measured, but it seems clear that, despite the limited successes of radical politics, one of its legacies is a generation of democratic theorists wary and weary of realism and narrow definitions of democracy. At the level of theory, democratic realism is decidedly on the defensive, if not defeated. Recent years have witnessed an outpouring of radical democratic theory by American political philosophers and social scientists, many of them seeking, as Dewey did, to develop hybrid forms of liberal-communitarianism and democratic-socialism, and some of them recognizing that Dewey was there before them.[18]

One of the most noteworthy developments in recent American democratic thought is the increasingly radical turn taken by such former realists as Dahl, one of the most sophisticated and subtle of American democratic theorists, who has considerably broadened his conception

---

(New York: Simon and Schuster, 1987), pp. 331, 317. One of the many virtues of Miller's fine book is that it reprints the full text of the "Port Huron Statement." For Arnold Kaufman's ideal of participatory democracy see "Human Nature and Participatory Democracy," in Carl Friedrich, ed., *Nomos III: Responsibility* (New York: Liberal Arts Press, 1960), pp. 266–289, and *Radical Liberal* (New York: Random House, 1968). For an astute estimate of the virtues and vices of face-to-face, consensual democracy—what she terms "unitary democracy"—see Jane J. Mansbridge, *Beyond Adversary Democracy*, 2d ed. (Chicago: University of Chicago Press, 1983).

18. A but partial list of recent work in participatory democratic theory (in addition to that already cited) would include: Benjamin Barber, *Strong Democracy: Participatory Politics for a New Age* (Berkeley: University of California Press, 1984) and *The Conquest of Politics: Liberal Philosophy in Democratic Times* (Princeton: Princeton University Press, 1988); Samuel Bowles and Herbert Gintis, *Democracy and Capitalism* (New York: Basic Books, 1986); John Burnheim, *Is Democracy Possible?* (Berkeley: University of California Press, 1985); Joshua Cohen and Joel Rogers, *On Democracy: Toward a Transformation of American Society* (New York: Penguin, 1983); Frank Cunningham, *Democratic Theory and Socialism* (New York: Cambridge University Press, 1987); Robert Dahl, *Dilemmas of Pluralist Democracy* (New Haven: Yale University Press, 1982), *A Preface to Economic Democracy* (Berkeley: University of California Press, 1985), and *Democracy and Its Critics* (New Haven: Yale University Press, 1989); Carol Gould, *Rethinking Democracy* (Cambridge: Cambridge University Press, 1988); Philip Green, *Retrieving Democracy* (Totowa, N.J.: Rowman and Allenheld, 1985); Amy Gutmann, *Democratic Education* (Princeton: Princeton University Press, 1987); Russell L. Hanson, *The Democratic Imagination in America* (Princeton: Princeton University Press, 1985); David Held, *Models of Democracy* (Stanford: Stanford University Press, 1987); James Miller, *Rousseau: Dreamer of Democracy* (New Haven: Yale University Press, 1984); William M. Sullivan, *Reconstructing Public Philosophy* (Berkeley: University of California Press, 1982); Michael Walzer, *Radical Principles* (New York: Basic Books, 1980) and *Spheres of Justice* (New York: Basic Books, 1983). Of these books, Barber's *Strong Democracy* and Sullivan's *Reconstructing Public Philosophy* are most explicit in linking their arguments to Dewey. For a time participatory democrats even had their own journal, the now defunct *democracy* (1981–1983), edited by Sheldon Wolin. Michael Walzer, ed., "The State of Political Theory: A Symposium," *Dissent*, Summer 1989: 337–359, is a useful summary of recent work in political theory which suggests that things might be moving in Deweyan directions.

of the nature and conditions of democracy over the last forty years. In an article titled "On Removing Certain Impediments to Democracy" (1977), for example, Dahl listed among those impediments inequality, constriction of participation, and ignorance he attributed to advanced capitalism, hierarchical and bureaucratic structures of decision making in large organizations, inaccessible experts, the imperial presidency, and an expansionist foreign policy. More recently, he has contended that the most closely guarded of elite prerogatives—the control of nuclear weapons—should be subject to popular authority.[19]

But whatever the triumphs of participatory democratic theory within the walls of the American university, democratic elitism remains ascendant in the halls of power and with those intellectuals who have the ear of the powerful. One of the most widely discussed documents in recent democratic theory was the report of the Trilateral Commission, *The Crisis of Democracy* (1975). This commission, funded by the wealth of the Rockefellers, was made up of the intellectual and policy-making elite of the United States, western Europe, and Japan. Its report argued that the trilateral nations were suffering from a bad case of "democratic distemper" which resulted from too much political participation by the masses and too many demands from below in the sixties and seventies. This participation and these demands, the report said, threatened the capacity of leaders in democratic nations to make the decisions necessary to ensure the stability of the international capitalist order. Democracies were becoming "ungovernable" and moving toward a crisis that only a further narrowing of the meaning of democracy and an assertion of elite autonomy and control could avert. And this, it should be said, was what passed for *liberalism* in the late seventies.[20]

The ascendancy of Reaganite conservatism in the eighties has served to enhance the dissonance between public and academic discourse on democracy and its discontents. As Michael Walzer has recently noted, radical political theory is thriving but "leftist and even liberal arguments these days are largely theoretical in character: professors writing for other professors." Without a significant nonacademic audience,

19. Robert Dahl, "On Removing Certain Impediments to Democracy in the United States," *Political Science Quarterly* 92 (1977): 1–20; Dahl, *Controlling Nuclear Weapons: Democracy v. Guardianship* (Syracuse, N.Y.: Syracuse University Press, 1985).

20. Michael Crozier et al., *The Crisis of Democracy* (New York: New York University Press, 1975). Two excellent studies of the antidemocratic politics of the last two decades are Thomas Edsall, *The Politics of Inequality* (New York: Norton, 1984), and Thomas Ferguson and Joel Rogers, *Right Turn* (New York: Hill and Wang, 1986). Harry Boyte discerns some rays of democratic hope in *The Backyard Revolution: Understanding the New Citizen Movement* (Philadelphia: Temple University Press, 1980) and *Community Is Possible* (New York: Harper and Row, 1984).

"political theory is a kind of alienated politics, an enterprise carried on at some distance from the activities to which it refers. The result, very often, is endless refinement, esoteric jargon, romantic posturing, and fierce intramural polemic." Very little of the sort of public philosophy that Dewey advocated and exemplified is being done these days, and we have no public intellectuals who can match him—or, indeed, his adversaries Randolph Bourne, Walter Lippmann, Lewis Mumford, and Reinhold Niebuhr. Perhaps the most pertinent suggestion one could make to help stem the decay of democracy in concluding a book that I am painfully aware is likely to find an audience made up mostly of professors is to call on that audience not only for more Deweyan theory but also for more Deweyan practice.[21]

A few years after Archibald and Lucina Dewey brought their family back to Vermont from the battlefields of the Civil War, Walt Whitman—whom their son John would later designate the "seer" of democracy—wrote, "We have frequently printed the word Democracy, yet I cannot too often repeat that it is a word the real gift of which still sleeps, quite unawakened, notwithstanding the resonance and the many angry tempests out of which its syllables have come, from pen or tongue. It is a great word, whose history, I suppose, remains unwritten, because that history has yet to be enacted"—yet to be enacted, he admitted, even in the United States of which he sang and in which he invested his hopes. But, as Dewey said fifty years later, "be the evils what they may, the experiment is not yet played out. The United States are not yet made; they are not a finished fact to be categorically assessed."[22]

Dewey himself devoted his life to continuing this experiment. In the process, he crafted a democratic philosophy of a depth and scope unparalleled in modern American thought. It would be a mistake (and most un-Deweyan) to recommend an uncritical or wholesale recovery of Dewey's philosophy. But it merits another, closer look. If we are to enact the history that Whitman envisioned, we could do worse than to turn to John Dewey for a full measure of the wisdom we will need to work our way out of the wilderness of the present.

21. Walzer, "The State of Political Theory," p. 337. On the decline of the public intellectual see Thomas Bender, *New York Intellect* (New York: Knopf, 1987), and Russell Jacoby, *The Last Intellectuals* (New York: Basic Books, 1987).
22. JD, *The Public and Its Problems* (1927), *Later Works* 2:350; Walt Whitman, "Democratic Vistas" (1871), in *Walt Whitman: Complete Poetry and Collected Prose* (New York: Library of America, 1982), p. 960; JD, "Pragmatic America" (1922), *Middle Works* 13:309.

Bibliographical Note

✳

I do not attempt here to reproduce all the citations in my notes or the bibliographical and historiographical commentary therein. This is but a guide to the most essential sources for those interested in the thought and career of John Dewey. Those in search of more comprehensive bibliographies should consult Milton H. Thomas, *John Dewey: A Centennial Bibliography* (Chicago: University of Chicago, 1962); Jo Ann Boydston and Kathleen Poulos, eds., *Checklist of Writings about John Dewey, 1877–1977*, 2d ed. (Carbondale: Southern Illinois University Press, 1978); and "John Dewey: A Guide to Correspondence and Manuscript Collections," available from the Center for Dewey Studies at Southern Illinois University.

Manuscript Sources

The papers of John Dewey and his family are housed in the Morris Library at Southern Illinois University in Carbondale, Illinois. This collection is rich in material for some periods of Dewey's career and sadly thin for others. Morris Library also is the depository for Sidney Hook's correspondence with Dewey which is not only significant in its own right but also important for students of Dewey's work, since Hook often kept copies of things that Dewey did not. Also at Southern Illinois is a valuable collection of documents that Joseph Ratner gathered when he was beginning work on a biography of Dewey he never completed. The Center for Dewey Studies at Southern Illinois serves as well as a secondary archive for Dewey papers in other collections. Although Carbondale is not easily accessible, it is indisputably the hub of Dewey studies.

Other manuscript collections (some of them available on microfilm) containing correspondence and other materials pertinent to a consideration of Dewey's social thought and political activism include the Henry Carter Adams Papers, Michigan Historical Collections, University of Michigan, Ann Arbor; James R. Angell Papers, Sterling Memorial Library, Yale University; Alfred Bingham Papers, Sterling Memorial Library, Yale; Boyd H. Bode Papers, Rare Books and Special Collections, Ohio State University, Columbus; Randolph Bourne Papers, Special Collections, Columbia University; V.F. Calverton Papers, Special Collections, New York Public Library; James McKenn Cattell Papers, Library of Congress; Merle Curti Papers, Wisconsin State Historical Society, Madison; Thomas Davidson Papers, Sterling Memorial Library, Yale; John Dewey Ms., Special Collections, Columbia; Sabino Dewey Papers, Morris Library, Southern Illinois University, Carbondale; George Dykhuizen Papers, University of Vermont Library, Burlington, Vermont; Max Eastman Papers, Lilly Library, Indiana University, Bloomington; James T. Farrell Papers, Van Pelt Library, University of Pennsylvania; Alexander Gumberg Papers, Wisconsin State Historical Society; Edward M. House Papers, Sterling Memorial Library, Yale; Horace M. Kallen Collection, American Jewish Archives, Hebrew Union College, Cincinnati; Scudder Klyce Papers, Library of Congress; S. O. Levinson Papers, Joseph Regenstein Library, University of Chicago; Library of Living Philosophers Papers, Morris Library, Southern Illinois University; Walter Lippmann Papers, Sterling Memorial Library, Yale; Benjamin C. Marsh Papers, Library of Congress; Agnes Meyer Papers, Library of Congress; Lewis Mumford Papers, Van Pelt Library, University of Pennsylvania; Max Otto Papers, Wisconsin State Historical Society; Presidents' Papers, Special Collections, University of Chicago Library; Raymond Robins Papers, Wisconsin State Historical Society; Herbert Schneider Papers, Morris Library, Southern Illinois University; Socialist Party Papers, Duke University Library; Swarthmore College Peace Collection, Swarthmore College; Harry Ward Papers, Union Theological Seminary, New York; Richard W. G. Welling Papers, Special Collections, New York Public Library; Howard Y.

Williams Papers, Minnesota Historical Society, St. Paul; and Woodrow Wilson Papers, Library of Congress.

Dewey Texts

John Dewey has been blessed with one of the finest editions of the collected works of an American author. In a modest building on the edge of the Southern Illinois campus, editor Jo Ann Boydston and her staff have established a remarkable enterprise that since the late 1960s has steadily churned out volume after volume. Now nearing completion, this edition of Dewey's works has been published in three parts (*The Early Works, 1882–1898, The Middle Works, 1899–1924*, and *The Later Works, 1925–1953*) and, when completed, will comprise thirty-seven volumes. Each volume has a short introduction by a leading student of Dewey's philosophy, and in many instances in which a piece by Dewey was part of an exchange or controversy with others it reprints the work of those with whom he was contending. The textual apparatus and editorial commentary that are so often intrusive in such "official" editions are both helpful and inconspicuous. Those like myself who have in the past spent countless hours tracking down Dewey's fugitive essays can perhaps best appreciate the gift that Jo Ann Boydston and her associates Patricia R. Baysinger, Richard W. Field, Bridget W. Graubner, Paul F. Kolojeski, Barbara Levine, Kathleen Poulos, Anne Sharpe, Harriet Furst Simon, and Bridget A. Walsh have provided to scholarship. It would have cut months off my effort to read everything Dewey wrote if all the volumes of this edition had been at hand ten years ago. Although it has taken me some time to find quotations in the collected works which I had copied from elsewhere, I have made every effort where possible to cite strictly from these texts. It is the very least of tributes I could pay to this outstanding project. These volumes should be in every American library.

Many of Dewey's major texts remain in print, some in inexpensive paperback editions. Those not in print can often be found in used bookstores in most cities and towns in the United States, as befits the work of a major public intellectual. There are a number of good collections of Dewey's writings, the best of which is the two-volume *Philosophy of John Dewey*, edited by John McDermott (Chicago: University of Chicago Press, 1981). The debates in which Dewey was involved in the pages of the *Journal of Philosophy* have been conveniently collected in

Sidney Morgenbesser, ed., *Dewey and His Critics* (New York: Journal of Philosophy, Inc., 1977).

Secondary Sources

The secondary literature on Dewey is enormous, though much of it is not worth reading. A very helpful guide to this literature is the Boydston and Poulos *Checklist of Writings about John Dewey*. A handy tour of the various aspects of Dewey's thought is provided by the essays in another volume published by the Center for Dewey Studies: Jo Ann Boydston, ed., *Guide to the Works of John Dewey* (Carbondale: Southern Illinois University Press, 1970).

There is no adequate intellectual biography of Dewey. George Dykhuizen, *The Life and Mind of John Dewey* (Carbondale: Southern Illinois University Press, 1973), offers more life than mind and in neither instance is interpretive or critical. It is, nonetheless, an indispensable source of biographical information. Morton White's *Origins of Dewey's Instrumentalism* (New York: Columbia University Press, 1943) and much of the analysis of Dewey in White's *Social Thought in America*, 3d ed. (Boston: Beacon Press, 1976) remain valuable. The best capsule summary of Dewey's thought is still Sidney Hook's *John Dewey: An Intellectual Portrait* (New York: John Day, 1939), but Richard J. Bernstein, *John Dewey* (New York: Washington Square Press, 1967), J. E. Tiles, *Dewey* (London: Routledge, 1988), and the relevant chapters in Paul Conkin, *Puritans and Pragmatists* (Bloomington: Indiana University Press, 1976), and Elizabeth Flower and Murray G. Murphey, *A History of Philosophy in America* (New York: G. P. Putnam's Sons, 1977), are also excellent. No library of Dewey basics is complete without Katherine Camp Mayhew and Anna Camp Edwards, *The Dewey School* (New York: Atherton, 1966).

The finest historical study of Dewey's work is Neil Coughlan, *Young John Dewey* (Chicago: University of Chicago Press, 1975), which examines his life and career to 1894. Although James Kloppenberg provides him with some strange bedfellows, his treatment of Dewey in *Uncertain Victory: Social Democracy and Progressivism in European and American Thought, 1870–1920* (New York: Oxford University Press, 1986), is the best analysis of Dewey's "middle period." The historical literature on "old John Dewey" is weaker, and one must rest content with specialized studies of his social commentary and activism that do not attempt, as Coughlan and Kloppenberg do, to make the connections between his philosophical concerns and his politics or even to consider his social thought in any depth. See Charles F. Howlett, *Troubled Philosopher: John Dewey and the Struggle for World Peace* (Port Washington, N.Y.: Kennikat Press, 1977); Gary Bullert, *The Politics of John Dewey* (New York: Prometheus Books, 1983); and the sections on Dewey in R. Alan Lawson, *The Failure of Independent Liberalism, 1930–1941* (New York: Capricorn Books, 1971), and Richard Pells, *Radical Visions and American Dreams: Culture and Social Thought in the Depression Years* (New York: Harper, 1973).

Bruce Kuklick's *Rise of American Philosophy: Cambridge, Massachusetts, 1860–1930* (New Haven: Yale University Press, 1977) and *Churchmen and Philosophers: From Jonathan Edwards to John Dewey* (New Haven: Yale University Press, 1985) are essential for an understanding of Dewey's intellectual context. The best history of pragmatism is H. S. Thayer, *Meaning and Action: A Critical History of Pragmatism*, 2d ed. (Indianapolis, Ind.: Hackett, 1981). John E. Smith, *Purpose and Thought: The Meaning of Pragmatism* (New Haven: Yale University Press, 1978), is also an excellent synthetic study. Given my central concerns, I found James Gouinlock, *John Dewey's Philosophy of Value* (New York: Humanities Press, 1972), and Alfonse J. Damico, *Individuality and Community: The Social and Political Thought of John Dewey* (Gainesville: University Presses of Florida, 1978), to be the most valuable books on Dewey by philosophers, though R. W. Sleeper, *The Necessity of Pragmatism: John Dewey's Conception of Philosophy* (New Haven: Yale University Press, 1986), which deals principally with Dewey's logic and metaphysics, is, of late, the most provocative. Robert Church and Michael Sedlak, *Education in the United States: An Interpretive History* (New York: Free Press, 1976), does a fine job of putting Dewey's educational ideas in the context of their more successful competitors as does Lawrence Cremin, *American Education: The Metropolitan Experience, 1876–1980* (New York: Harper, 1988), the third volume of his magisterial history of American education. Despite all the criticism directed at it, Cremin's *Transformation of the School: Progressivism in American Education* (New York: Vintage, 1964) remains valuable, as does Merle Curti's *The Social Ideas of American Educators* (Totowa, N.J.: Littlefield, Adams, 1968). The most rewarding book on the history of modern American democratic theory is Edward A. Purcell, Jr.'s superb *Crisis of Democratic Theory: Scientific Naturalism and the Problem of Value* (Lexington: University of Kentucky Press, 1973), which covers the interwar period.

The arguments I make here might be said to comprise an interpretation of Dewey's thought which sets itself against both the uncritical hagiography of such liberal Deweyans as Dykhuizen and Hook and the efforts of various radical social and intellectual historians, most notably some "revisionists" in the history of education, to deny Dewey his credentials as a radical democrat and convict him of complicity in the constriction of democracy in modern America. The latter range from the crude polemics in Clarence Karier et al., *Roots of Crisis: American Education in the Twentieth Century* (New York: Rand McNally, 1973), to the often tendentious readings in R. Jeffrey Lustig, *Corporate Liberalism: The Origins of Modern American Political Theory* (Berkeley: University of California, 1982), to the subtle arguments in Christopher Lasch, *The New Radicalism in America* (New York: Vintage, 1965). My conviction that these critics are, to different degrees, off the mark is perhaps more firmly held by virtue of the fact that theirs is a position I once took myself. The most recent study of Dewey's mature activism, Bullert's *Politics of John Dewey*, tries to enlist him on behalf of neoconservatism, but the book is filled with factual errors and misreadings that make it the mirror image of revisionist scholarship. I have noted my objections to the treatment of Dewey in Richard Hofstadter's *Anti-Intellectualism in American Life* (New York: Vintage, 1963), but it merits mention because of the influence it has exerted on those who have taken their Dewey second-hand.

When I began work on Dewey, I faced the widespread conviction that he was, in the worst sense, only of historical interest (if that). Recently, though, I have taken heart from the efforts of some philosophers to restore his reputation. Most prominent of these is Richard Rorty. See especially his *Consequences of Pragmatism* (Minneapolis: University of Minnesota Press, 1982) and *Contingency, Irony, and Solidarity* (New York: Cambridge University Press, 1989). Somewhat closer to my own convictions about where Dewey's relevance for our time lies are the views of John J. McDermott, Richard J. Bernstein, and Cornel West. See McDermott, *The Culture of Experience* (New York: New York University Press, 1976), and *Streams of Experience* (Amherst: University of Massachusetts Press, 1986); Bernstein, *Praxis and Action* (Philadelphia: University of Pennsylvania Press, 1971); *Beyond Objectivism and Relativism* (Philadelphia: University of Pennsylvania Press, 1983); and *Philosophical Profiles* (Philadelphia: University of Pennsylvania Press, 1986); and West, *The American Evasion of Philosophy: A Genealogy of Pragmatism* (Madison: University of Wisconsin Press, 1989). Among the numerous important works of radical democratic theory to appear in the last decade which might be said to be "Deweyan," Benjamin Barber, *Strong Democracy* (Princeton: Princeton University Press, 1984), and William Sullivan,

Reconstructing Public Philosophy (Berkeley: University of California Press, 1982), have forged the most explicit links to Dewey's thought.

Finally, in all fairness, I refer readers to two masterful biographies of Dewey's most important democratic-realist adversaries: Ronald Steel, *Walter Lippmann and the American Century* (Boston: Little, Brown, 1980), and Richard Wightman Fox, *Reinhold Niebuhr: A Biography* (New York: Pantheon, 1985).

Index

✶

Unless otherwise indicated, books and articles indexed here are by John Dewey.

Library of Congress Cataloging-in-Publication Data

Westbrook, Robert B. (Robert Brett), 1950–
    John Dewey and American democracy / Robert B. Westbrook.
    p. cm.
    Includes bibliographical references and index.
    ISBN 0-8014-2560-3 (alk. paper)
    1. Dewey, John, 1859–1952—Contributions in political science.
  2. Dewey, John, 1859–1952—Contributions in democracy. I. Title.
JC251.D48W47   1991
320'.01—dc20   90-55712